RASKA

Union Pacific Railroad

Platte River

Big Blue River

Little Blue River

Missouri River

IOWA

MISSOURI

Kearny

Republican River

*North Fork
olomon River*

olomon River

Solomon River

Fort
Riley

Manhattan

Fort
Leavenworth

Kansas City

ort Hays

Saline River

Abilene

Kansas River

Independence

Ft. Harker

Salina

Topeka

Lawrence

nut Creek

Ft. Zarah

N

e Fork

Ft. Larned

Arkansas River

KANSAS

Scale in miles

0   50

Cimarron River

INDIAN TERRITORY

nadian River

George Skoch

EYEWITNESSES TO THE INDIAN WARS, 1865–1890

ALSO BY PETER COZZENS

EYEWITNESSES TO THE INDIAN WARS, 1865–1890

Conquering the Southern Plains

EDITED BY PETER COZZENS

STACKPOLE BOOKS

Published by
STACKPOLE BOOKS
5067 Ritter Road
Mechanicsburg, PA 17055
ISBN: 0-8117-0019-4

Printed in the United States of America

For Ismael Alexander

CONTENTS

PART ONE:
Hancock's War and the Medicine Lodge Treaty, 1865–67

PART TWO:
The Battle of Beecher Island, 1868

PART THREE:
Sully's North Canadian Expedition, 1868

PART FOUR:
The Cheyenne War, 1868–69

PART FIVE:
Mackenzie and the Texas Frontier, 1866–73

PART SIX:
The Red River War, 1874–75

PART SEVEN:
Raids and Reprisals, 1865–81

PART EIGHT:
The Ute War, 1879

ILLUSTRATIONS AND MAPS

Maps

PREFACE

Eyewitnesses to the Indian Wars, 1865–1890: Conquering the Southern Plains is the third volume in a planned five-volume series that will tell the saga of the military struggle for the American West in the words of the soldiers, noncombatants, and Native Americans who shaped it. Volume Four will be devoted to the conflicts on the Northern Plains. Volume Five will include accounts of a general nature. Among the topics that narratives in the fifth volume will address are the Indian-fighting army, the army and Indian policy, prominent chiefs and warriors, prominent officers and their campaigns, officers and enlisted men, scouts and Indian auxiliaries, army wives, and forts and camps.

It is the intent of the present volume to offer as complete a selection of outstanding original accounts pertaining to the struggle for the Southern Plains and Texas as may be gathered under one cover. The Ute War of 1879 is also covered in this volume. Most of the accounts presented here are drawn from contemporaneous newspapers and magazines—a wealth of primary source material, much of which has remained unknown not only to the general reader, but also to serious students and historians of the Indian Wars.

For the benefit of readers new to the series, I will review the considerations that have guided my choice of material for inclusion in *Eyewitnesses to the Indian Wars*. First, the events described must have occurred between the end of the Civil War and the tragedy at Wounded Knee. Most of the articles in the series were first published during the authors' lifetimes, and none published within the last fifty years have been included, as they are for the most part readily available. I also have excluded accounts that later appeared in book form, as well as those of dubious reliability.

Manuscript sources account for a small but significant portion of the contents of the series. A third source of material is military reports, both official and unofficial, which, at the time they were penned, were considered sufficiently important that their authors or the War Department had them published outside of normal channels.

In the accounts presented in this volume, there is an unfortunate but unavoidable imbalance between white and Native American sources. The extant accounts of Southern Plains Indian participants consist largely of oral testimony and have formed the basis of several fine books. Col. Wilbur S. Nye interviewed Kiowa tribal elders in the early twentieth century and drew on similar interviews that Capt. Hugh Scott had conducted in the 1890s to produce *Bad Medicine and Good: Tales of the Kiowas* (Norman: University of Oklahoma Press, 1962). The forty-four stories collected in *Bad Medicine and Good* trace Kiowa tribal history from the 1700s to the New Deal of the 1930s. There are chapters on the organization and conduct of raiding parties, the martial deeds of war chiefs, and the treatment of white captives. Colonel Nye also authored two highly regarded works on the Southern Plains Indian Wars that drew on the testimony of Native American participants: *Carbine and Lance: The Story of Old Fort Sill* (Norman: University of Oklahoma Press, 1943) and *Plains Indian Raiders: The Final Phases of Warfare from the Arkansas to the Red River* (Norman: University of Oklahoma Press, 1968).

The Cheyenne story of the Southern Plains Wars is brilliantly told in George B. Grinnell's *The Fighting Cheyennes* (New York: Charles Scribner's Sons, 1915), a classic of western Americana. Grinnell (1849–1938) was a naturalist and ethnologist who knew the Cheyennes well. "A long association with the Cheyennes has given me a special interest in them, and a special wish that they should be allowed to speak for themselves," said Grinnell in the preface to *The Fighting Cheyennes*. "What the Indians saw in the battles here described, I have learned during years of intimate acquaintance with those who took part in them." Grinnell allowed the Cheyennes to speak without inserting critical comment of his own.

Charles J. Brill also used the testimony of Cheyenne participants in writing his *Conquest of the Southern Plains: Uncensored Narrative of the Battle of the Washita and Custer's Southern Campaign* (Oklahoma City: Golden Saga Publishers, 1938). Unfortunately, Brill's extreme hostility toward the army in general and to Custer in particular often obscures the valuable Cheyenne accounts that are interwoven with Brill's narrative.

A few words about editorial practice in *Eyewitnesses to the Indian Wars* are in order. My goal has been to present accurate and annotated texts of the articles, letters, reminiscences, and reports included in the series. I have added notes to correct errors of fact, clarify obscure references, and provide historical context where needed. Editing of the text has been light. Most nineteenth-century writers had a penchant for commas. I have eliminated them where their overuse clouded the meaning or impeded the rhythm of a sentence. I have regularized capitalization, punctuation, and the spelling of names and places. I also have standardized references to the ranks of army officers, using their Regular army rank at the time of the events described. Apart from these small changes, I have left the writings as I found them.

ACKNOWLEDGMENTS

Continued diplomatic service abroad with the Department of State made it particularly challenging for me to gather the articles and other primary accounts presented in this volume. Without the persons mentioned below, whose help I am pleased to acknowledge, it would have been impossible.

First, I thank my mother for her many trips to the Wheaton Public Library, submitting interlibrary loan requests and retrieving articles; my sincere thanks go also to the staff of the periodicals department of the Wheaton Public Library for their patience and diligence in filling these requests.

I also wish to thank the staffs of the following institutions for materials from their archives and, where necessary, for permission to reprint them: Harold B. Lee Library, Brigham Young University, Provo, Utah; Kansas State Historical Society, Topeka; University of Colorado, Boulder; and the U.S. Army Military History Institute, Carlisle Barracks, Pennsylvania.

Much of the material presented here I obtained during several visits to the Newberry Library in Chicago. The reference staff of that institution was most helpful on every occasion.

I am grateful to Perry Frohne of Oshkosh, Wisconsin, a noted collector and dealer in Civil War and Indian Wars images, for permission to reproduce a number of fine images from his stock.

I continue to be indebted to my editor at Stackpole Books, Leigh Ann Berry, for her enthusiastic support of this project.

INTRODUCTION

In the 1860s, most Americans knew the Southern Plains of the United States simply as the Great American Desert. Except for a smattering of white settlements, struggling against nature and Indian attacks for a foothold on their periphery, the Southern Plains were the domain of the bison, and of the Native Americans who hunted them.

A vast and monotonous region, the Southern Plains stretched from the Platte River south to the Rio Grande, and east from the Rocky Mountains to the ninety-eighth meridian. Interminable stretches of level, grassy sod rolled away to nearly treeless horizons. Water was scarce, and the weather volatile. Strong southerly winds blew blast-furnace heat across the Southern Plains in the summer, and harsh north winds brought blizzards of remarkable force in the winter.

The monotony of the landscape is more apparent than real. The Southern Plains are not flat, as they seem, but slope downward from the base of the Rockies, creating two distinct topographical divisions, the High Plains and the Low Plains. The High Plains reach elevations of nearly five thousand feet in eastern New Mexico and Colorado, while the Low Plains sink to sea level along the Gulf of Mexico. Across most of the Southern Plains, the decline is imperceptible. But in the Texas Panhandle, the High Plains yield to the Low Plains in a precipitous drop of stunning magnitude called the Caprock escarpment. The walls of the three-hundred-mile-long Caprock vary from two hundred to one thousand feet in height. Deep canyons—the most prominent of which are the Palo Duro and the Tule—penetrate the escarpment and give rise to the principal rivers of Central Texas.

The High Plains west of the Caprock are known as the Llano Estacado, or Staked Plains. One of the largest tablelands on the North American continent, the Llano Estacado stretches thirty-two thousand square miles, an area greater than that of all New England. Early white settlers shunned its arid and barren reaches, and Southern Plains Indians resorted to it principally as a refuge when pursued. The Spanish explorer Francisco Vásquez de Coronado dismissed the region in a letter to the king of Spain in 1541: "I reached some plains so vast that I did not find their limit anywhere I went, although I traveled over them for more than three hundred leagues, with no more landmarks than if we had been swallowed up by the sea. There was not a stone, nor bit of rising ground, nor a tree, nor a shrub, nor anything to go by." The harsh conditions Coronado described would prove the bane of U.S. troops operating against recalcitrant Indians three centuries later.

The Southern Plains were home to five Native American tribes: the Comanches, Kiowas, Kiowa-Apaches, Southern Cheyennes, and Arapahos. All were nomadic hunters, for whom the American bison not only provided food and shelter, but also underpinned their culture and religion. The Southern Plains Indian contemplated the disappearance of the buffalo with apocalyptic dread.

An inseparable adjunct to the buffalo in Southern Plains culture was the horse. The Indians gathered strays from Spanish herds, drawn to the rich grazing land of the Low Plains, and by the end of the seventeenth century, the Southern Plains warriors had become superb horsemen and formidable light cavalry. The horse extended both the range and effectiveness of the buffalo hunt and, not surprisingly, became a medium of exchange and a measure of wealth.

Raiding and warfare were central to the horse culture of the Southern Plains. Each tribe counted from four to twelve military societies. Tribal military societies varied in prestige and cohesiveness—from informal groups for untested boys to exclusive and highly regimented bodies to which only the greatest warriors were admitted. An entire tribe might fight, or individual bands within a tribe make war, but warfare was most commonly conducted by small war parties drawn entirely from volunteers. Discipline was loose, and individual prowess all-important. A warrior's standing derived from deeds of valor.

None of the five tribes of the Southern Plains were native to the region. The Comanches, Kiowas, and Kiowa-Apaches had dwelt there for less than 150 years, and the Cheyennes and Arapahos only drifted into the area in the 1830s. The struggle for the Southern Plains was less a battle of the indigenous Native American against the white interloper than a conflict between two vastly different emigrant cultures.

The preeminent Southern Plains tribe was the Comanche, a Shoshonean people numbering twenty-five hundred, who had migrated to the Southern Plains from the northern Rockies. The Comanches were widely admired for their courage and refined code of honor, and theirs was the language of intertribal trade. They returned these compliments with a smug certainty of their own superiority.

The Comanches maintained a loose tribal structure. The band commanded greater loyalty than did the tribe, and a band itself might coalesce or disperse according to the desires of its members. Five major bands constituted the Comanche tribe. The largest and most pacific was the Penateka, which roamed Central Texas. North of the Penateka ranged the Nokoni. Beyond the Nokoni was the Kotsoteka. The northernmost band was the Yamparika. The fifth and fiercest band was the Kwahadi, the only Southern Plains people to call the Llano Estacado home.

The democratic nature of Comanche society made meaningful negotiations with the entire tribe problematic. Each band had its own war and peace chiefs, who exercised only limited powers, and these at the pleasure of band members.

That the Comanches were more warlike than their neighbors may be deduced from their name, which is derived from the Ute word *Komantcia*, meaning "anyone who wants to fight me all the time." The Comanches had warred sporadically with Mexico since the early 1700s, conducting raids deep into Durango. Their initial encounters with Anglo-Americans had been amicable, but relations deteriorated after Mexico opened Texas to foreign immigration and land-grabbing Texans shoved the Comanches off their traditional hunting grounds.

The Republic of Texas treated the Comanches worse than had the Mexican government, pursuing a policy of betrayal and brutality that culminated in the slaughter of thirty-five members of a Comanche peace delegation in San Antonio in 1840. The Comanches afterward counted the Texans their bitterest enemies, and they regarded depredations against Texas settlers as just retribution for the massacre of their peace chiefs. Matters improved somewhat after Texas joined the Union in 1845 and the federal government took charge of Indian affairs. Between 1848 and 1853, the army established two chains of forts to protect the Texas frontier and keep the hostile parties apart, but settlers spilled over the cordon. The withdrawal of federal garrisons during the Civil War enabled the Comanches and their Kiowa allies to push back the Texas frontier. No sooner did the war end, however, than the outward migration resumed.

The tribal history of the Kiowas was similar to that of the Comanches. Also a northern people, the Kiowas had drifted southward from the headwater of the Yellowstone and Missouri Rivers. The Crow Indians taught them to ride horses and hunt buffalo, and the lure of large horse herds and good hunting drew the Kiowas deep into the Southern Plains. The Kiowas and Comanches confederated in about 1790, and thereafter their fate was entwined. Both peoples hated the Texans with equal intensity, and they raided, bartered captives, and made peace together. But it was not always an easy association. The free wheeling Comanches, who seldom if ever congregated as a tribe, found the formalized politics of the Kiowas frustrating, an impediment to the lightning raids at which the Comanches excelled. Questions of war or peace required the blessing of the Kiowa tribal council and were often postponed until the annual Sun Dance ceremony. The Kiowas assembled at the start of each summer for the ten-day ceremony, without which they believed the buffalo would vanish.

There were some thirteen hundred Kiowas in the midnineteenth century. The tribe was composed of six bands, each of which had played a unique role in the Sun Dance ritual. The tribe was further stratified into four distinct social levels, or ranks: the Onde, the richest warriors, principal chiefs, and the ten guardians of the sacred medicine bundles; the Odegupa, lesser chiefs, medicine men, and warriors of moderate means; the Kaan, the poor people of the tribe; and the Dapom, the misfits and the crazy.

Closely affiliated with the Kiowas were the Kiowa-Apaches, a small Athapascan-speaking group that owed its name to the erroneous assumption that it was a splinter band of Eastern Apaches. Kiowa-Apache tradition placed their origin in the eastern Rockies and recounted an association with the Kiowas since time immemorial. Believed never to have numbered more than 350

A Kiowa summer shelter. BUREAU OF ETHNOLOGY, *FOURTEENTH ANNUAL REPORT.*

persons, the Kiowa-Apaches had an oddly symbiotic relationship with the much larger Kiowa tribe. They lived together but spoke different languages and seldom intermarried. The Kiowa-Apaches participated in the Sun Dance and held the same religious beliefs as the Kiowas. The Kiowa-Apaches were more peaceably inclined than their protectors, who enjoyed a reputation as the most sanguinary warriors of the Southern Plains.

The last Native Americans to arrive on the Southern Plains were the Cheyennes and Arapahos, both tribes of the great Algonquin family. Like their Comanche and Kiowa neighbors to the south, the Cheyennes and Arapaho were closely allied peoples; indeed, their tribes had been so long linked that observers often spoke of them as one. Both tribes had once farmed the Red River Valley of Minnesota. The principal difference between them lay in their war-making proclivities: The Arapahos were an accommodating, peaceable people, whereas the Cheyennes were proud and turbulent, the members of their Dog Soldier military society being the finest and most intractable warriors on the Southern Plains.

Pressure from the Sioux, whom the Chippewas of Wisconsin were driving onto the Northern Plains, forced the Cheyennes and Arapahos southward. The construction of Bent's Fort on the Arkansas River in 1832 drew a portion of each tribe—perhaps thirty-five hundred persons in all—into Comanche and Kiowa country and led to eight years of bitter warfare between the two allied groups. Charles Bent helped broker a peace in 1840, and thereafter the Comanches, Kiowas, Cheyennes, and Arapahos acted in unison, particularly against white encroachment. Those Cheyennes and Arapahos who had

An Arapaho shelter. BUREAU OF ETHNOLOGY, *FOURTEENTH ANNUAL REPORT.*

remained on the Northern Plains made peace with the Sioux. Over the next twenty years, the Cheyennes and Arapahos separated into distinct yet closely related northern and southern branches.

As the growth of Texas forced the Comanches and Kiowas to fall back to the north and west, the displaced tribes vented their rage on the Santa Fe trade route and western Kansas settlements. Heavy migration to the California gold fields in the 1840s and to the Pikes Peak region of Colorado a decade later squeezed the Southern Cheyennes and Arapahos into western Kansas and eastern Colorado. In his annual report for 1859, Indian agent William Bent related the plight of the four tribes:

> The Kiowa and Comanche Indians have, for two years, appeared in full numbers and for long periods upon the Arkansas, and now permanently occupy the country between the Canadian and the Arkansas Rivers. This is in consequence of the hostile front opposed to them in Texas, by which they are forced towards the north, and is likely to continue perpetual. A smothered passion for revenge agitates these Indians, perpetually fomented by the failure of food, the encircling encroachments of the white population, and the exasperating sense of decay and impending extinction with which they are surrounded.
>
> These numerous and warlike Indians, pressed upon all around by Texans, by the settlers of the [Pikes Peak] region, by the advancing people of Kansas, and from the Platte, are already compressed into a small circle of territory, destitute of food. A desperate war of starva-

tion and extinction is therefore imminent and inevitable, unless prompt measures shall prevent it.[1]

Bent's warning went unheeded. In place of a comprehensive and forward-looking Indian policy, Washington relied on stopgap measures that only delayed the day of reckoning. With the naive assumption they would relinquish the buffalo culture in favor of farming, in February 1861, the government concluded the Fort Wise Treaty with the Southern Cheyennes and Arapahos, the terms of which confined the Indians to a small parcel of land in southeastern Colorado. Both tribes made good-faith efforts to keep the peace, but most Coloradoans wanted them out of the territory altogether. During the Civil War, territorial authorities stepped forward with a thinly veiled policy of extermination. The pretext for violence was a dubious complaint that an Indian raiding party had stolen cattle from the settlements. No matter that no one could say for certain which tribe was responsible; the commander of the District of Colorado, Col. John Chivington of the 1st Colorado Volunteer Cavalry, ordered that the Cheyennes be "chastised severely."

On May 3, 1864, a detail of the 1st Colorado attacked a peaceable Cheyenne village at Cedar Bluffs, near the South Platte River. The Cheyennes and their Arapaho, Kiowa, and Comanche allies retaliated, raiding outlying settlements and closing down the mail and stage routes. The territorial governor, John Evans, ordered all Indians to come in to Fort Lyon or face annihilation. Maj. E. W. Wynkoop of the 1st Colorado, a man of principle and courage who loathed the brutal Chivington, persuaded Black Kettle of the Cheyennes and Left Hand of the Arapahos to confer with the governor in Denver. But Evans refused to negotiate until all the Indians had surrendered. The one man in a position to inject some integrity into the proceedings, Maj. Gen. Samuel R. Curtis, commanding the Department of Kansas, instead told Chivington that he wanted "no peace until the Indians suffer more."

That was all Chivington needed to hear. On November 28, 1864, he led an expedition of one thousand volunteers on a forced march to Black Kettle's village on Sand Creek, near Fort Lyon. Committed to peace despite Governor Evans's rebuff, on the advice of Major Wynkoop, Black Kettle had brought his people into Fort Lyon to surrender. But at daybreak on November 29, Chivington descended on the Indian camp without warning. Black Kettle raised first the American flag and then a white flag over his tepee, but the Coloradoans ignored both, massacring five hundred of the seven hundred Cheyennes camped along Sand Creek. As the federal commission appointed to investigate the affair discovered, "Fleeing women holding up their hands and praying for mercy were brutally shot down; infants were killed and scalped in derision; men were tortured and mutilated in a manner that would put to shame the savage ingenuity of interior Africa."[2]

The specter of Sand Creek cast a sinister shadow over U.S.–Indian relations for a generation. Said Maj. Gen. Nelson A. Miles, "But for that horrible butchery it is a fair presumption that all subsequent wars with the Cheyennes and Arapahos and their kindred tribes might possibly have been avoided."[3]

The Southern Cheyennes and their allies returned to the warpath with unprecedented fury. As word of the Sand Creek massacre spread, other tribes took up the scalping knife, setting the plains aflame from the Red River of Texas to the Canadian border. Thousands of volunteer soldiers, expecting to be mustered out after the Civil War, were instead sent west to contain the outbreak until enough regular troops could be mustered in to replace them. The volunteers deserted in droves, and the effectiveness of those who remained was limited. Nonetheless, the warring tribes agreed to give peace another chance. On August 15, 1865, sixteen chiefs of the Southern Plains tribes, including the long-suffering Black Kettle, met Brig. Gen. John B. Sanborn, commanding the Military District of the Upper Arkansas, at the mouth of the Little Arkansas River to arrange a cease-fire and an autumn peace conference.

Horrified by the Sand Creek massacre, Congress had authorized a government commission to negotiate a lasting peace on the Southern Plains. Commission members included frontier legends Kit Carson, Jesse Leavenworth, and William S. Harney—all men of good intentions. The grand peace council convened at the mouth of the Little Arkansas River in October 1865. Representatives of the Cheyenne, Arapaho, Comanche, Kiowa, and Kiowa-Apache tribes affixed their marks to a treaty that accorded them a reservation covering much of eastern Colorado and southwestern Kansas, nearly all the Texas Panhandle, and a large segment of the Indian Territory.

What seemed a generous grant on paper turned out to be an empty gesture. Texas refused to relinquish any portion of the Panhandle, and Kansas similarly declined to permit a reservation within her boundaries. The only portion of the proposed reservation that the federal government controlled was that lying within the Indian Territory, which would not be open to the Southern Plains tribes until Washington was able to extinguish the land titles of the Five Civilized Tribes. In the meantime, the Southern Plains Indians were free to roam their old hunting grounds, so long as they stayed clear of the wagon roads and railroads.

Despite the fatal flaws in the treaty, during 1866 a tenuous peace held. This was good for the government, because the Regular army was ill prepared for war. The last of over 1 million volunteers were mustered out at midyear, leaving a Regular establishment with a paper strength of 54,641 officers and men, of whom perhaps half were available for field duty.

Administrative changes were made to accommodate the army's frontier responsibilities. The sprawling Military Division of the Missouri had been created the year before to encompass the entire Great Plains. Headquarters were at St. Louis, and the first commander was Brig. Gen. John Pope. The division was divided into departments, which were subdivided into military districts. The Southern Plains lay within the Departments of the Missouri and of Texas. Maj. Gen. William T. Sherman, who succeeded Pope in command, understood the magnitude of his task and the paucity of his resources. A chain of frontier forts protected the Texas and Kansas settlements and the principal wagon roads west, but their garrisons were too small for active operations. In the Department of Missouri, there were only three cavalry regiments, composed of raw recruits and Civil War retread officers, available to protect Kansas, New Mexico, Missouri, and the Indian Territory. It was a fragile barricade that Sherman had constructed against Indian incursions. As he confessed in his annual report at the end of 1866, "Were I or the department commanders to send guards to every point where they are clamored for, we would need alone on the Plains a hundred thousand men, mostly cavalry."[4]

Unfortunately for all concerned, Sherman's principal subordinate, the able but arrogant Maj. Gen. Winfield Scott Hancock, who knew little of the Indian or his ways and cared less about learning of them, upset the balance. Convinced that the spring of 1867 would see a major outbreak on the Southern Plains, Hancock concluded to lead a preemptive military expedition to overawe the Indians. Although he would march forth in peace, Hancock was prepared for—and probably wanted—war. "We go prepared for war," he told his subordinates, "and will make it if a proper occasion presents. No insolence will be tolerated." Hancock proposed to hold meetings with the chiefs of each tribe to tell them that peace could be had only if they stayed far from the white man's roads. As if to precipitate a conflict, Hancock forbade the issuance of arms and ammunition that the Indians had been promised under the terms of the Little Arkansas Treaty.

Evidence that the Southern Plains tribes wanted war was lacking, but there were troubling portents. Large bands of Sioux, tired of Red Cloud's war with the whites in the Powder River country, had migrated across the Republican River as far as Fort Larned, Kansas. Rumor had it that the Sioux had come to make common cause with the southern tribes in a general Indian war. The Plains Indians were quiet in the winter months, when the harsh cold and lack of forage for their ponies kept them close to their tepees. With the coming of spring and the return of the lush buffalo grass, the younger warriors—over whom the peaceable chiefs had little control—always grew restive. Comanche and Kiowa raids on the Texas settlements were a certainty, and the gradual encroachment of Kansas farmers and ranchers onto Cheyenne and Arapaho hunting grounds in the valleys of the Saline, the Solomon, and Republican Rivers also presaged trouble. Most ominously, the Cheyenne Dog Soldiers had declined to attend the Little Arkansas council or to surrender their preferred hunting grounds along the Smoky Hill road.

On April 3, 1867, Hancock started from Fort Harker with fourteen hundred troops. Colonel Wynkoop, who had labored in vain for peace in 1864 and who was now the agent for the Cheyennes and Arapahos, brokered a meeting between Hancock and the chiefs of Sioux and Dog Soldier bands encamped on Pawnee Fork. The council was to convene at Fort Larned on April 10, but a late-spring blizzard delayed the gathering. A handful of chiefs reached the post two days later. Their spokesman, Tall Bull of the Cheyenne, assured Hancock his people wanted peace, but he feared that the depletion of the buffalo and antelope would bring starvation upon them. Ignoring Tall Bull, Hancock demanded to know why so few chiefs had come. When told that the Indian ponies were too weak to travel, Hancock concluded to march to the Pawnee Fork encampments to continue the council. Wynkoop and Tall Bull tried to dissuade him, knowing the memory of Sand Creek would frighten the women and children, but Hancock persisted. As predicted, the Indians decamped upon Hancock's approach.

Hancock took this as a declaration of war. He sent Lt. Col. George A. Custer to bring back the Indians, who had fled northward, and made ready to burn the village and remaining Indian property. Wynkoop protested vehemently, and Hancock stayed the torch, pending Custer's report.

But Custer had lost the trail of the Pawnee Fork bands just after

*The Dog Soldier insignia—
the lance and sash.*

BUREAU OF ETHNOLOGY,
FOURTEENTH ANNUAL REPORT.

setting off. Not until he reached the Smoky Hill River on April 17 was he able to report anything. Settlers and railroad workers told him that Indians had attacked Lookout Station and were raiding all along the Smoky Hill route. Custer wired Hancock the news, then marched to Fort Hays to refit.

Custer could not say what Indians had committed the depredations, but Hancock destroyed the Pawnee Fork encampment all the same. After ordering Custer to the Republican River country, Hancock started for Fort Dodge to meet with Kiowa chiefs Kicking Bird and Stumbling Bear, both of whom said the tribes south of the Arkansas River were united for peace. Little Raven and other Arapaho chiefs repeated these assurances, as did Kiowa subchief Satanta, with whom Hancock met on May 1 at Fort Larned.

Well satisfied with the Kiowas and Arapahos, Hancock marched to Fort Hays, where he found Custer without supplies or forage. With Hancock's expedition concluded and Custer shackled to Fort Hays, Sioux and Cheyenne war parties from Pawnee Fork bands staged reprisal raids along the Smoky Hill route and the Union Pacific Railroad, among the settlements in the Solomon and Republican River Valleys, and against military posts, virtually laying siege to Fort Wallace.

Not until June 1 did Custer resume campaigning, starting with 350 troopers for Fort McPherson on the Platte River, and intending to scout along its south bank as far as Fort Sedgwick, where he was to receive further orders from General Sherman.

Over the rough and arid plains, Custer drove his men relentlessly to little avail. No fights were fought except on the Indians' terms. Custer found few hostiles, and scores of his men deserted. And at the end of June, a ten-man detachment under Lt. Lyman Kidder sent from Fort Sedgwick with orders for Custer to divert to Fort Wallace was wiped out.

When Custer limped into Fort Wallace in mid-July, he found the beleaguered garrison low on supplies and learned that cholera had stricken the posts farther east on the Smoky Hill road. Worried that his wife might have fallen ill, Custer hurried with a small escort to Fort Hays, covering the 156 miles in fifty-five hours and losing two men to hostile fire. From Fort Hays, Custer rode on with four men to Fort Harker. There he arranged for supplies for the Fort Wallace garrison and his own regiment, then went on to Fort Riley to see his wife. She was fine, but a court-martial sentenced Custer to a one-year suspension for having absented himself from his command. Custer departed, convinced Hancock had offered him up as a scapegoat.

Certainly there was need for one. Hancock's campaign had been a dismal failure. Any lingering doubt the Indians may have had of the innate perfidy of the white man after Sand Creek was removed when Hancock burned the Pawnee Fork village. And far from overawing them, Hancock's empty bluster in council and Custer's ineptitude in the field only emboldened the Indians. Dog Soldier and Sioux war parties ranged over western Kansas at will, shutting down travel and rolling back the settlements. A new government Indian policy clearly was in order.

━┈ ≊◆≊ ┈━

The Hancock and Custer fiascoes prompted Congress to extend the olive branch to the Southern Plains tribes. On July 20, 1867, an act was passed creating an Indian peace commission to confer with the hostile chiefs, learn their grievances, and make peace if possible.

The commission worked quickly. Gathering in St. Louis on August 6, its members elected Commissioner of Indian Affairs N. G. Taylor president of the commission. All agreed that lasting peace depended upon removing the nomadic Plains tribes from the lines of western travel and onto reservations, with liberal provision made for their maintenance. After an abortive meeting with the Northern Plains Indians in September, the commission joined the assembled southern tribes on Medicine Lodge Creek in mid-October. Maj. Joel H. Elliott accompanied the commissioners with five hundred troopers of the 7th Cavalry. A legion of newspaper reporters came along to cover the proceedings.

Preliminary discussions were held on October 15. Despite the absence of many prominent Cheyenne chiefs, the council opened in earnest on the nineteenth. The commissioners apologized for the burning of the Pawnee Fork village and absolved the Indians of blame for their subsequent raids. The federal government, they assured the chiefs, and not the Indians, had broken the Little Arkansas Treaty. As the commissioners later complained to Congress:

> If the lands of the white man are taken, civilization justifies him in resisting the invader. Civilization does more than this; it brands him as a coward and a slave if he submits to the wrong. Here civilization made its contract and guaranteed the rights of the weaker party. It did not stand by the guarantee. The treaty was broken, but not by the savage. If the savage resists, civilization, with the Ten Commandments in one hand and a sword in the other, demands his immediate extermination.[5]

The commissioners concluded a treaty with the Kiowas, Kiowa-Apaches, and Comanches on October 21. The tireless Black Kettle persuaded the Dog Soldier chiefs to come in, and a week later the Cheyennes and Arapahos signed a treaty. The terms of both agreements were similar. In exchange for surrendering a much larger area of their traditional hunting grounds, the Comanches, Kiowas, and Kiowas-Apaches were accorded a 3 million-acre reservation between the Washita and Red Rivers in the southwest corner of the Indian Territory. The Cheyennes and Arapahos received 4.3 million acres, largely between the North Fork of Red River and the North Canadian River. Liberal allowances of food, clothing, equipment, and—by implication— weapons and ammunition for hunting were promised. In exchange for agreeing to stay off the roads and away from white settlements, the Indians were granted permission to hunt north of the Arkansas River so long as the buffalo remained—a concession necessary to obtain the consent of the Dog Soldiers, but one that doomed the treaty from the outset. The Indians went away happy but, as most observers concluded, with no idea of what they had signed.

The promise of peace proved fleeting. Congress, which had been quick to appoint the peace commission, was unconscionably slow to ratify the treaty the commissioners had negotiated. The Senate and House differed on key stipulations, and neither was inclined to compromise. Months passed. The Indians grew restive. No annuities were issued during the winter months of 1867–68, when the Indians most needed them, and by spring they were nearly destitute. Game grew scarce, and women and children were starving. No one had come to show the tribes their new reservations, and while they lingered on their old hunting grounds, the Indians watched surveying parties, settlers, and railroad crews overrun the land and slaughter the buffalo.

The Kiowas were the first to return to the warpath. With the spring thaw, they crossed Red River to attack the Texas settlements. The implacable Kwahadi Comanches, who had absented themselves from the Medicine Lodge proceedings, fanned out from the Staked Plains to raid over hundreds of miles of west-central Texas frontier. Army efforts to punish them proved fruitless.

Despite their legitimate grievances, the Cheyennes and Arapahos remained faithful to the terms of the Medicine Lodge treaties, instead directing their ire against their longtime enemies the Kaws, who had stolen a herd of horses and killed several Cheyenne and Arapaho warriors the preceding fall. In early June 1868, a large Cheyenne war party rode east from Fort Larned to do battle with the Kaws. They passed peaceably through the Kansas settlements until they reached the Kaw reservation near Council Grove. There, with great fanfare but no bloodshed, the Cheyennes and Kaws engaged in what one witness called "three hours of harmless scrimmage." Their honor redeemed, the Cheyennes returned home.

Kansas governor Samuel J. Crawford visited Council Grove and found no harm had been done, but news of the raid became distorted as it traveled east. Believing that white settlements had been attacked, Commissioner of Indian Affairs Taylor forbade the Kansas superintendent, Thomas Murphy, to issue arms or ammunition to the Cheyennes and Arapahos. With eight troops of cavalry on hand to discourage unrest, Agent Wynkoop conveyed Taylor's decision to his wards when they gathered at Fort Larned in late July for their annuity goods. Sullen and mistrustful, the chiefs refused to accept any annuities, but promised nonetheless to "wait with patience [for] the Great Father to take pity upon them and let them have the arms and ammunition which had been promised them."[6] Wynkoop persuaded Murphy to release the arms after the chiefs promised him that they would never be used against the whites. A much-relieved Wynkoop doled out the complete issue of annuity goods on August 9.

But the time for reining in the bolder spirits among the Cheyennes and Arapahos had passed. On August 10, a large war party returning from an attack on a Pawnee village paused at an isolated homestead to beat a man and rape his wife and sister. Their blood up, the main party continued on to depredate the Saline and Solomon River Valley settlements, while a small band of warriors turned north to kill and pillage along the Republican River. Two army scouts sent out from Fort Hays to treat with the Cheyennes were fired upon; one was killed, and the other barely escaped to Fort Wallace with word of the Indian treachery.

Agent Wynkoop strove to avoid further bloodshed, but the die had been cast. Congress would extend no olive branch, and Superintendent Murphy, concluding that the Cheyennes and Arapahos were best left "in the hands of the military," told Wynkoop to advise the Comanches and Kiowas to gather at Fort Cobb in the Indian Territory until their new agent, Col. William B. Hazen, arrived. General Sherman, meanwhile, ordered department commander Maj. Gen. Philip H. Sheridan to drive the hostiles from Kansas by any means necessary. Said Sherman:

> If it results in the utter annihilation of these Indians, it is but the result of what they have been warned again and again. I will say nothing and do nothing to restrain our troops from doing what they deem proper on the spot, and will allow no more vague general charges of cruelty to tie their hands. These Indians, the enemies of our race and of our civilization, shall not again be able to begin and carry out the barbarous warfare on any kind of pretext they may choose to allege. These Indians will seek some sort of peace, to be broken next year at their option; but we will not accept their peace, or cease our efforts till all the past acts are both punished and avenged.[7]

But Sheridan could do little more than concur with Sherman's sentiments. He had scarcely enough troops to hold the forts, and what detachments he did send out failed to kill a single Indian. In late August 1868, a frustrated Sheridan directed his aide, Maj. George A. Forsyth, to hire fifty "first class handy frontiersmen," arm them with Spencer repeating rifles, and find the hostiles.

Forsyth found them—and almost lost his entire command in the effort. On September 10, Forsyth and Lt. Frederick H. Beecher led the scouts out of Fort Wallace to chase a war party that had attacked a wagon train near the town of Sheridan, Kansas. The Solomon Avengers, as Forsyth's scouts styled themselves, arrived too late to catch the Indians, but they did find a trail, which they followed to the bank of the Arikaree Fork of the Republican River. By the time they made camp beside the Arikaree on the night of September 16, what had begun as a faint trail had broadened into a wide and well-beaten path. Fearing an ambush, the scouts urged Forsyth to withdraw. He refused. They had enlisted to fight Indians, and fight Indians they would.

The next morning, a war party of at least 750 Sioux, Cheyennes, and Arapahos swept down upon the tiny command. The scouts escaped instant annihilation by falling back onto a sandy island in the center of the Arikaree and digging in. They repulsed three charges during the course of the day and killed the great Cheyenne warrior Roman Nose, but at a staggering cost. Forsyth was hit first, shot through both legs. Lieutenant Beecher took a bullet in the side

Maj. Gen. Philip H. Sheridan in the summer of 1865.
PETER COZZENS COLLECTION.

and died after hours of agony. Surgeon J. H. Mooers was shot in the head and never regained consciousness. Two scouts were mortally wounded, and sixteen others were hit. All the horses were dead, the rations were exhausted, and the Indians showed no signs of leaving. The only hope was to get help from Fort Wallace. Forsyth sent two details of two scouts each on the perilous, 110-mile journey, while the remainder of the command ate putrid horseflesh and withstood an eight-day siege.

Miraculously, all four scouts slipped safely past the Indians. Two reached Fort Wallace, and two stumbled upon a troop of the 10th Cavalry under Capt. L. H. Carpenter, who hastened to the island. Capt. H. C. Bankhead arrived a day later with a detail from Fort Wallace.

Although trumpeted as a stunning victory, the battle of Beecher Island, as the fight came to be known, was a dismal failure for the army. The Solomon Avengers had killed Roman Nose and dealt the Dog Soldiers and their allies their first check, but Indian depredations continued unabated from the Arkansas to the Solomon. Even Forts Wallace and Larned came under attack.

Having accomplished little with civilian scouts, Sheridan flailed away again with regulars. On September 7, Lt. Col. Alfred B. Sully led nine troops of the 7th Cavalry and three companies of the 3rd Infantry from Fort Dodge in an expedition south of the Arkansas River. After several indecisive skirmishes, Sully withdrew to Fort Dodge on September 18, hurried along by warriors who contemptuously thumbed their noses and slapped their buttocks at the troops. In October, seven troops of the 5th Cavalry, recently transferred to Kansas from Reconstruction duty, fought three separate engagements with Tall Bull's Dog Soldiers along the Republican and Solomon Rivers. Maj. E. A. Carr had greater success than did Sully, killing some twenty warriors and capturing 130 ponies, but Indian attacks on the settlements and wagon roads went on. The onset of winter accomplished what the army could not, driving the war parties back to the protective warmth of their villages—there, thought the hostiles, to rest until spring.

—————

But Sherman and Sheridan had other ideas. They would make winter their ally in a carefully orchestrated campaign to drive the Cheyennes and Arapahos onto the Fort Cobb reservation, pursuing and killing those who resisted. Rather than chase well-mounted war parties over the plains, as they had during the summer and fall, the army would strike their home villages, relying on the element of surprise and the weakened state of the Indian ponies for success.

During the last weeks of autumn, Sheridan made his plans and gathered men and supplies for a three-pronged drive into the Indian Territory. Four columns of troops would march in concert. From Fort Bascom, New Mexico, Maj. Andrew W. Evans was to lead six troops of the 3rd Cavalry and two companies of infantry eastward. Maj. Eugene A. Carr would march southeastward from Fort Lyon, Colorado, at the head of seven troops of the 5th Cavalry. Together they would sweep the Cheyennes off the Staked Plains and into the path of the principal strike force—eleven troops of the 7th Cavalry and five companies of infantry under Lt. Col. Alfred B. Sully. Sully was also to construct a cantonment on the Canadian River for the use of all troops in the field. Sheridan would make his headquarters with Sully's command. A fourth column, consisting of the newly recruited 19th Kansas Volunteer Cavalry under the command of Gov. Samuel Crawford, was to rendezvous with Sully on the Canadian.

Although the Indian Bureau concurred with the need for military action, it differed with the War Department as to its scope. The Indian Bureau believed that friendly Cheyennes and Arapahos should be spared. Sherman and Sheridan disagreed, arguing that all should be held accountable for the crimes of the Dog Soldiers and their allied bands. Only the Kiowas, Comanches, and Kiowa-Apaches were to be offered sanctuary at the Fort Cobb reservation; any Cheyenne and Arapaho bands encountered were to be attacked. "I am of the belief," Sheridan told Sherman, "that these Indians require to be soundly whipped, and the ringleaders in the present trouble hung, their ponies killed, and such destruction of their property as will make them very poor."

The intransigence of Sherman and Sheridan precipitated the tragedy that ensued. On November 1, Sheridan issued marching orders to his subordinate commanders. Eleven days later, Sully's column left Fort Dodge for the Canadian River, which it reached after a six-day march. While their troops set about constructing Camp Supply, as the cantonment was called, Colonels Sully and Custer, who was back in command of the 7th Cavalry, wrangled over rank. Sheridan settled the matter in favor of Custer, and Sully returned to Fort Dodge.

Meanwhile, winter had struck. Heavy snow and piercing winds obscured trails and confused guides, and by November 21, the 19th Kansas Cavalry had become lost on the plains of southern Kansas. After wandering four days longer among box canyons near the Cimarron River, Crawford called a halt. Gathering up the strongest horses, he and Lt. Col. Horace L. Moore set out with five hundred men on a desperate bid to find Camp Supply. Maj. R. W. Jenkins and the remaining six hundred stayed behind on a snow-piled flat, which the famished Kansans christened "Camp Starvation."

Impatient of delay, Sheridan unleashed Custer without the errant 19th Kansas. The 7th Cavalry left Camp Supply at dawn on November 23. Four days later, to the strains of "Garry Owen," Custer's command attacked an unsuspecting Cheyenne village—the camp of peace chiefs Little Robe, Little Rock, and Black Kettle—a hundred miles upriver on the Washita from Fort Cobb. A week earlier, the Indians had come to Fort Cobb seeking sanctuary. Black Kettle confessed to Colonel Hazen, whose responsibility it was to gather the friendly Kiowas, Comanches, and Kiowa-Apaches at Fort Cobb, that he had been unable to prevent some of his restless young warriors from participating in recent hostilities, but he assured the colonel that he and the majority of his people wanted peace. Big Mouth, speaking for the Southern Arapahos, said the same. Hazen believed the chiefs but had no authority to make peace; Sherman had branded them hostile. Reluctantly, Hazen told the chiefs to return to their people until such time as he might send for them.

Sheridan's orders to Custer had been simple. The 7th Cavalry was to "proceed south in the direction of the Antelope Hills, thence towards the Washita River, the supposed winter seat of the hostile tribes; to destroy their villages and ponies; to kill or hang all warriors, and bring back all women and children." Custer complied in grand style. Over one hundred Cheyennes were killed in the dawn attack on the Washita, among them Little Rock and Black Kettle. With half that number of women and children captives, Custer returned to Camp Supply and to congratulations from Sheridan. Custer had lost eighteen men, including a detachment under Maj. Joel H. Elliott, which warriors from nearby villages had ambushed while the troopers were in pursuit of fleeing members of Black Kettle's camp.

On November 28, Crawford and Moore reached Camp Supply with their starving Kansans; Major Jenkins and the remainder straggled in on December 1. Seven hundred of the regiment's horses had died from starvation or exposure. Nevertheless, on December 7, Sheridan himself took to the field with Custer and the 19th Kansas and the 7th Cavalry. He intended to return to the Washita battlefield, and from there march down the Washita to Fort Cobb, driving in or destroying any bands he might encounter. Sheridan pacified the Kiowas and Comanches without a struggle, and a few hundred starving Cheyennes and Little Raven's band of Arapahos also agreed to surrender, but the main body of the hostiles escaped southward toward the headwaters of Red River. Sheridan would have preferred to pursue and fight them, but the mixed success of the expeditions of Majors Evans and Carr during the month of December suggested that persuasion might now accomplish more than coercion.

Carr had scouted the North Canadian River for five weeks without locating a single Indian. Nearly two hundred of his cavalry mounts starved to death before Carr reluctantly returned to Fort Bascom. Evans fared better, destroying a hostile Nokoni Cheyenne village on the North Fork of Red River and killing twenty-five warriors at a cost of one man killed and two wounded.

What Carr and Evans had accomplished was to keep the Cheyennes and Arapahos on the run. Their ponies weakened and died; hunting was risky with troops always near; and their women and children grew hungry and sick. Through their Kiowa and Comanche friends, the Cheyennes and Arapahos signaled their desire for peace.

Sheridan authorized Custer to treat with them. With a small escort, Custer rode forth in early January 1869 from a newly established camp on Medicine Bluff Creek, which Sheridan would christen Fort Sill, in search of the Indian villages. He scouted through the Washita Mountains and onto the Texas Panhandle. There he found the principal band of Arapahos under Little Raven, who agreed to come into Fort Sill in three days time, but the Cheyennes had fled, presumably onto the Staked Plains. With his supplies low and horses weak, Custer returned to Medicine Bluff Creek, convinced that only a strong show of force would compel the Cheyennes to surrender. Sheridan concurred, and on March 2 Custer set out with eleven troops of the 7th Cavalry and ten troops of the 19th Kansas Cavalry. Skirting the southern base of the Washita Mountains, Custer paused at the site of old Camp Radziminski to divide his command. With eight hundred handpicked men from the 7th and 19th, Custer resumed the westward march on March 6. He sent Lt. Col. William Myers with the remainder of the men to meet the wagon train near the Washita battlefield. For two weeks Custer stalked the Caprock escarpment. Finally, on the morning of March 15, he discovered a recently abandoned Cheyenne camp on the North Fork of Red River. At noon his Osage trailers spotted a large pony

William T. Sherman as a lieutenant general.
NATIONAL ARCHIVES.

herd. With his weary command strung out behind him, Custer rode ahead with an interpreter and two officers to parley with the Cheyennes, who proved to be of Medicine Arrow's band. From them, he learned that the entire hostile tribe was encamped along the Sweetwater River, a short distance away.

With characteristic audacity, Custer accepted Medicine Arrow's invitation to continue the parley in his village. All went well until Custer's tardy troopers closed in. Nervous warriors faced off with the ill-disciplined Kansas volunteers, and for a time a fight appeared inevitable. But Custer, knowing that the Cheyennes held two white female captives at the village, withdrew his troops a safe distance, then invited Medicine Arrow to his campsite.

Medicine Arrow came, as did several lesser chiefs and heavily ornamented warriors, ostensibly to entertain the troops, but in fact to distract them while the Cheyenne village decamped. When his lookout reported the ruse, Custer seized four of the chiefs as hostages. In exchange for their release, he demanded the white captives. Little Robe promised to find them. After waiting forty-eight hours, an exasperated Custer threatened to hang the hostages and attack the Cheyenne camp if the white women were not delivered by sunset the next day, March 19. The Cheyennes yielded, surrendering their prisoners and promising to come in themselves as soon as their ponies were strong enough to travel. Custer rode into Fort Hays, Kansas, on April 10 to a tumultuous welcome. Little Robe led his band of Cheyennes to Fort Sill on April 8. Other bands straggled in during May and June, and in July Medicine Arrow surrendered at Camp Supply.

But not all the Cheyennes were prepared to walk the white man's way. Tall Bull, for one, refused to bring his people in. With two hundred warriors and their families, he set out for the old Republican River hunting grounds, where he hoped to join the Sioux and Northern Cheyennes.

Colonel Carr set out from Fort Lyon, Colorado, with seven troops of the 5th Cavalry to find him. He scouted the country between the Arkansas and Platte Rivers in the direction of Fort McPherson until, on May 13, he found and overran Tall Bull's village. Tall Bull escaped with five hundred warriors and their families, but at a heavy cost. Twenty-five warriors were killed and fifty wounded, and the village and its contents were burned. Carr took up the chase, but the Indians scattered. With further pursuit futile, Carr marched his column to Fort McPherson.

No sooner had Carr quit the field than Tall Bull unleashed his warriors on the western Kansas settlements. Again Carr started in pursuit, this time with eight troops of regulars and Maj. Frank J. North's famed battalion of Pawnee scouts. Carr swept the Republican River country for a month before finding the hostiles encamped at Summit Springs, Colorado. Carr attacked on July 10 and, at a loss of just one man wounded, captured the village and killed fifty-two warriors. Among the dead was Tall Bull.

Carr's stunning victory demoralized the Cheyennes, and all bands off the reservation came in. Sheridan was delighted. Now, he told Congress in his annual report for 1869, "the good work of civilization, education, and religious instruction" might begin.

＊＋ ᚎ᚜ ＋＊

The "good work of civilization" would be done in a new way. Fed up with the corruption and inefficiency of the Indian Bureau, both the president and Congress took decisive steps to restructure the management of Indian affairs. The newly inaugurated president, Ulysses S. Grant, acted on an October 1868 recommendation of the peace commission that a wholesale clean-out of superintendents and agents be undertaken, offering the jobs to religious organizations interested in the work. The Society of Friends stepped forward, and Quaker agents were assigned to the Southern Plains superintendency. Lawrie Tatum, a courageous Iowa farmer of unquestioned integrity, relieved Colonel Hazen at Fort Sill in July 1869 as agent for the Kiowa, Comanches, and Kiowa-Apaches. The capable Brinton Darlington replaced Edward W. Wynkoop, who had resigned in protest after the Washita massacre, as agent for the Cheyennes and Arapahos. Enoch Hoag, a doctrinaire Quaker, assumed charge of the superintendency.

Congress took Grant's reform measures a step further, authorizing the president to appoint a nine-member Board of Indian Commissioners to assist the secretary of the interior in overseeing the Indian Bureau. The secretaries of

HARPER'S WEEKLY.
A JOURNAL OF CIVILIZATION

Vol. XVIII.—No. 919.]   NEW YORK, SATURDAY, AUGUST 8, 1874.   [WITH A SUPPLEMENT.
PRICE TEN CENTS.

Entered according to Act of Congress, in the Year 1874, by Harper & Brothers, in the Office of the Librarian of Congress, at Washington.

THE MERE SHADOW HAS STILL SOME BACKBONE.
"OUR STANDING ARMY" STANDS IN SPITE OF POLITICAL FALSE ECONOMY.

"Our standing army." HARPER'S WEEKLY 1874.

war and the interior, in turn, met to reconsider the role of the army in light of the new "peace policy." They agreed that reservation Indians would be under the exclusive control of their agents, who would be at liberty to call upon the army when needed. All Indians off the reservations would be considered hostile and subject to the sole jurisdiction of the military.

The army could only hope that the Indians remained quiet and amenable to Quaker "conquest by kindness." Confident that the peace policy would resolve the Indian problem, in the army appropriation act of March 3, 1869, Congress slashed the number of infantry regiments from forty-five to twenty-five, which meant a drop in the standing army from fifty-four thousand to just over thirty-seven thousand officers and men. Of this number, fewer than twelve thousand would be available for duty in the vast Departments of Texas and Missouri.

That kindness alone would not conquer the Kiowas and Comanches became clear to Lawrie Tatum. They behaved well enough on the reservation, but raiding parties slipped across Red River and penetrated deep into Texas with alarming regularity. The military was prohibited from pursuing them north of Red River, so Tatum's agency became a "city of refuge," where war parties might draw rations and rest between raids.

The Kiowas were the worst offenders. Under the leadership of Satanta, Satank, and White Horse, they grew increasingly bold in their depredations until, in early 1871, Tatum concluded the Kiowas were intent on a general war. Over the objections of Superintendent Hoag, Tatum asked the army to patrol along Red River.

There were too few troops for the task, and the raiding went unchecked. A growing chorus of demands from Texans for greater federal protection brought William T. Sherman, now the commanding general of the army, to Texas on a personal inspection of the frontier posts in May 1871. His tour was uneventful until he reached Fort Richardson, where he learned that a Kiowa war party had waylaid a freight train belonging to Henry Warren twenty miles west of the post a few hours after Sherman's party had passed the same point.

Sherman responded decisively. He ordered Col. Ranald Mackenzie and his crack 4th Cavalry to pursue the raiders wherever their trail might lead—including the reservation itself—then traveled to Fort Sill to see Tatum, who offered to cooperate fully in tracking down the guilty.

When his band came to draw rations on May 27, the Kiowa chief Satanta obliged Tatum with a boastful confession of guilt. "If any other Indian comes here and claims the honor of leading the party he will be lying to you, for I did it myself," Satanta declared. Tatum penned a note to Col. Benjamin Grierson, the post commander, requesting the immediate arrest of Satanta and his cohorts Satank, Eagle Heart, and Big Tree. A swaggering Satanta repeated his boast to Sherman. After a brief but tense encounter in which the Kiowa Lone Wolf came close to shooting Sherman, 10th Cavalry troopers rounded up a dozen chiefs. Sherman placed Satanta, Satank, and Big Tree in irons and sent them to Texas to stand trial. Satank was killed trying to escape, but Big Tree and Satanta were delivered to civilian authorities, tried, found guilty of murder, and sentenced to hang. Acceding to pressure from religious and other humanitarian groups outside the state, Gov. Edmund J. Davis commuted their sentences to life in prison.

The capture of their chiefs split the Kiowas into a war faction led by Lone Wolf and a peace faction led by Kicking Bird, who prevailed, and for a time the Kiowas were quiet. With the reservation Indians in check, the military turned its attention to the Kwahadis, who maintained a lucrative trade with an unsavory group of New Mexican traders known as the Comancheros. In exchange for stolen cattle and horses and captive women and children, the Comancheros gave the Kwahadis guns, ammunition, and whiskey.

In May 1872, Brig. Gen. Christopher C. Augur, the commander of the Department of Texas, set about to break up the Comanchero trade and subdue the Kwahadis. He sent Colonel Mackenzie with the 4th Cavalry and Lt. Col. William R. Shafter with the 24th Infantry onto the Staked Plains after the Kwahadis. Neither expedition found any Indians, but they did demonstrate that operations on the arid tablelands were possible.

Mackenzie returned to the Staked Plains in September, and his renewed efforts were amply rewarded. On September 29, the 4th Cavalry surprised a Kwahadi village, seizing 120 women and children and 1,200 ponies, and burning 262 lodges. Although the Kwahadi warriors recovered their ponies, the confinement of their families at Fort Concho brought them to the agency. The winter of 1872–73 passed quietly on the Texas frontier, and peace seemed assured so long as Satanta and Big Tree remained in the penitentiary and the army held the Kwahadi captives.

But the government surrendered its advantage. At the urging of the Executive Committee of the Society of Friends, the commissioner of Indian Affairs promised a visiting delegation of Kiowa chiefs in October 1872 that Satanta and Big Tree would be freed if the tribe behaved for six months. General Augur, in turn, was prevailed upon to liberate the Fort Concho prisoners.

The release of Satanta and Big Tree disgusted both General Sherman and Lawrie Tatum. The latter resigned in protest, to the evident delight of the Quaker Executive Committee, which replaced him with James Haworth, whose thoroughly pacifist views coincided with those of Superintendent Hoag.

The pious, friendly treatment of Hoag and Haworth availed of nothing, as in 1873 Comanche and Kiowa war parties struck the Texas frontier with renewed vigor. Cheyenne warriors from the Darlington agency joined them. For nearly four years, the Cheyennes had kept the peace. But pressures were building on the reservation that even the most peaceably inclined could not resist. Unscrupulous white traders plied the Cheyennes with illicit whiskey, and white horse thieves from Kansas preyed upon their pony herds. Surveying parties fringed the reservation, and buffalo hunters decimated the great Southern herd—the cornerstone of the nomadic Indian's way of life.

The slaughter was staggering. Between 1872 and 1874, white hunters shot an estimated 4 million buffalo to feed an insatiable eastern market for robes. When the last bison vanished from Kansas, the more daring of the hunters ventured into the Indian Territory to prey upon bison that by treaty belonged to the Indians. In early 1874, a group of Dodge City hunters, tanners, and merchants set up a permanent camp at Adobe Walls on the North Canadian River, preparatory to a summer hunt on the Staked Plains.

The presence of buffalo hunters below the Cimarron River was in blatant violation of the Medicine Lodge Treaty, the terms of which compelled the army to keep poachers out of the Indian Territory. But the commander of the Military Division of the Missouri, Phil Sheridan, encouraged the buffalo hunters in their illegal work. The buffalo hunters, he told the Texas legislature in 1875, "have done more in the last two years to settle the vexed Indian question than the entire Regular army has done in the past thirty years. They are destroying the Indians' commissary. For the sake of lasting peace, let them kill, skin, and sell until the buffaloes are exterminated."[8]

Secretary of the Interior Columbus Delano agreed. In his annual report for 1873, Delano said:

We are assuming, and I think with propriety, that our civilization ought to take the place of their barbarous habits. We therefore claim the right to control the soil they occupy, and we assume it is our duty to coerce them, if necessary, into the adoption of our habits and customs. I would not seriously regret the total disappearance of the buffalo from our western prairies, regarding it as a means of hastening [the Indian's] sense of dependence upon the products of the soil.[9]

Though they abhorred the violence that might accompany the transition of their Indian wards from nomadic hunters to God-fearing farmers, Superintendent Hoag and his Quaker agents concurred with Secretary Delano's objective.

The depletion of the buffalo herds might have been easier for the reservation Indians to accept, and the white man's road easier to walk, had the government at least kept its promise to feed and clothe them. But heavy blizzards during the winter of 1873–74 prevented the private contractors upon whom federal authorities depended from delivering beef rations, and the Indians were compelled to slaughter their ponies to survive. Unseasonably cold weather prolonged their suffering well into the spring.

Anger grew apace with hunger. When a volatile young Comanche of strong medicine named Isa-tai proclaimed that the Great Spirit had chosen him to drive off the white man, the Southern Plains tribes listened. On June 27, 1874, Isa-tai and Chief Quanah Parker of the Kwahadis led a war party of between seven hundred and twelve hundred Comanche and Cheyenne warriors in an attack on Adobe Walls. The twenty-eight occupants of the trading post, most of them crack marksmen with high-powered rifles, repulsed the Indian attack. How many Indians fell is not known, but enough died to discredit Isa-tai's medicine. The large war party splintered into smaller bands, which fanned out across western Texas, Oklahoma, Kansas, and eastern New Mexico to raid and pillage with bloody abandon. Hostile Cheyennes prowled the Fort Dodge–Camp Supply and the Darlington-Wichita roads, effectively laying siege to the Darlington agency.

⌐•┤ ⊫◊⊨ ├•⌐

Adobe Walls marked the end of the peace policy. General Sherman demanded and received permission to pursue hostile Indians onto the reservations. On July 20, 1874, he instructed Sheridan to turn loose the troops.

Sheridan's strategy for the Red River War, as the conflict came to be known, paralleled that of the 1868–69 campaign, with the important exception that it was to be conducted in the summer months, rather than the winter. And the summer of 1874 was to prove unusually hot and arid. Temperatures soared above 110 degrees. On the Texas Panhandle, where much of the fighting was to take place, creeks dried up and waterholes vanished; swarms of locusts devoured the plant life, leaving bare, baked earth upon which not even the hearty Indian ponies could find sustenance.

As he had done in the fall of 1868, Sheridan now strove to separate the hostile from the friendly Indians, directing that the latter be enrolled at their agencies immediately. At Fort Sill, Agent Haworth enjoyed mixed success. More than half of his Comanche wards remained off the reservation and were presumed hostile, but nearly three-quarters of the Kiowa tribe followed Kicking Bird into camp near the fort. Matters were decidedly more delicate at the Darlington agency. Not only were nearly all the Cheyennes on the warpath, but Agent John D. Miles also feared that his employees would be massacred and the government property pillaged. Friendly Arapahos helped maintained order, as did a detachment under Col. Thomas H. Neill, and the threat quickly passed.

Trouble arose, however, at an unexpected location—the Wichita agency at Anadarko. There sixty lodges of Nokoni Comanches under Big Red Foot had appeared in mid-August demanding food. Lone Wolf and his band of hostile Kiowas also made camp at the agency among peaceable Wichita and associated tribes. With only one company of infantry on hand, the agent sent to Col. John H. Davidson at Fort Sill for help. Davidson arrived on August 22 with four troops of the 10th Cavalry. A melee ensued when Davidson demanded that the Cheyennes lay down their arms. After two days of skirmishing, the Kiowas and Comanches fled toward the western reaches of the Indian Territory. Some encamped with the Cheyenne confederates in the deep canyons of the Caprock escarpment; others pushed on to join the Kwahadis on the Staked Plains.

The Anadarko affair separated the hostile from the peaceable elements of the Kiowa and Comanche tribes to the satisfaction of the army. Field operations could now begin in earnest. Sheridan's instructions to his department commanders, Generals Pope and Augur, were general in nature: They were to conduct a campaign similar to his own 1868 offensive, with a combination of aggressive converging movements by separate mounted columns, designed to seek out the Indians and drive them onto the reservations. Nothing should fetter units in the field. Departmental boundaries were to be disregarded, and the reservations were no longer inviolate. Operations were to continue until the hostiles had been soundly defeated. Once subdued, they were to be stripped of their arms and ponies, and their leaders punished. Sheridan was determined to make this the last Indian war on the Southern Plains.

Pope and Augur adopted similar plans independently of one another. From the headquarters of the Department of the Missouri at Fort Leavenworth, General Pope ordered three commands into the field. He accorded the ambitious Col. Nelson A. Miles the principal role, directing him to strike southward into the Indian Territory from Fort Dodge with eight troops of the 6th Cavalry and four companies of his own 5th Infantry. Pope gave Miles wide discretionary authority to act as circumstances might dictate. To operate in conjunction with the main body under Miles, Pope ordered Maj. William R. Price to march east from Forts Union and Bascom in the New Mexico Territory with four troops of the 8th Cavalry. Price was to follow the South Canadian River as far as Antelope Hills, on the rugged eastern fringe of the Staked Plains. There he was to join Miles's column or act independently, as the situation required. A third column, under Lieutenant Colonel Neill, would operate out of the Darlington agency and strike any hostiles that Miles or Price might drive in his direction.

At Department of Texas headquarters in San Antonio, General Augur orchestrated three expeditions of his own. Col. John W. Davidson was to strike westward with six troops of the 10th Cavalry, three companies of the 11th Infantry, and a company of scouts from Fort Sill. Col. George P. Buell would move northeastward from Fort Griffin with four troops of the 9th and two troops of the 10th Cavalry, as well as two companies of the 11th Infantry. The fiery and gifted Col. Ranald Mackenzie, from whom Augur expected the most, would sweep northward from Fort Concho with his crack 4th Cavalry and five companies of infantry. Opposing the six army columns were some twelve hundred Cheyenne, Comanche, and Kiowa warriors, burdened with three times that number of women and children.

Miles drew first blood. Marching south from the Canadian River over a drought-stricken landscape, he clashed with two hundred Cheyenne warriors near Mulberry Creek on August 30. The hostiles gave way slowly, fighting from hill to hill as their ranks gradually swelled to nearly six hundred. Miles followed them into Tule Canyon, flushing them on to the Staked Plains beyond. He tried to resume the pursuit the next day, but his supplies had run out. Reluctantly, he retraced his steps to the Antelope Hills, where an advance supply depot awaited him.

Miles's return march proved a nightmare. Torrential rains swept the plains, temperatures plummeted, and streams that had been dry only a few days earlier overflowed their banks. As he slogged northward, Miles made contact with Price, who likewise was in search of supplies.

The Indians made common cause with nature to harass the soldiers. Kiowas and Comanches driven west after the Anadarko fight fell upon Miles's supply line. On September 9, 250 warriors struck his thirty-six-wagon supply train south of Antelope Hills. The train commander, Capt. Wyllys Lyman, corralled the wagons and deployed the escort—one company of the 5th Infantry and a detachment of the 6th Cavalry—to protect them. After a three-day siege, the warriors broke contact on September 12.

As they drew off, the warriors came upon Scouts Billy Dixon and Amos Chapman and their escort of four cavalrymen en route to Camp Supply with dispatches from Miles. Four of the six men were hit, but they dragged themselves into a shallow buffalo wallow and managed to hold off the circling Indians. Major Price found the men the next day. All but one survived the encounter.

The Lyman wagon train and buffalo wallow fights, combined with the rain and cold, took the spirit out of many of the Kiowas. Woman's Heart surrendered his band at the Darlington agency in October; among them were Satanta and Big Tree, both of whom earnestly wanted peace.

Neither Buell nor Davidson had contributed much to the Indians' discomfiture, and Miles was chained to his camp on the Sweetwater for want of supplies. But there was no respite for the hostiles. Colonel Mackenzie routed a huge Cheyenne, Kiowa, and Comanche encampment in Palo Duro Canyon on September 28. Only three warriors were killed, but Mackenzie captured the entire Indian pony herd and burned all the lodges and camp equipage. Faced with these catastrophic losses, and with winter approaching, many of the hostiles returned to their agencies and surrendered.

Mackenzie kept up the pressure on those still out. For five weeks he dogged the Kwahadis, who had broken into small parties for the winter. Mackenzie's 4th Cavalry visited every Staked Plains water hole known to be frequented by the Kwahadis, breaking up hunting camps and capturing ponies, until exhaustion and the relentless work of the winter "northers" compelled his return to Fort Griffin.

Colonel Buell did his share to demoralize the Indians as well. Working his way up the Salt Fork of Red River, he burned a deserted camp of 75 lodges on October 11, and the next day destroyed an abandoned village of 475 lodges.

Not to be outdone by Mackenzie, Miles took the field again in late October against the Cheyennes. On November 8, a detachment under his most trusted subordinate, Lt. Frank D. Baldwin, swooped down on Gray Beard's camp near the headwaters of McClellan Creek. The Cheyennes fled, and in the abandoned village Baldwin found two young white girls—Adelaide and Julia German, two of four sisters a war party had seized in Kansas two months earlier. As Gray Beard retreated to the northwest, Colonel Davidson took up the chase. He pursued the Cheyennes as far as the Canadian River, where his horses gave out. Sleet and snow killed one hundred animals; with the remainder, Davidson's column went back to Fort Sill.

Colonel Mackenzie broke up his command shortly before Christmas, and Davidson closed his operations on New Year's Eve. But Miles persisted. On January 2, 1875, he embarked on a final swing to the south and west. All trails led to Fort Sill, as Indians by the hundreds were coming in to surrender. When he learned that the two principal Cheyenne bands of Stone Calf and Gray Beard were about to give up, Miles returned to Fort Dodge in early February, ending six months of near-constant field operations.

On March 6, Stone Calf and Gray Beard surrendered to Colonel Neill near the Darlington agency. With the sixteen hundred Cheyennes were the other two German sisters, Catherine and Sophia. The last of the hostile Kiowas had capitulated to Colonel Davidson at Fort Sill a few days earlier.

The final phase of Sheridan's plan was now implemented. The warriors were stripped of their arms and ponies, and the ringleaders were culled for transfer to a Florida military prison. All went smoothly with the Kiowas and Comanches at Fort Sill, but the process was interrupted at the Darlington agency when 150 frightened warriors and a handful of women and children stampeded. Neill sent two troops in pursuit and wired General Pope that the Cheyennes were heading north. From Fort Wallace, Lt. Austin Henely set out with forty troopers from the 6th Cavalry to intercept the fugitives. He found their camp on the North Fork of Sappa Creek and attacked on April 23, killing nineteen warriors and eight women and children.

With this tragic denouement, the Red River War drew to a close. The proud Kwahadis of Quanah Parker surrendered on June 2 to Mackenzie, who confined the warriors only briefly and permitted them to keep five hundred of their horses.

A way of life had ended. The wild tribes of the Southern Plains had been conquered, and they knew it. Before starting for Florida, Chiefs Gray Beard and Minimic had asked their captor, Lt. Richard H. Pratt, to write a letter for them to their Indian agent. It contained this message to their people:

> Your Gray Beard and Minimic want me to write you to tell their people to settle down at their agency and do all that the government requires of them. They say, tell them to plant corn and send their children to school, and be careful not to get in any trouble; that we want them to travel in the white man's road. The white man are as many as the leaves on the trees, and we are only a few people, and we should do as the white man wants us to, and live at peace with him.[10]

PART ONE

Hancock's War and the Medicine Lodge Treaty, 1865–67

The Smoky Hill Route

JULIAN R. FITCH[1] AND ISAAC E. EATON

Junction City (Kansas) *Union,* September 9, 1865

D. A. Butterfield, Superintendent Overland Dispatch:
SIR. I have the honor to report that in compliance with Special
Order No. 143, Headquarters Department of Missouri, dated Fort
Leavenworth, June 9, 1865, I started on the morning of June 13 to
accompany the Butterfield surveying expedition on its route to Denver and the gold mines, via the Smoky Hill River, for the purpose of
testing the feasibility of building a central road directly west from
the Missouri River to the mountains. My party consisted of myself,
Charles H. Fitch and Daniel Clark as assistants; also Abner Coleman
and Joseph Cornell of the United States Signal Corps were detailed
to accompany me.

We joined the expedition, which we found under charge of Isaac
E. Eaton awaiting us at Leavenworth City. We started on the Fort
Riley road and arrived on the twenty-third at Fort Riley, 115 miles
west of Fort Leavenworth, having been detained somewhat by the
immense floods of rain, which had rendered most of the other roads
impassable. We went into camp at this point to await the arrival of
our escort.

The road from the river to this point is located through what is
known as the Kaw River Valley, being for the first fifty miles high
rolling prairie under a fine state of cultivation and intersected at distances ranging from ten to twenty miles with fine streams which are
easily crossed. Directly west of Soldier Creek, at a point just north
of Topeka, the capital of the state, we entered upon the Pottawattomie reserve on the broad bottom of Kaw, following it west thirty
miles, along the line of the Central Pacific road, crossing several fine
streams; we leave the reserve, still keeping up the river, pass through
Louisville on Rock Creek, and Manhattan on the Big Blue Fork, fifteen miles east of Riley. At this latter point I was informed it was the
intention of some parties to build a fine bridge. At present there is a

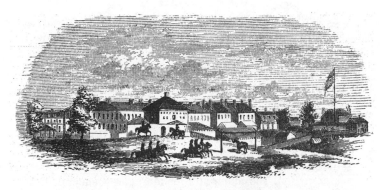

Fort Leavenworth, Kansas.

JOHN W. BARBER, *THE LOYAL WEST IN THE TIMES OF THE REBELLION.*

good ferry in operation. I have recommended to the U.S. government the bridging of all the streams west of the river to this point. Between this point and Fort Riley there are no bridges needed, and indeed, the road is now far superior to any other road leading west from the river.

At Fort Riley we were joined by Major Pritchard with two companies of the 3rd Wisconsin Cavalry under command of Captain Pond. On the morning of July 6 we started on our journey, taking the Fort Larned road. We crossed the Republican fork, which by its junction with the Smoky Hill River at this point forms the Kansas, then bearing a little south of west, across fine benchland lying between the Smoky Hill and Republican. At three miles we came to Junction City, the thriving county seat of Davis County. We here met with a very cordial reception by the inhabitants, who seemed disposed to do all in their power to aid us in our project. Passing through Junction City, we followed the beautiful valley of the Smoky Hill, which grows broader and broader as we leave the Republican; eleven and a half miles west from Junction City we crossed Chapman's Creek on a good rock ford; twelve miles farther west we passed through Abilene, the county seat of Dickinson County, situated on Mud Creek, nine miles west of which we crossed Solomon's Fork (a fine stream which bears southeast one mile into the Smoky Hill) on a ferry owned by Whitley and Hall. The road from this point extends across a high, level bottom formed by the Smoky Hill, the Solomon, and the Saline, extending as far as the eye can reach, skirted on all sides by heavy timbers. Seven miles west of Whitley's Ferry, we cross the Saline River at Woodward's Ferry, and once more touched the banks of Smoky Hill at Salina, the county seat of Saline County, situated on the eastern terminus of the

Great Bend of Smoky Hill. I would here state that I was positively assured by the county officers of Dickinson and Saline Counties that they had issued a sufficient quantity of bonds to secure the speedy erection of substantial structures across the Solomon and Saline Forks, and as I had already recommended to the government to bridge those streams, I think there is no doubt but that they will both be bridged in the course of six months.

The country from Junction City to a point twelve miles on our road west of Salina is the finest stretch of land by far in the West, noted for its heavy timber, its luxuriant grass, and the extraordinary richness of its soil. The country for the most part is under cultivation, and there are today sufficient quantities of corn and other produce to be had either at Junction City or Salina, as well as Abilene, to supply all emigration. This, of course, will increase as emigration increases, and furnishes the farmers with a permanent market.

Still following the old government road thirty-four miles west of Salina, we arrived at Fort Ellsworth, situated at the crossing of the old road on the western terminus of the Great Bend. Here we were joined by two companies of the 13th Missouri Cavalry under command of Captains McMichael and Snell. After resting a day, killing a few buffalo, which we had commenced to find in considerable numbers, we diverged from the old road, bearing a little north of west upon the north side of the Smoky Hill, near our old trail of 1860, which had at this time become entirely obliterated.

Our road from this point lay over a hard stretch of level benchland covered with a luxuriant growth of buffalo grass, intersected every three or four miles with fine streams of water. Our party at this time consisted of Colonel Eaton and his party of constructionists, twenty-six in number; eleven four-mule wagons loaded with tools, reapers, and everything necessary for putting the road in fine condition; Major Pritchard and 250 cavalry as escort; and the Engineer Corps. On July 14, with everything looking fair and all in good spirits, we started on our work. I was accompanied by [my] wife, and Captain West by his.

Five miles west of Fort Ellsworth, we were fairly in the buffalo range, and for miles in every direction as far as the eye could see, the hills were black with these shaggy monsters of the prairie, grazing quietly upon the richest pasture in the world. Should I estimate the number of buffalo to be seen at one view at a million, it would be thought an exaggeration, but better authority than myself has estimated them at millions, or as being greater than all the domestic cattle in America. Truly it has been said that the Smoky Hill is the garden spot and hunting ground of America. Following along on the high, level bench before spoken of, erecting mounds at every station, our route lay over a fine, rich, and fertile soil, with wood, water, grass, and everything necessary to make a good wagon road or railroad.

Finding fine springs as we traveled along, thirty-four miles west of Fort Ellsworth we found a fine coal bed on what we named Coal Creek. Parties that accompanied us on our expedition, and who were capable of judging, pronounced it as being a fine vein and capable of yielding in sufficient quantities to pay for working. Twelve miles farther west we came to Big Creek, a large stream having a beautiful valley with heavy timber. Here we made a good rock ford and erected a large mound and stake for a home and cattle station. We camped here over Sunday and Monday to rest and hunt. During our stay, a party under Lieutenant Bell, whilst exploring in the neighborhood, discovered a vein of coal on the south side of Smoky Hill seven feet in thickness. Specimens of it were brought into camp and gave indications of someday proving a source of great benefit and wealth to this part of the country.

On the morning of the eighteenth we left camp, bearing a little south of west over the same character of country, close to the Smoky (which, at this time, owing to the rains, would have floated a large steamboat), and at a distance of twenty-eight miles we came to a fine, large spring—one of the largest in the West. Fifteen miles farther we bore away from the river, and kept on high, level ground about three miles north of the river, which here makes a southerly bend. On the south side of the river, opposite this point, we discovered high bluffs covered with cedar. Twelve and a half miles west, we camped at the headsprings of a stream emptying south three miles into Smoky Hill. The water and grass at this place we found unusually fine. We called this place Downer Station. Nine miles west, we came to a splendid basin of springs covering an area of one mile square—one of the finest spots on the route. We called it Ruthton. Nine and one-fourth miles farther west, we crossed Rock Castle Creek. Camped two days to rest. The scenery here is really grand. One mile south is a lofty calcareous limestone bluff, having the appearance of an old English castle, with pillars and avenues traversing it in every direction. We named it Castle Rock.

Leaving Castle Rock Creek, we once more bore a little south of west on the divide between the Smoky Hill and the creek, keeping along the bench of Smoky, crossing streams at convenient distances for stations. At a distance of about fifty miles we found the largest springs on the route, situated at Ogallala Creek, in a pleasant valley one-half mile north of the Smoky Hill. Eight miles farther on, we crossed the North Fork, keeping up the south fork. The great difficulty on what was known as the old Pikes Peak road lay in the fact

The railroad bridge over the Kansas River at Topeka.
JOHN W. BARBER, *THE LOYAL WEST IN THE TIMES OF THE REBELLION.*

that emigration kept up this fork, then bore across a divide, eighty-five miles without water, to the Smoky, lengthening their route. We followed the south fork, finding wood, water, and grass all the way. Twenty-eight miles from the forks, we came to a bottom, extending to within two and a half miles of Big Cottonwood Grove, covered with grass six feet high, and containing some splendid springs. This we called the Meadows, and left a reaper in the grass. Two and a half miles west of the Meadows, we camped at Big Cottonwood Grove. This is a grove of large cottonwood trees and used to be a celebrated camping ground for Indians. Sixteen and a half miles west, we reached the Cheyenne well, at the head of the Smoky Hill. This well was built by our party in 1860 and is one of the finest of wells, yielding sufficient water to supply a heavy emigration.

At this point we left the Smoky Hill, bearing southwest across the divide between Smoky Hill and the Sand Branch of the Arkansas. At eleven miles we erected a mound for a well to be dug, and at twenty-one miles came to Eureka Creek. At its junction with the Sandy, here we found a large, living stream of water; also good grass. We bore from this place north of west up the Sandy, seventy miles, to its most northern bend, finding an abundance of water and grass, and some timber, though the latter is scarce.

Fourteen miles west of this point, we had our first view of the mountains, which we had been prevented from seeing on account of clouds. This morning the snow-capped mountains burst upon our view, looming far above the clouds. The long-expected view cheered our boys, and we pushed on with vigor, now that our work seemed almost done and our goal appeared within our reach.

Leaving the Sandy at the bend before mentioned, we bore northwest across the divide, crossing Beaver at nine miles, then the Bijou and Kiowa, with other well-watered streams, and struck the old Taos road at Cherry Creek, nine miles from Denver. This we followed into Denver, where we were received with congratulations. Our trip lasted, after leaving the old road, twenty-four days, six of which we rested. We lost but one mule and one pony, which died of colic.

The advantages of the Smoky Hill route over the Platte or the Arkansas must be apparent to everybody. In the first place it is 116 miles shorter to Denver, making 232 miles on the round trip; and emigration, like a ray of light, will not go around unless there are insurmountable obstacles in the way. In this case the obstructions are altogether on the Platte and Arkansas routes. Aside from the difference in the distance in favor of the new route, you will find no sand on it, whilst from Julesburg to Denver, a distance of 200 miles, the emigration or freighter has a dead pull of sand, without a stick of timber or a drop of living water, save the Platte itself, which is from three to five miles from the road; and when it is taken into consideration that a loaded ox train makes but from twelve to fourteen miles a day, and never exceeds sixteen, it will not pay and will double the distance to drive to the Platte (the only water in the country) for the purpose of camping, and all will admit that the Platte waters are so strongly impregnated with alkali as to render it dangerous to water stock in it. The carcasses now lining the road along the Platte bear evidence to its destructive qualities, whilst on the new route not a particle of this bane can be found.

Another advantage of the new route is that on the Platte from the Junction to Denver, a distance of eighty-five miles, hardly a spear of grass can be found to hide the sandy, desertlike appearance of the route; whilst on the new route an abundance of excellent buffalo grass and grama grass can be found all the way, and the approach to the mountains does not seem to affect it, as all kinds of grass can be found from one end of the route to the other.

On the new route we saw no signs of Indians or, in fact, any signs later than last fall. This can be accounted for from the fact that the Platte and Arkansas routes being so heavily garrisoned, Indians with their natural shrewdness will not wedge themselves into a narrow strip of country entirely surrounded by government troops. In addition to which, I have reason to suppose, in fact I know, that it is the intention of the United States government to protect that route, and I have, in compliance with my instructions, suggested places for U.S. military posts on the route.

Early Denver, Colorado.
JOHN W. BARBER, *THE LOYAL WEST IN THE TIMES OF THE REBELLION.*

In addition to the advantages above enumerated, the new route is located through its entire length along and directly parallel to the Central Pacific Railroad, which is now running daily trains as far as Lawrence, forty miles west of the Missouri River, and I have been confidently informed that the cars will be running as far as Topeka, the state capital, this fall, which will shorten the stage route over the new line 60 miles, making the distance to be traveled by coach but 526 miles, or 126 miles less than by the Platte, and 276 shorter than by the Arkansas, as it is 700 miles from Leavenworth city or Atchison to Denver, by the Platte route, and 800 by the Arkansas.

Further, should emigration ever increase to such an extent as to cause a scarcity of timber, nature has supplied bountifully the Smoky Hill with an abundance of <u>borse de vache,</u> which is always cheerfully chosen by the tired emigrant in preference to cutting timber for a fire.

Accompanying this report you will find a copy of my notes; also a correct map, which I hope will show truly the relative positions of the two routes, as I have endeavored to describe them in this, my report, fairly and impartially, and having just returned by coach over the Platte route, I think I am fully qualified to decide between the two routes.

I am, sir, very respectfully,
Your obedient servant,
JULIAN R. FITCH

Junction City *Union*, September 30, 1865

ELLSWORTH, Sept. 12, 1865

Hon. Thomas Carney, Mayor, Leavenworth City, Kan.:

DEAR SIR—I have returned from Denver, via Smoky Hill River route, to this point with the men, without a military escort [and] without molestation from the Indians or any other sources. Two hundred fifty mules belonging to Butterfield's Overland Dispatch reached here a few days since, with which I returned and stocked the road to Denver. The road has been fully stocked for a daily line from here to Leavenworth, and with the stock I have with me, it will be complete to Denver in fifteen days.

The following is a table of distances on the Smoky Hill route, with the stations from Leavenworth to Denver:

		Miles	Miles
Leavenworth to	Junction City*	—	118
	Herseys	16	—
	Solomon River*	17	—
	Salina*	16	—
	Spring Creek	15	—
Leavenworth to	Ellsworth*	14	196
	Buffalo Creek	14	—
	Lost Creek*	15	—
	Fossil Creek	14	—
	Forks Big Creek*	14	—
	Downer Station	14	—
	Ruthton**	10	81
	Blufton	11	—
	Bridgens Raisin	18	—
	Grannell Spring	12	—
	Chalk Bluffs	13	—
	Monuments*	14	—
	Four Crossings	12	—
	Eaton**	11	91
	Henshaw's Springs	13	—
	Pond's Creek*	11	—
	Fitch's Meadows*	14	—
	Blue Mound Creek	9	—
	Cheyenne Wells*	13	—
	Eureka Creek	21	—
	Dubois*	13	—
	Cornell Creek**	11	105
	Coon Creek	12	—

	Miles	Miles
Hedinger's Lake*	18	—
Big Bend Sandy	10	—
Reed's Springs*	17	—
Beaver Creek	10	66
Bijou Basin**	12	539
Box Elder	10	—
Parkhurst*	11	—
Cherry Valley	14	—
Denver	14	—
Total distance, Leavenworth to Denver		688

The stations designated by one star are home stations, and those by two stars, cattle and home stations. At the home stations, passengers procure their meals and are always kept by a family. At the cattle stations, trains change their cattle and drivers the same as horses and mules are changed on a mail and passenger line.

The cattle stations are selected with reference to the large quantities of hay that can be procured in their immediate neighborhoods. At all the cattle stations, the amount of hay that can be procured is limitless, and along the whole route there is [an] abundance of grass and watering places.

At fifteen of the stations named, there are large springs of water, varying from five to twenty feet in depth, and these springs or pools formed from the springs are filled with bass and other panfish sufficient to supply all the demands of the stations. There is no alkali whatever on the route, and if all the sand (include the crossings of streams) was put together, it would not reach five miles. The roadbed itself is the best natural one I have ever seen, and I fail to do the Smoky Hill route justice when I say it is one hundred percent superior to either the Platte or Arkansas routes in every respect. I have no doubt of the verification of my prediction when I say that in twelve months from now, there will not be a wheel turn destined for Colorado, New Mexico, and Utah from St. Joseph and points south of it except by this route.

The Butterfield Overland Dispatch Company is making arrangements to build a road from Pond's Creek on the Denver route, via Fort Lyon and the McFerren Trail to Santa Fe, and thus save one hundred miles in distance over the route now traveled between Leavenworth and New Mexico. The company will also during the coming season extend their Denver route via Berthoud's Pass, over the Rocky Mountain range—the Middle Park, down White and up the Uinta Rivers, through Provo Canyon to Fort Crittenden, and thence to Salt Lake City.

This route, the Smoky Hill, is the natural track for the Pacific railroad and the only one in which the people of Kansas, Missouri, and the middle and central states are particularly interested.

This company is erecting the most substantial kind of buildings for stations, and also bridges over all the streams and ravines. The stations are frame made of yellow pine timber, one and a half stories high, thirty-two by sixteen feet in front, and kitchen attached eighteen by twenty feet. The stabling is made of the same material and substantiability. These will all be completed by the first of November. The stations and bridges from the Saline west are all framed in the pine ties near Parkhurst Station and in close proximity to the sawmills of Colorado and shipped down the road by the returning freight trains of the company, and are erected at less expense per station than the miserable hovels erected on the Platte route.

As Leavenworth City has always felt a deep interest in the opening of the Smoky Hill route, and has contributed liberally towards it, I have thus given you, as the official head of the city, as briefly as I could, the position of the route now and Butterfield's Overland Dispatch in relation to it. You will please furnish the Times, Bulletin, and Conservative this letter for publication, and oblige.

Yours truly,
ISAAC E. EATON

Eleventh Indiana Cavalry in Kansas in 1865

FRANK DOSTER[1]

Collections of the Kansas State Historical Society 15 (1919–22): 524–29

I first saw Kansas in the summer of 1865. The wind of chance that blew me into the state that early time was an erratic gust from the calming tempest of the Civil War.

At the close of the war, my regiment, the 11th Indiana Cavalry—my whole brigade, in fact—was sent from Mississippi for service on the western plains. The 3rd Illinois went up into Dakota; the 12th Missouri elsewhere; my own command went out on the Santa Fe Trail in Kansas. Newly mounted and armed at St. Louis, we rode through the Ozark hills of Missouri, through Rolla, Sedalia, and smaller towns, crossing the line into Kansas at the now unknown hamlet of Little Santa Fe, thence through Olathe, Lawrence, Topeka, Fort Riley, and Council Grove, the last then the jumping-off place of civilization into the great mysterious land of legend and adventure. Beyond was distance and sunset only.

May an old soldier's vanity be pardoned for pausing at this introduction to his story to indulge in the reminiscence, and irrelevance too, of the printed notice given his command on its entrance into the state.

Said the Lawrence *Tribune* of July 2, 1865:

> The 11th Indiana Cavalry passed through our city en route from Rolla, Missouri, to Fort Riley. They are a fine body of men, somewhat tattered and worn by long marches and the smoke of hard-fought battles; and as they marched through our streets led by their gallant colonel, [Abram] Sharra, presented an imposing appearance. This regiment was with General Wilson before Nashville and thence through the southern Confederacy, and has made a splendid record.

Why we came to Kansas, we could only conjecture. The common soldier never knows why he is sent, and not always does the highest of his officers. Our supposition was we were ordered out in anticipation of an Indian uprising. Some said (an improbable story) we were to be held in readiness to move

across the Rio Grande to repel the Maximilian invasion of Mexico; but whatever the object of our going, the services thus conjectured were not performed.
There was no Indian uprising save some desultory marauding up north on the
Platte; nor were we sent to Mexico. Looking back now in the light of an event
presently to be noted, my supposition is our business was to take part in what
the military strategists call "a demonstration in force"—an armed parade to
impress the Indians with the fact that he "was up agin it." He had been troublesome during the war, and there now being troops to spare, the design was to
scare him—lick him, if need be—into good behavior.

A general condition of apprehension of the Indians existed throughout the
trans-Missouri country. Fanciful rumors were spread, and fantastic stories having small foundation in fact were told. The Leavenworth *Daily Conservative* of
July 1 stated that

> a letter from Senator Doolittle[2] at Fort Larned to the Hon. James Har-
> lan, secretary of the interior, expresses apprehension of an extensive
> Indian war on the upper Arkansas. The Cheyennes, Kiowas,
> Comanches, and Arapahos, numbering five to seven thousand war-
> riors, are banded together to make war on the exposed settlements.
> The senator believes that peace can be made with the chiefs if justice
> is done them. They have lost confidence in the whites from the cow-
> ardly butchery of the Cheyennes on Lance Creek, an affair in which
> the blame was on our side.

June 17 the Junction City *Union* said, "Indian attacks on the Santa Fe
Trail all the way from Zarah to Dodge, capturing a wagon train and killing a
couple of drivers." July 18 the same paper reported, "On the Santa Fe Trail
eighteen miles east of Cow Creek, five soldiers, dispatch bearers belonging to
the 13th Missouri Cavalry and 2nd Colorado Cavalry, were found killed and
scalped." These were false reports, but August 2 the Leavenworth *Conservative* published what really was a substantially truthful item: "On the North
Platte west of Fort Laramie, the 11th Kansas and 11th Ohio were attacked by
Sioux, Cheyennes, Arapahos, Blackfeet, and Comanches, and a number were
killed and wounded." However, on the tenth of the same month, the *Conservative* gave credence to the following extravagant estimate of the troops mobi-
lized for the demonstration in force: "There are now about 12,000 cavalry at
Fort Larned preparatory to a grand hunt after the predatory redskins, who have
been so long the terror of emigrants on the plains." We rode through the camp
at Larned twice, first in July and next a few days before the date of the above
item, and there were not twelve hundred, if that many, troops there. That these
newspaper reports were in the main hysterical exaggeration is evident.

Viewing it now in the perspective of two generations of time, what seems to
me the greatest excursion that could then be taken by a tough, healthy boy was
a summer's horseback ride out the Santa Fe Trail on the Arkansas. Blazing hot

it was, dusty from the tramp of innumerable hoofs and the rolling of many wheels; but on each side of the worn track of travel were the freedom of the unfenced greensward and the stretches of limitless distance. There, too, was restful sleep with the bare grass for a couch and the stars for covering, the opal and crimson sunrise of morning, the shimmering heat of day with its curious and deceptive mirage, the gorgeous sunsets of red and gold, seen only on the open plains and open sea, followed again by the untroubled oblivion of night. Then, too, there was the dramatic sense of adventure, pleasing to a boy of ardent disposition—a sort of fanciful, make-believe challenge to the fates that might be lurking just out of sight on the nearby stretches of the plains.

Buffalo there were, seemingly by the million. We first struck into them about what is now the line between Marion and McPherson Counties and, day or night, were not out of sight of them the entire journey. At various places along the trail, companies or other detachments were dropped off to do escort duty for the mail coaches and trains of merchandise wagons bound for Santa Fe and other points. Most of my own company were left at Moore's ranch in the northwest corner of Marion County, where the trail crossed the headwaters of the Cottonwood. By some mischance, as I then thought it, several of us continued on with the main command until it dwindled down to scattering details from several companies. How far we went, and why we went, are unknown to me to this day; but we went, seemingly at courier speed, past Forts Zarah, Larned, Dodge, to Lyons and beyond and, halting overnight, turned back the next morning and retraced our way to our respective companies. Nearly a month was consumed in the journey out and back. I suppose we were dispatch bearers and had a message to deliver to someone about something. There were other soldiers all along the trail as far as we went, and why our message was not carried by relays of riders from one camp to the next was one of the inscrutable things of military orders.

The morning we turned back on our journey, [there] occurred a mirage of an unusual and interesting kind. We distinctly saw, elevated above the plain, a collection of adobe houses and corrals. We knew the name of the illusion, but not the name of the place. Someone said it was Santa Fe, and in our Wabash ignorance of the geography of the West, we accepted the idea as true. It probably was Trinidad, possibly Pueblo, each of which then had a cowboy and Mexican existence.

The Kansas newspapers of 1865 were not only given to sensational stories of Indian raids and scalpings, but to tales about the resources and riches of the state, particularly its distant and unsettled parts, so fantastic as to appear ludicrous to us now. One which appeared in the Junction City *Union* of September 2, probably in the newspapers of the state generally, stated that "the Butterfield exploring party on the Smoky Hill route discovered a vein of coal along the Smoky Hill seven feet thick, extending for sixty-five or seventy miles. The supply to all appearances seems inexhaustible. There are also acres upon acres of iron ore. The mineral wealth of the extreme western part of this state is of immense value." How seriously this grotesque yarn was received, we have no means of knowing.

Glad indeed were we when the tiresome journey up the Arkansas and back was ended, but we had not more than comfortably settled ourselves in camp when another trip, though a shorter one, was entered on.

One hot August afternoon, some dignitaries riding in a government ambulance, one or two dressed in military uniform, came in on the trail from the east and, after staying overnight, were furnished with an escort to go somewhere. As ill luck had it, so I thought, I was one of the detail. A soldier never agrees that it is his turn to do duty. The sergeant has made a mistake or has it in for him, so he thinks. Had I known where we were going and why, and could have looked forward along the path of the years to come, I would have gladly accepted the service. We were going to meet the chiefs of the Plains tribes of Indians to effect a treaty to make the great green prairies stretching to the west safe for the white man's travel and habitation. However, we started ignorant and unwilling, and only after our arrival came to know the object of our going. Even the little lieutenant commanding the escort, whose dashing lead we had followed on many a bushwhacking raid, rode morose and inwardly insubordinate at being sent no telling where, to do no knowing what, to return no guessing when.

Two days' ride brought us to the junction of the Big and Little Arkansas Rivers, where Wichita now stands. To what transpired there I was not, of course, a party—was not even a witness except as my uninformed and incurious eyesight glanced out over a dirty herd of blanket Indians, a hundred or more in number, a few frontier scouts, two or three military officers, and one or two in civilian clothes. These, together with my own party of fifteen or twenty and a company or two of soldiers already on the ground, made up the aggregation, besides which, though not all immediately present, were the Wichitas, a peaceful tribe about a thousand in number, scattered up the valley.

In a vague, uninterested way, I came to understand that our officers were holding a treaty conference with the chiefs, but to what precise end I didn't hear; and had I heard, would not have cared. Someone said the ambassador we had escorted down was General Sanborn[3]—and it really was he, so I have since learned by reading—but I didn't care; I had seen a score of generals higher than he. Someone said Kit Carson was there. I don't think he was; but if so, he was only a name to me. Indians—even chiefs—had been common sights for many weeks past, so I lay on the grass under the shade of the cottonwoods and fought flies and cussed the powwow for not hurrying through to an end.

A few words in excuse of my ignorance and indifference. I was a boy, scant eighteen years old. I had been away from home more than a year and a half. The war was over and I wanted to return. But a short while back, I had been where the drama of great events was played. I had seen the blossoming flags of ten thousand on parade and had heard the "shouting of the captains." A convocation of filthy Indian bucks grunting a jargon I could not understand, about something I did not know, consuming the time I wanted to put in going home, was not of a nature to excite my interested attention. It had in it neither the thrill of adventure nor the charm of sightseeing.

Only one thing do I remember with distinctness. They told of one of the scouts, then present, who unaccompanied had gone out on the prairies among the wild Indians with a message for them to come to the conference. It was thought to be a daring venture, as it must have been, because recently the red devils had been much in the mood to go on the warpath and had given no assurance of safety to the white man's envoys. Years afterwards, relating the story to George Coble, an old Kansas pioneer, himself a participant in the events of the time, he told me the man's name was Charley Rath; "the bravest man of all the plains," he said. This Charley Rath was he who a few years afterwards settled down to the prosaic life of a village storekeeper, going into partnership with Bob Wright, another old-timer, at Dodge City.

Of course, it is not possible for me now to pick out from among the industrial plants and skyscraper buildings or the pleasant homes and tree-bordered streets of Wichita the spot where our tents were pitched, but it was on the east bank of Little River, and must have been about opposite the park, because over there was most of the shade, and the officers and Indians and interpreters monopolized that ground. Somebody—I don't know who, most likely Bill Griffenstein—kept a frontier trading store there, but having no taste for his firewater, nor, in fact, any money to buy that or anything else, I didn't learn about him or his place. In about a week, perhaps less time, we returned to our camp at Cottonwood crossing.

What was done at the meeting I only know from reading. I supposed we had effected a treaty with the Indians. That was what everybody who didn't know said. It turned out, however, that the paper signed was not a formal treaty, but a preliminary agreement to meet at a later date and negotiate a treaty. In the report of the commissioner of Indian affairs for 1865 will be found an epitomized statement of the results of the conference, made by General Pope[4] to Secretary of the Interior Harlan:

ST. LOUIS, August 21, 1865

General Sanborn reports that on the fifteenth instant he met the chiefs and headsmen of the Comanches, Kiowas, Arapahos, and Apaches[5] at the mouth of the Little Arkansas. He gives his opinion that this is the end of hostilities south of the Arkansas River. In conformity with the above arrangement, I suggest the immediate appointment of commissioners to meet the Indians at the time and place specified.

I was not present at the making of the formal treaty. Before that time, my command was returned home. For some reason, the meeting for the treaty proper was not [*sic*] held on October 4, at a point said to be "six miles above the mouth of the Little Arkansas."

An important stipulation of the treaty—the most important, indeed—was an agreement by the Indians to abandon all the region between the Platte and the Arkansas Rivers. This area was subsequently enlarged until all the tribes were located in what is now Oklahoma.

There are few now living who can connect their lives with the Wichita of the middle sixties, nor even the next few years. To those who can, memory holds no nobler sight than the great circle of primeval wild which there converged. There never was a panorama that excelled the valleys of the two Arkansas rivers in their virgin sod. The present generation has a landscape, the only one it has ever seen, made over from that of the earlier day, but one so different as to be unrecognizable in comparison with it, and one, too, which will change but little as the years go by. For those of this later time, there are orchards, and groves of trees, and hedged fields, and fruitful farms, churches, schools, swift highways of travel, electric lines, all the conveniences and arts of the world's highest civilization, and the security and peace of an established order. For us of the sixties, there are in memory the waving grass, the billowing prairie sea, the illusive mirages, cooling shade and water, the lordly buffalo and the nimble antelope, the coyote's dismal howl, the sinister and uncertain red man, the tiresome and dusty trail across the plains, the expansiveness of soul which a gaze on illimitable distance gives, and that voiceless "call of the wild" heard by the primal instinct of the race. In which of these contrasting environments the higher gratification can be found I would not undertake to say. Certainly the nobler purpose can be wrought in the former one, and it is with some degree of satisfaction that I can claim to have been a witness, at least, though not performing any conspicuous part, in events which made for the civilization that presently grew into the great state of Kansas and the great city of Wichita.

The Indians

WINFIELD S. HANCOCK[1]

Army and Navy Journal 5, no. 3 (September 7, 1867): 43

The following extracts from letters from General Hancock and others give additional information on the Indian question.

On March 13 last General Hancock addressed a letter to Colonel Wynkoop,[2] agent for the Cheyennes, Apaches, and Arapahos, at Fort Larned, Kansas, in which he says:

> I have the honor to send you this communication for the purpose of informing you that I have about completed arrangements to move a force to the plains, and only await a proper condition of the roads to march. My object in making an expedition at this time is to show the Indians within the limits of this department that we are able to chastise any tribes who may molest people who are traveling across the plains. It is not my desire to bring on difficulties with the Indians, but to treat them with justice and according to our treaty stipulations, and I desire especially in my dealings with them to act through their agents as far as practicable. In reference to the Cheyennes of your agency in particular, I may say that we have just grounds of grievance. One is that they have not delivered up the murderer of the New Mexican at Zarah. I also believe that I have evidence sufficient to fix upon different bands of that tribe whose chiefs are known to have been in several of the outrages committed on the Smoky Hill last summer. I request that you will inform them in such a manner as you may think proper that I expect shortly to visit their neighborhood, and that I will be glad to have an interview with their chiefs; and tell them also, if you please, that I go fully prepared for peace or war, and that hereafter I will insist on their keeping off the main lines of travel, where their presence is calculated to bring about collision with the whites. If you can prevail upon the Indians of your agency to abandon their habits of infesting the country traversed by our overland routes, threatening, robbing, and intimidating travelers,

Winfield S. Hancock as a major general of volunteers.
CENTURY MAGAZINE 1886.

we will defer that matter to you. If not, I would be pleased by your presence with me when I visit the locality of your tribes, to show that the officers of the government are acting in harmony.

Maj. H. Douglass,[3] under date of March 14, writes to Maj. Henry E. Noyes:[4]

I have received from Little Raven, head chief of the Arapahos,[5] a message to the effect that no more wood must be cut by this command on the Pawnee Fork, and that the troops must move out of the country by the time the grass grows. Mr. [F. F.] Jones, the interpreter at this post, brought me a message from Satanta, the principal chief of the Kiowas,[6] to the effect that all white men must move out of Council Grove by the spring; that he gave me ten days to move from this post; that he wanted the mules and cavalry horses fattened, as he would have use for them, as he intended to appropriate them; that all the Indians had agreed to stop the railroads and roads at Council Grove; that no roads or railroads would be allowed west of that point. Capt. J. H. Page, 3rd Infantry,[7] brought me a message from the same chief: "Tell the chiefs on the road that they must gather their soldiers and leave; if they do not I will help them to leave. No wagons will be allowed on the road except those that bring presents; if any are found they will be taken." Subsequently, in council Satanta stated in substance the same, but not in the insulting manner which has already been reported to the district headquarters. It has also been reported to me that eight Arapahos, apparently friendly, stopped on the tenth at the camp of a Mr. Gilchrist, a wagon master for a Mr. H. Wadello of Moro, New Mexico, on the other side of Fort Aubrey, 125 miles from here, shot at the herder, and ran off forty head of mules and one mare.

One of the letters above referred to by General Hancock acquaints Colonel Wynkoop that the object in preparing an expedition to the plains is to convince the Indians that we are able to punish any of them who may molest travelers across the plains, or who may commit other hostilities against the whites. He says:

We desire to avoid any trouble with them and to treat them with justice according to the requirements of treaties with them, and I wish specially in my dealings with them to act through the agents of the Indian Department as far as it is possible to do so. Concerning the Kiowas of your agency, we have grave reasons for complaint. Among others, it is officially reported to these headquarters that that tribe has been making hostile incursions into Texas, and that a war party has very recently returned to Fort Dodge from that state, bringing with them the scalps of fourteen colored soldiers and one white man. I am also informed that the Kiowas have been threatening our posts in Arkansas; that they are about entering into a compact with the Sioux for hostilities against us, and that they have robbed and insulted officers of the United States Army who have visited them, supposing that they were friends. It is well ascertained that certain members of that tribe (some of whom are known) are guilty of the murder of James Box, a citizen of Montague County, Texas, last summer, and of the capture and barbarous treatment of women in his family. I desire you to particularly explain to them that one reason why the government does not at once send troops against them to redress these outrages against our people is that their Great Father is averse to commencing a war upon them (which would certainly end in destroying them) until all other means of redress fail. I request that you will inform the Indians of your agency that I will hereafter insist upon their keeping off the main routes of travel across the plains, where their presence is calculated to bring about difficulties between themselves and the whites. If you, as their agent, can arrange these matters satisfactorily with them, we will be pleased to refer the whole subject to you. In case of your inability to do so, I would be pleased to have you accompany me when I visit the country of your tribes, to show that the officers of the government are acting in harmony. I will be pleased to talk with any of the chiefs whom you may meet.

A large number of other documents show the hostile character of the Indians and their massacres and depredations. General Ord,[8] in a communication dated March 5, says, "The wild Comanches are bent on mischief. From the fact that they steal from the frontier and have supplied themselves with large caballadas,[9] that they supply horses to the northern Indians on the mail routes, I think it important to put a stop to their wholesale plundering. I propose building posts in their country, as that demoralizes them more than anything else except money and whiskey."

Among the documents is a letter from General Hancock, dated Fort Leavenworth, Kansas, July 31, 1867, addressed to headquarters of the army of the United States, in which he says he has the honor to acknowledge the receipt of certain communications named by him, and continues:

In reply to the letters of Colonels Wynkoop and Leavenworth herein referred to, and to a telegram dated May 23, 1867, from General Grant, upon the subject of the burning of the Indian villages at Pawnee Fork, April 29, 1867, I have the honor to submit the following statement, first premising that I have replied to General Grant's telegram of May 23[10] by a telegram of the same date, and that in my official report of the operations of the expedition made last spring to the plains under my command, forwarded to General Grant by General Sherman, a full and accurate history is given of the objects of that expedition and the military movements connected with it, together with my reasons for destroying the villages of the Sioux and Cheyennes on the Pawnee Fork.

The report in question touches on all the main points mentioned in the copies of the letters from Colonels Wynkoop and Leavenworth, referred to me by General Grant, May 23, 1867, and is believed to be sufficiently full in details to cover the questions mentioned therein; yet there are a few statements made in some of them which are inaccurate, and which I desire to correct. They are as follows:

Among the letters enclosed is a copy of one from Colonel Wynkoop, dated Headquarters, District of the Upper Arkansas, March 14, 1867, stating that "Wilson Graham, the Cheyenne boy who was captured from that tribe some time since, is now en route to this post (Fort Riley). As soon as he arrives he will be sent to you, in order that he may be delivered to his nearest relatives. Please inform this office of the name and band of his nearest relatives."

No authority was ever given by me to the commanding officer of the District of the Upper Arkansas to transfer the child in question to any agent of the Indian department whatever. On the contrary, I informed the commanding officer at Fort Larned, through headquarters, District of the Arkansas, in a letter dated these headquarters, March 11, 1867, that the boy in question, who was then under my charge at Fort Leavenworth, would be sent to that post (Fort Larned) for delivery to his nearest relatives, and that he had been obtained from the persons who had had possession of him since his capture through the exertions of the military authorities, this action on my part being in accordance with the instructions I had received on that subject from headquarters, Military Division of the Missouri, in a special order dated St. Louis, Mo., February 23, 1867. The boy being too unwell to travel as soon as was anticipated, I detained him here until I started with the expedition to the plains, March 25, when he accompanied me, and was delivered by me to the commanding officer at Fort Larned, leaving him with the following instructions:

HEADQUARTERS, DEPARTMENT OF THE MISSOURI,
NEAR FORT LARNED, KANSAS, April 12, 1866
To the Commanding Officer, Fort Larned:
SIR: On leaving the camp it is the intention of the major general commanding to place in your charge the Cheyenne boy now in his possession known by the name of Wilson Graham. You will retain him until an opportunity presents for the delivery of him to his nearest relative. His mother is said to be living, and is said to belong to the Black Kettle band. When you deliver him to his relatives, you will take a receipt for him. I am, sir, very respectfully, your obedient servant,

W. G. MITCHELL,
Captain and Acting Assistant Adjutant General

In a conversation which I had with Colonel Wynkoop on this subject while I was at Fort Larned, I informed him that my instructions required me to deliver the boy to his nearest relations through the military authorities, and not through the Indian agents.

A copy of a letter from Colonel Leavenworth,[11] United States Indian agent for the Comanches and Kiowas, to the Hon. N. G. Taylor, commissioner of Indian affairs, dated April 9, 1867, states that he (Colonel Leavenworth) was directed by instructions from the Indian bureau to proceed to St. Louis to receive from General Sherman Wilson Graham, the Cheyenne boy in question, and to deliver him to Colonel Wynkoop at Fort Larned. Upon his arrival at St. Louis, General Sherman informed me that the child had been sent to me with instructions to deliver him to the Cheyennes in the presence of the agent. These instructions would have been carried out while I was present at Fort Larned had the band of Cheyennes to which his relatives belonged (Black Kettle) been in that country at the time. It was reported to be in Texas, and I left the boy with the commanding officer at Fort Larned with instructions before referred to. Shortly after that time (April 16) the Cheyennes commenced the present war against us, which has thus far rendered the delivery of the child to his friends impracticable.

In the letter of Colonel Wynkoop, dated at my headquarters on Pawnee Fork, April 18, 1867, addressed to the Hon. N. G. Taylor, commissioner of Indian affairs, he states that a courier had arrived in my camp from Colonel Custer[12] (then in pursuit of the Sioux and Cheyennes from Pawnee Fork) with the information that the Cheyennes had turned and gone toward the Arkansas River, while the Sioux had continued northward. He followed the Sioux trail, and the last dispatch from him (Colonel Custer) is to the effect that the Sioux, upon crossing the Smoky Hill road, had destroyed a mail station and killed three men.

Colonel Wynkoop then goes on to state that, as there was yet no evidence of the Cheyennes having committed any overt act of hostility, he made an appeal to me to preserve the village belonging to that tribe, as it was distinct from that of the Sioux.

There is no evidence in Colonel Custer's report of the pursuit of the Sioux and Cheyennes from the village on the Pawnee Fork, which would go to prove that they had separated or that the Cheyennes were not implicated in the killing and burning of the three men at Lookout Station on April 15, and burning of the station; on the contrary, in Colonel Custer's report to Bvt. Maj. Gen. A. J. Smith, commanding District of the Upper Arkansas, of April 19, received after the destruction of the village and too late to be considered in that connection, in reference to the outrage at Lookout Station on the Smoky Hill, he says expressly that, after a careful examination by himself and the Delaware scouts who were with him, it was found impracticable to discover the slightest clue as to what tribe had committed the act, but says in his report to General Smith of April 17 that the outrages were certainly committed by the Indians who abandoned the village on Pawnee Fork. They were a portion of the same body of Indians, about eight hundred strong, who crossed the Smoky Hill road on April 16 and reported themselves to be Sioux, Cheyennes, and Pawnees. They were all stripped and painted for war at that time, and in addition to the previous killing and burning at Lookout Station, they fired into Stony Hollow mail station and ran off stock from that point belonging to the mail company; threatened the mail station east of Stony Hollow, and ran off stock belonging to the Union Pacific railway, Eastern District, a few miles further north.

Lt. Col. George A. Custer.

NELSON A. MILES, *PERSONAL RECOLLECTIONS AND OBSERVATIONS.*

My official report of the operations of the expedition last spring shows conclusively that I did not determine to destroy the Indian villages until I had learned officially of the outrage committed on the Smoky Hill by the Indians (Sioux and Cheyennes) who had treacherously left their camps on Pawnee Creek on April 14, or during the previous night.

In none of the reports which were received from Colonel Custer of his pursuit of the Indians from Pawnee Fork was there any facts going to show that the Cheyennes had left the Sioux and gone south. All of the information contained in the dispatches of Colonel Custer at that time was to the effect that the Indians from Pawnee Fork (Sioux and Cheyennes) remained together, with probably a few exceptional small bands, until they arrived at the Smoky Hill, when they committed the murders and depredations on the mail stations and then pursued their flight northward.

In reference to the statement of Colonel Wynkoop that the village of the Cheyennes was distinct from that of the Sioux, I can only say that the villages stood upon the same ground, and I was unable after an inspection which I made in person to distinguish with any certainty the lodges of the Cheyennes from those of the Sioux; nor could any of the officers who were with me say positively where the line of separation between the villages commenced, although it was understood that the Sioux were on the north side and the Cheyennes on the southern and eastern sides.

It is not seen on what grounds "the Indians became fully impressed with the belief that General Hancock had come for the purpose of murdering their women and children, as had been previously done at Sand Creek." (See same letter from Colonel Wynkoop to Hon. N. G. Taylor of April 18, 1867.) Nothing which I said to the Sioux and Cheyenne chiefs whom I had met at Larned on April 12, nor at the meeting near the villages on the fourteenth of that month, could have led the Indians to such a conclusion or have given them apprehensions of such murderous inclinations on my part, for I had certainly assured them that my intentions were peaceful and that I had only marched into their country for the purpose of having a conference with the different tribes, so that they might have a full and just understanding of the views and intentions of the military authorities in reference to their future conduct and their interference with the railways and other routes of travel, emigrants passing through that country, and the treatment of our frontier settlers. Such were well known to Colonels Wynkoop and Leavenworth to be the objects of the expedition, and they constantly assured the Indians, when in my presence, that my intentions were peaceful, and it was not until after the hostilities on the Smoky Hill subsequent to their abandonment of the village on Pawnee Fork, which compelled me to destroy their village, that the assertions were made that the Indians had actually been forced into a war. (See Colonel Wynkoop's letter of April 21 to Hon. N. G. Taylor, commissioner of Indian affairs.)

While on the subject, it is proper to state that none knew better than Colonels Wynkoop and Leavenworth that I did not march to the plains last spring for the purpose of commencing a war with the Indians, for before my departure from Fort Leavenworth I had written to each of them, informing them of my instructions and of the objects of the expedition, and stating that no Indians would be arrested or called to account by me for past outrages and depredations unless upon the application of the agents themselves.[13] In his letters of April 21 and 24, the first from Fort Dodge, the latter from Fort Larned, Colonel Wynkoop again reiterates the statement that the village of the Cheyennes on Pawnee Fork was burned without provocation or any overt acts on the part of that tribe. Notwithstanding, he must surely have known when he was at Fort Dodge with me, from the reports which I had received from Colonel Custer, the contents of which were made known to him, and these were the only possible sources of information at that time, that the Cheyennes generally had not gone south of the Arkansas when they deserted the villages at Pawnee Fork, but had fled north of the Smoky Hill with the Sioux, and were parties with the latter to the murders and burning at Lookout Station and the other outrages committed on the Smoky Hill about the same time. I consider the evidence as to the participation of the Cheyennes in the massacre of Lookout Station and the depredations on the Smoky Hill after they had abandoned the village on Pawnee Fork, contained in Colonel Custer's reports of his pursuit of the Cheyennes and Sioux, conclusive and beyond question, their conduct on that occasion being, in my opinion, only a continuation of the outrages which they had been previously committing against the whites in this department ever since I had assumed command of it in August 1866.

To show the temper of the Cheyennes toward us, and the feelings of hostility which animated them before the expedition to the plains last spring, I enclose herewith the reports of former outrages perpetrated summer and fall, with evidence which it is considered fixes the guilt of these outrages upon that tribe beyond any question of doubt:

September 19, 1866—A party of savages ran off fourteen horses and two mules.[14]

September 29, 1866—Two employees of the Overland Mail Company murdered at Chalk Bluff mail station.

October 12, 1866—A band of Indians burned the mail station at Chalk Bluffs.

November 10, 1866—An unprovoked murder of a New Mexican was committed at Fort Zarah by a Cheyenne, Fox Tail, a son of Medicine Arrow, a prominent man of that tribe. That murder has never been denied even by the Cheyennes.

I also enclose a copy of a statement from Mr. John Smith, United States Indian interpreter, dated July 14, 1867, in reference to the killing of six white men by the Cheyennes in the month of June 1866 on one of the tributaries of Solomon's Fork; and a copy of a letter dated February 22, 1867, from Mr. F. R. Page, United States agent for the Kansas Indians, stating that about January 1, 1867, a part of the Cheyennes attached to Kaw Chief (Katiaugah) captured forty-four horses and wounded one man. I have also on record at my headquarters the official report of various outrages and depredations committed before the present war by other tribes belonging to the agencies of Colonels Wynkoop and Leavenworth—Arapahos, Kiowas, and Comanches—some of which Indians themselves, when in council with me last spring, acknowledged to have been justly charged to them. The reports in all such cases were promptly reported by me to the Indian Department as soon as they were received, and though I had constantly informed the department through the agents that I was ready to assist them with the troops under my command in arresting the offenders, I have never in a single instance been called upon to render such assistance, and in all cases (even in that of the murder of the New Mexican at Zarah, when the name of the culprit was known), the guilty ones have been permitted to go unpunished.

Colonel Wynkoop's letter of April 21 also contains the following: "I have just arrived with General Hancock's column at the post—Fort Dodge—and learn since my arrival here a few days ago that six Cheyenne Indians on foot were attacked by 135 cavalry about twenty-five miles west of this post, and all of them killed. I also learn that they had done nothing to provoke an attack, but were of the party that had fled before Hancock's approach."

In reply to this passage, I will merely quote that portion of my official report which referred to this matter. It contains the facts, which I drew from the report of the late Maj. W. Cooper, 7th Cavalry, who commanded the detachment which had the encounter at the Cimarron Crossing[15] with the Indians referred to in Colonel Wynkoop's letter:

On my arrival there (Fort Dodge) on April 19, a party of Cheyennes (evidently runners from the north) had approached the Cimarron Crossing and were discovered skulking around the bivouac of a detachment of the 7th Cavalry, which was at that point under command of Maj. Wickliffe Cooper of that regiment. When the Indians were perceived, they were endeavoring to steal up on some herders, who were in charge of the cattle of the command; it is supposed they were not aware of the presence of the troops. Major Cooper directed Lieutenant Berry of the 7th Cavalry, with twenty men, to advance and demand the surrender, which was done through the interpreter. In reply, the Indians fired upon the troops. They were attacked and pursued across the river, and six of them, all that were seen, were killed. One of our men was wounded and one horse killed.

In concluding this letter, it is proper for me to say again that before the expedition of last spring set out, I informed Agents Wynkoop and Leavenworth fully of its object, telling them that war was not intended against the Indians, and that it was my earnest desire to act through them in all matters connected with the tribes under their agencies. I also invited them to accompany me on my march from Fort Larned to Fort Dodge, so that they might be present at my interviews with the chiefs of the various tribes and hear what I had to say to them during the time they were in my camp. They must have observed that all of my conferences were with a view of preserving peace on the plains, and all of my actions friendly until the treachery of the Sioux and Cheyennes at Pawnee Fork, and the murders and depredations committed by them on the Smoky Hill route after they ran away from their village, compelled me to take hostile measures against them.

It is worthy of remark in this connection that while in my camp, Colonel Leavenworth stated to me in conversation that the tribes of his agency had been greatly wronged by having been charged with various offenses which had been committed by the Indians of Colonel Wynkoop's agency. In the opinion of Colonel Leavenworth, as expressed to me, the Indians of Colonel Wynkoop's agency, especially the Cheyennes, deserved severe punishment for their numerous misdeeds, very many of which had been laid at the door of his innocent tribes (the Comanches and the Kiowas). But Colonel Wynkoop informed me in conversation, about the same time, that the Arapahos, [Kiowa-]Apaches, and especially the Cheyennes, were peacefully inclined and rarely committed offenses against the law; but most unfortunately, they were charged with crimes which had been committed by other tribes, and that in this respect they had suffered heavily from the Kiowas of Colonel Leavenworth's agency, who were of the most turbulent Indians on the plains and deserved punishment more than any others.

More recent events have shown that all the tribes above referred to (save, probably, a portion of the Comanches), including the Sioux, were determined upon a general outbreak this summer, and that the abandonment of the village on Pawnee Fork and the murders committed immediately afterward on the Smoky Hill were but the commencement of a war which had been threatened to our post commanders on many occasions during the winter, and which is now waged with savage fury on the part of the Indians throughout my command and the Departments of the Platte and Dakota.

This reply to the statements of Colonels Wynkoop and Leavenworth, contained in the copy of their letters referred to me by order of General Grant, May 23, would have been transmitted promptly after the date of their receipt but for the fact that since that time until the fifteenth instant [July], I have been constantly on the plains, marching almost every day.

I am, Major, very respectfully, your obedient servant,

WINFIELD S. HANCOCK, Major General,
United States Army, Commanding

Across the Plains
with General Hancock

JAMES W. DIXON[1]

Journal of the Military Service Institution of the United States 7, no. 16
(September 1886): 195–98

An expedition was organized in the early spring of 1867 to operate against
the hostile Indians in the geographical section known as the Department
of the Missouri, and commanded by Maj. Gen. W. S. Hancock. Constant
reports of unprovoked and brutal murders committed rendered decisive action
necessary, with a view to punishing the guilty parties. General Hancock
wished to show the Indians within the limits of his department that the government was able to bring to justice those who committed hostilities and wantonly
murdered travelers across the plains in direct violation of the stipulations of
their treaties.

Those who had committed the outrages of the most aggravated nature
were Sioux and Cheyennes. They had attacked the stations of the Overland
Mail route, killed many of the employees, burned the stations, and run off the
horses. They had also killed a considerable number of the settlers of the frontier
of Kansas. The agents, although aware of the identity of many of the offenders,
took no notice of their misdeeds. Threats were boldly made that "as soon as
the grass was up," a general war would be inaugurated along the entire frontier,
especially against the main routes of travel.

General Hancock took six companies of the 37th Infantry and Light Battery B, 4th U.S. Artillery, together with eleven troops of the 7th U.S. Cavalry
commanded by Lt. Col. and Bvt. Maj. Gen. George A. Custer, and proceeded to
march from Fort Riley, Kansas, into the heart of the Indian country. Accompanying the expedition were fifteen Delaware Indian scouts under the celebrated
Chief Fall Leaf; the distinguished artist Mr. Theodore R. Davis[2] as representative of *Harper's Weekly*; and the since famous Henry M. Stanley, the great
African explorer.

From Fort Riley, the command marched to Fort Harker, a distance of
ninety miles. Halting only long enough to replenish the supplies, the column
was headed towards Fort Hays. From Fort Hays to Fort Larned was but the
march of a few days and was accomplished between April 3–7. The agent of

Watering horses in an adobe hole. HARPER'S NEW MONTHLY MAGAZINE 1895.

the Comanches and Kiowas accompanied the command to this point, and the agent of the Cheyennes, Arapahoes, and [Kiowa-]Apaches here joined it.

On April 9 a terrible snowstorm occurred. The cold was intense. Runners had been sent out to the chiefs of the various specified tribes by the agents, inviting them to a council, and they had agreed to assemble on the tenth of the month. Of course, the council had to be postponed.

The Sioux and Cheyennes were located on Pawnee Fork, some thirty miles above Fort Larned. They wished to avoid coming in, and also, by all the arts of Indian diplomacy, to prevent the nearer approach of the command to their village.

On the twelfth two chiefs of the Dog Soldiers,[3] the most bloodthirsty band of Indians of the plains, came in and intimated that they, with their followers, desired a conference. The general gratified their desire. A large fire was built, and the officers of the command assembled around it. The Indians approached the council fire in silence and, seating themselves around it, proceeded to smoke the inevitable pipe, passing it from one to another in solemn silence, only broken by an occasional grunt.

General Hancock opened the conference with a speech, which was interpreted to the Indians by [Ed] Guerrier, the half-breed interpreter. He told them why he had come among them; what he expected of them in the future; that he was not there to enforce war, but to administer justice; that he regretted that more of the chiefs had not come to the council; and that he would proceed to the immediate vicinity of their village on the following day. Tall Bull,[4] a large, fine-looking Indian, replied, but his speech contained nothing pertinent to the occasion and referred principally to the growing scarcity of the buffalo.

Accordingly, on the following morning the command was marched up Pawnee Fork toward the Indian village. Indians were seen all day in the distance, watching the movements of the troops. They set fire to the grass and burned it for miles between themselves and the command. On April 14 we were met by a number of chiefs and warriors belonging to the Sioux and Cheyenne tribes, among them the famous chief Pawnee Killer[5] of the Sioux and White Horse[6] of the Cheyennes.

These chiefs remained with the command during the night. Pawnee Killer left us in the morning with the promise that he would bring in the active chiefs, but he did not return. A little later Bull Bear,[7] a chief of the Cheyennes, came in and reported that the chiefs were on the way in for a council, but that they could not arrive for some time, being engaged in a buffalo hunt. General Hancock, who was in no degree deceived by the "diplomacy" of the Indians, informed Bull Bear that he would move his troops up the stream to meet them.

The march was resumed at 11:00 A.M., and soon thereafter a scene was witnessed never to be forgotten by any member of that command. Suddenly there appeared upon the crest of a divide an Indian line of battle of the most imposing nature, according to the Indian art of war. It was drawn up directly across our line of march and seemed to imply, "thus far but no farther." Nearly all were mounted upon war ponies. All were in war paint and bedecked with feathers of the brightest colors. Upon their heads they wore war bonnets of bright crimson, and their lances bore flaming pennants. Their bows were strung and their quivers bristled with long, steel-pointed, barbed arrows. Besides these each had a breech-loading rifle and one or more large-sized Colt revolvers. To this armament were added a tomahawk, a scalping knife, and various other warlike weapons. About fourteen hundred Indians composed this line of battle, while as far as the eye could reach, Indians could be seen watching the opposing forces. The chiefs rode madly along the line as if exhorting their braves to deeds of valor.

A finer battleground could not have been selected throughout the broad state of Kansas.

General Hancock, riding at the head of the column, as was his invariable custom, came suddenly upon this most imposing display. The infantry was in the advance, followed by the battery, the cavalry marching on the right flank. The general ordered the command to form line of battle, and the command was executed in less time than is required to write it, the cavalry coming into line at a gallop and drawing sabers at the word without waiting to align the ranks.

General Hancock was forbidden by superior authority at Washington to strike the first blow. Innocent settlers had been murdered in vast numbers. Arms and ammunition had been sold by agents and traders to Indians in direct violation of orders, but United States soldiers must wait until first fired upon before retaliating.

General Hancock, accompanied by the members of his staff, rode forward and, through the interpreter, invited the head chiefs to meet him midway between the lines.[8]

The celebrated chief Roman Nose,[9] bearing a white flag (the significance of which Indians totally ignore), accompanied by Bull Bear, White Horse, Gray Beard, and Medicine Wolf of the Cheyennes, and Pawnee Killer, Tall Bear, Bad Wound, Tall Bear that Walks under the Ground, Left Hand, Little Bear, and Little Bull of the Sioux, rode forward. The general inquired the meaning of the warlike display, saying that if war was their desire, he was ready then and there to gratify it. Their answer was that they did not want to fight but were peacefully disposed. Upon this the general informed them that he would continue his march towards their village and encamp near it. The interview ended, the line of battle vanished almost as suddenly as it had appeared, and the troops continued the march in the direction of the village. A few miles farther on, the tepees appeared in sight. Upwards of four hundred of them were erected upon the banks of the forked stream, and no more beautiful spot could have been selected in that generally barren and treeless country.

Our camp was situated some half a mile distant. At about 9:30 P.M. that night, Guerrier, the half-breed interpreter, reported that the Indians were "lighting out." General Hancock sent an aide with orders to Colonel Custer to pursue them with the cavalry. All haste was made, but the trail spread out like a gigantic fan, and the Indians escaped.

Guards were posted around the village to prevent its destruction by the soldiers. A tepee of marvelous workmanship was packed and sent to Washington. Some days later news arrived from Colonel Custer that the Indians were murdering all the whites who came in their way, and General Hancock ordered the destruction of the village, with all its contents, by fire.[10]

Had he been free to act, how many valuable lives would have been spared that were sacrificed in subsequent Indian wars, and what vast sums would have been saved to the government?

A Summer on the Plains

THEODORE R. DAVIS[1]

Harper's New Monthly Magazine 36 (February 1868): 292–307

The last touches were being given to the sketch that opens this article[2] when, glancing over the picture, my thoughts wandered back to that bright morning of April 2 [1867], when the commander-in-chief of *Harper's* met me on Broadway and demanded, with a tone of surprise, "Why are you not with General Hancock's Indian expedition?"

That was all. The commander continued his constitutional walk down Broadway, and the special artist—the writer hereof—did not find it requisite to devote more than a half hour to getting ready his baggage, i.e., sketchbook, pet "Ballard," and a few minor necessaries. Then away over Erie, Atlantic and Great Western; Ohio and Mississippi; Pacific; and Union Pacific, Smoky Hill Division. The third morning after, I was at Junction City, Kansas, nearly two thousand miles from New York.

Hancock's command had left Fort Harker and was beyond Zarah; probably at Fort Larned, a military post on the Arkansas route to Santa Fe. The coach for Santa Fe was about to leave, which it shortly did, with a number of mailbags filled with public documents.

The company's special messenger and the special artist—not the company's—completed the contents of the hack. At dawn on the following morning, the coach had arrived in the center of the Smoky Hill River, at a point near Fort Harker. We remained in the river until a team was obtained from the fort to pull the public documents' coach across. A freezing snowstorm had set in; the [driver] was wet and became very profane in his allusions to public documents; the messenger was in a soaked condition, and so was the artist, for we had all taken a lift at the wheels of the coach and a bath in the Smoky. The snow came faster and faster; the undulations of the plains were in bridal costume and were beautiful to me, but not to the driver, for he exhausted his stock of condemnatory oaths, and had just recommenced the list, when the ranch where we were to breakfast became visible—a black speck far in the distance.

The breakfast was poor, though expensive to the dental organs as well as to the pocket. I mention this fact as it will tend to increase the interest in the sketch of the coach in the storm.

Breakfast over, we pulled out for the next station. The coach and mules were soon as white as the plains, and the road was so completely hidden as to be easily lost; add to this the weight of the public documents, and it is not wonderful that we made that day but twelve miles' travel before our coach was stuck fast in a snowdrift; then darkness sent its twilight message that it would soon be night.

That it would be impossible to get the coach out of the drift before morning was too evident; that the mules would freeze if they were left out in that storm was apparent also. It was speedily decided in council that the driver should attempt to take his stock to the next station, while the messenger and the special artist should stay by the coach to guard the treasure and the public documents.

On leaving us, the driver gave vent to the longest, most emphatic, and unsurpassable bullwhacker oath that it has ever been my bad fortune to listen to. Coming as it did from a man who had nine chances out of ten of freezing to death before morning, it was simply horrible. The driver gone, we turned our attention to the making of our coach more comfortable, which we did by lining it with our blankets to keep out as much of the wind and snow as possible. Then came the question of food. We had corn in two states: the liquid extract, bottled, and one single hermetically sealed can of the corn in a solid state, half cooked. By means of the coach candles, which unfortunately were not of the edible kind, we cooked the corn, a little of it at a time. A snowball melted with each installment of corn furnished the liquor for our soup.

Housewives, do not fail to preserve this recipe, and if it be possible to add such appetites as we had, be assured that you will have a most enjoyable dish. It should be served hot. The corn eaten, we undertook a hot punch, which resulted in being one of the best that I ever tasted.

By this time the wolves had gathered about the coach, and such music as we had that night was not conducive to sleep, so we neglected to court the drowsy god, but we did some talking.

I wish there were space in this article to give the story told by the messenger. He had traveled over the route for several years, had been very lucky, and was not averse to mentioning the fact. There had never been, he said, such preparations for an Indian outbreak as the redskins had been making during the past winter. All they are waiting for now is the grass, and when that is sufficiently grown to subsist the ponies, you will see the Indians out on the warpath. They have their arms and ammunition ready. They'll talk peace to Hancock and the others now—that's to gain time—but before the summer is over, you will see some Indian deviltry, and the soldiers will learn what nonsense it is to undertake to fight Indians during the summer season. Now is the time to go for their villages. They know that they can't escape because their ponies are too poor to carry them, so they will stay and fight. If the Indians are whipped at this time of the year, there will be some show for peace for the rest of the summer, otherwise they will fight all summer and make peace in the fall.

This is from my diary, written up that night in the stagecoach, and the statement seems rather too near the truth, as shown by the experience of the past summer, to have been guessed at by the messenger.

So the night passed, and when we dug our way out through the drift that had enveloped the coach during the night, we saw a morning the full glory of which it would be difficult to describe. The air was strangely clear, and the cloud effects were [as] fantastic as they were magnificent. Over the snow-clad billow of land, there danced and sparkled fresh colors from the brilliant palette of nature, ever changing, always new. But what was all this sublimity to us when our situation was considered? Hungry mortals in a snowdrift can hardly be in a frame of mind to enjoy the cold beauties of nature.

Teams and men came in sight and were not long in rescuing our coach from the drift. We were soon on the route again, and the following morning reached Fort Larned, near which the command of General Hancock was encamped to await the arrival of a number of Indian chiefs, with whom a council was to be held.

A day or two passed before the chiefs arrived. Late one afternoon[3] the Indians came. Ten or twelve were chiefs,[4] all of whom announced themselves as hungry and unwilling to talk until they had been fed. A Sibley tent was arranged for them and food provided. When night came, a large log fire was built near General Hancock's tent, and the several officers of the command were notified that they were expected to don their loudest garments and assemble at the council fire. The artillery officers were the most successful in their getup, and I may say, on the authority of more than one Indian chief, that their clothes showed them to have been successful warriors.

Two hours after dark, the Indians came out of the tent, formed in line— their agent, Colonel Wynkoop, being on the right—and marched toward the council fire, where they seated themselves on logs provided for them at the right hand of General Hancock.

A handshaking ensued; pipes were filled and lighted by the Indians; then Hancock made a speech, which was interpreted, sentence by sentence, to the Indians. Hancock's speech was a simple statement of the reason of his presence there. He had heard that some of the tribes had bad hearts and would go on the warpath—those Indians he should fight. The Indians would not be permitted to kill white people and stop travel over the overland routes. He wanted all the Indians to be at peace and to be friendly with the white men, who would then be kind to them and would see that they were well taken care of.

The Indians then proceeded to talk. They wished for peace, but did not like the idea of having railroads built through their country. Their words were good enough, but there was a certain something in the manner of the Indians which indicated that they were only talking to gain time.

Hancock asked why more of their chiefs were not present. The Indians replied that their ponies were too poor to travel. The general then told them that he would move nearer their village so that all the Indians could see his soldiers, and all the chiefs could come for a talk.

This did not seem to please the Indians. They did not care to have the white men near their village and gave unsatisfactory accounts as to its location.

On the following morning Hancock broke camp and moved his command up the Pawnee Fork. At evening a number of Indians came to the camp.[5] They received a hospitable welcome and went off promising to bring the head chiefs of the Cheyenne tribe to see General Hancock when the sun should be "so high" the next morning—pointing to that part of the heavens which would indicate about 9:00 A.M.

The Indians did not come, though Hancock waited until noon for them. Then he moved toward the village and, at a distance of five or six miles from it, met Roman Nose, the war chief of the Dog Soldier band of Cheyennes, with about three hundred of his warriors. They were drawn up in line of battle and formed one of the most picturesque arrays possible. Hancock halted his command, formed line, and accompanied by Colonels A. J. Smith and Custer, rode forward to meet the war chief, Roman Nose.

I have never seen so fine a specimen of the Indian race as he—quite six feet in height and finely formed, dressed in the uniform of a United States officer and provided with a numerous quantity of arms, he rode his well-formed pony up to Hancock and proposed to talk. From his manner, it was quite evident that he was indifferent whether he talked or fought. His carbine, a Spencer, hung at the side of his pony, four heavy revolvers were stuck in his belt, while his left hand grasped a bow and a number of arrows—the bow being strung and ready for instant use.

Hancock told Roman Nose that he would go into camp at the first good place, and then he would talk; he could not camp where he was, as there was neither wood nor water. A few Indians remained with Hancock, but Roman Nose rode back to his braves, or in Plains parlance, "bucks," and they all moved off toward their village.

Hancock did not move forward for some time, as he expressed himself anxious that the Indians should reach the village and inform the inhabitants of his peaceful intentions before the command came in sight of it. While waiting for this, the Indians who remained produced their pipes, seated themselves in a half circle, and proceeded to smoke. They faced toward the south, the owner of the pipe filled and lighted it, then passed it to the Indian at the eastern end of the semicircle; this party took the pipe, made several motions with it, the purport of which was that he had not forgotten his friends who had gone to the "Happy Hunting Ground." Then he took a long draw at the pipe and blew the smoke upward—an obligation to the Great Spirit. Next, three or four whiffs were taken and inhaled; then the pipe was passed to the next Indian, who made his signs, took his whiffs, and passed the pipe. It was smoked by each Indian in turn till the western end of the half circle was reached; the pipe was then passed back to the eastern end, and the smoke commenced again.

Sometimes more than one pipe is in circulation at the same time, but the pipe is always passed in the same manner. The Indians do not care to smoke the white man's tobacco until it is mixed with their preparation of roots, herbs, bark, and marrow from the bones of buffalo. An Indian will light a match, and with it his pipe, in a wind that a sailor would consider too great to think of attempting the feat. The Indian strikes and holds the match as near the ground as possible, then holds the pipe along the ground and lights it.

As the command moved toward the point where the Indian village was supposed to be located, it became evident that the redskins had made preparations for visitors. Every particle of grass had been burned off the country, making it necessary for Hancock to march his command to a point less than a mile distant from the Indian village before he could go into camp. A small party rode to the village and found that the squaws and children had all left it, and that the Indians that remained were enjoying a dog feast.

I will simply state that dog is not such bad eating, but the quantity which the Indians insist on one's consuming is discouraging in the extreme. You eat a reasonable meal to assure your host that you appreciate his hospitality, when another Indian secures you, and more dog must be eaten. This is continued till you have satisfied yourself of the flavor of various canines and are absolutely incapable of enduring more dog.

Two of the chiefs went to Hancock's camp and told him that all the women and children had become frightened and had gone away; also that some of their young men were hunting buffalo up on the Smoky Hill, and that they could not say what they would do. All this looked suspicious, and Hancock set a watch upon the village. Shortly after 9:00 P.M., it was discovered that the Indians were abandoning it.

Custer was ordered to take his command—about 600 men of the 7th Cavalry—and surround the village, but not to enter it or to attack the Indians. The surrounding was effected with great celerity; no noise whatever could be heard in the village, and closer examination revealed the fact that the Indians had abandoned it and moved northward toward the Smoky Hill.

Many of the tepees, or lodges, had been cut in such a manner as to render them unserviceable. From some, large pieces had been cut and carried off, to be used as temporary shelters. The only human beings that we could discover were an old Sioux, lame and helpless, and a little half-breed child of not more than nine years. The child was covered with blood and moaned terribly, having suffered a most abominable outrage from the Indians before they left.

A guard was at once placed over the village, and strict orders were issued that nothing should be disturbed. Custer was ordered to have his command ready to move at daylight for the purpose of overtaking the Indians and forcing them to return. He moved with the greatest rapidity and reached Lookout Station on the Smoky Hill while the station was still burning. There he discovered the half-consumed bodies of the station men among a pile of ashes. He at once dispatched a messenger to Hancock stating these facts, and also that he would find it necessary to go to Fort Hays, twenty miles east, to procure rations for his men and forage for his horses before he could continue his pursuit of the Indians.

Upon the receipt of this intelligence, Hancock ordered Smith to burn the Indian village and destroy all the articles that could be of any use to the Indians. A number of articles were found in the village which the Indians had taken from the bodies of the soldiers killed near Fort Phil Kearny. The village was burned, but not before a careful inventory had been taken of all the property to be destroyed. I have heard some estimates of the value of this property that were ludicrously large. The loss inflicted upon the Indians could easily be made good by them in a single summer.

It may be well to give some general facts with reference to the Indians and their idea of the value of different articles. An Indian tepee is usually composed of from ten to twelve buffalo hides, from which the hair has been removed and the skin nicely dressed. A fair average of the number of Indians to a tepee is seven, and of this number, two are probably warriors. A nicely dressed buffalo robe is to be had from the Indians for ten or twelve cups of sugar, or about seven pounds' weight. A ten-dollar bill is also equal to the value of a buffalo robe. A pony is worth ten or twelve robes (sugar currency), and a tepee is valued at two ponies. The poles over which the skin is stretched are more difficult to obtain than the robes for covering and appear to be quite as.valuable to the Indian.

There is no recognized price for squaws, as their qualifications are taken into consideration, and a price is demanded in accordance with their capability to render service. The general run of them may be purchased for a pony, a small quantity of flour and sugar, a little tobacco, and a bottle of whiskey. But woe betides the purchaser if he should locate at any point convenient of access to the Indians of the tribe to which the squaw belonged. While she is with the band, the squaw is kicked about and whipped by any buck that takes a notion to do so. When she becomes the white man's squaw, affairs are changed. There is not an Indian in the tribe who does not claim relationship with her. She is sister to the majority of them, and as near as cousin-german to the rest. They meet her with an embrace, and she feels that she must give each one some token of her regard. The result of all this is that the white man soon discovers that he has married the whole tribe—that is, so far as his property is concerned.

One of the favorite diversions of the Indian is to set the squaws to fighting; this done, he sits down and enjoys the sight. If any particular squaw does not "come to the scratch" with sufficient energy, the possessor of her takes his whip to encourage her to renewed exertion. No slave was ever more abused than is the squaw, and yet she does, without complaint, all the drudgery; and I have frequently seen them armed with rifle and revolvers, riding man-fashion on a sorry beast, keeping at a very respectful distance behind their lords.

I remember the extreme anxiety of one Indian to effect a trade with an army officer. The Indian came into Fort Dodge and saw the wife of the officer and, like many others, was greatly charmed. The following day he came into the post with a pony, two squaws, and a quantity of other merchandise, included in which was a fat canine. All of this the Indian would give for the white man's squaw. When he found that no trade could be made, a more disgusted Indian would be difficult to imagine.

After burning the Indian village, Hancock moved south to Fort Dodge, where he met a number of chiefs of the Kiowa and Arapaho tribes. They all talked peace and asked for presents. From Fort Dodge, Hancock marched to Fort Larned, where he held a council with Satanta, the war chief of the Kiowa tribe. Satanta's talk was the finest specimen of Indian oratory that I ever listened to. His talk opened with an allusion to the fact that Colonel Leavenworth, agent of the Kiowa tribe, and who sat near him, had misappropriated the goods of the tribe and had not dealt justly with them. "Satanta wants an honest agent." He then proceeded to tell what an excellent friend Satanta was of the white man, and showed how much better peace was than war. The talk impressed Hancock and Smith so favorably that they felt impelled to do something for so good an Indian. Hancock gave him a coat with the insignia of the rank of a major general of the United States Army, adding thereto a rather grandly plumed military hat and a yellow silk sash. Besides these tokens of esteem, Satanta secured rations and a few other things that make glad the heart of an Indian.

Hancock was disposed to think well of Satanta and resolved to make an example of his case. "If it should prove that Satanta was only talking to gain time," said he, "we shall have the satisfaction of having given him all he asked, and of having treated him with the utmost kindness. There are neither soldiers nor other white men near the range of the Kiowas, so that they can have absolutely nothing to complain of."

The ranchmen and others conversant with Indians were certain that Satanta was only endeavoring to gain time, and this proved to be the case, for on the morning of June 1, Satanta, dressed in the good clothes that he had received at the council, made a raid on Fort Dodge and stampeded nearly every animal that belonged to the post. He had the politeness, however, to raise his plumed hat to the garrison of the fort, though he discourteously shook his coattails at them as he rode away with the captured stock. There is more Indian in this performance of Satanta's than one would at first imagine. Satanta went off, after the council at Fort Larned, boasting that "he had outtalked the big white chief, and the white chief had the first talk to. Satanta goes to his village to have a dance now."

From Fort Larned, Hancock marched north to Fort Hays, where he found Custer awaiting the arrival of rations and forage, which should have been ready for him weeks before. Hancock remained but two days at Fort Hays, then started east with the battery that had formed a portion of the expedition.[6] During the greater part of the month of May, Smith and Custer waited for the promised rations. The men were suffering from scurvy to an extent that was positively frightful. The officers, one and all, depleted their purses to procure from sutlers and others the antiscorbutic food for which the soldiers were suffering. Buffalo hunts were organized, and every possible exertion made to secure for the soldiers a beneficial change of rations.

Meantime, the men were deserting to the number of fifty a month, and despite all the efforts made to overtake them, they escaped with their horses, arms, and accoutrements. There seemed but one way of accounting for this persistent desertion. Many of the men had enlisted under assumed names and gone out on the plains just to see the country, proposing, no doubt, to take advantage of any chance that might appear to afford them a bettering of condition. They were perfectly aware that the extent of the punishment which could be inflicted, in the event of capture, would be six months in the guardhouse, and in all probability not even that. In less than one year the 7th Cavalry had lost by desertion nearly eight hundred men. Some of these men were killed by the Indians, a number escaped south to Council Grove, where they joined the bands of desperadoes which infest that region; others are now among the mines of Colorado; and a few are busy among the breaks of the Platte, cutting ties for the Union Pacific Railroad.

By the last of May, the grass had become well grown in every place except the immediate vicinity of Fort Hays. Accounts of Indian depredations were brought in continually from the stage ranches along the Smoky Hill. Some of these reports were based on facts; others were the stories of frightened ranchmen, after the following style:

One afternoon a man came galloping into camp with the story that there were more than two hundred Indians in the immediate vicinity of Lookout Station; a wagon proceeding toward Downer's Station with an escort of five men had barely escaped capture by them. He had gone out immediately to make sure of the number of Indians and, if possible, to determine to which tribe they belonged. He was satisfied that they were Cheyennes, and numbered about four or five hundred. There could be no doubt of it, as he had been within sixty yards of the Indians and had narrowly escaped being captured by them. I will mention here that distance on the plains is very deceptive, but hardly to the extent the investigation of this individual's story would lead one to suppose.

Custer determined to make a night attack on these Indians, and at sunset left camp at the head of three hundred troopers. About midnight the command reached the vicinity of Lookout Station. Custer and one or two of the scouts rode up to the stockade occupied by the few soldiers who composed the garrison of the station. The men were all on the alert, but those who had seen the Indians were not discoverable. The colonel then went to a cave which was occupied by the stage men and carpenters who were rebuilding the station. Here he found a social game of draw poker going on.

"Have you seen any Indians near this place?" asked the colonel.

"What's that, stranger? I raise that blind," said one of the gamesters.

"Indians? I chip two better. Dang me if I know," remarked another. "I'm a rare horse if I care."

It was too evident that there was no valuable information to be obtained here, so the colonel withdrew. A moment after, one of the poker players remarked, "Fellers, did you ever see 'Wild Bill?' That was the chap; purty boy, wasn't he? Looked as if he wanted a hand in, didn't he though."

A man was found who had seen what he took to be Indians. Then one of the men who had been with the wagon was discovered. A careful examination of the ground where the Indians had been seen showed that it had been lately traversed by a herd of buffalo. The night ride had been for nothing.

On June 1 Colonel Custer left the camp at Fort Hays with about three hundred men and a train of twenty wagons. The plan of campaign, as then proposed, was to move north to Fort McPherson, thence up the south bank of the Platte River to Fort Sedgwick, where rations, forage, and a few fresh horses were to be obtained before starting southward to Fort Wallace on the Smoky Hill. It being considered certain that there were considerable bodies of Indians somewhere near the forks of the Republican River, there seemed to be no doubt that they could be found during the march between Forts Sedgwick and Wallace.

The march from Fort Hays to Fort McPherson was made over one of the most interesting portions of the plains. The country is broken into bluffs and canyons, never flat and uninteresting, as seems to be the general supposition of persons not familiar with the physical geography of that particular section of our country. The banks of the little streams are fringed with trees of all descriptions, ash and walnut being as plenty as cottonwood. Game was abundant and furnished a continual and much-needed supply of meat for the command. On the Saline River, a campground was discovered that had been lately occupied by the Indians. From the number of elk bones which were strewn about, one might have thought that the Indians had done little else than kill and eat elk during their sojourn in that place.

At some little distance from the village site, and on a prominent knoll, we discovered a small scaffold. It was evidently the last resting place of some Indian; its investigation proved very interesting. The scaffold was constructed of small saplings; the body was placed on the top, where it was carefully covered from the weather with the canvas cover of a captured wagon. The Indians had left with the body what they consider the necessary outfit for a trip to the Happy Hunting Ground, such as arms, ammunition, food, clothing, a number of carefully braided lariats, and a small portion of the scalp of some murdered white woman. The white man's clothing seemed to have been highly valued, for several articles of his wearing apparel were found with the body.

The Indians say that the white man cuts down and burns all the trees that he finds, and in this manner will soon deprive the Indian of the wood with which to cook his food; also that an Indian can find beneath the tree all the fuel that he needs. This is not the only thing of which the Indian complains in the destruction of the few trees on the plains. There are numerous cottonwood groves which for years have been used by families or bands of Indians as the last resting place of their dead. It is not in the ground, shaded by the fine old grove, but among the branches of the trees that the Indian deposits his dead. The body is covered with different wrappings, the first usually a blanket, and the last a mat made of small willows.

When the contracts are let for the supply of wood needed at the different government posts, the contractor and his men repair to some favorably located grove and proceed to cut and haul the wood to the fort. It is not difficult to imagine that the Indians object to this and proceed at once to attack the men who are engaged in the destruction of their burial places. This is the only real wrong to the Indians that has come under my observation, and for this there are many palliating circumstances. In many instances the wood used for fuel at government posts is only to be obtained at a distance of fifty or sixty miles from the fort, and even then the supply is limited.

During the march from the Saline River to Fort McPherson, the command was camped for one night on ground that was subsequently discovered to be perforated with the holes of rattlesnakes. The shelter tents were just pitched when the snakes made their appearance. The soldiers were quickly at work with sabers and sticks. As this is no "snake story," I prefer not to mention the number of rattlers that were placed *hors de combat.* My tent companion, Major Elliott,[7] murdered five good-sized rattlesnakes in the vicinity of our tent; but inasmuch as the major was the caterer of our mess, it was in a measure his duty to secure all the prairie eels that might come within reach. The cook for our mess was a character, by the way, whose recent importation from Schleswig-Holstein is a sufficient assertion to indicate his slight acquaintance with the English language. This individual was averse to snakes of all kinds, and particularly to rattlers. On this occasion he was rushing wildly from one point to another to escape the neighborhood of snakes, and finally returned to the mess tent to discover five or six large snakes lying at length on the mess chest. His horror knew no bounds. He was absolutely frightened out of his wits.

With the exception of ours, there was not a mess in camp that afternoon that did not enjoy broiled or fried rattlesnake. "Schleswig-Holstein" could not be brought to cook the snakes, so we dined out. About 11:00 P.M. the occupants of our tent were startled by an energetic yell from the region of the cook's tent. We rushed out and met our Teuton. Words came faster than ideas, but we gathered from the jangle that a snake had got into his tent and tried to make a hole of his mouth. The affair was too ludicrous to refrain from laughter. The major rushed into the cook's tent and found a large snake rattling away as if he were as badly frightened as the cook had been. The snake was killed and boiled for breakfast. Schleswig took revenge on the bones, which he pronounced "so tam good as de eel." From that time there was not a more energetic snake hunter in camp than our dog robber Schleswig.

The mention of dog robber brings to mind a scene that occurred in our tent while we were encamped on Walnut Creek. We had laid in a store of provisions of different descriptions and were well satisfied that so long as we retained possession of the mess chest containing them, we should not suffer for lack of food, but in this instance we reckoned without our key, for the detailed men who were employed as orderlies took advantage of a dark night to desert. They carried with them our entire stock of provisions, as well as four of the best horses that belonged to the command. Lieutenant Brewster,[8] at that time one of our mess, made the discovery. No one of the party who saw the lieutenant that morning, as he came into the tent to announce the fact, will ever forget the expression which decorated his ordinarily cordial face. He did not say damn, but his whole countenance expressed it.

"Gentlemen," he remarked, "the dog robbers have gutted our mess chest. The white sugar, nutmeg, and lemons are gone!"

The situation required an explanation, when information was gained that "dog robbers" was the name by which the soldier designated the cooks and detailed soldiers who were the occupants of the second table of an officers' mess.

During the march northward, the distance traveled each day would not exceed an average of twenty-three miles. No Indian trail of sufficient freshness to follow was discovered until the command reached the vicinity of the Republican River, and then the trail indicated too small a body of Indians to make it worthwhile to pursue, as it was evident that the horses of the pursuing party would be worn out in a futile endeavor to overtake the well-mounted scouting parties that had made the trails.

On the morning that the command crossed the Republican, a war party of thirty or forty Indians was discovered about two miles distant from us. Two companies were sent after them. The Indians moved off across a small creek that flowed through deeply cut banks. In crossing this, or rather in clambering up the steep banks after the stream was crossed, a considerable number of men and horses fell back into the water. Before a crossing could be effected, the Indians were far away. Upon a close examination of the trail, it was ascertained that the Indians were mounted on stage horses, and this alone was sufficient to make the abandonment of the pursuit the wisest course to pursue.

The horses which are used by the Overland Stage companies to take their coaches over the plains are, as a general thing, the best that can be secured. On the Smoky Hill route, the stage horses are worth about $250 each. They are selected by very knowing horsemen, and when captured by the Indians are considered great prizes.

Between the Republican and Platte Rivers, a great number of antelopes were killed, and many of the young ones captured. These were quickly tamed and became the favorite pets of the camp. Several juvenile coyote wolves were also held as captive, but they could not be brought to the same degree of sociability that the little antelopes evinced.

As the command marched out of the breaks, or bluffs, of the Platte into the broad valley through which the river flows, we saw a large train of wagons moving hastily into corral. It was evident that the bullwhackers took the cavalrymen for Indians and were making preparations for a fight.

The next movement was up the valley of the Platte to Fort McPherson, where rations and forage were secured; then the march was continued twelve miles farther up the river to a campground near Jack Morrow's ranch. Abandoned ranches all along the Platte showed that the Indians had been at work. Grave after grave was passed. Some had a rude board with a simple inscription, "Unknown man killed by Indians," and the date; but more frequently the simple mounds of earth near an abandoned ranch were all that told of the fate of the poor mortals who had ventured to make a home on the plains.

While in camp near Jack Morrow's, Colonel Custer was visited by Pawnee Killer, a Sioux chief, who brought with him five or six braves. Ostensibly the visit was for the purpose of having a talk, but in reality to obtain rations, information, and if possible, ammunition. Pawnee Killer said that the Cheyennes were bad Indians; he was tired of them and would be glad if Colonel Custer would let him bring his band to a campground near some fork, so that they might be fed and enabled to keep away from the Cheyennes until they were whipped and at peace again. He was anxious to know where Custer would go next, but failed to discover.

While the talk was going on, "Little Bill," one of the pet antelopes, was making a careful investigation of the beadwork on the clothing of the Indians, dividing his attention between them and a pail of water which, for the refreshment of the thirsty, was placed in the center of the tent. The tameness of the antelope seemed to strike the Indians as peculiar; but when they saw the little fellow attack one of the dogs that came into the tent, their astonishment was too great to be contained, and they complimented Little Bill with a succession of "how-how-hows!"

Pawnee Killer departed with a generous supply of sugar, coffee, and hard bread, promising to bring his band to a point near Fort McPherson, and to remain there peacefully until the trouble with the Cheyennes should cease.

The day following, General Sherman arrived. He was doubtful about the intentions of Pawnee Killer and expressed his belief that there was no reliance to be placed on what he had said.

On June 15 Custer marched away from the Platte, moving southward. For fifty miles the country was the most broken that we had met with. The undulations were abrupt, and but for the absence of timber, one might have thought it the very broken country directly in the rear of Vicksburg.

When Custer reached the forks of the Republican after a four-days' march, he went into camp to await further instructions from Sherman, under whose direct orders he was then acting.

On June 23 Major Elliott left camp with an escort of ten men and proceeded toward Fort Sedgwick with dispatches to Sherman and Augur.[9] On the same day, sixteen wagons were sent under escort of Lt. Sam Robbins to Fort Wallace, where they were to be filled with rations and returned as quickly as possible.

Just at dawn on the twenty-fourth, Custer's camp was attacked by Indians, who attempted to stampede the animals. They were discovered in time and driven off. One of the vedettes was badly wounded and lost his carbine and ammunition, both of which were carried off by the Indians, who suffered no loss whatever. Immediately after this attempt the main body of Indians withdrew to a prominent knoll about a mile from the camp. Here they formed in line, flashed their signal mirrors, and were soon joined by parties of Indians who seemed to come from all directions.

One of Custer's scouts, an interpreter named Gay, rode out and made first "peace," then "circle" signs. The peace sign is made by riding toward the party with whom it is desired to communicate, making the horse take a zigzag course. I do not know how to describe it better than to say that the course of the horse would resemble a Virginia rail fence. The council sign is made by riding in a circle, then forward, circling again, and so on.

A small party of Indians rode toward Gay and told him that they would talk if the white chief would only bring a few of his officers with him. Gay replied that in such event, there must [be] only as many Indians come as there were white men who came toward them. Returning to Custer, he told him that it was Pawnee Killer and some other Sioux chiefs, who were anxious to "talk."

There is a point which now enters into the case that it may be well to mention. Sherman told Custer, while on the Platte, that he hoped that he would be able to see Pawnee Killer; and if he did see him, he thought it would be advisable to send a company of cavalry with him to his village to make an effort to bring the Indians to the vicinity of some military post.

The attempt that Pawnee Killer had just made to stampede the animals, and the full paint with which the warriors had decorated themselves, the tied-up tails of the ponies, and other signs were not very favorable endorsements of the talk which had been held only a week previous at the camp on the Platte. Nevertheless, Custer determined to hear what Pawnee Killer might have to say; so, accompanied by five or six persons, he rode out to meet him. The Indians, true to their natural instincts, had double the number to meet the party, and others were continually advancing nearer and nearer. Pawnee Killer would give no reason for his recent attack and continually demanded that Custer should tell him why he had left the Platte. Finding that he could discover nothing from Pawnee Killer as to the location of his village or his present intention, the colonel told him that he should follow him. Pawnee Killer then said his hearing was good. Thunder Lightning and The Man Who Walks beneath the Ground—two chiefs who were with Pawnee Killer—also remarked that their hearts were good. Then all of them requested that Custer would give them "sug" (sugar), coffee, and some ammunition, none of which they received, however.

Returning to camp, Custer had the "general" sounded, and in twenty minutes was moving off after the Indians. The chase was soon found to be useless, and the command returned to its lately abandoned location.

Half an hour after the return, a small party of Indians were discovered on the bluffs near. Capt. Louis Hamilton was ordered to take twenty men and pursue them. After a chase of nearly eight miles, the band of ten or fifteen Indians suddenly increased to nearly three hundred. These in a few moments completely surrounded Hamilton's little party, who succeeded in beating off the Indians and in holding their ground. Their skirmish lasted over an hour. The Indians rode rapidly about the party, yelling and shooting but doing no other damage except killing one horse. The loss to the Indians was three killed and several wounded. Hamilton succeeded in bringing his men into camp in safety.[10]

On the morning of the twenty-sixth, the wagon train, under the escort of Lieutenant Robbins, was attacked while on the return from Fort Wallace to the camp on the Republican. The attacking party was composed of Cheyennes and Sioux, to the number of seven or eight hundred. The manner in which Robbins handled his little force against this large body of Indians was admirable. Lieutenant Cooke,[11] acting commissary, had charge of the wagons and kept them moving forward in double column. The horses of the cavalrymen were placed between the wagons, and were thus in a great measure sheltered from arrows and bullets. The fight was kept up for nearly fifteen miles, when Robbins had nearly reached the two companies of Captains West and Myers,[12] which Custer had sent to meet the train, fearing that an attack would be made upon it.

We afterward learned that on the same morning, a hard fight took place near Fort Wallace by a company of the 7th Cavalry under Captain Barnitz.[13] On this occasion the Indians abandoned their old style of circle fighting, formed in line, and charged after the manner of a squadron of cavalry. This made the fighting desperate, it being mostly hand to hand. In this fight some of the bravest and most efficient noncommissioned officers of the 7th Cavalry were killed, and their bodies mutilated in the most horrible manner.[14] When an Indian was shot off his pony, two redskins would ride their ponies up to him, pick up the body, and carry it to a place of safety. Those who were in the fight state that they never saw such excellent riding as the Indians exhibited on this occasion.

On June 27 Major Elliott returned from Fort Sedgwick, having made his trip of over two hundred miles in safety. Lieutenant Robbins came into camp on the morning of the twenty-eighth, also the companies of West and Myers. It was amusing to listen to the accounts which the men had to give each other. During the past few days, they had all seen service of some kind, and each had his experience to relate. The different yelps of the Indians were imitated, and all the newly learned characteristics were canvassed, and as far as possible accounted for. When the men mounted at the "water call," some were seen to mount from the right-hand side, Indian fashion; others to get on their horses' backs by catching hold of the animals' tails and giving a spring—also an Indian fashion. There was not a trooper in camp who had not made an effort to ride beneath his horse instead of above him.

Will Comstock[15] deserves more than a passing notice, for he was the character of the expedition. No Indian was ever half so superstitious as Will. He had his medicine horse, medicine field glass, medicine everything, in fact.

Even Will's evil-looking dog was medicine, and had a medicine collar. If he had bad luck, his medicine was bad, and something must be done to change the condition of things. While on the Platte, Comstock saw a locomotive for the first time. His surprise was inexpressible.

"Good medicine! Good medicine!" shouted Will. "Look! Look at the tu-te!"

The telegraph wires which stretch along the valley of the Platte hum and sing like the strings of a large harp as the wind sweeps across them. Will hears the sound and avers directly that the wires are talking medicine. If, during the march, Will arrives first on the bank of a stream, he locates himself in the most favorable spot and indulges in a monody. This he declares to be the best kind of medicine. Yet for all this, Will Comstock is fearlessly brave. He is quiet and unassuming in manner, small in size, and compact in proportion. He is one of the best riders on the plains, with which he is probably more familiar than any other white man who roves over them. Learning one day that there were buffalo in Central Park, he came to me to know whether there were any good buffalo horses in New York; "for," said he, "when I come to New York, you and I will have to run them buffalo in the park, sure."

It must seem strange that the Indians so seldom molest the telegraph wires, which bear our messages across the plains to the Rocky Mountains, and thence to the Pacific Ocean. This is another case of medicine. Shortly after the wires were erected, the attachés of the telegraph company invited a number of Indian chiefs to meet at a certain point, and from thence to travel, one party east and the other west. When they were separated by nearly a hundred miles, they were permitted to dictate messages, which were flashed from one party to the other. Two days subsequently, the chiefs met and compared notes. Naturally they were greatly astonished and expressed themselves that it was the Great Spirit's talk which the wires did. At all events, it was decided that it would be well to avoid meddling with the telegraph wires.

As if to strengthen this opinion, an affair occurred soon after which made it evident that there was a potent something connected with the iron string. A young Sioux Indian determined to show that he had no faith in the Great Spirit's connection to the wires, so he set to work with his hatchet to cut down one of the telegraph poles. A severe thunderstorm was going on at a distance; a charge of electricity being taken up by the wires was passed to the pole which the Indian was cutting, which resulted in the instant death of the Indian. For a long time thereafter, the telegraph line was not molested.

While remarking on this medicine idea, it may be of interest to mention the fact that the Indians have many very excellent remedies for the various diseases to which flesh is heir. These are generally applied by the squaws. If they fail, the sick Indian is turned over to the medicine men, who proceed to kill or cure the patient as quickly as possible. Some idea of their method of treating a case may be formed when it is known that an Indian suffering with a sore throat has had his palate extracted with a pair of bullet moulds handled by an expert medicine man. Naturally the patient died, but then it was evident nothing could have saved him, for the medicine man under whose care he departed for the Happy Hunting Ground was one of the most famous in the tribe.

The counting coup that an Indian always does when he has time is, next to scalping, the most satisfactory thing to him that can be accomplished. If a pony is captured, or a wagon, or in fact anything but a human being, each Indian present at the capture is not content until he has struck the object a blow with his whip, bow, or the end of the lariat. "It makes their hearts strong," they say, "and that is very good for the Indian."

When an enemy is slain, a number of the Indians present will at once shoot arrows into the body. If a band of thirty or forty Indians kills one white man, it is pretty certain that when the body is discovered, as many as thirty or forty arrows will be found in it. I have seen the bodies of white men who had been killed by Indians, and counted in them from fifty to sixty arrows. From the circumstances, there could be no reason to doubt that a majority of the arrows had been shot into the body after the victim was dead.

Occasionally the Indians use poisoned arrows, but this is not very frequently the case. The poisoned arrow is dangerous, and death frequently results from a slight wound by them. There are many different methods employed by the Indians to poison their arrows. Rattlesnake poison is frequently used, but this is not nearly so fatal as when the head of the arrow is poisoned with meat. The wound made by these arrows is much like that to which surgeons are exposed at the dissecting table.

The way in which the arrows are prepared is simple. The liver of a deer or antelope is kept in some moist place until it reaches a state of putrefaction. Into this the iron head of the arrow is thrust, and a small quantity of the decayed matter is taken up; the arrow, then carefully dried, is ready for use. I remember to have seen a horse that had received a slight wound from one of these arrows. The animal died in a very short time, suffering the greatest agony.

For signaling, the Indians have a simple and effective code which they work by means of small mirrors, from which they flash the sunlight, first in one direction, then in another. In this way, they communicate intelligence from bluff to bluff a distance of eight or ten miles. I do not know that the code used by them has ever been deciphered. The sign language used by the Indian is very complete. Their pantomimic power seems perfect. There are no two tribes of Indians that use the same oral language, but all are conversant with the same pantomimic code.

Their ideas of the life hereafter present some strange coincidences with those of Christendom. The Indian has his paradise, or Happy Hunting Ground, and his inferno, the abode of bad spirits; also his purgatory. His medicine arrows are his Bible. He is convinced that a good record in this world, particularly as a warrior, will entitle him to a favorable location in the Happy Hunting Ground; but he must be buried in good state and receive a proper outfit at his burial to enable him to make a respectable appearance when he presents himself at the gate.

If an Indian loses his scalp, he has little chance to obtain the hoped-for entrance to the Happy Hunting Ground. He would rather be burned alive than be hung, for in the latter case, the spirit goes straight to the abode of bad spirits and has no hope even of so good a place as purgatory. It seems to be generally supposed that in scalping, the Indian removes all the fleshy covering of the skull on which hair grows. This is erroneous; usually, the portion of the scalp removed does not exceed four inches in diameter. He may take more, and sometimes does, but it is when the victim has fine hair, such as will be of use in decorating a hunting shirt or a pair of leggings. One reason why the Indians have such an aversion to fighting against Negro troops is because of the penchant which the darkies have for taking their hair. One scalp will meet with nearly as great a powwow in a Negro camp as it would among the tepees of the Indian.

The Negroes make admirable Indian fighters and seem to enjoy the sport. Moreover, they do not desert, and as a general thing are under an excellent state of discipline—that is, if the officers who are over them are of the proper stamp. It is but just that the colored soldier should have his due. They did capital fighting last summer and won the commendation of all the frontiersmen who saw them while engaged in an Indian fight.

A word should be said with reference to the half-breed Indians that are to be found with every band of warriors. Charley Bent[16] will be a good example. He is the son of Col. Bill Bent by a Cheyenne squaw. Charley was well brought up and received a good education at the academy in St. Louis. Shortly after the Sand Creek affair, he joined the Dog Soldier band of Cheyenne Indians, with which he has ever since continued to roam. He makes occasional visits to traders' camps but does not care to frequent government posts, as there are too many crimes laid at his door to make such localities entirely safe for him.

The last visit that he paid to his father's ranch on the Purgatory River was not of the most peaceful character. The colonel tells the story:

My daughter saw something that looked like an Indian's head sticking up over the bank of the main irrigating ditch, through which the water ran past the house. She went out to look at the object and discovered Charley. She told him to stay there until she went to the house and got him some clothes. He said no, that he was after the old man, meaning me. I was off in New Mexico at the time, and she told him so and asked the durn'd scoundrel to come to the house. "No," he said, "I only wanted the old man," and uncocking his rifle, he went off. That's the last that we've seen of him.

Charley Bent speaks English perfectly and is quite intelligent, but there is no doubt that he is one of the worst Indians on the plains.

From the camp at the forks of the Republican River, Custer marched his command up the south bank of the river some fifty or sixty miles, and from thence north to the Platte, which he struck at Riverside Station, forty miles west of Fort Sedgwick, from which place he learned by telegraph that orders had been sent out to him from Sherman, and that these orders had been entrusted to Lieutenant Kidder,[17] who with an escort of ten men had started out to deliver them. Copies of the orders were, however, transmitted to Custer. The new instructions directed that he should proceed direct to Fort Wallace, where he would in all probability meet Hancock. The fact that Lieutenant Kidder had not succeeded in overtaking the command occasioned very considerable uneasiness in the minds of the officers, for it seemed certain that some misfortune had befallen him.

The stay of a single day on the banks of the Platte River cost the command a loss of thirty-five men by desertion. This out of a force numbering less than three hundred men was a serious misfortune. Halting at noon to graze the animals, ten more men attempted to desert—five mounted, five dismounted. Custer ordered Major Elliott and one or two officers to pursue the deserters and shoot them if any resistance was offered to being captured. As Major Elliott rode up to one of the men on foot, he was met by a lowered carbine. The major shot the man down and continued the pursuit. Two more of the deserters were wounded before their capture could be finally effected. The five mounted men escaped. During the afternoon march, it was discovered that a general mutiny had been arranged by the men to take place that night. As it did not occur, it was evident that the summary measures of the afternoon had a salutary effect. For days after this, there were no more desertions in the 7th Cavalry.

The morning following, the command reached the "prickly pear country." By some this portion of the plains is called the "Cactus Country." As far as the eye could reach, the plains seemed as if covered with a most gorgeously colored tapestry carpet of the most brilliant crimson and yellow. Mile after mile the column marched through this strange scene, beautiful to the eye but dreadfully uncomfortable to the feelings. The dogs were placed in the wagons, out of which they persisted in jumping; then they went howling along the column, pricked at every step by the sharp thorns. For two days' march we moved through this sharp country. Once out of it, I do not think that there was a man in the entire command that would have willingly gone through it again.

Chief Creek, one of the heads of the Republican, was reached and crossed at a point fifty miles west of the forks near which the command had camped for so long a time. Two days more, and the wagon trail—made at the time of Lieutenant Robbins's trip to Fort Wallace—was struck. Here, too, was discovered the trail of Kidder's party. They had mistaken the Fort Wallace trail for the route taken by the command. On the following day, the bodies of Lieutenant Kidder and his party were found, but in such a mutilated condition that it was impossible to distinguish the body of the lieutenant from those of the men. One thing was evident: They had been killed almost without a fight. Why this should have been the case was impossible to understand. The party numbered twelve in all. They had each a Spencer carbine and a hundred rounds of ammunition, two revolvers, and a liberal supply of cartridges. The only account of

The ambush of the Kidder party. W. F. BEYER, *DEEDS OF VALOR.*

the affair that can ever be known we gathered by a careful examination of the trails. From these we learned that the party was moving at a walk along a high divide, about a mile from Beaver Creek. When they first discovered the Indians, Kidder left this divide at once, and at a gallop made for the basin, where he was surrounded and forced to fight at a disadvantage.

The Indians had attacked in two parties, numbering something over a hundred each. But very few shots could have been fired by Kidder's party with their carbines, as there were not more than ten or a dozen cartridge shells to be found. They may have used their revolvers, but there was every reason to believe that they had been overpowered by the Indians in the first attack. From appearances one or more of the men had met death by torture.

One of the bodies we recognized as that of Red Bead, a friendly Sioux who had accompanied the party as a guide. The body had been scalped, but the hair trophy had not been carried off—a fact that made it certain that the attacking Indians had been Sioux—probably Pawnee Killer and his band. Indians will scalp one of their own tribe who is found with an enemy, but the scalp is invariably left near the body. The remains were buried by Custer's command. Then the column moved on, reaching Fort Wallace on the evening of the day following. The garrison of the fort had fought two fights with the Indians, in both of which they had lost a few men killed and wounded. The loss of the Indians was unknown.

The Smoky Hill stage route might be considered as closed, there having been no coaches through for a number of days. Indians were known to be in great numbers along the entire route. Colonel Custer was determined to rest the command for a few days, when he would take a sufficient escort and push through to Fort Hays. This would enable him to ascertain the actual condition of affairs along the route. On the evening of July 15, he left Fort Wallace with an escort of seventy-five picked men and horses under the command of Captain Hamilton. With these he marched rapidly and reached Fort Hays, more than a hundred and fifty miles distant, in a little less than three days' time.

At every station along the route, we received intelligence of Indians; sometimes they had been seen in large bands, sometimes in small. They had made but few attacks, as they seemed anxious to avoid too close proximity to the mud monitors that had been constructed for the defense of the ranches used as stations. The mud monitors are simply covered pits located a short distance from each corner of the ranch, and communicating with it by means of tunnels. While in these monitors, the station men were perfectly protected, but an attacking party was exposed to fire from all directions.

Near Downer's Station, a small party of the escort, which had lingered a few miles in the rear, were attacked by a large band of Indians. Two of the men were killed, but the remainder reached the command in safety.

The Indian campaign was over, and at Harker an individual clad in ragged buckskins took the cars for the East. It was the special artist, leaving the plains after a horseback ride of nearly three thousand miles. A peace has lately been made with the Indians. This they will keep through the winter. If, when the grass is come again, they are not out on the warpath, it will be contrary to the teachings of all previous experience.

The Indians feel that they are rich when at war and poor while at peace. Naturally they prefer war; that is, when they can have it, as they invariably do, entirely in their own way—war when there is good grass for their ponies to subsist on, and peace when there is none. Riches and glory are the Indian's sure means of reaching the Happy Hunting Ground. These are nowhere to be secured so easily as on the warpath against the whites.

There are many old chiefs who prefer peace, but the young men are invariably for war. The chiefs cannot control the bucks, who take the warpath as naturally as the quail does the bushes, or the young ducks the sedge.

I have yet to meet the frontiersman who does not prefer peace with the Indians to war, and it is due these hardy men to say that few can realize the outrages that they suffer at the hands of the redskin before they reach the trusty rifle that hangs in the antlers over the mud fireplace of the ranch, which is their home only so long as they are suffered by the Indians to occupy it.

The 18th Kansas Volunteer Cavalry, and Some Incidents Connected with Its Service on the Plains

HENDERSON L. BURGESS[1]

Collections of the Kansas State Historical Society 13 (1913–14): 535–38[2]

A t the close of the Civil War, a large amount of territory embracing what is now central and western Kansas, eastern Colorado, and the Indian Territory was inhabited by numerous tribes of hostile Indians. The general government at Washington had turned its attention to the development of the West [and] the opening up of a public thoroughfare across the continent to the Pacific coast. To this end aid was being granted by the government in the construction of a line of railroad across the plains, and the Eastern Division of the Union Pacific Railroad in the spring of 1867 had been completed to Fort Harker, Kansas, and was in course of construction from that point west.

The hostile Indians, and especially the Cheyenne, Kiowa, Arapaho, and Comanche tribes, were upon the warpath and determined to prevent the building of the railroad and travel and transportation across the plains by the method then in use; to wit, ox and mule teams with long wagon trains. The United States mails were interrupted. Men, women, and children were being massacred, stock stampeded, wagon trains captured, and contents burned and destroyed by these hostile tribes to such an extent that the United States government troops then on the frontier were inadequate to afford protection. Therefore, by order of the War Department at Washington, the first battalion of the 18th Kansas Volunteer Cavalry[3] was organized and enlisted between July 5–15, 1867, and on July 15 was mustered into the United States service at Fort Harker, Kansas. It was armed, uniformed, and equipped by the United States government, and within three days after it was mustered into service under command of the late Horace L. Moore,[4] of Lawrence, Kansas, entered upon an active campaign of four months' duration against these hostile Indians.

On the day the regiment was mustered in, the command was attacked by Asiatic cholera, and a number of deaths occurred at Fort Harker on July 15, 16, and 18, 1867. Major Moore, who had recently been mustered out of the United States service as colonel of the 4th Arkansas Cavalry, being a man of excellent judgment and having at heart the interests of the troops under his command, took the best method of preventing a greater loss by disease by putting the command immediately into active service and moving it from Fort Harker across the country by way of Pawnee Rock to Fort Larned.

While en route to Fort Larned, a detachment of twenty-two men under the command of Lt. Henry L. Hegwer of Company D was sent in pursuit of a band of hostile Indians that had stampeded a train and run off some stock belonging to freighters. Three fine horses were recaptured and later returned to the owners by the government.

At Fort Larned we lost the regimental surgeon; one commissioned officer, Lt. Samuel L. Hybarger of B Company; and a number of enlisted men from cholera. However, the troops fit for duty were immediately sent forward from Fort Larned to Fort Hays to cooperate with the 7th and 10th United States Cavalry regiments in an expedition against the Indians in the north and northwest part of the state. At our camp on Walnut Creek, while en route to Fort Hays, more deaths occurred from cholera. I remember at this point a boy belonging to Company C was sick with the cholera. When the four companies broke camp early in the morning, this young soldier was breathing his last, and as Company D passed by where he lay on a stretcher, he expired. A detail was made to dig a grave. He was taken from the stretcher, wrapped in his blanket, and buried on the banks of Walnut Creek, and the four companies continued the march to Fort Hays, where we sustained no further loss from cholera.

About the middle of August, Companies B and C, under the command of Capt. Edgar A. Barker and Capt. George B. Jenness,[5] with Company F of the 10th United States Cavalry, the entire command being under Capt. George A. Armes of the Regular army, were ordered on a scouting expedition to the northeast in pursuit of Indians who were making raids from the northwest, killing and scalping those engaged in surveying and building the Union Pacific Railroad. A number of men had been killed near what is now Bunker Hill Station west of Ellsworth, and along the line of the road, and a large force was necessary to drive these Indians out of the country.

Major Moore, with Companies A and D under command of Henry C. Lindsey and Capt. David L. Payne, was sent upon this expedition, his command to move to the northwest from Fort Hays. The troops carried three days' rations, and the two commands under Captain Armes and Major Moore were to cooperate in the campaign against the hostiles. The rations proved to be entirely insufficient for the raid, which lasted for eight days. The buffalo had been driven out of the country by the Indians and a large part of the prairie burned over to prevent our obtaining forage for our horses and mules. The herds of buffalo that usually ranged through this district would have afforded an abundance of fresh meat. Both men and animals suffered greatly for want of food and water, it being exceedingly hot and dry during the entire summer.

After reaching the Saline River, Captain Armes with his three companies of cavalry proceeded to follow the river until he formed a junction with Major Moore, with A and D Companies of the 18th. Major Moore with his command proceeded to the northwest, while Captain Armes with his three companies took a northeasterly course, each of the two commands intending to cut off the possible escape of the Indians and to form a junction on the Solomon River.

By this movement the Indians were driven farther to the northeast, where a part of Captain Armes's command engaged them, and the battle of Beaver Creek ensued.[6] The battle was a most bloody fight. The small detachment of troops separated from the command were placed at every disadvantage and exposed to the greatest danger from their relentless and savage foes. Captain Jenness was severely wounded in the thigh. The chief scout, Capt. A. J. Pliley, was twice wounded by the Indians, and a number of troops were wounded, some dying from their wounds, while several were killed. The soldiers fought bravely and, when finally joined by Captain Armes and the rest of the command, succeeded in forcing the Indians to retire with a severe loss in killed and wounded. The exact number, of course, could never be ascertained, as Indians carry their dead and wounded with them when it is by any means possible to do so. On the other hand, they rarely fail to torture and kill their enemies when they fall into their hands.

This account of incidents of the service of the 18th Kansas Cavalry is prepared from memory. It is impossible now to recollect the names of all those killed and wounded. In fact, I never knew the names of all the brave men who fell during the campaign, but I remember, in addition to Captain Jenness and Chief Scout Pliley, the name of Thomas G. Masterson, of Company C, who was killed in the fight on Beaver, or Prairie Dog, Creek, and of James H. Towell of the same company, who was wounded several times and afterwards died of his wound in the latter part of August at Fort Hays; also the name of Thomas Anderson of Company B.

Of those who died of cholera at Fort Harker, I remember the name of Bailey McVeigh and William P. Maxwell of Company D. Maxwell was a fine young man and had been promised promotion; he was in perfect health, a man of splendid physical development. He was taken sick in the evening and was dead and buried the next morning. I helped to care for comrade Maxwell during his very short illness. His body is buried at Fort Harker on the Smoky Hill River, as is also the body of Bailey McVeigh and many others belonging to the battalion who died of the cholera. Others are buried at Fort Larned on Pawnee Creek, on Walnut Creek at Fort Hays, and on the Beaver. Some were killed in action; others died of wounds received in action in various places between the Republican River on the north and the Arkansas River on the south.

The 18th was constantly engaged in drilling. Marching by day and by night, fighting Indians, guarding government trains, making its basic operations at Fort Hays, Fort Larned, and Fort Dodge, from which government posts it received its rations, ammunition, and supplies, it marched over two thousand miles in four months and engaged the Indians on several occasions, affording protection to government property and the United States mail, as well as to private citizens. It greatly aided in making safe the then unoccupied plains for settlement by the sturdy and industrious farmers who have for the last forty years planted and reaped golden grain over the graves of these brave men who gave their lives in the protection of the frontier. They suffered all the hardship endured by the soldiers of any war. The last service rendered, in October and the early part of November 1867, was in guarding a train of provisions, arms, and ammunition together with four hundred head of native cattle, sent by the government to the peace council at Medicine Lodge for the use of the Indians. Here most of the Indians agreed to the unmolested occupation by white men of this great agricultural territory. But this agreement was wholly disregarded and violated the very next year by these same hostile tribes. The 18th Kansas Cavalry served with the 7th and 10th United States regiments during the summer of 1867. These were brave soldiers and entitled to a large degree of credit. At one time the entire command was with the 7th Cavalry in the northwest part of the state and, under the command of Colonel Custer, pursued the Indians and drove them out of the country. The 7th Cavalry afterwards, on June 25, 1876, made a record as a fighting regiment that can never be exceeded. Like old Roman Nose, every man in the command laid down his scarred body fighting the red man.

The uncoffined clay of the soldiers of the 18th Kansas Cavalry who died of disease, who were killed or died of wounds in the summer and fall of 1867, have been moldering back to Mother Earth for forty-seven years, and although this command served its country faithfully from the day it was mustered into the United States service until it was mustered out and discharged on November 15, 1867, a grateful government has never provided a service pension for its members, nor for the soldiers of the 19th Kansas Volunteer Cavalry. The soldiers of every other war from the time this government was organized down to the present have been most generously dealt with.

Be it said, however, to the credit of the representatives of the state of Kansas now in Congress, that at least three bills are now pending before the Committee on Pensions in both the House and Senate, the object of which is to do justice to these soldiers by placing them on the pension rolls of the United States and extending the laws now in force applicable to other soldiers to them, their widows, and minor children. The government cannot afford to do less. It is due to the state of Kansas. It is due to the officers and soldiers who so bravely and earnestly defended the frontier and made it possible that broad fields of waving grain should be grown over this territory, then inhabited by a hostile and relentless foe.

Under the present law, every soldier who served in the Mexican War for a period of sixty days and was honorably discharged from the United States service is entitled to a service pension. Every soldier who served in the late Civil War for a period of not less than three months is entitled to a service pension, and every soldier who served in any Indian war up to and including the year 1860 for a period of not less than thirty days is entitled to a service pension.

The Battle on Beaver Creek

GEORGE B. JENNESS[1]

Collections of the Kansas State Historical Society 9 (1905–6): 443–52

The Indian depredations on the Kansas frontier during the spring of 1867 early developed the inadequacy of the Regular army efficiently to protect so great a range of country as was then exposed upon the Kansas border. After repeated and most urgent solicitation of the War Department, Gov. Samuel J. Crawford finally received authority to raise and muster five companies, which were to be armed and equipped by the general government.

Under the call, each volunteer furnished his own horse, and within two weeks from the date of the governor's proclamation,[2] four companies of fine men were in camp, mounted upon horses well used to frontier duty and considered in every way equal to the Indian ponies. Owing to the exigencies of the situation and the immediate demand for troops, it was thought proper not to attempt the organization of the fifth company, but to push the battalion of four companies already in camp immediately into the field. Upon consultation with Maj. Gen. Philip H. Sheridan, the territory to be guarded by the volunteers, respectively, was duly agreed upon, and under the efficient command of Maj. Horace L. Moore[3] of Lawrence, the Kansas battalion was ordered into service. The companies were commanded respectively by Capt. Henry C. Lindsey, A; Capt. Edgar A. Barker, B; Capt. George B. Jenness, C; and Capt. David L. Payne, D.

The first experience was not very encouraging for the future usefulness of the battalion, for while in camp at Fort Harker, the Asiatic cholera broke out among the troops and came very near demoralizing the command. Each company lost more or less men by death, while desertion through panic became altogether too common. Company C alone, in two weeks, lost thirteen men who died from cholera and seven deserters. Finally, upon moving camp, the cholera disappeared and the campaign began in earnest. Several weeks were spent in scouting between the Arkansas and Saline Rivers before the companies were separated. Companies B and C were ordered to Fort Hays and about August 18 were directed to prepare for a grand scout toward the headwaters of the Solomon and Republican Rivers, where a large body of Cheyenne and

Arapaho Indians were reported to be encamped. This expedition was to be participated in by Company F, 10th United States Cavalry, and Companies B and C, 18th Kansas, the whole under command of Brevet Maj. George A. Armes of the 10th.[4]

Starting from Fort Hays on August 20, and with but few wagons and two ambulances, the company provisions mostly carried on pack mules, the force marched rapidly in a northwesterly direction. On the evening of the twenty-first, the command camped on the Solomon [Prairie Dog] River, about eighty-five miles northwest of Hays and at a point twelve miles from the Republican, the two streams running almost parallel. Indian signs, fresh and clear, had been discovered during the day, and that night a bright light was visible some distance to the east. Captain Jenness volunteered to take a file of men and investigate the matter. This meeting the approval of Captain Armes, he selected Sergeant Stringer and Corporal Campbell and started in the direction of the light, the distance to which proved greater than was at first supposed, it being nearly midnight before they approached near enough to investigate the cause. It was then discovered to be an old log burning, where the Indians had evidently stopped the day before. Turning back, the party became bewildered in the darkness, and finally, giving up all hope of finding the trail, they bivouacked for the remainder of the night on the open prairie.

Early in the morning they were in the saddle, and traveling in a northerly direction, they soon reached the river, perhaps eight miles below the camp from which they had started. From a high hill here, they discovered the camp of the wagon train, which had been ordered to move parallel to the command, some three miles further down the river. This opportunity to breakfast was not to be missed; so galloping thither, they were soon enjoying a bountiful supply of rations. The train was guarded by thirty men under Lt. John W. Price of Company B, 18th Kansas, a very efficient and brave officer. Upon learning of the Indian signs, he made preparations to continue his march with due caution. Captain Jenness, being joined by Pvt. Thomas G. Masterson, who had just arrived from Fort Hays with the mail, left the train at about 8:00 A.M. and pushed up the river to rejoin the main command. He reached the camp about noon, to find the troops gone, and after a short rest crossed the river and proceeded to follow the trail. Here he was met by three dismounted men, sent back by Captain Armes to join the wagon train. Not thinking it safe to allow them to continue in the face of the many Indian signs, he ordered them to follow him forward. The day was exceedingly warm, and all the men had taken off their coats, those mounted strapping theirs behind their saddles. No particular order was maintained, and no immediate danger apprehended.

Proceeding in this way for about three miles, they were suddenly startled by hearing the most unearthly yells ever dropped on mortal ears, and looking up to the west, they saw about five hundred Indians swooping down upon them from a ridge about a half mile away.[5] At the same time, they saw, to their intense relief, a party of cavalry, twenty men and a sergeant, coming towards them from the direction of the command. Putting their horses on a gallop, after taking up the dismounted men, they formed a junction with the sergeant and his squad just as the Indians had approached within three hundred yards. Captain Jenness assumed command, dismounted his men, formed a hollow square in the time it takes to tell it, and they began to pour volley after volley into the Indians from their Spencer carbine seven-shooters.

The Indians began the fight by forming a complete circle around the detachment and just within range of the guns. They were promiscuously armed with Springfield and Mississippi rifles, shotguns, and bows and arrows. Had they been armed as well as Indians generally were several years later, not a white would have escaped. Their tactics appeared to be to stampede our horses, and the shaking of blankets and lances with streamers attached, and their unearthly whoops and yells as they circled around, were calculated to make the horses uneasy. As they continued riding, each alternate Indian would from time to time wheel his horse inside their circle, rein up, and discharge his piece at the square.

After the formation of the square of skirmishers by Captain Jenness, the horses were wheeled "fours right" into column, and each set of fours put in charge of number four of each file, and under a determination to push on and attempt to reach the main command, which Sgt. George W. Carpenter reported about four miles north, in the bottomlands of Beaver Creek, we started forward. We moved slowly, keeping up a constant firing on the Indians, who also continued a perfect shower of balls and arrows. Occasionally we would be compelled to halt for a moment or so, and at such times squads of Indians would dismount, creep up behind prairie dog hills and buffalo wallows, and pour in flight after flight of arrows. Several of the men were struck with arrows, while scarcely a horse remained which had not been wounded. As for the execution from the square, many Indians were seen to fall from their ponies, while others would drop on one side of their saddles or topple backwards, as though fatally hit, but were tied to their horses. This plan of strapping themselves to their trappings is a common one with Indians, as in case of being shot their bodies will be borne off with their party and not fall into the hands of their enemies.

Occasionally Indians would rally in a squad of one hundred or more, suddenly face the whites, and come dashing down on a full charge. At such critical times the threatened side of the square would be reinforced by running up each alternate man from the other side of the square, when this front would kneel down and empty the full seven shots of their carbine magazines into the approaching Indians. The red devils had never before encountered troops armed with seven-shooters, and these repeated volleys without any perceptible intermission for reloading would stagger them before they reached the square, and they would break and retreat in all directions, yelling like demons. The rapid succession of shots appeared to work upon their superstitious notions, and after each such charge they would draw off and huddle together, as though for consultation over the strange phenomenon. Many Indians could be seen to fall, and at one time eleven dead bodies were counted lying in the track of their futile charge. In one of their most daring charges, one Indian, mounted upon a splendid white animal, led his band.[6] He never looked behind, but with a revolver in hand dashed on, giving encouraging commands to his warriors until within pistol range, when he opened fire. At this point, his followers were staggered by a telling volley from the square and, wavering for a moment, broke and ran. The chief, however, came on, dashing his spurs into his horse and flourishing his revolver. He rode over one man who essayed to stop him, to the square, and on to the farther side. Probably fifty shots were fired at him, but all were apparently ineffectual. He bore a charmed life and had made a most daring ride.

The detachment carried two hundred rounds of ammunition per man, and no fears were felt for our safety upon that score.

After advancing about half a mile in this manner, fighting incessantly, Scout Allison J. Pliley informed the commander that another and still larger body of Indians could be seen through his glass on the hills, and between us and where the main command was supposed to be. At the time, all thought them to be warriors, but subsequently we learned that they constituted the inactive force of the camp—squaws, old men, and children. Being then satisfied that they were fighting men, and having no hopes of being able to cut our way through them, the plan of joining Captain Armes was given up.

Upon consultation with Scout Pliley, Captain Jenness determined to return to the river, and there erect a breastwork of driftwood and prepare for the coming darkness. Changing the front and turning the horses around caused something of a halt, during which the Indians redoubled their firing and showers of arrows, until only four horses remained unwounded. Many had been killed, and all except those four were badly hurt and fairly bristling with arrows. They were restless and enraged, and it took more men to care for them than could be spared from the lines. Under this condition of affairs, it was decided to kill all but the four whole animals, and as they were turned out of the square, they were shot by men selected for the purpose. At this point, Cpl. James H. Towell received seven balls in his body, and Thomas G. Masterson was also mortally wounded. This was the man who had brought out the mail from Fort Hays to the wagon train. One of the 10th Cavalry, the dismounted man who was picked up at the river, was killed instantly. Mounting five badly wounded men, who were too badly hurt to be able to use their arms, the return movement was begun. Before killing the horses, all the saddle pockets containing the ammunition had been taken off, and these the men carried across their shoulders. Leaving the high ground, the detachment entered a ravine, and for the first time since the beginning of the battle, the men here got water.

Three hours of constant fighting, with the nervous system strained to the utmost, had almost exhausted the energies of even these hardy westerners. The fearful odds against them and knowledge that no quarter was ever given by those red devils had created a desperate energy which made each man perform the deeds of five. Add to this their intense thirst, for by some oversight on the part of Captain Armes, the canteens of all the men sent to meet Captain Jenness were empty, and you have some conception of the condition of the men when they left the ridge and entered the ravine. Already fourteen men were wounded, two of them mortally. Nine of these were so severely shot that they were unable to use their guns. Of these, five were mounted upon the four remaining horses, and their intense groans increased the gloom of the situation.

Upon entering the deep ravine before mentioned, a fine spring was discovered, and regardless of the rapid and close-range firing of the Indians gathered on the high ground surrounding, the men broke in disorder for drinks and to fill their canteens. The ground was so broken that the squad was protected from a charge of the hostiles, and as fast as a man satisfied his thirst, he would retake his position and resume firing with redoubled vigor.

The sun was sinking slowly in the west, and upon marching farther down the ravine, here cut by the little stream running from the spring, the men found cover among a stunted growth of cottonwoods and willows. From this time until dark, we remained in the same position, having a good range at the Indians, and not another man wounded.

After dark the savages drew off, and the firing suddenly ceased. The rest from combat was a grateful one and gave us time and opportunity to care for the wounded men. Taking those from the horses, the captain tore up the shirts and blankets, washed and dressed all the wounds as well as possible, and gave the sufferers a short rest upon the remaining blankets.

A reconnaissance made by Scout Pliley and Sergeant Carpenter proved the position to be a short distance from the river. They also reported another little stream running into the river a quarter of a mile east, which appeared to run from the northeast and in a line parallel to the river.

Scout Pliley had been twice shot through the calf of his left leg, the balls passing through within three inches of each other. Captain Jenness had received a large ball in his right thigh but, binding it up with a handkerchief twisted tight with a piece of a gun wiper, continued on foot, though his boot full of blood would squash as though he had waded in water. Pliley, notwithstanding his two wounds, heroically kept his feet and was ever ready to second the plans of the commander. The balance of the wounded men, including Sgt. Henry H. Campbell, who was shot in the shoulder, and Sergeant Carpenter, shot in the left arm, showed a valor seldom equaled by any men.

As full darkness fell upon the squad, the signals of the Indians could be heard upon every side—now the yelp of the coyote, and again the hoot of the owl—showing that they were posting their vedettes.

Just before entering the ravine, which we had followed down to this point, and after leaving the body of the colored man of the 10th Cavalry, who had been instantly killed, the Indians had taken his scalp, tied it to a lance, and giving it to one daredevil, sent him as close as he dared come, to insult us. He would flaunt it at the men and yell out, "This is the way we will serve you all." Others spoke good English and would shout insulting epithets from time to time during the fight. Said one, "We have killed all the balance of your men and propose to have you." Upon no occasion did they get the best of the brave boys, for they would reply as spiritedly as though a thousand men were present.

At no time could any firing be heard from the direction of the main command; but as the wind blew from the south, it bore our firing to them, as we subsequently learned. The silence, however, from the main force was ominous to us, and fears were entertained that the boasts of the Indians, or the white men with them, might be true. Everything combined to make the situation desperate, but still there was a fixed determination to fight to the last.

Resting in the cottonwoods until about 10:00 P.M., with pickets thrown out to guard against surprise, time was given to decide upon the next step for escape from the unpleasant dilemma. An examination made by Pliley discovered a buffalo path leading from the ravine in which we were situated through a dry creekbed out to the little stream before mentioned as running parallel with the river. This path ran through quite thick underbrush, and the steep, stony bluffs upon either side were inaccessible to the Indians. From the top of the bluff, where their pickets could be heard, this path could not be seen. Evidently the Indians knew nothing of it, and had no vedettes stationed to guard it. Upon consultation, it was decided to avail ourselves of this avenue to gain the river, and perhaps get to the wagon train. Muffling the feet of the horses with shirts torn into suitable strips to prevent the noise of their iron shoes striking the stones, and covering one white horse with a blue blanket, we prepared to move. The nine men who were badly wounded were mounted on the four horses—three on the first, three on the second, two on the third, and Tommy Masterson, who was already slowly dying, upon the fourth—and a dreary march was begun. The suffering men agonized under the smarting of their wounds, shut their teeth, and most heroically abstained from groaning during the whole of this midnight march. Scout Pliley and Captain Jenness, leaning upon each other for support—one wounded in the left leg, the other in the right, and each using a carbine for a cane—led the file; five men followed; then came the horses, led by careful comrades; and the balance of the detachment followed, Sergeants Carpenter and Campbell acting as rear guard. Silently they crept forward, keenly watching the flanks and whispering encouraging words to each other and the wounded boys. Tommy Masterson, with all hope gone, was whispering his dying message for his mother to Cpl. John A. Kirkland, who walked by his side. It was a solemn procession, yet hopeful of the end.

For over two miles this silence and strain were maintained; and then, feeling that the Indian vedettes had been successfully passed, a more cheerful spirit took possession of the party. Even Masterson brightened up, and Corporal Towell, with seven wounds, talked of our future plans.

On crept the file, until five or six miles had been traveled, when the rippling waters of the Solomon were heard upon the right. Turning towards the welcome sound, the squad soon stood upon its banks. In the dim moonlight, the high bluffs on the opposite side could be seen, and thinking that they would afford a better protection in case of another attack, the detachment found a shallow place and crossed over. Here a small canyon was selected—one which had the appearance of a natural redoubt—and the wounded men were taken from their horses and laid upon blankets, and as comfortably fixed as possible under the circumstances. The balance of the command, tired beyond endurance, refused all duty and threw themselves upon the ground for rest. Sergeant Carpenter was the only man who could be induced to remain awake, and posting him upon an elevation to the east of the position, Captain Jenness himself ascended the slope on the west to keep a lookout until morning. Scout Pliley was left in charge of the men and busied himself assisting the wounded. This solemn vigil was kept until the east became tinged with red, when, by great exertion, the men were aroused to eat the remnants in their haversacks. While assigning the men positions and making suitable preparations for another fight, the Indians were discovered in full force upon the north side of the river. There was but one hope under the circumstances. Pliley, who knew the country, must find the wagon train and bring reinforcements or, if that was captured, go to Fort Hays. Mounting the best of the remaining horses, he bravely set out, going down a ravine leading south and out of sight of the Indians. In twenty minutes from his departure, we were again surrounded by the demonically yelling savages, who appeared to fairly cover the hills upon every side. Our ammunition was still plentiful, and an active fire soon began.

Covered as the detachment was by the friendly canyon, the random, though quite rapid, fire of the Indians was wholly ineffectual. The men, though confident of an ample supply of cartridges, were careful in their firing and never wasted a shot. Whenever an Indian presented his form above the summit of the high ridges surrounding us, he received a shot. There were no means of knowing whether such firing was any ways effectual, but as the men were all westerners, and many of them fine marksmen, it cannot be doubted that the Indians lost quite a number during this morning's fight.

About 8:00 A.M. the attention of the captain was called to a column of men moving toward us on the high ground to the south. At first this new force was supposed to be another body of Indians, but as they came more plainly into view, two cavalry guidons could be seen. As this was reported, a loud and joyful cheer broke from the men, and as hearty a three times three as we ever heard echoed among those sterile hills and doubtless startled the savages themselves. They had seen the newcomers also, and quickly withdrawing, the next we saw of them was in the stunted timber on the riverbank and broken ground beyond.

Coming into sight for a few moments only, the friendly guidons disappeared. We waited anxiously for another hour, when a few rapid volleys below us and towards the river called our attention in that direction. A few of the Indians broke from the underbrush upon this side, and soon a dismounted detachment led by Pliley, our faithful scout, still on his horse, was in our midst.

Handshaking and the warmest congratulations ensued. They were a part of the main force under Captain Armes and had been sent to our relief. It appeared that the Indians had surrounded his command at about the same time they attacked the detachment of Captain Jenness and had been fighting them every hour of daylight since. The command had just fallen back to the river and joined the wagon train, which, unbeknown to us, was camped a mile west of where we had taken position in the canyon.

Pliley, after wandering around through the bleak hills for several hours, eluding the Indians, had finally struck the trail of the wagons, and following it up, reached it but a few minutes before Captain Armes came in. As quickly as possible, he had secured a detachment and had come to the relief of the badly demoralized party in the canyon. As soon as practicable, the wounded men were mounted on horses and a line of march taken up for the train. The fresh men formed a large square around their worn-out companions, and in this way they proceeded to the train. The Indians, with reckless bravado, would ride out from their cover in the timber and attempt to scare the squad. Several brisk little skirmishes took place in this way, but no one was hurt upon the side of the soldiers.

Reaching the train, there ensued a scene of cordial greeting such as is experienced nowhere except among comrades in battle. The detachment under Captain Jenness, and especially himself and the two men with whom he had originally started, had been given up for lost. Their firing had been heard on the day before until nightfall, when it had suddenly ceased, and it was supposed the entire detachment had been massacred. Their escape had indeed been miraculous. Their fighting, twenty-nine men against five or six hundred Indians, was unparalleled in the history of Indian fighting on the plains. That it was desperate the wounded evinced—fourteen men wounded and one killed out of twenty-nine. Tommy Masterson breathed out his life a half hour after the train had been reached, while Jimmy Towell only lived to be taken back to Fort Hays two days afterwards.

During the interchange of congratulations, the Indians, emboldened by the fact that no attack was made upon their stronghold, came out in small detachments and surrounded the little valley in which the train was parked. As soon as possible, a systematic line of picket skirmishers was organized and thrown out, and a large party, to be mounted on the best horses, was selected for a charge upon the hostiles.

In the meantime, it became necessary to procure water from the river, now held by the Indians, and for this purpose volunteers were called for from the dismounted men. A sufficient number were soon secured, and they, led by Ed Paramore, company clerk of F Troop, who volunteered to conduct this perilous duty, deployed in line and advanced cautiously under a heavy fire, which was briskly returned. Reaching the outskirts of the timber, Paramore saw that his men, some fifteen or sixteen, were taken at a disadvantage by Indians from behind a tree, and gave the order for a charge. This movement was executed gallantly and sent the Indians flying to the opposite side of the river. The water here was very shallow and the stream narrow, though the riverbed itself was 150 feet wide. Our boys reached the bank with but one man slightly wounded, and while the water squad filled their kettles, the others kept the Indians on the other side completely under cover in the small growth of timber. The water squad returned in safety with an ample supply for all immediate purposes, and the company cooks began the preparation of the first regular meal the command had eaten for three days.

Soon after dinner, Captain Armes organized his party for a charge upon the Indian lines. The savages were posted upon the high ground and nearly surrounded the canyon in which the troops were situated. Upon a gentle slope to the west was their main body of warriors. The air was so clear that almost every command of their chiefs could be distinctly heard. At intervals some of them who spoke good English would yell out, "Come out of that hole, you white sons of bitches, and give us a fair fight," or other insulting expressions. At one time three of their warriors on foot came down towards the troops bearing a white flag. They were dismounted and apparently unarmed. Thinking that they wanted a conference, Charlie Cadaro, a half-breed who was with the command in the capacity of a scout and spoke several Indian dialects, was sent out towards them. Cadaro was up to Indian tricks and carried a Spencer carbine beneath his overcoat. Advancing slowly and cautiously towards the now stationary savages, he had no sooner approached within good range than they threw aside their blankets, leveled their guns, and fired. Cadaro saw their motion and, anticipating their shot, dropped quickly to the ground. Uncovering his carbine, he poured seven shots after the now-fleeing savages, finally bringing one of them to the ground. The wounded Indian's companions returned to him quickly, slung him over the back of the tallest, and again made off. Cadaro, unfortunately, had no more cartridges with him, and his carbine being empty, nothing remained for him but to return. This little episode put a stop to flags of truce.

When Captain Armes had formed his picked squad, he ordered an advance toward the river, with a view to cover his intention of an assault upon the hill where their main body was stationed. The advance caused a very perceptible commotion among the hostiles along the river, and as Armes's move threatened their left flank and rear, they could be seen running back and to the opposite side of the river. Finally, he reached a proper distance on the left of their position on the hill, and giving the order to change front, the men came into line on a gallop. Heading for the summit of the hill, they went up the slope with a hearty cheer and in gallant style. The steady and regular volleys from the carbines were too much for the random and slow firing of the Indians, and they soon broke and fled in all directions. Their fleet ponies and their scattered condition rendered pursuit impossible. As soon as the squad would make a dash for a knot of Indians, another party of hostiles would rally in their rear and thus threaten to cut them off from the train. After an hour or so of this ineffectual skirmishing, Captain Armes withdrew to the canyon, and the Indians could be seen gathering at one point. Here they remained until darkness hid them from our view.

Thus ended the battle of Beaver Creek, for the next morning the Indians were gone.

The command, after sending out a few scouting parties to scour the country, soon got under way for a return to Fort Hays. The wounded who were unable to mount their horses were crowded into the two ambulances. Tommy Masterson, who had died the day before (August 22), was that night buried in a bank by the river. The men, in the absence of spades, dug out the dirt to a sufficient depth with their sabers, and here was left the body from which had flown as brave a soul as ever actuated the drawing of a saber. A week afterwards, Captain Jenness visited the scene of the battle and found that this grave and that of one of the 10th Cavalry, who died from his wounds the same day, were desecrated. The body of Masterson had been disinterred and most fiendishly mutilated. Another and a better resting place was prepared for the body, and the remains of brave Tommy were left alone amid the wild grandeur of those rugged cliffs. James H. Towell died of lockjaw in the hospital at Fort Hays on the third day after the return.[7] His body was interred in the post cemetery, and a neat headboard, cut out by his captain, marked the quiet spot.

This properly concludes the battle of Beaver Creek, as participated in by the detachment under Captain Jenness.

The official report of this fight gives the following mortality of this small command in this miraculous escape from such an overpowering force of Indians: one man, Company C, 18th Kansas Volunteer Cavalry (K.V.C.) killed; one man, Company F, 10th U.S. Cavalry, killed; six men, Company C, 18th K.V.C., wounded; four men, Company B, 18th K.V.C., wounded; four men, Company F, 10th U.S. Cavalry, wounded; Allison J. Pliley, scout, wounded; Capt. George B. Jenness, Company C, 18th, wounded—out of a total engaged of twenty-nine enlisted men, one scout, [and] one commissioned officer, leaving only twelve men unhurt. The men, with no exception, displayed coolness and bravery, and were prompt and willing in the execution of every command.

Letter from Fort Dodge

"BART"

Army and Navy Journal 5, no. 9 (October 19, 1867)

FORT DODGE KANSAS, October 3, 1867

To the Editor of the *Army and Navy Journal:*

SIR: I am able to communicate the following particulars relative to incidents in this vicinity of late. On September 22 a Mexican train of twenty-eight wagons was attacked by Indians on the Santa Fe and Overland Southern Stage Route, some thirty-seven miles west of Fort Dodge, Kansas. Two Mexicans were killed and over a hundred whites captured by the savages. On the twenty-third Col. R. B. Marcy,[1] inspector general, U.S.A., was attacked. He was accompanied by Company K, 5th Infantry, recently from Albuquerque, New Mexico, officered by Bvt. Maj. D. H. Brotherton and 1st Lt. E[phraim] Williams. We lost one man killed and Lieutenant Williams severely wounded by a rifle ball in the left leg above the knee. The Indians were repulsed; loss not known. This affair took place near the Nine Mile Ridge, ten miles west of Cimarron Crossing.[2] Lieutenant Williams was conveyed to Fort Dodge, Kansas, where amputation was found necessary. He is doing well and will recover.

On the twenty-fourth Lt. Philip Reade, 3rd Infantry, with sixty men was sent from Fort Dodge to relieve the Mexican train and to, if possible, force an engagement with the Indians. He was gone four days and returned, reporting that the country was cleared of hostile Indians, having killed the only Indian he saw. His party sustained no loss. Immediately after, he was ordered to Cimarron Crossing to investigate the cause, which resulted in a conflict between the citizens at that station and the soldiers on escort duty there. The report has not yet been made known, but it is believed will bear heavily on the noncommissioned officer in charge of the escort, who has been arrested as being mainly responsible for the death of three men and wounding of others.

On September 25 three Indians made a dash for a man herding cattle within a mile of this post. He was unarmed and paid the penalty of his indiscretion by the loss of his life. On the twenty-seventh a train of about a score of wagons, escorted by twelve colored soldiers,[3] was attacked twelve miles east of here by a large party of Indians. A teamster killed, and a large amount of quartermaster and some ordnance stores captured and destroyed. The goods and stores were invoiced to 1st Lt. G. A. Hesselberger, 3rd U.S. Infantry, A.A.Q.M., at post. Capt. William Thompson, 7th U.S. Cavalry, is now stationed here, and Lt. Philip Reade, 3rd Infantry.

October 2 a detachment of one hundred cavalry belonging to the 18th Kansas Volunteers, commanded by Major Moore, passed through here on a western tour.

The Medicine Lodge Treaty, Sixty Years Ago

EDWARD S. GODFREY[1]

Winners of the West 6, no. 4 (March 1929): 8

I joined Troop G, 7th Cavalry, Capt. Albert Barnitz, at Fort Harker, Kansas, in the fall of 1867, having graduated from West Point in June. A few days later Troops D, G, and H, Maj. Joel H. Elliott commanding, were detailed as escort to the Indian peace commission.

About three hundred army wagons had been assembled on the south bank of the Smoky Hill River at the crossing of the stage road, opposite the site of old Fort Ellsworth; some timbers of buildings were still there, evidence of the site. These wagons were loaded with annuities or gifts for the Indians and supplies for the peace commission. Also, there were four Gatling guns hauled by two mules each, with civilian drivers. Against my wishes, I was detailed to command them. I receipted for the guns, mules, harness, etc., to Maj. Henry Inman, depot quartermaster at Fort Harker.

The only Gatling guns I had ever seen were in the ordnance museum at West Point. My first problem was to get men to man the guns. I finally found two men, one a sergeant who had served in the field artillery during the Civil War. We three worked out the minimum number of men to man the guns, and the necessary number of men was detailed. My second problem then was to improvise a drill to work the guns. On the march, I drilled my teamsters.

There were no howitzers with this expedition. Ambulances and Dougherty wagons were sent to Ellsworth City for the commissioners, and these joined us on the first day's march. On arrival at Fort Zarah (Great Bend), near the mouth of Walnut Creek, nearly all the commissioners left the expedition and went to Fort Larned, where the Indian agency was then located.

The next day we camped on the Arkansas River, near the mouth of Pawnee Creek. I well remember our astonishment to find that we could cross the great Arkansas dry shod at some places and find it a running stream above and below.

The next day we were joined by the parties who had gone to Fort Larned, the personnel of the Indian agencies, including guides, interpreters, and several officers from Forts Larned and Dodge.

Edward S. Godfrey (center) as a member of the West Point Class of 1867.
COURTESY OF PERRY FROHNE.

I recall that our army mess was increased to thirteen. At our midday luncheons, a case of twelve canned peaches was opened, and there was a drawing of "cuts" for the cans, the successful ones contributing to the "short cut." Later Major Page and other visiting officers established their own mess.

After crossing the Arkansas River, we ascended the sand hills. I rode to the highest hill, and there to my surprise found the wind had blown out a crater, exposing the top of a tree, which upon examination I found to be oak. Up to that time we had not seen any buffalo, but from my high sand hill I could see the rolling prairie to the south and miles and miles of buffalo. It occurred to the Indians to drive these herds to that vicinity in anticipation of the assembly for the treaty conference on October 12, 13, and 14—sixty years ago—so that their people could prepare their winter supply of dried meat.

That day, while at a halt, an army ambulance drove up to where a group of us were. Lt. Tom Wallace[2] called out, "Hello, Satanta!" A bleary-eyed, drunken Indian wearing the uniform of a colonel raised up from his bed, looked out from the rear entrance, and not seeing any of his particular friends, gave a grunt and settled back on his bed. Then the ambulance drove to where the commissioners were grouped.

During the day several of us, including Major Elliott, engaged in runs on the buffalo. That aroused the ire of Satanta, and he complained to General Harney,[3] the senior of the commission present. General Harney sent for Major

Elliott and placed him in arrest, but on arrival in camp released him. That stopped our sport.

Satanta's complaint was that we killed more buffalo than we needed for food. A number of times at our camps the command had to be turned out to keep stampeding buffalo from running into our camp, for some reason or no reason, and stampeding our stock. They were particularly troublesome on Rattlesnake Creek.

I will remark here that General Sherman, who was chairman of the peace treaty commission, was at no time present at this Medicine Lodge conference.

The day we reached the treaty grounds, the escort and supply train was halted a couple of miles from the place while the commission and followers went ahead to meet an escort of warriors from the assembled tribes—the Arapahos, [Kiowa-]Apaches, Kiowas, and Comanches. The Cheyennes had not yet arrived. The commission was received by a vast array of chiefs and warriors in panoplies, with shouts and shoots of firearms, and escorted to a large, open space near the left bank of Medicine Lodge Creek above the villages.

The escort and wagon train then advanced, and on arrival were placed in camp by General Harney—the troops in line facing upstream, officers' tents on the right, above the camp of the commission. My detachment of Gatling guns was camped behind the right of the line, facing toward the creek. The supply train was parked behind the commission camp. The commission had two hospital tents facing, with two flies between for the conference. Daily conferences were held with the chiefs and subchiefs, or delegations from the various tribes and bands.

Almost daily visits to these conferences left the impression of monotony in the welcomes by the officials and the replies by tribesmen. No doubt, though, that some of the speeches by the chiefs, [of] dignified bearing and gestures and well-modulated voice, lost much of their eloquence through the monotonous translation by the interpreter.

I recall one amusing incident. Kicking Bird, a subchief of the Kiowas who later became the famous head chief of the tribe, had made his speech and remained standing, but had his gaze fixed on the high silk hat in front of one of the commissioners.

The commissioner, not thinking of the hat but that some trinket had attracted his fancy, asked, "What do you want?" Kicking Bird, without changing his gaze, replied, "I want that hat." The commissioner, thinking he only wanted to satisfy his curiosity, handed over the hat. Kicking Bird took it and walked away. Later, he appeared in the immediate vicinity of the council tents arrayed in moccasins, breechclout, and the high hat. He stalked back and forth, telling the tribesmen to look at him; that he "was walking in the white man's ways," and using other set phrases that had been used in the councils. Finally he grew tired of his burlesque, set the hat on the ground, and used it as a football until he had battered it out of shape, then stalked away.

*An army wagon train on
the plains.* RUFUS F. ZOGBAUM,
HORSE FOOT AND DRAGOONS.

These councils continued for more than a fortnight,[4] according to my recollection, and there was considerable anxiety because the Cheyennes had not come in, and what the attitude of Charley Bent would be.[5]

One day word came that the Cheyennes would arrive the next day. Later word came that they would camp about three miles upstream for the night and arrive on the morrow. There was serious anxiety as to the meaning of this delay when so near, and that night guards were instructed to be particularly on the alert.

Stumbling Bear,[6] a subchief of the Kiowas, became a constant visitor at our camp, and became particularly friendly with Major Elliott; he was sure to be there about supper time and got the "leavings" of the supper. He would give us instructions in the sign language. The morning that the Cheyennes were to arrive, Stumbling Bear came to our camp, but not in his usual jolly mood. He told us to be on our guard when the Cheyennes came in, then went away.

As the Cheyennes approached our camp, we could hear occasional shots and shouts. Stumbling Bear and a few of his tribesmen came walking rather hurriedly and, without a word to anybody, squatted in close vicinity to Major Elliott's tent.

All the troops had instructions what to do in case of demonstration of hostile intent, but stood in front of their tents with everything in readiness to jump to their places fully equipped for dismounted defense.

The nearer the Cheyennes approached, the more demonstrative they became. Shooting, shouting, and blowing of trumpets; of the latter they had two or three. When about two or three hundred yards from our camp, they gave several loud shouts and dispersed.

Stumbling Bear and his followers left in high good humor. A year later, November 27, 1868, at the battle of Washita, Major Elliott was killed. In January 1869 the Kiowas came to their agency at Fort Sill. Stumbling Bear came to see me. I noticed that he had his hair cut off, and there were other unmistakable signs of mourning. I asked him if he was in mourning for losses in his band or family. He replied, "No," and gave me to understand that he was in mourning for the loss of his good friend Major Elliott. I never saw him again.

The conferences were closed soon after the arrival of the Cheyennes, the treaties signed ("touching the pen"), and then the wagons were unloaded and gifts of supplies were distributed—food, tobacco, clothing, blankets, pots, kettles, skillets, and trinkets. When we left there, the plain where the commission had camped was strewn with the despised, leftover, shoddy Civil War uniforms, issued by the bale to them.

At Fort Larned, Kansas, these same tribes were assembled (in August 1868) less than a year after signing the treaties to receive the annuities promised by the treaties. The next day of the issuance of these annuities, as if concerted, warriors of these same tribes attacked the frontier settlements in the Saline, Solomon, and Republican Run Valleys; killed men, women, and children; outraged and made captive women; burned homes; and stole stock.

The outcries of consternation and indignation with protests for protection resulted in the winter campaign of 1868–69 under General Sheridan, including the attack, capture, and destruction of Black Kettle's village of the Cheyennes by the 7th Cavalry, who later rescued two of the captive white women, Mrs. Morgan and Miss White. Then these tribes went on their agreed reservation, and for some years there was peace.

The Medicine Lodge Peace Council

HENRY MORTON STANLEY[1]

Daily Missouri Democrat (St. Louis), October 19, 1867

FORT LARNED, Oct. 13, 1867

You have already received in a former letter of mine[2] the gracious reception we met at [Fort] Harker. Did I tell you of the thundering salute that greeted our awakening in the morning? Have I already informed you how they serenaded us up to a late hour? How the ladies at Harker, bless them, did their utmost for our comfort. If so, then I will not repeat the tale.

About 2:00 P.M. the train of ten ambulances containing the commissioners and the press gang, a battery of Gatling guns of the 4th Artillery, and thirty wagons containing stores roll off westward, escorted by three companies of the 7th Cavalry, commanded by Major Elliott.

In the ambulances are Generals [Alfred H.] Terry, [William S.] Harney, [James A.] Hardie; Senator [John B.] Henderson; Commissioner [of Indian Affairs, Nathaniel G.] Taylor; Colonel [Samuel F.] Tappan; Governor [Samuel J.] Crawford; Senator [Edmund G.] Ross; A. S. H. White, secretary commission; John D. Howland, *Harper's Weekly*; [Solomon T.] Bulkley, New York *Herald*; S. F. Hall, Chicago *Tribune*; George Center Brown, Cincinnati *Commercial*; H. I. Budd, Cincinnati *Gazette*; William Fayel, St. Louis *Republican*; George Willis, photographer; [Milton W.] Reynolds, editor *Kansas State Journal*; correspondent Chicago *Times*, one from the Chicago *Republican*, and from the Leavenworth *Bulletin*; and your own inimitable "Stanley."

A march of one mile, across the Smoky River, and we camp. We have gained a start.

The reason that we have such an escort may be seen by reading the subjoined letter:

MEDICINE LODGE CREEK, Oct. 5, 1867

SIR: I have the honor to inform you that as far as I am concerned, I feel perfectly safe among these Indians without soldiers, yet if the honorable commissioners feel otherwise, it might be better to have an escort with them, and in this event I would suggest that you bring

Henry Morton Stanley.
FRANK LESLIE'S ILLUSTRATED WEEKLY 1867.

regulars, and in number not exceeding two hundred. I make this suggestion for the reason that the strictest military discipline will have to be enforced while these soldiers are among the Indians. This discipline is not often found outside the Regular army. It would be wiser to come without any soldiers than to come with a few; hence I name two hundred as a sufficient number for an escort, and few enough not to alarm the Indians. I will meet you at Fort Larned and will have some of the chiefs of each tribe with me. Do not leave that post until I get there.

    Your obedient servant,

THOS. MURPHY,
Superintendent of Indian Affairs

HON. N. G. TAYLOR, Commissioner of Indian Affairs

    Just one mile away to the northward across the river stands Fort Harker, looking this evening like a city with its row of tents dwindling down to the size of headstones laid with regularity by an experienced sexton. A tall, strong flagstaff towers above all the buildings, and even from here the beautiful American flag can be seen waving and flapping protectingly from its peak. A low ridge intervening between the fort and our camp prevents us from seeing the garrison moving about, but along the road which ascends the hill come trooping some cavalry, advancing towards us. They halt at the river and allow their horses to drink, and then retire with the same steady gait and discipline as they advanced.

Well, our camp is situated on the brow of the hill looking lovingly across the river and into the old fort, now dilapidated, and only distinguishable from where we stand by two solitary adobe chimneys, which last winter saw a group of exiled soldiers begging them for the friendly warmth of their homely hearths. At the west end of our camp are the tents of three companies of the 7th Cavalry under the command of Major Elliott. The wagons of their regiment are clustered near, loaded with green, red, and blue blankets, gaudy printed calico, blue cloth, workhouse hats, beads, and silver medals for the friendly chiefs that we intend to visit. Then comes the artillery, two Gatling guns belonging to Battery B, 4th Artillery commanded by Capt. [Charles C.] Parsons. The tents of the artillerists flank the north side of the battery and therefore were parallel with the other tents. Eastward are ranged the ambulances, ten in number. These, while on the march, contain the commissioners and the members of the press. The whole camp is flanked at the eastern end by the tents of the commissioners. Those exposed to the everlasting shrieking wind sway like drunken beings, their flaps like human arms beating to the fierce whistling gusts which threaten momentarily to give way before its power. Like the impetuous Provencal mistraon or the levanter, this American simoom comes down upon this exposed spot without a warning, sometimes leveling every forward object to the ground. It is the first thing the residents at Fort Harker will complain of.

Fronting their tent in a social circle, even while the wind is making such a terrible racket, the commissioners, now composed of Henderson, Taylor, Harney, Tappan, Terry, and Hardie, discuss the long mooted and most detested Indian question. Like philosophers, like astute geometricians do these gentlemen look the question in the face patiently and kindly. Though their efforts fail in perfecting a peace between the white and red men, no person catching a glance at this extemporaneous council would attach blame to them. This knotty enigma, which grew more knotty and warty day by day, is gradually being unraveled, and now bare lines, straight facts easy to be satisfied are all that is left. Just look with me between the wheels of this wagon, at the circle, examine each feature and tell me what you see.

We will first take Harney, who is now bending forward, seated on his camp stool, his broad face marked with the traces of busy years; his kindly blue eye beams brighter now, as he is engaged in an animated discussion; he lifts a forefinger to emphasize a point. When he stands erect, he towers above all like Saul the chosen of Israel. It does not require a remarkable degree of acuteness to see that underneath that calm, smiling, venerable exterior of Harney, there lies a wonderful power of vitality and passion not quite dead. Really a goodly man, a tried soldier, and a gentleman.

Opposite Harney you will see another Missourian of Pike County, John B. Henderson, known here as Senator Henderson.[3] He is the businessman of the commission. He is forever endeavoring to sift evidence concerning the Indians we intend to visit. One of forcible utterance in speech; possessed of a dogged perseverance to obtain light upon a dubious subject; never forgetful of western interests; a cool head, courteous in deportment, patient, affable to all, ever eager to oblige and always thoughtful of the wants of others. Any points that are necessary for publication, we all feel an inclination to ask Senator Henderson about.

On the senator's right sits Sanborn, a general who has served with some distinction on many a hard field. A garrulous, good-natured, and jovial gentleman, fond of good living and good company, an air of bonhomie all about him. Pleasant to converse with, free of access, and pretty thoroughly posted on Indian matters. Those are the prominent points of Sanborn. The general has been selected on account of his tact in business to superintend the movements of the commission.

On the senator's left sits Colonel Tappan[4] of Colorado, an agreeable companion, always smiling, but a gentleman of few words. He is also very well acquainted with Indian affairs.

And there is Commissioner N. G. Taylor, the president of the commission, a man of large brain, full of philanthropic ideas relative to the poor Indian. He is undoubtedly earnest in his opinions. Formerly a Methodist minister, he has turned his attention to secular matters, devoting his life to an improvement of the social status of the American aboriginal.

And lastly there is Terry,[5] the gallant and genial; his praises and his good deeds have been recorded by nobler pens than mine, and therefore I will not essay the task. The country remembers him.

Sherman is mysteriously absent. A telegram recalled him to Washington.

But the council is ended now, and they all adjourn for supper. The press gang follow and enter the tent. The cook, Ernest Michael, formerly employed at the Southern Hotel, has spread himself out. Why, here are excellent viands, food fit for the gods, delicious ham, unctuous sardines, assorted pickles, loaf sugar, and butter, Switzer cheese and light bread, tea and coffee, cakes and pies, excellently cooked and temptingly provided. Crimini! Cri! Here is a feast spread out in the most *recherche* manner in the most heaven-forsaken spot of Kansas. Annoyances vanish; smiles reign instead. Jokes and repartees are freely exchanged through the exhilarating influence of hot Bohea and strong Java coffee. I say Java because it was so good, even excelling in my opinion the best mocha I ever drank in an Egyptian Kahn. Who would not sell a farm and become a reporter?

But such a night as we passed the first on the march. Till almost dawn, we, the press gang, enlivened the long night hours with songs and glees. Jack Howland, the skillful, amusing, entertaining, good-hearted, brave Jack Howland, the artist of *Harper's Weekly,* told funny stories, and Chamberlain, our worthy caterer, sang funnier songs. Witty, hilarious, eccentric, but gentlemanly Brown of the Cincinnati *Commercial* exerted himself to the utmost to make everybody agreeable. Jovial Budd of the Cincinnati *Gazette* strained himself in cudgeling his brains to propound a conundrum *en passant.* I may remark that Budd can write a letter; a good letter; an entertaining one, not ponderous or tiresome. He never drives his readers crazy with theorizing, nor does he inflict a stale pun. Fayel enjoyed himself like a philosopher of Samos. Fayel, the correspondent of the *Republican,* has a fund of dry humor underneath his waistcoat, and some common sense, a qualification rarely met with in a literary Gitano camp. Bulkley of the *Herald* almost fell into convulsions with laughing at everybody's eccentricities. Bulkley is the best fellow out of Jericho, always polite, never sulky. Good souls, all of them, but I am getting prosy and must turn my attention to business.

We started next morning, the ninth instant, on our march to Larned. Sanborn is on horse, moving about, directing the movements, and having heard the order "March," the train is in motion. We present quite an imposing appearance, and with the formidable number of newspaper correspondents, the expedition to the Indian sachems becomes important.

The following letter you will find very interesting, as it contains in detail some valuable information:

MEDICINE LODGE CREEK, Oct. 5, 1867.

SIR: Having been selected by the Honorable Peace Commission to proceed to the Indian country and put myself in communication with the Indians of the Plains, Cheyennes, Arapahos, and [Kiowa-] Apaches, with a view of congregating them at some point near, at south of Fort Larned, there to await the arrival of the commissioners at Full Moon in October and, if possible, have the Indians, now on the warpath, come in and cease fighting. I have the honor to report that I have now completed this duty, and for a more full report of my operations in endeavoring to carry out your wishes, I respectfully refer you to my correspondence with you on this subject, and for your future information I now state that I have at this time assembled at this place the following number of Indians:

Arapahos, number of lodges 171
[Kiowa-]Apaches 85
Cheyennes 25
Kiowas 150
_____

Making in all 431

Little Big Mouth of the Arapahos, who has twenty-one lodges, is far away south and will not be here with his lodges, but is represented. The Cheyennes sent in word last night that they were moving their whole village, numbering some two hundred lodges, and would be here in a few days. The Comanches, who I am informed number one hundred lodges, are in camp about thirty miles below here, and would be present now, but that they have made some arrangements with Colonel [Jesse H.] Leavenworth and were waiting to see him. They sent me word to that effect yesterday, and also that they would be here in two days.

We count now on the ground 431 lodges. Those coming in and who will be represented, 421 lodges; making in all 852. Averaging each lodge at six persons, we have over five thousand Indians.

In the performance of this service, both myself and those with me have taken considerable risk so far as our persons and lives were concerned. We were compelled to go into their country in order to gather the Indians together, or go home and abandon the whole project. And in order to make our mission a success were obliged to come without soldiers. These Indians have been so often deceived by whites and sought by soldiers that they are very suspicious of the former, and cannot see why people calling themselves friends of the Indians cannot come among them without bringing their enemies the soldiers with them. So far our mission has been a perfect success, and I hope the honorable commission will crown our efforts by making with the Indians such a treaty as will ensure peace in the future to the Indians, and security to the frontiersman and pioneer.

I had considerable difficulty in getting communication to the camps of the hostile Cheyennes. I sent first Mr. Isaac N. Butterfield, who knew many of them, with a half-bred Cheyenne. The half-breed lost his way, and Mr. Butterfield was shot at in the camps of the Arapahos by a returning band of hostile Cheyennes. His horse, saddle, bridle, and pistol were taken from him. The other messenger sent out, for one reason and another, failed to reach them, and until Roman Nose and White Beard, with ten of the warriors, made a dash into our camp, I was unable to talk with them. Since that talk, the Cheyennes have been gathering in their war parties and, as they say, are "shoving" for peace. Everything now looks well.

Respectfully,

THOS. MURPHY

Daily Missouri Democrat, October 21, 1867

On [October] 12 we arrived at Larned. A complete change has been effected since Hancock's army swept by in pursuit of Roman Nose and Tall Bull's legions. The shabby, dilapidated, vermin-breeding adobe and wooden houses have been torn down, and new and stately buildings of hewn sandstone are in their stead. The comfort of the troops has been taken into consideration by the architect and builder. The fort is now garrisoned by six companies of infantry and one company of cavalry. Major Kidd[6] is the commandant.

Generals Harney and Sanborn paid a visit to the fort, accompanied by the correspondents. Like many other institutions, this place has also a whole squad of "bummers," who seemingly do nothing but imbibe a wretched infusion of rye and smoke "Virginity" and "Bird's Eye" tobacco. These gentlemen gathered around the new arrivals and did their level best to stare them out of countenance. But, being public characters, they stood it pretty well.

While we were in the private room of the sutler, discussing the merits of some of Hohnecke's beer, a number of Indians walked in, led by the redoubtable Satanta himself, followed by Little Raven, head sachem of the Arapahos; Stumbling Bear, a Kiowa chief; and two noble Apache chiefs.

Satanta seemed beside himself with joy on recognizing your correspondent and gave him a gigantic bear's hug. He was introduced to the other members of the press, who looked upon him with some awe, having heard so much of his ferocity and boldness. By his defiant and independent bearing, he attracted all eyes. A solid chest; a large head, with busy, glittering orbs; fine ears, not too large; long, wavy, shining black hair; straight, broad nose, with expanded nostrils; heavy jawbones, large mouth, square chin, and short, muscular neck. He is little above the ordinary height. His person is compact throughout. Agile and strong, he would certainly be a most formidable enemy to encounter alone on the prairie, especially with the words of "Wild Bill" ringing in the ears, "that man has killed more white men than any other Indian on the plains, and he boasts of it."

Little Raven is a fat, good-natured, peaceable-looking cacique; one who doubtless loves to smoke his pipe peacefully in his lodge, surrounded by his dusky concubines; one who would prefer to be at peace because it required exertion to go to war. There was one [Kiowa-]Apache chief, a tall, wiry fellow, and if I may trust to my knowledge of physiognomy, a cunning unprincipled Indian. A little firewater was given to them, which opened their hearts, like a knife opening a bivalve. Recklessness mounted every feature, and all reserve was swept away. For the nonce, Satanta, ever ready with his tomahawk, allowed his enmity of the paleface to sleep, and laughed like a child.

Three of the reporters were introduced to Major Wynkoop, the agent for the Cheyenne and Sioux. The major is a genial soul and a polished gentleman. He is a skillful concoctor of drinkable beverages, and in his company we whiled away a social hour.

The major narrowly escaped with his life two or three days ago at the camps of the Indians now on Medicine Lodge Creek. Roman Nose, with ten warriors, rode up to the lodge in which Wynkoop was then staying. Wynkoop heard that Roman Nose, a Sioux [Cheyenne] sachem, had threatened his life, and was even then hurrying to his lodge for that purpose. Though there were three or four thousand warriors then at the camp kindly disposed towards the "Tall Chief," Wynkoop, still it was evident that Roman Nose, with his fierce eloquence, could command aid and carry his point. Behind the lodge was a racing horse, which he quickly mounted, and putting spurs to him, left the village at the very moment Roman Nose had a revolver drawn on him. The animosity of this chief towards Wynkoop originated from a suspicion that he entertained that Major Wynkoop—then agent—was the very person who informed Hancock of the whereabouts of his people's lodges, thus causing their entire destruction.

It is thought best to relieve the major from his agency, as he has lost the confidence of Sioux and Cheyennes, for whom he was agent, and the peace commissioners have held several sessions in discussions of the plan.

After we had glanced over the fort, we started for camp and for the first time crossed the celebrated Arkansas River, three miles south of Fort Larned. At this point, the river was very shallow, at no place over two feet in depth. The southern banks of the river were covered with luxuriant grass, into which the pedestrian sunk up to the midriff. The mules, on being released from the harness, plunged into it and reveled in the rich pasture, constantly braying their intense delight and rearing their heels at each greedy fellow who would insist upon a too near neighborhood.

Here our train was increased by sixty wagons, containing stores and presents. The number of wagons and ambulances with the expedition is now 165. Six mules to each wagon and 200 cavalry horses make the number of animals 1,250. The number of men on this trip, including the camp followers and scavengers, is six hundred. Thus when on the march, we present quite a formidable appearance.

In our company are now Colonel Leavenworth, Major Wynkoop, Superintendent Murphy, Captain Rankin,[7] Capt. John W. Smith, interpreter, with a host of camp followers, who pretend to have special commissions, but who really follow out of mere curiosity, and to live on the bountiful rations doled out by the commission. They all live sumptuously, with no expense to themselves. It is rather an imposition on good nature.

On our first day's march south from the Arkansas River, we saw about ten thousand buffaloes. In herds of about a thousand, they grazed, with sentinels and vedettes marching isolated far away from the herds, watching our advance suspiciously and snorting their alarm to the main body.

At night we fared on buffalo. Jack Howland, *Harper's* artist, mounted on a bay nag, brought down a fine buffalo expressly for the Bohemians' mess.

Jack is a fine fellow and is rapidly becoming acclimated in the West. He has traveled for that enterprising paper *Harper's Weekly,* from Montana to Chihuahua, from San Francisco through Arizona, New Mexico to Texas. The Rio Colorado, Rio Grande Del Norte, Rio Pecos, and the Rio Gila he has traversed from their mouths to their rise in the Rocky Mountains. The Mexican language is as familiar to him as the English; and it was with a feeling akin to gratitude to "our special artist" that we ate the rare delicious steaks cut from the hump of the slain buffalo. That night was a pleasant one, long to be remembered, for we invited to the feast several supernumerary strangers who were around, and passed the night chanting and storytelling.

The next day we came to a place where the prairie was on fire. Stretching before us in a long, and seemingly impenetrable, column was a gloomy funeral pall of smoke, raising its voluminous front up to the very heavens. But through the smoke, through the fire we traveled, lost for a short time to each other, and our advent from the cloud was hailed by gratified expressions.

General Augur caught up with us at night. He was ordered by the president to join the Indian commission vice General Sherman, the latter having received a telegram to return to Washington.

This country through which we travel south of the Arkansas has been selected by the commissioners for the Indian reservation. There is a serious difficulty arising against this course. The state of Kansas stretches away over one hundred miles to the southward of Medicine Lodge Creek,[8] and this portion south of the Arkansas is about as fertile a country as the state can boast of. The representation of the state, now with the commissioners, object to this division of their state, and therefore that proposition will fall to the ground. The reservation must be selected somewhere in the neighborhood of the salt plain, and no collision between the authorities can take place.

Monday morning about 10:00 P.M., we came in sight of the great encampment of the Southern Indians. A natural basin, through which meandered Medicine Lodge Creek, with its banks extensively wooded, was the place selected for their winter camp. The basin, hedged in commanding elevations, was intersected by small, undulating hills, deep ravines, pyramidical mounds. On the extreme right was the Arapaho camp, consisting of 171 lodges. Next to these, and close to the creek, almost buried in a dense grove of fuel timber, was the camp of the Comanches, numbering 100 lodges, adjoining which was the Kiowa camp, 150 lodges. At the western extremity of the basin were the camps of the [Kiowa-]Apaches, numbering 85 lodges, and the Cheyennes, 250 lodges. Thousands of ponies covered the adjacent hills, while in the valley grazed the cattle, making the whole resemble a cluster of villages. All these camps were pitched so as to form a circle, in the center of which sported the boys and girls, and little papooses in a complete state of nudity.

Thousands of warriors, braves, young bucks, papooses, damsels, and squaws from the different villages hurried up to satisfy their curiosity, viewing the commissioners. The escorts were all left to come on after us in an hour or so. This was a wise plan, as so many treacherous deeds have been done whenever the troops have come up that the Indians have come to regard the whites as snakes. By this seeming confidence, this apparent trust in their good faith, we found all the Indians there expectant and willing to see us. During the march, though, several little things occurred which many feared would disturb the general serenity. The graceless, vagabond followers, who insisted on joining the expedition at Fort Larned on the pretense that they were relatives to some commissioners or that they knew some Indian agents who were going there, or that they had especial commissions for some business not down on the list of commissions issued, shot down buffaloes simply that they might boast that they killed one. This multitude of bummers not only entailed expense upon the government at the rate of a good round sum per diem, but by their indiscriminate shooting and reckless use of firearms fostered ill will between the Indians and the whites at a time when so much tact and diplomacy were needed to reconcile both parties. Satanta, never backward of speech to assert his rights, burst forth at last and said, "Have the white men become children, that they should kill meat and not eat? When the red men kill, they do so that they might live."

This speech produced the desired result. Two or three of them were put under arrest, and the major commanding the battalion[9] was also arrested for not preventing the shooting. Satanta is no double-faced Janus that can talk with a forked tongue.

When we arrived at the camp, the Indians were engaged in the important ceremony of "making medicine." Shields of tanned buffalo hides were slung on poles, facing the sun, to propitiate it. The unsophisticated aboriginals believe that the sun will aid them by turning their shields towards it while it shines, and covering them by night from dew. The medicine man, whom they revere so much, whom they regard as prophet, priest, and king, is absent, engaged in devout incantations.

There are five thousand Indians present. We are camped within half a mile of the Indian villages. After a cursory glance at the neighborhood, a preliminary council was held at noon in front of our tents with the Arapaho and Cheyenne chiefs. At this council there were several gray heads, and men afflicted with various distempers. When all were seated, Commissioner Taylor asked, "Were all the Cheyennes present?" He was answered, "No. Most of the Cheyennes are on the south bank of the Cimarron with Medicine Arrow." The commissioner then said, "Tell these men here present that the Great Father has heard there is trouble, and he has sent us to look for ourselves and see what the matter is, and to make peace if possible; that we have a good many military men with us to protect us as we are traveling through a wild country. We have heard that there is trouble north and we must be there by the new moon, so it is important that we should be as expeditious as possible down here, that we may keep our word up there. We have made peace with the Oglala and Brule, and we hope to make a full and lasting peace with you. How soon can your people be here?"[10]

(At this point the departure of the courier makes it necessary to break off short. Will resume in my next.)

—◆—

The great medicine lodge on Medicine Lodge Creek.
FRANK LESLIE'S ILLUSTRATED WEEKLY 1867.

Daily Missouri Democrat, October 23, 1867

MEDICINE LODGE, October 17

A council was held this morning at which the commissioners, Colonel Leavenworth, Col. Wynkoop, Dr. Root, A. S. H. White, and the reporters were present, with twenty-five chiefs of the Kiowas, Arapahos, Cheyennes, [Kiowa-] Apaches, and Comanches. In the front row sat Kicking Bird, Little Raven, Spotted Wolf, Fishermore, Heap of Birds, Black Kettle, Elk Poor Bear, Satanta, Satank, and Mrs. Adams,[11] interpreter for the Arapahos. This woman came in dressed in crimson petticoat, black cloth cloak, and a small coquettish velvet hat, decorated with a white ostrich feather. She appears intelligent and rather refined. She speaks fluently the English, Kiowa, and Arapaho languages.

Before the council commenced, the village crier, in a loud voice, gave command to the nations sitting around "to be good, and behave themselves." At this period, Fishermore, the Kiowa's council orator, stepped up, his dirty face beaming with joy, and loudly shouting out "a-how, a-how," insisted upon shaking hands with all. Fishermore is a stout Indian of ponderous proportions and speaks five languages. He is a favorite with all the tribes. When the calumet came to him, he directed the stem north, south, east, and west, and then took three deliberate whiffs and passed it to his neighbor.

When all were ready, Commissioner Taylor said that he had distributed twenty suits of clothes to the Arapaho runners; he was ready to distribute twenty suits to each of the different tribes, and if they could agree upon terms of peace at the general council, he had many more presents to give away. The clothes were immediately brought in the center and distributed around.

The commissioners were called to order, and the meeting was organized. Commissioner Taylor said, "We understand that you are tired of staying here, and in the talk yesterday you requested us to defer the council for eight sleeps. To that proposition we assented, supposing that you would all be willing to wait. We have found, however, that delay does not please some, the Arapahos, [Kiowa-]Apaches, Comanches, and Kiowas having waited here so long; therefore, we have agreed to hold the general council at your village when the council circle is prepared." At this juncture, [Philip] McCusker said that if the commission excused him, he would go and bring the Comanches to the council, that they might also hear the proposition of the commission.

Ten Bears, head chief of the Comanches, Iron Mountain, [and] Little Horn, son of Ten Bears, were introduced to the commission. Powerful warriors! I thought of the wonderful stories of Mayne Reid[12] and other authors, and the various battles said to have taken place between this warlike nation and the invincible Texas Rangers. When they were seated, McCusker, their interpreter, related the late talk to them. They were all well pleased.

Mr. Taylor again spoke:

> My friends, these commissioners have come from Washington to make peace with all of you. We desire to make treaties with you all together. Now, we are anxious, therefore, that all of you chiefs should agree together upon what day the grand council takes place. We are also anxious to have it over as soon as possible, that we may do justice to the Northern Indians. If you can agree among yourselves upon what day you will hold the council, we will be willing to treat with you; if not, we must treat with each tribe as they are ready. We are done, and we hope the chiefs will let us know upon what they agree.

Black Eagle rose and said, "I know Generals Sanborn and Harney of old when there was no blood on the path; when the whole country was all white. I speak for the Kiowas now. We would like to stop until four sleeps have passed before we speak."

The Comanche chief Ten Bears, a good-natured old warrior who had the honor of once being introduced to President Lincoln, said, "I had a talk with the Great Father himself when I was at Washington. I am willing to repeat it here. Since I have made peace with the white men, I have received many presents and my heart has been made glad. My young men look upon you with gladness. I have not much to say, except it be to say that we are willing to travel any road you lay out for us." Then the Kiowa chief said, "We would like to hold the council tomorrow and then wait four days before receiving the goods." Satanta said, "I don't want to say anything at this talk. I will say what I have to say at the grand council." Ten Bears, angry at this vacillation of the

Kiowas, here made the remark, "What I say is law for the Comanches, but it takes half a dozen to speak for the Kiowas."[13] After a few more retorts of this kind, it was finally agreed that the Comanches and Kiowas should meet in grand council after the night.

Poor Bear, a [Kiowa-]Apache chief, stepped up and, after a long pause, said, "When the grass was green I was on the Washita, and I heard that the commissioners wanted to see me. I am glad. The [Kiowa-]Apaches, though few, are all here. I have been here some time. I would like to get my annuity goods as soon as possible, as I understood they were here. I will wait four days for the talk. I have spoken."

After this speech, Satanta stood up before the warriors who had gathered together to witness the ceremony of the powwow. There were fully five hundred of them, splendidly dressed in the most gorgeous Indian costume. His remarks were universally applauded, if one might judge by the frequent bursts of gratified "ugh, ugh."

Satanta's style of delivery is well calculated to please a savage multitude. Presenting a formidable appearance himself, and gifted with native eloquence, he commands all attention. His name is a thing to swear by. His many acts of prowess the young Indian maidens sing, while the young braves endeavor to emulate.

Black Kettle, chief of the Cheyennes, got up now and addressed the multitude of Indians present as follows: "We were once friends with the whites, but you nudged us out of the way by your intrigues, and now when we are in council, you keep nudging each other. Why don't you talk and go straight, and let all be well? I am pleased with all that has been said." Little Raven followed in the same vein, appealing to them "to behave themselves and be good."

The council was then adjourned, to meet again on the morning of the fifth day in grand and solemn council at the council place specially prepared for the occasion.

Senator Henderson is remarkable for his businesslike faculties. He urged upon Taylor to make the "talks" as short as possible, while Taylor, out of pure habit alone, enlarged and explained, thus making the powwow tediously and unnecessarily long. While the talk was being interpreted, the honorable gentlemen were engaged in different things. Harney, with head erect, watched with interest each dusky and painted face of the Indians around the tent. Sanborn picked his teeth and tried to break forth into one of his usual horselaughs. Tappan read Indian reports about the destruction of the Indian village. Henderson, with eyeglass in his hand, seemed buried in deep study. Terry busied himself in printing alphabetical letters, and Augur whittled away with energy. Leavenworth examined his children, and made by-signals to old Satank, the oldest chief of the Kiowa nation. Under the table sat Commissioner Taylor's papoose, making wry faces at some pretty squaws sitting astride, behind some aspiring youths on ponies, in the background. The correspondents sat on the ground, their pencils flying with lightning speed over the paper.

At dusk Gray Head came to camp from the warpath with fifty Dog Soldiers. His band looked ferocious enough, and just the kind that a person might
expect to see on the warpath. Gray Head presented the following letter to General Harney:

HEADQUARTERS, COTTONWOOD SPRINGS,
July 15, 1858

This is to show that the bearer, Gray Head, a chief of the
Cheyennes, has voluntarily visited my camp and made promises of
peace toward the whites. And believing that these promises are made
in good faith, I commend him to the friendship of our people and the
troops.

W. S. HARNEY,
Brigadier General U.S.A.

Black Kettle lately received a message from Medicine Arrow's band that
if he did not make his appearance at their camp on a certain day, they would
come in and kill all his horses.

Towards night, Colonel Wynkoop was called up before the commission
to testify as to the cause of this Indian war, which he gave in the following
manner:

Wynkoop said that Governor Evans[14] blamed him for bringing the
Indians to Sand Creek, but Wynkoop insisted that he should see them,
as the Cheyennes were desirous for peace and he had brought them to
Sand Creek for that purpose. The massacre took place two days after
he had left Fort Lyon, of which he was in command. Directly after the
massacre, two hundred Sioux Indians went on the warpath, attacked
Mexican trains, killing everyone they came across, and since that
massacre the Indians have been on the warpath.

(In answer to a question which Henderson asked, Wynkoop said
Chivington's reply at the council in Denver was that his business was
to kill Indians and not to make peace with them.)

After Sand Creek, the Indians were at war everywhere, mostly on
the Platte. Property was destroyed, horses were stolen, and emigrants
were killed.

Some annuity goods which Commissioner Goodall bought in New
York, three-point blankets, which are used as wrappers and which
were charged in the bill at $13 per pair, were the most worthless
things that I ever saw. The Indians told me that they would not have
taken those goods from anybody else but myself. It was a most
shameless affair. They were not only killed, but the friendliest were
cheated.

Concerning the disposition of the Sioux, I [Wynkoop] will state that they were under the impression, previous to the destruction of that Cheyenne village by Hancock, that as the Cheyennes had made peace, they will also. I asked Pawnee Killer, a Sioux chief, and he said they said the same thing.

The Mexican killed at Fort Zarah was killed by an Indian who was under the influence of liquor. But the Indians generally were satisfied with keeping the peace, and save that murder at Zarah, they had kept it. They had certainly done nothing after the treaty was made in 1865 until Hancock made his appearance with his army. There was a report that the Indians had run off stock near Fort Wallace. General Hancock has various statements from his officers of several depredations, but these could not be fixed upon any particular band. I know of one affair, viz., a young chief attempted to run off some stage horses, but he did not succeed.

Concerning Hancock's expedition, the first I knew of the expedition, I received a communication from him dated Leavenworth, stating that he was coming with a large body of troops. He intended to make peace, but at the same time was prepared for war. He also wished me to accompany him on his expedition. He stated that he was going to make a demand for the parties who committed the depredations on the Smoky Hill, and also for the Indian who killed the New Mexicans at Zarah. I received another letter, stating that his orders from Sherman were not to make the demands.

As soon as I received this communication, I sent out runners to gather in the chiefs. When Hancock arrived at Larned, they had not reached there. But two days afterward, seven arrived. Amongst them were Tall Bull, White Horse, and Bull Bear, chiefs of the Dog band. The night of their arrival, a council was held, and Gen. Hancock made a speech. After him, Tall Bull spoke and said that his tribe were at peace, and he wished to remain so; they hoped he would not go to their village, as he could not have any more to say to them there than where he was. General Hancock answered that he was going to see them at their village on the morrow.

The next day he started for the village. That night we camped twenty-three miles from the fort. The day after, we met a body of Indians on the Plains. As soon as they saw us, they started to run away but Edmund Guerrier[15] made signs with his horse that we were peaceable. So they came back. Hancock told them he wished to see them at the village that night and talk with them, to which they agreed.

Roman Nose and his party started back towards their village. The troops took up the line of march for it. Bull Bear remained behind with the column, and he then told me that it would produce no good to march up to the village; that the women and children would be afraid. This I communicated to General Hancock; but he did not agree with that view of it.

They still marched on, and at last camped within three hundred yards east of the village. About 5:00 P.M. Hancock sent interpreters to fetch the chiefs to the council. They returned immediately and informed Hancock that the women and children had fled. He then sent them back and ordered them to send the headmen to him. Bull Bear and Tall Bull came accordingly. General Hancock appeared very angry and asked them why they had acted so mean towards him.

About 11:00 P.M. Guerrier returned from the camp and stated that the chiefs had come back from the pursuit of their women. Hancock sent for me and told me when I reached his tent that he had ordered Colonel Custer to surround the camp and retain all that were found in it. He asked for my opinion upon the order. I told him that if there were only ten men found there, when they saw the cavalry they would have a fight. Hancock said it mattered not. The cavalry marched up and surrounded the camp. A little while after that, General Hancock ordered Colonel Custer to pursue the Indians and bring them back. Custer immediately started in pursuit.

About 2:00 A.M. Hancock stated in my presence that he intended to burn the village next morning, as he considered that they had acted treacherously towards him and they deserved punishment. Upon hearing this, I wrote him a letter urging him to do nothing rash, but to ponder well on what he was about to do. Hancock did not burn that village next morning as he promised. I also urged Colonel Smith to endeavor to show the general that it would be wrong to burn the village. Colonel Smith did so.

The night of April 16 a courier came from Colonel Custer, bearing a letter stating that two men had been killed and burned and Lookout Station destroyed, on the Smoky Hill. That same night General Hancock gave orders to Colonel Smith to burn the village next morning.

The next day, as the troops were leaving Pawnee Fork, the order of General Hancock was obeyed. The village was set on fire, and everything in it was burned.

A courier was dispatched to the commandants of Forts Larned and Dodge, ordering them to prevent the Indians from crossing the Arkansas River. Two days after that, a party of Indians were intercepted at Cimarron Crossing, and ten killed.

The old Indian and young girl who had been in the deserted village, and who had been taken to Fort Dodge by General Hancock, died a few days after the expedition left, at that post.

In answer to a question by General Sanborn, as to whether he (Wynkoop) had any idea who had committed the outrage upon her,

Wynkoop said, "I firmly believe that the soldiers ravished the child. It was the conclusion I arrived at when I heard that she was ravished. It is my belief now."

The Cheyennes I have seen lately gave me to understand that the war this summer was in retaliation for the destruction of their village by General Hancock.

There are several little inaccuracies in Colonel Wynkoop's testimony, as I was with Hancock and I know whereof I speak. *First.* War was already declared when Hancock appeared with his army. *Second.* He did not burn the village until the nineteenth, four days after his arrival at Pawnee Fork, and not until he had received positive proofs that the Indians were at war. Nor did he then burn it until he had counseled with his officers. *Third.* The soldiers were not the persons who violated the young girl found at the Cheyenne village.

—•— ≍◆≍ —•—

Daily Missouri Democrat, October 25, 1867

MEDICINE LODGE CREEK,
October 18, 1867

Last night the party of correspondents connected with this expedition resolved to go in a body to the camp of the Arapahos to witness a grand war dance. Through the camps of the infantry, cavalry, and the mulewhackers we plunged, and out into the Egyptian darkness, without one friendly light to guide us on our way, through the crackling ferns and dry stalks, down ravines and unceremoniously into slimy marshes, over a long, blackened ridge of scorched prairie, and plump against an Indian vedette.

We thus found ourselves in the Arapaho village, a fearful din of tom-toms, beating of gongs, tin kettles, howling of the watchful Indian dogs, shrill singing of children, of squaws, the guttural voices of braves, and the energetic jingling of brass bells. Directing our steps over the offal and refuse of the village towards the lodge from which the sounds proceeded, we found ourselves before a chief's wigwam.

Peeping in without so much as asking permission, we saw seated around a fire, built in the center of the lodge, a double circle of Indians. The first was composed of warriors, mostly young, chanting lustily, while a few were beating tom-toms with all their might, one especially endeavoring to outrival the rest by his ferocity of countenance, the ludicrous interest in the ceremony which beamed in his features, the pomposity of his bearing, and the exhilarating beat of his drum. Next to those engaged in gong beatings were three youngsters holding a string of brass bells, and jingling them in harmony with the voices of the squaws, [which] rose high and clear on the night air. The squaws occupied the rear circle, joining in the chorus with all their might, their flashing, dark eyes lit with excitement. A louder beat of the gong, a shriller cry, a fiercer jingling of bells, and four warriors leaped up with the animated tones and commenced dancing, each one adding his voice to the swelling chorus, singing his "eya-eya-ooh-eya-ooh-eya-woo-woo-o-oo-ah," which closed the first performance.

On the commencement of the second tune, four correspondents, Willis the photographer, Hall of the Chicago *Tribune,* Smoot of the surveying party, and Fayel of the *Republican,* partaking of the intense excitement, joined in the war dance and flung their heels after the manner of dancing dervishes until the per- spiration rolled down their bodies in living streams. This extravagant show of excitement on the part of Bohemians quite melted the hearts of the dusky war- riors. They embraced each other, and tears rolled down the cheeks of the spec- tators, who were tenderly affected by the scene. This war dance lasted until midnight, and when we parted, there were eternal protestations of love and friendship on both sides.

In Little Raven's lodge, I encountered the young brave, the lost Arapaho child, Wilson Graham, whom Sherman found dressed as a gymnast in a circus, the boy who accompanied Hancock on his expedition, and who was left by that general at Fort Larned, to be delivered over to his kindred. Two months ago his friends applied for him, when he was given up with great regret, hav- ing made many friends during his sojourn among the whites. This boy is rapidly forgetting the English language. He is efficient in the use of the bow and arrow and has acquired prominence among his many playmates on account of his varied accomplishments. His feats of leaping and wrestling command the respect of the Arapaho elders. His knowledge of the English lan- guage is a source of constant admiration, and his many-bladed jackknife is an object of envy to his brother braves.

To illustrate how peaceably inclined the much-abused Indian is, I will relate an incident which occurred during our visit to the village. "Our Special Artist" had buckled to a strangled waist a very fine navy revolver. While our artist was engaged in trading beads and paint for a bow and arrow, an Indian *gamin,* a reckless urchin, having not the fear of a pale face in his bosom and utterly regardless of the result of his indiscretion, put forth his digits in a very sly manner and abstracted "Our Special Artist's" fine navy revolver, and sneaked away with his plunder under his blanket. When the artist recovered himself and stood up, he found too late that his "peacemaker" was gone. Great was his dismay, unutterable his anger, indescribable his woe. He scratched his head for light on this most dark subject, but no light came. He looked to the right, to the left, to the front and rear; he saw nothing but profound darkness and the outlines of a lodge with a few human forms near it. He inquired of his confreres about what was the best thing to do in the premises. A legal fledg- ling, who for the nonce belonged to our fraternity, remembering his legal edu- cation, uttered a few Latin quotations, which translated into English meant "Go and inform the chief, Little Raven." Acting upon this sententious advice, the artist forthwith proceeded to the chief's lodge and made him acquainted with his loss. Little Raven was very sorry and offered one of his own in its place. He also promised to have a thorough search instituted for the weapon, and, if recovered, returned to its rightful owner. "Our Special Artist" returned to his camp loaded with compliments and Indian curiosities.

The press tent is the Bourse, the exchange, which everyone disposed for argument enters. Commissioners, officers, soldiers, bullwhackers, mule drivers, Indian chiefs, squaws, and papooses pass in and out the whole day long. Itinerant pretenders, interested Indian agents, political aspirants, reliable interpreters, and *soi-disant* correspondents love its cool shade and merry, jovial inmates. Those who have the entree to the press tent consider themselves highly honored with such aristocratic acquaintances and forthwith reckon up how many papers they will buy which mention their names, that they may preserve them and hand them down to their posterity.

Colored scavatores also darken the entrance with their presence now and then, listening to the elegant debates carried on with animation, upon the topics of the day. The scholastic portion of the press gang dive deeply into the classics frequently, and then all the little world stands back astonished at the learning displayed; the romantic members, giving full rein to their vivid imaginations, soar away on eagle's pinions beyond the ethereal dome above, and come down again gently gliding, sailing over regions unknown to the dull few till they alight on Mother Earth, and find themselves only in the press tent, but still admired by the wondering crowd around.

Our matter-of-fact reporters delight in ridiculing both but still, between themselves, discuss the merits of the Indian question. One has for his standard "my policy," which he is consistently defending with facts. The others have no policy whatever, but content themselves with reporting facts, leaving the public to draw their own conclusions. There is also one who talks "in whispers." His whispers are louder than a clown's; his laugh can be heard a mile off, but all declare him the best fellow in existence. The commissioners make much of him, the redskins laugh at him, while he remains a target for all their shafts.

Outside our tent is the promenade, the Broadway of the camp. The most motley set of people saunter up and down. Unbaptized redskins with unpronounceable names—self-betitled chiefs who will swear to you that they are the biggest chiefs in America—air their feathers, war paint, and gaudily dressed carcasses. Unchristianly "woa-woa chiefs" (whites) in their enormous felt hats, heavy top boots, and plaid shirts. Bewhiskered long-haired hangers-on, with knife and pistol slung to their waists, follow copper-colored squaws clad in dingy gray blankets. Naked boys and girls of aboriginal parentage greedily look on at the delicious viands in course of preparation by our *chef-de-cuisine* with watery eyes and greedy stare. On the other side of our Broadway are piles of annuity goods in plethoric bales and capacious boxes, [and] slaughtered beeves, around which congregate the cooks of the different messes, waiting for their portion of the meat.

Forming a group by themselves, chatting incessantly, are a lot of young officers, their attention divided between Satanta's favorite papoose Saliaso, and Miss Julia Bent, daughter of Colonel Bent. Saliaso is mounted on a magnificent pony, dressed in the most elegant manner, with blue jacket decorated with a cavalry captain's epaulettes, rows of bright buttons, armlets of beaten silver, and a gold ring or two. From his neck hang necklaces of pearl-like shell, a grizzly bear's claw, and a long silver cross. Leggings of the most fancy style encase his legs, while his feet are covered with the most exquisite moccasins. Waving masses of raven black hair are confined behind the ears, exposing a tall forehead of clear olive complexion. His features indicate intelligence. An aquiline nose, with finely arched nostrils, a well-cut mouth, not too large, and an oval chin make up the picture of Saliaso, or "Flying Eagle," the pride of the Kiowa nation and their future chief. He is about twelve years old and is a perfect young Adonis.

Miss Julia Bent was dressed in a long "smock frock" of blue cloth, adorned with six rows of elk teeth sown across the bosom. She is of medium height and rather coarse features, but has a charming, ringing laugh, which in a measure atones for other drawbacks to an otherwise interesting figure. Her feet are of the most diminutive size, and a peep at her trim ankles might drive an anchorite insane. She is very modest and is evidently regarded as a treasure. She appears to be about fifteen years old. George and Charley Bent are also in the camp.

There is very little news afloat. The grand council comes off tomorrow, and we are all bracing ourselves for the task.

Last night the Arapahos lost a hundred head of ponies. It is presumed that they were stolen by the Pawnees. Testimony was taken this morning, but nothing was elicited further than the supposition given.

Yesterday Maj. Henry Douglass, former commandant of Fort Dodge, was examined relative to what he knew of the origin of the Kiowa troubles. Being sworn, he testified as follows:

> The information which I sent to the War Department concerning Indian raids and their dissatisfaction with Colonel Leavenworth, I received from traders and interpreters. All the leading chiefs were dissatisfied with him. They have affixed their names to a letter sent to me, containing a list of their grievances.
>
> I held several councils with Satanta, the great chief of the Kiowas, and To-haw-son, the second in importance, in which they stated over and over that their agent did not treat them well; that he refused to give them annuity goods when due, as per treaty.
>
> Col. David Butterfield[16] and Charley Rath, a trader at Zarah, have issued guns, pistols, and ammunition, the consequence of which was that before Hancock appeared with his army, Satanta openly boasted

that they had plenty of arms and ammunition and were not afraid of the whites.

The accounts of the depredations committed by the Kiowas before Hancock came along were based upon affidavits, and I believed them to be true, and therefore transmitted them to General Hancock. The Kiowas brought three women, the Misses Box, daughters of farmer John Box of Texas, to me at Fort Dodge, and upon payment of money and provisions, they were given up.

(Question by Sanborn: "Do you not think that these Indians made that boast of cleaning out the whites in a joke?" Before an answer could be given, General Harney said, "I never knew the Indians to jest. In their boasts there is always a meaning.")

According to information received by me, the Kiowas scalped seventeen colored soldiers and stole two hundred head of horses early in February 1867. They also abused Captain Page,[17] an officer of the United States Regular army, in the month of March.

It seems that these statements of Major Douglass, which he sent to General Hancock, were the main causes of the expedition being sent to the West; and yet, in a cross-examination which he underwent, he deliberately said that he would not believe [Fred] Jones, his interpreter, unless some person was there to check him; that he did not believe those statements when he sent them, but would not contradict them though he received contradictory proofs strong as Holy Writ. Captain Page denied his being abused by the Kiowas twenty-four hours before Douglass sent his dispatches to Hancock stating that Page was abused. Douglass never saw the scalps of these colored soldiers, but still he sent the account of the deed to Hancock.

◄—• ≃�◆≥ •—►

MEDICINE LODGE CREEK, OCT. 19, 1867

A vast amphitheater had been cleared in the center of a grove of tall elms as the place where the grand council should be held. Logs had been arranged so as to seat the principal chiefs of the southern nations. Tables were erected for the accommodation of the various correspondents. Before these tables were the seats ranged in a semicircle for the commissioners. Facing the commissioners were a few of the most select chiefs of the different tribes. Beyond all were the ponies of the chiefs, forming a splendid background to a picture. Above the space allotted to the commissioners and the press were placed boughs to shelter them from the sun.

At 10:00 A.M. the council was opened by Fishermore, the lusty crier of the Kiowa nation, exclaiming loudly and counseling the tribes to do right above all things. Satanta, their chief, sits proudly on a camp chair, and behind him are his band of principal warriors. Little Raven aspires to be next in importance. He is seated on a stool, a fat, short, asthmatic fellow, but possessing features stamped with native dignity. Near him sits Mrs. [Margaret] Adams, dressed in a new crimson gown, specially worn for this important occasion. She is the interpretess for the Arapahos—a pleasant-faced, intelligent woman enough, bearing about her face indications of her origin and descent.

The commissioners look amiable and are dressed in their best—Sanborn especially. He sports a suit of purple cloth and laughs immoderately; whether at his jokes or appearance it is impossible to state. He looks around for applause—none greets him, but a certain air of scorn is visible upon the taciturn face of Satanta. Harney is dressed in full uniform and looks the warrior chief. Taylor is quiet and dignified. Augur and Terry appear gentlemanly.

Looking around, Commissioner Taylor found that all was ready. Telling the interpreter that he was going to speak, he rose and thus addressed the assemblage of chiefs: "We have selected a great peace man—a member of the peace council at Washington—to tell you what we have to say. Listen to him. (Cries of "ow-how-ugh.")

Senator John B. Henderson then rose and addressed the chiefs in the following manner:

Our friends of the Cheyenne, Comanche, [Kiowa-]Apache, Kiowa, and Arapaho nations, the government of the United States and the Great Father has sent us seven commissioners to come here and have a talk with you. Two years ago the government entered into a treaty with you at the mouth of the Little Arkansas, and we hoped then that there would be no war between us. We are sorry to be disappointed. During the last year we heard several times that persons belonging to your tribes were committing war against us. We heard that they were attacking peaceable persons engaged in building our railroads, that they were scalping women and children. These reports made the hearts of our people very sad. Some of our people said that you commenced the war. Some of them denied that you commenced it. Some of our people said that you and other Indians were going to wage a general war against the whites; others denied the charge. In this conflict of opinion we could not find the truth, and therefore the Great Father has sent us here to hear from your own lips what were those wrongs that prompted you to commit those deeds, if you had committed those acts of violence. We do not like war, because it brings bloodshed to both sides; but we do like brave men, and they should speak the truth, for it is an evidence of their courage. We now again ask you to state to us, if you have at any time since the treaty committed violence.

What has the government done of which you complain? If soldiers have done wrong to you, tell us when and where, and who are the guilty parties. If these agents whom we have put here to protect you have cheated and defrauded you, be not afraid to tell us. We have come to hear all your complaints and to correct all your wrongs. We have full power to do these things, and we pledge you our sacred honor to do so. For anything that you may say in this council, you shall not be harmed.

Before we proceed to inform you what we are authorized to do for you, we desire to hear fully from your own lips what you have done, what you have suffered, and what you want. We say, however, that we intend to do justice to the red man. If we have harmed him, we will correct it; if the red man has harmed us, we believe he is brave and generous enough to acknowledge it, and to cease from doing any more wrong. At present we have only to say that we are greatly rejoiced to see our red brethren so well disposed towards peace. We are especially glad because we as individuals would give them all the comforts of civilization, religion, and wealth, and now we are authorized by the Great Father to provide for them comfortable homes upon our richest agricultural lands. We are authorized to build for the Indian schoolhouses and churches, and provide teachers to educate his children. We can furnish him with agricultural implements to work, and domestic cattle, sheep, and hogs to stock his farm. We now cease and shall wait to hear what you have to say, and after we have heard it, we will tell you the road to go. We are now anxious to hear from you.

Grayhead got up and said that as there were only two of the Cheyennes present, they could not speak until the rest were present. Satanta became uneasy, buried his hands in the ground, and rubbed sand over them, after which he went round shaking hands with all, and then stood in the circle dignified and ready with his speech:

The commissioners have come from afar to listen to our grievances. My heart is glad, and I shall hide nothing from you. I understood that you were coming down here to see us. I moved away from those disposed to war, and I also came from afar to see you. The Kiowas and Comanches have not been fighting. We were away down South when we heard that you were coming to see us.

The Cheyennes are those who have been fighting with you. They did it in broad daylight so that all could see them. If I had been fighting, I would have done so also. Two years ago I made peace with General Harney, Sanborn, and Colonel Leavenworth at the mouth of the Little Arkansas. That peace I have never broken. When the grass was growing this spring, a large body of soldiers came along on the Santa Fe road. I had not done anything, and therefore was not afraid.

All the chiefs of the Kiowas, Comanches, and Arapahos are here today. They have come to listen to the good word. We have been waiting here a long time to see you, and we are getting tired. All the land south of the Arkansas belongs to the Kiowas and Comanches, and I don't want to give away any of it. I love the land and the buffalo, and will not part with any. I want you to understand also that Kiowas don't want to fight, and have not been fighting since we made the treaty. I hear a good deal of fine talk from these gentlemen, but they never do what they say. I don't want any of these medicine homes built in the country; I want the papooses brought up just exactly as I am. When I make peace, it is a long and lasting one; there is no end to it. We thank you for your presents.

All these chiefs and headmen feel happy. They will do what you want. They know that you are doing the best you can. I and they will do so also. There is one big chief lately died—Jim Pockmark of the Caddoes—he was a great peacemaker, and we are sorry he is dead.

When I look upon you, I know you are all big chiefs. While you are in the country, we go to sleep happy and are not afraid. I have heard that you intend to settle us on a reservation near the mountains. I don't want to settle there. I love to roam over the wide prairie and when I do it, I feel free and happy, but when we settle down, we grow pale and die.

Hearken well to what I say. I have laid aside my lance, my bow, and my shield, and yet I feel safe in your presence. I have told you the truth. I have no little lies hid about me, but I don't know how it is with the commissioners; are they as clear as I am? A long time ago this land belonged to our fathers, but when I go up to the river, I see a camp of soldiers, and they are cutting my wood down or killing my buffalo. I don't like that, and when I see it, my heart feels like bursting with sorrow. I have spoken.

Satanta's speech produced a rather blank look upon the faces of the peace commissioners. Satanta has a knack of saying boldly what he needs, regardless of what anybody thinks. On the close of his speech, he sat down and wrapped a crimson blanket around his form.

Little Raven said that he had nothing to say, as his young men had been dispatched after the Pawnee horse thieves. "God damn them mean squaws!" said he. After Little Raven delivered himself of his wrathful speech, Ten Bears, chief of the Comanches, after putting on his spectacles, commenced in a shrill voice as follows: "Of myself I have no wisdom, but I expect to get some from you—it will go right down my throat. I am willing to do what you say." After saying which, the old chief hobbled around the circle and shook hands with the commissioners with as much gravity and unimpressibility as a Turk.

Tosh-a-way, another Comanche chief,[18] stood up and in a calm, argumentative voice, said:

I have come from away down South to see and hear you. A long time ago the band of Penateka Comanches were the strongest band in the nation. The Great Father sent a big chief down to us and promised medicines, houses, and many other things. A great, great many years have gone by, but those things have never come. My band is dwindling away fast. My young men are a scoff and a byword among the other nations. I shall wait till next spring to see if these things shall be given us; if they are not, I and my young men will return with our wild brothers to live on the prairie. I have tried the life the Great Father told me to follow. He told me my young men would become strong, but every spring their numbers are less. I am tired of it. Do what you have promised us and all will be well. I have said it.

Poor Bear, chief of the [Kiowa-]Apaches, a poor-looking, superannuated warrior, next got up and in a hurried manner said:

Some time ago the president sent for me. I went to see him and heard what he had to say. I remember it well. What he told me I repeated to the [Kiowa-]Apache braves. What I promised to him, I and my young men have kept, even until this hour. Many whites travel the Santa Fe road, but no [Kiowa-]Apaches have troubled them, for I am chief among the warriors and I know what I say. My young men recognize me alone as chief, and they listen and obey. At my bidding they came with their squaws and papooses to listen to your good words. We will listen attentively to them and will follow the straight road. I am very tired of staying here. I wish you would get through as soon as possible, and let me and my braves go to our homes south. As we have never broken any treaties, I think we might get our annuity goods without delay. Since I was a child, I loved the paleface, and until my departure to the happy lands, I hope to follow in their footsteps. I have said it.

After delivering his speech in a very effective manner so far as regards delivery, he said he had some presents to give the "Great Peace Chief of Washington." A shield was brought to him by a select warrior, which he presented to the commissioner with these words: "I have slain many an enemy; this shield has saved me many a time from death. When my foe saw this shield, he trembled and I triumphed—go you and do the same."

This ended the first day's proceedings, after which the council adjourned to meet again at the same spot, at the same hour, next day. The Arapahos and

Cheyennes could give no definite answer, as their principal chiefs were not present. The Comanches and Apaches will doubtless accede to the wishes of the commissioners.

━━ ⇥◆⇤ ━━

Daily Missouri Democrat, October 28, 1867

MEDICINE LODGE CREEK, Oct. 20, 1867

Before the council commenced, twelve Osage chiefs made their appearance at the council ground. They had been traveling for ten days to see the commissioners. They appeared very tired and hungry. Their ponies were also lame from excessive traveling and had buckskin wrapped around their feet. Little Bear, the principal chief, requested an introduction to the commissioners. After a shake of the hand all around, he said that he had come from the Osage reservation to see the great peace chiefs.

Ten Bears, Comanche chief, said:

> My people do not trouble the white man at all; but two years ago, on this road, your soldiers commenced killing my young men, and on the Canadian also. My young men returned the fire and fought your soldiers. Your men then attacked our villages; we retorted as well as we could, but we finally made peace, and there was an end of it. We have been at peace since.
>
> There is one thing which is not good in your speeches; that is, building us medicine houses. We don't want any. I want to live and die as I was brought up. I love the open prairie, and I wish you would not insist on putting us on a reservation. We prefer to roam over the prairie when we want to do so. If the Texans were kept from our country, then we might live upon a reserve, but this country is so small we cannot live upon it. The best of my lands the Texans have taken, and I am left to shift as I can best do. If you have any good words from the Great Father, I shall be happy to hear it. I love to get presents, for it reminds me that the Great Father has not forgotten his friends the Comanches. I want my country to be pure and clean.

Another shaking of the hands, and then Ten Bears sat down and was followed by Satanta, who spoke as follows: "The Kiowas have no more to say. We have spoken already. When you issue goods, give all that is our due to us; do not hide any from us. Keep none back. I want all that is mine." After saying this, he went and dragged Black Eagle up before the commissioners, that he might speak. Black Eagle had nothing to say.

Commissioner Taylor said that the council chief would speak to them their reply and that their annuity goods would be distributed to them the next morning. Upon hearing this, Satanta seemed to get sulky. Folding his blanket about him, he deliberately mounted his horse and rode off. In a short time he returned and made another speech: "We need two agents—one for the Kiowas and Comanches. There are so many hearts in the two tribes that it requires two. I have no objection to Colonel Leavenworth or anybody else in the commission, but it requires two to distribute our goods properly. For myself and my band, we will take John Tappan (a cousin of S. F. Tappan); the other Kiowas may take Leavenworth if they will."

Although he said that he had no objection to Leavenworth, still there was a current of hatred or dislike against him which attracted attention.

Senator Henderson next spoke. His speech is of the greatest importance, and I therefore copied it verbatim:

> To our Kiowa and Comanche friends who spoke to us on yesterday through their chiefs Satanta, Ten Bears, and Tosh-a-way, the commissioners say they have listened to your words and considered them well. We are glad to hear you express confidence in us, and to be assured that you will follow the good road we shall give you. We will not abuse that confidence. What we say to you may at first be unpleasant, but if you follow our advice, it will bring you good and you will soon be happy.
>
> Through your great chief Satanta, you say you desire to hold this country south of the Arkansas River. By your treaty of the Little Arkansas, two years ago, you received into your country here the Cheyennes, Arapahos, and [Kiowa-]Apaches. We agreed you might continue to hunt up the Arkansas River. We are still willing to stand by that treaty.
>
> You say you do not like the medicine houses of the whites, but you like the buffalo and the chase, and that you wish to do as your fathers did. We say to you that the buffalo will not last forever. They are now becoming few and you must know it. When that day comes, the Indian must change the road his father trod, or he must suffer and probably die. We tell you that to change will make you better. We wish you to live, and we will now offer you the way.
>
> The whites are settling up all the good lands. They have come to the Arkansas River. When they come, they drive out the buffalo. If you oppose them, war must come. They are many, and you are few. You may kill some of them; but others will come and take their places. And finally, many of the red man will have been killed and the rest will have no homes. We are your best friends, and now, before all the good lands are taken by whites, we wish to set aside a part of them for your exclusive home. On that home we will build you a house to hold the goods we send you; and when you become hungry and naked, you can go there and be fed and clothed. On that home we

will send you a physician to live with you and heal your wounds, and take care of you when you are sick. There we will send you a blacksmith to shoe your ponies, so that they will not get lame. We will send you a farmer to show your people how to grow corn and wheat, and we will send you a mill to make for you meal and flour.

Every year we will send to the warehouse a suit of clothing for each of your men, women, and children so they shall not suffer from cold. We do not ask you to cease hunting the buffalo. You may roam over the broad plains south of the Arkansas River and hunt the buffalo as you have done in years past, but you must have a place you can call your own. You must have a home where we can send your goods, and where you can go and see your physician when you are sick. You must have a home where all your people who wish may farm, and where you may bury your dead and have your medicine lodges. We propose to make that home on the Red River and around the Wichita Mountains, and we have prepared papers for that purpose. Tomorrow morning at nine o'clock we want your chiefs and headmen to meet us at our camp and sign the papers.

This last speech ended the proceedings for this day. It was understood before the council broke up that the Kiowa and Comanche chiefs would be up at our camps [at] 9:00 A.M. tomorrow to sign the treaty. Thus far so good; though the business of the commission is not half completed yet. The Cheyenne and Arapaho braves will be here at the end of three days from date. The proceedings of that council will be more important than any we had yet, as the Cheyennes are those who have been at war. If peace is not made with this tribe, then the peace commission is a failure, and it only remains to carry out the last section of the act of Congress relating to the peace commissions, viz., the raising of four thousand additional troops for the vigorous prosecution of the war.

We have been waiting eight days for the Cheyennes. The commissioners are tired, and they talk of splitting up the party: one part to go up to Fort Laramie to give presents and make arrangements with the Indians to meet again next spring, another to go up to North Platte to settle with the Oglala and Brule [Sioux], and then they go for dividing after they have spent already for the government over $250,000. Senator Henderson uses all his influence to bind and cement together the commission for the settlement of the Indian question.

The treaty with the Kiowas and Comanches cannot be made public until the president has proclaimed it. But to satisfy the public, it may be well to state that it contemplates no cession of any lands except the removal of the tribes ten miles southward of Medicine Lodge Creek.

Over $150,000 worth of provisions have been distributed to the tribes, also two thousand suits of uniforms, two thousand blankets, fifty quarter boxes [of] tobacco, twenty bolts of Indian cloth, three bales domestics, one bale linseed, twelve dozen squaw axes, one bale ticking, fifty revolvers (navy size), besides an assortment of beads, butcher knives, thread and needles, brass bells, looking glasses, and sixteen silver medals worth $250.

※◆※

MEDICINE LODGE CREEK, October 21
The treaty was signed this morning. Satanta said:

This building homes for us is all nonsense; we don't want you to build any for us. We would all die. Look at the Penateka. Formerly they were powerful, but now they are weak and poor. I want all my land, even from the Arkansas south to the Red River. My country is small enough already. If you build us houses, the land will be smaller. Why do you insist on this? What good can come of it? I don't understand your reason. Time enough to build us houses when the buffalo are all gone; but tell the Great Father that there is plenty of buffalo yet, and when the buffalo are all gone I will tell him. This trusting to the agents for my food, I don't believe in it.

Tosh-a-way, Comanche chief, said, "For my tribe, the Comanches, I speak. I like those houses built, but if they are not completed before next summer, I don't want them. So many things have been promised us."
Tonaenko's speech:

Two years ago the whites made a treaty on the Arkansas; that treaty has not been broken by us. It promised annuities—let us have them. I don't see any necessity for making new treaties. You are piling more papers here, one after another. Are you ever going to get through with this talk? When you came here, we were glad to see you because you came with presents, but our squaws and papooses are tired. You told us yesterday, in council, to come up here to sign papers. We have come here, why don't you let us sign?

The following chiefs signed the treaty: Satanta, Satank, Black Eagle, Tonaenko, Fishermore, Manietyn, Sitemgeah, Satpaga, Cauvois, [and] Satamore, Kiowa chiefs, and ten Comanche chiefs.[19] All the commissioners signed it and the reporters witnessed it.

※◆※

MEDICINE LODGE CREEK, October 22, 1867
Last night Little Robe, Black Kettle, Minnick, and Gray Beard, four chiefs of the great Cheyenne nation, came to camp and said they wished to talk with the peace chiefs. Admitted into a special council, they gave their excuses for

their nonappearance. They had advanced one day in their medicine-making work. They had three days more; ordinarily it takes four days to renew medicine arrows, but as this was an urgent necessity, they will only take three.

Taylor spoke to them thus: "We are glad to see you; we have been anxiously expecting you. We would like to know how soon your people could be here."

Little Robe replied:

> It may be four or five nights after this. I was requested by the Cheyenne nation to communicate their wishes to you. I came here for that purpose. If you can detain the chiefs of the other tribes, we would be very well pleased, as we have something of importance to discuss in general council. The Cheyenne soldiers have all got together; no more shall leave their village until we arrive there. It has taken us a longer time to collect the men of this nation together, as they were scattered. Do not be in too much of a hurry to leave. We want to see you very bad and want to shake hands with you. If you have anything very particular to send back to our village, one of our men shall be a runner and start back tomorrow.

The commissioners consulted together about using their influence to request the other tribes to stay till the arrival of the Cheyennes.

General Harney said: "Well, I am in favor of making the tribes to stay [*sic*]."

Henderson: "Well, I suppose that asking us to stay is to test our endurance."

Harney: "Well, let us show the Cheyennes that we can endure."

Henderson: "We do not see why the Cheyennes could not be here sooner. It does not usually take five days to travel twenty-nine miles."

Augur: "That is not the point, Judge Henderson; it is this—these tribes have engaged in certain ceremonies, and they cannot cut them short any more than a man would leave church to take a drink." [Laughter.]

Henderson: "Many a man has done it, and you know it, General. I think these men might cut short their ceremonies. I must be home by November 1, and I cannot wait here five days; we have waited here eight days already, and they had promised to be here tonight."

Harney: "Well, Judge, you cannot go home. We cannot do without you, and if you go, I fear I will have to arrest you." [Great sensation.]

Sanborn: "Tell the chiefs that if they want to see us together, they must be here at the end of three days."

Taylor: "Tell them also that these other tribes have finished their business with us. We can request them to stay, but we can do no more. We can tell also that is the Cheyennes' wish."

Little Robe: "We are in as much of a hurry as yourself. We have thrown away one day to please you. You have your engagements, we have ours. We want to do all in our power to meet together. If we can't meet, then we must abide the consequences."

Black Kettle: "I give you my word I will not ask you to stay here six or seven or eight days. When I look to my left, I see you, and that you intend to do right; and when I look to my right, I see my men, and know that they intend to do right. I want you both to touch and shake hands."

Henderson (to commissioners): "Ah! I see what is the matter—they are afraid to come in. Tell them, interpreter, that they have our full pardon and forgiveness for past offenses."

Harney: "Oh, no! Don't tell them that. I am sure they will come here. I'll bet my life on their keeping their word."

Henderson: "Bah! This medicine is all humbug."

Augur: "Oh no, it ain't. It is life and death with them. It is their religion, and they observe all the ceremonies a great deal better than the whites theirs."

Henderson: "It must be. I never knew a white man that would not put aside religion for business."

Taylor (to interpreter): "Tell them that they must send a runner to their villages; that we can wait four days, and that is all."

At this point Murphy, of the Central Superintendency, requested to make a remark. On being permitted to do so, he said that Little Raven had informed him that he was ready to go into council and sign a treaty tomorrow at 9:00 A.M. Little Raven wished to dissolve their confederation with the Cheyennes and go with the [Kiowa-]Apaches instead. The Cheyennes had always got them into trouble, and by that trouble had prevented them from getting their annuities. Besides, the Cheyennes had made threats against them, and they did not wish to be with them anymore. "Little Raven also told me to tell you that his young men would be in camp in the morning; they had caught up with the Indians who had stolen their ponies and had killed some of them, and when they returned to camp tomorrow not to be alarmed, as they would give some startling whoops, yell, and fire, and he hoped the soldiers would not get alarmed and fire on them."

"Hurrah!" said Harney. "I hope they killed them all. What were they, Pawnees?"

"No, sir," said Murphy; "they were Kaws."

"Well done," replied Harney. "The Arapahos ought to have killed them all, darn them!"

I have endeavored to give, in the above, a synopsis in dialogue form of the proceedings in the council tent last night. Everyone looks with anxiety to the arrival of the Cheyennes, as they are the Indians who have been at war, and we may expect some interesting disclosures when they arrive. It were well for the commissioners to stay and see this affair out, and do it well. But your correspondent will be at his post.

Daily Missouri Democrat, November 2, 1867

COMMISSION CAMP, MEDICINE LODGE CREEK,
October 24, 1867

This month is a time of treaty making. Our time is agreeably divided between looking at squaws bedizened in their artless finery, at nude forms of children romping with infantine glee about the camp, listening to sentimental speeches from the commissioners, and reporting Indian orations. Much breath has been expended, and many fine poetical sentiments wasted on the prairie air. Councils have broken up time and again with eternal promises of love and friendship on both sides, many a shaking of hands and mysterious gesticulations, the meaning and the true interpretation of which is only known to the favored few.

We have a daily exhibition at our camp of either the Arapaho, Kiowa, Comanche, or [Kiowa-]Apache villages turning out en masse and promenading up and down, followed by hundreds of dogs of all sizes, breeds, and colors, howling, yelping, or snarling incessantly. While the Indian boys give eclat to the scene by indulging in sundry war whoops, the little papooses are heard yelling with all their might, their squaws uttering forcible remonstrances at their obstreperous conduct.

Two days ago the treaty of peace was signed by the Kiowa and Comanche chiefs. Yesterday was the day of the distribution of presents and annuity goods. The two tribes, numbering about three thousand souls, came up to our camp and seated themselves in great circles around their respective chiefs, the Kiowa circle on one side and the Comanche on the other. The goods were rolled into the center—boxes of soap, beads, brass bells, long strings of tin cups, dozens of iron pans, bales of red, blue, and black blankets, bolts of domestic and printed calico, a pile of revolvers, caps and ammunition, and dozens of packages of butcher knives.

Then the chiefs, divesting themselves of their cumbersome robes, took out their knives and ripped open the bales. As the bright red blankets are exposed to view, cries of admiration simultaneously burst from all quarters of the savage circle.

Then braves stepped up with beaming faces to receive the blankets and distribute them around, and each squaw, surrounded by a numerous progeny, stretches out her hand for the rich gift. Another brave receives beads, bright buttons, and bells, and starts around the circle with the coveted treasure. Another and yet another receives coats, hats and pants, and to each male adult gives his portion. The bolts of gaudy calico are then cut open, and three yards are measured off and given to each female over fifteen years old. Over this calico there is a discussion, and angry voices are heard. The squaws pick up their ears, a sharp cry is uttered, and the circle is a circle no longer. All, with a rush, hurry to the male disputants and sweep off everything as if by magic. Over the spoils they fight and tug, and several of them turn somersaults in the air, exposing

Issuing clothing to the Comanche Indians. FRANK LESLIE'S ILLUSTRATED WEEKLY 1867.

lusty legs and naked hips. Into the midst of this scramble, where their wives have forgotten their maternal dignity, the chiefs dart, plying their thongs without regard to age or sex. Quietness reigns again, but the calico, the beads, the bright buttons and brass bells are all gone. One old deaf squaw, more avaricious than the rest, had pounced upon a sack of brown sugar and had almost dragged it to her place, but as the noise subsided, she was seen by a chief with her saccharine plunder, who straightway strides up to the elderly thief and belabors her well with his rawhide. Piercing shrieks are uttered by her, testifying to the energy with which the lash was applied, and her ill luck is a source of amusement to the other offenders. Over $100,000 worth of goods is reckoned to have been distributed the last two days to the Kiowas and Comanches.

The sight of so many gifts seems to have good effect upon their untutored minds; universal good temper is apparent among them all, and many little presents have been given by them to the commissioners. I am of the opinion, and so are all, that the peace thus so opportunely concluded with them will ultimately prove of great benefit to the West. Satanta cannot now have a shadow of a cause to justify his digging up the hatchet. The lands that they formerly owned they retain for hunting purposes, and a splendid country for agricultural purposes has been given these tribes forever as reservation.

Satank, the old chief of the Kiowa Nation, preparatory to commencing his long journey to Coahuila, rode up to the council tent, accompanied by a few of his best warriors, to take a final leave of those who had been so good to him. Alighting from his gaily caparisoned horse, he turned round to where the peace commissioners stood and addressed them thus:

> It has made me very glad to meet you, who are the commissioners sent by the Great Father to see us. You have heard much talk by our

chiefs and no doubt are tired of it. Many of them have put themselves forward and filled you with their sayings. I have kept back and said nothing—not that I did not consider myself the principal chief of the Kiowa Nation, but others younger than I desired to talk, and I left it to them.

Before leaving, however, as I now intend to go, I come to say that the Kiowas and Comanches have made with you a peace, and they intend to keep it. If it brings prosperity to us, we of course will like it the better. If it brings prosperity or adversity, we will not abandon it. It is our contract, and it shall stand. Our people once carried war against Texas. We thought the Great Father would not be offended, for the Texans had gone out from among his people and become his enemies. You now tell us that they have made peace and returned to the great family. The Kiowas and Comanches will seek no bloody trail in their land. They have pledged their word and that word shall last, unless the whites break their contract and invite the horrors of war. We do not break treaties. We make but few contracts, and them we remember well. The whites make so many that they are liable to forget them. The white chief seems not to be able to govern his braves. The Great Father seems powerless in the face of his children. He sometimes becomes angry when he sees the wrongs of his people committed on the red man, and his voice becomes loud as the roaring winds. But like the wind, it soon dies away and leaves the sullen calm of unheeded oppression. We hope now that a better time has come. If all would talk and then do as you have done, the sun of peace would shine forever. We have warred against the white man, but never because it gave us pleasure. Before the day of oppression came, no white man came to our villages and went away hungry. It gave us more joy to share with them than it gave him to partake of our hospitality. In the far-distant past there was no suspicion among us. The world seemed large enough for both the red and the white man. Its broad plains seem now to contract, and the white man grows jealous of his red brother.

The white man once came to trade; he now comes as a soldier. He once put his trust in our friendship and wanted no shield but our fidelity. But now he builds forts and plants big guns on their walls. He once gave us arms, and powder and ball, and bade us hunt the game. We then loved him for his confidence; he now suspects our plighted faith and drives us to be his enemies; he now covers his face with the cloud of jealousy and anger and tells us to be gone, as an offended master speaks to his dog. Look at this medal I wear. By wearing this I have been made poor. Formerly I was rich in horses and lodges— today I am the poorest of all. When you put this silver medal on my neck you made me poor.

We thank the Great Spirit that all these wrongs are now to cease and the old day of peace and friendship to come again.

You came as friends. You talked as friends. You have partially heard our many complaints. To you they may have seemed trifling. To us they are everything.

You have not tried, as many have done, to make a new bargain merely to get the advantage.

You have not asked to make your annuities smaller, but unasked you have made them larger.

You have not withdrawn a single gift, but you have voluntarily provided more guaranties of our education and comfort.

When we saw these things done, we then said among ourselves, these are the men of the post. We at once gave you our hearts. You now have them. You know what is best for us. Do for us what is best. Teach us the road to travel, and we will not depart from it forever.

For your sakes, the green grass shall no more be stained with the red blood of the palefaces. Your people shall again be our people, and peace shall be between us forever. If wrong comes, we shall look to you for right and justice.

We know you will not forsake us and [will] tell your people also to act as you have done, to be as you have been.

I am old, but still am chief. I shall have soon to go the way of my fathers, but those who come after me will remember this day. It is now treasured up by the old and will be carried by them to the grave, and then handed down to be kept as a sacred tradition by their children and their children's children. And now the time has come that I must go. Good-bye!

You may never see me more, but remember Satank as the white man's friend.

The above speech is a gem. There is a good deal of truth in it which strikes home. This old chief has been a desperate fighter, and only three years ago, he stole up in the dead of night to the fortifications at Larned and shot a sentinel dead at his post. Colonel Leavenworth was then commander of the fort, and this act created great alarm to the garrison at the time. But as no more such occurrences happened, the affair was soon forgotten.

Today a treaty of peace with signed with the [Kiowa-]Apaches.[20] Their reservation is located near the reservation of the Kiowas and Comanches. Before the treaty of October 17, 1865, this tribe confederated with those two tribes, but by their own request at that treaty, they were numbered with the Arapaho and Cheyenne tribes, and their former confederation was dissolved in the presence of Harney, Sanborn, and Kit Carson. But this union, it seems, did not prove acceptable, for the Arapahos assumed a belligerent attitude, and the Cheyennes dug up the hatchet and broke out into open war. The [Kiowa-]

Apaches, few in number though the bravest warriors on the plains, got into trouble. Their annuities were withheld, and [they] finally were reduced to great impoverishment. In spite of all these difficulties, the [Kiowa-]Apaches still maintained friendly relations with the government, even while they found themselves isolated from other tribes.

At the council which they held previous to signing, they declared their intentions of uniting their fortunes with the Kiowas and Comanches. To all the benefits to which those two tribes were entitled according to treaty, the [Kiowa-]Apaches have also a right, and besides their annuities are allowed the sum of five thousand dollars annually.

Governor Crawford and the other gentleman representing Kansas have left for home. Before they started, Governor Crawford made some very serious charges against the Indian agents, Snow[21] and Leavenworth. Snow he charged with having withheld from the Osage Indians one year's annuities and with living away from his agency. Leavenworth he charged with being "a bad man generally."

The Osage Indians have sent a delegation of twelve chiefs, under the leadership of Little Bear, to see the commissioners. The result of the conference is that the commissioners have told Little Bear that his tribe possesses a reservation too large for their purposes.

These Osages are about three thousand strong, and they possess a tract of land 230 miles in length by 30 miles in width, thus allowing to each soul 1,371 acres. This tribe has already in the Treasury of the United States the sum of $300,000, drawing five percent interest per annum. It is now proposed to sell a tract of land on which the whites have encroached already for the distance of four miles on their lands, for their especial benefit, and then to make a law excluding all white men from settling on their lands.

In two days the Cheyennes, it is thought, will be in to make a treaty. The Arapahos have entered into a confederation with the Cheyennes, and this treaty to be made will include both tribes, and then our business on Medicine Lodge Creek will have been finished.

Daily Missouri Democrat, October 31, 1867

MEDICINE LODGE CREEK, October 27, 1867

A treaty has just been concluded with the [Kiowa-]Apaches, who have entered into a confederation with the Kiowas and Comanches. Where those tribes will be placed on the reservation adopted for agricultural purposes, is situated on the southwest corner of the Indian Territory, in the region known as the Wichita Mountain country. The [Kiowa-]Apaches, in lieu of their annual sum of fifteen dollars, receive annually one suit of clothes for each male adult, one flannel dress for each female over twelve years old, and enough material to make each child under twelve a proper covering for the body. Exclusive of this annuity, the [Kiowa-]Apache tribe, consisting of eighty-five lodges under Poor Bear, shall receive the sum of five thousand dollars annually, which, including the twenty-five thousand dollars to be annually paid the Kiowas and Comanches, makes the total sum to be paid this confederation thirty thousand dollars.

Until such time as the [Kiowa-]Apaches choose to go upon their reservation, they are permitted to range at pleasure over the whole Indian Territory, stretching from the southeast corner of New Mexico, thence north to the Wichita Mountains, thence northerly along the ninety-sixth degree of longitude to the Arkansas River, thence westward to the northeast corner of New Mexico—an area of sixty thousand square miles, covered with game of all kinds, and over which roam thousands of buffalo.

Formerly this tribe confederated with Arapahos and Cheyennes, but owing to the hostile attitude of the latter towards the whites, which prevented them from getting their annuities, they dissolved the compact at this last treaty.

Yesterday Little Raven made a speech exonerating himself from any charges that may be against him. He represented himself as having been the friend of the whites and wished to continue so when the Cheyennes appear. The Arapahos desire to have a treaty drawn only for themselves. They also wish to dissolve connection with the Cheyennes. The Cheyennes are expected here tomorrow night, when they will advance with war whoop and sound of gong. They are coming in force with their wives, children, and substance, to the number of four hundred lodges, or about two thousand five hundred souls. Their medicine arrows are renewed with satisfaction; everything is auspicious for a peace council. We have waited thirteen days for this tribe, and will wait for them until Monday noon[22]; if they are not here, then we will put off. The commissioners will go east. Gray Head, subchief of this nation, gave some interesting facts concerning the burning of their village by Hancock, which I will send you by mail. Two wagonloads of ammunition are at Larned, which are to be distributed among the Arapahos and Cheyennes.

Daily Missouri Democrat, November 2, 1867

MEDICINE LODGE CREEK, Oct. 27, 1867

Tired of the fruitless, tokenless life which we waded through with many anathemas upon the universal sameness of each passing day, we anxiously looked for an end to this unprofitable existence by an abrupt termination to our dreamy proceedings here by the arrival of the Cheyennes. A change of weather would have been an event worth rejoicing at, or a massacre for the sake of indulging in a sensational description of a bloody scene. We hankered for the fleshpots of St. Louis, and we harped upon the joys of city life. But the longest day has an end, and so did we experience an unwelcome termination to paradisiacal weather.

This morning dawned clear and bright. The sun came forth in all its royal glory from its purple pavilion. The feathered songsters warbled sweet melodies in the groves hard by; the zephyrs lightly sighed. Nature was radiant. Towards noon a gradual change passed over all. A tempest was brooding in the western horizon. Men called it a "norther." Banks of black clouds lay piled one upon another, and out of their depths others rose higher and higher, until the whole firmament was completely overshadowed. The prairie for ten miles around leaped into flame, and its lurid light framed the long clouds that hung low in the west with reddish streaks, which added to the gloomy beauty of the skies. Far behind the struggling tempest, the setting sun was casting its evening rays through the restless heavens, shooting out his vivid light on either side of the rising storm, flinging his silver lining around the wrathful elements and breaking out into sparkling flashes upon the quartz rocks south of the Nescotongwa. For a while the storm seemed spellbound, while the erratic lightning shot lambent flames around. Another moment, and the storm has burst. It hurries along the earth with speed; it drives a funeral pall of smoke and a long wave of crimson flame towards our camp; an icy chill heralds its approach; a moaning sound is heard in the air, and then a cloud of sand obscures every object from view. The tents reel and stagger, and full well we know the tempest—the "norther" of the plains is upon us. For ten hours it has lasted already. Summer is turned into winter. Fire has become absolutely necessary. Overcoats are in requisition, and warm gloves are in high demand. We bribe our chef de cuisine to make us a cup of hot, steaming coffee, and while we sip delicious draughts of this decoction of Rio and inhale its delicate aroma, the cheery song is heard from one of our lighthearted mess, and the blinding, chilly storm and the gloomy darkness is forgotten.

Before the storm set in, Gray Head, an old, venerable Cheyenne chief, was requested, through the interpreter, John S. Smith, to state what he knew of the burning of the Cheyenne village by Major General Hancock last April.

Gray Head was one of the runners who came in yesterday, announcing the day on which the Cheyennes would arrive.

The following story of Gray Head will serve to throw light upon the other side of a subject which has lately been in this camp an all-day theme:

> A tall chief came along the Arkansas road when the grass was not yet green last spring, with many soldiers and many big guns. He came as far as Larned. Our chiefs held counsel together, and they said he came to war against us. By and by a courier came direct from him inviting us to big council at Larned. Bull Bear, Tall Bull, White Horse, Slim Face, and I went with him. The tall chief had many other great chiefs about him; one a graybeard (Colonel A. J. Smith) whom the tall chief said was next to him. At the council he asked us if we wanted to go to war. He said he was ready to fight us. Tall Bull said that we had been at peace, and that we did not wish war. The white

chief said that he was going to visit us in our villages. Then we were afraid. We remembered Chivington, and we asked him not to go there, that we could talk to him where we were as well as at our villages. The next day he started and we chiefs went with him. On the second day I went ahead and told Roman Nose that the white chief was coming. Roman Nose called a lot of his warriors together and went to meet the white chief. When the tall chief saw us, he drew up his soldiers in a long line before us. Then our people got afraid and ran each way. Some hid themselves in the woods (on the banks of the Pawnee). Roman Nose and myself stood still with a few of our young men. We had a white flag up, which we waved above our heads.

The tall chief rode towards us and shook hands with the chiefs. I was so afraid that I shook hands with all his chiefs. I kept shaking hands all the while, for by that means I thought I would conciliate them. The white chief said that he was going to our village. We went straight to our village and told our women that the big chief was coming. Then they were afraid. Some cried out and got ready to go off. Our chiefs did all in their power to keep them in the village. They got their ponies, packed up, and scattered over the prairie. The papooses were screaming, and we had to let them go.

After this the chiefs were afraid to meet the white chief. They feared he would be angry and kill them all, and they wanted to leave also. But Roman Nose said, "No, we will meet him and talk to him." Towards evening the white chief came near our village and camped. Roman Nose went to him and told him that the women and papooses had all gone because they were afraid. The white chief got angry and told Roman Nose and Bull Bear to take his horses and bring them back. I went to these chiefs and said good words to them, but they would not come. I told Ed Guerrier to take the chief's horses back to him and tell him we could not do what he wanted. We next day, while camping, saw the soldiers of the white chief after us. Then the women and papooses commenced to scream, but Roman Nose beat them and made them stop, lest the soldiers should see us. By his orders the Cheyennes made a rush to the Sioux and laid down. They passed by, and they did not see us. We turned off in another direction, while the soldiers went north towards the Smoky Hill. Some of the Sioux followed them. When we saw these soldiers follow us, we knew the white chief came to make war. We held solemn council that night, and the chiefs decided that the white chief only came for war, and Roman Nose said we should go to war also.

Two days afterwards, a Cheyenne runner came into our camp and said that the white chief had burned our village. Then the chiefs got angry and resolved to go to war.

Question by Sanborn: "Did you leave any of your people in the village?"

Gray Head: "Yes, one old man with his knee broken and a little Cheyenne girl who was not right in her mind. She would not come with us, and we had to leave her there."

Sanborn: "Was she hurt by anyone before you left?"

Gray Head: "I was the last one that left the village, and she was not hurt then."

Sanborn: "Are you sure that she was a Cheyenne?"

Gray Head: "Did I not know her parents; did I not see her as she grew up, day by day?"

This ended Gray Head's plain story of facts concerning the burning of his village. Throughout it bears the stamp of truth and ingenuousness. It must be admitted that General Hancock was deceived for a purpose:

First by Major Douglass, who sent official information relative to sundry depredations said to have been committed by Indians; the massacre of seventeen colored soldiers; and a meditated confederation of the five tribes of Indians—Cheyennes, Sioux, Arapahos, Comanches, and Kiowas.

Second, by interpreters who wished to curry favor with the general, and to give him some good cause for war.

Third, by interpreters who said that the girl captured by the village was either a white or a half-breed.

It is proposed to compromise the affair by paying the Cheyennes the sum of $100,000, the entire value of the village and property burnt. It is also proposed to turn over to them the forty-five lodges which Hancock ordered to be stored at Fort Dodge. Exclusive of all these, the accrued annuities are stored here ready for distribution, amounting to some $80,000 worth. There are also five thousand dollars' worth of presents to be given to the Cheyennes.

Yet we have been delayed nine days on their account; runners have been dispatched time and time again with most pathetic messages of love and regard—manifold promises of presents and wishes for peace. The major part of the chiefs reply in the same strain, but Roman Nose remains stern and indifferent to all promises. Only a warrior—a common brave in his tribe—by his very recklessness and audacity, he has more influence today over the Cheyennes than any chief. His promise to his chiefs at Pawnee Fork was, "I will talk once more to the white chief (Hancock), and if he will not listen, this knife shall be wet with his best blood." By the utmost combined exertions of the headmen, this desperate threat was prevented from being carried into execution. His reply to the proffered condolences of the peace commissioners is, "I am but a brave; let the chiefs speak. I will obey." Having lost faith in the whites since the massacre of his people at Sand Creek by Chivington, he stands aloof from messengers and the soothing words of his chiefs; and the young men, always emulating bold deeds, follow him en masse. They are not quite assured that we will not repeat that sanguinary deed of Sand Creek, or some such action as that of the destruction of their villages. Their medicine business, some of the commissioners are disposed to believe, is a pretense to gain time. The military portion of them place implicit reliance on their words of peace. Harney stakes his life on their honor, while Henderson believes the medicine arrow "all poppycock."

The Cheyennes are a keen, shrewd, diplomatic nation. When once assured that we mean to make peace, they will come in and ratify it.

Since April 19, a memorable day to them, a detachment of them went to the mountains and hewed down eight thousand tall saplings, in daily peril of their lives killed over four thousand buffalo, skinned them, and converted their hides into lodges. They have now four hundred new lodges and plenty of robes to sell. This is an evidence of their industry.

Another band has roamed from the Arkansas River, up the Republican and along the Platte, killing, mutilating, and destroying as they went, pillaging trains, burning ranches, attacking forts, abducting women and children, and creating constant alarm through a country eighty thousand square miles in extent. Who then will not pause and consider a little, even amid the fret, fever, and bustle of political life, how much better it is to make peace with such a tribe, than waging war against them?

Although we have strong hopes of making peace with this warlike nation, all fears of personal safety are not banished from the mind. Not quite five paces to our right is the commissioners' tent. A lively discussion is going on as to whether the Cheyennes will make peace or not. The time is night, of pitchy darkness. Commissioner Taylor argues, "But look for an instant at the provocation which they have received," to which Sanborn replies: "Oh, pshaw, have they not retaliated in full," and chiming in with a clincher, Senator Henderson's voice is heard: "To be sure, have we not thousands of dollars' worth of presents to give them?"

The city reader will suppose that everybody was satisfied after that. Not so. Harney redoubled his pickets and ordered vigilance, while the careless sang, "Away with retrospects and dark forebodings. If we die, why we'll die with merry morals on our tongues. Let us sleep."

MEDICINE LODGE CREEK, Sunday, October 27, 1867

Today has been throughout a beautiful day—a real Indian summer's day. Over the dark green foliage of the woods bordering the pellucid waters of this creek, a filmy haze swam in the air. Out of the earth issued a vapor, in which distant objects seemed to float and assume monstrous proportions. It was a day which invited rest.

About 10:00 A.M. the whole camp was considerably exercised over the news that the Cheyennes were coming. The news spread like wildfire throughout the camp. Everyone, from the commissioners down to the jenny driver, was on the alert. The teamsters clambered on top of the ambulances to catch a view of the long-expected Cheyennes. The Arapaho, Comanche, and Kiowa criers passed through the camps warning everyone to his wigwam, something after the manner and style of the ancient Israelite criers. "To your wigwams, oh ye Arapahos, ye Kiowa braves, and Comanche warriors. To your wigwams, the dreaded Cheyennes are coming!" Away skedaddled the papooses and squaws, and ingloriously the braves ran, each to his camp. The vaunted Kiowa, the terrible Comanche, and the redoubtable Arapaho paled before the echoed name of the invincible Cheyennes, the scourge of the plains.

In a second, almost, our camp was deserted of the Indians. The Cheyennes were coming! "What will they do?" "Will they fight?" "Let's get ready!" And with such words as these, we got ready; loaded our rifles, our revolvers, and our derringers; and then awaited their coming with what patience we could command.

An hour elapsed, and between the ravine which divided the odd-looking plateaus from each other, a cloud of sand was seen rising into small spiral columns, "for sure the Cheyennes are coming." A few moments pass and we see emerging from under the cloud of sand several dark forms. But they descend into the valley, and we are prevented from seeing them again by the clump of timber. Dinner is piped, and we leave the scene to attend to that most necessary meal. "The Cheyennes are coming," shouts a gaddling gaberlunzje of the camp, and we hastily rush out to view the approach of the dusky caballeros. Simultaneously with that movement, their voices are heard breaking out into a chant, and away to the right of the timber is seen a column of the long-expected Cheyennes on the double trot. At the same moment, Black Kettle is seen making his way towards us on a full gallop, his horse covered with foam. The commissioners meet him, and Black Kettle, the head chief, informs them that all his tribe are approaching. The blow of a bugle and the peculiar exciting shout of the Indian is heard nearer, and a second column of a hundred men is seen issuing from the timber. Black Kettle gallops back to meet them, and a third, a fourth, and a fifth column emerges into view. A wave of Black Kettle's hand, and the four last columns debouch to the left, swinging into divisions, marching obliquely on the double trot, in most admirable order. Another wave, and they all approach in line of battle, singing as they come. The first column swings around on the left flank and dash down towards us to the rear of the Arapaho warriors, drawn up under the leadership of Little Raven on the hill, expectant and ready for demonstrations. On the left, posted on a hill, are the Kiowa and Comanche warriors under Satanta, looking with jealous eyes upon this magnificent display of the Cheyennes. Up to within fifty paces the Cheyennes ride, and then halt in a long line two files deep. The chiefs advance twenty paces nearer, and the commissioners direct their steps towards them.

Then commences the shaking of hands, Taylor taking the lead. This ceremony is concluded, which General Harney declares upon his honor is very wearisome. Soft words pass between the two high parties, and they separate, the Cheyennes to their camping ground, and the commissioners to their tents. To show you what sort of an impression the meeting made upon the great peace commissioners, I subjoin the following conversation:

General Harney: "Well, by God, I am glad that this wearisome task is over."

Augur: "So am I."

Harney: "Let's go and wash our hands."

Terry: "I wonder if these fellows have got the itch."

Harney: "Gad, shouldn't wonder."

We will leave the august representatives of the government of the United States while we take the thread of the story.

The Cheyennes undoubtedly presented a fine appearance. For this grand occasion, they had arrayed themselves in their most gorgeous costumes. All the silver in the tribe seemed to be conspicuously displayed on the breasts of the chivalry of the nation, the "Dog Soldiers." The Cheyennes who thus made their appearance numbered fully five hundred stout men, the rank and file of the power of the nation. Within about an hour after their arrival, another exciting scene occurred. A few miserable Kaws, desirous of increasing the wealth of their tribe by capturing a few horses, made a raid on the Arapaho shekels. Some Arapaho braves discovered them in the act of driving away their stock, upon which they gave instant pursuit. The Cheyenne Dog Soldiers, having buried the hatchet, galloped to the scene of action and prevented the deeds of blood about to be committed. The Kiowas, the Comanches, and the Apaches, urged on by curiosity, also galloped up, until over fifteen hundred warriors were assembled. Imagine for one instant so large a body, dressed in the most fantastic manner, their dresses made of every color, riding the sinewy, fleet mustangs of the prairie, galloping in every direction, giving utterance to their quick, yelling whoops, and you may form a better idea of the scene we witnessed, than I can give by attempting a description of the subject. It was exciting in the extreme. Suffice it to state the Kaws were not killed, they were merely driven ignominiously away with a significant warning.

At dusk the Cheyennes again visited our camp and were regaled with a plentitude of coffee and hardtack, after which they expressed themselves satisfied with their treatment. Early next morning they would be willing to hold a powwow and make a lasting peace, which should prove beneficial to both. Before departing to their village, they presented General Harney with a pony.

The Cheyennes number about two thousand souls. Medicine Arrow and Roman Nose are absent, and neither will be present at the council. Tomorrow I shall have, I expect, enough items to form another letter.

Daily Missouri Democrat, November 1, 1867

MEDICINE LODGE CREEK, Oct. 28, via

JUNCTION CITY, KANSAS, Oct. 31

A treaty of peace has been concluded with the Cheyennes and Arapahos. The reservation of the Cheyennes covers an area of nine thousand square miles and is bounded east by the Arkansas River, south and west by the Cimarron, north by Kansas.

Peace has been declared with all the Southern Indians.

The Arapaho reservation is not definitely located as yet, but Little Raven signed the treaty leaving the reservation to be settled at some future time.

We go from here to North Platte via St. Louis. The commissioners will be in St. Louis at 10:00 A.M. Friday, November 1.

◆—◆ ≋◆≋ ◆—◆

Daily Missouri Democrat, November 2, 1867

MEDICINE LODGE CREEK, October 28

Ten o'clock this morning the Cheyennes, according to their promise of yester eve, came to the council. This, of course, was to be the most important council of all. The Cheyennes had been at war; it was desirous to make peace. They gathered in number—chiefs, braves, and warriors, old and young.

The spokesman of the nation, while the chiefs were seated in a semicircle, delivered a long harangue to them, urging on them forbearance, picturing the blessings of peace and the horrors of war, to which they listened with open ears.

The five principal chiefs—Black Kettle, Big Jake, Big Head, Tall Bull, and White Horse—were also presented, and occupied the front circle. Behind these came the chivalry, the famous Dog Soldiers, a band of braves with iron hearts and desperate-looking physiognomies—modern Spartans, who knew how to die but not to be led captive; the same people who, when at Sand Creek their best warriors fell, stabbed themselves rather than be taken captives. So the story goes.

Braves sitting astride their ponies, watching with fierce eyes every movement that is going on, their heads adorned with nodding plumes, their breasts with large silver crosses, their faces painted red, blue, black, or yellow, they present in my mind the safeguard of a nation, the forlorn hope of the Indians. In this band, haughty and obstinate, are to be found the best representatives of the American aboriginal who are still extant. Even now, their hands are on their gleaming tomahawks, ready to ply with certain aim whenever summoned by the swarthy chiefs, who squatted on the ground, gravely inhale the calumet preparatory to the opening of the grand council.

These plumed riders are the celebrated "Dog Soldiers," the elite of the Cheyenne nation, who look with scorn and contempt upon all other bands. None but warriors tried can enter the ranks of this band. They are allowed to enter any council of the tribe they please. They are a privileged set. Their wishes are consulted upon any subject connected with affairs of the government of the tribe.

A chief of the Dog Soldiers was absent when Hancock swept along the Arkansas River last spring. With a few of his choicest warriors, he had gone on the warpath against the Utes, the hereditary enemies of his tribe. He started on his return after Hancock destroyed the village.

The chief, White Buffalo, was flushed with victory; to his girdle hung several reeking scalps. He threaded with unwearied patience his long way across the plains to his village on the banks of the Pawnee, followed by his trusty band. He thought of his gentle wife and little papooses, and as he thought, shot wistful glances towards the hill which shut the village from his view. He pictured to himself the triumph he would receive upon displaying his ghastly trophies, and then fancied the walls of his conelike lodge hung with them. The hill was in sight, from the top of which the village could be seen. He spurred onward and at last gained its summit.

He looked around; rubbed his eyes; he could see nothing. A deep and incomprehensible dread took possession of him. What had become of his home, his wife and children—his gray-haired father and his nation? Whither had they gone? If they were still alive; and while agitated by these conflicting thoughts, he galloped down the hill to solve at once his doubts and fears. Oh, well; what did he find? He found his home a ruined place—the wigwams of his people in ashes, and his people gone he knew not whither. What was to be done? The chief veiled his sorrow and his agony, girded his loins tighter, and followed fast on the trail of his people. On the third day he came up with them and heard the story: "A white chief came along with many soldiers and burned the village." Blame not, then, the unfortunate Cheyennes, if in any part of this letter you find enough to judge them obstinate. They have had reason—twice deceived and twice suffered.

When quietness was restored all around, Commissioner Taylor announced the council in session and requested interpreters Smith and Mrs. Adams, interpreters of the Arapahos, to inform their respective tribes that as the joint council of the Cheyenne and Arapaho chiefs was opened, he would state that Senator Henderson, one of the great council at Washington, had been chosen to deliver the words of the peace commission.

Our friends, the chiefs and the headmen of the Cheyenne and Arapaho nations, we come out among you to determine the most important question in human affairs, that of peace or war. Three of us are appointed by the Great Father at Washington, and four of us by the great council. Two years ago, at the mouth of the Little Arkansas, we made peace with you and wished it to last forever, but bad men on one side or the other broke the peace. We believe that falsehood was brought to us about your people in regard to your feelings and intentions, and no doubt, falsehoods were carried to you in reference to the feelings of the whites. We have among us wicked men who wish to profit by the calamities of both sides. And these bad men continually seek war. Many tell you lies to excite you, and in the same way to us. We now think these bad men told wicked lies to General Hancock and caused him to march with his soldiers last spring into this country. The great council and the Great Father both asked him for the reasons of his march, and he informed them that you had broken the peace, and he said that you had committed many outrageous acts upon our people before he had commenced his march. Some of our people said that General Hancock was right, some said that he was wrong. Some said that you wanted war and proposed that we should send soldiers among you to cover the plains like grass. Others said that peace commissioners, and not soldiers, should be sent among you to talk with you.

Those of us who wanted the commissioners were in the majority, and we are those commissioners. We are now ready to hear your complaints and take them to Washington, that the president and council may redress them. We do not want war, but we have to accept it sometimes, when we cannot have honorable peace. Some of our bad people mock and scoff at us because we want to have peace with the red man. Perhaps some of your young braves with more blood than brains will oppose your making peace with us, contrary to the express wishes of the nation. Such men on both sides must be cast away; their councils are black with death. Why should we war against each other? The world is large enough for us all. Peace makes us happy, and war brings sorrow to the lodge of the red man and the house of the white man.

War long continued must result [in] total destruction to the Indian, because his numbers are less. As long as the buffalo ranges on the plains, we are willing that you should hunt him, as long as you keep to the treaties made at the Little Arkansas. But the herds of buffalo are becoming fewer and thinner every year. You can see this for yourselves; therefore, you should prepare for the day when he shall cease to be. When that day comes, we want you to be prepared to live. In lieu of the buffalo, you must have herds of oxen, and flocks of sheep, and droves of hogs, like the white man. In order to have them, you must now select a rich piece of land for a reservation, that it may be set aside for you before the white man settles upon it. We will help you select it, and we pledge our words and the honor of our Great Father that it shall be set aside for you. On that reservation we will build a house to store your goods that shall be sent to you every year. Your agent shall be sent among you, to live with you, that he may hear your complaints. At the same place, you will have your trading houses; also, a physician to cure you of sickness; also, a farmer to cultivate your soil. We will send you a mill to grind your corn, and teachers to educate your children. In addition to these things the Great Father will send you every year such other things as you may need. Now, in return for this, we only ask that you will not molest our railroads (cries of "ha-ow-how"); that our white settlers be permitted to live in peace; that our stagecoaches, mule trains, and other wagons may pass along the Cimarron and other roads without being attacked.

In other words, we propose a firm and lasting peace. We want the red and white man to be friends forever. If one of our people breaks the peace, you must tell your agent, and we will see you righted. If any of your people break the peace, deliver him up to your agent, that he may be punished according to the laws of the great council. If he be innocent, no harm will be done him. When we have written down this peace, we must trust each other as friends. We must cast aside suspicion and defend each other from harm (smiles and universal cries of "ugh, how"). We have now done, and wait to hear your reply.

The steatite hookah, quaintly decorated, was passed around, after which the Cheyennes made answer that as the Arapahos had been at peace, they ought to speak first; that before giving a decided answer, they would like to hear from them first.

Little Raven, chief of the Arapahos, then got up and addressed the assembled chiefs and commissioners as follows:

I am glad to see my brothers of the Cheyennes present. We Arapahos have been waiting a long time to see you, and I hope you will sign the peace which we wish. We should not go to war with the whites. They have been very kind to us; they give us warm clothes and good food. They don't want to go to war. There's the Utes, make war upon them as much as you please, they are your enemies, the whites are your friends. I have heard that you have been offended at me for protecting some whites who fled from your way to my camp for protection. Would you have me behave like a dog? Would you not have done so also? Do not be children, but be men and consider this thing well, and you will find nothing to blame.

And now, you commissioners, I hope that what you have said is the truth. But you should also tell your young men at these forts on the Arkansas roads their duty. They are mostly children, and you must not allow them to run wild, for that provokes war. Keep them within bounds. Tell the white settlers also to behave themselves, and then there will be peace. And now that I see all the Cheyennes, let me congratulate you upon your success. It will be a good thing to tell the whites in the states. The news of peace will make their hearts glad. You have done a wise thing in not mentioning anything about the mules they have taken from the whites. Let the Cheyennes have them.

I and my nation have been driven from near the mountains and our country. I hear the whites are getting much gold, cutting fine timber. I make no fuss about it. Let me have my reservation near Fort Lyon. Keep the whites away from it.

This winter, when the annuities are sent to us, send out ammunition and guns that we may hunt game. You will by that means convince all my people that you will do right.

Even if you ever want a railroad to go through, I am willing. There shall be no noise about it. Let the medicine lodges (schools) be built on our reservation. By the time my tribe settles down, I shall be in my grave, but these young men, it will do them good.

By placing my reservation apart from the rest, you cannot possibly attach any blame to my young men, should anything be wrong. My hands, and those of my people, shall be clean and white.

We shall want a trader at our village who will do right. I believe it is the traders that do all the mischief. You should caution them. They are very dishonest people, and you should warn them to do right lest evil should come. I have spoken.

The old gentleman, having finished, walked around the peace commission, and after saying his genial "How" to each, sat down.

Little Raven was followed next by Buffalo Chief. A Cheyenne chief rose next and said he wanted to talk to Henderson alone. Henderson sat in front of all, and the chief addressed him in the quick, vigorous spasmodic manner of the Cheyennes:

I ask you if it is as you say. Have you come from the Great Father with these good words? Are you to make peace to with us? (On being told that he was, he continued.)

Well then, I take you by the hand, and my soldiers shall take you also. Here you are chiefs. You sit in the front, your soldiers at your backs. Here I am chief, my young men are all around me. You spoke about the railroads; well, we will hold it together. We will both have a right in it. I believe you are sent by the Great Father to make peace with us. We sprung from the prairie, we live by it, we prefer to do so, and as yet, we do not want the blessings of civilization. We do not claim this country south of the Arkansas, but that country between the Arkansas and the Platte is ours. We are willing, when we desire to live as you do, to take your advice about that, but until then we will take our chances. It were well that those on the Arkansas road were out of the country, that we might roam over the country as formerly; the bones of our forefathers may rest then. You think that you are doing a great deal for us by giving these presents to us, but we prefer to live as formerly. If you gave us all the goods you could give, yet we would prefer our own life. You give us presents and then take our land; that produces war. I introduce to your notice Col. David Butterfield. I want him for our trader. He is a good man. I have said all.

This was the last speech delivered by anybody. It was the speech of a Cheyenne chief, a tribe which had been at war all summer and had now come at the invitation of the commission to ratify a peace. They had been conquerors, and we wished for peace. They did not wish any peace, but since we asked it, they, as brave men, were willing to accord it. As a recompense for this action, we might, if we chose, build them schools, but they could not occupy them. They preferred the life they led, the wild, free, roving life of nomadic tribes, here today and there tomorrow.

After this speech, they started to leave without signing the treaty. John S. Smith was in a perfect state of living excitement. Hither and thither he flew in pursuit of the Indians, and by his industrious efforts, the following chiefs were induced to sign: Bull Bear, Black Kettle, Little Bear, Spotted Elk, Buffalo Chief, Slim Face, Gray Head, Little Rock, Whirlwind, Tall Bull, White Horse, and Little Robe, all Cheyenne chiefs.[23] The following Arapaho chiefs, as it was a joint treaty, then signed: these were Little Raven, Yellow Bear, Storm, White Rabbit, Spotted Wolf, Big Mouth, Young Colt, and Tall Bear.

It took a long time to convince Little Robe and Bull Bear of the propriety of signing the treaty of peace. "One is enough to sign for our nation," said they, but by dint of infinite coaxing, they finally consented.

Subjoined is a summary by Senator Henderson:

By the treaty of [1851], concluded at Fort Laramie with the Sioux, the Crows, the Assiniboines, Gros Ventres, Arickarees and Mandans, Blackfeet, Bloods, Pequins, Cheyennes and Arapahos, and others, the Cheyenne and Arapaho reservation commenced at the forks of the Platte and continued up the North Platte to the summit of the Rocky Mountains, thence southward along the summit of said mountains to the Arkansas River, thence down the Arkansas to a point thereon due south of the forks of the Platte, and thence north to the place of beginning.

By examining the map, it will be seen that this reservation covered the larger part of the present state of Colorado, a larger portion of western Kansas, and a part of Decotah. By the said treaty, as originally made, the United States was to pay the said tribes (all combined) $50,000 per annum for fifty years. When it went to the Senate, that body struck out "fifty years" and inserted twenty years, and for a further period of five years, if the president so willed it.[24]

By the year 1861 the gold mines of Colorado had been developed to such an extent as to make it absolutely necessary to obtain the right of the Cheyennes and the Arapahos to the lands on which not only mining operations were being conducted, but even the city of Denver and other important towns had been built.

Hence, a treaty was concluded on February 18, 1861, with the Cheyennes and Arapahos at Fort Wise, in Kansas, by which they ceded all their lands except a small reservation lying on both sides of the Arkansas River, southeast of Denver, between the Purgatory River on the south and the Sandy Fork of the Arkansas on the north. The said district includes Fort Lyon and the post of Reynolds, recently established. They deny consenting to the treaty.

After the terrible massacre by Chivington at Sand Creek in November 1864, the Cheyennes and Arapahos were driven out, and in October 1865, after a most terrible, and to us disastrous and extensive, war, the commissioners—Sanborn, Harney, and others who were appointed to hunt them up and endeavor to make a peace with them— found them at the mouth of the Little Arkansas, below Fort Zarah.

It was thought best to remove them to a reservation as far as possible from the Colorado people, who seemed to be so much excited and embittered against them. The district selected for them commenced at the mouth of Red Creek, where it empties into the Arkansas River, and extending up that creek to its source, passed westward to the Cimarron River, opposite the mouth of Buffalo Creek, which is about the meridian of Fort Larned, thence north to the Arkansas River, and then down that stream to the place of beginning. It will be observed that the reservation included about seventy miles of southern Kansas, lying between the longitude of Fort Larned on the west and the Arkansas River on the east. When this treaty went to the Senate, it was amended so as to require the reservation should be in the state of Kansas, and no part of it to be on other Indian lands, unless the tribes interested should consent.

In said treaty it was stipulated that the Indians should not be required to remove to their new reservations till conflicting titles had been adjusted. Those titles have not been settled as yet. It was further stipulated that the Indians should be permitted "to range at pleasure throughout the unsettled portions of that part of the country they claim as originally theirs, which lies between the Arkansas and Platte Rivers." The country referred to, of course, is that described by the treaty of 1861, herein before alluded to. It was further agreed to pay them an annuity of $20 per capita prior to their locating permanently on their reservation, and $40 per head after they should have settled thereon.

The two tribes were estimated at 2,800. After the treaty had been signed, the [Kiowa-]Apaches were incorporated with them and received into all the benefits of their treaty, they numbering about 700 persons.

Since General Hancock marched on the Cheyenne village in April 1867, war has been waged by the Cheyennes in a most relentless manner. They take upon themselves the responsibility of all that has since been done and expressly exempt other tribes. The treaty just concluded leaves out the [Kiowa-]Apaches, who prefer a confederation with the Kiowas and Comanches.

The reservation given drops off all lands lying in Kansas and extends the southern boundary, as defined by the treaty of 1865, from Red Creek down to the Cimarron River, sometimes called the Red Fork of the Arkansas. Hence it is bounded, east by the Arkansas River, south and west by the Cimarron River, and north by Kansas, comprising eight or nine thousand square miles.

It is agreed to build for them an agency house and other necessary buildings for a physician, farmer, miller, schoolteacher, blacksmith, etc. Also, it is stipulated to give them each a suit of good, substantial woolen clothing each year or the necessary material to make it; and in addition thereto, to expend thirty thousand dollars annually for their benefit in such articles as they may need.

The Cheyennes positively refuse as yet to yield the right to hunt north of the Arkansas and south of the South Platte. They are willing to yield it whenever the buffalo leave it, but not before, unless they shall previously try to live by agriculture. They agree, however, to take the right subject to the terms of the treaty of 1865; that is, to carry the permit of their agent and keep away ten miles from roads and forts. They withdraw all opposition to white settlements, and agree to protect and defend the white man as they would their brother. They withdraw all opposition to the Cimarron road to New Mexico and to the Smoky Hill and Platte railroads and all other roads.

All they ask is a hunting right, and they are willing that any conditions be imposed to keep the peace; but for the commissioners to have demanded an absolute concession of this right would have been to continue the war.

If white settlements drive away the buffalo, they say they will not want to hunt, but they cannot imagine why the white man would forbid them hunting on an unoccupied country filled with game.

They said, "Give them the right to hunt, and the white man might fill up the remainder of the treaty, and whatever it might be, they would abide by it and be his eternal friend."

To the commissioners' assertion that the game would soon be gone, they answered invariably that when gone on account of settlements, railroads, or any other cause, they would cease to ask the privilege.

The presents and annuity goods, which lay piled up near the watchful, prudent Colonel Chamberlain's tent, were then sorted out for distribution.

The Cheyennes and Arapahos hurried up from the council tent and, with their wives and little ones, squatted down on the ground in two vast circles. The chiefs of their respective tribes marched up the center with eyes beaming with good temper and excitement. Ripping up the huge bales and knocking off the lids of the boxes, the various goods were exposed to view, eliciting from the many thousand Indians present guttural expressions of pleasure. The red blankets and variegated beads seemed to be special objects of their desire. Each chief endeavored to allay all envious feelings that might be created by the fairness and impartiality with which they doled out each article. In an incredibly short space of time, fifty thousand dollars' worth of goods were distributed between the Cheyenne and Arapaho tribes, which caused universal satisfaction to all parties.

At night the Arapaho braves treated us to a war dance, a description of which I have already given in a former letter.

The commissioners thus far have been eminently successful in their work. Commissioner Taylor, Senator Henderson, and Generals Harney and Sanborn have shown themselves well adapted to the task of making peace with the warlike tribes of the south. Mr. Taylor, especially, has manifested an ardent sympathy with the poor, persecuted Indian. The Indians are quick to discern kindly feelings, and they will long remember the uniform kindness of the "Great Peace Chief" of Washington.

During his many years of arduous service on the plains, General Harney became thoroughly initiated into the feelings, superstitions, and ceremonies of the Indians of North America, and his experience thus gained proved an important aid in this last great work of reconciliation with the powerful Cheyennes. The general was the recipient of a fine pony from the Cheyennes, as a testimony of the great esteem in which the old veteran of the West was regarded by them.

General Sanborn, through his long experience on the border, aided in a very material manner towards effacing from the memory of the eight thousand warriors then and there assembled the wrongs they had silently endured for months, and towards effecting a lasting peace.

Senator Henderson also, with his keen knowledge of the world and business ability, was a very efficient auxiliary of the peace commissioners. He drew up the several treaties that were to heal up old wounds and reconcile both white and red man to inevitable fate.

Peace has been concluded with all the southern tribes. Civilization is now on the move, and westward the Star of Empire will again resume its march, unimpeded in the great work of progress.

Universal malediction light upon the man who will cause the Indian to dig up his hatchet, and all blessings shower upon those who keep the peace.

Tomorrow we start on our journey to North Platte via St. Louis to finish the work in the north, so propitiously begun in the south.

STANLEY.

PART TWO

The Battle of Beecher Island, 1868

A Frontier Fight

GEORGE A. FORSYTH[1]

Harper's New Monthly Magazine 91 (June 1895): 42–62

More than twenty-five years ago, it so fell out that I was an actor in one of the most important Indian campaigns of the last half of the present century—the second of a series of four such campaigns, all fought since our Civil War, that finally broke down the power of the various semiunited tribes, compelled them to accept the reservation system, and has practically ended savage warfare within the present limits of the United States.

Upon the reoccupation of the southern and western frontier by government troops at the close of the war, the Indians, who had grown confident in their own strength, were greatly exasperated; and the construction of the Union Pacific Railroad across the continent to the Pacific coast, directly through their hunting grounds, drove them almost to frenzy. The spring of 1868 found them arrogant, defiant, and confident, and late in the summer of that year, they boldly threw off all concealment, abrogated their treaties, and entered upon the warpath. I have lying before me, as I write, a tabulated statement of the outrages committed by the Indians within the Military Department of the Missouri from June until December of that year, and it shows 154 murders of white settlers and freighters, and the capture of numerous women and children, the burning and sacking of farmhouses, ranches, and stagecoaches, and gives details of horror and outrage visited upon the women that are better imagined than described.

As soon as it became evident that war was the only alternative on the part of the government, I made up my mind to try for a command in the field. The regiment to which I belonged was serving in another department; as a major in the line, I was conspicuously a junior. To displace any one of my seniors for the purpose of giving me a command in the field would have been rank favoritism, a thing not to be thought of by the commanding general or myself. Still, I could not give up the idea of an active command. After several days' cogitation, I went to General Sheridan, told him that I thought I could do better service both for him and the government in the coming campaign if I had an active command than I could possibly render as a staff officer; that I did not

Maj. George A. Forsyth.
NELSON A. MILES, *PERSONAL RECOLLECTIONS AND OBSERVATIONS.*

see how he could provide me with a command of any kind under the existing condition of affairs, but I wished that, in case opportunity offered, he would kindly consider my request for the first field vacancy.

An hour later I was handed the following order:

HEADQUARTERS DEPARTMENT OF THE MISSOURI
FORT HARKER, August 24, 1868

Brevet Colonel George A. Forsyth, A.A. Inspector General,
Department of the Missouri:

COLONEL—The general commanding directs that you, without delay, employ fifty first-class hardy frontiersmen to be used as scouts against the hostile Indians, to be commanded by yourself, with Lieutenant Beecher,[2] 3rd Infantry, as your subordinate. You can enter into such articles of agreement with these men as will compel obedience.

I am, Sir, very respectfully,

Your obedient servant,
(Sgd.) J. SCHUYLER CROSBY,
A.D.C. & A.A. ADJUTANT GENERAL

In the year I write of, there was little trouble in obtaining capable and competent men for my new command. Hundreds of men who had served through the bitter civil strife of 1861 to 1865, either for or against the government, had flocked to the frontier and were willing, and even anxious, to assist in punishing the Indians, while many a frontiersman was only too glad to have an opportunity to settle an old score against the savages. In two days I had enrolled thirty men at Fort Harker, and marching from there to Fort Hays, sixty miles westward, I completed my complement in two days more, and on August 29, five days from the time I had received the order, we took the field.

Our equipment was simple: a blanket apiece, saddle and bridle, a lariat and picket pin, a canteen, a haversack, butcher knife, tin plate, and tin cup. A Spencer repeating rifle (carrying six shots in the magazine, besides the one in the barrel), a Colt's revolver, army size, and 140 rounds of rifle and 30 rounds of revolver ammunition per man—this carried on the person. In addition, we had a pack train of four mules, carrying camp kettles and picks and shovels in case it became necessary to dig for water, together with four thousand extra rounds of ammunition, some medical supplies, and extra rations of salt and coffee. Each man, officers included, carried seven days' cooked rations in his haversack.

As of late years there has been some discussion as to who were the men who were with me in the fight on the Arikaree Fork of the Republican River. I herewith append the list, as copied from the original roll. All but four of these men were native Americans, and a number of them college graduates, and I never saw but one company of enlisted men who I thought exceeded them in general intelligence: 1st Lt. Fred H. Beecher, 3rd Infantry, U.S. Army; Acting Assistant Surgeon J. H. Mooers, Medical Department, U.S.A.; Abner T. Grover, chief scout; Wm. H. H. McCall, first sergeant; W. Armstrong, Thomas Alderdice, Martin Burke, Wallace Bennett, G. W. Chalmers, G. B. Clark, John Donovan, Bernard Day, Alfred Dupont, A. J. Eustler, Louis Farley, Hudson Farley, Richard Gantt, George Green, John Haley, John Hurst, Frank Harrington, J. H. Ketterer, John Lyden, M. R. Lane, Joseph Lane, A. B. Nichols, George Oakes, M. R. Mapes, Thomas Murphy, Howard Morton, H. T. McGrath, Thomas O'Donnell, A. A. Piatt, A. J. Pliley, William Reilly, Thomas Ranahan, Chalmers Smith, J. S. Stillwell, S. Schlesinger, Edward Simpson, William Stewart, H. H. Tucker, Isaac Thayer, Pierre Trudeau, Fletcher Vilott, William Wilson, A. B. Whitney, John Wilson, Eli Ziegler, Louis McLaughlin, Harry Davenport, [and] T. K. Davis.

My lieutenant, Frederick H. Beecher of the 3rd U.S. Infantry, was a most lovable character. He was a nephew of the distinguished divine Henry Ward Beecher, and I think his father was also a clergyman. He served through the Civil War with great gallantry and was lamed for life with a bullet through his knee at the battle of Gettysburg. Energetic, active, reliable, brave, and modest, with a love of hunting and a natural taste for plains craft, he was a splendid specimen of a thoroughbred American, and a most valuable man in any position requiring coolness, courage, and tact, and especially so for the campaign we were about entering upon.

My guide [was] Sharp Grover, a plainsman of somewhere between forty and fifty years of age, who had passed his life in hunting and trapping along the Northwest border.[3] He was well posted in Indian craft, spoke the dialect of the Sioux, and knew many of their tribe personally; a keen eye, a good shot, and a cool head made him a valuable man. As my scouts were to serve as soldiers, I organized the command as a troop of cavalry. My first sergeant was a man of about thirty years of age, who had served throughout the Civil War with more than ordinary distinction. He was [Bvt. Brig.] Gen. William H. H. McCall. [He] had been colonel of a Pennsylvania regiment and had been brevetted a brigadier-general for his brilliant services at the time [Maj.] Gen. J. B. Gordon, of the Confederate forces, early one morning in the spring of 1865, during the siege of Petersburg, assaulted and carried Fort Stedman. Martin Burke, one of the privates, an Irishman, had served in the English army in India and throughout the Civil War. Of the others, to the best of my recollection, Bennett, Clark, Donovan, Dupont, Green, Haley, Hurst, Harrington, Ketterer, Joe Lane, Oakes, Murphy, Piatt, Pliley, Chalmers, Smith, Simpson, Stewart, Thayer, Whitney, Ziegler, McLaughlin, and Davenport had served in either the Regular army or the United States or Confederate volunteers. The two best shots of our troop were Louis Farley[4] and his young son, Hudson Farley,[5] both frontiersmen, and I think farmers by occupation—men of great coolness and unsurpassed bravery.

Early on the morning of August 29, 1868, I received the following at the hands of the acting adjutant general, Col. J. Schuyler Crosby:

FORT HAYES, KANSAS, August 29, 1868
Brevet Colonel George A. Forsyth, Commanding Detachment of
Scouts:
I would suggest that you move across the headwaters of Solomon (River) to Beaver Creek, thence down that creek to Fort Wallace. On arrival at Wallace report to me by telegraph at this place.
Yours truly,
P. H. SHERIDAN, Major General

Shaking hands with the genial colonel, who wished me all sorts of good luck, I sprang into the saddle with a light heart and no little elation at the thought of having a field command and a roving commission—a state of affairs that any true cavalryman can thoroughly appreciate. In less than ten hours' time, we were practically beyond civilization and well into the Indian country. Looking back at this late day, after more than twenty-five years have passed since the morning we left Fort Hays for the headwaters of the Solomon River, I find it almost impossible not to rhapsodize somewhat over the freedom of the life we led: the fresh air of the plains, the clearness of the atmosphere, the herds of buffalo, which scarcely raised their heads from their feeding grounds as we passed, the bands of antelope that circled around us, the chirping bark of the prairie dogs as they dived headlong into their holes as we approached, the shout that startled the sneaking gray wolf into a run, the laugh that followed the antics of our pack mules, the half haze, half vapory mist that marked the line of the Smoky Hill River, and above all, the feeling that civilization was behind us, and the fascination that the danger of campaigning in an enemy's country ever holds for a soldier was before us.

Crossing the Saline River and South Fork of the Solomon, we struck Beaver Creek where Short Nose Creek empties into it. Here the Indians had evidently held a great Sun Dance, where probably they had finally decided to go to war with the whites. Moving thence up Beaver Creek beyond timberline, I struck trail directly for Fort Wallace, reaching there the night of September 5, not having seen an Indian during the march. Here I found a messenger from the governor of the state of Kansas, urging me to move to the protection of some settlers in Bison Basin. This I decided to do, with the cooperation of Captain Bankhead,[6] the commanding officer at Wallace, and so telegraphed the commanding general of the department; but as the command was about starting, word was received from the little town of Sheridan, thirteen miles east from Wallace and then at the end of the Kansas Pacific Railroad, that the Indians had attacked a freighter's train near there, killed two of the teamsters, and captured some of their teams. Leaving two of my command sick in hospital at Wallace, I started at once for the scene of action. On my arrival there, I carefully examined the ground in the vicinity and soon reached the conclusion that the attack had been made by a war party of not more than twenty or twenty-five Indians. This from the fact that there were not more than thirty or thirty-five different-sized pony tracks to be seen; and as the ground near where the wagon train had been fired upon was slightly marshy, the impress of the hoofs of the horses of their assailants was very distinct and easily compared, and the result was as I have stated. Little as I then knew, in comparison with what I have since learned, of Indian habits, I knew that it was customary for a war party to drive with them a few extra horses, and I therefore made up my mind that while this party was probably not less than twenty, it did not exceed twenty-five men. This being the case, I assumed that the attack had been made by a scouting party, and not improbably by a war party who had cut my trail and followed it towards Fort Wallace, and stumbling upon this freight train, had at an opportune moment attempted its capture, but finding that the drivers were armed, and plucky enough to defend themselves, concluded not to risk a heavy loss, and accordingly drew off after killing and scalping two poor teamsters, who had incautiously fallen behind the train a few moments before the attack was made. We followed the trail until dark and camped upon it. Resuming our march at early dawn, we again took the trail, but within two hours it began to become less and less distinct; every few hundred yards it was a little less clearly apparent, and I realized that the Indians were dropping out here and there, one by one, wherever the ground hardened and their individual trail could not be easily followed. Riding together fifty yards ahead, Beecher and Grover kept their eyes fixed on the fast-diminishing trail; and knowing that either man was my superior in this especial line of plains craft, I quietly followed on at the head of the command, content to await developments. Within an hour they halted, and as the command overtook them, Beecher sententiously remarked, "Disappeared!"

Halting and dismounting the command, we held a consultation, in which Grover, Beecher, McCall, and I took part. On one point we were all agreed, and that was that the Indians had seen us, knew they were being followed, and had scattered on the trail, and it was reasonable to suppose that they would rejoin their main body sooner or later. One thing was certain—they were not strong enough to fight us. The question now was would they willingly give us a trail to their main body? Evidently not, as their object was to throw us off the scent. If this conclusion was correct, was it not probable that if we could pick up their trail and find the rendezvous of the main body, we could successfully give them battle? Beecher said little and refused to express an opinion. Grover and McCall were inclined to think that before we could overtake the war party, it was more than probable that they would be able to mass several of the tribes against us, as the general trend of their trail was north, towards the Republican River.

Now I had already determined in my own mind that it was in that section of country we would eventually find the Sioux and Northern Cheyenne who had recently done so much damage to the settlers near Bison Basin, and I therefore cut short the discussion by saying that I had determined to find and attack the Indians, no matter what the odds might be against us. If we could not defeat them, we could show them that the government did not propose that they should escape unpunished for want of energy in their pursuit. I thought that with fifty-one men, even if we could not defeat them, they could not annihilate us. Furthermore, it was expected that the command would fight the Indians, and I meant it should do so. Pushing on to Short Nose Creek, and seeking for trails in every direction, on the fifth day out from Wallace, on the north bank of the Republican River, we stumbled upon an abandoned "wickiup," a shelter formed by pressing over young willows or alders growing about three feet apart, interlacing the tops of their branches, and covering the top with hides or long swamp grass. It had evidently been occupied by two dismounted Indians the preceding night, was carefully concealed in the swamp willows, and an attempt of one of our party to push through the willow copse on the riverbank to get a drink for his horse discovered it. We took up the trail here, and followed it a couple of miles, and were rewarded by finding a place where three mounted Indians had encamped within twenty-four hours; and following their trail, we ran into that of a small war party, possibly some of the Indians who had given us the slip a few days since.

From this on, the trail was easily followed. It led up to the forks of the Republican River, where it crossed to the north side of the stream and grew steadily larger as various smaller trails from the north and south entered it, until finally it was a broad beaten road, along which had been driven horses, cattle, and trains carrying heavy loads of Indian tent poles that had worn great ruts into the earth, showing that all the paraphernalia of one or more large Indian villages had passed that way. Coming to what we then believed to be Delaware Creek, but which we knew later to be the Arikaree Fork of the Republican River, we found the trail leading up it along the south bank of the stream. Encamping at nightfall, we again took up the march the next morning and pushed steadily ahead. So far we had not seen an Indian, but the trail grew steadily broader until it was a well-beaten road, and some of the men of the command ventured to approach me with a protest. They said that if we followed the Indians to their villages, we would be met with overwhelming numbers and stood no show whatever for our lives. I listened to them patiently, told them that they were assuming no risk that I was not taking myself; that they had enrolled to fight Indians; and that in my opinion there was less danger to advance and attack than there would be now to attempt to return. This ended the discussion, and apparently satisfied that they had entered a protest, they fell back into the little column. The fact that probably half or more of my men had served as soldiers was, at this particular juncture, of great moment. These men recognized the value of implicit obedience without discussion, a truth that emphasizes the difference between an army and a mob. Each hour we progressed established the probability that we were following close on the heels of a large body of Indians, who could not be far ahead of us on the well-beaten trail. Here and there they dropped tent poles, pieces of half-dried buffalo meat, now and then little articles of clothing, an old moccasin, a worn-out basket, and various odds and ends that attested their rapid flight; furthermore, no game had been seen for two days, an indication that it had been hunted away, and I now moved slowly and cautiously, fearing an ambush or a sudden attack. It was about 4:00 P.M. on September 16 that, as we followed the sinuosity of the trail, at a little distance from the south bank of the stream as it wound in and out among wild plum thickets, alder bushes, and swamp-willows, a bend in the river, as we passed through a little gorge, opened out upon a small, well-grassed valley of perhaps two miles in length and nearly the same in width. From our side of the water, the land sloped slowly down to the stream from the rolling plain on the south, while upon the other side, it receded from the water at almost a dead level for nearly three-quarters of a mile, and then terminated in a line of low hills or bluffs, varying from forty to fifty feet in height, which shut out the view of the plains from that direction.

We were nearly out of supplies, save a little salt and coffee, and my animals had to subsist upon such grazing as we could find. As the grass at this spot was good upon each side of the stream, I decided to go into camp, graze my horses, refit my command as well as I could, and take the trail again early in the morning, feeling convinced that before the close of another day we would meet Indians. Dismounting about the middle of the valley, we encamped on the bank of the stream, opposite the center of a small island, which had been formed in the sand in the middle of the bed of the stream, owing to a gravelly rift at its head, at which point the water divided and gently rippled along each side until it again united about two hundred fifty feet below. It made a pretty break in the landscape, lying out in the bed of the main stream, perhaps seventy yards away from the riverbank on either side.

All, or nearly all, of these western and southwestern streams are peculiar in one thing. In the spring and early summer, when the snows melt in the hills and mountains, they are wide, deep, and even majestic rivers. Late in the summer, they dwindle to almost the merest thread of water. This stream formed no exception to the rule, and the little island in the center of its bed was fully seventy yards from the bank on either side. It was raised about a foot above the water at its head, while on either side of it was a flowing stream of say fifteen feet in width, and with an average depth of less than five inches, that came together at the foot of the island, which here sloped down to the level of the bed of the main stream. Long sage grass grew on its head, and a thicket of alder and willows shot up four or five feet in height about the center, while just at its foot stood a young cottonwood tree of about twenty feet in height.

In western Kansas and Colorado, while the September days are generally hot, the nights are at times decidedly cool—in fact, cold would not be an exaggeration of the truth—and in my wakeful hours of this September night, as I paced the ground to and fro along the riverbank in front of the line of my sleeping men, I felt that the coming winter's campaign in the Indian country would result in much hardship outside of actual fighting. I had seen personally to the posting of our sentries and had given especial instructions not only to hobble the horses, but directed that every scout should be especially careful to see that his horse's lariat was perfectly knotted; and further than that, before lying down to sleep, he was to inspect his picket pin and see that it was firmly driven into the ground. In case of an attack, each man was to seize his horse's lariat as soon as he grasped his rifle, and to stand by his horse to prevent a stampede, for I was somewhat apprehensive of an attack at daylight. Several times during the night, I rose and visited the sentries, for I was restless, anxious, and wakeful.

At early dawn, as I was standing by a sentry near one of the outposts, closely scanning the skyline between ourselves and the rising ground to our right which lay furthest up the stream, I suddenly caught sight of an object moving stealthily between us and the horizon. At the same moment, the sentry saw it, and simultaneously cocking our rifles, we stood alert, with straining eyes and listening ears. An instant later the soft thud of unshod horses' hoofs upon the turf came to our ears, and peering just above the crest of the rising ground between us and the horizon, we caught sight of waving feathers crowning the scalp locks of three mounted warriors. The sharp crack of our rifles rang out almost simultaneously, and with the cry of "Indians! Turn out! Indians!" we ran backwards towards our camp, firing as we ran at a group of mounted warriors which instantly surmounted the hill, where, pausing for a few seconds, evidently for re-enforcements, they broke into a gallop and came rushing down on our camp, shouting, beating Indian drums, and rattling dried hides in an endeavor to stampede our horses; but by this time nearly every man was standing with his horse's lariat wrapped around his left arm and ready for a shot at the stampeding party as they bore down upon us. A scattering volley from the scouts dropped one of their number from his saddle, and they sheered off, carrying with them two of our four mules and two horses that had not been

The surprise. HARPER'S NEW MONTHLY MAGAZINE 1895.

securely picketed, in violation of orders. The attempted stampede had proved a failure. "Saddle up quickly, men," was my next order, and in an incredibly short time the command was saddled and bridled, and in another moment every man was fully and completely equipped.

It had begun to be light enough by this time to see dimly surrounding objects within a few hundred yards, when suddenly Grover, who stood by my side, placed his hand on my shoulder and said, "Oh, heavens, General, look at the Indians!" Well might he say look at the Indians. The ground seemed to grow them. They appeared to start out of the very earth. On foot and on horseback, from over the hills, out of the thickets, from the bed of the stream, from the north, south, and west, along the opposite bank, and out of the long grass on every side of us, with wild cries of exultation they pressed towards us. A few sharp volleys from the command, who stood coolly to horse, each man having his bridle thrown over his left arm, staggered them for a moment, and then they hastily fell back out of range. It was scarcely so much of a surprise party as they had planned, and they were somewhat astonished to find an active and responsive reception committee promptly on hand and ready to accord them a warm and enthusiastic welcome on their very first appearance.

I now saw clearly that there was but one course to take. So completely were we surrounded, and so greatly outnumbered, that our only hope lay in a successful defense, and I determined, in any event, that they should pay dearly for the lives of my scouts before ornamenting the ridgepoles of their lodges with our reeking scalps.

The command was ordered to lead their horses to the little island just in front of us, to form a circle facing outwards, securely tie their horses to the bushes just outside of the circle so formed, throw themselves on the ground, and entrench themselves as rapidly as possible, two men working together, protecting each other in turn as they alternately threw up the earth to cover themselves.[7] As we moved in almost a solid front to the little island, leading our horses, a few of our best shots—under Beecher, Grover, and McCall—kept up a rapid and steady fire from our flanks to cover the movement, which seemed for a few moments to puzzle the Indians, for they had apparently left the way open on the east, down the stream, and, I think, looked to see us mount and attempt a retreat that way; but I knew enough of Indian craft to be certain that the little gorge just around the bend of the stream in that direction would be lined with warriors, and I knew, furthermore, that once established on the island, there was no direction from which they could take us unawares during daylight. Three of our best men remained temporarily in the long grass on the bank of the river, covering the north end of the island, thereby holding in check any unusually adventurous warriors who might be inclined to attempt to crawl up that way through the river bottom.

Scarcely were the horses tied in a circle when the men threw themselves on the ground and began firing from beneath the animals, when it seemed to suddenly dawn upon the savages that they had been outgeneraled; for as we started towards the island, judging by their actions in signaling their comrades on the opposite bank, they fully expected that we would cross the stream. Now they saw their error and also realized, too late, the mistake they had made in not occupying the island themselves. Apparently infuriated at their blunder, and almost instantly comprehending the advantage we would have should we fortify ourselves, they made a desperate onslaught upon us, their various chiefs riding rapidly around just outside of rifle range and impetuously urging their dismounted warriors to close in upon us on all sides. Many of the mounted Indians sprang from their horses also, and running forward, they lined both banks of the river, and from the reeds and long grass poured in a steady and galling fire upon us. A few of our men had been hit, one killed, and several more badly wounded; our horses were being shot down on all sides, the poor animals plunging and rearing at their tethers, and adding their cries to the wild shouts of the savages and the steady crack of the rifles on every side.

At the height of this crisis—for to us it was the crisis of the day—one of the men shouted, "Don't let's stay here and be shot down like dogs. Will any man try for the opposite bank with me?"

"I will," answered someone from the opposite side of the circle.

"Stay where you are, men. It's our only chance," I shouted as I stood in the center of the command, revolver in hand. "I'll shoot down any man who attempts to leave the island."

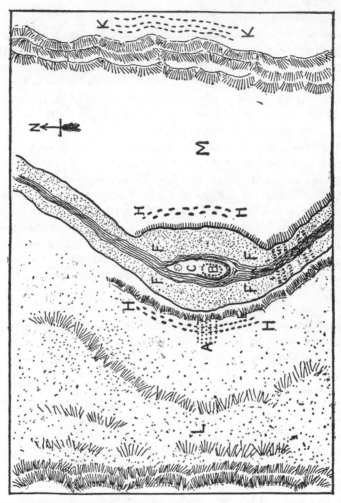

MAP OF FORSYTH'S DEFENSE OF BEECHER'S ISLAND, ARIKAREE RIVER, COLORADO
(Drawn by the author from rough sketches and maps furnished by General Forsyth)

Explanation of Map: A. Forsyth's camp before attack. B. Rifle-pits on island. C. Low, unoccupied land on island with solitary cottonwood at end. D. Indian charge led by Roman Nose and Medicine Man. EE. Low banks fringed with trees. FF. Dry sandy bed of the river. HH. Indian riflemen on the banks. KK. Indian women and children on bluffs, half a mile from river. L. Ground sloping gently to river. M. Level grassy plain to bluffs.

Forsyth's defense of Beecher Island.

CYRUS T. BRADY, *INDIAN FIGHTS AND FIGHTERS.*

"And so will I," shouted McCall.

"You addle-headed fools, have you no sense?" called out Beecher, whose every shot was as carefully and coolly aimed as though he was shooting at a target.

"Steady, men! Steady, now! Aim low. Don't throw away a shot," was my oft-repeated command, in which I was seconded by Beecher, McCall, and Grover. "Get down to your work, men. Don't shoot unless you can see something to hit. Don't throw away your ammunition, for our lives may depend upon how we husband it."

This was my constantly iterated and reiterated command for the first twenty minutes of the attack. And now discipline began to tell. Many an Indian had fallen to the rear badly wounded, and some had been borne back dead, judging from the wild wails of the women and children, who could now be seen covering the bluffs back of the valley on the north side of the stream. So hot had the scouts made it for the Indians close in on the riverbank that they had crawled back out of short range, evidently satisfied that it was safer, as far as they were concerned, to send their bullets from a longer distance. During this comparative lull in the fight, the men were not idle, and with their butcher knives to cut the sod, and their tin plates to throw up the sand, most of them had already scooped out a hole the length of their body, from eighteen inches to two feet in depth, and piling up the sand on the side facing the enemy, had an ample cover against rifle bullets. I still stood upright, walking from man to man, but from every side came appeals for me to lie down. As we were now in fairly good shape, and the men cool and determined, I did so.

Scarcely had I lain down when I received a shot in the fore part of the right thigh, the bullet ranging upward; and notwithstanding it remained embedded in the flesh, it was by far the most painful wound I have ever received. For a moment I could not speak, so intense was the agony. Several of the men, knowing I was hit, called out to know if I still lived, but it was at least a full minute before I could command my voice and assure them I was not mortally hurt.

In the meantime, one or two Indians had crawled up on the lower end of the island and, hidden by a few bushes, were annoying us very much. However, the elder Farley, who, with Harrington, Gantt, and Burke, had temporarily taken position close under the bank of the river, saw the flash of one of their rifles from the center of a little bush, and the next instant a bullet from his rifle went through the very middle of the bush and crashed into the brave's brain, and a wild, half-smothered shriek told us that there was one less of our enemies to encounter. As we heard nothing more from the other one, I concluded that he dare not again risk exposing his position by using his rifle. As I was now about the only man of the command unprotected by a rifle pit, Doctor Mooers (who had been doing splendid service with his rifle, as he was a capital shot) suggested the enlarging of his pit to accommodate us both. Several of the men promptly went to his assistance in enlarging and deepening it; but while they were doing so, in leaning over to caution one of the men, who I thought was firing a little too fast for really good shooting, I was obliged, in order to ease my wounded thigh, to draw up my left leg as I lay prone on the earth, and unfortunately for me, one of the Indians sent a bullet through it, breaking and shattering the bone badly about midway between the knee and ankle. Three minutes later I was pulled down into the now enlarged pit and was under cover.

Meanwhile, a steady fire was kept up by the Indians, who, as one of the men expressed it, were fairly frothing at the mouth at our unexpected resistance, for with their experience at Fort Fetterman in 1866, where they annihilated a detachment of eighty-one soldiers in forty minutes, who advanced fresh from the post to attack them, the determined defense of our much smaller and rather worn party in the very heart of their own country was to them decidedly exasperating. In my present condition, with my left leg broken and a bullet in my right thigh, I was for the nonce, save for the fact that I still retained command, something of a spectator. Gradually working myself to one end of the pit on my elbows, dragging my body along with no inconsiderable pain, I was able to partially sit up and, by resting my elbows against and upon the fresh earth, crane my head forward so as to obtain a clear view of the field. The pit occupied by Surgeon Mooers and myself was at the lower end of the island; consequently, it commanded a view of the whole field. A glance over my own command was most reassuring. Each man was fairly well sheltered in a rifle pit of his own construction, generally two men in a pit, and the various pits were in an irregular circle, about six feet apart, and fortified by an embankment of sand fully eighteen inches in thickness both front and rear, for the enemy's bullets came from all points of the compass. Some of the wounded men, with bandages around their heads, were quite as active and alert as their more fortunate companions. Only one man of the command had failed me. When we had been attacked at dawn, he seemed paralyzed with fear, had been among the first to finish and occupy his rifle pit on the island, and after firing a single shot, had lain sheltered in his pit, face downward, claiming that one of the Indians kept a bead drawn on him.

And now I cautiously took in a complete view of the field. Nearly all of our horses lay dead around us; a few of them, badly wounded, still plunged and moaned and strained at their lariats as bullet after bullet entered their bodies, and had I been certain that I could spare the ammunition, I would have directed my own men to put the poor beasts out of their misery. Meanwhile, the dead bodies of their companions stopped many a bullet intended for us. It must have been nearly or quite 8:00 A.M. The cover of any kind that commanded our island, such as reeds, long grass, trees, turf, plum thickets, and in some places, small piles of stones and sand thrown up hastily by themselves, was all fully occupied by the Indian riflemen, and here I desire to say that in the matter of arms and ammunition, they were our equals in every respect. The Springfield breechloaders they had captured at Fort Fetterman formed part of their equipment, as well as Henry, Remington, and Spencer rifles, for upon their withdrawal from the field, notwithstanding the fact that they generally keep their discharged shells for reloading, my command found scattered around in the grass many hundreds of the empty shells of fixed ammunition of all these different makes of guns.[8]

Riding around just out of range of our rifles were several hundred mounted warriors, charging here and there, shouting, gesticulating, waving their rifles over their heads, and apparently half frenzied at the thought of the blunder they had made in permitting us to obtain possession of the island. Riding up and down their line was a warrior, evidently chief in command, of almost gigantic stature. I was almost certain who it must be, so calling out to Grover, I asked the question, "Is not the large warrior Roman Nose?"

"None other," was the reply. "There is not such another Indian on the plains."

"Then these are the Northern Cheyenne."

"Yes, and the Oglala and Brule Sioux, and the Dog Soldiers[9] as well. There are more than a thousand warriors here."

For the next hour or so, matters in our immediate vicinity were comparatively quiescent. A steady fire against us was constantly kept up by the enemy, but only returned by the scouts when they saw an opportunity to effectively use their cartridges, and the Indians at length began to perceive this, for as it was, they were playing a losing game. Our men were now better protected than they were, and were also better shots; the consequence was that many a badly wounded brave fell to the rear, while very few of our people were being hurt. At this juncture, the last of our horses went down, and one of the Indians shouted in English, "There goes the last damned horse, anyhow!" This rather confirmed me in the idea I had somehow imbibed during the action that either one of old Bent's sons (the half-breed Indian trader), who had been educated in the East, was with the Sioux, or else there was some white renegade in their ranks, for twice since the opening of the engagement, I had distinctly heard the notes of an artillery bugle. Leaning too far forward to get a better view of the mounted warriors, who seemed to be moving towards the canyon below us from where we had on the preceding day debouched into the little valley we were now besieged in, I rather rashly exposed my head, and some one of the Indian riflemen promptly sent an excellent line shot towards it. The bullet struck me just on the top of my soft felt hat, which, having a high crown, was fortunately doubled down, so it glanced off, cutting through several thicknesses of felt, but nevertheless knocked me almost senseless to the bottom of my rifle pit. It was some seconds ere I could completely recover myself and crawl back to my sitting position. At the time of this occurrence, I thought little of it; of course, a large lump swelled up at once, but as the skin was hardly broken, and just then I had many other things to occupy my attention, I took little heed of the intense headache that for a short time half blinded me. A month later, however, the surgeon's probe disclosed the fact that my skull had been fractured, and he removed a loose piece of it. About this time, several of the mounted Indians, for some cause that I was not able to determine, dashed up within rifle range and, from their horses, took a sort of potshot at us. Doctor Mooers, who had been closely watching their approach as they careered around the island, gradually lessening their distance, watched his opportunity and shot one of them through the head. As the brave fell dead from his horse, he remarked, "That rascally redskin will not trouble us again." Almost immediately afterwards, I heard the peculiar thud that tells the breaking of bone by a bullet. Turning to the doctor, I saw him put his hand to his head, saying, "I'm hit," his head at the same time falling forward on the sand. Crawling to him, I pulled his body down into the pit and turned him upon his back, but I saw at once that there was no hope. A bullet had entered his forehead just over the eye, and the wound was mortal. He never spoke another rational word, but lingered nearly three days before dying.

Once more placing my back against the side of the rifle pit, and again raising myself up on my elbows, I peered over the little earthwork with rather more caution than before. On looking towards the opposite bank and down the stream, I saw most of the mounted warriors had disappeared, and those who remained were slowly trotting towards the little gorge I have before mentioned, and again I distinctly heard the clear notes of an artillery bugle. Others of the mounted warriors now moved towards the gorge, and it flashed upon me that Roman Nose was forming his warriors for a charge just around the bend of the river, out of sight and beyond rifle range. I accordingly called out to Lieutenant Beecher, who was near the head of the island, stating my opinion. "I believe you are right," was his reply, and both Grover and McCall coincided with us. "Then let the men get ready," was my order. Accordingly each Spencer repeating rifle was charged at once, with six shots in the magazine and one in the barrel. The guns of the dead and mortally wounded were also loaded and laid close at hand, the men's revolvers carefully looked to and loosened in their belts, and word was passed not to attempt to return the fire of the dismounted Indians in case a mounted charge was made; but the men were told to turn towards the quarter from whence the charge came, and to commence firing at the word of command only. In the meantime, the fire of the Indians lying around us had slackened and almost ceased. This only confirmed us in our anticipation, and word was again passed cautioning the men to lie close until the fire of the dismounted Indians slackened.

We had not long to wait. A peal of the artillery bugle, and at a slow trot the mounted warriors came partially into view in an apparently solid mass at the foot of the valley, halting just by the mouth of the canyon on the opposite side of the river from which we had emerged the preceding day. I had placed my back firmly against my little earthwork; my rifle lay across my chest, and my revolver on the sand beside me. I could not do much, wounded as I was, but I recognized the fact that even a chance shot or two might possibly do good service in the work that the savages were about to cut out for us. Closely watching the mounted warriors, I saw their chief facing his command, and by his gestures, evidently addressing them in a few impassioned words. Then, waving his hand in our direction, he turned his horse's head toward us, and at the word of command, they broke at once into a full gallop, heading straight for the foot of the island. I was right in my surmise; we were to be annihilated by being shot down as they rode over us.

As Roman Nose dashed gallantly forward and swept into the open at the head of his superb command,[10] he was the very beau ideal of an Indian chief. Mounted on a large, clean-limbed chestnut horse, he sat well forward on his bare-backed charger, his knees passing under a horsehair lariat that twice loosely encircled the animal's body, his horse's bridle grasped in his left hand, which was also closely wound in its flowing mane, and at the same time his rifle at the guard, the butt of which lay partially upon and across the animal's neck. He was a man over six feet and three inches in height, beautifully formed, and save for a crimson silk sash knotted around his waist and his moccasins on his feet, perfectly naked. His face was hideously painted in alternate lines of red and black, and his head crowned with a magnificent war bonnet, from which, just above his temples and curving slightly forward, stood up two short, black buffalo horns, while its ample length of eagles' feathers and herons' plumes trailed wildly on the wind behind him; and as he came swiftly on at the head of his charging warriors, in all his barbaric strength and grandeur, he proudly rode that day, the most perfect type of a savage warrior it has been my lot to see. Turning his face for an instant towards the women and children of the united tribes, who literally by thousands were watching the fight from the crest of the low bluffs back from the river's bank, he raised his right arm and waved his hand with a royal gesture in answer to their wild cries of rage and encouragement as he and his command swept down upon us; and again facing squarely towards where we lay, he drew his body to its full height and shook his clinched fist defiantly at us; then, throwing back his head and glancing skywards, he suddenly struck the palm of his hand across his mouth and gave tongue to a war cry that I have never yet heard equaled in power and intensity. Scarcely had its echoes reached the riverbank when it was caught up by each and every one of the charging warriors with an energy that baffles description, and answered back with blood-curdling yells of exultation and prospective vengeance by the women and children on the river's bluffs and by the Indians who lay in ambush around us. On they came at a swinging gallop, rending the air with their wild war whoops, each individual warrior in all his bravery of war paint and long, braided scalp lock tipped with eagles' feathers, and all stark naked but for their cartridge belts and moccasins, keeping their line almost perfectly, with a front of about sixty men, all riding bareback with only a loose lariat about their horses' bodies, about a yard apart, and with a depth of six or seven ranks, forming together a compact body of massive fighting strength and of almost resistless weight.

Boldly they rode, and well, with their horses' bridles in their left hands, while with their right they grasped their rifles at the guard and held them squarely in front of themselves, resting lightly upon their horses' necks.

Riding about five paces in front of the center of the line, and twirling his heavy Springfield rifle around his head as if it were a wisp of straw (probably one of those he had captured at the Fort Fetterman massacre), [Bad Heart] led the charge with a bravery that could only be equaled but not excelled, while their medicine man, an equally brave but older chief, rode slightly in advance of the left of the charging column. To say that I was surprised at this splendid exhibition of pluck and discipline is to put it mildly, and to say, further, that for an instant or two I was fairly lost in admiration of the glorious charge is simply to state the truth, for it was far and away beyond anything I had heard of, read about, or even imagined regarding Indian warfare. A quick backward glance at my men was most reassuring. Each scout had turned in his rifle pit towards the direction from which the charge was coming, crouching low and leaning forward, with their knees well under them, their rifles grasped with a grip of steel in their brown sinewy hands, their chests heaving with excitement, their teeth set hard, their nostrils aquiver, their bronzed countenances fairly aflame, and their eyes flashing fire, they grimly lay waiting the word of command, as brave and gallant a little company of men as ever yet upheld the reputation of Anglo-Saxon courage. No sooner were the charging warriors fairly under way than a withering fire was suddenly poured in upon us by those of the Indians who lay in ambush around us intently watching our every movement, in the vain hope that they might sufficiently cow us to protect their charging column against our rifles. I had expected this action, but I well knew that once their horsemen came within a certain radius, their fire must cease. For eight or ten seconds it seemed to rain bullets, and then came a sudden lull. Sitting upright in my pit as well as I was able, and leaning backward on my elbows, I shouted "Now," and "Now" was echoed by Beecher, McCall, and Grover. Instantly the scouts were on their knees with their rifles at their shoulders. A quick flash of their eyes along the barrels, and forty good men and true sent their first seven successive volleys into the ranks of the charging warriors.

Crash!

On they came, answering back the first volley with a ringing war whoop. Crash!

And now I begin to see falling warriors, ay, and horses too; but still they sweep forward with yet wilder yells.

Crash!

They seem to be fairly falling over each other; both men and horses are down in heaps, and wild shrieks from the women and children on the hill proclaim that they, too, see the slaughter of their braves; but still they come.

Crash!

They have ceased to yell, but yet come bravely on. What? No! Yes, down goes their medicine man; but [Dry Throat] still recklessly leads the column.

Bad Heart leading the first charge.
CYRUS T. BRADY, *INDIAN FIGHTS AND FIGHTERS.*

But now I see great gaps in their rank, showing that our bullets have told heavily among them.

Crash!

Can I believe my eyes? [Dry Throat] is down! He and his horse lie dead together on the sand, and for an instant the column shakes; but a hundred yards more and they are upon us!

Crash!

They stagger! They half draw rein! They hesitate! They are breaking! Crash!

And like an angry wave that hurls itself upon a mighty rock and breaks upon its rugged front, the Indians divided [on] each side of the little breastwork, threw themselves almost beneath the offside of their chargers, and with hoarse cries of rage and anguish, break for either bank of the river and scatter wildly in every direction, as the scouts spring to their feet with a ringing cheer, pour volley after volley from their revolvers almost in the very faces of their now demoralized and retreating foe.

"Down, men! Lie down!" I fairly shriek. "Get down! Down for your lives!" cries McCall. And the men, hurling bitter taunts and imprecations after the retreating savages, throw themselves, panting, flat on their faces inside of their rifle pits just in time to escape a scorching volley from the Indians still lying in ambush around us, who have been anxiously watching the charge and, naturally enough, are wildly enraged at its failure.

As for myself, a single shot from my rifle, and a few from my revolver just at the close of the charge, was all that I could do in my crippled state; but the fact that I had to lie flat upon my back, craning my head forward, had, by placing me below the plane of fire, enabled me to watch every phase of the Indians' desperate charge.

But now to me came the hardest blow of the whole day. Lieutenant Beecher rose from his rifle pit and, leaning on his rifle, half staggered, half dragged himself to where I lay, and calmly lying down by my side, with his face turned downward on his arm, said, quietly and simply: "I have my death wound, general. I am shot in the side and dying."

"Oh no, Beecher—no! It can't be as bad as that!"

"Yes. Goodnight." And then he immediately sank into half-unconsciousness. In a few moments I heard him murmur, "My poor mother," and then he soon grew slightly delirious, and at times I could hear him talking in a semiunconscious manner about the fight; but he was never again fully conscious; and at sunset his life went out. And thus perished one of the best and bravest officers in the United States Army.

Once more I slowly worked my way back against the end of the pit and, leaning my elbow back against its side, craned my head forward for a view of the field. Close to our pits—so close that the men by leaning forward could touch their bodies with their rifles—lay three dead warriors; just beyond these lay several more, while for six or seven hundred yards in the direction from which the charge had been made, the ground was strewn here and there by dead Indians and horses, singly and in little groups, showing clearly the effect of each one of the seven volleys the scouts had poured into the charging column.

Turning towards where my guide Grover lay, I somewhat anxiously put the question, "Can they do better than that, Grover?"

"I have been on the plains, man and boy, General, for more than thirty years, and I never saw anything like that before. I think they have done their level best," was his reply.

"All right, then," was my response; "we are good for them." And again glancing to where lay the dead bodies of [Dry Throat] and the medicine man,[11] I felt that the outcome of the battle would be decided by the staying powers of the combatants. In the meantime, the valley was resonant with the shrieks of the women and children, who, from their [point] of vantage on the hills, had safely but eagerly watched the result of [Bad Heart's] desperate charge, and now, as their fathers, sons, brothers, and lovers lay dead on the sands before them, their wild wails of passionate grief and agony fitfully rose and fell on the air in a prolonged and mournful cadence of rage and despair. And as for a short time many of the Indians rode circling around, yelling and waving their arms over their heads, hither and yon, apparently half dazed at the death of the medicine man and their great war chief, as well as at the disastrous failure of their charge, the whole scene, combined with the steady crack of the rifles of the Indians in ambush, the reply of scouts, the smoke of the powder, and the view of the dead warriors and horses lying on the sand before us, seemed for a moment or two almost uncanny and weird in the extreme.

And now came another lull in the battle. The mounted Indians drew off to the little canyon where they had before formed for the charge, and for the next few hours were evidently in close consultation; but the wailing of the women and children never ceased, and the Indians in ambush fitfully fired now and then at our breastworks, but with no results so far as any loss to us was concerned.

About 2:00 P.M., under new leaders, they essayed another charge, this time in open order, and half surrounding us as they came on. It was an abject failure, for they broke and ran before they came within a hundred yards of the island, and before they had lost more than eight or ten men killed and wounded; not a man of my command was hit.

Renewed wails from the women and a desultory fire from the Indians surrounding us were the outcome of this fiasco; but between 5:00 P.M. and 6:00 P.M., they again formed up in the little canyon, and with a rush came on *en masse* with wild cries for vengeance, evidently wrought up to frenzy by the wails and taunts of their women and children; but scarcely had they come within range when the scouts (who during the lull in the battle had securely covered themselves by deepening their rifle pits and strengthening their earthworks, so that they were well protected from the Indian riflemen) began picking them off as coolly and deliberately as possible. It was simply death to advance, and they broke and fled just as the boldest of them had reached the foot of the island; and as they turned back and sought safety in flight, I felt satisfied that it was the last attempt that would be made by mounted warriors to carry our little breastworks.[12]

Night came slowly down, and as darkness overshadowed the land, it began to rain; and never was night or rain more welcome, for during the day the sun had been intensely hot, blisteringly so, and our fight had been from early dawn without water or food of any kind, and we were well nigh spent with the work and excitement of the day. As the Indians never attack at night, we were comparatively safe until morning; so as soon as we had obtained water from the stream and quenched our thirst, I called McCall and Grover to me and asked for a list of the killed and wounded, and in a few moments I had the result of the day's fighting, as far as we were concerned. Considering the fact that my command, including myself, only numbered fifty-one men, the outlook was somewhat dismal. Lieutenant Beecher, Surgeon Mooers, and scouts Chalmers Smith and Wilson were dead or dying; scouts Louis Farley and Bernard Day were mortally wounded; scouts O'Donnell, Davis, Tucker,

Gantt, Clark, Armstrong, Morton, and Vilott severely; and scouts Harrington, Davenport, Haley, McLaughlin, Hudson Farley, McCall, and two others slightly wounded. As for myself, with a bullet in my right thigh, my left leg broken below the knee, and an inconvenient scalp wound that gave me an intense headache, it was all I could do to pull myself together and set about getting out of the dangerous position into which I had led my command. I had an abundance of ammunition and still twenty-eight fairly sound men, and at a pinch, all but six or seven of the wounded could also take a hand if required in a hot fight. I had little fear that the Indians would again assault our works, and I knew that water within our entrenchments could be had for the digging; in fact, scout Burke had already dug a small well at the bottom of his rifle pit and, with a shout, had just announced that the water was rapidly seeping through the sand. The dead horses and mules would furnish us food for some days if we could keep the meat from putrefying, and I believed I could rely upon some of the men to steal through the Indian lines and make their way to Fort Wallace, which I judged to be about one hundred ten miles distant.

Accordingly, orders were given to strengthen and connect all the rifle pits; unsaddle the dead horses and use the saddles to help build up our parapet; to dig out and fortify a place for the wounded, and dress their wounds as well as could be done under our adverse circumstances; to deepen Burke's well; to cut off a large quantity of steaks from the dead horses and mules; and to bury all the meat that we did not immediately need in the sand. The men worked with a will, and before midnight we were in very good shape. I had volunteers in plenty to go to Fort Wallace, and of these I selected two—Pierre Trudeau,[13] an old and experienced trapper, and a young fellow named Jack Stillwell,[14] a handsome boy of about nineteen, with all the pluck and enthusiasm of an American frontier lad, who afterwards became one of the best known and most reliable scouts on our northwestern frontier.

Two better men for the purpose it would have been difficult to find. I gave Stillwell, as he was by far the more intelligent and better educated man of the two, my only map, told him about where I thought we were, and gave him directions to get to Fort Wallace as quickly as possible, tell Captain Bankhead, the commanding officer and an old friend, our situation, and as he would probably send, or more likely come at once to our rescue, to return with him and guide him to us. A little after midnight he and Trudeau stole out quietly, walking backward in their stocking feet, and carrying their boots slung around their necks, that the impress of their feet in the sand might make a similar mark to that of a moccasin and deceive the Indians, should they discover the sign.

(These two men eventually reached the post of Fort Wallace three days after leaving us. They had to lie concealed during the daytime, as they almost ran into several Indian scouting parties, and at one time they had to conceal themselves by hiding inside the dried-up, year-old carcasses of two dead buffaloes. Trudeau died a few years afterwards, but Jack Stillwell grew to be one of the ablest and best-known scouts on the plains.)

After they had started, I ate a few mouthfuls of raw horse flesh, drank nearly a canteen of water, dressed my wounds as well as I could with water dressings, and a strong guard having been mounted, I dozed away until nearly daylight. Then we prepared a reception for our foes, who I knew would be likely to renew the attack at dawn.

All night long we could hear the Indians stealthily removing the dead bodies of their slain, and their camp resounded with the beat of drums and the death wail of the mourners. I had cautioned the men to lie close and not to fire until the Indians were fairly upon us, as I thought they would make a rush on us at the first flush of dawn. In this, however, I was mistaken, for from their actions, they evidently believed that we had escaped under the cover of night, and accordingly a large party of mounted warriors rode up to within a few hundred yards of our works, and about twenty dismounted and came running forward to pick up our trail. At this juncture, some one of the men, probably by accident, discharged his piece. Instantly the dismounted Indians threw themselves flat on the ground, and the horsemen galloped off. Of course, we opened fire upon them, but to little effect. I think we killed one man, but no more. I was much disappointed, as I felt we had lost an opportunity of crippling them badly.

At daylight they again took up the fight from their former position in ambush, but as we were now fully protected, they did us no particular harm. It was now apparent that they meant to starve us out, for they made no further attempts to attack us openly.

As the second day wore on, our wounded suffered very much. As I have mentioned in the preceding pages, the nights in southern Colorado during the month of September are really cold, but the clear sunny days in the sheltered valleys are intensely hot, and already the bodies of the dead horses lying around us began to swell and decompose. Our surgeon was senseless and slowly dying, and unfortunately, in our rush to the island, we omitted to take the medical supplies; in fact, it was all we could do in our haste to throw the boxes containing our four thousand extra rounds of fixed ammunition on the saddle of four of our horses and get them over with us. The surgeon, in the panniers that were abandoned, had some bandages, his instruments, a few simple medicines, and some brandy; but these had fallen into the enemy's hands, and assuredly he had ample need of them.

All day long the Indian women and children kept up a dismal wailing and beating of drums, the death chant over their slain braves. In the meantime, our men kept watch and ward, and rarely returned the fire of the besiegers unless opportunity offered to make the bullets count, and during this day but one of the command was hit, and the wound was a mere scratch, and as nightfall drew on I felt satisfied that the score was quite a long one in our favor. Two more of my company were sent out at 11:00 P.M. to try to make their way to Fort Wallace, but they found the Indians guarding every outlet, and returned to the command about 3:00 A.M. the next morning.

The third day, fortunately, was slightly cloudy, and consequently the wounded had something of an easier time of it; besides, we had begun to get used to our injuries. Desultory firing was kept up by both sides from early light, but with no damage to either side, as the Indians had dug out rifle pits for themselves and were about as well protected as we were.

At midday Scout Grover called my attention to the fact that the women and children, who had been such interested spectators of the fight since its commencement, had ceased their chanting and were beginning to withdraw. To me this emphasized an idea that had taken possession of my mind since daylight, viz., that the Indians had about decided to give up the fight, and this was still further confirmed by an attempt upon their part to open communications with a white flag. This was, as I knew, merely an effort on their part to get near enough to our works to see the condition of my command; consequently, I directed several men to warn them, by waving their hands and shouting, not to attempt to come near us. They understood what was said to them, without a doubt, especially as Grover addressed them in their own dialect; but affecting not to comprehend, they slowly advanced. I then ordered half a dozen shots sent in close to them. This action on our part convinced them that their ruse was useless; so, falling back out of range, their riflemen promptly sent several volleys into our works, probably as an evidence of their appreciation of our astuteness.

During the day, I took out my memorandum book and penciled the following dispatch:

> On Delaware Creek, Republican River, September 19, 1868
> To Colonel Bankhead, or Commanding Officer, Fort Wallace:
>   I sent to you two messengers on the night of the seventeenth instant, informing you of my critical condition. I tried to send two more last night, but they did not succeed in passing the Indian pickets, and returned. If the others have not arrived then hasten at once to my assistance. I have eight badly wounded and ten slightly wounded men to take in, and every animal I had was killed, save seven, which the Indians stampeded. Lieutenant Beecher is dead, Acting Surgeon Mooers probably cannot live the night out. He was hit in the head Thursday and has spoken but one rational word since. I am wounded in two places—in the right thigh, and my left leg is broken below the knee. The Cheyennes alone number four hundred fifty or more. Mr. Grover says they never fought so before. They were splendidly armed with Spencer and Henry rifles. We have killed at least thirty-five of them and wounded many more, besides killing and wounding a quantity of their stock. They carried off most of their killed and wounded during the night, but three of their men fell into our hands. I am on a little island and still have plenty of ammunition. We are living on mule and horsemeat, and are entirely out of rations. If it were not for so many wounded, I would come in, and take the

chances of whipping them if attacked. They are evidently sick of their bargain. I had two members of my company killed on the seventh, namely, William Wilson and George W. Chalmers.[15] You had better start with not less than seventy-five men, and bring all the wagons and ambulances you can spare. Bring a six-pound howitzer with you. I can hold out here for six days longer if absolutely necessary, but please lose no time.

Very respectfully, your obedient servant,
GEORGE A. FORSYTH, U.S. Army,
Commanding Company Scouts

P.S.—My surgeon having been mortally wounded, none of my wounded men have had their wounds dressed yet, so please bring out a surgeon with you.

At nightfall I confided it to two of my best men—Donovan and Pliley—with the same general instructions I had given Stillwell two days before. Shortly after midnight they left our entrenchments, and as they did not return, I felt satisfied that they had eluded the Indians and were on their way to Fort Wallace.

On the fourth day our sufferings were intense. It was very hot, our meat had become putrid, some of the wounded were delirious, and the stench from the dead horses lying close around us was almost intolerable. As the ball in my right thigh had begun to pain me excessively, I decided to extract it. I appealed to several of the men to cut it out, but as soon as they saw how close it lay to the artery, they declined doing so, alleging that the risk was too great. However, I determined that it should come out, as I feared sloughing, and then the artery would probably break in any event; so taking my razor from my saddle pocket, and getting two of the men to press the adjacent flesh back and draw it taut, I managed to cut it out myself without disturbing the artery, greatly to my almost immediate relief.

At dawn of this day the Indian riflemen had sent in quite a volley, and at odd times kept sending in shots from their ambuscade; but they grew gradually less, and in the afternoon almost ceased. In the meantime, but few Indians could be seen in the vicinity, and I began to suspect the entire body was withdrawing. Accordingly, I asked several of the men to lift me upon a blanket, as by this time numbers of scouts were standing upright, and two of them had crawled over to the south bank of the stream and reported that there were no more Indians on that side. Just as the men had lifted me up that I might judge of the general condition of things from a more extended view than I could obtain lying upon my back in the rifle pit, about twenty shots were suddenly sent in among us, and the man who had the corner of the blanket which supported my broken leg dropped it and took to cover. The result was that the bone parted and partially protruded through the flesh. To say that I was angry is hardly doing the subject justice, and I fear the recording angel had no easy task to blot out the numerous expletives with which I anathematized the startled scout. This volley, which did no particular harm, was about the last sent in upon us; there were a few more stray shots sent at us now and then, and we could see Indian vedettes posted on the crest of the adjacent hills; but save a few warriors that lingered around in ambush to watch our movements, we did not again see any large force of the savages.

Up to this time I have said nothing of the individual heroism of my men. It was worthy of all praise. Young Hudson Farley, who was shot through the shoulder, fought straight through the first day's fight, never speaking of his condition until the list of casualties was called for. Howard Morton lost one of his eyes by a bullet that lodged just behind it, but wrapped a handkerchief around his head and fought on steadily. The elder Farley, though mortally wounded, lay on one side and fought through the entire first day's fight. Harrington, with an arrow point lodged squarely in his frontal bone, never ceased to bear his full share in the fray, and when a bullet ploughed across his forehead and dislodged the arrowhead, the two falling together to the ground, he wrapped a rag around his head and, though covered with blood, fought to the very close of the three days' fighting. McCall never once alluded to the fact that he was wounded until after nightfall; and so of Davis, Clark, Gantt, and others.

There were, as a matter of course, queer episodes during the siege. On the third day a large and very fleshy Indian, having, as he thought, placed himself just out of range, taunted and insulted us in every possible way. He was perfectly naked, and his gestures especially were exceedingly exasperating. Not being in a happy frame of mind, the man's actions annoyed me excessively. Now we had in the command three Springfield breech-loading rifles which I knew would carry several hundred yards farther than our Spencer rifles. I accordingly directed that the men using these guns should sight them at their limit—1,200 yards—and aim well over the sight, and see if by some chance we might stop the antics of this outrageously insulting savage. At the crack of the three rifles, he sprang into the air with a yell of seemingly both surprise and anguish, and rolled over stone dead, while the Indians in his vicinity scattered in every direction, and this almost unexpected result of our small volley was a matter of intense satisfaction to all of us.

And now came a time of weary waiting and comparative inaction that was hard to bear, and under our peculiar circumstances well nigh intolerable. We were out of food of any kind; the meat cut from the dead mules and horses had become putrid, and although we boiled it and sprinkled gunpowder upon it, it was not palatable. One of the scouts succeeded in shooting a little coyote, and not long ago one of my men told me that the head of the little gray wolf was boiled three successive times to extract the last shred of nutriment it contained. On the fourth or sixth day, two of the command quietly stole away down the stream in the hope that they might possibly get a shot at some game, but their quest was in vain. However, they did find a few wild plums. These they brought back, boiled, and gave to the wounded, and I know that the few spoonfuls I received was by far the most delicious food that ever passed my lips. As the days wore on, the wounded became feverish, and some of them delirious, gangrene set in, and I was distressed to find the wound in my leg infested with maggots. The well men, however, did all they could for us, and we tried to keep up our spirits as best we might.

On the evening of the sixth day, I called the sound men around me and in a few words stated the facts in the case as they knew them. I told them that possibly the scouts who had been sent out from the command had failed to get through, and that we might not get the succor we hoped for. Furthermore, I thought that by moving out at night and keeping together, they could make Fort Wallace, and even if attacked, they had plenty of ammunition with which to defend themselves, and I believed that no ordinary scouting party of Indians would dare to attack them after their recent experience with us; furthermore, I did not believe that any Indians, other than those whom we fought, were in the vicinity, and I doubted if those who might still be watching us were in any great numbers. Those of us who were wounded must take our chances. If relief came in time, well and good; if not, we were soldiers and knew how to meet our fate. For a few seconds there was a dead silence, and then rose a hoarse cry of "Never! Never! We'll stand by you, General, to the end!" and McCall voiced the sentiment of the men by saying, "We've fought together, and by heaven, if need be, we'll die together!"

The next two days seem to me to have been almost intolerable. The well men of the command moved up and down the stream within sight of our earth-works, seeking but not finding game; at night the crests of the hills were dotted with wolves, who, attracted by the carrion yet not daring to come within range of our rifles, sat upon their haunches and howled the night through; and during the day the sun beat down upon our devoted heads with a strength that I had not deemed possible in that latitude during the month of September.

On the morning of the ninth day since the attack by the Indians, one of the men near me suddenly sprang to his feet and, shading his eyes with his hand, shouted, "There are some moving objects on the far hills!" Instantly every man who could stand was on his feet gazing intently in the direction indicated. In a few moments a general murmur ran through the command. "By the God above us, it's an ambulance!" shouts one of the men; and then went up a wild cheer that made the little valley ring, and strong men grasped hands, and then flung their arms around each other, and laughed and cried, and fairly danced and shouted again in glad relief of their long pent-up feelings. It was a troop of the 10th Cavalry, under Captain L. H. Carpenter,[16] the advance of Captain Bankhead's command from Fort Wallace, which that officer had fairly hurled forward as soon as news of our situation reached him through Donovan and Pliley. An hour later he was at my side with his infantry, and in less than another hour Major Brisbin of the 2nd Cavalry was there with the advance of Colonel Bradley's command, which had also hurried to my aid.[17] When Captain Carpenter rode up to me, as I lay half covered with sand in my rifle pit, I affected to be reading an old novel that one of the men had found in a saddle pocket. It was only affectation, though, for I had all I could do to keep from breaking down, as I was sore and feverish and tired and hungry, and I had been under a heavy strain from the opening of the fight until his arrival.

During the fight I counted thirty-two dead Indians; these I reported officially. My men claimed to have counted far more, but these were all that I saw lying dead, and I have made it a rule never to report a dead Indian I have not seen myself. The troops who came to my rescue unearthed many a one, and several years later I met one of the younger chiefs of the Brule Sioux at a grand buffalo hunt given by General Sheridan to the Grand Duke Alexis of Russia. It was a superb affair, and a large number of Indians participated in it and afterwards gave a war dance for the entertainment of the distinguished guest.

One evening one of the government scouts asked me if I would see this young chief, a man of about twenty-seven or twenty-eight years, who wished to talk to me about the fight on the Republican. We had a long, and to me, at least, an interesting, conversation over the affair. He asked me how many men I had, and I told him, and gave him a true account of those killed and wounded, and I saw that he was much pleased. He told the interpreter that I told the truth, as he had counted my men himself; that for four days they had been watching my every movement, gathering their warriors to meet us from far and near, and that I stopped and encamped about two miles below, where they lay in ambush for me. He said that had I continued my march for another hour the day I encamped at 4:00 P.M., every man of us would have been slaughtered. My occupation of the island was a surprise to them all, and it was the only thing that saved us. I then questioned him regarding their numbers and losses. He hesitated for some time, but finally told the interpreter something, and the interpreter told me that there were nearly a thousand warriors in the fight. He said he thought the number about nine hundred and seventy. Regarding their losses, the chief held up his two hands seven times together, and then one hand singly, which, the interpreter told me, signified seventy-five. I asked the interpreter if that meant killed and wounded. "That," said the interpreter, "signifies the killed only. He says there were 'heaps' wounded." Just as he started to go, he stopped and spoke to the interpreter again. "He wishes to know whether you did not get enough of it," said the interpreter.

"Tell him yes, all I wanted," was my reply. "How about himself?" As my words were interpreted, he gave a grim, half-humorous look, and then, unfolding his blanket and opening his breast of his buckskin shirt, pointed to where a bullet had evidently gone through his lungs, nodded, closed his shirt, wrapped his blanket around him, turned, and stalked quietly from the tent.

Withstood the Siege: The Story of Col. George A. Forsythe's Brave Defense at Arikaree Fork

FLETCHER VILOTT[1] [as told to A. Bailey, Mankato, Kansas]

National Tribune 26, nos. 4 and 5 (November 5 and 12, 1896)

A mong the many men now living in Kansas whose courage has been tried on the battlefield, none is more deserving of notice than a certain quiet, unassuming farmer seen weekly on the street of Mankato, whose home is about seven miles southwest of the city. This man deserves a place of honor in our list of heroes, for he was one of that little band of fifty-one men who, under the command of the brave Maj. George A. Forsyth, on a little island in the Arikaree Fork of the Republican River, withstood a siege lasting nine days, surrounded by hundreds of Sioux and Cheyenne warriors under the leadership of the great chief Roman Nose.

Fletcher Vilott has for many years been a resident of Jewell County. So diffident and unpretending is he that scarcely a man of his acquaintance had ever heard that he was one of Major Forsyth's command. He doubtless might have continued to reside here for many years to come without men ever dreaming of what he had passed through had not the writer learned by accident that twenty-seven years ago he was a scout on the plains. A few questions revealed the fact that he was a participant in the battle mentioned, an account of which is here given substantially as narrated by him.

Vilott was born in Indiana in 1831, and in 1856 removed to Kansas. In the summer of 1868, he was living in Lincoln County, on a ranch near the Saline River. One afternoon in August, he was engaged in making hay, when a recruiting officer rode up and, accosting him, asked if he was willing to join Major Forsyth's company as a scout, whose duty it would be to range the frontier between the Platte and Republican Rivers, to protect the settlers from the incursions of hostile Indians.

Vilott announced his willingness and was instructed by the officer to furnish his own horse and equipment and to report at once at Fort Harker. The team was at once unhitched from the wagon, the stock turned loose upon the ranch, and that night Vilott reported at the fort. 10:00 P.M. found the company on board the cars, bound for Fort Hays, which was reached the next morning, where they remained for two days waiting for horses and equipment necessary in a campaign of this kind.

August 29, at about 3:00 P.M., they left the camp on Bug Creek, about one mile below the fort, and with Lieutenant Beecher at their head, rode at full speed for the post. As they dashed past headquarters, the scouts caught sight of General Sheridan standing on the portico, and near him their leader, Major Forsyth. In their wild dash, some of the scouts followed the streets, while others swept through the parade grounds.

A few minutes later Major Forsyth shook hands with the general and, mounting his horse, gave the command, and the company rode away from the post, their course being due north. The day had been dark and threatening, and soon after sunset a rain began falling, which increased at sunset, continuing through the night.

About 10:00 P.M. the next day, they went into camp on the banks of the Saline. Nothing eventful occurred during the day; the country passed over was a monotonous stretch of rolling prairie, varied only by the Saline and its tributaries.

The next day, August 31, the range of the buffalo was entered, thousands of these animals appearing on the divides to the north and west. Every man now wished to try his marksmanship on the great game, but the order was given that no shooting would be allowed except by a few regularly detailed hunters.

From morning until darkness set in, the command was at no time out of sight of buffalo; as far as the eye could reach, they were seen, some of the herds calmly grazing, while others were scurrying over the hills with that peculiar rolling gait that distinguishes them from every other inhabitant of the prairie. Occasionally a drove of timid antelope, startled by the invaders, would dash away to the right or left until, a safer distance gained, they would turn and gaze for a moment, then bound away to halt again, mere specks on the horizon; here and there droves of elk were seen stalking majestically at a distance, curiously regarding the strange objects that had so suddenly appeared in their native haunts. The men detailed as hunters being expert marksmen, there was no scarcity of game in camp. With Lieutenant Beecher acting as guide, the line of march led to the northwest, in the direction of Beaver Creek, which was reached about September 2.

Up to this time no Indians had been seen, and the abundance of game throughout the country traversed indicated to the scouts that this section had not been lately visited by them; but when the Beaver was followed for a short distance, signs of the enemy were apparent, the trained eye of Lieutenant Beecher discovering a spot where they had lately held a war dance. From here Major Forsyth enjoined more caution.

Acting under orders, the valley of the Beaver was followed to the southwest, and September 5 the command came in sight of Fort Wallace. Before entering the fort, however, a line of objects was seen away on the bluffs to the southeast, which Beecher thought to be Indians. Major Forsyth decided to charge them, and preparations were at once made.

The level stretch of prairie was quickly crossed, but when the summit of the bluffs was gained, the supposed enemy was found entrenched behind a long line of government wagons. It proved to be a hay train on its way to Fort Wallace.

The only mishap caused by this charge was occasioned by one of the horses stepping into a prairie-dog hole and stumbling, throwing its rider to the ground with such force as to disable him for the time, compelling him to remain at the fort. From this point a plain beaten road led to the post, where they arrived at about 10:00 P.M. that night, remaining there for three days, making final preparations for the campaign. When fully equipped for the march, each man was mounted on a good horse and carried with him rations for a seven days' campaign. There were no wagons, but a pack train of five mules answered for the purpose.

At Fort Wallace the company was joined by "Sharp" Grover, a scout who had passed several years on the frontier and understood all the wiles practiced by the Indians. He was at this time a man of about thirty to thirty-five years of age, above the medium height, rather spare, sinewy, and active. He was a perfect sleuthhound in pursuit, riding his horse at a gallop along a trail perceptible to none of the command except himself and Beecher. When the hoof marks of ponies were no longer visible, then Grover and Beecher would ride away, leaning forward in their saddles, carefully scanning the ground and picking up a trail where no evidence could be seen by those who followed.

Lieutenant Beecher was a nephew of the Rev. Henry Ward Beecher. He too had spent several years on the plains, much of the time at frontier posts, a life to which he seemed to have taken a peculiar liking. He was a silent man, talking but little, but possessing the confidence and esteem of all who knew him.

Another, Jack Stillwell, deserves special mention here. He was a boy of not more than eighteen or nineteen years of age, fair complexion, rather tall, slender, and straight. He was young in years but old in experience; a stranger to fear and always acting where duty called him, taking upon his young shoulders responsibilities under which those much older than himself would have shrunk.

As the company was about to pull out for a week, a dispatch was received ordering Major Forsyth to hurry to Sheridan, then the terminus of the Kansas-Pacific road (distant from Fort Wallace about seventeen miles in a northeasterly direction),[2] as the Indians had put in an appearance there in some force and made an attack upon a train.

The company arrived at Sheridan about 10:00 A.M., to learn that the enemy had made a quick dash, killing two Mexican teamsters and driving off about thirty head of cattle; but a few minutes had elapsed since they disappeared over the hills to the north. The trail, made plain by one wagon which they had taken away with them, was easily followed, and at a place about two miles distant from the scene of their depredations, the wagon was found at the bottom of a deep gulch, broken to pieces, and, lying near, two or three dead cattle. After leaving this place, the trail grew gradually dim, and at last battled the best efforts of Beecher and Grover, becoming wholly lost in the rough ground traversed by them in their hurried retreat. It was decided, however, to keep a northwesterly direction toward the Republican River, where it was believed the enemy would be found in considerable numbers.

Nothing of importance occurred during the next two days. Occasionally, at a distance, objects were seen which Grover pronounced Indians, and this led to the belief that every movement of the company was watched and communicated.

Major Forsyth now announced his intention to follow this straggling band to its hiding place and to attack them, no matter where found or what their numbers; that they were not out for recreation but to fight Indians; and that the command should not return until a blow had been struck.

On reaching the Republican, indications of the enemy became apparent, although nothing to denote the presence of any great number; but as the march continued toward the forks of the river, these signs multiplied, until it no longer required the practiced eye of Grover or Beecher to know that at no great distance the scouts would find work to do; pony tracks were seen, and occasionally the print of a moccasin in the sand, and finally a spot was found among the willows where two or three Indians had spent the night. It was noticed also that the herds of buffalo which had been encountered everywhere for the last three days had disappeared—a very significant fact, as the Republican Valley was the favorite range of these animals, and their absence told plainly that some foe had been annoying them.

Soon a trail was struck leading directly up the river, a path that grew plainer and broader at every mile traversed. Grover here warned Major Forsyth that when the enemy was found, it would be in large force and doubtless in a position to offer strong resistance, but this did not shake the major's determination to try them, and he again reiterated his intention of attacking them at the first opportunity offered.

The path was followed leading up the Arikaree Fork of the Republican until September 16. At an early hour in the afternoon, the company went into camp on the north bank of the river, at a few rods distant from the stream.

The last three days had been clear and warm, the sky without a cloud, and as the spirits of men are influenced to a great extent by the weather, so on this September evening the camp gave evidence of cheerfulness scarcely to be expected among men enduring a forced march and for the last two days subsisting on half rations. Since reaching the Republican, however, an abundance of wild plums and grapes had been found growing in profusion on either hand in every canyon and ravine, and this had assisted to a great extent in preserving the scanty rations allowed each man.

The place chosen for a camp at first appearance did not seem to be the strongest position for a defense, and some of the scouts supposed that the camping place was not intended as a permanent one, but that before night the march would be resumed and a position taken somewhat farther up the river. Had this been done, the story of the battle would never have been told by a survivor.

To the north of the camp, there stretched a level plain of perhaps one hundred rods in width, terminating in a bluffy ridge rising to the height of two hundred feet or more. This ridge furnished a fine hiding place for the enemy, gashed here and there as it was by deep ravines and canyons. South of the stream was a tract of level bottomland of two miles in width, rising gradually to the line of hills which away to the east marked the windings of the Republican. Directly opposite the camp, in the middle of the stream, was an island about three hundred yards in length and from fifty to one hundred feet in width. On either side of the island, a sandy riverbed of perhaps one hundred feet in extent separated it from the mainland, while a shallow stream of water a few inches in depth worked its sluggish way through the sands, encircling the island and uniting in one channel some distance below. There were a few willows and cottonwood trees growing there, together with a shrubby undergrowth sufficient to hide men when lying prostrate.

Major Forsyth formed the camp parallel with the riverbank, the fires only a few feet apart. The horses were carefully picketed, and the usual preparations made for the night. No extra precautions were taken, although the feeling was general that the enemy must be close at hand.

As night drew on, Grover, Beecher, and Major Forsyth were seen in frequent conversation. Beecher would from time to time slowly scan the horizon, following carefully the line of bluffs marking the river on the north, while Major Forsyth paced slowly back and forth, halting occasionally, while his eye swept the surrounding country up and down the valley, and from the bluffy ridge to the distant foothills on the south.

In selecting guards for the night, John Wilson, one of the bravest men in the command,[3] was stationed to the east of the camp near a plum thicket, which terminated a long ravine running down from the hills and was regarded as the spot of greatest danger to the camp. About an hour after dark, while the men were seated around in groups, suddenly there appeared away to the southeast a bright light; it rose above the foothills, blazed brightly for an instant, and as quickly died out. Vilott happened to be looking in that direction and called out, "Major! Look quick! See that signal!"

All watched intently, but it was not repeated.

Soon after this there arose in the distance what seemed to be the howling of coyotes, but which the more experienced believed to be Indians signaling each other, as they can imitate very closely the howling of this animal; but in a short time silence settled about the camp, and all except the guards lay down to sleep.

A little before daylight, the howling of the coyotes was again heard, much nearer than at dark and from every direction. Vilott called out to his mate, "Greene,[4] those are not coyotes; they are Indians."

About this time, John Lyden[5] started a fire, declaring that he was going to have a cup of coffee, but as it blazed up, the clamor increased. Someone yelled, "Put out that fire," and Lyden emptied the contents of his coffeepot over the blaze, quickly extinguishing it. At that instant the rattling of horses' hoofs was heard to the east of the camp, followed by the cry of "Indians, Indians, Indians!" from Wilson, who, after firing two or three shots at the enemy, rushed into camp, arousing every man with the alarm. Obeying the command of the major, each scout seized his carbine and ran to his horse, as it was well known that the effort of the Indians would be to stampede the horses. The attacking party, some seven or eight in number, came on with loud yells until within easy shooting distance, when a fire was opened up on them, checking their advance and tumbling one of their number to the ground. They swerved to the right but succeeded in approaching near enough to sweep up three horses that had not been securely tied, together with two or three of the pack mules, with which they dashed out of sight beyond the bluffs.

In his efforts to thwart the Indians, the major ran in their direction until he was more than fifty yards from the camp, all the while calling on the men to assist in heading off the stampeding animals, but for the time each scout seemed intent on saving his own horse. The order was given to saddle up, as an attack from a large force was anticipated.

By this time it was light enough to distinguish objects quite clearly. The few Indians who had alarmed the camp, whose only object was to stampede the horses, had disappeared to the north; but now above the nearest hills, feathered heads and painted faces suddenly appeared. Every man now understood the situation; it was apparent to all. They were surrounded by the Sioux and Cheyennes, and fifty-one men must contend against hundreds of the enemy, who within five minutes would be down on them.

Grover, in whom all placed such reliance, became restless and anxious; he knew they must act quickly. All at once, away to the northwest upon the highest hill, appeared a solitary Indian.

"Has he a flag with him?" asked Grover.

"Yes," was the reply.

"My God! There will be a thousand Indians down on us in less than five minutes," was Grover's answer. "Major, what shall we do?"

Major Forsyth, after studying the little island opposite the camp for a moment, gave the order to repair to it at once, as it seemed to be the only place offering a refuge at such a time.

Just as the order was given, up the river three-fourths of a mile away there came in sight a long line of mounted warriors, riding down at a gallop—a thousand savages in all the panoply of barbaric war, hideously painted, their war bonnets fluttering in the breeze, their weapons glittering in the morning sun, sweeping on in savage pride upon this little band of scouts.

———— ✠ ————

Down came the redskins, a solid unbroken line, encouraging each other with loud yells until, at a distance of about four hundred yards from the camp, the column opened like a fan and, dividing, the right wing crossed the river and extended its line around the island to the south, while the left, entering the defiles to the north, stretched away until, uniting on the east, a circle was formed, completely hemming in the scouts and effectually closing every avenue of retreat. In the meantime, the company had gained the island, tethering the horses as compactly as possible to the bushes there growing.

At this moment Major Forsyth, looking back, saw one of the pack mules, Old Black Kettle, as she was called, close to the bank but showing no disposition to follow farther. As this mule carried valuable supplies, including the surgeon's medicines and instruments, he called for two volunteers to lead her over; Vilott and Henry Tucker[6] responded. Reaching the north bank, Vilott made an attack in the rear, and between the two, they soon had her on the way to the island, accelerating her movements at every jump by prodding her with a carbine. The attacking party from up the river opened a sharp fire on them, but although the bullets dropped in the sand all about them, and several struck the pack, the return was made in safety, all three gaining the island without a scratch.[7]

By this time, lining the hills to the north in all directions, emerging from the canyons, thickets, and ravines, were seen the savages, some on foot, creeping stealthily from one hiding place to another; some mounted on their ponies, dashing across the level bottomlands, intent on intercepting the scouts in what they thought was a hurried retreat; while away on the bluffs here and there could be seen those whose duty it was to signal those engaged in the attack. Major Forsyth ordered each man to construct a rifle pit for himself as hurriedly as possible, which was quickly done by scooping out the sand to the depth of a foot or two. Three men were stationed so as to keep a careful watch to the south, a like number to the west and north, while the main body operated from the center. Jack Stillwell was placed at the lowest point on the island.

Permission having been granted by Major Forsyth, Louis Farley, Tucker, Clark, and Vilott recrossed to the north, taking up a position under the riverbank at a place thought to be secure from the fire of any prowling Indians, and from whence they could operate to good advantage against the enemy in that direction, the immediate danger coming from the Indian marksmen who were fast securing positions from which they could at their leisure pick off the scouts one by one.

But a few minutes elapsed when Clark received a rifle ball in the ankle, crippling him; a second shot from the same direction struck Farley in the thigh, shattering the bone. Tucker was lying flat upon his face when a bullet passed between him and the ground. He sprang to his feet, crying out that he was shot through the body, but the next moment discovered that he was unharmed. Vilott was resting upon one knee when a fourth shot from the same source as the three preceding struck him in the leg, severely wounding but not crippling him. These four shots, coming at regular intervals and from the same direction, led Vilott to believe that they were fired by one Indian in hiding.

Watching carefully, he saw, partially screened behind a small bush, the movements of an arm, as if engaged in ramming down a ball. Leveling his carbine directly at the center of the screen, he pulled the trigger. At the report, the Indian went down and was seen no more.

Farley had received the severest wound and now called out, "Boys, I shall be dead before night; you may save yourselves by returning to the island. Take my gun with you and keep it; do not let it fall into the hands of the Indians."

This request was refused, Vilott and Tucker reminding him that he might have good use for his rifle before the day closed.

Poor Farley! He had been fatally shot but remained where he was throughout the day, doing wonderful execution with his carbine, killing three Indians who, in spite of all precautions, had gained a lodgment on the island. After dark that day, Clark crawled on his hands and knees across the sand to his companions, while Lyden carried Farley over on his back. Nine days later Farley died and was buried on the island.

But while these four men were battling under the riverbank, the fire from the savages had proved most destructive among their companions on the island. Most of the horses had fallen; some remained on their feet, struggling and groaning, even after being pierced by three or four rifle balls. If a scout showed head or hand, it became a target for a half dozen of the secreted foe.

Mooers was lying in his rifle pit, a bullet through the head and slowly dying. Lieutenant Beecher had received a mortal wound and was unconscious; several of the command were dangerously wounded; the younger Wilson was lying dead; and Major Forsyth was suffering terribly, one ball having perforated his ankle, and another inflicted a dangerous wound in the thigh.

Vilott and Tucker, believing that their only safety lay in a return to the island, determined to take their chances by running the gauntlet. Watching for a favorable moment, when there came a lull in the firing, Tucker sprang forward across the sands. When about halfway over, a big Indian beheld him, and some distance from the river set up a derisive yell. Tucker halted for an instant and turned his head to look behind him. A shower of bullets followed, but he escaped, joining his comrades in safety. Vilott remained a few minutes, firing a shot or two, and then followed Tucker. He too escaped unharmed, the wound in his leg not being of such a nature as to impede running.

It was now about 11:00 A.M. But one horse, Vilott's mule, remained standing, and a few minutes later another ball struck her, and she went down. As she fell, from across the river in plain English came the shout, "There goes the last damned horse."

About this time, the fire of the enemy slackened, and soon nearly ceased. Major Forsyth regarded this as ominous, presaging an assault, and gave orders to each man to make preparations for resisting an attack, which he felt would soon be made.

Half an hour elapsed, when from away off among the bluffs to the north-west came the clear notes of a bugle. Here and there, mounted Indians were seen in motion, coming over the hills from the north, issuing from the ravines and canyons, or speeding across the river bottom, all converging upon a deep gulch leading down from the rough lands and at a distance of about six hundred yards from the island.

Soon they reappeared, pouring from the ravines and forming in line, while riding back and forth along their front was a leader who harangued them and issued orders in a voice of such volume that he could be heard distinctly by the distant scouts. At times he wheeled his steed as if determined to dash down alone, gesticulating savagely and shouting his commands to the Indians, who heard and obeyed, though some of them were more than half a mile away. Grover recognized him and called out, "That big fellow is Roman Nose. There is but one such Indian living. They are going to ride over us, and Roman Nose will lead them."[8]

He had scarcely spoken when a bugle again sounded and "Here they come" ran along the line. But they were not coming. Darting from their midst, and alone, came [Dry Throat]. He was riding a magnificent horse, an animal of fine appearance and great speed, stripped for the race, without saddle or bridle, naked save a lariat noosed about the lower jaw, thence passing once or twice around the body and that of his rider.

As the giant chief swept across the space intervening between him and the river, from time to time a yell escaped him such as was never before heard, a savage cry which was replied to by the warriors as they watched their leader in his daring ride.

On he comes. He gains the riverbank and plunges over into the sandy bed. He is headed straight for the island, determined to ride over the scouts as they lie hidden in their rifle pits. Every scout has his eye upon him, and carbines are raised to wait his nearer approach. He is within one hundred yards of the head of the island when his horse swerves to the right. [Dry Throat] means to show his contempt for the scouts by riding around the island, but in doing this he must pass within one hundred feet of the rifle pits.

Save a gorgeous war bonnet covering his temples and a narrow sash about his loins, he is nude; his left arm wears a shield, while his right hand grasps a heavy revolver. He reaches a point opposite the head of the island before a shot is fired; two or three carbines are discharged. [Dry Throat] answers with a yell and, slightly raising his shield, opens fire with his revolver. With the speed of a whirlwind, he passes the center of the island, his headdress of eagle feathers streaming in the wind, his savage face scowling defiance. Puffs of smoke leap from the rifle pits, but rider and horse sweep on unhurt. Is he going to succeed in his mad undertaking? A few seconds more and he will pass the lowest pit; but Jack Stillwell is there. Suddenly the mighty chief raises his shield and weapon above his head; his tall form straightens to its full height; a second more, and

The defense of Beecher Island. HARPER'S NEW MONTHLY MAGAZINE 1895.

with a convulsive movement, he pitches forward and falls into the shallow stream. His riderless horse hurries on, gains the bank, climbs it, and disappears.

The assembled Indians, on seeing [Dry Throat] fall, seemed for a time confused and lost; the body of the warriors that had remained watching their chief in his mad ride now broke up into small bands and were seen riding away at full speed, some of them crossing the stream at a point some distance below the island, while others began assembling on the south bank, but at a place beyond carbine range.

Wailing and howling arose from the squaws over the death of [Dry Throat], lamentations that lasted throughout the rest of the day. From noon until 4:00 P.M., desultory firing was kept up on the part of the Indians, but little harm resulting from it. But at about the hour mentioned, reinforcements appeared away to the north, which, crossing the river at some distance above, formed in line on the south bank at a distance of about six hundred yards from the island. It was surmised that they contemplated a charge, and precautions were at once made to receive them.

At the sound of the bugle, the column started.[9] On they came, several hundred of them maintaining an unbroken front until one half of the intervening space was passed over, when two volleys poured into them in quick succession scattered them to the right and left; but a few seconds, and the last one disappeared beyond the bank on either side.

The afternoon had been intensely hot, and all had suffered from thirst. There was water within a few feet, but none dared to venture outside the rifle pits, for behind every bush and bank lurked an Indian sharpshooter.

Murphy, holding a favorable position, commenced digging for water and soon had a shallow well, into which the water seeped through the sand. When

Dry Throat charging the island. CENTURY MAGAZINE 1893.

a supply had accumulated, canteens were thrown to him from one rifle pit to another, which, after being filled, were returned in the same manner.

As soon as it was dark, the wounded were made as comfortable as possible, and Major Forsyth, knowing that the Indians would attempt to starve them into surrender, prepared for a long siege by ordering the men to cut steaks from the horses, as the flesh would become tainted before morning. Accordingly, strips were taken from the dead animals and hung across the lariat ropes to dry, and in this way enough was secured to keep the scouts from starvation.

That night Major Forsyth called for volunteers to go to Fort Wallace, distant 110 miles, for help. Jack Stillwell and Pierre Trudeau were selected for the perilous undertaking and at once made preparations to depart.

There was still a small store of crackers on hand, and each scout furnished of his scanty share until it was thought that this, with the fruit that could be obtained on the way, would prove sufficient for the journey. With this meager ration, and each man carrying about one hundred fifty rounds of cartridges, about 10:00 P.M. they shook hands with their comrades and crept quietly from the island. Stillwell's words at parting with his companions were "Boys, keep up good courage; you will see me back again. I will bring you relief." Before morning they had succeeded in getting through the lines, but when daylight came, they were so near the enemy that they were compelled to remain secreted during the entire day within sound of the firing on the island. But when darkness came, they hurried away, and before the next morning dawned, they had left the Indians far behind.

On the island, the forepart of the night was spent in burying the dead, caring for the wounded, preparing food, and still further strengthening defenses.

Double guards were thrown out, and about midnight the scouts lay down in their rifle pits, and those not suffering from wounds slept until morning.

At about daybreak, the neighing of horses across the river gave notice that the Indians were again on the move, and the warning ran along the line to get ready for them. The enemy moved cautiously along in the twilight until they arrived at the camping ground on the north bank, where they halted and one shot was fired. But as it brought no response from the island, they advanced to the riverbank, where they remained for a few minutes in perfect quiet. Then came the sound of horses' feet as they slid down the bank into the yielding sand.

It was now light enough to distinguish the mass of horsemen, and a volley from twenty-five or thirty carbines was poured into them; evidently this proved a surprise, for without waiting for a second greeting, they fled in great confusion until, a safer distance attained, they sent in a few scattering shots, which were not replied to by the scouts. It was impossible to determine the loss to the enemy, but had the order to fire been withheld for a few minutes, they doubtless would have approached much nearer, and in consequence received a terrible chastisement. As it was, a few riderless horses galloped off, but the killed and wounded were carried away by their companions. The body of [Dry Throat], which at dark lay in front of Jack Stillwell's rifle pit, had disappeared, his warriors having quietly taken possession of it within the night.

There was no more fighting on the second day; the Indians could be seen in all directions, but they carefully kept out of range, and it now became evident that they were not desirous of making any more charges, their object being to starve the scouts out. The day was spent in caring for the wounded, giving them every attention possible. Still, their sufferings were most trying, the death of Surgeon Mooers leaving the command without a man capable of setting a fractured limb or properly dressing a wound.

That night, not knowing the fate of Stillwell and Trudeau, Major Forsyth sent out two more men[10] with dispatches, but they were unable to elude the enemy and returned the next morning.

About dawn of the third day, the Indians again assembled with a pretense of charging, but contented themselves by firing a few shots from a safe distance, after which they rode slowly away.

During the day, a fire was kept up from one point on the riverbank where a daring warrior had secreted himself, and from whence at regular intervals the smoke of his rifle was seen, followed by the whizzing of a bullet, each time passing uncomfortably close to the concealed scouts. Major Forsyth called out, "Look out for that fellow; he will do mischief." Not being able to determine his exact locality, as the next puff of smoke arose, a volley was fired in his direction, when the Indian sprang to his feet and ran for some distance, dropping his blanket and feigning that he was shot. "Give it to him," cried the major, "he is not hurt." Another volley followed, but he escaped, disappearing with the speed of an antelope.

Still uncertain of the fate of Stillwell and Trudeau, on the third night two more scouts, Pliley and Donovan, were selected to carry a message to the fort, and as these men did not return at daylight, it was hoped that they had been successful in getting through the lines.

On the fourth day,[11] no Indians were seen except an occasional one on the distant hills, and men were now detailed to cross to the mainland in quest of fruit, four being sent out at a time. They met with fair success, returning with grapes and plums, which were greatly relished by their starving companions.

The next four days were a repetition of the one just described, the scouts venturing a little farther each day but encountering none of the enemy. This gave rise to the hope that they had taken the alarm and were leaving. Still, a careful watch was kept up to guard against a surprise.

On the morning of the ninth day,[12] Eli Ziegler and Vilott volunteered to repair to a high bluff about a half mile to the northwest, which they named Point Lookout, there to keep watch for help and to signal their companions at the first approach. This height is near the place where Roman Nose and his warriors assembled on the first day and commands an extensive view of the valley to a great distance.

About 10:00 A.M., away on the southern hills, some six or eight miles distant, appeared a line of objects that at once arrested the attention of the two scouts, coming into view as they did in the direction from whence succor was to come.

Vilott called out, "Ziegler, I see something. What is that away yonder?"

Ziegler replied, "Buffalo."

The two men shaded their eyes, watched the moving objects intently for a few moments until, as they gained a point more favorable for observation, the conviction came to the minds of both that it was a government train from Fort Wallace.

Waiting until they were fully convinced that help was at hand, they swung their hats above their heads as a joyful signal to their distant comrades.[13] The scouts on the island, mistaking this demonstration as a warning of the approach of the enemy, at once made preparations for defending themselves; but soon, on the hills to the south, and not more than two miles away, several horsemen came in sight, riding directly toward the island, where they arrived at the moment Vilott and Ziegler appeared on the north bank.[14] They were Captain Carpenter and staff, Dr. [Jenkins A.] Fitzgerald, and the two scouts, Pliley and Donovan, the advance of Carpenter's men, who arrived an hour or two later.[15]

It is impossible to describe the meeting that now took place. Men rushed into each other's arms; some cried, some danced and sang; the wounded set up a faint cheer as they once more saw horsemen among them, realizing that they were saved.

Major Forsyth was lying in his rifle pit, wasted and worn from nine days of terrible suffering, when Captain Carpenter sprang from his horse and walked quickly to the spot pointed out to him by one of the scouts. Major

Forsyth reached out a trembling, emaciated hand, which was grasped by his companion, and the two remained silent for a moment, looking into each other's eyes.

The rugged scouts had endured nine days of war and famine [and] had seen their companions shot down by their side, some of them lingering long hours before death came. They had borne up under all and had shown no signs of weakness; but when that meeting took place in Major Forsyth's rifle pit, they turned away with bowed heads.

Following close after Captain Carpenter came a wagonload of supplies, on the arrival of which the camp was removed to the south side of the stream, where the wounded, under the care of Dr. Fitzgerald, received the attention so much needed.

The next morning, Captain Bankhead and Jack Stillwell rode into camp an hour in advance of the command, which they left a few miles down the valley. As they rode up at full speed, Stillwell dropped the reins on his horse's neck and, leaping to the ground, rushed with arms extended to greet his comrades, who now crowded around him, cheering and shaking hands.

He had been true to the promise made on the night he left the island; he and Trudeau appeared at the post in advance of Pliley and Donovan, but Captain Bankhead took the Custer trail directly north to the Republican River,[16] thence up the valley, while Carpenter, at the time twenty miles west of Fort Wallace, led by Pliley and Donovan, started in a straight course for the island, arriving one day in advance of Colonel Bankhead.

The loss to the Indians during the siege was never accurately determined but was known to be severe.

Lieutenant Beecher, Surgeon Mooers, George Chalmers,[17] William Wilson,[18] and Louis Farley were buried on the island.

On the return to Fort Wallace, some twenty miles from the scene of the battle, on the bank of a small stream, the scouts discovered a white buffalo lodge. On entering, they there found the body of Roman Nose on a scaffold four or five feet in height. About him were placed his weapons, drum, and trophies of war, while lying around outside were several of his horses, which in accordance with their peculiar rites had been strangled and left for the use of their chief on his journey to the Happy Hunting Ground.

Owing to the condition of the wounded, progress was necessarily slow, and three days were required in the return to Fort Wallace, where, on their arrival, the wounded remained and the company, recruited, joined Lieutenant Colonel Custer in the valley of the Arkansas.

Reminiscences of a Plainsman

ALLISON J. PLILEY[1]

Olathe (Kansas) *Mirror,* March 19, 1931

These reminiscences were written after two interviews with the veteran scout and Indian fighter Allison J. Pliley in the summer of 1909. After being written, they were submitted to him for correction and verification. Captain Pliley has long since "hit the long trail," and his type is extinct. The record of his exploits is worth preserving and is printed that the present generation may read of how the West was won.—S. T. Seaton.

— ⚬ ━✦━ ⚬ —

One would scarcely suspect the reserved, mild-mannered man, now past sixty-five, who lives at 1908 Cheyenne, Kansas City, Kansas, of having been a real Indian fighter and an important figure in the savage warfare which was waged on the plains of Kansas, Colorado, and Texas in 1867, '68, and '69. Nevertheless, "Capt. Allison J. Pliley was in those days one of the last romantic figures in Kansas," writes Hadley,[2] the historian of the Indian-fighting 19th Kansas Cavalry; "One of my best scouts," Maj. George A. Forsyth wrote of him; Custer, who knew him on the Texas expedition, invited him to go with him on his last trail; and General Sherman, without solicitation, secured him a captaincy in the 19th Kansas.

At first Captain Pliley was reluctant to talk of himself and his exploits, but when his interviewer began to ask questions about the fights at Beecher Island, Prairie Dog Creek, the Texas expedition with Custer, and his old comrades, Jack Stillwell, French Pete Trudeau, Jack Donovan, and others, the old man's eyes brightened, he straightened up in his chair, and for two hours told a thrilling story of scouting and fighting on the plains with men to whose names an historic and romantic interest will always attach.

— ⚬ ━✦━ ⚬ —

I was on the plains from the time I was seventeen, and I knew the prairies and the ways of the Indian pretty well when Maj. H. L. Moore employed me to scout for the battalion of the 18th Kansas Cavalry, which was organized in July 1867.

Almost my first experience in this service was a sort of duel with an Arapaho Indian up on the Saline. The Kansas Pacific was then in course of construction and had been completed to a little town called Rome, beyond where Hays City now stands. The Indians had been harassing the parties of hunters who were furnishing the construction gangs with buffalo meat and had killed several of them. A detachment of the 18th was sent up there to protect them. One night the soldiers were hidden in some adobe houses three or four miles out from camp, and the next morning I was directed to ride out on the breaks of the Saline and see if I could stir up something red.

I had a fine black horse—the fastest-mile horse on the plains—called "Nick," and I soon ran onto a bunch of about twenty Arapahos. I turned Nick's head for the adobe houses and had no trouble in keeping a safe distance ahead. After a while the Indians either became suspicious of an ambush or became discouraged, and they fell back—all but one fellow, who was bolder and better mounted than the rest. I let him think he was gaining upon me until I got him far enough away, and then I began to circle around him Indian fashion, and presently he began the same tactics, and out there on the prairie we fought it out, circling about at full speed, all the time drawing closer and shooting to kill. After a few shots, the Arapaho reeled from his horse and fell to the ground. I rode to him and, dismounting, took off him a medal about three inches in diameter which he wore around his neck. On one side it had the image of Lincoln, and on the other a representation of an Indian village. That was all I had time to take, as the rest of the band, hearing the firing, was hastening to the rescue. Nick soon got me beyond the danger line, and although I gave them every encouragement to follow, the Indians came no further.

My next experience of importance was not so fortunate for me. It happened on Prairie Dog Creek, in Phillips County, Kansas, near where the city of Phillipsburg now stands. Bvt. Maj. George A. Armes of the 10th U.S. Cavalry, with two depleted troops of the 10th, two companies of the 18th Kansas, a train of thirteen wagons, and a number of pack mules, set out from Fort Hays on August 21, 1867, ostensibly to hunt for a large body of Cheyenne and Arapaho Indians who were reported to be camped on the headwaters of the Solomon and Republican Rivers. The real object of the expedition, I have every reason to believe, was Armes's desire to get to Fort McPherson, where the woman in the case was located. At all events, our course was laid on a beeline for that point.

On the night of the twenty-first, a night march was made. When we started, Captain Armes sent me out on the left front with instructions not to get more than a half mile from the command, and if I found Indian signs, to come in and report.

It was a beautiful night, and all went well until we got near the breaks of the Prairie Dog, in the after part of the night. Then I saw signal arrows going up, the object of which I well knew. I reported to Captain Armes, who said that he did not apprehend that there was any considerable body of Indians in that vicinity, but he ordered the train to go down to the right and go into camp on the Prairie Dog, some five miles from where we were, with a guard of sixty-five men under Lieutenant Price of the 18th.

I was sent out on the left front again, Captain Armes telling me that he would move directly north and if I saw further signs to report. In the course of an hour or so, I found fresh signs and plenty of them. I turned to the right for the purpose of reporting to Captain Armes and kept riding on, although I thought it strange that I did not meet up with him. Thinking that I might have gotten farther from the command than I intended, I kept on until I rode into the camp of Lieutenant Price and the wagon train, just about daylight. I afterwards found that Captain Armes had turned sharp northwest and passed behind me to the left. I got breakfast with the train, and while talking with the lieutenant, a detachment of ten cavalrymen from Fort Hays came in with orders for Captain Armes to return there with his command. I took this detachment and went up the Prairie Dog until I found the trail of Captain Armes's command. That was about noon. Meantime, we had picked up enough stragglers to make twenty-seven men, including Captain Jenness of the 18th Kansas, who, having gone out for a little scout with a few of his men, had succeeded in getting lost. I am aware that Captain Jenness's account of what followed,[3] both as to location and incident, differs materially from mine, but I think that the captain is as badly astray in his narrative as he was that day when I found him and his companions on the banks of the Prairie Dog; besides, there is enough glory in it for all of us just as it happened.

Captain Jenness, being the ranking officer, was of course thenceforth in command. We took the trail and bore north up a tributary of the Prairie Dog about a mile. Here the trail bore to the right, away from the creek,[4] and we stopped to water our horses. Mine had finished drinking before the rest, and I rode out on the bank of the creek and looked the field over with my field glasses. Half a mile away was a band of at least 300 Indians come for us full tilt. I called Jenness and handed him the glasses. He ordered the soldiers to mount and follow him. I caught his bridle and called his attention to the fact that not all of the boys were well mounted, and that in a run for it, only a few of us would get away. He saw the point at once and ordered the soldiers to form a hollow square and fight up the trail. The Indians fought in their customary way, dashing past at full speed and firing at us. We kept them off until we came to a place where the trail led down into a depression. Here we planned to get across part at a time, one division remaining behind to cover the crossing of the rest. However, the Indians pressed too hard, and we all got down into the depression at once.

At this point, several of the men were badly wounded, and I myself got two bullets in the calf of my right leg in quick succession. Finally we got out of this hole and had gotten about a half mile up the trail when we saw a cloud of dust in front, and the boys, thinking it was Captain Armes's command to the rescue, began to cheer, but out of that cloud of dust came a whoop that made us think the devil had turned all his imps loose. It was another body of about 400 warriors, who had been repulsed by Captain Armes and, hearing the firing down our way, had come to help finish an easier job.

※✦※

Olathe (Kansas) *Mirror,* March 26, 1931

Now we had to fight back over the same ground amidst a rain of bullets and arrows. As it began to get dark, the Indians made a desperate attempt to finish the job, and at times got almost among us. Finally we reached a dry canyon running down into Prairie Dog Creek. By this time we had one man killed and fourteen wounded. I told Jenness that our only salvation was to turn loose our horses, that is, all of them that had not been killed. We turned loose all but two of the best.

The Indians for the time seemed to forget about us and grabbed the horses within fifty yards of us. As they rushed in a bunch, it was like shooting quail, and before they had time to realize what had happened, we poured several volleys into them. They hurriedly withdrew, and this gave us time to get our wounded and ourselves into the canyon, where behind the banks, we fought them off. They then went down and attacked Lieutenant Price at the wagon train.

We dressed our wounds as best we could. Captain Jenness was shot in the right thigh but fought on just the same, as did all the wounded men who were not entirely disabled.

We remained in this canyon until morning,[5] when we made a wide detour and crossing the Prairie Dog at least three miles below the camp, crossed the first ridge of hills, and went up to a point opposite the train, where I left them and started to the camp for help. At daylight the Indians had resumed their attack on the wagon train. I waited until they withdrew to prepare for a charge, and made a run for it on one of the horses which we had kept. The reds saw me and gave chase, firing a hail of bullets after me. My horse fairly flew, and as I lay over his side, I heard the bullets singing above me like a swarm of bees. I reached camp without being hit, but I was convinced of the old doctrine that you can't kill a man before his time. Later Captain Armes came up with his command, and Captain Baker of the 18th took his company, and we brought in Captain Jenness and the men from the hills. I dressed my own wound, which was very painful, and although my leg was very much swollen, I rode that evening and night to Fort Harper with Captain Armes's report to Col. A. J. Smith,[6] a distance of seventy miles. I would not have done that, however, had not Armes taunted me with being afraid to go. I went, but that report and what I told Colonel Smith about Captain Armes got that gentleman court-martialed a little later.

In September 1867 I was at Medicine Lodge Creek, where Colonel Thomas Murphy[7] was trying to round up the Indians for a grand powwow and preparing for the coming of the commission, which came soon afterwards, consisting of Generals Sherman, Harney, and Sanborn, and Commissioner of Indian Affairs [N. G.] Taylor, father of Senator Bob Taylor of Tennessee. Most of the big chiefs were there. Satanta and Kicking Bird, chiefs of the Kiowas, [and] Roman Nose, chief of the Arapahos,[8] were among the most prominent. Roman Nose was the finest specimen of manhood I ever saw. He was over six feet in height and built from the ground up. There was a natural impressiveness and dignity about him such as I have never seen in any other man. He was graceful even in the way he wore his blanket. I heard him make a speech which was both eloquent and forceful. I remember particularly his references to what had been said about the "Great Father at Washington."

"The Great Spirit is my father, the earth is my mother, and some day I will lay myself down on her bosom, still fighting the white man." He made good, for I saw him killed at the fight at Beecher Island just about a year later, and no Indian could desire a more dramatic finish than he got.

Little Raven of the Arapahos became a great friend of mine during the two weeks I was at Medicine Lodge Creek. He took a fancy to my horse Nick and would ride him proudly about during the day, returning him to me promptly at nightfall. He offered me six mules for Nick, but as the mules had "U.S." branded on them, I declined. Finally he offered me his daughter and membership in the tribe, but I diplomatically declined that also by telling him that he was making too great a sacrifice and that I was as loath to take too much as too little for Nick, and as Little Raven could not make the exact change, the trade fell through.

After leaving Medicine Lodge Creek, I went to Dodge. Arriving there, I bargained to carry an important dispatch from Washington back to the peace commission, which was then due at Medicine Lodge Creek. They wanted it to go by the short and dangerous route south of the Arkansas River instead of the long and comparatively safe route via Larned.[9] Thinking I could make the ride in a night and a part of a day, I took only one feed for the horse and myself, besides the usual pound plug of navy tobacco.

Next morning I ran plumb into Charley Bent's village of Cheyennes. Charley Bent was the renegade son of Colonel Bent by his Cheyenne wife, Owl Woman, and for being disowned by his father, had sworn to take the old man's scalp. But he was perfectly willing to take the scalp of any white man who gave him the opportunity. I had a good mount, furnished by the government authorities at Dodge, where I left Nick, and I ran for safety.

Charley Bent's Indians chased me seventy-five miles south, across the Cimarron River, and once got close enough to shoot a chunk out of my hat. They kept me out five days. There was grass for the horse, but my plug of navy tobacco was all I had. I could have shot buffalo and antelope, but I did not dare. The second night out, there was a terrible storm. It thundered, rained, and hailed. The buffalo stampeded, and with them ran every animal known to the prairie. Everything seemed privileged to run except me. That I was not run over and trampled to death was only one more confirmation of my faith in the doctrine of predestination. On the fifth day I rode into General Sherman's camp, fifteen miles from Medicine Lodge Creek, and delivered my dispatch.

I was with Maj. George A. Forsyth and Lt. Fred Beecher, nephew of Henry Ward Beecher, at Beecher Island in Arikaree River, in Yuma County, Colorado, in September 1868, when fifty-one of us were surrounded by a thousand Northern Cheyenne, Oglala, and Brule Sioux under Roman Nose. This terrible battle began on September 17, 1868, and the siege lasted nine days. All the horses were killed the first day, and putrefied horse and mule meat was all the men had to live on during that time. The most dramatic incident of the battle was the charge of Roman Nose and his warriors.

Roman Nose believed that his life was charmed and no bullet was ever made to kill him, and this made him unmindful of personal danger.[10] The charge began about 10:30 A.M. Roman Nose had on a magnificent war bonnet, and his Indians were in full war paint, their scalp locks braided with eagles' feathers. Roman Nose led the charge, spear in hand. Yelling like exulting demons, they dashed straight for the island.

Jack Stillwell and the scouts at the east end of the island poured a deadly fire into them from their rifle pits, dug with butcher knives, but on they came, yelling like devils and firing as they came. As they reached the middle of the island, the main body of scouts at the west end opened fire. Roman Nose's spear fell from his hands, [and] he grasped convulsively at his horse's mane to keep from falling. His braves gathered round him and held him on his horse, and thus they carried the great chief from the field under a deadly fire from our own rifle pits. Thus he kept the promise which I heard him make a year before at Medicine Lodge Creek. The island, which was nothing but a sandbar at that time, was covered with blood. Dead men and horses were scattered in every direction. Half our men were killed or wounded, and our surgeon was crazed with his own wound. Young Beecher was mortally wounded and died that night, and lies buried at the foot of the monument which now stands on the island.

That night Jack Stilwell and Pete Trudeau left camp with instructions to reach Wallace, 100 miles away, for relief. On the third night, no relief having come, Forsyth sent Jack Donovan and myself out. We robbed two dead Indians of their moccasins and stole down the bed of the river under the willows and grass. Out on the prairies, we discovered our mistake in taking the moccasins. The cacti which covered the ground pierced the wet leather and inflicted painful wounds. We had to tear up our shirts and tie up our injured feet. We traveled by night and hid in buffalo wallows by day. We suffered for water and lived on rotten horseflesh, with which we had filled our pockets before leaving camp.

When we reached Fort Wallace, we found that Stilwell and Trudeau had been there and gone with Captain Bankhead and a relief column three days before. Donovan tried to find Captain Carpenter, who was out on a scouting expedition, and I started to hunt Major Brisbin, who was reported to be near the mouth of the Frenchman's Fork of the Republican River with two companies of cavalry. I rode eighty miles that night and intercepted him. Strange to say, Donovan found Captain Carpenter's command and led them to the party at Beecher Island, arriving there at 10:00 A.M., September 25. An hour and a half later, Major Brisbin arrived. Captain Bankhead, with Stilwell and Trudeau, did not get there until twenty-six hours later. After finding Major Brisbin, I returned to Fort Wallace with dispatches for General Sheridan at Fort Hays. Of the four scouts who went through the lines at Beecher, I am the only survivor.

Shortly after the battle of Beecher Island, I went to Topeka, and when I got there, Governor Crawford sent for me. To my surprise, he showed me a letter from Gen. Phil Sheridan asking him to make me a captain in the 19th Kansas Cavalry, then being organized to fight Indians in the Southwest with Sheridan and Custer and his famous 7th Cavalry. I got my commission before I left the statehouse. I have always thought that Major Forsyth did not forget me and asked Sheridan to write that letter.

The Story of the Beecher Island Battle

ELI ZIGLER[1]

Robert Lynam, ed., *The Beecher Island Annual: Sixty-second Anniversary of the Battle of Beecher Island, September 17, 18, 1868* (Wray, CO: Beecher Island Battle Memorial Association, 1930): 61–66

The first night, we camped on the little bottom on the north side of the river opposite Beecher Island on the Arikaree, as we went into camp early on September 16, 1868. The game had been pretty scarce the last few days, and we were about out of rations. We unsaddled our horses and picketed them out to graze, and built our fires and went to rustling our suppers, such as we had. As we were pretty tired after supper, we kept pretty quiet and saw nothing until about dusk, when we saw a signal light go up south of us and a little east, and then we saw more go up in different directions, so we were pretty certain we would have more for breakfast than we had had for supper.

We kept pretty good watch out, and the major put on more guards that night and ordered us to be ready at any moment, but I thought there would not be any danger until daylight anyway, and as my horses and Mr. Culver's were picketed out close to the river, we took our blankets and went out close to our horses and spread them down, and said we would wake up early in the morning before there was any danger; but we did not wake quite as early as we expected we would, and they came a little earlier than we had expected them and woke us up.

I believe I heard the first whoop they gave, but I was so sleepy I thought it was a flock of geese; just then the guards fired. I gave a jump and said to Culver, "They are here."As we were all dressed and our revolvers and cartridge boxes all buckled on and our carbines lying by our sides, we were ready for action as soon as we raised up.

It was hardly daylight yet, but we were so close we could see them by the flash of their guns and ours. Culver and I made for our horses as they rode by; they were whooping and yelling and shouting and shaking their blankets to make a stampede. I don't believe there were many went past on the side where Culver and I were—probably six or eight, and the next thing I saw was a few of our horses going over that little raise out of the bottom with quite a little band of Indians closed in behind them. I think most of the stampede went on

176

the north side. They came from the east and came together on the west of us. It was still dark, and that was as far as we could see them.

We all rushed our horses together, and the major ordered us to saddle up, so we saddled up. There were no more orders given just then, so we went rustling for a little breakfast, and when we had got that it was quiet light, and our major and lieutenant and chief scout were standing together on a little higher ground watching the movement of the things. We could see the Indians scattered all around us and quite a number of little parties riding down the river on the south side at some little distance away. We kept firing at them now and then. Culver, George Clark, and I, and one or two others were standing close together watching them.

There soon was quite a stir. It seemed as if the whole valley kind of raised, and then they commenced riding and whooping around there, and in a movement they all started down the river. Our commander moved us across the river to the island. I tied my horse to a bush, then I looked around to see what spot I would take, and I saw George Clark and Farley and a couple of others running across the river; they got behind a bank on the north side, so I thought that would be a good place to go. As I started the Indians made a charge down through that way, so I had to stop. I stopped where there was a little bunch of brush and a few horses tied; some of the horses were hit by the flying bullets and commenced charging and jumping, so I had to get away from there.

I started again, thinking that maybe I could cross. Just then the major saw me and asked me where I was going. I told him I was going across the river where Farley and some of the boys were. He said, "You can come with me; I want you on this side." We went a few steps toward the east; the Indians were making another heavy charge from the southeast, and he said, "We will have to get down here," and as we got down on our knees, he said, "Hold your fire till they get close." As we shot a time or two, I heard something strike, and the major said, "I'm shot," and put his hand on his leg and said, "They hit me in the leg." He turned over a time or two and said, "I am shot again." I told some of the boys that the major was shot, so they came, and the first chance we got, we carried him farther in, near the center of the bunch.[2] He said, "My lieutenant is shot too, and Sharp will have to take command."

The command was given for every man to dig holes in the sand and make breastworks [in] what time we had to spare, and to hold our fire and not shoot until they were close to us, and hold our ammunition, for we knew we had a long fight in front of us.

We all went to digging when we could and shooting when we had to. I moved a little south of where we left the major and got down and tried to dig some, but they kept coming so fast and so close that it did not seem that there was much chance to dig.

About the time I had dug a hole that I could partly lie in, I heard Tucker say, "I'm shot through the arm and I would like to have someone tie this handkerchief around it to stop the blood." John Haley[3] was nearer to him and went to tie the handkerchief around his arm, but before he got it tied, a bullet struck him. I told him to come over where I was and I would tie it up. He came over, and we both got down together, and before I got it tied up, an arrow struck him in the leg. I pushed the arrow on through and finished tying up his arm. I told him to take the old hole I had and make it a little larger so he could get into it, and I would find another place.

I started north toward the river again, passed by where the major was lying, thinking I might yet get across the river, but just as I came to where Jack Donovan was lying behind a little bunch of grass with a little sand thrown up around, he said, "Where are you going? You'd better keep down." I said I thought I could get across the river where Farley and George Clark were, but he said, "No, you stop here. One of us can dig while the other shoots, and we will soon have the hole big enough for both of us," and I have always been glad that I stopped there, because I believe that Jack was as good and grave a boy as we had on the island. He was very cheerful and cool and certainly did good work, but made me do most of the digging.

Our location was about on the northwest corner of our pits, and it gave us a fine chance at them. I know of several that we made good Indians out of on the upper end of that little bottom we camped on, for when they got on the island, they were so close. They rode back and forth north of us on the island all the afternoon. We got word about noon from across the river saying they were all wounded. The Indians had been riding between us and them all afternoon, and we supposed they were all dead before night. Our last horse fell about soon, and some men among the Indians shouted in plain English, "There goes their last damned horse." We knew from that there was a white man or two with the Indians and probably urging them on the harder.

It was a very warm day, and the sun beat down upon us hot; we had had nothing to eat or drink all day; a well had been dug near us, but we could not get to it, so we had to hold out the best we could until sundown.

About dark the Indians fell back and quit fighting. One of the party came from across the river and said the rest were alive but badly wounded; we went over and found them. Farley's leg was badly broken, and we carried him over. We then counted up to see how many were dead and how many wounded. A number of the boys were very badly wounded. This weakened our little party considerably. We first cared for the wounded the best we could, and then prepared our supper. We had plenty of it, such as it was. We built small fires in the rifle pits, and then went to the horses and cut off small pieces and roasted them; we had to eat it without salt. I made out a very fair meal, but I don't know how the others liked it.

After supper we held a council to decide what was best to do. We knew that the Indians would try either to starve us out or wait until we ran out of ammunition, so we thought our best show was to try to send a dispatch to Fort Wallace. It looked almost impossible for anyone to get out, but Jack Stillwell came forward and volunteered to go if they would let him pick a man to go

In the rifle pits. HARPER'S NEW MONTHLY MAGAZINE 1895.

with him. The major talked with him and told him it looked nearly like certain death to start on such a trip, and thanked him very much for his bravery in volunteering his services in such a dangerous mission. Stillwell chose Pierre Trudeau to go with him, and as Pierre was older and a good Indian fighter, the major agreed. Trudeau said, "I will go with you, Jack. We have never yet got into a place that we could not get out of, and I think we can go through with this." The major then wrote a dispatch to Fort Wallace. Jack was the best imitator of an Indian that I ever saw, so they fixed themselves up as Indians as best they could, and took off their boots and tied some rags and blankets on their feet, so that if the Indians saw their tracks next day, they would think it some of their own party and not follow them and try to head them off before they got to the fort. We went to work while they were getting ready and roasted them some horse meat, enough to last three or four days, as we thought it would take them about that long to get to the fort. At a late hour, they gave us their hand and crawled out. We listened, expecting to hear them run into some Indians and fire, but we heard nothing.

The next thing in order was to fix our rifle pits. We had been keeping in our holes as much as possible; we commenced digging to one another so as to connect them all together, and by working hard all night, we got all connected together and enlarged our hospital, as we called it, where we kept the worst wounded. As we had our well, we cut off a few hams from the horses and got in a little wood, so we would be prepared for the next day. Not having had any rest or sleep, we were not all in the best of humor, but as we expected company early, we commenced our roasts, so as to have breakfast over and dishes washed before they got there.

They did come early—just before the sun rose. It seemed to me there were just as many and as bad as the first day, and the squaws took their places on the hills just the same as the day before. Our orders were about the same: "Hold your fire till they get close, but don't let them ride over us."

We were in a good deal better position and could all be together, which gave us a better show than we had had the day before. It seemed to me that the Indians were more determined than ever to get us out, as they charged in from every direction and it seemed to take more than one volley to stop them. A great many times their commanders urged them hard to try and ride over us, and while they were making these hard charges, we would have to raise up to check them; then their sharpshooters in the grass would pour in a deadly fire upon us, but we always succeeded in turning them around and leave several behind, so finally they thought they would try some other plan to get us out. They stopped fighting and sounded the bugle and put up a white flag, but most of us were too old to be scalped alive that way, and we showed no signs of a white flag, so that did not last long with them. They soon commenced again and poured in on us as hard as ever the rest of the day. After sundown they fell back and camped around us as they had done the night before. When we summed up the day's work, we had one man killed and one wounded, so we got off easy from a hard day's fighting, and I think we broke their backbone that day. We heard nothing from Stillwell and Trudeau, and feared they had not succeeded in getting through. Jack Donovan and friend attempted to go out the second night, and after having been gone three hours, returned saying they could not get through the Indians' line.[4]

We went out and cut some more steak off our horses; it was not quite as fresh but more tender, and we made our supper out of this as best we could. We had not had any sleep and very little rest for the last two days, so we took turns at sleeping and watching, so we fared better that night than we had the night before.

The next morning about daylight, a smaller party of Indians charged down on us. There were not as many as the other two mornings. We laid low and let them come close, then we raised up and gave them a couple of volleys and started them back. As Roman Nose and their medicine man had been killed, they had started with a powwow instead of that sharp war whoop. They continued their fight all day, but not as strong, I did not think, as it had been the other two days. The fight continued until sundown, and again they fell back as they had the previous days and quit fighting. As soon as it was dark, we commenced rushing our supper. When it was good and dark, the talk was again about Fort Wallace. We still did not believe that Stillwell and Trudeau had got through. So Jack Donovan and Pliley said they would try it again. The major talked to them as he had to the other two and wrote a dispatch. They fixed themselves up to imitate the Indians as well as they could, as the first two had done. We cut them off some of that poor, rotten horsemeat, enough to last three or four days, and at a late hour they crawled out.

Some of us tried to nap again while the others kept watch. The night passed quietly, and we heard nothing from Donovan and Pliley.

We got up early the next morning to look for something to eat. Our horses lay just where they were shot down the first day and were getting pretty badly spoiled. The smell was not very pleasant, but our appetites were good, so we made out a fair breakfast.

The Indians commenced fighting a little later, and there did not seem to be nearly so many of them. They did not come so close, and there were more small dashing parties. We could see no squaws around, so we were sure they were moving out their families anyway. The most we feared then was that they had captured the two parties we had sent out for relief, and that they would gather reinforcements and come back on us.

We skirmished along with them all day. By night the Indians had nearly all disappeared. We got our supper from the same source, only now it was a little more tender. More of us lay down to rest that night and put fewer out to guard, as everything seemed quiet, and we rested pretty well that night.

In the morning when we arose, the Indians' campfires were all out, everything was quiet, and no Indians were in sight. We rustled around for our breakfast, which still came from the same place and was getting very tender by this time. After breakfast we moved out around the island and could see a few Indians scattered around over the hills at a distance to show us that they still were on guard. We kept close to the island that day, and it passed quietly. When night came, we could see nothing more of the Indians, and we again rested well considering our circumstances.

On the morning of the sixth day,[5] everything was quiet except the howling of the wolves, and [the] sour horsemeat was so rotten and alive with maggots we thought we would try to find some game or something to live on, so we rustled out a little and found nothing much but prickly pears. We soon found out that they would not do entirely for food, so we lingered along on our old butcher shop until the eighth night.

We had heard nothing of either party we had sent out and thought it nearly time for them to return if they had succeeded in getting through. I stood guard the latter part of that night, so it was a little late when I got up the next morning.

After I got up and was sitting by our little campfire, Fletcher Vilott came up and said, "Eli, let's take a little walk and see what we can find." I told him I had not been to breakfast yet and for him to wait till I could rustle something. So I went to the old slaughterhouse, and after looking over several, I found them all of the same material and the same price, so I cut off a slice and laid it on the coals and roasted it and ate it; then we took our guns and started north across the river.

When we got across the river, Fletcher said to me, "There is going to be a chance today, that is why I wanted you to take a walk with me. I wanted to tell you about it."

"What makes you think so, Fletch?"

"Well, I'll tell you. Last night I had a dream."

"Well, I don't care nothing about your dreams. I don't believe in dreams anyway."

We walked on up toward Squaw Hill. Fletch was telling me his dream. He said either the Indians were coming back on us or we would get relief. As we got nearly to the top of the hill, we came to a big rock and sat down a moment to rest. Fletcher was still telling his dream. He looked way over to the south on the far hills and asked, "What is that?"

I said, "That is some rock—some more of your dream, Fletch."

He said, "All right, you will see before night."

We sat there talking a few moments; my eye caught an object on the far hills to the south. I said, "There is something moving out there."

He said, "That is what I saw."

We jumped to our feet and walked up the hill a little farther, where we could plainly see that they were coming over the hill toward us. As some of the boys were out trying to find something to eat, we fired a shot and motioned them in toward camp. We could not make out what it was, so we hurried back to camp to make ready in case it was Indians. We reported in camp that there was quite a large force of something coming over the hill from the south. The major said, "I think it is the relief, but get the men all in and we will be ready for anything."

We hurriedly got things into shape. I thought there were two of the boys out of sight around the hill to the south of us, so I went across that way. In a short while, I saw a man at full gallop. When he got a little closer, to my great surprise, it was my old friend Jack Peate.[6] He asked, "How are the rest of the boys?" And I said, "Have you got anything to eat?" He reached in his saddle pockets and brought me out a hardtack and a little piece of bacon about an inch thick and about two inches long. Then he put spurs to his horse and rode on to the island.

I followed him up as close as I could, thinking he might drop another crumb that I could pick up. I suppose you people think you have had something good to eat in your life, but you never had anything as good as that was. When I got there, the boys were laughing and cheering, and the tears were running down their cheeks. Peate said that Donovan was coming right back there, and Captain Carpenter and his command, and that there were ambulances and wagons and plenty of provisions. In a very few moments they drove in, and soon we all had our mouths full of raw bacon and hardtack, so we could hardly speak. I think that was the happiest time there ever was or ever will be on the Arikaree, and as the wounded had been lying around suffering with their wounds nine days without treatment, it was pretty hard for them to keep from breaking down. There were plenty of doctors, and they encouraged them and went right to work to dress their wounds. We still lay in our pits right among the dead horses; the scent was so bad that we had to be moved right away. They moved us right out on the high ground south of the island and put up tents and made the wounded as comfortable as possible.

That night they amputated Farley's leg, and he died soon after. Some of the colored troops sang a few songs. We went to bed early, and as there was no guarding for us to do, we passed the night very quietly, except those who had eaten too much.

We stayed there a couple of days so that the wounded would have a chance to get a little stronger before starting for Fort Wallace. During that time, John Stillwell led in his command,[7] so that made a large command, and when the wounded were strong enough, we started for the fort. We camped the first night on the South Fork of the Republican, and then continued our journey. Our wounded stood the trip fairly well, and we left them in the hospital at Fort Wallace.

Scout John Hurst's Story of the Fight

JOHN HURST[1]

Robert Lynam, ed., *The Beecher Island Annual: Sixty-second Anniversary of the Battle of Beecher Island, September 17, 18, 1868* (Wray, CO: Beecher Island Battle Memorial Association, 1930): 68–73

My Dear Comrades of the Battle of Beecher Island:

I have been requested to write a letter to help make up your annual, which will contain a brief account of my life just previous to the battle, an account of the battle, and my life just after the battle. I must state right here for the benefit of the general reader that the battle of Beecher Island was fought September 17, 1868, by Maj. George A. Forsyth and his company of fifty men on one side, and a great band of Indians of different tribes, estimated at one thousand, on the other side, commanded by the noted chief Roman Nose of the Sioux tribe.[2]

During the Civil War, I enlisted in the 1st California Volunteer Infantry and served three years. The greater part of that time was spent fighting Indians in Arizona and New Mexico, and I was mustered out of service September 21, 1864, at Los Penos, New Mexico, and immediately started across the plains for Kansas by ox train, which was returning after unloading their freight at Fort Union. They were glad of our company, as the Indians were on the warpath. We arrived at Fort Leavenworth just after the noted Price's raid through Kansas[3] and went to work for Uncle Sam driving mules, which were then used in hauling supplies to frontier posts, and continued in that business with more or less scrimmages with the Indians.

I joined the scout sometime the last of August 1868 at Fort Harker, Kansas. Love of adventure, which is inherent in all American frontiersmen and becomes kind of a second nature, prompted me to go. If I remember correctly, we went to Fort Wallace with eight days' rations[4] and four pack mules, which were loaded with the doctor's medicine boxes, axes, shovels, and picks. We made a circuitous route as far north as Beaver Creek and followed that up some distance, and then bore south to Fort Wallace, where we rested for a few days. We were hurried away on account of a party of Indians making an attack on a freight train, killing two men and running off some stock. The train was encamped between Fort Wallace and Sheridan. Sheridan was about four miles east of Fort Wallace[5] and at that time was the terminus of the Kansas Pacific Railroad, and all freight going west was hauled from there by wagons.

As soon as the news of the killing reached Fort Wallace, we started in pursuit with six days' rations. We found their trail and followed it up for some time, but soon lost it on account of the Indians scattering, as they generally do, when they do not want to be followed; however, we kept traveling north, as that was the direction the trail went as far as we found it, thinking that we would run onto some trail or Indians, but saw nothing until we reached the Republican River. After scouting around until the morning of the fourth day, we found a small trail running up the river, which we followed until evening, when we went into camp. The trail continued to grow all the time by other trails leading into it. Next morning we started on the trail, which kept enlarging, and soon we discovered the trail of the lodge poles; then we knew that they had their families with them. The lodge poles are strapped on each side of the ponies, one end dragging on the ground, and their movables are fastened to the poles behind the ponies.

On the fifth day, the trail kept enlarging. Some of us became somewhat concerned as to the wisdom of following such a large party of Indians, knowing they could not travel very fast with their families and we would therefore soon overtake them, and we knew that they would fight desperately for their families, and our company being so small, we would likely get whipped. We made known our anxiety to Major Forsyth, who asked us if we did not hire with him to fight Indians. That ended the matter but did not convince us as to the wisdom of the course. We went on in silence until the evening of the fifth day out, when we went into camp early on the north side of what we thought was the south branch of the Republican River, but which proved to be Arikaree Creek. It was a beautiful place opposite a small island.

Aside from the trail we were following, we saw nothing that would indicate there were Indians in the country. A sure sign, say old Indian fighters, that they are planning mischief. Divine Providence, I think, had a hand in our camping there, as well as in a great many other incidents connected with the battle, which I will now try to give the reader as I remember it.

I was on guard the night before the battle, and Thomas Murphy[6] was my partner. We had what we called running guard; that is, in place of being on duty two hours and off four, half of us stood the forepart of the night and half the after part. Murphy and I were on

The defiance of Dry Throat. HARPER'S NEW MONTHLY MAGAZINE 1895.

duty the forepart. We cooked some beans for the fellows that were to
relieve us and had a good square meal to go to sleep on, the last
meal we had for nine days. We lay down with our saddles for pillows and our guns at our sides, and were soon fast asleep, not knowing the danger that threatened us. The next thing we heard was the
guards shouting "Indians" and shooting off their guns, which awoke
all; we grabbed our guns and got onto our feet in quick time. We
could see three or four Indians driving off three or four of our horses
that had gotten loose in the night. Major Forsyth gave orders to saddle up, which we did, and were standing by our horses awaiting further orders when some of the men got permission to drive off some
Indians that were hiding behind rocks on the side hill north of us.
When they got onto the high ground, they shouted to us to look up
the creek, and by this time the Indians were in full view, and such a
picture! It would be grand to look at in the moving picture show, but
to know that they were after our scalps, it was appalling. All were
mounted on their war horses, in war costume, with feathers and
plumes flying, shouting the war whoop, their horses running at full
speed and seeming to have partaken of the spirit of the fray. Was it
any wonder that some of our men were overcome by the sight? But
there were only three. I sometimes wonder that there were not more,

but thank God the rest of us measured up to the duty of the hour.
There is an old saying that such things try men's souls, but you must
experience them to fully know the meaning. This terrible trial
brought out latent heroic qualities which many of our men did not
know they possessed, fortitude which enabled them to bring into
action all their energies for our defense and protection.

We soon took in the situation and knew that we would be no
match for that army of red men in the open, and as we were close by
the small island before mentioned, which was covered with long
grass and scrubby trees, Forsyth gave orders, at the suggestion of
Jack Stillwell, to move onto the island. I do not know how the order
affected the other men, but to me it was the most welcome and
timely one I had received. We made a grand rush for the island,
without order, and tied our horses to the trees. Some ran across to
the south side and crouched down in the long grass at the roots of
the small trees and were hardly located when the Indians were
charging through us. Comrade Armstrong[7] was close by my right
and another comrade on my left, each one by a tree. John Stillwell
and his party were on the east end of the island, Jack Donovan and
his party were on the west end, and some were in the central part, all
pretty well hid, and all shooting when the Indians came in close
range. It was a great surprise to our enemies how we got out of sight
so quickly, and our bullets coming from all directions seemed to
bewilder them. One of their ponies, whose rider had been shot, came
among our horses, stayed with them, and was shot down with ours.
After many charges and attacks upon us, they changed their tactics
and tried sharpshooting, and when they could not see men to shoot
at, they shot our horses. When the last one fell, one of them shouted,
in good English, "There goes their last damned horse."

About this time in the fight, our dear Surgeon Mooers was killed,
and also Lieutenant Beecher. It was unfortunate that some of our
men were located near the horses, as it brought them in range of the
bullets coming from a certain direction that were intended for the
horses. Thereby some were killed and many wounded. Major
Forsyth stood up giving orders until shot down twice.[8] The last order
I remember him giving was "Men, dig holes in the sand and make
banks for protection." A warrior coming from the north almost ran
over me, and would have but for his horse shying to one side, which
saved me, as the Indian had to make extra efforts to keep his seat
until he was past me. It rather surprised me, as my attention was
directed toward the south, and [I] did not see him until he was right
near me. However, I was glad his horse took him away from me, for
had he fallen off his horse, it would have meant death for one of us;
but as he rode straight away from me, I had a good chance to shoot,

which I improved immediately, and while I did not see him fall, I think I must have hit him.

My near neighbor, Armstrong, and the other comrade were both wounded in the early part of the battle and ran to the other comrades, which made me feel rather lonely. I was afraid the Indians would get between me and the other men. There was much shooting on the east end, and I thought it was the Indians, as I did not then know that Stillwell and his men were there. I kept close watch that way and soon saw an Indian creeping through the grass toward our horses, then I felt sure that the much shooting was done by the Indians and [that] they were closing in on us. The idea proved to be erroneous, but I am giving the reader my impressions, and this conviction was burned into my memory, never to be forgotten. I thought then we would all be scalped, and I think this belief was quite general with all the comrades. Major Forsyth called out and wanted to know if anyone could pray, for he said, "We are beyond human aid, and if God does not help us, there is no help for us." But no one responded. I have thought since, in the light of subsequent events, what an awe-inspiring thing it would have been to the Indians if a man of God had broken out in loud appeal to the Great Spirit for help. This thought came from the answer that the wife of Roman Nose made when taken prisoner about a year after and asked why they did not rush in and kill all. "Oh," she said. "We thought the Great Spirit was protecting you, and we were afraid." Divine providence again! Well, I did not want to be scalped out there on the island alone, so fired at the Indian that I saw creeping through the grass, and without waiting to see the effect of my shot, jumped up and ran to where some of the comrades were located. Some had dug holes and made banks of sand around them, and some were using the dead horses for protection, and so I dropped down beside an unoccupied dead horse and went to digging with my hands and throwing up the sand. Digging was easy when we got through the grass roots, and I soon had a place large enough to sit up in. While I was busy digging, comrades McCall and Culver came in and got down beside another dead horse and went to work digging. They had not been there but a short time when the comrades on the inside of the circle shouted, "If you fellows on the outside don't get up and shoot, the Indians will be charging us." McCall and Culver got up to look for Indians to shoot, and some sharpshooter fired at the exposed heads. The bullet grazed McCall's neck, stunning him for a short time, and hit Culver in the head, killing him. That was the last exposure of heads made during the fight.

About this time in the fight, comrade Harrington[9] came in covered with blood from head to foot, and with the head of an arrow sticking in the top of his head. One of the comrades tried to pull it out and could not, but strange to say a bullet knocked it out during the fight. Comrade Burke[10] then came in and dug a hole nearby us, and kept digging until he came to water. He filled his canteen and passed it over to the next, and so on until it was emptied and passed back again and refilled, which was done many times until all in reach had been supplied. Water at that time was a boon to us, especially to the wounded, who had become feverish and very thirsty. Burke then told us his experience. Somehow he did not get onto the island with the rest of us, and during the fight he saw an Indian some distance away— too far, he thought, to make sure of him, but as there was a hummock between him and the Indian, he thought he would crawl to it, and then he would be sure to hit the Indian. He crawled along until he reached the hummock, and raising himself, almost bumped noses with the Indian, and it so surprised him that he did not know where he was. He punched his gun at him, shouted "Boo," and ran for us. He said he thought the Indian ran the other way, as he did not hear him shoot.

Well, we were in a pretty hard place, not knowing how soon we would be scalped, but the way that droll Irishman told his story made us laugh.

The next excitement we had was the white flag held up by the Indians. We had quite a controversy over the question of recognizing it and concluded it would not do to trust them, as they might take advantage of the armistice and rush our lines, but it might have been all right, for there were two of their warriors killed so close to our lines that they did not dare attempt to get them away, and as they hated to have their dead fall into the hands of the enemy, they might have taken that way to get them, but at that time we did not know there were any of their dead near us. These two warriors had been shot by Louis Farley as he lay on the north side of the stream with a broken leg. They were in full view of him as they crept along a ridge of sand made by the water where it divided to go around the island. Both were shot through the head, and each had a rifle and bow and quiver full of arrows. The killing of these two warriors had an intimidating effect on the rest, and so stopped that mode of warfare. I believe it was divine providence that Louis Farley did not get onto the island with the rest of us.

After the white flag incident, the fight was renewed with sharp-shooting but no more charging across the island. The songs of their women, which in the early part of the fight were joyful and exultant, expecting victory, were changed to sorrow and lamentation for the loss of their fathers, brothers, and husbands. Night came at length as a welcome shadow to hide us more securely from our enemies and enable us to care for our wounded comrades. It was a dark, rainy night, and our first work was to get the wounded all in and dig a place for them; the next was to get the saddle blankets and make as good beds for them as the material would allow. We dug a large square hole, which we called the hospital, and placed all the wounded there. We then secured the cartridges, which were in our saddlebags, and cut the hams of our horses and hung them on the limbs of the trees to dry, for that was all we had to live on until we got relief. In that climate, beef hung in the open air would soon dry, so that the flies could not harm it, and [it] would keep indefinitely. Next we dug trenches connecting all the rifle pits. Major Forsyth called a council to determine what was to be done. Our guide was Sharp Grover, and Major Forsyth inquired of him the prospects of sending men through the Indians' lines to Fort Wallace for reinforcements, a distance of about one hundred miles. Grover said it was impossible to get through and went on to tell how the Indians did in such cases.

We all stood there listening to the dark picture he was painting. When he got through, Jack Stillwell spoke up and said, "If I can get someone to go with me, I'll run the risk." A comrade by the name of Pierre Trudeau said, "I will go with you, John." Major Forsyth wrote a dispatch to Captain Bankhead, commanding officer at Fort Wallace, and then, turning to Grover, wanted to know if wagons could be brought directly across the country from Fort Wallace to us. Grover told him that the country was so rough it would be impossible, and Stillwell was directed to come by way of Custer's Trail, which ran directly north from Fort Wallace to the Republican River, and then follow the river to us, which made a distance of about 130 miles. This accounts for Stillwell being so long on the road. Sharp Grover was the man that should have volunteered to go, but he was afraid to risk it, and the description he gave of the country was all wrong, for we returned to Fort Wallace with all our wagons straight across the country. We expected to get relief in about six days, and when our scouts left us, we just settled down to business, for we did not know what the Indians might do before morning, so [we] kept diligent watch all through the long night.

The next day was a day of watching; no fighting, but some shots by sharpshooters, and when night came, Major Forsyth thought it wise to send two more scouts to Fort Wallace, not knowing whether the others would get through or not. Two men volunteered, but I do not remember their names;[11] they could not get through and came back. We watched another night and another day, and when the third night covered us with its mantle, Forsyth called for two men to go to Fort Wallace. Jack Donovan and Captain Pliley started with directions to come back straight across the country with a few soldiers, an ambulance, doctors, and such supplies as we needed. Their experience has been told in other articles, and I will not attempt to give them here further than to say that after many privations in the way of sore feet, hunger, and thirst, they succeeded in getting through.

Donovan started back the next day with the ambulance and a few soldiers. Pliley was so used up that he could not travel.

While the scouts were making their way to Fort Wallace, we were having a serious time on the island. The Indians left us after the fifth day, and some of the comrades were prompted to advise saving our lives by attempting to strike out for Fort Wallace and leaving the wounded to their fate, thinking the scouts had never reached their destination. When the talk of abandoning the wounded came to Major Forsyth, he called us together and made a nice address. It was very touching and soldierlike, so much so that I never heard another word about leaving the wounded. Our dried meat gave out in six days, and we had nothing then but our horses that had been dead six days, and when we would cut into the meat, we found it had green streaks through it and was fast decaying. The only thing we could do was to sprinkle it with powder while it was cooking, which partially took away the bad odor, but we could only eat it when we were starving. We had no salt, and our systems were crying for it. One of the men found a small piece of pork rind in his haversack and chewed it until he thought he had all the good out of it and spit it out, when another comrade took it up and chewed it for a while and spit it out, and then I took it and chewed it up and thought it tasted delicious on account of the salt. On the eighth day, we made quite a march around the camp and found a prairie-dog town, but none of them came in sight, and I made up my mind that I would come up in the morning and try to capture a dog. The next morning being the ninth day, I went out to the dog town and watched it for quite a while, but no dog came out. I had kept up pretty well until this time, but I began to think I would starve to death and was having the blues pretty bad when I started back for camp. I had not gotten far when I saw some of my comrades running towards me and motioning to me to come to them, and the thought that Indians were coming took possession of me, and I started to run as fast as I could but soon got tired and thought they would surely get me before I could make camp, so I thought I might as well die fighting, and turned around and sank down on the ground and saw three horsemen coming directly toward me, but I thought they did not look like Indians, and the closer they came, the more they looked like white men.

It proved to be Jack Donovan with a relief party. Well, I never was so glad to see the face of a friend before or since, and the sudden transition from despair to safety was too much for me, and I wept like a child. We had great rejoicing in camp that day when the relief party came to us, for Donovan had run into Captain Carpenter on his way back and brought him directions from Fort Wallace to go to the relief of Forsyth. The poor wounded comrades got the medical aid they needed so much, but one of them was too far gone. Louis

Farley, the old hero, died after his leg had been taken off. If I remember correctly, we stayed three days after the relief party came before we started for Fort Wallace. Stillwell arrived the next day after Donovan, so we had a great company to escort us back.

On the first day's march home, our advance guards came onto two Indians, one riding a pony and the other walking. The walking one saw us first and shouted to his pal; when he saw our men so close to him, he whipped up the pony and got away; our men got the one that was on foot. We found thirteen fresh graves on scaffolds on the first stream of the Arikaree. In due time we arrived at Fort Wallace, where we were received joyfully and had the freedom of the fort. General Sheridan issued an order to give any of Forsyth's men any position they were qualified to fill in the Quartermaster's Department. In a few days I went to Fort Harker and secured the position of wagonmaster, and hauled goods and camp supplies all winter while Custer was operating farther south. I ran this train for two years, until 1870, when I went into the police force in Hays City, where I was ambushed and shot by a man named George Clinton and have been a cripple ever since. Clinton was caught and hung by the vigilantes. I was taken to [the] Fort Hays hospital when shot and was treated by Dr. Delano, the army surgeon, for three months. As soon as I was able to travel, I came home here to Ogdensburg, New York, and lived here until 1873, when I went to Renville County, Minnesota. I married an old schoolmate and lived here until 1881, when I moved with my family back to Minnesota on my old homestead, where I lived until 1900, when we came back here, and here I expect to live until I hear the last call. I am seventy years old, and with the infirmities caused by my wound, I am pretty well used up.

And now, my dear comrades, and all who read these lines, I wish to add a few words to what I have already written about God having a hand in the battle of the Arikaree. At the time of the battle, I was like Samuel, the judge in Israel, when a boy. I did not know the Lord, but the Lord knew me, and knew that I would believe and be saved, as I hope He knew a great many more of my comrades would believe and be saved; therefore He interposed and saved us from the Indians.

And now, my dear comrades, while I would love to meet with you and all the good people who meet there to commemorate the battle, circumstances will not permit, and while we may never meet again on earth, I hope through the atoning merits of Jesus Christ to meet you all where parting will be no more.

Your old comrade,
JOHN HURST

An Interview with Scout John Hurst

WALTER M. CAMP[1]

Mss 57, Box 4, Walter M. Camp Papers, Interview Notes, Special Collections and Manuscripts, Harold B. Lee Library, Brigham Young University

An amusing incident happened to Martin Burke. He did not succeed in reaching the island before the Indians were upon us, and lay under cover, fighting as best he could. Finally he saw an Indian crawling along in broad view about two hundred yards off, and wanting to make sure of getting him, he decided to crawl up to a hummock, from which he thought he could get a better shot. Accordingly, he began crawling up toward the hummock on hands and knees, very cautiously, and when he got to the hummock, he cautiously raised himself up on his hands to take a look, when to his surprise and consternation, the Indian on the other side of the hummock was in the act of doing the same thing.

Both were frightened at each other, and evidently discomfited also, for instead of shooting at the Indian, he merely poked his gun at him and cried, "Boo," then took to his heels as fast as he could and ran to the island, where the rest of the men were. He did not look back to see what had become of the Indian, but hearing no shot from that direction, presumed that the Indian had run the same as he did. Whenever Burke would tell this story of himself, in his comical way, it always created laughter.

I heard no command to go to the island, but when Jack Stillwell said he was going there, we all went instinctively, as it were. After the Indians had ridden through and the guard had fired at them, and some of our stock had stampeded, we began to look around in all directions for Indians. Finally someone saw a few Indians up in the hills to the northwest, and two or three of the men asked Forsyth [for] permission to go up there and chase them out. Forsyth consented, and no sooner had these men gotten up where they could overlook the valley than they shouted to us to look up the creek. As we did so, we suddenly beheld the whole force of Indians mounted and coming down upon us. It was at that instant that we, as one man, started for the island.

We walked to the island leading our horses. My horse having been wounded, I was riding a mule that hung back and did not lead well. I kept pulling on him and letting out rope, and when I got to the first tree, I had got to the end of the rope. I just managed to get enough of the rope flung around the sapling to tie it, as the mule held back stubbornly, and then at once saw that the tall grass on the island was in our favor. I saw Indians going around to the south and thought I ought to crawl that way, where I could shoot out of the tall grass, and did so.

The first Indian I fired at was on a horse coming directly toward me. I took careful aim and fired, but noticed that he did not fall from his horse. The next Indian I caught sight of came near riding over me, and would have done so if his horse had not swerved. I think the sudden side motion of his horse prevented him from firing at me, for he had a gun in his hand and the sudden action of the horse seemed to momentarily throw him out of balance. He went on past me, and I took good aim and fired, but he also did not fall off his horse.

While this was going on, I heard a lot of firing to the north of me and wondered whether it could be that of white men or Indians. All of a sudden it dawned on me that if it were the firing of Indians, I might soon be cut off from the rest of the party, and just then a skulking Indian came along, and I concluded the rapid firing to the north of me must be by Indians, so I blazed away at the Indian. Not waiting to observe the effect of my shot, [I] ran as fast as I could and came to a group of about a dozen near some horses still standing. It occurred to me at this moment that it was a dangerous place to be in, as the horses were drawing the fire and were fast being shot down. I jumped in behind a dead horse and began to dig up sand to protect myself from the other direction. My cartridge box was in my way, and so I took it off, and in my haste to burrow in, I covered it up. While I was digging, McCall and Culver had dug in beside another dead horse that lay almost touching the one I had taken refuge behind.

When I got dug in, I called to McCall and asked him how he was doing, and he replied, "McCall is wounded." I then asked for Culver, and he said that Culver was dead, in a voice so faint I could hardly hear him. I had thought he was joking and reminded him that we were in no situation for joking, when he assured me that he meant what he said.

In my haste to dig in, I had thrown off encumbrances, and among these my cartridge box, and had covered it up and did not dare to pull down my fortification to look for it. I then said that if Culver was dead, he [McCall] might throw over to me his cartridge box, and he flung it over to me.

About that time, some of the men called out that the Indians were getting thick around us, and that if we did not rise and fire more rapidly and drive them off, they would soon be running into us. That was how Culver was killed. He would rise up to get shots at the Indians, and thus exposed himself. After the Indians left us, there were not enough able-bodied men among us to carry off the wounded, and we had to stay.

The steaks that we at first cut from our horses and hung up to dry lasted six days and were palatable, but when these gave out, we had to eat the putrefied meat of horses that had lain dead six days and more. The only way we could do this was by sprinkling it with gunpowder and roasting it in the coals.

After the Indians quieted down, we took shovels and dug connecting trenches between the pits we had scooped out in the early part of the fight, enlarging these pits. We took the blankets from our horses to make beds for the wounded, and took all the extra ammunition from our saddle pockets and prepared for a siege.

When Forsyth the first night inquired of Sharp Grover, the guide, as to the chances of sending word to Fort Wallace, Grover magnified the danger all he could, saying the Indians in such cases would be on the watch, and that no one could get off the island. Grover pictured the situation as darkly as he could and seemed to be discouraging any attempt to send word for relief.

After his talk was over, young Stillwell spoke up and said he didn't care how alert the Indians might be—if someone was willing to accompany him, he would go. Old man Trudeau at once spoke up and said he would go with him, and Forsyth at once gave consent and began to plan the trip and to write dispatches.

I must frankly confess that this readiness of Stillwell to go on such a dangerous mission at once raised my estimate of him very much. He had been a gabby fellow, apparently careless in his ways, and he was the man I would least have expected to volunteer for such a dangerous mission. When he showed himself not only willing but eager to go, I thought to myself that Stillwell after all was a much worthier man than I had ever taken him to be.

Scout Schlesinger's Story

SIGMUND SCHLESINGER[1]

Robert Lynam, ed., *The Beecher Island Annual: Sixty-second Anniversary of the Battle of Beecher Island, September 17, 18, 1868* (Wray, CO: Beecher Island Battle Memorial Association, 1930): 75–82

To relate my experiences while a member of Forsyth's scouts during the fight with Indians on Beecher Island in September 1868, I am obliged to refer to the tablets of memory which Father Time may have somewhat obliterated, and if my recital should seem contradictory in some respects, it must be attributed to this fact.

At my home in New York City in 1865, at the age of sixteen years, I was engaged by a merchant from Leavenworth, Kansas, and taken by him to his western home. I remained in his employ as clerk for over a year. At this time the Union Pacific Railroad was being built across the plains. The end of [the] track reached Junction City, or Fort Riley, when rumors of fruitful trading with the railroad builders and military guarding the workers influenced me to join the throngs drifting towards the frontier along the surveyed line of proposed track. From Junction City, we traveled by wagons to a settlement called Salina. When I reached this place, the citizens were preparing to defend a threatened Indian attack, but the rumor seems to have been a false alarm.

From there, after a time, I moved with the tide along the grading of the proposed railroad. This was a new country. Towns sprang up overnight. Communities moved houses and effects in a few days to any locality that seemed promising to become the end of track and a prospect for trade with the railroad employees. I found employment of various kinds and natures. I was clerk in a clothing store, barkeeper in a tent liquor house, waiter in a tent hotel, clerk in a grocery, shoveled on the railroad, cooked for a mass of teamsters, night herded mules for contractors, and teamstered driving mules hauling stone from a quarry. In this latter occupation, I had my first experience with Indians. I obtained this job of mule driving from contractor Fish at Fort Hays because he wanted me to vote for him in an election, the nature of which I did not understand, but I voted as directed.

One day I was ordered with the team to take some woodchoppers to Big Creek about twelve miles east of Hays. About this time, there was no general outbreak of Indians, but occasionally rumors reached the settlement of small bands attacking travelers or isolated settlers, evidently on pilfering bent. No general alarm was felt; my party had guns and revolvers, but were not provided with ammunition. I was driving alongside of the railroad up an incline nearing our destination at some distance to the other side of the summit, where a troop of cavalry were stationed to guard this portion of track workers. In my wagon box were seated the woodchoppers talking and joking. One of them was sitting on a hardtack box and by this means had a higher view of the surrounding country. All at once he called our attention to some moving objects several miles away. It was not very long before we could discern that those were mounted Indians coming our way at a rapid gait. Needless to say that the scare nearly paralyzed my senses, and that I was impelled to lay the whip in no gentle manner on the backs of my mules, urged on by my companions. We soon reached the top of the incline, the Indians, about one-half dozen of them, coming fast. We started downward toward Big Creek, yelling with all our might to attract the attention of the soldiers at their camp. When we were about halfway down the incline, the Indians reached the top and began to shoot, their few bullets raising the dust as they struck the ground around us, but the soldiers, being attracted by our commotion, suspected trouble. Quickly mounting, they came full tilt towards us, and their proximity to our predicament saved us. The Indians moved off leisurely, and we watched them disappear around the bluffs.

I do not remember the succession of events as they happened from time to time, but gradually I became acclimated. When I came to Hays, there were very few buildings up; the most prominent was the J. D. Perry house, a big barnlike building. Most of the housing was in tents. The day I arrived, most of the townspeople were out on the prairie watching William F. Cody chasing a buffalo and bringing him down with his rifle. We gathered around the carcass, from which came my first meal of buffalo meat. Here I entered upon several ventures, such as a bakery with a capital of a few dollars. I procured a piece of tent cloth and a couple of store boxes and fitted up a storeroom. About a dozen loaves of bread and as many pies represented my stock. A few of each were sold, the rest eaten. This wound up the business. I obtained a recipe to brew beer, which I brewed in a wash boiler on a wood fire on the open prairie, the product proving a menace to the health of venturesome customers. With others I hunted coyotes one winter. I peddled papers among the soldiers of the 7th and 10th Cavalry and railroad employees. Colonel Custer was one of my customers, also "Wild Bill" Hickok, who was one of the finest gentlemen I met on the plains. By these means I became acquainted with some of the government scouts at Fort Hays and of other posts, whom I sometimes accompanied on their trips of carrying dispatches between military posts and camps.

One winter's day, I took a construction train to the end of the track about seven or eight miles west of Hays with papers, magazines, etc. The day was very stormy and no train went back, so I had no alternative but to remain overnight. The sleeping quarters in the cars for the men were all so full that I could find no room. I obtained permission from the head cook to sleep on the floor of the cooking car, where they were baking and cooking all night for the three hundred or four hundred employees. The floor was wet from the water they used, also from melted snow that blew in under the sliding doors of the car. So in order to overcome this inconvenience, I piled up cordwood, one stick alongside the other and two for a pillow. I slept all night on this contrivance with an army overcoat for covering. Next morning the number of sticks I was sleeping on could, by the ridges, be counted on my body. This was the hardest bed I ever had.

I also worked on a wagon train plying between Forts Hays and Dodge. On one of these trips, we camped on Walnut Creek about thirty miles south of Hays. Here we were visited by some Indians who came begging for coffee, sugar, or anything in the line of grub. We were told that there was a large Indian village in the vicinity, which was an incentive to break camp sooner than intended. Later I understood that the following fall a portion of these Indians were of the attacking party upon Major Forsyth at Beecher Island.

In the summer of 1868, I was entirely out of funds, living on hardtack and coffee most of the time, going from camp to camp looking for something to turn up, but no chance for employment came. About this time, Major Forsyth was organizing a company of frontiersmen to scout for Indian warfare. I eagerly sought an engagement and succeeded through the influence of C. W. Parr, post scout at Fort Hays. His interest in my obtaining membership in the command was due to the fact that the pay of scouts, who had their own horses, was to be $75 a month, and those who drew horses from the government were to receive $50. Parr loaned several of his own horses to a few of the men, myself among these, for which he drew $25 per month of our pay.

Although I had no military experience, I was fairly well inured to prairie life, acquired by my two years of knockabout on the frontier, so that the prospect of this campaign did not deter me from entering cheerfully upon the expected adventure, perhaps because I did not know what was coming. When Forsyth's command left Fort Hays for the first scout of the country, we started in a northwesterly direction, Lieutenant Beecher acting as guide. We traveled all day, except a short rest for lunch, and did not go into camp until we reached the Salina River late that night. I will never forget this first day's ride. I was not used to the saddle; my equipment, consisting of carbine, revolvers, saddlebags, roll of blankets, etc., were always where they should not have been. I could not adjust them so they would be comfortable; my horse would not stay with the column, but forged ahead, being a fast walker, causing me to be ordered back into line several times. My bridle arm became stiff and lame in the effort to obey; every bone in my body began to ache; the ride and the day seemed never to end, and with every mile of travel my misery was bordering on torture. I was chafed by the saddle, and some parts became swollen to twice their normal size; my gun would never stay in place, and to add to my troubles, my clothes became wet from a drizzling rain, making the skin tender where belts attempted to hold the equipment in place. At last we reached camp. I was too exhausted to enjoy my supper, and to cap the climax and fill my cup of misery to the brim, I was detailed for guard duty. But human nature could stand the strain no longer; the old saying in ordinary phrase "I'm tired to death" proved a literal exemplification in my case. I was directed to my post, but no sooner left to myself than I dropped to the ground and fell asleep. If there had been thousands of Indians around us, my physical condition could not have prevented them exercising their vocation, and I can solemnly declare that I was not disturbed by anybody all night in an attempt to relieve me, and the suspicion still abides that all the rest of our comrades must have had troubles of their own. But it did not take many days for everybody, myself included, to become so hardened and fit to meet emergencies incidental to life on the prairie.

After being out about a week, we rode in a southerly direction towards Fort Wallace without any incident. Those of us that may have been apprehensive about the danger of meeting Indians became reassured, and the scout assumed the nature of a pleasure outing.

One day we were descending into a valley, traveling in an irregular formation, Indian fashion, when we beheld in the bottom a camp of haymakers. They were spread out in the valley at their work. When they discovered us, they took us for Indians, as they had no idea that white men in such numbers were within many miles of their camp. We watched them hasten to their camp and make ready to corral their stock. Major Forsyth at once ordered two or three of our men to hasten forward to inform them of our identity. The man in charge was Charley Christy, known to many of our company. Their pleasure was great to have us as guests, and we, too, were glad to partake of their hospitality. When we left this camp, we had to ascend a hill. As we proceeded, we noticed heads of men peering from behind the brow of the hill. We suspected them to be Indians. At an order from Major Forsyth, we at once charged up the hill at a gallop. When we reached the top, we found some haymakers returning from Wallace. They were ready, corralled to receive the supposed Indians. In our charge, one of our men was thrown by his horse and was injured to an extent that he had to have medical attention when we reached Fort Wallace and could not join the command when we were ready to take the trail again. When we left Fort Wallace, refreshed and provisioned, it was under orders to relieve a Mexican train at Sheridan that had been attacked by Indians. Two men joined our company. Jim Curry, whose name does not appear anywhere as a member of Forsyth's scouts or as a participant in the battle at Beecher Island, but he was with us, of that I am sure, for I was well acquainted with him and knew him better than anyone else.[2] The other was Abner T. "Sharp" Grover, who assumed the position of guide for the command. He just had recovered from wounds received from Indians in an encounter in which Bill Comstock,[3] the noted scout, and he had participated, and in which Comstock was killed.

How we left Fort Wallace and arrived at the scene of the attack on the Mexican train; how we took the trail; and incidents leading up to and reminiscences of the battle of Beecher Island, I have already described in a letter to

Rev. Cyrus Townsend Brady, which he published in his book, *Indian Fights and Fighters.* When I looked at the two dead Mexicans at Sheridan, killed in an engagement, looking death in the face, my mind seemed as on the brink of the infinite, and to still the flutter of the heart required the greatest self-control. Our enterprise included such possibilities, however, and I determined to do my best regardless of what might happen.

We were too late at Sheridan, and after losing the Indian trail next day, we continued our scout into the northern country, where there was no road or defined trail, scanning remains of old or recent campfires on the lookout for Indian signs, hunting buffalo and antelopes for food, but otherwise without incident, until finally our flankers reported finding signs of a trail. This we took up and followed until it became so distinct and broad that there was no longer any doubt of a fight ahead. Everybody was on the *qui vive.* Remarks of possibilities as to numbers of Indians, when and how we would come into contact, and probable results were debatable subjects under discussion. Some of the older and experienced scouts made predictions to which I at least (the most inexperienced) gave attentive ear, and everybody was tense in expectation. Game was no longer in our path, and hunting was inadvisable, so our meals became very circumscribed, and as we rode hard and steady, our horses, being too tired to graze much at night, became fagged, so that on September 16, 1868, Major Forsyth decided to camp on a spot that looked inviting as to good grazing much earlier than usual. The circumstances undoubtedly proved to be an act of providence. Had we traveled about a half mile further, we would have fallen into an ambush, ingeniously prepared, and the scheme favored by topographical formation of the country, so that had we passed that way, not a mother's son would have escaped alive, but we were ignorant of the fact at that time.

The next morning (September 17, 1868), we were awakened long before daylight by a commotion among our picketed horses and pack mules. When fully awake, we found that a band of Indians had attempted to stampede our mounts and had succeeded in driving off a portion of our stock. We realized that this act was merely the beginning of our trouble. We were camping on the north bank of the Arikaree River, opposite a flat plateau which formed an island by the overflow of the river in flood seasons, being dry at this time, and a sandy bottom. Major Forsyth and his advisers, Lieutenant Beecher, Sharp Grover, General McCall, Jack Stillwell and others, at once chose this island to be our best position to give battle. It was so situated that we were far enough removed from the zone of gunfire directed from surrounding hills. To reach us, the Indians had to come down nearer to our level, and here the sandy bottom proved our protection.

As we had expected, just about daybreak the plain to the west was literally covered with Indians forming leisurely for attack. It appeared as if they were sure of their prey, judging from the fact that they had their squaws and papooses with them, a circumstance unusual with Indians on the warpath. They placed them upon the north hill, where they could watch the battle and

The first attack on Beecher Island. W. F. BEYER, *DEEDS OF VALOR.*

enjoy the expected fun, and perhaps run in and participate in the finish. This contingent manifested their presence by chanting, singing, and other expressions of encouragement to their brave bucks. This was at the beginning of the battle, but as the fighting progressed, the scouts stubbornly refused to ratify the program of extermination; on the contrary, when they delivered the blow with most telling effect, even if they were outnumbered twenty to one; when their terrific gun play mowed down the bravest of the assailants, then the tone on the hill changed to wailing and lamentations. Human nature is the same in effect on the heart, be the outer coloring white or red. The sight of slaughter of our dear ones is grievous.

We were placed in position, lying flat on the ground, our horses tied to the brush in our center. The Indians, after showing off in massed formation, began circling around us, displaying splendid horsemanship. Soon thereafter they charged, and kept up those tactics all day. With every repulse, they seemed to gather new acquisitions and strength. The fighting began to tell on us. Every once in a while the cry went up that this one or that one was hit, and that Wilson, and later Culver, was killed. Our horses were being killed in rapid succession. The fierce attacks and repulses kept on. In the beginning of the battle, we began to dig in the sand, scraping holes with our hands, kicking with our toes while fighting, and eventually we dug trenches deep enough to afford partial protection from Indian bullets that poured into our camp like hail.

The first day's battle ended by the Indians withdrawing overnight. Our toll of the day was two men dead, two men mortally wounded, twenty more or less wounded, and all our horses killed. Next day was a repetition of the first, with the difference that there were fewer casualties among our men, due to the fact that we worked nearly all night to strengthen our trenches.

For four days the Indians kept charging in every conceivable way and from every direction, only to suffer repulses, until finally they realized the futility of trying to capture our position. They withdrew on the fifth day, leaving us more exhausted than they suspected, for we had no food other than meat cut from our horses, and this supply soon became putrid, yet we had to subsist on this ration for nine days. It became worse from day to day. The dead horses lying in the sun became softer, and oh, the stench! At last relief came, summoned by our four men, who were dispatched by Major Forsyth. They stole out of our camp at night and could only travel afoot at night to Fort Wallace. Forty-five out of fifty men composing Forsyth's command, of which number about half were wholly disabled or more or less wounded, were fortunate to be rescued from a siege, the parallel of which there are few, if any, to equal, according to the records in the annals of border Indian warfare, considered from a standpoint of men engaged, fifty scouts against an estimate of about a thousand Indians, both sides about equally armed.

I have often been asked whether I have killed any Indians, to which my answer must truthfully be that I don't know. The conditions were such, speaking for myself, that I did not consider it safe to watch the results of a shot, the Indians being all around us, shooting at anything moving above ground. At one time I threw a hatful of sand that I had scraped up in my pit to the top of the excavation, exposing myself more than usual, when a hail of bullets struck my hill of sand, almost blinding me! This will explain why I did not look for results!

My plan of observation was to work the barrel of my carbine, saw fashion, through the sand from the edges on the top of my hole downward, obtaining by these means a sort of loophole through which I could see quite a distance; also taking a general observation by suddenly jumping up and as quickly dropping back into my hole, which enabled me to take a shot, or as many as the size of the target warranted, without undue exposure and yet be in touch with the general situation. In such instances I have seen Indians crawl behind a knoll, and saw several times two horsemen drag a body away between them. Indian boys came from behind a knoll shooting arrows at us. I saw bodies of Indians both on foot and horseback coming toward us. These I considered good targets.

Only in one instance do I suspect of having done personal execution. In the south channel of the then dry creek was a tree trunk, evidently floated there by a flood. From this stump came many shots, to the annoyance of Lou McLaughlin and myself. McLaughlin was wounded and *hors de combat* for the moment. I employed my tactics of suddenly going up in the air and firing at the stump. After several shots, the sniping from that direction ceased. I have also seen an Indian, evidently a chief, standing on a high elevation a little south by west of our position, talking loudly and giving commands. He was in sight of all of us. Grover, who was in the next pit east of ours, and next to Major Forsyth, interpreted to us the chief's orders, stating that he wanted his young bucks to persist in charging, as we had only a handful of cartridges, etc. Grover yelled back at the chief, telling him in his language to "send on the bucks; that we each have a hatful, which we will give them." I have no idea who the chief was, nor do I remember hearing anybody mention names. I did not know who was in command of the hostiles, and therefore was unaware when a chieftain fell.

Owing to the fact that I considered it dangerous to remain long above ground at any one time, I was not in position to observe the behavior or doings of our men during action, so after our rescue and return to Wallace, I was surprised to learn that there were one among us who did not do his duty, and that Lane was discharged for cause. There was a peculiar incident connected with Lane in his pit. During the first day of the fight, a mule with a partial pack on his back got loose and wandered around the vicinity of our pits; he had several arrows sticking in his body and seemed wounded otherwise, which caused him to rear and pitch to such an extent that Jim Lane, my neighbor, and I decided to kill him. Upon being shot, he fell and lay between us. He served a double purpose as a barricade and food. Two or three days later, when Jim was cutting meat off the mule, he must have cut deeper than he intended, for he cut an intestine and received its full contents over himself, nearly filling his pit! This was one of the humorous incidents, but of course not to poor Jim, judging from the blue streaks in the air around him.

When the Indians left our vicinity after the fifth day of fighting, we improved the opportunity to leave our trenches and look around the neighborhood in search of some change of diet other than the rotting horse meat on which we had subsisted so long, and which began to tell on our bowels. One day, while searching for prickly pears, about half a dozen of us were climbing the hill to the north, and while about halfway up to the summit, we were startled by the sudden appearance of an Indian on horseback riding leisurely down the hill toward us. We perceived each other simultaneously. Only for a moment we looked at each other. He seemed as surprised as we. Like a flash he turned, and lying low on his pony, he whipped him to his utmost speed and soon was out of sight. When we first caught sight of him, he was no more than about fifty yards from the nearest of us. As soon as we recovered from our surprise, we began to shoot at the vanishing rider. Each of us fired at least twice, but strange as it may seem, he got away, and if he was hit at all, we never knew it, for when we got to the top of the hill, there was no sign of an Indian in sight. We did not dare to go too far from camp, therefore did not hunt, and there was no game in the vicinity outside of a coyote killed during one night, that had prowled and howled around our camp, attracted by our dead horses. We had nothing else but putrid horse meat for food, and would have been glad to feast on coyotes, as bad as their meat tasted, but they only appeared at night, and while we shot in the direction from where the howls came from, we were not lucky enough to make a hit, so we had no alternative but to continue cutting meat from the horses for our food supply, even if their condition was nauseating, until the ninth day, when Captain Carpenter came to our relief, augmented by Captain Bankhead the next day.

This most momentous event in the career of Forsyth's scouts I have described in my letter to Reverend Brady; only those that have faced death in a desperate cause can appreciate such a rescue and the joy of a new lease on life. The rescuers delighted in feeding us with the best they had, and their kindness continued all the way back to the fort, which journey we undertook as soon as our wounded were made comfortable for the trip over the rough prairie without roads. Some of us were given mules to ride, and the rest rode in wagons.

The first day's travel we reached the Republican River. Clark[4] and I were flanking on the left and reached the river a little ahead of the main column, there forming a flat plateau of about seventy-five to one hundred yards before reaching the riverbed. Here we camped that night. Before Clark and I descended to the bottom, we looked around and saw four Indians running towards three horses. Three of them jumped on the horses and in great agitation galloped away through the water to the other side of the river, and kept on to the south as fast as their ponies could carry them, leaving their companion behind, who ran after them, but of course could not overtake them. Before the three Indians had crossed the river, we noticed two or three of our company who were flanking on the right hasten down to the bottom towards the Indians. I don't remember what shooting was done, but about this time the main body of soldiers came upon the scene and swarmed down, surrounding the lone Indian, so that we two lost sight of him, and when we got there, we could not get near for the crowd. I heard that he defended himself bravely before he died, and that it was because his revolver missed fire that none of our men were hurt. Here also we found an Indian burying ground, which the four Indians evidently were guarding. There was one mound composed of stones piled up around a body, and this was covered with a buffalo hide. When this was removed, another such layer was revealed, but I could see no more, being crowded aside. Then there were about six or eight scaffolds composed of four poles stuck in the ground, and a buffalo hide stretched across to each pole, on top whereon lay a corpse fully dressed and wrapped in blankets. All the bodies were pulled down from their lofty perches. This may seem like a wanton sacrilege, but not to those who have suffered bodily torture and mental anguish from these very cruel savages. I had no scruples to roll one out of his blankets, which were still soaked in the blood from the wounds evidently that had caused his death, and appropriated the top one that was least wet. This Indian had on a headdress composed of buckskin, beautifully beaded and ornamented, with a polished buffalo horn on the frontal part and eagle feathers down the back. When I took this off, maggots were on the headpiece. I also pulled off his earrings and finger rings, which were of tin. He was so far decomposed that when I took hold of the rings, the fingers came along, and these I shook out! I also got his beaded knife, scabbard, and other trinkets. The blanket, one earring, and scabbard are still in my possession, but I had great trouble in carrying these things away, owing to the awful stench. No one would tolerate me near him. When I was mounted, I tied the bundle to the saddle girt under the mule's body, and when I rode in a wagon, I tied it to the axle, but in spite of these expedients, I had to put up with remonstrances until we finally reached Fort Wallace, where I immediately soaked my trophies in a creek, weighing them down with stones. At Wallace, we naturally were objects of interest to the populace, and our souvenirs no less so. My Indian headdress was an especial curiosity. Jack Donovan interceded for one of the officers and offered me $50 for the headdress, but I refused to part with it. Next morning it was missing from my tent.

We remained at Fort Wallace for some time. Major Forsyth, with our other wounded, were in the hospital doing well, we were told. A good many members of our company resigned from the command, and new recruits were taken in to fill the original quota, Lieutenant Pepoon[5] taking command of the reorganized scouts. I remained with this command and was on two more scouts with them. Nothing of importance happened, so I resigned and, at the earnest solicitations of my family, returned to my former home in New York City, and later moved to Cleveland, Ohio, where I engaged in the cigar and tobacco business.

My experience on the plains furnished a theme of many tales to the edification of my friends, and on several occasions incidents recalling my adventure presented themselves by contact with former participants of either direct or indirect frontier life. One incident in particular will no doubt be of interest. William F. Cody, who had obtained the soubriquet of "Buffalo Bill" since I had known him at Hays, and who sometimes called on me at my place of business when in Cleveland, gave a performance in the open for the first time on the show grounds. He had two camps, one for white performers, and one for the Indians. Thinking that perhaps I might meet someone in the white camp whom I may have known on the plains, I took a stroll in that direction. I came across one who seemed a typical frontiersman. I said to him, "Beg pardon, did you live in Kansas in 1868, and if so, do you know any of Forsyth's scouts?" "Yes," he said, "I was at Forsyth's rescue." His name was John Nelson. This information made him an object of great interest to me. I inquired about some of my former comrades and acquaintances, and after a mutually pleasant visit, he invited me to go with him to the Indian camp. Arriving there, he entered a tepee and asked me to walk in. Sitting on a buffalo robe on the ground was an old squaw surrounded by papooses. She was his wife. He said something to her in the Indian tongue, whereupon she looked up at me, grunted, started up towards me, and grabbed my hands. Although the manifestation seemed friendly, I got scared. She kept up her chatter in her language. I asked him what all this meant. He answered, "She is glad to see you, for she was on the north hill watching your fight with her people." He acted as interpreter, for she would not talk English, although she understood it. I invited them to come downtown next day after the performance. When they came, a bunch of them, my store was a place of curiosity to a crowd on the sidewalk. While at my place, the squaw and her husband had some conversation, at the conclusion of which he turned to me and asked me to do him a favor, which was to tell his wife who it was of Forsyth's scouts that wore a buckskin shirt. I reflected a moment and remembered that Jack Stillwell brought such a garment to camp before we started from Fort Hays. I helped him hem a seam around the collar. I informed Nelson that Jack Stillwell wore such a shirt, wondering what the inquiry meant, and asked the reason thereof. He replied, "Do you remember the three dead Indians your people scalped on the edge of the island? One of them was a relative of my wife, and a man wearing a buckskin shirt was seen to shoot and kill this Indian. All these years my wife and her people have been under the impression that I was with you during the fight, and accuse me because I happened to be there with the rescue party; and because I usually wore a buckskin shirt, that was conclusive evidence that I was the guilty one. It would please me much," he continued, "if you would testify to my innocence," or words to that effect. Of course, I cheerfully gave testimony without any compunction and expressed the hope that such little matters might cease to cause a bone of contention between two loving hearts. This was a sensational episode in which I was a corroborative participant in the establishment of connubial felicity after a lapse of about a quarter of a century. I was in correspondence with Jack Stillwell, and in my next letter I told him of the incident. His reply was, "If you have a chance, tell John Nelson to handle the truth more carefully, for I know him well." I never had the chance.

The Battle of the Arikaree

THOMAS B. MURPHY[1]

Kansas History Collection, Manuscripts Department, Kansas State Historical
Society, Topeka

The Forsyth scouts were made up at Fort Harker and Fort Hays in the summer of 1868. The occasion for this organization was the repeated raids and depredations of the Indian tribes on the frontier settlements, in spite of the peace treaty signed at Medicine Lodge the year previous.

This troop of brave Indian fighters, under the command of Maj. George A. Forsyth, consisted of fifty-one picked men, selected from available material stationed at these two forts on the western frontier, the western part of Kansas being at this time the front line of western civilization. Qualifications essential to acceptance into this command were indomitable courage, wonderful endurance, perfect marksmanship, and a knowledge of the Indian character, as well as the plains over which he roamed.

Major Forsyth had for his lieutenant F. H. Beecher of the 3rd Infantry, a particular friend of Forsyth and a nephew of the celebrated Brooklyn preacher Henry Ward Beecher. Our surgeon was J. H. Mooers, a man of ability both as a surgeon and as a fighter. First sergeant was William H. McCall, who had been colonel of a Pennsylvania regiment in the Civil War.

The expedition was fitted out at Fort Harker, and no unnecessary equipment formed any part of our supplies. No tents or wagons were taken; pack mules carried the commissary stores, which were of the simplest character. Maj. Henry Inman was quartermaster in charge of the Commissary Department as well as paymaster at Fort Harker at this time.

Each man was mounted on an excellent horse, his arms consisting of a breech-loading rifle or a carbine and a revolver, and in some instances, two. I myself had a trusty carbine and a Colt .44 pistol. In our belts we carried probably from fifty to seventy-five rounds of ammunition, and in our saddle pockets a reserve quantity, the general supply of ammunition being carried on pack mules.

On the first trip out, we worked between the Republican and Smoky Hill Rivers for several days, until our provisions gave out. Between the two rivers, we had investigated all tributaries of any size for signs of Indians, over a wide scope of country about one hundred fifty miles in length.

We then went to Fort Wallace for supplies. In a few days we went to Sheridan, then the terminus of the Union Pacific Railroad, where the Indians had recently made a raid. The redskins had all disappeared before we reached Sheridan. We went from here north until we were near the Republican River, then northwest until we came to the confluence of the three streams that make the Republican River. We crossed this and went across the valley and got on higher land. We found where an Indian village had been close to a big spring of fine water. All indications were that there was a large number of Indians, and that they had been there in camp all summer. This was in the center of a fine buffalo range, as far from civilization as they could get, not less than one hundred miles from any human habitation in any direction you could go.

We continued west on the north side of the river five or six miles. The trail crossed the North Fork of the river and went across to the Arikaree Fork. All indications pointed to the fact that a great number of Indians had recently passed over the trail.

When we found the summer camp, we knew that there was a large body of Indians, and in following the trail, facts corroborated this conclusion. To follow this trail without provisions was extremely dangerous. Our commander, Major Forsyth, proved to be unacquainted with the western country and Indian warfare in particular. We followed the trail until night and went into camp just north of the little sandy island. The last of our provisions had been consumed the preceding morning, so we went into camp and to rest, hungry and tired. To meet a large body of savages in our destitute condition was very unwise. There was a long hill or ridge just west of the camp; a rough elevation with some scrubby timber at the east side. Both elevations reached close to the south bank of the island, the space between the hills being about fifty yards, the open space running north, with slight elevation, on smooth ground. Our camp gave the Indians a chance to hold the scouts there with very little exposure.

In the early dawn of the morning of September 17, 1868, our little camp was suddenly aroused. With wild whoops, a small group of Indians rushed into our camp, making all the commotion possible to stampede our horses and locate our camp in anticipation of their attack soon to follow. Every scout was on the alert. We dashed to our picketed horses to quiet them and save them from stampede and loss. A stampede is always the Indians' customary preliminary attack. In this instance they were successful in driving off one horse and six pack mules, which later proved a most serious loss to us.

After pacifying and saddling our horses, we were standing in a group, holding our horses and awaiting orders. One man said, "What are we going to do?" Another answered, "We are going after those pack mules." At this, we looked up the river to the west and over the hills and saw Indians—hundreds of them—rushing toward us, their camp being about a mile above ours. It was

The Indians massing for the attack on Beecher Island.

CENTURY MAGAZINE 1893.

at this time that Jack Stillwell and I called simultaneously, "Go on to the island." Instantly every man made a dash for the island, only one stopping to mount, the other scouts leading their horses on the run.

That horde of savage Indians, nearly one thousand strong, had overlooked one thing, and that was they failed to anticipate any thought or desire of ours to occupy the island as a means of defense.

The Indians had divided their forces into two groups, the smaller one coming down from the west, crossing the river, and sweeping across the island to the northeast. The main body of Indians came down the open canyon from the north, between our camp and the island, and continued down the valley between the long line of hills running parallel with the valley on the west.

It is evident their idea was to surround us in our camp and thereby make short work of our annihilation. They had miscalculated their prey.

While we were in the little stream, that was about six times as wide as it is now, the water being shallow—not more than four or six inches at the deepest place—the Indians that crossed just west of where the monument now stands went on to the island, sweeping onto the east side, riding in a swift gallop and firing as they ran. They came upon the island from the west, then turned to the northeast side, right in front of us, while we were in the stream that runs north of the island. They kept up this movement until about two or three hundred of them had all passed and left a gap, which the scouts took advantage of and rushed onto the island, losing no time in doing so.

If the Indians had stopped there on the island while we were in the stream, we could not have been successful in securing our location, which we had thought of for defense—another instance of Anglo-Saxon ingenuity pitted against savage tactics.

Fortunately, not one of the scouts or our horses was wounded while getting onto the island. Providence seemed to be with us that day.

Upon reaching this little stronghold, we quickly tied our horses to the cottonwood saplings which grew plentifully on the island at this point, there being a fringe of willows growing on the outskirts of the island, which proved a great protection to the Indians, as it concealed their movements in the battle. We secured our horses in a group, as near together as we could, to form a circular enclosure which would afford us some protection in the fray, which was imminent.

Just here began one of the fiercest and most unequal contests ever waged in human warfare. The conflict was for the possession of this place, and was as fierce and furious as it was possible for both sides to make it, the firing being at very close range.

Soon after the battle began, our horses began to fall, and not many hours elapsed before they were all killed except one that had been tied about fifty yards from the main group. When this horse, the last of our fifty, fell, we heard someone from the enemy ranks say, "There goes the last damned horse, anyway." Whether this was from an Indian or from a white renegade among them, we did not know.

During the first hour of the battle, scout Harrington, with Pat [Martin] Burke, myself, and two others, were fighting from the shelter of a little bank when an arrow from an Indian close by hit him [Harrington] in the middle of the forehead and stuck fast. The man nearest Harrington[2] jerked the wood of the arrow out, leaving the spike intact, and within a few minutes a bullet hit the spike remaining and dislodged it. The blood from the wound flowed profusely down and over his beard and covered his face, body, and [flowed] into his shoes. Such a bloody man I never saw in any other battle or out. In spite of the annoyance and suffering occasioned by this, Harrington was game for the full day's battle and never flinched from duty on the firing line, but fought to the finish. When surgeons in the relief party, eight days later, dressed this wound, they found it infested with multitudes of screw worms. Such fortitude and nerve as displayed by this hero in the defense of civilization is worthy of the admiration of all. This brave man passed the declining years of his life at his home in Mountain View, Oklahoma.

For several hours this fierce and furious fighting continued. Then our savage foe perceived that we had some advantage in outwitting them in regard to occupying this strategic point.

Now came a lull in the fight; the Indians evidently decided to resort to heavy charges, thinking to crush us with numbers and combined strength in the savage onrush of their charges.

The great horde of Indians scattered about the hills; in our camp, which we had so hastily quitted in the early dawn; and all those about the valley had taken part in the attack of the morning. We had been able thus far to keep them back with the accurate work of our rifles and the grim hardihood of our men.

This lull was only a check to prepare for the charges to follow. The charges were organized in the little sand hills to the south of the island. Farther back in the hills, the squaws, with their wails and war cries, were using every means to get their warriors to the front and ready for the charge.

Roman Nose, reputed to be the most perfect savage chief in respect to physical superiority as well as cruel hate, wearing his great war bonnet of eagle feathers and heron plumes, crested with two shining black buffalo horns. Wearing his moccasins and a scarlet sash, and painted in hideous barbarity, [he] led the charge.[3] He urged his warriors on to furious onrushes, thinking to exhaust our ammunition.

The fact that their formation in battle front was in the nature of single file, the warriors dashing down upon us, one following another, gave the scouts a wonderful opportunity for their skill in marksmanship. With wild war whoops, riding as fast as their horses could run, they charged upon us at such close range that our rifles did a telling slaughter. Every charge proved a heavy loss to the Indians. Roman Nose, superb and wicked Cheyenne chief, fell leading his bravest warriors in their grandest charge. We could have executed double the fatalities in the ranks of our foe had it not been for our shortage in ammunition, for as they were driven off and shied off, we ceased firing to save our ammunition, which we knew would be badly needed before the siege was over. The charges continued up to midafternoon, when the Indians, after the loss of their leader, realized that they were getting the worst of their bargain.

When the charging ceased, the Indians fell back to sniping all around us. This continued until the darkness of evening made it impossible to shoot a rifle with effect. When the battle ceased, we immediately sought out our dead horses for the ammunition stored in our saddle pockets. I recall that I was aware of the extreme shortage of my own supply on my person.

We then took inventory of our little band to determine the casualties and relieve the suffering as best we could among our wounded comrades. Seventeen of our men were wounded and five were dead. Twenty-two of our little band of fifty-one out of commission, and five of them forever.

Our surgeon, Mooers, fell early in the battle, and our medical and surgical supplies had been left behind, so there was little we could do to alleviate the suffering of the wounded men. Lieutenant Beecher suffered a broken back and, after intense suffering, died a few hours after the close of the first day's battle. Major Forsyth received two severe wounds, one a scalp wound, the other a rifle ball through his ankle.

No man engaged in this battle knew the number of Indians killed except the Indians themselves. Only three dead Indians were left on the battlefield, and they were close together and so near the scouts that they could not be gotten away with their other dead.

The next day after the battle, a large number of Indians—warriors, squaws, and children—came up under a flag of truce. We made no reply but lay quietly in our rifle pits. They came within 150 yards of us and remained for a half hour at least, hoping to secure their three dead warriors. One of our men fired a shot at them. At this they rallied and seemed to be getting ready for another charge, but gave this up as they had had enough of a losing game. The loss of 360 of their bravest warriors—a fact I learned from their interpreter later—was a terrible execution,[4] proof that our plainsmen scouts were expert riflemen. I am confident the execution would have been doubled if we had not felt the necessity of saving our ammunition, our only lifeguard in this fearful contest for the mastery of the plains.

The loss by serious wounds of our commanding general from duty, of our lieutenant and our surgeon by death in battle, more than one-third of our command wounded, and all of our horses killed, left us in very bad straits, to say the least. And to this, add the lack of food, medical supplies, and tools, and you have a tragic situation. One hundred miles from the nearest help! Comrades whose suffering we had no means to alleviate! An ambushed foe all around about us! This was the grim situation for our men to face.

The next thing to do was to fortify ourselves as best we could for the siege we knew was to follow. The island was almost a clear bed of sand, so we dug out with our hands, the only tools at our command, the loose sand and made holes or pits to be ready for the morning. We worked throughout the night at our improvised entrenchments. The dead bodies of our horses had served us well as a screen or breastworks all throughout the battle, where they fell.

At dawn the next morning, a small band of Indians came upon the island to ascertain the strength of our position. They readily saw how we were fortified and made no attempt afterward to come upon the island, nor within such close range of our rifles. However, sniping was continued throughout the day; in fact, for the next two or three days. It was our fortifications that saved us.

Being without rations, the scouts had suffered about as heavy a load as they could carry. Fighting throughout the day with no food, and no supper the previous night, was telling on the endurance of the strongest.

The night following the battle was dark, cloudy, and rainy. The second night was also dark and stormy. The scouts were scantily supplied with clothing and bedding. We had nothing in this line except what we wore and carried on our horses. Being hungry and tired, we were in a pitiful condition to withstand the rain and storm, and suffered much from the effects of it.

Many of us divided our scant supplies of both clothing and bedding with the badly wounded men. I gave the only coat I had to a scout named Armstrong, who was severely wounded in the back. This left me with an ordinary army shirt for protection from the cold and rain these mid-September nights on the western plain. The two dark nights were greatly to our advantage in getting scouts out with messages for relief. However, we suffered much in our ill-protected condition from the inclement weather with our sandpits our only shelter.

During the two days following the battle, little was done in the way of warfare except the continual sniping by Indians on every side. The scouts kept on the alert, sending many an Indian to his happy hunting ground by means of our trusty rifles. We suffered few injuries from this sniping, as our fortifications, made with arduous labor the night following the battle, afforded us ample protection from the enemy's fire, for we observed all caution and kept ourselves concealed in our sandpits behind the breastworks of the bodies of our fifty cavalry horses that fell during the first half day of the battle.

On the third day, we saw on the ridge about a mile away a group of horsemen whom we knew to be Indians taking observation. Scout Louis Farley, raising the sights of his rifle, gave them a parting shot.[5] The Indians immediately beat a hasty retreat. Farley's aim was true even at that range. This was the last appearance of Indians during our eight anxious and weary days of waiting for relief from the fort. The remainder of the fight was for life from starvation, from infection, and [from] contamination.

An empty commissary is a hardship at any time, but to us, in our dire distress, [it] was appalling indeed. It was after breakfast of the morning we consumed the last of our provisions that we found the location of the Indians' summer camp, where they had been tanning robes and drying meat.

We followed the trail all day,[6] going into camp without anything for supper, and commenced the battle at daylight the next morning without anything to eat, and fought all day without food. It was endurance and reserve energy that carried us through. No time was there to try to secure any food that night or the day following, as our time was consumed in beating off Indians.

The third day we began to eat the flesh of our fallen horses, and were hungry enough to relish such unsavory food in our dire need. We built fires in our pits and broiled the meat. We had no salt nor seasoning for this meat from carcasses three days dead, but starvation must be avoided and our strength reserved for whatever was to follow.

After the departure of the Indians on the third day, we cut from the carcasses the meat and dried this, hoping to have enough to subsist upon until relief should reach us. The dried meat did not contain nourishment enough to satisfy our hunger, and too, our supply of this was exhausted two or three days before relief came, so we had to fall back upon the remains of the dead carcasses, such as the wolves and flies had left for us, and select the best of this putrid flesh. Such a ration was well nigh impossible, but life was dear to us. Some of our men tried eating the seed balls of the cactus growing on the island, but with very unsatisfactory results.

In spite of the fact that this was considered a big-game country, all living animals of food value were driven out except prairie dogs, and these, when shot, would fall back into their holes, so it was impossible to get them, our tools having been left in our old campsite. One man was successful in getting a yellowhammer; another, a prairie wolf, the meat of which was scarcely more wholesome than the putrid horseflesh which had been our daily ration while awaiting the relief we were trusting soon to come.

Jack Stillwell, one of the youngest scouts, a fair-haired boy of eighteen, and Pierre Trudeau went out the night following the battle with messages from Major Forsyth to Fort Wallace for help. We were in doubt about their safety or success in running the gauntlet of the watchful savages, and during the second night, two more men tried to get through, but came back reporting that they had run upon Indians close by.

On the third night of our siege, Jack Donovan and Pliley went forth with dispatches to Colonel Bankhead at Fort Wallace. Several hours out, they came upon an Indian herd near an Indian camp and met up with the Indian in charge of the herd. Donovan, knowing that dead Indians tell no tales, of necessity made short work of him and hastened on his perilous mission.

Time dragged heavily in our famished and suffering plight on the island during the last four days of our waiting for help. We spent considerable time in searching for food, but without success.

Being accustomed to scouting about the frontier with a small amount of food in my saddle pockets, I thought to investigate to see if by chance I might find some morsel of nourishment in my saddle pocket. To my great satisfaction, I found a small piece of bacon, probably two inches in length and very hard. I chewed this hard scrap of cured bacon until it was white, with scarcely anything left of it. I then tossed it into a sandpit. My friend, John Hurst, seeing it and noting its resemblance to food he so much craved, said, "I believe I will chew this awhile." He did so, and others of the scouts, observing the satisfaction derived from it, chewed on this poor bacon rind until a dozen of the poor fellows in turn had a chance at it. Such were the pangs of hunger that beset us in our siege.

The decaying carcasses of our one-time splendid cavalry horses made our location almost unbearable. Added to this tragic dilemma was the torture of our wounded comrades, whose wounds were badly infested with screw worms.

The burning heat of the September sun at midday was torture indeed to those of our fevered and languishing party who were unable to move about. However, the coolness of evening gave welcome respite to this hardship.

Jack Donovan, who had gone out with dispatches from Major Forsyth to the fort on the third night after the battle, was returning to us four days later. He came upon Captain Carpenter and his company of colored troopers twenty miles to the south of us. Captain Carpenter had received the information that we were surrounded on the Republican River instead of the Arikaree. Donovan piloted Captain Carpenter and his command to our little stronghold on Beecher Island, he being the first to reach us with aid of those who had gone for relief.

Reuben Waller[7] of Eldorado, Kansas, is the only living survivor of Captain Carpenter's 10th Cavalry. He is a man eighty-nine years of age, in excellent health and spirit. He says that had Captain Carpenter and his men been a few hours later, help would have been of no avail to the famished scouts.

Jack Stillwell and Pierre Trudeau, the first messengers sent with dispatches by Major Forsyth, arrived at Beecher Island in the evening after Captain Carpenter's arrival in the morning of September 24, 1868. Stillwell conducted the wagon train with supplies, ambulances, and several companies of soldiers from Fort Wallace under the command of Colonel Bankhead. A small relief party from the Platte River arrived the same evening.

The wounded, suffering, and emaciated scouts were cared for as well as possible by the surgical and medical staff of the rescue party. They were removed from the contaminated atmosphere of the island to an eminence overlooking the valley. Tents were erected for their comfort, food provided, and after another day of rest prepared to return to Fort Wallace. The wounded rode in ambulances, the rest of us in government wagons, with the exception of a few of the scouts, who came in on cavalry horses.

On the way back to Fort Wallace, the advance guard of mounted soldiers and a few scouts met up with three Indians, two on horse and one afoot; he evidently had lost his horses. These Indians carried packages from a well-known store in Denver. In the skirmish which ensued on meeting them, the two horsemen got away, but the soldiers shot the one afoot. He fell near the scaffold

(Indian tomb) of a fallen chief, who wore on his breast a large silver medal awarded in President Madison's administration. One of the scouts took possession of the medal, which was three or four times larger than a silver dollar.

While at Wallace, our little band of scouts, now numbering forty-five (Farley passed [on] before we started back to Wallace), were scattered. The wounded were placed in government hospitals; some of us went to Fort Harker after a few days rest, where Major Inman[8] was paymaster, after which some of us went south and engaged in what was called the winter campaign, quieting the hostile tribes.

It was two years after that I learned something of the results of this battle on the Arikaree. In December 1870, while in camp one evening on Bluff Creek, near the present site of Caldwell, Kansas, I met up with Phil McClusky, interpreter for the Comanche Indians. We talked for an hour or two around the campfire. The subject came up about the number of Indians killed in the battle on the Arikaree, and the various estimates made by different individuals of the loss to the tribes engaged. The unauthentic estimates, with complacent indifference to evidence, ranged from fifty up. The Indians said there was never before anything like it—360 killed. A very unequal contest it was in respect to the numbers engaged.

We knew while in battle on the Arikaree that our rifles were calling [forth] a heavy sacrifice from our enemy, but not until I met Phil McClusky did I learn the truth in regard to their heavy losses. McClusky's long life among the Indians [and] his intimacy with them in the capacity as interpreter is proof of the authenticity of the statement. The Indian's native reticence in respect to his suffering shows that his calculation in this is bound to be conservative and exact. Anyone with broad acquaintance with Indian life and character will vouch for the reliability of this statement.

Wounded at Beecher Island

HOWARD MORTON[1]

Robert Lynam, ed., *The Beecher Island Annual: Sixty-second Anniversary of the Battle of Beecher Island, September 17, 18, 1868* (Wray, CO: Beecher Island Battle Memorial Association, 1930): 99–100

The following brief account of Major Forsyth's fight with Indians at Beecher Island, September 17, 1868, was written by Howard Morton from the hospital at Fort Wallace, Kansas, a short time after the fight, to his brother in the East:

We were attacked by the Indians just after daybreak, September 17. First, a small party tried to stampede our horses and succeeded in getting six or seven which were not well picketed. Then in about twenty minutes a large part of them came over the hill, charging right for us. We were encamped on a dry, sandy fork of the Republican River. There was a kind of a sand island nearly covered with tall grass and clumps of small cottonwood trees. There we led our horses as quickly as possible, tied them to the trees, and threw ourselves on the ground.

By this time the Indians were all around us, firing from all sides. They made a charge, intending to run over us, but we knocked over a few of them and kept up such a steady fire that they broke and circled around us. Then they began to dismount and crawl up in the grass on all sides, others charging on horseback all around us. We had about fifty-three men all told, and there were at least five hundred of them, well armed with hunting rifles, Spencers, carbines, and revolvers. In one hour fifteen of us were wounded.

The only way any of us escaped was by digging holes in the sand with our hands. The Indians kept crawling up in the grass, and if they had made one grand rush upon us, they could have killed us all in ten minutes; but we killed and wounded so many of them that the chiefs could not bring them up to the work.

We think we killed and wounded more than our number. We had five men killed, counting Farley, and sixteen wounded.

When night came in, we collected our little force and worked until morning digging with our hands and knives, cups, etc., making quite a respectable fortification.

The Indians came again at daybreak, but we gave them a volley, knocking over a few of them, and the rest broke. They crawled up in the grass and popped at us all day but hit no one. They tried it again the next day, but we drove them away, and they troubled us no more.

We were out of rations when we went into camp when the Indians attacked us. All our horses and mules were killed. We must eat or starve, so we cut up and jerked enough to last a week, then we went to cooking and eating. We had no salt—only the bare meat.

The first night we started two men to crawl through the Indian lines and foot it to Fort Wallace. The third night two other men started. At the end of seven days, our horse and mule meat gave out and we began on the horses again, cutting and jerking a large quantity of it. It tasted strong but, as the boys said, it beat nothing a long way.

The men began to get discouraged. There was no certainty that our men sent to the fort, from eight to one hundred miles distant, had ever reached it. Some of our well men found prickly pears on the hills, which we ate with a relish. We were a disconsolate-looking crowd. It was cold and wet most of the time, and one morning it snowed. We hovered over our little fires, made soup from the strong horsemeat, putting in powder to deaden the taste.

On the ninth day, about 10:00 A.M., a few horsemen appeared on the hills. We had a field glass and tried to find out whether they were Indians or white men. Some said one, some the other. The horsemen kept coming. Everybody who could get up was watching them, our hearts in our mouths. They saw us and rode toward us on the run. There was no doubt any longer—we were saved. Such shouting, swinging of hats, laughing and crying you never saw.

In an hour teams came with rations. A doctor had come in advance and had examined our wounds; and last but not least, we were cooking coffee and eating hardtack as though they were the greatest of dainties.

We were put into a government wagon and, after three and a half days jolting, arrived at Fort Wallace.

Beecher Island Diary

CHAUNCEY B. WHITNEY[1]

Collections of the Kansas State Historical Society 12 (1911–12): 296–99

August 29, 1868—Left Hays at 2:00 P.M.; marched until 11:00 P.M. and camped among the hills.

August 30—Started at 7:00 A.M. for the Saline River; reached it at noon and camped for dinner. Rained all last night.

August 31—Rained part of the day yesterday. Killed some buffalo. About 4:00 P.M. a scout, Joe Lane,[2] reported Indians a mile or two away; false report. Camped at dark on the South Fork of the Solomon.

September 1, 1868—Crossed Solomon yesterday morning. Marched until nearly sundown and camped on Prairie Dog Creek. Was on guard last night with A. J. Pliley, my "bunky."

September 2—Camped last night on Beaver Creek; followed its course about ten miles for grass. The country is almost a barren desert. Prairies covered with thousand of buffalos. About 10:00 A.M. yesterday, as a few of us were on rear guard, a sudden volley brought us to the front in double-quick time. As we came over the bluff, a poor, frightened antelope was seen, and all unharmed.

September 3—Broke camp at 8:00 A.M. Country very broken. Followed Beaver [Creek] to its source, then crossed to Little Beaver, on which we camped last night. Are making for Sheridan or Wallace. Rations played. The country along the creeks is covered with wild plum and grape.

September 4—Broke camp at 8:30 A.M. Marched until 11:30 A.M. and fed the horses. No breakfast or dinner yesterday. Marched about forty miles and camped at 11:00 P.M.; made a kettle of soup for supper. Guards all asleep last night.

September 5—Broke camp at 8:00 A.M.; marched forty-five miles. Reached Fort Wallace at 11:00 P.M. last night. Horses all tired out. About 5:00 P.M. last night, Indians were reported among the bluffs. A charge was ordered. Away all went as though the devil had rocked us, and charged upon a Mexican train. One man was thrown and badly hurt. Fort Wallace is situated on the broad level prairie, one hundred eighty miles west of Fort Harker and about five miles east of the Colorado state line, on the South Fork of Smoky Hill River. The buildings are built of a pink sandstone, dressed and polished.

September 6—Lay at Wallace all day.

September 7—In fort today; up to Pond City tonight, about three miles from the fort.

September 8—In fort today, and up to city again.

September 9—In fort today. Wrote some letters, but did not receive any.

September 10—Orders to march this morning. As we were ready to move, received a telegram from Sheridan that the Indians had surrounded the town. Made a hasty march and found some dead cattle and two dead Mexicans, but the Indians had decamped. Followed the Indians about twenty miles and camped in a ravine.

September 11—Marched today about twenty-five miles and camped on the head of Beaver Creek about 3:00 P.M.

September 12—Marched about forty miles without water; camped at night on Big Timber.

September 13—Marched down Big Timber to South Fork of Republican until found an Indian camp; then struck across the country. Camped on middle branch of Republican, or Chief Creek, at dark. Marched about thirty miles.

September 14—On guard last night. Marched down Chief Creek and camped. Marched about twenty-five miles.

September 15—Marched up the Republican yesterday. Struck an Indian trail and followed it until near sundown. Camped on Republican. Marched thirty miles.

September 16—Struck camp at sunrise. Followed Indian trail until sundown and camped on Dry Creek.

September 17—About daylight this morning was aroused by the cry of Indians. Eight tried to stampede the stock; got seven horses. In a few moments the bottoms were completely filled with red devils. Went across the river onto an island when the fight commenced. About five hundred attacked us on all sides, with their unearthly yells. The balls flew thick and fast. The major was the first man wounded. Lieutenant Beecher was wounded twice, as was also the major. In a few moments eight or ten were hurt, some fatally. The ground on which our little squad was fighting was sandy. We commenced to scoop out the sand with our hands to make entrenchments for ourselves. In a few moments I was joined by two others, who helped me. With a butcher knife and our hands, we soon had a trench which completely covered us from the enemy. Behind the works, we fought the red devils all day till dark. Only two men were hurt after we entrenched ourselves. Culver[3] was killed and McCall wounded. William Wilson was also killed early in the morning.

September 18—This morning the Indians made a slight charge on us but were speedily repulsed. They were after three of their dead, who lay about twenty yards from us. About fifty of the red devils were killed and wounded. They kept firing from the hills and ravines all day. No one hurt today. Two men started for Wallace.

September 19—The Indians made another attack this morning but were easily driven off. About 10:00 P.M. this evening, myself and A. J. Pliley were requested by the major to go to Fort Wallace. We started, but a few rods from the battleground, we found the Indians had surrounded the camp and forced us to return. Was awake all night. It rained all night steady, and everybody was wet and cold. Am very lame with rheumatism today.

September 20—Sunday, and all is quiet. No attack this morning. Last night I slept for the first time in three nights. Our surgeon, Doctor Mooers, died this morning about daylight. He was shot in the head. He did not speak from the time he was shot until he died. We have twenty men killed and wounded; four dead.

September 21—No Indians seen today; all dined and supped on horsemeat.

September 22—No Indians today. Killed a coyote this morning, which was very good. Most of the horsemeat gone. Found some prickly pears, which were very good. Are looking anxiously for succor from the fort.

September 23—Still looking anxiously for relief. Starvation is staring us in the face; nothing but horsemeat.

September 24—All fresh horsemeat gone. Tried to kill some wolves last night but failed. The boys began to cut putrid horsemeat. Made some soup tonight from putrefied horsemeat. My God, have you deserted us?

September 25—A day long to be remembered by our little band of heroes. Arose at daylight to feel all the horrors of starvation slowly but surely approaching. Got a light breakfast on rotten meat. Some of the boys wandered away to find something to satisfy and appease their hunger. About 10:00 A.M. the cry of "Indians" rang through the works. Some of the men being out, eight or ten of us took our guns to rescue them if possible. The word was given that it was *friends*. In a few moments, sure enough, our friends did come. Oh, the unspeakable joy! Shouts of joy and tears of gladness were freely commingled. Such a shaking of hands is seldom witnessed. Soon our hands were filled with something for the inner man, both in the shape of victuals and stimulants. The day passed off in joy and gladness among friends, who condoled with us over our hardships and shouted for joy at our success against the enemy.

September 26—Very little sleep was done in our camp last night. Today several hundred men came on with two field pieces. Tomorrow we are to start for Fort Wallace, where I shall bid good-bye to our brave band of scouts to prepare to return east, where I will try to forget in a peaceful home the scenes of the past two years. One man very sick tonight.

September 27—Arose early this morning to prepare to start for Fort Wallace. Rolled out about 10:00 A.M., marched twenty miles and camped at four on the south branch of the Republican. Five of our boys killed and scalped a Cheyenne about one-half mile from camp.

September 28—Marched thirty miles today and camped on a branch of Beaver. Had buffalo for supper and cooked on buffalo chips.

September 29—Broke camp at 7:00 A.M., marched thirty miles, and camped within seven miles of Fort Wallace; [the] wounded [are] very bad.

September 30—Broke camp at 7:30 A.M. and reached the fort at 10:00 A.M. Helped get the wounded into the hospital. Drew and set up tents.

The Story of a Rescue

LOUIS H. CARPENTER[1]

Winners of the West 2, no. 2 (February 1925): 6–7[2]

About the middle of September 1868, my troop (H of the 10th Cavalry) was sent to take station at Fort Wallace, located on the western border of Kansas. The Cheyennes had broken out during the summer and devastated the line of settlements on the Solomon and near the center of the state, but the troops, after rapidly concentrating in that vicinity, compelled the savages to retreat, and they were next heard of attacking travelers and trains on the roads farther to the west.

The garrison consisted of two troops of the 10th Cavalry and three companies of the 5th Infantry under command of Bvt. Col. H. C. Bankhead, captain 5th Infantry, a soldier of experience who had graduated in 1850 and had served in the Civil War.

Reports came to the post that the Indians were seriously interfering with travel on the road to Denver; that carrying the mail was dangerous, and its delivery uncertain and unreliable.

On September 22[3] I left the post under instructions to proceed on the Denver road to where it was crossed by the Sandy Creek, about sixty miles from Wallace, and there establish a camp. From this point we were to scout in every direction and take measures necessary to keep off the Indians and protect the trains passing through the country.

In addition to H Troop, 10th Cavalry—which was about seventy strong—there were attached seventeen frontiersmen,[4] who had been enlisted for the campaign; a self-reliant and fearless party under the leadership of Victor Clark, a dashing, handsome-looking man, and a fine specimen of the frontier scouts who came into the service and figured prominently in the Indian campaigns which occurred soon after the war.

The officers who accompanied me were 1st Lt. Charles Banzhaf[5] and 2nd Lt. L. H. Orleman, 10th Cavalry,[6] with Dr. Jenkins A. Fitzgerald of the medical corps as surgeon.

As we were to go into camp for at least a month, thirteen wagons were furnished to carry the forage, rations, extra ammunition, and tentage required.

On the evening of the twenty-second, the command bivouacked near Cheyenne Wells on the road to Denver, and early on the twenty-third resumed the march to the westward. We had reached a point on the old stage road about forty-five miles from Fort Wallace, from which Pikes Peak could be seen and the range of the Rockies, including Longs Peak and the mountains back of Denver, when a courier from the post, who had ridden all night, overtook us bearing the following dispatch:

Headquarters, Fort Wallace, Kansas
September 22, 1868, 11:00 P.M.

Bvt. Lt. Col. L. H. Carpenter,
10th U.S. Cavalry. On scout.
Captain:

The commanding officer directs you to proceed at once to a point of the Dry Fork of the Republican [Arikaree Fork] about seventy-five or eighty miles north, northwest from this point, thirty or forty miles west by a little south from the forks of the Republic, with all possible dispatch.

Two scouts from Major Forsyth's command arrived here this evening and bring word that he (Forsyth) was attacked on the morning of Thursday last by an overpowering force of Indians (700), who killed all the animals, broke Major Forsyth's left leg with a rifle ball, severely wounded him in the groin, wounded Doctor Mooers in the head, and wounded Lieutenant Beecher in several places. His back is supposed to be broken. Two men of the command were killed and eighteen or twenty wounded.

The men bringing the word crawled on hands and knees two miles, and then traveled only by night on account of the Indians, whom they saw daily.

Forsyth's men were entrenched in the dry bed of the creek with a well in the trench, but had only horse flesh to eat and only sixty rounds of ammunition.

General Sheridan orders that the greatest dispatch be used and every means employed to succor Forsyth at once. Colonel Bradley[7] with six companies is now supposed by General Sheridan to be at the forks of the Republic.

Captain Bankhead will leave here in one hour with one hundred men and two mountain howitzers.

Bring all your scouts with you.

Order Doctor Fitzgerald at once to this post to replace Doctor Turner, who accompanies Colonel Bankhead for the purpose of dressing the wounded of Forsyth's party.

I am, Captain, very respectfully, your obedient servant,

HUGH JOHNSON

1st. Lt., 5th Infantry,

Acting Post Adjutant

Having read this communication hastily, I mounted the command and proceeded to consider the matter. I knew Forsyth personally very well. We had served together in the Shenandoah on the staff of General Sheridan. After the battles of Winchester and Fisher Hill, I accepted the command of a regiment of volunteers in the West and had not been thrown [in] with him since. He was, at the time of which I write, a major in the 9th Cavalry and a brevet colonel, remaining on the staff of General Sheridan after the war.

We had heard at Wallace that he had raised a company of scouts under special authority, and that he was operating somewhere to the north of that post, but had no further information regarding his movements.

Neither of the two scouts bringing word from Forsyth's party had been sent to assist in guiding me to the place where the fight occurred, and I had nothing but the general direction contained in the letter.

The map in my possession was very unreliable, as no accurate surveys of this part of the country had been made. On inquiry, I found that no man among the scouts had ever been through the country to the north, and in fact, I doubt if many white men had visited that locality, as it was the camping ground and home of the tribes of the Northern Cheyennes and certain affiliated tribes of the Oglala and Yankton Sioux, and it was not safe for anything less than a considerable force to venture in the vicinity.

A point "north, northwest" from Fort Wallace, upon being protracted on the map, showed about north ten degrees west from my present position, and I finally concluded to take that course, hoping for something favorable to turn up.

I also concluded to keep my wagons with me, as in the first place, I did not wish to detach any men to escort them back to Wallace; then, there was no other way of carrying the supplies required; and finally, if attacked in the open by a large force of Indians, the wagons would serve as a fort.

Upon further consideration of the dispatch, it seemed probably that Bankhead had really no expectation that we would succeed in rescuing Forsyth but had sent the instructions contained therein to carry out the general directions received from General Sheridan.

I could not help being impressed with this, because no guide had been sent who could conduct us, and the order to return the surgeon, Dr. Fitzgerald, back to the post so as to allow Bankhead to take Dr. Turner with him seemed strange under the circumstances.

As I made up my mind to use every effort to help the beleaguered party in distress, it struck me that if attacked on the way, or if so fortunate as to find Forsyth and his party before the others reached them, we would need a surgeon and would be nearly helpless without one. I had always been trained to obey orders without questioning, but in this case determined to risk the chances and retain Dr. Fitzgerald. The doctor clinched the resolution by expressing a great desire to go along.

A glance showed the greatest interest and expectation on every face. The scouts had crowded around, and the troops were on the "qui vive," as all felt certain that something unusual had occurred. Having explained to them in a few words the purport of the news, and that we would have to make every exertion to relieve the party in distress, a cheer broke forth, and we left the stage road and struck across the open country. To Lieutenant Orleman was given the task of running the course upon which it was decided to travel, as he was very efficient and reliable in every way. The wagonmaster was told to keep his train close in rear of the cavalry column and was instructed that if any of the mules gave out through weakness, they were to be left, and if necessary, the wagon abandoned. However, the mules seemed strong and in good condition, and I judged that they would stand the distance we would probably have to make even if they were pushed considerably.

The gait was an alternate walk and trot, making about five or six miles an hour. We left the stage road nearly at noon and marched steadily over a rolling country, finding no difficulty in selecting a good trail for the wagon train. After traveling about thirty-five miles, when it became too dark to move, we bivouacked for the night near some waterholes.

In the morning, we started as early as possible and moved on the same course for about twenty miles, when we arrived at a large and impossible-looking dry river of creek, with a wide bed of sand. As my instructions described Forsyth as being located on the "Dry Fork of the Republican," and as the map showed a South Fork, the Arikaree Fork, and the North Fork, I could not tell which was the Dry Fork, and I was therefore afraid to pass this stream without a thorough investigation. I think this tributary is now known as Dry Creek on the later maps. We scouted up the creek about fifteen miles, but finding no result, pushed on to the northward, and at a short distance came to a stream with plenty of flowing water in the midst of a wide, grass-covered valley, with hills on either side of beautiful meadow bottomlands.

As we passed into the valley, a large and fresh trail of Indians was discovered. At least two thousand head of ponies had been driven or ridden over it but a few hours before, and the signs showed that a large village were on the move. The tracks indicated that the savages were traveling down the river, and they were so fresh that we were apprehensive that the hostiles were near at hand and that there was danger of an attack at any time. Influenced by this evidence, a spot was selected on the banks of the river so as to be sure of water, and the train corralled with the tongues of the wagons inward, so as to present a formidable obstacle in case the enemy should assault us. Having made all of the dispositions necessary to make an effective defense, I took a small party and rode to a high hill, from which a good view could be expected. We could see far down the river but did not discover any moving object. Having surveyed the landscape, our attention was directed to several Indian scaffoldings erected on the hill, upon which bodies were placed after the Cheyenne method of burial, to keep them from the wolves. These scaffoldings must have had a new look, for something instigated a close examination. A body was taken down, unrolled from the skins enveloping it, and it was discovered that the Indian warrior had evidently died from a recent gunshot wound. Another was examined with the same result, and another and another. Five Indians all killed recently by bullet wounds. Everyone was satisfied that these men had met their death in some fight fought at no great distance within the last few days, and as the Forsyth fight was the only one likely to have occurred, they had probably taken part in that affair.

Standing on the hill and gazing across the valley, we saw something white in a ravine on the opposite side. This turned out to be a tepee built of new, freshly tanned white skins. Inside on a little platform lay the body of an Indian warrior, evidently a chief or man of consequence, wrapped in buffalo robes. An Indian drum, similar to those used by the Indians for medicine purposes, a shield, and some other equipment were placed at the head and feet. This chief had also been killed recently by a bullet wound.[8]

A scout sent down the river returned with a report that the trail was found to leave the river some miles down and led across the country in a southeasterly direction toward Beaver Creek, but that no Indians had been seen. The signs seemed to show that a large portion had remained in camp in the vicinity for about two days. We were convinced that the trail was that of Indians who had participated in the attack made upon Forsyth, and it began to look as if they had left after killing and scalping the whole party. As my mission was to find them, whatever might be their condition, I came to the conclusion that following the trail of the Indians would lead farther and farther away from the object, and that it would be better to take the back trail and go where they came from, with the hope that this would bring us into the vicinity of the later conflict and give a chance of extending a helping hand to our friends if by good fortune we found any alive.

But the sun was down, and we were compelled to pass another night before we could take any further measures. Early in the morning, and while we were packing up, some mounted men appeared on the hills to the south and rode rapidly towards us. We soon discovered that they were white men, and on their joining us found it was a party of five, one of whom was a man named Donovan, one of Forsyth's scouts. Donovan and another had been sent out the day after Stillwell and his companion had succeeded in getting through the Indian lines. Stillwell carried the information which resulted in the efforts now being made for Forsyth's rescue, but Donovan, arriving at Wallace after

Bankhead's departure, had collected four adventurous spirits and started out, expecting to overtake him. Not knowing the trail, he had taken a wrong course, and by a wonderful piece of luck had happened on my command.

I gathered from a talk with Donovan that the fork or branch that Forsyth was on was probably more to the north, and that the stream where we were was the South Fork of the Republican.

As we expected, the back trail of the Indians soon left the South Fork and led to the northward. It was evident that the main force of the Indians had gone to the eastward, and we felt there was little to fear. I took thirty men with me and the ambulance, leaving the remainder of the force and the wagons to follow under Lieutenant Banzhaf. Some hard bread, coffee, and bacon were thrown into the ambulance to give immediate relief in case we found any of the beleaguered party alive. The Indian trail was as plain as a wide road and conducted us over a good practical country for wagons, generally the case with the routes laid out by the Cheyennes and Sioux. At all events, their trails followed as good ground as the country will afford.

Marching at a rapid gait for about eighteen miles, we came to broken and rugged ground, evidently the breaks of a large stream. Finally we came to a spur, from which the country could be seen for a long distance. The ground fell away below us, and far down in a valley a large stream appeared running east and west. To the right, the valley opened out, and we could see what appeared to be an island in the midst of the river. Donovan recognized the place at once and said that was the island upon which Forsyth and his party were entrenched. We could make out moving objects near the island but too far off to distinguish them clearly. The ambulance was sent to follow a safer route, and we then picked our way down the stream, which was a dry bed of sand with here and there a little water on both sides.

As we clambered over the rough ground, we saw the men near the island run towards their comrades as if apprehensive of our character, but as we neared them, they recognized us and received us with evidences of the wildest joy. I could not help noting the haggard, wolfish look on their countenances, which indicated hunger and starvation, but did not stop, rushing forward to where Forsyth was. He was lying in an excavation made in the sand, unable to move from the nature of his wounds. He maintained his nerve wonderfully but was much affected when he saw me. I grasped his hand and told him that I was sorry to see him in his present condition, but was glad to be able to render him assistance.

The island was surrounded by rifle pits, affording complete protection and connected with each other. The Indians had very little to show against men entrenched in this way, and they could have been reduced only by starvation.

It was high time that succor was given to the wounded. We relieved them on the twenty-fifth, the eighth day after the first day's attack, and many had wounds which had not been properly dressed for seven days. Forsyth had three

The rescue. HARPER'S NEW MONTHLY MAGAZINE 1895.

wounds, and Dr. Fitzgerald informed me that in his case blood poisoning had already commenced.

Banzhaf and the remainder of the command arrived with the train in a short time, and the tents were erected on a grassy spot a quarter of a mile from the island in order to get away from the terrible stench which filled the air from the dead horses which lay in a circle around the trenches. As soon as the tents were in shape, the wounded were carried to them and made as comfortable as possible. Forsyth's men were soon cooking bacon, munching hard bread, and drinking coffee. One of them showed me a piece of horseflesh that he had cut off to use for his dinner that day, but it was so offensive that I could not bear it near me.

That night Dr. Fitzgerald amputated the leg of a scout named Louis Farley, who had been shot in the thigh, the ball breaking the bone. I assisted all that I could in the operation, but the poor fellow was so far gone that he could not stand the shock and died the following morning. Forsyth was wounded in the leg below the knee, the ball shivering the bone and making a comminuted fracture. The doctor thought the leg should come off, but its owner strenuously objected, and after many weary months the leg was finally saved and has been, I believe, serviceable ever since.

On the morning of September 26, we began to wonder what had become of Bankhead. According to my letter of instructions, it will be seen that he left Fort Wallace with one hundred men and two howitzers about midnight of the twenty-second, or about twelve hours before I left the Denver stage road, and with the advantage of having two of Forsyth's scouts to lead him directly to the objective point. In order to be sure, he had evidently gone north from Fort Wallace to the forks of the Republican and then followed up the Arikaree Fork. Some scouts were therefore sent down the Arikaree to look up the missing troops. Shortly after, I received word that they were at hand, and about 12:00 P.M. on the twenty-sixth, Captain Bankhead arrived with his column. He was not alone, however. At the forks of the Republican, he had met Major Brisbin[9] with two troops of the 2nd Cavalry, who had been sent forward by Colonel Bradley, and the troops of Captain Bankhead and those of Major Brisbin arrived together, learning with some surprise that Forsyth and his party had been relieved by our force twenty-six hours before.

Forsyth and the wounded men were conveyed to Wallace. The former lay in a critical condition for three months, and I was informed by Dr. Fitzgerald that if medical attention had been delayed in his case twenty-four hours longer, he would not have lived, as blood poisoning had already set in.

The chieftain whose body was found on the South Fork of the Republican was satisfactorily identified as Roman Nose, a famous Cheyenne warrior, the most prominent leader in the fight with Forsyth's party, and I brought back his medicine drum and presented it to the Historical Society of Pennsylvania.

The following dispatch was sent by Captain Bankhead relative to this affair to department headquarters:

Detachment U.S. Troops,
Dry Fork of the North Fork of the Republican River,
September 26, 1868

Major Forsyth sends his love. He is badly wounded but will be able to travel tomorrow. Lieutenant Beecher of the Third Infantry and Dr. Mooers died of their wounds and are buried.

Captain Carpenter arrived here yesterday at 10:00 A.M. His promptness and celerity of movement deserve credit.

The scouts sent from Wallace I met on Beaver Creek, they having been driven back by the Indians. I started them again, but they did not find the command of Colonel Bradley, who did not reach the forks until yesterday.

Forsyth's men fought desperately, the details of his fight I leave to him. His spirited and noble conduct encouraged his men. There are few cases on record of more desperate fighting and continued endurance without food, except horseflesh, and surrounded by the dead and dying.

I cannot remove the dead, but the doctors say I can remove the wounded tomorrow to Fort Wallace. Major Forsyth estimates the number of Indians at six hundred. He takes this estimate from the judgment of Sharp, an old and experienced scout. They were Cheyennes, Arapahos, and Sioux.

Captain Carpenter reports that he struck the trail and place where they had encamped, probably for two days after leaving here, and the trails show that they are going southeast toward Beaver Creek.

He found the bodies of five Indian warriors (Cheyennes) about eighteen miles from Forsyth's camp, evidently some of the killed in the fight with Forsyth.

I have the honor to remain,
Your obedient servant,

HENRY C. BANKHEAD,
Brevet Colonel, Commanding

After the campaign was over, Major Forsyth was brevetted brigadier general for the fight on the Arikaree Fork of the Republican, and Captain Bankhead was brevetted brigadier general for his energy in relieving Forsyth.

The Relief of Beecher Island

JAMES J. PEATE[1]

Robert Lynam, ed., *The Beecher Island Annual: Sixty-second Anniversary of the Battle of Beecher Island, September 17, 18, 1868* (Wray, CO: Beecher Island Battle Memorial Association, 1930): 89–92

Owing to a misunderstanding of orders by the commanding officer at Fort Hays, I with seven others who were members of the Forsyth scouts were not with the company at the time of the battle on Beecher Island. When I reported at Fort Hays for orders, we were ordered into camp and remained there several days, when we should have been sent direct to Fort Wallace, there to await the arrival of Major Forsyth. When the error was discovered, we were sent at once by rail to the end of the Kansas Pacific (now the Union Pacific) railway and arrived at Fort Wallace about thirty-six hours after Major Forsyth had left on the Arikaree campaign.

The evening after our arrival, Captain Bankhead, the commander at Fort Wallace, concluded to send us to overtake Forsyth. We were reinforced by nine Wallace scouts, were given ten days' rations and pack animals, and we reported for duty after dark at the quartermaster's office, where we remained for several hours while Bankhead talked by wire with [Maj.] Gen. P. H. Sheridan. Bankhead wanted us to go that night to where the Indians had attacked a train and killed two teamsters, that being Forsyth's first objective point; then at daylight we could find Forsyth's trail and follow it. Sheridan would not allow us to go. Had we gone, it is not at all probable that we would ever have reached Forsyth, owing to the large number of Indians in that country.

We remained at Fort Wallace doing escort duty and sometimes going after marauding bands of Indians, but were not able to get near enough to make good Indians of them.

September 21, 1868, we were ordered out on a scout with Captain L. H. Carpenter and his troops of the 10th U.S. Cavalry (Colored). The command consisted of Captain L. H. Carpenter, 1st Lt. Charles Banzhaf, 2nd Lt. L. H. Orleman, Dr. J. A. Fitzgerald, about seventy troops, nine Wallace scouts, eight Forsyth scouts, thirteen wagons, and one ambulance. We were to scout along the Smoky Hill road, as the Indians were doing considerable damage there. We were to establish a camp where the road crossed Sand Creek, and from this point we were to scout in every direction. We had traveled for two days without any incident worthy of note and were in camp on Goose Creek, north of the stage road and about the Kansas line, when four troopers came to us with a dispatch from Fort Wallace.

They told us that they had met two of Forsyth's men, that Forsyth had had a battle with the Indians, [and] that half of his men were killed or wounded and all his horses were dead.

A little before noon the next day, while traveling west on the stage road, we saw horsemen approaching from the east at a rapid gait. They proved to be couriers from Fort Wallace with orders for us to go to the relief of Forsyth. The dispatch directed Carpenter to proceed at once to a point on the Dry Fork of the Republican "about seventy-five or eighty miles north, northwest (from Fort Wallace), thirty or forty miles west by a little south from the forks of the Republican, with all possible dispatch."

Not a man in the company knew the country north; it was so far from the usual routes of travel that it is doubtful if many white men had ever been there. Thirty or forty miles west by a little south from the forks of the Republican, it seemed to us, would be south of the south fork. Carpenter communicated the dispatch to all and ordered the wagon boss to leave any mules that could not keep up and, if necessary, to abandon wagons. The whole command was eager to do all that was in their power to crown our efforts with success. Not a man, horse, or mule but did all that was required of him. We left the stage road at noon, going in a northerly direction. Our gait was an alternate walk and trot, making five or six miles an hour—a gait that seemed far too slow for those in the command who had friends on the island.

Captain Bankhead had started from Fort Wallace twelve hours before we left the stage road. We were thirty or forty miles west of Fort Wallace. The twelve hours on a forced march should bring him as near Forsyth as we were, and he had two of Forsyth's men who had crept through the Indian lines the night after the first day's fight. Why had not Bankhead sent us one of these men? It looked as if he thought we would not be able to reach Forsyth. Bankhead also ordered Dr. Fitzgerald back to Fort Wallace; but, fortunately for the wounded men, [Carpenter] disobeyed orders.

The night of the twenty-third, we camped by some holes of water, and at daylight the twenty-fourth, we were again forging ahead as fast as we could with the train. Our order of travel was scouts well in advance and on the flanks, troops next, with the train close up.

We had traveled about half a mile when we found three Indian saddles and fresh pony tracks. The Indians evidently heard the bugle that morning and left in a hurry. About the second blast of the bugle, Carpenter stopped it, and we had no more bugle calls that march that I remember of. About noon we came to a large, sand-bottomed dry creek and hunted on it for miles for signs of Forsyth. But finding none, we resumed our march northward. The first sign we found of a battle was a dead horse that had died of gunshot wounds. This was about a mile south of the South Fork of the Republican. Half a mile south of the river, we found several dead Indians on a scaffold about eight feet above the ground. They were wrapped in blankets and buffalo robes and had their hunting and war paraphernalia beside them. Horses had been killed by the side of the scaffold so the departed warriors would have horses to ride in the Happy Hunting Grounds. We examined the dead warriors and found they had died recently of gunshot wounds. This was about 3:00 P.M., and we felt sure we were near where the battle had taken place. We found several other scaffolds with dead Indians upon them that afternoon. We saw where a large band of Indians had been encamped on the river but a short time before. There was a large, fresh trail near the river, and the Indians had traveled east. Some of the scouts were sent down the river on this trail, and they followed it till it left the river and went in the direction of the Beaver. We kept up the hunt until dark, intending to take the back trail of the Indians the next morning, believing by so doing we would be going in the direction of Forsyth and would find him if he was still alive, or if he was dead, find where the unequal contest had taken place.

Just before day the morning of September 25, we saw five mounted men coming over the hills from the south. We supposed them to be Indians and went out to meet them. We were glad to find it was Jack Donovan, one of the second two to leave the island for help, and four other fearless men, who were returning with him to the island. Donovan told us that Forsyth was twenty miles further north. Only twenty miles, and we had lost so much time yesterday afternoon that we would have been there by dark had we known that Forsyth was on the Arikaree. Carpenter took one lieutenant, the doctor, Donovan and his comrades, fifteen scouts, fifteen troopers, the ambulance, a few rations, and away we went. Even our horses entered into the excitement of the hour and needed very little urging. We traveled at a run until almost over this canyon, and when Carpenter ordered us to fall back, we went to a ridge that we could follow down until we could see up and down the Arikaree. We could see the sandy channel of the river as it crossed and recrossed the narrow bottom. Not a living being at first met our eyes. After looking down the river a few moments, Donovan followed with his eye the stream to the west and said, "I am not quite sure, but I think it (meaning the battleground) is a little farther up the river." Just at this moment, I was looking in a northeast direction and saw two objects that looked like men walking down a hill a mile and a half away. I called Donovan's attention to them, and he said, "Yes, by God! There is a camp!" Looking at a point on the river toward which the men were going, where there were a few small trees and bushes, I saw for the first time Beecher Island and quite a number of men at the west end of the island, where the rifle pits afforded complete protection.

The hill on which we were had been the Indians' vedette post, and the watchers on the island took us for Indians. They looked for relief to come from the east or southeast. Down that steep hill we rushed as fast as we could urge our horses. Soon we were out of sight of the island, as there was a long, low ridge between, but we were over in a moment and could see several men running toward us. Nearer us was a man running toward the island. We were fast overtaking him when he stopped and raised his gun to fire at us. We separated, waved our hats, and he came running toward us. Soon we met the others, but as I did not know them, I put spurs to my horse and rode into that bloodstained island alone.

Crowned king nor conquering general ne'er received so royal and hearty a welcome as I did when I rode into that island among those staunch-hearted men, who lifted me from my horse, embraced me, and, strong men though they were, wept as cheer upon cheer arose. How they cheered, again and again, while manly tears coursed down their cheeks; these, nature's true noblemen, who would have heroically died upon that island without a murmur rather than left it while there was one of their wounded comrades who needed their attention and care.

All had that wolfish, haggard look on their countenances which indicates hunger. We relieved them at 10:00 A.M., the eighth day after the first day's battle. None of the wounds had been properly dressed, as the doctor had been killed in the battle. A terrible stench from the dead horses, which lay where they had fallen during the battle, filled the air. We carried the wounded to the camp a quarter of a mile from the island. Meals at all hours was the order of the day: hardtack, bacon, and coffee, all free. Forsyth's men were welcome at the campfire and could have the best we had.

Louis Farley was the most desperately wounded and died that night after his shattered leg had been amputated. Dr. Fitzgerald said that blood poisoning had already commenced in Forsyth's wounds, and had medical attention been delayed twenty-four hours, he could not have lived. Twenty-six hours later, Captain Bankhead with his command and Major Brisbin with his two troops of the 2nd Cavalry arrived.

Jack Stillwell and Pierre Trudeau, the first two men to leave the island for help, returned with Bankhead. A. J. Pliley, Donovan's partner, could not return with him, as his feet were wounded with cactus thorns.

After the campaign was over, our government gave Major Forsyth the star of brevet brigadier general for the fight on the Arikaree Fork of the Republican.

I have never heard that our government gave Captain Carpenter anything for the part he took in the rescue. But I think a whole nebula of stars would have been none too much as a brevet reward for his tireless energy during our forced march to the rescue.[2]

ON THE RETURN

Sunday, September 27, 1868

"Up by daylight, preparing to move the boys back to Fort Wallace, where they can get better attention and care, that it is impossible to give them on the march. Went back to our old camp on the south branch of the Republican River. Killed and scalped an Indian within a mile of camp."

This is after the battle on Beecher Island and when we were returning to Fort Wallace with the men that were wounded in that battle. This leaf brings many memories to my mind of the comrades that were with me in those days—grand, fearless fellows—and of the closing scenes of that Indian's life. It was a race for life, and he lost.

The scouts with this command (Captain Bankhead's) were the advance and flank guards. This day eight or ten of us were in advance, and after riding about twenty miles, we were several miles in advance of the main column, they traveling very slow on account of the wounded men. Just before we came to the South Fork of the Republican River, we discovered an Indian lodge in a canyon and went to investigate. The banks of the canyon were very steep, being a hundred or more feet high. The lodge was placed on a small bench or shelf of flat ground on the east side and about fifty feet from the bottom.

We went into the lodge and found that it was the tomb of a medicine man who was killed in the late battle. The lodge was in shape like a Sibley tent; it was fifteen feet in diameter, made of buffalo hides tanned with the hair off. The Indian was placed on a scaffold that was eight feet high. Fastened to the scaffold was his war bonnet and a large drum. He was wrapped in blankets and a buffalo rode and [was] tied on the scaffold. The posts on one side of the scaffold were torn away by the boys so we could have a better look at the good Indian. The body was then rolled to the edge of the canyon, and it rolled from there to the bottom. This investigation had taken but little of our time, and we went down the canyon to the river.

About half a mile up the river, we saw three horses, and as we had not seen any Indians or fresh signs of Indians that day, we supposed that they were loose horses; so we went into the river and watered our horses (not a good thing to do when there is a race on), then started after the three horses. We went along in a walk for perhaps a hundred yards, when up jumped four Indians right by the horses. Three of them mounted the horses and lashed them to their utmost speed, the other Indian doing his best to keep up with them on foot. The Indians had the advantage in the race at the start, as there was not a long stretch of sandy bottom for them to go over before they came to the higher ground on the south side of the river. The Indians ran towards a deep canyon to the southwest. We did not hold our own with the mounted warriors but were gaining a little on the other. Just before he came to the river, he dropped a woman's white skirt, and soon after a calico dress; then, as the race grew warmer (we were on the rolling ground south of the river now), he dropped his blanket.

The sport, to us, was now becoming exciting, the boys shooting at the Indian whenever they could. The Indian was running very fast, but we were gaining on him slowly. He would not run in a straight line; he would jump several times to the right, then back to the left, still rushing ahead at what seemed to us to be a tremendous speed for one on foot to attain. The bullets were striking the ground all around him.

His medicine for a short time was good—the charm may have kept the bullets away. Our horses were winded by our urging them through the sand on the river bottom. It looked as if the Indian would get to the deep canyon still half a mile away, where his comrades had passed out of sight, when a shot from a Henry rifle in the hands of Pierre Trudeau (one of the first two men to leave Beecher Island for help) broke the Indian's right leg above the knee. He falls to the ground; he gets up and attempts to go on on one leg; after hopping a few feet, he sits down and faces the foe. The few hundred feet that still separate us is soon passed over. As soon as the Indian faces us, he commences to fire, being armed with a Colt's navy revolver. Before we get him, he fires five shots at us. Then something seems to be the matter with his revolver; he looks into it and throws it on the ground. Not a shot was fired by our party while advancing after the Indian discarded his revolver.

He was a young man, perhaps twenty-five years of age, and was arrayed in the lovely simplicity of nature and a breechcloth. He was chanting a weird song and did not offer any resistance. He knew what his fate would be and showed no fear, although if his belief was the same as that of some Indians, he thought that in the Happy Hunting Grounds he would be the slave of the one that took his scalp.

In examining the discarded revolver, we found that the cylinder would not revolve, and the cause was a bullet from a revolver the same size in the hand of Jack Donovan (one of the second two to leave Beecher Island for help and the first to get back) going into the barrel of the Indian's revolver and about half of it passing into the cylinder, thereby stopping its revolving, and the Indian could not fire his last load.

Now that the trouble was over and we had made another good Indian, we commenced to look around. Had we gone into the canyon, we would have been surrounded by a hundred or more Indians. Over the hills, on three sides of us, we could see warriors. This may have been ambush laid for us; we did not know, but it looked that way. We held a council of war and decided to return to the bluffs on the north side of the river and there await the arrival of the troops.

It was nearly night when they came up, and as our wounded comrades required our first care, no attempt was made to follow the Indians. The next morning I rode by where we had left the good Indian. The wolves had held a banquet there, and a few bones was all that remained of the warrior of yesterday.

JAMES J. PEATE

Beverly Kansas, May 17, 1905

PART THREE

Sully's North Canadian
Expedition, 1868

Some Reminiscences, Including an Account of General Sully's Expedition against the Southern Plains Indians, 1868

EDWARD S. GODFREY

Cavalry Journal 36 (July 1927): 417–25

A s was the custom from time immemorial, when winter approached, the troops in the field were ordered to posts for the cold season. After our return from the escort of the Indian peace commission at Medicine Lodge, Kansas, October 9 to November 20, 1867, six troops and headquarters of the 7th Cavalry were ordered to Fort Leavenworth, Kansas; two troops to Fort Harker, Kansas; one to Fort Dodge, Kansas; one to Fort Wallace, Kansas; one to Fort Lyon; and one to Fort Reynolds—the last two being in what was then Colorado Territory.

At that time there was great unrest among the enlisted men. As long as the troops were in active fieldwork, the men appeared contented and there were few desertions, but while we were in winter quarters, and after each bimonthly payday, the desertions were appalling, hundreds leaving at a time. At one post in Colorado, the first sergeant, after tattoo roll call, went into the barrack room and designated thirty men to saddle their horses for detached service, armed and equipped, and had the cooks issue each man rations for a period of days. The sergeant mounted the detachment, marched it quietly out of the post, and when some distance away, moved rapidly until about thirty miles from the post. Then he halted the detachment and informed the men that they were all deserters and it was then every man for himself, said good-bye, and started south for the mining region. Two or three at once turned back, returned to the fort and gave themselves up, and told the story of their deception.

Many of these deserters had served in the Civil War, and many of those who were captured said that they had enlisted for adventure or to get transportation to the West, intending later to go to the vicinity of the mining camps. The inaction and routine of garrison duty and, too, the strict discipline hastened their determination to get to the mines.

Every few weeks detachments of recruits would arrive from the Carlisle, Pennsylvania, Depot. This, of course, greatly handicapped instruction. I heard an inspector (who was with Sheridan in the Civil War), after he had inspected the records, state that the recruit assignments to the regiment during the first two years after its organization would total the strength of a cavalry division during the Civil War.

As was the custom of the service and of the Indians, when the grass began to grow, active operations stirred the garrisons of the army and the nomads who had wintered along the streams, where cottonwood was abundant to feed, and plenty of underbrush to shelter, the ponies.

On April 4, 1868, five troops of the 7th Cavalry under the command of Maj. Joel H. Elliott left Fort Leavenworth and marched to the Kansas frontier, encamping near Ellis Station on the then Kansas Pacific Railroad.

Ellis Station, at the crossing of Big Creek by the railroad, consisted of one house for the section hands and a water tank. The terminus of the railroad track was then near the mushroom canvas town or "city" of Coyote. The western limit of civilization on the Kansas frontier at that time ran approximately from Scandia through Solomon Grove, Ellsworth, and Wichita. Soon after our arrival at Ellis, one troop (or company) was ordered to Wichita to protect the settlements, and one troop from Fort Wallace, Kansas, arrived at our camp. About the middle of July, the command was ordered to march at once to Fort Larned.

Due to the fact that the Indians had signed a peace treaty only a few months before at Medicine Lodge, we had anticipated a peaceful summer cantonment, and officers and men had gone to considerable trouble to make themselves comfortable by constructing bunks, "bush verandas" in front of their tents, and bush canopies over their kitchens and dining tables—the latter made with puncheons or split logs. Hence this summons for active fieldwork came as quite a surprise. We had no information that indicated such an emergency. Anticipating only a temporary absence, we left most of our canvas standing and took only such supplies as were necessary for the trip; a detail from each organization and the laundresses were left in charge of the cantonment. The next morning we were on our way to Fort Larned.

Our arrival seemed to have a quieting effect. On August 1, I was ordered to take the wagon train and bring the property and laundresses from our former camp. These I found had been moved to Fort Hays for safety.

One afternoon we heard loud moaning and cries of distress. The belated war party of the Cheyennes had returned, reporting the loss of several of the party. The next night there was a scalp dance, so they had some consolation for their losses. The annuities were issued by the Indian agent, and then there was feasting and dances throughout the Indian camps. Among the annuities issued were muzzle-loading rifles, revolvers, lead, caps, bullet moulds, and powder. At the battle of the Washita, we found quantities of these issues.

Soon after the annuities were issued, many of the camps broke up and moved away south of the Arkansas River. Several days later there was a sudden and hasty move of all the camps to the south bank, or south of the Arkansas. It was generally understood that troops were not to operate south of the Arkansas except in pursuit of hostiles; the peaceably disposed were not to be molested. It is my recollection that this promise was made by the Indian peace commission at Medicine Lodge. This move was made two or three days before we learned of the raids on the Saline, Solomon, and Republican River settlements.[1] Apparently the Indians had timed their move to the south of the Arkansas with that of the raids. Our first information came with the official announcement, and that the two troops of the 7th Cavalry stationed at Fort Harker (now Kanapolis), Kansas, and also the troops of the 10th Cavalry at Fort Hays, had been ordered to the scenes of trouble.

On August 28 I was sent to Fort Larned to get the mail, and Lt. J. M. Bell, the regimental quartermaster,[2] went with me, as he wanted to close up some business transactions at the post. In this mail I received my commission promoting me to first lieutenant, 7th Cavalry, to date from February 1. Because of the political quarrel between Congress and the president, the Senate had refused during this long period to go into executive session, and all appointments were held up. I purchase from Lappan and Company, post sutler, a case of wine to "wet my commission," as was the custom of the service at the time.

This mail brought orders from Lt. Col. Alfred Sully,[3] commanding the District of the Upper Arkansas, for Major Elliott to move his command to Fort Dodge, Kansas, up Walnut Creek by way of Saw Log Crossing.

On our way back to camp, the sun was suddenly obscured, and Lieutenant Bell and I got out of the ambulance to see if a storm was brewing. To our great astonishment, we discovered that the obscuration was made by millions of grasshoppers. The glint of the sunlight on their flickering wings gave the appearance of a snowstorm high up in the air. Our march to Fort Dodge was in the midst of this pest. The trees and bushes were denuded of their leaves; in fact, every living green thing was subject to their attack. They invaded our tents; they ate the nap off our blankets. Fortunately for our animals, the hot, dry summer had "cured" the buffalo grass on which we depended for grazing.

On arrival at Fort Dodge, we received orders from Colonel Sully, the district commander, then at post, to equip and supply ourselves for the expedition against the Indians. Our command was joined by Troop B, Capt. William Thompson, stationed at the post; Troop C, Capt. L. P. Gillette, from Fort Lyon, Colorado; Troop F, Capt. G. W. Yates, from Fort Leavenworth, Kansas—making nine troops of the 7th Cavalry under Major Elliott. Three companies of the 3rd Infantry under the command of Capt. J. H. Page; also, the medical staff, Capt. Henry Lippincott, assistant surgeon, U.S.A.; Dr. Renick, contract surgeon, and I think one other contract surgeon, completed the expeditionary force. We had an ample wagon train loaded with supplies.

I recall three guides, civilians—John Smith, Ben Clark, and Chapman.

About 4:00 P.M. of September 7, the command pulled out. The 7th Cavalry was organized with four squadrons, two troops each. Troop K, to which troop my promotion assigned me, was detailed as headquarters guard and escort. Two troops had the advance, two on each flank, and two as rear guard. The infantry, loaded in wagons, was at the head of the wagon train. We marched up the Arkansas several miles to the Cimarron Crossing on the Dry Route of the

Pursued by a war party. W. F. BEYER, *DEEDS OF VALOR.*

old Santa Fe Trail. Colonel Sully and escort halted on the south bank and waited until the wagons and rear guard had crossed, when he said, "Now we have crossed the Rubicon." Orders were given to observe the greatest silence possible, and that no bugle signals should be sounded. Smoking was prohibited. The wagon train was formed two abreast, and the cavalry was to regulate its march on the wagon train. The lieutenant colonel in his ambulance, followed by his escort, rode at the head of the train. After two hours' march, the lieutenant colonel sent word to the advance squadron to halt for a rest. Captain Thompson,[4] in command of the advance, rather prided himself on his lung-power; he had been a territorial delegate to Congress from Iowa and was the colonel of the 2nd Iowa Cavalry in the Civil War. When he received the message, he gave the command in stentorian tones, "Battalion, halt!" Then a mule brayed. The lieutenant colonel was very angry; he said he was satisfied the Indians had been watching our preparations form hidden outlooks, and he had moved after dark and in silence to outwit them, but Balaam's ass had thwarted his scheme! Thereafter, silence was observed as far as practicable, and commands were given in low tones. We marched southward till sometime after midnight, when orders were given to rest on arms till daylight, the cavalry to hold their horses. Of course, the animals tugged at the reins to get grass, and the cavalrymen got little rest.

With the dawn, the march was resumed and continued till we came to some water holes near the head of Crooked Creek, where we halted to cook breakfast. There were some dead bushes, left from a fire of some past year, and the plainsman's never failing fuel of those days, "buffalo chips," with which to prepare our coffee and bacon.

Our marches were in a southwesterly direction to the Cimarron River. A short time before we reached the Cimarron, some buffalos were seen on the bluffs south of the river. Contrary to the expectations of Colonel Sully, we had not as yet seen any Indians or signs of them, and Sully gave permission to a couple of officers to give chase to the buffalo. As they approached the herd, they saw a mounted Indian hunter riding full speed toward the same herd. As soon as the Indian discovered the character of his contestants, he reversed his direction and, followed by a few long-distance shots, disappeared down a ravine. The officers returned to the command and reported their adventure.

We camped that night in the valley at the foot of the bluffs of the second bench. Sometime after dark, the command was startled by the "swish, swish" of arrows through lighted tents and at campfires. Shouts of "Put out the lights, put out the fires," then a few shots from firearms. Troops were hastily formed and rushed up the bluffs, but the enemy had fled.

At the time the arrows were shot into camp, several Indians tried to get at our horses, but the vigilance of the guards and the quick formation of troops at their rendezvous thwarted their attempt, and the scare was soon over. This was the first and only night attack. Fortunately there were no casualties. Thereafter our camps were selected more carefully.

Orders were issued forbidding anyone going outside the limits of the camp guards, or going beyond the limits of the advance or rear guards or flankers on the march without authority of headquarters.[5]

Contrary to our expectations, no Indians were seen the next day. We struck a single travois trail that led down the valley, but it was old, and no particular significance was attached to it except that it eventually would lead to the main tribes. We camped on the south side of the river on a bench above the bottom.

The next morning[6] we broke camp in our usual leisurely manner. A short distance below our camp was a deep, dry arroyo that led back into the hills beyond our camp. After the train had crossed this arroyo and gone some distance, Capt. Louis McLane Hamilton (a grandson of Alexander Hamilton), in command of the squadron of the rear guard, mounted his squadron and started to join the trains. At the lower camp limit, near this arroyo, were two men (Captain Yates's mess cook and his striker), who were cautioned by Hamilton not to delay and to join their troop as soon as they could mount. As their horses were saddled and ready, he passed on and paid no further attention to them. After he had gone several hundred yards beyond the arroyo, he heard the war whoop of the Indians and the screams of men, and then saw several Indians making away with the men and their mounts. The Indians had stealthily moved down the arroyo until opposite the old camp, and then swooped on the unsuspecting, terrified men; two Indians to each man had thrown them across one of their horses in front of the rider, and the others had seized the horses.

Captain Hamilton at once gave pursuit, and Lt. A. E. Smith,[7] acting adjutant of the cavalry, ordered one of the flank-guard troops to follow in support. The facts were at once reported to Colonel Sully, who was at the head of the train in his ambulance. He was furious and at once sent a staff officer to stop the pursuit and order the immediate return of the troops.

Hamilton's pursuit had so gained on the pursued that one of the captives had been shot and abandoned as killed, and he was gaining on the other party when he reluctantly halted and returned. An ambulance was sent for the rescued, wounded man. The wound proved to be not serious.

Hamilton and Smith were placed under arrest for disobedience of orders in assuming to make pursuit without proper authority, but that evening upon arrival in camp, they were released from arrest and restored to duty. Hamilton was never reconciled to the abandonment of the pursuit.

This episode had a demoralizing effect on the command. We of the cavalry had been imbued with the principle to take any risk to attempt the rescue of a comrade in peril.

For five days the command was under attacks, some quite determined, the hostiles fighting to allow time for the flight of their families. Our marches down the Cimarron and Beaver followed the trail of the villages, which grew fresher and larger as the camps of the various bands scattered along the streams joined the flight. As we advanced, the abandonment of property at campsites and on the trail indicated something of a panic on the part of the Indians in their haste to escape. There was no indication of haste in the pursuit.

It was during one of our engagements that the horse ridden by Captain Keogh[8] was shot in the rump. Keogh christened him *Comanche* and adopted him as his field mount. This horse was ridden by Captain Keogh at the battle of the Little Bighorn with Custer's command; he was found after the battle on the site of the Indian village, severely wounded. Later he was retired and the subject of much sentimental poetry.

When we arrived about three miles above the fork of the Beaver and Wolf Creeks,[9] where later Camp Supply was located, the hostiles had selected a good defensive position and put up a stiff fight, detaining the command for nearly two hours.[10] Finally, Colonel Sully formed a strong dismounted skirmish line, advanced, and when about two hundred yards of their position, ordered the charge. The hostiles mounted and fled into the sand hills. No attempt was made to use the cavalry for mounted charge and pursuit.

On arrival at the forks of the rivers, the command, except the advance guard, was halted. The advance guard followed the hostiles for over a mile, when it was recalled, and the command went into camp.

That evening the one man killed in the engagement was buried on the picket line to hide the grave from the Indians. Two months later, when we returned, we found that the wolves had burrowed to the corpse, as shown by the scattered remains. Then we understood why the Indians placed the remains of their dead on scaffolds or trees.

That evening, as several of us were sitting around the headquarters camp-fire, Colonel Sully emerged from his tent and announced that the command would begin its return march to Fort Dodge and ask for reinforcements and to refit for another expedition. Later in the evening, when he and I were alone, I asked him why he gave up the pursuit. He replied, "Oh, those sand hills are interminable." The expedition was a failure.

The next day we began our return. We crossed the Beaver Fork, and not an Indian in sight. Not until we were leaving the valley for higher ground did they make their appearance. At first a few scouts; most of these soon left, and later returned largely reinforced. A few shots were exchanged. Then, at a distance from the flanks of the train, they rode in groups for several miles, as if giving safe conduct. Finally, about noon, the groups approached near, "thumbed their noses," spanked their buttocks, and made other contemptuous manifestations, then rode away.

The following morning, a soldier of Troop I, Captain Keogh's, was return-ing to his picket post from camp, missed his post in the darkness, and wan-dered some distance beyond his post. The corporal in charge of the post saw him in the dawn, mistook him for a lurking Indian, shot and mortally wounded him. He died that afternoon. At our next camp, Captain Keogh invited the offi-cers to attend the funeral on the picket line after retreat. At the appointed time, Captain Keogh read the burial service, and at the conclusion of the funeral thanked the officers for their attendance, then added, he "hoped soon to return the compliment."

Lieutenant Gibson's[11] quick wit and humor sensed the "bull" and exploded, echoed by the group. Keogh blushed, stammered a lame explana-tion, and then emphasized a "good-bye!"

We arrived at Fort Dodge about September 18.

General Sully reported his return, asking for reinforcements and recruits and horses to fill the 7th Cavalry to the maximum. He had canvassed the qual-ifications of the various field officers to command the cavalry, and concluded by requesting the restoration to duty of Lt. Col. George A. Custer, then absent, serving a sentence of suspension from command.

Fighting Indians
from an Ambulance

ANTHONY C. RALLYA

Winners of the West 4, no. 5 (May 1927): 8

Dear Comrade Webb:[1]

I will now relate a few things that I remember in the Sully campaign of 1868. Troop I, 7th U.S. Cavalry, left Fort Wallace in the spring of 1868,[2] being ordered to join the regiment at Fort Hays. Arriving there in good shape, we were surprised to find that the 7th U.S. Cavalry had a new commander, Colonel Sully, as Colonel Custer had been suspended from the army for one year, and let me say right here that I think it should have been for all time, and I think it would, had it not been for General Sheridan. No doubt you know why.

We stayed at Fort Hays only long enough to be fitted out for the warpath. Before leaving we were told that I Troop would have a new commander, as Keogh would be on Colonel Sully's staff. This was sorrowful news, as every man in the troop idolized Captain Keogh. However, we were not going to lose him entirely and would see him every day; and did, as he kept close touch with us to see that we were properly treated. Captain Cox[3] was our new troop commander; don't know where he came from, but did not amount to much.

We did not know where we were going but were on our way, bringing up at Fort Dodge. After a short stay there, we crossed the Arkansas River and started south.[4] On our way, we were told that this was to be known as the Sully campaign after Indians, and right here let me say that it will never be forgotten by those who took part in it, and will be remembered as at least the worst the 7th U.S. Cavalry took part in.

We did not have much fighting to do until we got into the sand hills, and there and then we were up against it proper. In trying to cross forks of Canadian and Cimarron Rivers, we lost several wagons and mules swamped in the quicksand. The only one of the scouts and guides, in my estimation, that amounted to anything was

247

California Joe,[5] and he knew
but little of that part of the
country.

California Joe was a tall,
rawboned, red-headed, old
scout, whose appearance and
makeup would indicate that
soap, water, comb, and brush
had been forgotten for a long
time. What he lacked in
makeup, he more than made
up in bravery, as he was like a
tiger in that respect. His only
aim during life was to kill
Indians in revenge for the
massacre of his wife and children. He joined our expedition at Fort Dodge and
wanted nothing for anything
that he might do to help us
along, which he did on many
occasions. His only wish was
to be given a free hand in
killing Indians.

He said, "Give me a horse
and mule, something to eat,
also plenty ammunition, and
when you see the smoke from

Cavalry officer in campaign dress.
CENTURY MAGAZINE 1890.

my old Long Tom, you can reckon there is one Indian less to fight."
We did see the smoke from that Long Tom many a time. He usually
wore an old blue army overcoat and government boots, with cartridge box, saddle pockets, and nosebag full of ammunition. He had
a quart bottle of "forty rod" in his overcoat pocket, and you can
imagine perhaps his appearance riding a small mule and his number
fourteen boots almost touching the ground. I never saw him take a
drink of water, and one day I asked him why it was. His reply was
that water would rot your boots, and he would not take any chances
with his stomach.

The only man lost on the trip that I can recall was Captain Hamilton's orderly. He was allowed to lag behind the rear guard one morning as we were starting our day's march.[6] A bunch of Indians
swooped down on the poor man and took him off. That morning our
troop was at the head of the column and close to headquarters.

Sergeant Andrews of our troop hastened to Keogh and requested permission to take a detail and try to rescue the man. Keogh requested permission of Colonel Sully, and he reluctantly gave consent. Andrews grabbed a dozen or so of us kids that had the best horses and we were off, not giving a thought of our own lives, as the hills and ravines were lined with Indians.

They had perhaps two miles the best of us, but we gained on them rapidly. My horse was not fast but could run all day, so I was at the head of the party. After a few miles' run, we got so close to them that they drew their bows and arrows, and thinking that we would rescue our man, they shot several arrows into his body. He did not fall from his horse, as I think he was tied on, but loped down in the saddle badly hurt. At that time the Indians did not have many firearms, and this bunch did not seem to have any. However, I would prefer a bullet to an arrow anytime.

Colonel Sully had gotten out of his ambulance and was keeping tabs on us. He perhaps thought we were getting too far from the command, so he had his bugler sound the recall. Andrews called our attention to it and said the only thing to do was turn back or get into trouble, so you can imagine the status of our minds when turning back and leaving our comrade to his fate. Maybe you think I did not say some hard words for a long time after that, and yet we cannot tell what might have happened to us if we had kept going. There might have been another Kidder or Major Elliott slaughter. However, on occasions like that, we never thought of danger but would ride through hell to rescue a comrade.

The Indians seemed to think they had us licked, and every day they would receive reinforcements. They became more daring, and when they became too numerous and daring, Colonel Sully would craw out of his ambulance, have his orderly help him on his horse, then look things over and perhaps order a charge made. This state of affairs continued from day to day for some time, and finally the Indians commenced disappearing. Don't know why, unless they thought we were not worth wasting any more ammunition on.

We went into camp not far from where Camp Supply was established a little later. We stayed here until Custer was restored to command, and poor old Sully went back in his ambulance to his former command at Harker, and so ended the Sully campaign.

Sully's Expedition to the Canadian: A Huge Joke

JOEL H. ELLIOTT[1]

Miscellaneous Collection, Theodore R. Davis, Manuscripts Department,
Kansas State Historical Society, Topeka

Camp, 7th U.S. Cavalry
Near Fort Dodge, Kansas
October 31, 1868

My Dear Davis,

Yours of September 21 reached me a short time ago. I fear I can
give you but little satisfaction in most of your queries but will
answer as much because <u>I feel out of humor</u> and so am fit for nothing but writing as from any other cause.

A grand winter campaign is being planned. One column of the
seven companies of the 5th Cavalry, commanded by Brevet Major
General Carr,[2] are to go south from Fort Lyon.[3] One of ten companies of the 7th Cavalry to go south from Fort Dodge, and one of five
or six companies of the 10th Cavalry under Captain Byrne[4] from
Fort Larned. Colonel Custer is to command our column. He is
already here. The regiment is in much better shape than I ever saw it
before. Colonel Custer and Captain West[5] seem to agree in letting
the "dead past bury its dead."[6] Both the 5th and 10th have been having a little brush or two with the Indians. These, with Forsyth's fight
on the Republican, which by the way was about the best thing that
has been done for some years in the way of Indian fighting, make all
the <u>real war</u> we have had.

I recently read a long article in the *Herald* from some scribbler
who was trying to make some reputation for Colonel Sully out of his
expedition to the Canadian in September. I had the honor to command the cavalry on that expedition, and if that was <u>fighting,</u> then
Indian wars must be a huge joke. (Don't allow this to become public,
if you please, for "Old Sully" is an amiable fellow, and I would not
like to hurt his feelings.)

I see some of the papers are pitying the "Poor Indian" as usual,
while the peace commissioners are making heroes and saints of them

again. I only wish some of the most enthusiastic of their admirers, both male and female, could have been the recipients of the "Noble Red" kindnesses instead of the unfortunate settlers on the Saline and Solomon. One of the women brought into Fort Harker was ravished by twenty-three of the villains and then shot through the body. Strange to say, she bids fair to recover from all this. Ed Wynkoop is out in a letter defending the Indians. If he were not so insignificant, I would like to see him "touched up" in good style. Comstock was one of the first victims to the savages. He and a scout named Grover had visited the camp of Black Kettle, a Cheyenne chief then sup- posed to be friendly, and were leaving it when they were followed and shot. Grover feigned death and escaped with his life. Comstock was killed [in] the first fire. From some cause, the Indians did not scalp him. He is the only one of our scouts who have been killed to my knowledge. Under present circumstances, I think my chances of getting coyote skins are at least no better than they are of being eaten by the coyotes. We are in the field and <u>move light,</u> which latter means as uncomfortable as possible.

When I began this letter, I had an idea of conveying to you my <u>grumblings</u> about "army life on the border," but have already written a tolerably long letter and haven't begun my subject yet. So I'll wait for a more favorable opportunity. Many thanks for those stamps. If you owed me any, you have a better memory than I have, but I was just as glad to receive them as though you had been my debtor for a thousand.

Very truly yours,
Joel H. Elliott

The Fight on Prairie Dog Creek

ANONYMOUS[1]

Army and Navy Journal 6, no. 13 (November 7, 1868)

A correspondent writing from Fort Hays, Kansas, under date of October 28, 1868, gives the following account of a recent expedition against the Indians in the Department of the Missouri:

On Thursday, October 22, the general commanding the department received a dispatch from Buffalo Spring[2] that the 5th Cavalry had come in and was encamped four miles from the railroad on the Saline.[3] Immediately the general gave orders to Bvt. Lt. Col. A. J. McConnigle, quartermaster, and Bvt. Brig. Gen. Michael B. Morgan, commissary of subsistence, both of the department staff, to hasten forward twenty days' supplies. About the same time, the two companies of the 10th Cavalry had returned home from a more successful visit to the country toward the north and bringing in the important intelligence of the location of the Indians [Cheyennes].[4] While these two companies immediately received orders to refit for another expedition, Bvt. Maj. Gen. Eugene A. Carr, major 5th Cavalry, was advised of the whereabouts of his command, which he joined immediately, reaching it on Friday, October 23. The command by this time was ready to move.

During its presence on the Saline, the general sent forward the few reinforcements which he had, which made this entire force, when it moved out the same day, to consist of Companies A, B, F, I, L, and M of the 5th Cavalry, Bvt. Col. William B. Royall, major 5th Cavalry, commanding, and the company of Forsyth's scouts, Lt. Silas Pepoon commanding; Bvt. Maj. Gen. Eugene A. Carr, major 5th Cavalry, commanding the expedition. Bvt. Lt. Col. Thomas W. C. Moore,[5] captain 40th Infantry and aide-de-camp to General Sheridan, also accompanied the movement. It was Friday, October 23, when the command started afresh. The line of march lay in a northwesterly direction across Prairie Dog Creek toward the Little Beaver. The weather was delightful, clear, and bracing. The plain, hardened by recent rains, made the march of the column less uncomfortable than had characterized its movements but a few weeks before.

On Saturday, October 24, the column continued its march, and more rapidly. The preceding day the encumbrance of the train was severely felt, and the rapid movements of the troops were necessarily held in check for the secondary purpose of saving a few wagons. Orders were given to destroy fifteen of the wagons, and all the tents were also disposed of in the same manner. Eight mules were now attached to the remaining wagons. The column thus disembarrassed now found less to delay its movements, and by forced marching covered the ground rapidly and were evidently gaining on the enemy.

The trail grew more distinct, but had not the appearance of the entire body of savages passing that way. All Saturday had passed until 4:00 P.M., when, as the advance of the column reached the summit of a ridge, it was confronted by two hundred savages on the hills opposite. They made no direct attack, but relied upon demonstrations calculated to bring the troops into formations to make or repel an attack, and as the troops advanced, the savages withdrew. The latter, evidently concerned at the formidable nature of the column, were particularly uneasy at its steady progress. Several times they ignited the dry grass on the plain to the windward in hopes of checking the march and gaining time. But the column held on its way, the savages receding as it approached. Detachments of men mounted on the fleetest horses made several dashes upon the savages, but their vigilance was superior to the activity of their pursuers, and [they] escaped all harm.

From the skill and determination with which the savages declined an engagement, it was apparent that their main force had not yet come up, and that until then there was little left to be done but to hurry forward, driving back the force in front and carefully guarding the flanks and rear from a surprise attack. The column moved on, the savages fell back, and at long range the two hostile bodies fired at each other without effect. The same night, after making an examination in different directions and traveling forty-two miles, the column encamped near the camp of the night before, forty-one miles north of the starting point of the movement. It was now 8:00 P.M., the body of the savages withdrew, the stock having been carefully placed under guard and pickets posted. The night was spent in quietude and speculation upon the chances of securing a fight on the next day.

It was still early in the day when the signs of the presence of the Indians were again discernible. The trail was fresh and had not long been passed over. These appearances encouraged a quicker movement. There was a keen relish in the appearance of all for the excitement now almost within reach. A light advance party moved ahead of the column at a distance of a quarter of a mile. Next came the advance guard, then came the train, and in the rear another strong guard to repel any attack from this quarter. On the flanks were small detachments prepared to sound the alarm should any demonstration be made in that direction.

Ten miles had been compassed when a strong body of the savages ranged themselves in front, determined to dispute with firmer resolution the further progress of the column. Proper dispositions were made of the troops, and the entire force advanced. A body of the 5th Cavalry consisting of Company H,

Bvt. Capt. John H. Kane[6] commanding, and Company M, Lieutenants Schenofsky and Forbush commanding,[7] were formed for the charge and at the word of command dashed for the savages on the hill. The savages withdrew, keeping a fair distance ahead, but keeping up a fire as they went. For three miles the pursuit was kept up, when the cavalry fell back. The Indians with unusual boldness pursued and frequently dashed within easy range. The Forsyth scouts, commanded by Lt. Silas Pepoon, 10th Cavalry, were next in turn ordered to charge. Pepoon shouted to his men, "Come on boys, pick your men; give them hell and let the devil take care of the rest." This was not the first time these scouts had tackled these Indians, and in they went.

By this time the engagement became of a more general character. A number of the men were dismounted and advanced in a heavy skirmish line. The Indians, in their open order of fighting, were dashing hither and thither without regard to discipline or order, shooting as they got an opportunity and then dropping behind their horses. Upon reaching the summit of a commanding eminence, many miles in the distance an immense cloud of dust indicated another large body moving in an opposite direction. The Indians who were engaging the troops were now positively concluded to be a strong covering party, and that the dust indicated the flight of their lodge poles and families, with the stock and whatever else they had necessary to escape the hostile white men.

With this appearance of the proximity of the bulk of the hostile Indians, a rapid movement was made, which forced back the savage warriors. This sudden advance brought the troops in possession of some hundreds of abandoned lodge poles of cedar, which from this reason were known to have come from Texas. Four hundred buffalo skins, having been subjected to the first stage of preparation for tanning, were also captured and destroyed; cooking utensils and everything unnecessary were discarded by the Indians and picked up or destroyed by the troops. The day was thus consumed. The savages with fresh animals kept harassing the advance, and the main body of the [Cheyenne] nation, with a strong guard, were still on the move miles ahead. The troops were exhausted, and much of the stock was completely unfit for further usefulness. Without the power of moving ahead, late in the evening the column went into camp, to refresh and resume the advance in the morning. During the day, ten Indians were killed and seventy ponies were killed or captured. On the side of the troops, several men were wounded and fifteen horses and twenty-two mules were lost, either by the bullet or the exertions of the day. The engagements of the twenty-fourth and twenty-fifth instant constitute as yet the most decisive that have taken place. Major Carr is still pursuing, and though the body of the Indians were still in flight, he was after them, they moving in a northerly direction, burning the prairies to impede the march of their pursuers. Major Carr has fifteen days' provisions, but the Indians have the advantage and any number of fresh ponies. On October 27 a dispatch by courier from the major announced a vigorous pursuit and still hopeful of overtaking the savages.

PART FOUR

The Cheyenne War, 1868–69

Sheridan's Indian Campaign

WILLIAM C. CHURCH[1]

Army and Navy Journal 6, no. 14 (November 21, 1868)

For some time past, the copies of departmental orders, which have reached this office from General Sheridan's[2] headquarters, have indicated beyond doubt that preparations were making for an important hostile movement against the Indians of the plains. Not only the sending forward of troops and the assignments to important posts and positions of competent officers, but the large transportation to certain points of Spencer carbines and Spencer and Springfield ammunition, with twelve-pounder shell and canister, and supplies and accoutrements of various sorts, made it clear that a vigorous prosecution of the campaign was at hand.

Last Monday, the sixteenth, General Sheridan, with his staff and escort, left Fort Hays for Fort Wallace. He announces that his headquarters are in the field, and the inference has been drawn that he would proceed as far south as the Canadian River, and there assume command in person of the troops operating in that region against the hostile Indians. There are several points in connection with this enterprise of interest to set forth.

The middle of November is commonly regarded by those most experienced in the warfare of the plains to be the time when the Indians cease to roam at will over the open prairies. Henceforward, to about the last of April or first of May, mindful of the pitiless winter storms that sweep the plains with almost resistless fury, they betake themselves to their winter quarters. In summer they can live carelessly anywhere in Nebraska and Dakota and plunder or fight with great relish, secure of their final retreat before the winter winds and snows come. But then, if pressed, they are forced to retreat southerly, beyond the Arkansas and its southerly tributaries, through Colorado and Kansas to the Indian Territory, or perhaps to New Mexico and Texas.

Now, whereas our forces have hitherto taken the middle of November as about the time to cease campaigning, Sheridan seems to have selected it as the time to *begin.* And in this difference of plan we see the augury of success. During the summer, it has been like looking for a needle in a haystack to get at the

Indians. Mounted on swift ponies, and with abundance of food and forage all about them, their movements have never been restrained by necessities of climate or of hunger. They could move north, east, south, west—to whatsoever quarter they chose—in order to escape our troops. They could fall upon ranches or outposts, upon trains, settlers, or forage parties of soldiers with impunity, sure of making good their escape in any direction, with abundance of game around them. And even if our troops pressed them closely, they had only to scatter, and it was harder work even than Sheridan found in the Shenandoah among the innocent "farmers," who had the day before been in Early's raiding columns, to tell who was the hostile and who the "loyal" man.

But in winter these advantages are gone. The hostile Indians can no longer live in this free-and-easy way. They must go to their lodges; they must betake themselves to their winter's huts and provisions; they can be found clustered around the wooded regions, where they find fuel for the cold months and shelter from the bleak storms. Driven out of these haunts, they will perish. Ordinarily our preparations have been made in winter for a summer's campaign, but now they have been made in summer for a winter's campaign.

We found, after a while, during the Rebellion that the best way to fight the enemy was not where he wished to fight us, but where we wished to fight him. And again, we learned by the same experience that if a winter's campaign was better than a summer's, to make it in winter, as Grant did that of 1864–1865, and not politely wait for spring to open. The Indian can only be hunted down in his own fixed abodes—in the bottomlands whither he betakes himself, and we must act against his *base,* namely his lodges and his winter supplies, if we would conquer him. A defeat in midwinter would be ten times more valuable than one in midsummer; and in the former alone can enough Indians be collected to fight against to advantage.

Next, as regards the number and equipment of our forces: The latest telegram from Fort Hays represents that General Sheridan's forces number about 2,700 men and that small expeditionary columns from Fort Lyon and from New Mexico will cooperate with him. Our readers may safely accept this estimate for general purposes, and it is force enough. When, in addition, we are informed that the hostile Indians now on the warpath number about seven thousand, it may at first appear that the odds are too great. But the difficulty hitherto has not been in too great odds, as the "salty dose" that Forsyth with fourscore men administered to six or eight times their number of Indians will attest. The trouble is that we hitherto have not often had the right *kind* of men, or even of officers. We have needed fewer bad ox-teams and more good officers for success; we have needed, in place of "raw recruits from a country town" or well-meaning but thick-skulled and untrained bumpkins, good soldiers habituated to a frontier life, familiar with the weapons they use, whether Springfield rifles or Spencer carbines, alert, adroit, used to the hardships of campaigning, a match for Indian tricks, and, in a word, fitted for the service in which they are engaged.

Two or three thousand men, *well mounted,* are sufficient for a successful campaign. This force, properly provisioned, properly armed, properly equipped, and provided with good officers, are all that are needed. The trouble has been, in some former campaigns, that the men were not well fitted for the service they undertook. In some cases, too great a reliance was had upon infantry—a force utterly inadequate to the work in hand; in some cases, they were fettered by the matter of supplies. Even our cavalry have been often unable, with their heavy mounts, to compete with the light-mounted, flying Indian. The nature of the force required is that of cavalry, armed with breechloaders and ready to act as infantry on reaching the enemy—the "mounted infantry" of our late war. They have every advantage which the Indian has in the way of food, clothing, forage, and protection from storms, and when once brought face-to-face with the enemy, 2,500 picked men, armed with breechloaders, will be equal to ten times their number, badly selected and badly armed. The advantages of the body of Indian scouts now in our service will also be apparent in this campaign.

Cut off from grass and from game by the season, and from their winter's store of dried buffalo meat and of fuel by the foray of our troops upon their villages, the Indian warriors will soon find that this campaign is entirely different from those to which they have been accustomed. Our troops will fare forth, prepared for the inclemency of the weather and with minds made up to the fact that they have no luxurious task before them. Their shelter and their comforts will be only such as they carry in their columns.

Precisely what tribes are now on the warpath, or rather what lodges of particular tribes, is not made officially known. We presume that the bulk of the hostile force south of the Arkansas consists of Kiowas, Comanches, and Arapahos. Probably our old foes the Sioux and Cheyennes furnish some bands to the enterprise, though Red Cloud, Big Bear, and some other chiefs were not long ago at Fort Laramie, it is said, on rather friendly terms with the whites, but rather sour regarding the Crows. However, all this will appear in good time.

We need hardly add that General Sheridan possesses in an eminent degree the force, dash, endurance, and determination necessary to bring this undertaking to success. If he can do nothing for us, we had better cast about for some other way of accomplishing our ends. We believe, however, that he will be successful, and at all events, it is a good omen that he has apparently gone to work in the right way.

General Sully's Winter Expedition

"SOLDAT"

Army and Navy Journal 6, no. 20 (January 2, 1869): 310

IN THE FIELD, INDIAN TERRITORY,
NOVEMBER 22, 1868

To the Editor of the Army and Navy Journal.

SIR: Colonel Sully's Indian expedition started from Fort Dodge, Kansas, and Fort Lyon, Colorado, on the twelfth instant [November], prepared for a winter campaign against the savages of the plains, whose persistent and consistent treachery has hitherto procured for them, almost annually, renewed treaties, presents, and annuities as rewards (virtually) for renewed hostilities.

The writer accompanied the cavalry army of the outfit—viz., the 7th regiment, commanded by Colonel Custer, when it broke camp on the Arkansas River below Fort Dodge on that day. The regiment moved off in column of divisions or platoons, in which the horses were arranged by colors—as chestnuts, blacks, bays, grays, sorrels, browns, etc.—presenting a magnificent appearance in the bright sunlight of a clear, cool morning, with just enough breeze to display the flags and guidons to the best advantage and to waft down the column the strains of music from the 7th Cavalry band, which was mounted on fine grays in advance.[1] The music mingled with the roar of an immense wagon train, which moved in a quadruplicated column in the same course and recalled to mind the scenes of yore, "way down in Old Virginia."

The band took occasion to remind us of the girl we left behind us—a period now quite too remote and obscure in the past to excite any tearful regrets in this instance.

Everybody marched off, seemingly cheerful—the men in the ranks particularly so—giving vent to their exuberant spirits in different ways quietly. While riding near the column this morning, I heard a trooper humming a version of "Out of the Wilderness," which ran in this wise:

If you want to smell hell,
Just join the cavalry, join the cavalry;
If you want to smell hell,
Then join the cavalry,
We're not going home.

The expedition consists of the entire 7th Cavalry; parts of the 5th and 10th Cavalry regiments; the 19th Kansas Volunteer Cavalry under Colonel Crawford,[2] the present governor of the state; and parts of the 3rd, 5th, 27th, and 38th Infantry regiments.

The huge supply train of several hundred army wagons contains materials and implements for constructing a new fort near the mouth of the Middle Fork of the Canadian River, 104 miles south-southeast from Fort Dodge, and is designed for a base of supplies during the campaign.[3]

Riding near Colonel Sully are some Osage Indians from a peaceful tribe, who are employed to hunt up and trace the enemy's trails. They are well mounted and are adorned with the usual amount of paint, feathers, leggings, blankets, etc., and look as savage as the enemy we seek.

Our ponderous, imposing column ploughs its way across the Arkansas River, where we fill our canteens with water, and when fairly over and under way, with the hills about to shut out the view, we turn to take a last look at its restless surface, wondering what scenes and incidents will come to us before we look at it again.

The march is varied by an occasional chase after buffalo, wolves, and antelope, all of which are abundant hereabouts.

We have reveille and breakfast before daylight, and the column is in motion at the first peep of day. We go into camp early in the afternoon, and all the animals are then allowed to graze until retreat. And all this movement is on account of "Lo,"[4] who costs us millions annually through other and more peaceful channels.

It is not surprising, perhaps, that a magnanimous spirit should prevail among the American people, and particularly among those who are least informed, concerning the Indians of this continent—as for instance through the eastern and middle states, where such ignorance certainly does exist. But this feeling of magnanimity is not well directed for several reasons.

Five of these Plains Indians against whom the troops are now moving—the Arapahos, Cheyennes, Kiowas, Comanches, and Kiowa-Apaches—were assembled together around Fort Larned in August last, numbering from twelve to fifteen thousand. There was every opportunity then for even the most philanthropic to observe that those Indians are not the most object beings in existence.

Indeed, it is not generally known how much the government does for the "noble red man." Instead of the suffering, squalor, and misery, which according to the prevailing belief, they present, the scenes witnessed at Fort Larned more resembled a stupendous circus. The Indians were mounted on fine horses and ponies caparisoned with handsome showy equipment, and themselves clad in bright-colored raiment, warm and durable.

One tribe in particular attracted my attention; the Cheyennes (whose butcheries last summer were the most merciless) looked remarkably clean and ostentatious, with a plethora of the best blankets and cloth and the finest trappings to their horses, indicating anything but destitution, while well supplied with robes and furs for traffic. Moreover, every tribe is now rich in the possession of large numbers of horses and ponies, which form their most valuable stock in trade. They murder and scalp, first in one region, then in another, always increasing their worldly possessions (never missing an opportunity, however, to augment their *spiritual* acquisitions), and always aiding to their increasing comforts by bartering their captured property at points where it will not be identified after the inevitable treaties, and with other peaceful tribes during war. So that, adding to these facilities the annuities and presents from the government, poor Lo manages to eke out a successful, chivalric, wandering existence, such as thousands of aimless white vagabonds in all countries would be satisfied to accept, if highwaymen's occupation were as leniently and respectfully tolerated as a misguided policy has hitherto sanctioned and enforced toward the treacherous, cowardly "brave," known as the noble red man of the American continent, who is the most bloodthirsty of all highwaymen.

When after truce is declared this petted creature, in quest of novelty and refreshments, stalks into your tent unasked and proceeds to inform you (after quietly taking a seat with a gravity and dignity really stunning) that he will then condescend to accept your most bounteous hospitality without affront, you very naturally stare at the impudent, sensual lump of red statuary and give him something to eat. He decks himself to feed your curiosity while you feed his stomach. Patience, generosity, and a fat larder are required, however, to do this, demanding a fortitude on your part worthy of a better cause.

Briefly, the Indian is cunning; he knows it, and knows we do not give him credit for one half his cunning, and this he takes advantage of in all his transactions with us, as he does when on the warpath. And yet one experiences a feeling of curiosity, although mingled with disgust, when meeting this monster whose hands are ever stained with the blood of the whites, remembering always that the fiend is wishing to scalp us the instant he dares to do so.

No person has ever been in this region for several years past, probably, with facilities for learning the actual state of affairs, without arriving at the conclusion that our whole system of treaties with Indians is a downright farce. Our government, with spasms of warped philanthropy and corrupted generosity, has rarely refused these ignorant, indigent, ingenious, indignant Indians any request, unless we except perhaps their recent demand for a battery of artillery. At least if this has been granted, it has not been made known to the public yet.

There are some who defend the Indians' cause. Do they know what efforts and proffers have been made to induce them to adopt even a semicivilized life?

Meanwhile, our grand expedition moves on through the deceiving mirage and prairie-dog holes, while we wonder how many people in the United States know that an undertaking is on foot, which from its importance would, before the late war, have engrossed the whole nation's attention.

An Indian Campaign

HORACE L. MOORE[1]

N.p., n.d.[2]

During the summers of 1868 and 1869, the western part of Kansas, the southeastern part of Colorado, and the northwestern part of Texas were raided over and over again by war parties of what were called the Plains Indians. The Indians engaged in these forays were the Cheyennes, Arapahos, Kiowas, Comanches, Northern Cheyennes, Brule [and] Oglala Sioux, and the Pawnees.[3]

On August 10, 1868, they struck the settlements on the Saline River. On the twelfth they reached the Solomon and wiped out a settlement where the city of Minneapolis is situated. In this raid fifteen persons were killed, two wounded, and five women were carried off. On the same day, they attacked Wright's hay camp near Fort Dodge, raided the Pawnee, and killed two settlers on the Republican. On September 8 they captured a train at the Cimarron Crossing of the Arkansas River, securing possession of seventeen men, whom they burned. And the day following, they murdered six men between Sheridan and Fort Wallace.

On September 1, 1868, the Indians killed four men at Spanish Fork in Texas and outraged three women. One of these women was outraged by thirteen Indians and afterwards killed and scalped. They left her with the hatchet still sticking in her head. Before leaving, they murdered her four little children. Of the children carried off by the Indians from Texas in 1868, fourteen were frozen to death in captivity.

The total losses from September 12, 1868, to February 9, 1869, exclusive of the casualties incident to military operations, were 158 men murdered, 16 wounded, and 41 scalped. Three scouts were killed, fourteen women outraged, one man was captured, four women and twenty-four children were carried off. Nearly all these losses occurred in what we then called western Kansas, although the Saline, Solomon, and Republican do not seem so very far west now.

In 1867 the Union Pacific Railroad was built as far west as Fort Hays, and as the graders were constantly being attacked by Indians, the 18th Kansas

Cavalry (a battalion of four companies) was mustered into the service of the United States for the purpose of furnishing protection to the laborers on the railroad and to keep the Santa Fe Trail clear for the passage of wagon trains and the overland coaches.

The battalion was rendezvoused at Fort Harker, near where Ellsworth is situated, on July 15, 1867. I was mustered with the rank of major, in command. At that time the Asiatic cholera was epidemic on the plains, and the hospitals at Harker were full of soldiers and laborers sick with cholera. As soon as the command was mustered into the service, and transportation and supplies could be obtained, it marched to the southwest to strike the Arkansas River near Fort Zarah, at the mouth of the Walnut Creek. The sick were left at Harker.

The afternoon march of July 15 developed no new cases of cholera. On the sixteenth a long march was made and camp pitched on the left bank of Walnut Creek, about ten miles above Zarah (Arkansas City now). The day brought no new cases and everybody felt cheerful, hoping that the future had nothing worse in store than a meeting with hostile Indians. By 8:00 P.M. supper was over, and in another hour the camp became a hospital of screaming cholera patients. Men were seized with cramping of the stomach, bowels, and muscles of the arms and legs. The doctor and his medicine were powerless to resist the disease. One company had been sent away on a scout as soon as the command reached the camp, and of the three companies remaining in camp, the morning of the seventeenth found five dead and thirty-six stretched on the ground in a state of collapse. These men had no pulse at the wrist, their hands were shrunken and purple, with the skin in wrinkles, and their eyes wide open. The doctor pronounced them in a state of hopeless collapse.

By sunrise a grave had been dug and the dead buried. Commissary and quartermaster stores were thrown away, and two of the sick (the most favorable cases) were put into the single ambulance with the command, and the remaining thirty-four were put into the wagons with blankets under them. A government wagon is wide enough for three men to lie side by side, and long enough for two men at the side, so that each wagon would carry six. In this way the sick were all taken along. It was necessary to follow up Walnut Creek three or four miles before a crossing could be effected. While this was being done, the sick were examined, and not one was found to have died since the cholera camp was left. On this the doctor took new courage, and during the balance of the day he was unremitting in his attentions. He went from one wagon to another, giving stimulants where it was possible to get the patient to swallow, and details were made to assist him in chafing the hands and feet to restore if possible circulation.

A long march was made on the seventeenth, and camp was finally made on the Arkansas River above Pawnee Rock. Not a man had died during the day. A buffalo calf was shot, soup was made, and the sick taken from the wagons and made as comfortable as possible under the circumstances. The night was spent in the most assiduous care of these sick men, and in the morning a detachment was sent to Fort Larned to notify the commanding officer of the post of the condition of the command. On arriving at the crossing of Pawnee Fork, now Larned, the sick were turned over to the United States surgeons who had established a hospital at this place. Although these thirty-six men were in a state of collapse when they were loaded onto the wagons at the camp on Walnut Creek, every one of them lived to be turned over to the doctors at Fort Larned at noon on September 18. The circulation had been restored, and they were able to take nourishment. I think this favorable result is entirely unprecedented in the treatment of Asiatic cholera.

The doctor, a young contract surgeon by the name of Squire from New Hampshire, was attacked with cholera during the night of the nineteenth. As the command had to move in the morning, the doctor was given his choice, to move with it or remain in the hospital. He chose the latter, and on the second day his case terminated fatally.

The command moved up Pawnee Fork without a medical attendant, and on the second day after leaving Fort Larned, one of the sergeants was attacked and died of cholera that night. This was the last fatal case in the command. The hospital steward was attacked at the same time but recovered.

The battalion served four months on the plains, marched about 2,200 miles, and fought a battle with the Cheyennes on Prairie Dog Creek, a branch of the Republican, in which it suffered a loss of fourteen officers and men, killed and wounded.

The depredations of the Indians during the fall of the following year, 1868, satisfied the War Department that something more effective than a summer campaign would have to be resorted to, to protect the frontier settlements and teach the Indians that the army was able to punish any tribe that made a pastime of robbery and murder. General Sheridan, who was then in command of the Department of the Missouri, determined on a winter campaign. If there is anything that strikes terror into the heart of a soldier, it is a winter campaign. There is no feed for his horse except what he can haul in the train, and the roads are generally impassable for trains and artillery. His camp equipage must be cut down all that is possible to save transportation. Tents, camp stores, and clothing must give place to commissary stores, and as a general statement the impedimenta of the army must be reduced to the lowest point possible.

In a winter campaign was the only hope of subduing the Indians. In the summer, the plains were covered with grass and buffalo. The Indians' forage and rations were everywhere. In the winter, the buffalo were in the canyons and mountains, snow covered the grass, and blizzards swept the plains.

On October 9, 1868, General Sheridan called on Gov. S. J. Crawford of Kansas for a twelve-company regiment of cavalry to be mustered into the United States service for this winter campaign. On October 15, General Sherman wrote as follows to General Sheridan:

Gov. Samuel J. Crawford.
COURTESY OF PERRY FROHNE.

As to extermination, it is for the Indians themselves to determine. We don't want to exterminate or even fight them. At best it is an inglorious war, not apt to add much to our fame or personal comfort; and for our soldiers, to whom we owe our first thoughts, it is all danger and extreme labor, without a single compensating advantage.

As brave men and as the soldiers of a government which has exhausted its peace efforts, we, in the performance of a most unpleasant duty, accept the war begun by our enemies and hereby resolve to make its end final. If it results in the utter annihilation of these Indians, it is but the result of what they have been warned again and again, and for which they seem fully prepared. I will say nothing and do nothing to restrain our troops from doing what they deem proper on the spot, and will allow no mere vague general charges of cruelty and inhumanity to tie their hands, but will use all the powers confided to me to the end that these Indians, the enemies of our race and of our civilization, shall not again be able to begin and carry on their barbarous warfare on any kind of pretext that they may choose to allege.

I believe that this winter will afford us the opportunity, and that before the snow falls these Indians will seek some sort of peace, to be broken next year at their option; but we will not accept their peace, or cease our efforts till all the past acts are both punished and revenged.

You may now go ahead in your own way, and I will back you with my whole authority, and stand between you and any efforts that may be attempted in your rear to restrain your purpose or check your troops.

This letter of General Sherman will be understood when it is remembered that the Indian Bureau is a part of the Department of the Interior. The Indian [Bureau] appointed Indian agents, bought and issued supplies, and had entire control of the Indian affairs till an outbreak occurred, when the War Department was called on to force the hostiles into submission. As soon as the army struck the Indians, the charges of cruelty and inhumanity mentioned by General Sherman were made and reiterated from one end of the country to another, with the result that the army was called off. Now Sherman promised Sheridan to back him with his whole authority and stand between him and the querulous and impracticable humanitarians of the East.

The 19th Kansas Cavalry was called into the United States service under instructions received by his excellency, S. J. Crawford, governor of Kansas, from Maj. Gen. P. H. Sheridan, dated October 9, 1868. The proclamation of the governor calling for volunteers was dated in October 1868, and the regiment was mustered, armed, and the organization completed at Topeka, Kansas, on November 4 by the muster in of Samuel J. Crawford as colonel. I was mustered in with the rank of lieutenant colonel.

In obedience to orders from General Sheridan, Captain [J. Q. A.] Norton, D Troop, and Captain [Richard D.] Lender, G Troop, were sent by rail to Fort Hays on November 5 with their commands, and under instructions from the same source, the remaining ten companies broke camp at Topeka and marched en route to the mouth of the Beaver Creek (the north branch of the North Canadian), where a depot of supplies was to be established by colonel Sully on the fifteenth. Our route was via Camp Beecher, now Wichita, at the mouth of the Little Arkansas, distant one hundred fifty miles, which distance we were to make with a new organization supplied with five days' rations and depend on procuring forage from the country through which we were to pass, as our limited transportation of fifteen wagons precluded the possibility of carrying any supply with us.

The command arrived at Camp Beecher on the twelfth. This was the first experience of the regiment in making five days' rations do the work of ten, and like all first efforts, it was not a complete success. General Sheridan says, "On November 15, I started for Camp Supply to give general supervision and to participate in the operations. I deemed it best to go in person, as the campaign was an experimental one—campaigns at such a season having been deemed impracticable and reckless by old and experienced frontiersmen, and I did not like to expose the troops to great hazard without being present myself to judge of their hardships and privations."

The regiment marched from Camp Beecher on November 14 with five days' rations en route to Camp Supply, supposed distance 140 miles. On the night of the sixteenth, the command camped on the Chikoskie, and the last of the forage was fed to the animals. On the night of the eighteenth, the regiment camped on Medicine Lodge Creek. A stampede of the animals of B, I, and K Troops occurred here, and about eighty horses were lost.

The regiment moved out of camp on the morning of the nineteenth without forage for the animals or subsistence for the men, marching through an unexplored region in search of a camp of supplies supposed to be situated somewhere on the Canadian River, and on the night of the twenty-second camped on Sand Creek during a heavy fall of snow, in sight of the bluffs of the Cimarron. Buffalo were abundant, and thus far the command had subsisted on them. Captain Pliley, A Troop, and Lieutenant [Jesse E.] Parsons, C Troop, with fifty of the best mounted men of the command, were sent forward from this point to find General Sheridan if possible and cause supplies to be sent back to the regiment.

November 23. A blinding snowstorm continued all day. The guides found it impossible to keep the direction, and the command was forced to lie in camp.

November 24. The snow this morning was fifteen inches deep. The horses had subsisted on cottonwood bark and limbs and were by this time so much exhausted that the men walked and led them. The country was so broken that in some instances the miles were traveled winding around the canyons to make two miles on the line of march. The regiment camped that night at "Hackberry Point" on the Cimarron, so named by the men from the abundance of hackberries in the vicinity, which were used for food.

The canyons of the Cimarron are not like those of Arizona, which are cut in the solid rock and have perpendicular walls, but are like the canyons of the Llano Estacado, or the Staked Plains. The Cimarron cuts its way through a plateau of clay, and the main stream together with the innumerable side streams have cut the whole country into a labyrinth of canyons, or deep gulches, that are almost impassable. The snow was from a foot to eighteen inches deep everywhere. The guide knew no more about the country than any man of the regiment, and the only course left was to continue the march, keeping a southwest course as nearly as possible, and keep going until the command got out of the canyon country. It happened that about sundown of the twenty-fourth, a bunch of buffalo bulls were seen among the bluffs. The command was halted while the guide stole upon them and shot the whole number.

The train failed to come up at night, and the command bivouacked on the snow without the usual small supply of blankets.

November 25. The train got in by morning and the regiment was divided. Four hundred fifty men (the best mounted) crossed the Cimarron at 1:00 P.M. and marched in a southwest course in search of Camp Supply. Those horses which were most nearly exhausted, together with the train and sick, were left in camp under command of Major [R. W.] Jenkins, with orders to remain until supplies reached them.

The country on the south side of the Cimarron at this point is much broken, and the command was forced to reach the tableland above by following up the dry bed of a stream which had cut its way down through the inaccessible bluffs. The men dismounted and, leading single file, wound their way around cliffs and over broken banks for several miles, till a little after sunset and just as the moon came up, they emerged from the canyon, and by climbing a precipitous cliff were enabled to overlook the inhospitable tableland, covered with snow.

Tonight we bivouacked in a small ravine with the never-failing buffalo meat for supper; no salt.

November 26. Still southwest over rolling prairie and through deep canyons, horses perishing by the way, but with stout hearts the command moved forward, one company after another taking their place in front to break the road through the deep snow. The crust today in some places was strong enough to hold up the men. Bivouacked on a nameless stream fifteen miles north of the Canadian.

November 27. Crossed Captain Pliley's trail at noon and bivouacked at night on the Canadian at a point supposed to be twenty-five miles below the mouth of Beaver Creek. Made supper from wild turkey.

November 28. Moved up the Canadian, and at 3:00 P.M. the advance came back to the regiment with the welcome news that Camp Supply was in sight. The advance of the command took up the shout, and it was carried back along the column with a vigor which evinced the fact that each had felt more anxiety for the safety of the command than he cared to express. Made camp at sundown, canvas being furnished from the post by General Sheridan.

Captain Pliley had arrived on the twenty-fifth, and supplies had been sent to the detachment left at Hackberry Point on the twenty-fifth. The detachment arrived at Camp Supply on December 1. The camp where the train was left was always known among the men as Camp Starvation.

After leaving Camp Beecher, the regiment marched 205 miles on three days' forage and five days' rations, consuming fourteen days in making the trip; seventy-five horses perished from the cold and want of food. The health of the regiment was good, and it endured the hardships of the march without a murmur. We did not lose a man.

Touching the loss of the regiment in the Cimarron canyons, General Sheridan says in his memoirs, "Instead of relying on the guides, Crawford had undertaken to strike through the canyons of the Cimarron by what appeared to him a more direct route, and in the deep gorges, filled as they were with snow, he had been floundering for days without being able to extricate his command. Then, too, the men were out of rations, though they had been able to obtain enough buffalo meat to keep from starving."

This was written in 1888. It is better to quote from the general's official report made at the time, twenty years before he wrote his memoirs: "On November 25 I was relieved from great anxiety by the arrival of Captain Pliley and about thirty men. The regiment had lost its way, and becoming tangled up in the canyons of the Cimarron and in the deep snow and out of provisions, it could not make its way out and was in a bad fix. Provisions were immediately sent and good guides to bring it in. It had been subsisting on buffalo for eight or nine days."

The word "good" is important, as it implies that the one sent to Topeka was no good, and the statement that Colonel Crawford did not rely on the guide till the guide got lost is entirely without foundation. The report was current in the command that when the guide met Sheridan, the said guide picked up considerable information as to the way English was spoken by the British Army in Flanders on a certain occasion. The general reported of the regiment, "Officers and men behaved admirably in the trying condition in which they were placed."

When the regiment arrived at Camp Supply, it found a camp prepared. The snow had been cleared off the ground, "A" tents pitched for the men, and wall tents for the officers, with hay in every tent for bedding. This was a palace hotel compared with the canyons of the Cimarron, and Sheridan had captured the regiment at one blow.

On December 6, D Troop reported at Camp Supply and was ordered to the command. Captain Moody's M Troop being detailed for escort duty in his place, Captain Norton reached Fort Hays on November 4 and escorted a train to Camp Supply, arriving on the twenty-second; returned to Fort Dodge and escorted a train to Camp Supply, arriving on December 5. On the same day Maj. Charles Dimon, with one captain, three lieutenants, [and] 250 men, were detached from the command and left at Camp Supply. This detachment was employed during the winter in garrisoning the post and escorting supply trains.

On the morning of November 23, Custer had been ordered to follow on the back track a trail that came up from the southwest and crossed the Fort Dodge road between Supply and Dodge. The trail led to an Indian camp on the Washita, some seventy-five miles south of Supply. Custer attacked the camp at daylight on the morning of November 27 and had a hard fight. He lost nineteen officers and men killed and wounded, with Major Elliott and fifteen men missing. He killed 103 Indian warriors,[4] and some of the squaws and children were killed and wounded in the excitement. He captured saddles, buffalo robes, provisions, and 875 horses. These were surrounded and shot. Colonel Custer returned to Camp Supply November 30, and on December 7 the whole command marched for Fort Cobb. This included the 19th Kansas [and] 7th U.S. Cavalry and a company of Osage Indian scouts. The first day's march was to the south bank of Wolf Creek, a distance of ten miles. The snow was still deep, and when the command left Camp Supply, the temperature was below zero. The second day's march was a little more than thirty miles, and camp was made on Hackberry Creek, with plenty of wood for fires.

During the night the wind rose, and by morning a full-fledged norther or blizzard was on the boards, billed for two nights and a matinee. The country seemed to be full of blizzards. The first had struck the regiment in the canyons, the second while it was in camp at Supply. This was the third. General Sheridan says of number three:

We camped in excellent shape on the creek (Hackberry), and it was well we did, for a norther or blizzard struck us in the night. It would have been well to remain in camp till the gale was over, but the time could not be spared. We therefore resumed the march at an early hour next morning, with the expectation of making the south bank of the main Canadian and there passing the night, as Clark[5] the guide assured me that timber was plentiful on that side of the river. The storm greatly impeded us, however, many of the mules growing discouraged, and some giving out entirely, so we could not get to Clark's "good camp," for with ten hours of utmost effort only about half a day's distance could be covered, when at last, finding the struggle useless, we were forced to halt for the night in a bleak bottom on the north bank of the river. But no one could sleep, for the wind swept over us with unobstructed fury, and the only fuel to be had was a few green bushes. As night fell a decided change of temperature added much to our misery—the mercury, which had risen when the norther began, again falling to zero. It can be easily imagined that under the circumstances, the condition of the men was one of extreme discomfort; in truth, they had to tramp up and down the camp all night long to keep from freezing.

Anything was a relief to this state of things, so at the first streak of day, we quit the dreadful place and took up the march.

The next morning the command crossed the Canadian, which was about half a mile wide, by first breaking up the ice with axes, and then marching the cavalry through. It took till noon to get the command over. Luckily there was timber on the south side of the stream. Fires were built and clothes thawed out and dried. General Sheridan says in his official report, "We moved due south until we struck the Washita near Custer's fight of November 27, having crossed the main Canadian with the thermometer about eighteen degrees below zero." The command marched in the afternoon and made camp on the Washita about dark. As wood was abundant, it was decided to lay over here till the storm subsided.

The next day, December 11, General Sheridan, with several officers of the 19th and 7th, visited the battlefield to determine if possible the fate of Major Elliott and his men. It took but a few minutes to discover the bodies on a bank of a tributary of the Washita called Sergeant Major Creek (as the sergeant major of the 7th was one of the killed)[6] on the south side of the battlefield. They were lying in a circle, feet to center, and a pile of empty cartridge cases by each man told how dearly he had sold his life. The bodies were stripped of clothing except a knit undershirt, and the throat of every one had the appearance of having been cut. This was caused by the Indians having cut out the thyroid cartilage. None were scalped, and none of the bodies had been molested by wolves. The men all lay there with their face down, and the back was shot full of arrows. Wagons were sent for and the dead buried that night in a grave dug on the north bank of the river opposite the scene of the battle.

On his way back to camp, Dr. Bailey of Topeka, surgeon of the 19th, discovered the body of a white woman and a little boy two years old. The woman had been shot in the forehead and the child killed by striking his head against a tree. The mother had a piece of bread concealed in her bosom as though she had attempted to escape from the camp. The next morning the woman was laid on a blanket on her side and the boy on her arms, and the men ordered to march by to see if possibly someone might identify her. It was Mrs. [Clara] Blinn,[7] captured by the Kiowas October 9 with a train going from Lyon to Dodge. Her husband was killed at the time. The bodies of the woman and child were taken along and finally buried in the government cemetery at Fort Arbuckle.

On November 2 a number of Mexican traders had been in the Kiowa camp, and she had taken the opportunity to send out a letter by them. It is dated Saturday, November 7, 1868, and reads as follows:

> Kind friends, whoever you may be, I thank you for your kindness to me and my child. You want me to let you know my wishes. If you could only buy us off the Indians with ponies or anything and let me come and stay with you until I could get word to my friends, they would pay you, and I would work and do all I could for you. If it is not too far to their camp, and you are not afraid to come, I pray that you will try. They tell me as near as I can understand they expect traders to come and they will sell us to them. Can you find out by this man and let me know if it is white men? If it is Mexicans, I am afraid they would sell us into slavery in Mexico. If you can do nothing for me, write to W. T. Harrington, Ottawa, Franklin County, Kansas, my father; tell him we are with the Cheyennes, and they say when the white man makes peace we can go home. Tell him to write to the governor of Kansas about it and for them to make peace. Send this to him. We were taken on October 9 on the Arkansas, below Fort Lyon. I cannot tell whether they killed my husband or not. My name is Mrs. Clara Blinn; my little boy, Willie Blinn, is two years old. Do all you can for me. Write to the peace commissioners to make peace this fall. For our sakes do all you can, and God will bless you. If you can, let me hear from you again; let me know what you think about it. Write to my father; send him this. Good-bye.
>
> Mrs. R. F. Blinn
>
> [P. S.] I am as well as can be expected, but my baby is very weak.[8]

The command marched on the morning of the twelfth, following the Indian trail down the Washita. This was a hard day. It is well to see what so old a campaigner as General Sheridan thought of it:

> At an early hour on December 12, the command pulled out from its cozy camp and pushed down the valley of the Washita, following immediately on the Indian trail, which led in the direction of Fort Cobb, but before going far, it was found that the many deep ravines and canyons on this trail would delay our train very much, so we moved out of the valley and took the level prairie on the divide. Here the traveling was good, and a rapid gait was kept up till midday, when, another storm of sleet and snow coming on, it became extremely difficult for the guides to make out the proper course. Fearing that we might get lost or caught on the open plain without wood or water—as we had been on the Canadian —turned the command back to the valley [and] resolved to try no more shortcuts involving the risk of a disaster to the expedition. But to get back was no slight task, for a dense fog just now enveloped us, obscuring the landmarks. However, we were headed right when the fog set in, and we had the good luck to reach the valley before nightfall, though there was a great deal of floundering about and also much disputing among the guides as to where the river would be found. Fortunately, we struck the stream right at a large grove of timber and established ourselves admirably. By dark the ground was covered with twelve or fifteen inches of fresh snow, and as usual the temperature rose very sensibly while the storm was on, but after nightfall the snow ceased and the skies cleared up. Daylight having brought zero weather again, our start on the morning of the thirteenth was painful work, many of the men freezing their fingers while handling the horse equipment, harness, and tents. However, we got off in fairly good season and kept to the trail along the Washita, notwithstanding the frequent digging and bridging necessary to get the wagons over ravines.

Three days' march brought the command within striking distance of the Kiowa camp. The Indians did not suppose it possible for soldiers to move in such weather and were taken by surprise. While the command was being got across a bad ravine, some of them appeared with a flag of truce and delivered a letter from Colonel Hazen[9] saying the Kiowas were friendly. The soldiers represented the War Department and Hazen the Indian [Bureau]. It was exactly this backfire and this influence that General Sherman had promised to guard against. There was no way out of it now, however, and Sheridan accepted the promise of the chiefs, Satanta and Lone Wolf, to move their families to Fort Cobb at once and said the warriors would go with the command. So the march was resumed. In a little while the warriors began to drop out one by one. At last Satanta tried to get away, when he and Lone Wolf were both put under guard.

The command reached Fort Cobb on the evening of December 18, and General Sheridan reported only two men sick in the 7th Cavalry and six in the 19th Kansas. He said, "The whole command is in shelter tents, as we could not spare transportation for others, but the men now prefer the 'shelter' even at this season of the year. Everybody is feeling well and enthusiastic."

On the march from Camp Supply to Fort Cobb, the command lost 148 horses, perishing from cold and want of food. [Brevet] Brigadier General Forsyth, assistant inspector general, Department of the Missouri,[10] inspected the regiment on November 22 and said in his report:

> The soldierly bearing and military appearance of this regiment has made rapid and marked improvement since my inspection at Camp Supply; for this favorable condition of affairs, the field officers are entitled and are deserving of especial mention and praise. I have the pleasure in concluding this report to mention particularly the military bearing and soldierly appearance of Captain Norton's Company D of this regiment. Next to Captain Norton's company, I have the pleasant duty of bringing to your notice Captain A. J. Pliley's Company A. By reference to the table before given, it will be seen that Captain Pliley was the only officer either in the 7th Cavalry or 19th Kansas that made the march through from Camp Supply to this post without losing a single horse.

Perhaps some of you have never made the acquaintance of a shelter tent. During the war, it was always called a dog tent. It is made of ducking, very thin, [and] is about six feet long and five or six feet wide. To pitch his tent, the soldier must first hunt up a couple of sticks with a fork or crotch, [then] stick them in the ground with the fork a couple of feet from the ground. Now he hunts another stick that will reach from one fork to the other, and then stretches the cloth over this, pinning the edges as close to the ground as he can. This leaves his tent open at both ends, with an open space of three or four inches between the cloth and the ground on each side. It always seemed to me that in zero weather this tent sacrificed a great deal in the interest of ventilation.

When the command reached Cobb, they found no Kiowas, but Sheridan told Satanta and Lone Wolf that he would hang them both on the day following if the tribe did not report by that time. Satanta was put into a Sibley tent and an armed guard around it. He would wrap his blanket around himself and come out and sit down by the side of the tent, then swing back and forth [and] chant the most doleful and monotonous death song. Then stooping over, he would scoop up sand and dirt and put [them] into his mouth. Then he would go around to the southwest side of the tent and, shading his eyes with his hand, would sweep the horizon to discover if possible the approach of his people.

But Satanta's hour had not yet struck. Before sundown the advance of his tribe came in, and before morning the Kiowas were camped around Fort Cobb, ready to obey orders. This settled the Kiowas, and the Comanches had all reported except one small band. Major Evans struck this band on the western base of the Wichita Mountains on Christmas day, killing twenty-five warriors, when what was left reported, some at Cobb and some at Fort Bascom.

Messages were sent to Yellow Bear of the Arapahos and Little Robe of the Cheyennes to report, and the former finally got his band in. This left nothing out but the Cheyennes.

The command now moved south to the Wichita Mountains and established Fort Sill on Cache Creek. The Indians were all required to accompany the command. It was impossible to obtain forage for the animals that had survived the severe winter and hard service, and after the arrival of the command of Cache Creek, the horses of the 19th were turned in to the regiment quartermaster, Capt. L. A. Thrasher, and taken to Fort Arbuckle. While we were in camp at Fort Sill, Colonel Custer took a scout of about fifty picked men and, passing along the southern foot of the Wichita Mountains, marched to the west a distance of one hundred miles or more. He got into a desolate country of sagebrush and mesquite entirely destitute of game and almost without water. As he could discover no signs of the Indians, he returned to camp.

On February 12, 1869, Colonel Crawford received a leave of absence for twenty days and resigned his commission as colonel, to take effect at the expiration of his leave of absence. He left the command on February 15, taking with him the best wishes of both officers and enlisted men.[11] I assumed command of the regiment by virtue of seniority of rank.

On March 2, 1869, the 19th Kansas and the 7th Cavalry marched from Fort Sill with intention to find Little Robe's band of Cheyennes. The command marched to the west and on the second day out camped at old Camp Radziminski, a camp where the 2nd Dragoons under Colonel Van Dorn wintered long before the war. The course was still west across the North Fork of Red River and across the Salt Fork of Red River, till the command reached Gypsum Creek. Here the command was divided. Most of the train and all the footsore and disabled were sent to the north up the North Fork and along the state line, with orders to procure commissary stores and halt on the Washita till joined by the balance of the command.

The 7th and 19th then pushed on up the Salt Fork and on March 6 struck the trail of the Indians. It was as broad and easy to follow as an ordinary country road. The scanty rations were now reduced one-half, and the pursuit began in earnest. At the headwaters of the Salt Fork, the trail turned north and skirted along the foot of the Llano Estacado. The trail led through a sandy mesquite country entirely without game, although the streams coming out of the Staked Plains furnished [an] abundance of water. By March 12 rations were reduced again. The mules were now dying very fast of starvation, as they had nothing to live on except the buds and bark of cottonwood trees cut down for them to browse on. Every morning the mules and horses that were unable to travel were killed by cutting their throats, and the extra wagons were run together and set on fire.

On the seventeenth the command came onto Indian campfires with the embers still smoldering. The rations were all exhausted on the eighteenth, and the men subsisted from that on on mule meat without bread or salt.

On the afternoon of March 20, the 19th Kansas came in sight of a band of ponies off to the west of the line of march, which was now in a northeast direction. In a few minutes Indians began to cross the line of march in front of the command, going with all haste towards the herd. The regiment quickened its pace, and I directed the line of march to the point from which the Indians were coming. In another mile the head of the column came upon a low bluff overlooking the bottom of the Sweetwater and saw a group of two hundred fifty Cheyenne lodges stretching up and down the stream and not more than one hundred yards from the bluff. The men thought of the long marches, the short rations, the cold storms, of Mrs. Blinn and her little boy, of the hundred murders in Kansas, and when the order "Left front into line" was given, the rear companies came over the ground like athletes. But "there is many a slip twixt cup and the lip." Lieutenant Cook, 7th Cavalry, rode up to the commanding officer and, touching his hat, said, "The general sends his compliments with instructions not to fire on the Indians."

It was a wet blanket saturated with ice water. In a minute another aide came with orders to march the command a little way upstream and down into the valley and rest. The order was executed, and the regiment formed in columns of companies, with orders to rest. The men laid down on the ground or sat on the logs, but always with their carbines in hand.

Custer was close by, sitting in the center of a circle of Indians chiefs holding a powwow. In two or three minutes, an officer of the 7th came up and in a low tone asked that a few of the officers put on their sidearms and drop down one at a time and listen to the talk. While Custer talked, he watched the officers as they gathered around, and in a few minutes he got up and said, "Take these Indians prisoners." There was a short but pretty sharp struggle, and a guard with loaded guns formed a line around these half a dozen chiefs, and Custer continued the talk.[12] But he had pulled out another stop. The tone was different. He told them they had two white women of Kansas and they must deliver them up to him. They had denied this before, but now they admitted it and said the women were at another camp fifteen miles further down the creek. He told them to instruct the people to pick up this camp and move down to the camp mentioned, and we would come down the next day and get the women. As soon as the chiefs were taken prisoners, the warriors mounted their ponies and, armed with guns or bows and arrows, circled around the bivouac of the troops. They looked very brave and warlike. They wore headdresses of eagle feathers, clean buckskin leggins and moccasins, and buckskin coats trimmed with ample fringe. Lieutenant Johnson, commissary of the 19th, watched them awhile and then remarked, "This is the farthest I ever walked to see a circus."

In a surprisingly short time after Custer gave them permission, the whole camp was pulled down, loaded onto the ponies, and not an Indian was in sight except the half dozen held by the guard. Another night of stout hearts but restless stomachs, and in the morning the command began the march of fifteen miles down the Sweetwater to the other camp. The trail was broad and fresh for five miles, and then it began to thin out and get dimmer and dimmer, till at the end of ten miles not a blade of grass was broken. At the end of fifteen miles, an old camp was reached, but no Indians had been there for two months. The regiment bivouacked for the night, and Colonel Custer had the head chief[13] taken down to the creek, a riata put around his neck, and the other end thrown over the limb of a tree. A couple of soldiers took hold of the other end of the rope and, by pulling gently, lifted him up onto his toes. He was let down, and Romeo, the interpreter,[14] explained to him that when he was pulled up clear from the ground and left there he would be hung. The grizzly old savage seemed to understand the matter fully, and then Custer told him if they did not bring those women in by the time the sun got within a hand's breadth of the horizon on the next day, he would hang the six chiefs on those trees. He let the old chief's son go to carry the mandate to the tribe. It was a long night, but everybody knew the next afternoon would settle the matter in some way.

As the afternoon drew on, the men climbed the hills around camp, watching the horizon, and at about 4:00 P.M. a mounted Indian came onto a ridge a mile away. He waited a few minutes, and then, beckoning with his hand to someone behind him, he came onto the next ridge, and another Indian came onto the ridge he had left. There was another pause, then the two moved up and a third came in sight. They came up slowly in this way till at last a group of a dozen came in sight, and with a glass it could be seen that there were two persons on one of the ponies. These were the women. The Indians brought them to within two hundred yards of the camp, where they slid off the ponies, and Romeo, the interpreter, who had met the Indians there, told the women to come in. They came down the hill clinging to each other as though determined not to be separated whatever might occur. I met them at the foot of the hill, and taking the elder lady by the hand, asked if she was Mrs. Morgan. She said she was and introduced the other, Miss White.[15] She then asked, "Are we free now?" I told her they were, and she asked, "Where is my husband?" I told her he was at Hays and recovering from his wounds. Next question, "Where is my brother?" I told her he was in camp, but I did not tell her that we had to put him under guard to keep him from marring all by shooting the first Indian he saw. Miss White asked no questions about her people. She knew they were all dead before she was carried away. Custer had an "A" tent, which he had brought along for headquarters, and this was turned over to the women. I forgot to say that on the trip, a scouting party had chased an Indian, who got away from them, but he lost a bundle, which was thrown into one of the wagons. On

examination it proved to be some stuff that he had bought of some of the
traders at the forts. It contained calico, needles, thread, beads, and a variety of
things. The bundle was given to the women, and in a surprisingly short time
they had a new calico dress apiece.

The story the women told us of their hardships—the cruelty of the
squaws, the slavery to which they were subjected, their suffering during the
long flight of the Indians to escape the troops—ought to cure all the humanitarians of the world. The women told us the Indians had been killing their dogs
and living on the flesh for the last six weeks.

At retreat that night, while the women stood in front of their tent to see the
guard mounted, the band played "Home, Sweet Home." The command
marched the next morning[16] for the rendezvous on the Washita. It was a couple
of days' march, but when the end came, there was coffee, bacon, hard bread,
and canned goods. Any one of them was a feast for a king. From Washita to
Supply, Supply to Dodge, Dodge to Hays, where the women were sent home
to Minneapolis, and the 19th was mustered out of the service. The Indian prisoners were sent to Sill, and soon after, the Cheyennes reported there and went
onto their reservation.

The generals had a good word for the Kansas volunteers and the work
they had done. General Sheridan:

> I am now able to report that there has been a fulfillment of all the con-
> ditions which we had in view when we commenced our winter's cam-
> paign last November; namely, punishment was inflicted, property
> destroyed, the Indians disabused of the idea that winter would bring
> security and all the tribes of the Platte forced onto the reservation set
> apart for them by the government, where they are in a tangible shape
> for the good work of civilization, education, and religious instruction.
> I cannot speak too highly of the patient and cheerful conduct of the
> troops under my command. They were many times pinched by
> hunger and numbed by cold; sometimes living in holes below the sur-
> face of the prairie, dug to keep them from freezing; at other times
> pursuing the savages and living on the flesh of mules. In all these try-
> ing conditions, the troops were always cheerful and willing, and the
> officers full of esprit.

Colonel Custer says in his official report:

> The point at which we found the Cheyenne village was in Texas, on
> the Sweetwater, about ten miles west of the state line. Before closing
> my report, I desire to call the attention of the major general com-
> manding to the unvarying good conduct of this command since it
> undertook the march. We started with all the rations and forage that
> could be obtained, neither sufficient for the time for which we have

already been out. First it became necessary to reduce the amount of rations; afterwards a still greater reduction was necessary; and tonight most of my men made their suppers from the flesh of mules that have died on the march today from starvation. When called upon to move in light marching order, they abandoned tents and blankets without a murmur, although much of the march had been made during the severest winter weather I have experienced in this latitude.

The horses and mules of this command have subsisted day after day upon nothing but green cottonwood bark. During all these privations, the officers and men maintained a most cheerful spirit, and I know not which I admire most, their gallantry in battle or the patient but unwavering perseverance and energy with which they have withstood the many disagreeable ordeals of this campaign.

As the term of service of the 19th Kansas Cavalry is approaching its termination, and I may not again have the satisfaction of commanding them during active operations, I desire to commend them—officers and men—to the favorable notice of the commanding general. Serving on foot, they have marched in a manner and at a rate that would put some of the regular infantry to the blush. Instead of crying out for empty wagons to transport them, each morning every man marched with his troop and—what might be taken as an example by some of the line officers of the regular infantry—company officers marched regularly on foot at the head of their respective companies, and now, when approaching the termination of a march of over three hundred miles on greatly deficient rations, I have yet to see the first straggler.

In obtaining the release of the captive white women, and that too without ransom or loss of a single man, the men of my command, and particularly those of the 19th Kansas, who were called into service owing to the murders and depredations of which the capture of these women formed a part, feel more fully repaid for the hardships they have endured than if they had survived an overwhelming victory over the Indians.

The expedition resulted in forcing the Kiowas, Comanches, Cheyennes, and Arapahos onto their reservations, and since then the frontier settlements of Kansas have been free from the depredations of Indians.

The campaign was a most arduous one, prosecuted without adequate camp equipage in the midst of winter, and much of the time with an exhausted commissariat. The regiments of Kansas have glorified our state on a hundred battlefields, but none served her more faithfully or endured more in her cause than the 19th Kansas Cavalry.

The 19th Kansas Cavalry and the Conquest of the Plains Indians

JAMES A. HADLEY[1]

Collections of the Kansas State Historical Society 10 (1907–8): 428–56

A ll summer previous to the council of 1867, the Plains Indians had been unusually active. Raids and outrages were constant. The 7th Regulars and 18th Kansas Cavalry swept back and forth, to and fro, in that vast uninhabited empire between the Platte and Arkansas Rivers, but rarely caught their enemies. The 18th was but a squadron of four troops, commanded by Maj. Horace L. Moore of Lawrence. The four captains were Henry C. Lindsey of Topeka, Company A; Edgar A. Barker (not Baker) of Junction City, Company B; George B. Jenness of Ottawa, Company C; and David L. Payne of Atchison, Company D.

In four months this squadron marched 2,200 miles, was nearly wrecked at the outset by cholera, fought Indians several times, lived chiefly on buffalo, lost about ten percent of its members by death—two out of thirteen officers—and at the end of four months, its muster rolls were seventeen percent of its original strength. It services were substantial, if not distinguished, and both Sheridan and Custer commended it highly. Its history abounded in dramatic and tragic elements, and if told would fill a volume. The ghost of its long-faded trail haunts almost every county west of Ellsworth. It is unfortunate that so interesting a story should remain untold and its landmarks lost. It is forty years since Moore's hard-riding squadron marched by day and night, fought cholera, Indians, and alkali water, and though its veteran commander still lives, the youngest of its members is approaching sixty years of age.

To secure the necessary force for the main cavalry column, the governor of Kansas was asked to furnish a full regiment on a war footing. Samuel J. Crawford, then governor, published his proclamation calling for the organization of the 19th Kansas Regiment on October 11, 1868, in the Topeka *Record*. Henry C. Lindsey, late captain of A Troop, 18th Kansas Cavalry (since colonel of the 22nd Kansas Infantry), received his commission Monday and began recruiting in the office of the adjutant general in the old Kansas capitol. Monday morning, October 19, one hundred forty recruits had been passed by the examining surgeon, Dr. Mahlon Bailey of Topeka, afterward regimental surgeon. The same morning, the men learned that Captain Lindsey was not to receive the appointment of major, as they had expected, and were angry. Many of the best men, practically all who had served with Lindsey, announced their determination not to muster. Captain Lindsey himself persuaded them not to carry out their threat. He was a fine officer, energetic, capable, thorough, and exceedingly popular with his men, who had unbounded confidence in his judgment. Tuesday afternoon, October 23, one hundred eight men were selected from these recruits and mustered into the United States service as "A Troop, 19th Kansas Cavalry." The original officers were Allison J. Pliley, captain, Benjamin D. Wilson and Raleigh C. Powell, lieutenants.

Captain Pliley was at that time one of the most romantic figures in Kansas. He was fresh from his hard-won honors at Arikaree Fork, where, with Jack Donovan, he had crawled out into the darkness among the swarming warriors to make his way afoot, if he could elude the alert Indians, to Fort Wallace, over 100 miles away, to bring help to the otherwise doomed scouts. Their only food for the trip was decayed horseflesh. Jack Stillwell and Trudeau, who started the first night, happily reached Wallace, and Captain Bankhead started to the rescue. Pliley and Donovan encountered Capt. Louis H. Carpenter with his troop of the 10th Cavalry, who at once moved swiftly to Beecher Island, reaching Forsyth a day before Bankhead.

Recruits from outside points soon began to arrive at Topeka. The recruits of Lindsey not needed for Pliley's troop were used to fill up others. All these men were quartered in the two legislative halls in the old statehouse on Kansas Avenue, north of Fifth Street. Wednesday morning, October 21, Camp Crawford was established and named for the governor. Two farms were rented in the bottom between the river and the Shunganunga for this purpose. Supplies, clothing, camp and garrison equipage, and arms were soon arriving from Fort Leavenworth, trainload after trainload, and the camp was soon a city of white. On the city side, the guard line of Camp Crawford was parallel to and about 150 or 200 yards east of the main track of the Santa Fe Railroad, built a year later. The camp extended north and south approximately from Second Street to Fifth, though there were no buildings in the bottoms. The headquarters tents were about 250 yards northeast of the first Santa Fe passenger station.

The horses soon began to arrive. A strong and high fence had been built on the Shunganunga, opposite the end of Sixth Street, and into this the horses were turned when inspected and branded. They were from the stables of Kansas, Iowa, and Missouri, and were as fine a body of cavalry horses as ever were collected on such short notice.

Horace L. Moore, of Lawrence, assumed command as lieutenant colonel. His experience as a field officer of cavalry was large from the Civil War, and his record as commander of the 18th Kansas Cavalry was fine. He could lead men for a longer period without rest, on a single ration of cheerful good humor, than any other officer. Though not given to jokes, he was the reputed author of as many astonishers as the great Lincoln. Late one night he was heard in the darkness of the tent calling his orderly. The man, who slept on the floor, was finally wakened, when the colonel, in a voice of mingled curiosity and solicitude, said, "Now, orderly, be honest and tell the truth; did you ever hear it actually *thunder?*" The soldier, in surprise, said, "Yes, sir." "What a hell of a clap it must have been!" exclaimed Moore, hopelessly lost in wonder and admiration at the bare thought of so tremendous a noise. Another time, on the march, he sent an orderly with a message to an officer at some distance. Before the man was out of hearing, Moore shouted, "Hey, Orderly! Come back here!" He came galloping back, sitting limply in the saddle. "Sit at attention! Give the proper salutation!" shouted the colonel, and as the trooper came to attention, Moore dropped his voice and, assuming a half-confidential manner, inquired, "Orderly, in the course of your life, have you ever seen a snail?" "Yes, sir," said the astonished orderly. "You met him then, for you'd never overtake one!" These are only specimens. Moore himself never smiled, and this, with the rasping, nasal voice he kept in stock strictly for such occasions, made his short dialogues irresistible.

The work of organization, drill, and discipline went on rapidly under the experienced eye of Colonel Moore. Probably no like body of men, before or since, was so quickly whipped into shape. This was due to the large number of officers and men who had recently served in the Civil War—many of them in the cavalry.

The first few days, before hard work began at camp, the streets were thronged with recruits, mostly sober and well behaved, a gang of Leavenworth hoodlums and street pirates being the only exception. These spent the time hunting down Topeka Negroes. When one was caught alone, the gang gave him a vigorous beating. The day camp was established, James M. Conwell and myself started to the adjutant general's office and found this gang had the Negro porter of the Gordon House at bay against the statehouse wall and were threatening him. He was covered with blood, and we gathered that he had sought refuge in the state offices but had been dragged out and punished. The leader of the hoodlums, a blasphemous young ruffian, called on an older man to prove that they two had served four years in the Rebel army together. "I'm a Rebel yet," said the younger man. "I hate and spit on this country of damned nigger-lovers, and never see the flag that I don't want to tear it to pieces." After the regiment had been on the march over a week, I saw this young ruffian and was astonished indeed to see that he was an officer in the 19th Kansas. Inquiry developed the fact that he was Charles T. Brady, lieutenant in E Troop. How he got there is still one of the unsolved problems of life. Three days after he came to Topeka, he never dreamed of such a thing. It was the very opposite of all his tastes and ambitions. He was often selected to serve as adjutant the first three months and surely must have believed in the fairy godmother. After he was mustered out with the regiment, he immediately returned to the tastes and companions of former days, and three days later was shot to death by the men of Hays, his body tossed into a freight car, and there found a few days later in the Kansas City yards.[2]

The officers of the 19th, as a whole, were the equals, mentally, morally, and socially, of a like number of like rank anywhere. Many were exceedingly capable. A number were as fine officers as ever drew the sword, and those of the so different variety could only slightly lower the average and exasperate the commander. The regiment's fortitude in a winter so severe that it swept off the entire mount in less than three months proves that officers and men were of substantial material.

The 19th was uniformed, armed, mounted, drilled, and so far disciplined as the brief time allowed, at Camp Crawford. Urgent necessity brought marching orders, and the night of November 4, the two troops of Captain J[ohn] Q. A. Norton of Lawrence (D) and Capt. Richard D. Lender of Fort Scott (G) were embarked on a special train by the way of the then Kansas Pacific Railroad, with all their horses and equipment, for Fort Hays, for escort duty between that point and another field depot, Camp Supply, Indian Territory.

At 10:00 A.M., November 5, 1868, the remaining ten troops moved out of Camp Crawford on their overland march to Camp Supply.[3] The column entered Kansas Avenue at Fourth Street, turned south in platoon formation, filling the broad avenue from curb to curb. The twenty-one buglers, in the showy uniform of that era, riding abreast as one platoon, followed Colonel Moore and his staff, and following them, platoon after platoon, troop after troop, a steady stream of horsemen a mile in length poured along the street, while sidewalks, doors, and even housetops were black with people to see the last of the men who were to be pitted against that hitherto unconquered terror—winter on the plains. The column soon left the little city behind. During that day's march on the prairie south of Topeka, six or seven houses were seen, mostly from one to three miles from the road.

Midafternoon, camp was made on the Wakarusa, not far from the crossing of the Burlingame road. Here Governor Crawford overtook us on horseback. The boys of the regiment now learned for the first time that Samuel J. Crawford, serving his second term, had resigned as governor of Kansas to become their colonel. He now assumed command. An hour later, a carriage approaching from the city over the lonely prairie road attracted considerable notice. At the guard line, the two occupants proved to be Adjutant General McAfee and "Jake" Smith, a wealthy and popular citizen of Topeka.

Next morning the regular and persistent bugles had the regiment in column and on the road by the gray light of early dawn, headed southwest. During two hours' steady marching that forenoon, not a settler's house was seen—near or far. The Santa Fe Trail was entered and followed through Burlingame. Again the route was southwest. It now began to rain as only Kansas knows how, and all were quickly wet to the skin. We crossed the great prairie where Osage City was built later, and if there was a house near, it was out of sight. At dark, tired, wet, and sore from the long march, camp was made in the heavy timber of the Neosho, two miles east of Emporia. The blankets from the wagons were nearly as damp as the soaked clothing. Great fires failed to dry them, for the rain turned to snow, and the wall tents of the officers were no better shelter than the dog tents of the men. It was a wet, melting snow, and an epidemic of hoarseness and sore throats resulted.

On the seventh, when the column emerged from the heavy timber, it encountered a piercing wind that set both men and horses aquiver. Though the rain and snow were stopped, the mud—the long, ropy, stringy, sticky, Kansas mud—clung affectionately to man and horse. What a bed of black mortar was left behind those 1,150 horses and 110 mules.

The head of the column entered Emporia from the east about 9:00 A.M. It was a town of about 800 people. The day was cloudy and cold, and the place looked so discouraged and homesick that the soldiers floundering through the miry streets felt sorry for it. Three men stood in front of the office of the Emporia *News,* published by Jacob Stotler, then speaker of the Kansas House of Representatives—the biggest crowd we saw. There were scattered settlers in the edge of the timber all the way to Cottonwood Falls. Scarcity of wagons had limited the rations carried to five days between Topeka and Fort Beecher, while all forage was bought on the line of march. To regulars or veterans, this sub-sistence would have been ample, but our new regiment nearly starved. Food was bought by the men on the route, but the kind people along the Cottonwood rarely would take pay. Five miles west of Emporia lived John Moon, one of the very first settlers in all that region. His wife, born Lavina Burnside, was a famous cook. As she was my mother's own cousin, I had reason to be thankful that her hospitable and kindly heart was on the line of march.

Again the camp was in thick timber, near Cottonwood Falls, and the cloth-ing and beds were dried out. The morning of November 8, the march was south over the high prairie to the headwaters of the Walnut. Along that rich valley were settlers near the timber, but the high prairies, as elsewhere, were as nature left them. The night of the eighth, the camp was again and for the last time in heavy timber. Camp Four was near El Dorado. Here we left the settle-ments, though there was one house between El Dorado and Fort Beecher. Here we camped on November 9, and it was the last house seen till the members of the 19th began to see them from the car windows homeward bound late the following April. This solitary homestead was Towanda, the place of Doctor Graham, and was in the neighborhood of our fifth camp.

The column marched out into the great valley of the Arkansas about three miles above the mouth of the Little Arkansas, whence, turning south, the route was straight to the fort, crossing as it did so the ground on which the heart of Wichita now stands. There was at this time a very thin fringe of cottonwoods along the smaller stream, but none on the banks of the big river except at their junction. The surface where the city stands was broken by the most remarkable network of buffalo wallows I ever even heard of. Fort Beecher was a collection of huts and tents, with one company of infantry as a garrison. It stood on the banks of the Little Arkansas, not half a mile above its mouth. The cavalry camped below the fort, between the rivers, a flank resting directly on each. It was expected that Crawford would be able to secure ample transportation, subsistence, and forage here to carry his command to the base in the field. This proved to be a snare. There were not enough commissary stores in the whole place to feed so large a force a week, while there was practically no forage, and a wagon was not to be had. The five days' rations from Topeka had been eked out by private purchases on the way. When the command crossed the river here, it not only entered a desolate and uninhabited land, but one to a large extent unexplored. Hence the food for man and beast must be carried by wagons. November 12 was spent in camp shoeing horses and tightening the screws that always work loose in the trial run of new machinery. Letters were also written, for Uncle Sam had no dickering with "that land across the river whence no traveler had returned."

Up to this time, the United States had, as a settled policy, kept the white man out of the country now known as Oklahoma. Few army officers had of late years crossed its mystic boundaries. Hunters and plainsmen had kept studiously to the north of the Arkansas. Those only directly connected with the Indian service, including traders, were permitted to enter. Communication between Texas and the states north must be made by Arkansas and Missouri. All of Kansas southwest of the Arkansas River shared the same fate. Not an officer or man in Crawford's command had ever been south of the Arkansas River. Even Simmons (Apache Bill) and Jack Stillwell, whom Sheridan had sent as guides, had never entered the forbidden land. Their general knowledge of the Great Plains, the lay of the land, of signs and of watercourses, were relied on to find the way. This was often the case with guides in that untracked region, and it would have answered well under ordinary circumstances. But conditions unforeseen and unprovided for—conditions that would have confused anybody—were met. The very maps were wrong and added to the confusion. If in such cases a commander proves impatient and demands immediate information, the confusion is apt to be increased. It is the cold, hard fact that the weather and the absurd lack of stores were the causes of the catastrophe that followed. The universal ignorance of that country, including that of Sheridan himself, was at the bottom of it all.

At Fort Beecher, Colonel Crawford was confronted with a grave danger, and he knew it. He could only secure five days' rations and three days' forage with which to march through a desert land for what was supposed to be 160 miles. With 1,100 partly disciplined men and nearly that many horses, untrained and unseasoned, his officers and men scarcely knowing each other's faces, and at the beginning of a season hitherto regarded as fatal to man—it was enough to sober the most reckless officer. But his orders were peremptory. He had no choice. With what stores he could get, he manfully did his best and left the worry and swearing to the general who gave the orders.

November 13, early, Crawford began to transfer his command to the south bank of the Arkansas. Though very wide, the whole riverbed was not covered with water at the time. Vagrant currents ran here and there, alternating with sandbars, the whole a quaking, shivering quicksand. Horsemen had already surveyed and marked a winding route, avoiding the deepest water and worst quicksand. The cavalry column crossed with little difficulty, but the train was not so easy. The "leaders" and "swings" were taken from each wagon, leaving only the "wheel" mules. A rope cable was then attached and carried forward between two lines of mounted soldiers, who seized it with their hands and snaked the wagon over the route to the distant shore with a swiftness and vigor that left the two mules nothing to do but guide the tongue. In a land of broad and bridgeless rivers, this was very effective.

Safely on the south bank, Crawford wasted no time. The horses were now grazed, groomed, and nursed with persistence. Every grain of the pitiful forage procured at Beecher was of vital import. When the column was well on its way in this land of silence and desolation, a change was noticed in the horses. They were uneasy, and there seemed a smoldering excitement among them. John Linton, Captain Pliley's farrier, a fine horseman, said the night of the thir-teenth, "If I was superstitious, I would look for something terrible to happen, the horses act so queer. I believe there is something this side of the river that makes them homesick." Something did happen! Those horses all perished within two months. Though carefully husbanded, the last forage was fed to the horses the night of the November 16. Discreet officers afterwards sent out a double force of men with them to graze.

A little before sundown on the November 18, the column swung into posi-tion in camp on Medicine Lodge Creek, somewhere near the place now located [on] the map as Kiowa. Although six days had elapsed since beginning on five days' rations, the men had fared reasonable well—buffalo having been killed daily. It was different with the horses. Out of forage for three days, the taste-less grass, bleached by rains, holding no nutriment, they were starving. Here the troopers had dismounted and unsaddled, when a belated man of Capt. Roger A. Elsworth's Troop I came galloping in hurriedly and threw off his sad-dle. Against orders, he had folded the picket rope on his saddle and left the end around the animal's neck. While removing accoutrements, the horse stepped backward and, seeing the saddle move, took fright and ran amuck among the thronging men and horses, the saddle following and receiving a resounding kick at every leap. The effect on horses was electrical. The mounts of troop after troop, in a frenzy of excitement, tore away and were carried off in the storm. The same jarring, grating roar as when a cyclone hurries along within a few miles was in air. The horses of five troops were swept away, heavily loaded ammunition wagons were overturned, and hundreds of men narrowly escaped death. By a miracle no one was seriously hurt. Systematic effort was at once inaugurated to recover the runaways, for time was too precious to lose in hunting them during marching hours. Fortunately the silent desert, or other mystery, brought the fugitives back, and before "Boots and Saddles" next morning, 450 had been recaptured and less than eighty horses were at large. Governor Crawford says all but six of these were brought in later.

The morning of the nineteenth was very warm, and I left my overcoat in a wagon. Before noon it began to rain, and rained steadily all day. During this day's march, we crossed the southern Kansas line into the [Indian] Territory. Toward night the wind changed and it grew cold. The train was far in the rear and deep in the mud. A bivouac was made just before dark on a crooked, sluggish stream, probably Salt Fork. Soon after, the wind increased to a hurricane, the temperature lost its grip and fell to zero and under, and the wet clothing stiffened and whitened with the frost. Not a stick of wood was found, and the buffalo chips were saturated with water. The wind was so furious that fires were impossible except in holes, and spades as well as axes were with the train. The night was moonless and very dark. Every available man was clinging to the horses. These, still excited by the late stampede—nervous, frightened, starving, freezing, confused by the darkness and the roar of the storm—were well nigh frantic. All night they were led up and down, up and down. The sudden lurch of a horse, or an unexpected movement of a man, would have carried every animal out onto the plain a fugitive—trampling men to death as they went.

Personally, I was in a sad plight. My overcoat back in the wagon, my saddle blanket used to keep my quivering horse alive, clothes wet and frozen, without fire or hope of fire; my only wrap, a light cloak, served the same purpose as a streamer at the top of a flagpole. About 11:00 P.M. some restless spirits of Troop A found the end of a big log protruding from the riverbank, two miles from camp. Some old flood had floated it down, time had covered it deep with alluvium, and the mutations of channels had brought one end again to the light. With infinite labor, it was dug out and on the shoulders of many men was carried through the darkness to camp. Attempts were then patiently made with knives and swords to split off pieces for a fire, but it was not until after 3:00 A.M., when the train arrived, that a pit was dug and a good fire started safe from the rude storm. These men remembered my predicament of the night, and though I had a dry overcoat, they sent for and placed me in a snug corner of the "portable cellar," as Jack Curtis of North Topeka scornfully called it. Overcoat and fire put me to sleep, and I was only roused by a hand on my shoulder and the shout, "Kirby's dead—wake up!" The buglers were recklessly getting off the accompaniment to that ancient and disreputable cavalry doggerel:

> *Come all that are able*
> *And go to the stable,*
> *To give your horses some corn and some hay;*
> *For if you don't do it*
> *The colonel will know it,*
> *And you'll go to the guardhouse this very same day.*

Such expectations could no longer be realized by the horses, and it was base to mock them. It was now light enough to see, and the storm had somewhat abated. One tent had been erected at headquarters, and a number of fires had been started in holes, behind screens, and other shelter.

A ford had to be found, and on account of my horse being a good swimmer, I was ordered to investigate the river above camp. I found the streambank full, a swift current running thick with mush ice, the water too salty to solidify. My horse suddenly stepped off into deep water, and we both went under. Just as this happened, the cloak of my overcoat was wrapped around my head by the wind. As the horse came to the surface, the cloak stuck to my face. The sudden cold and surprise caused the horse to plunge and struggle, while I, disconcerted by the ducking and blindness, was not for the moment sitting firmly in the saddle, so was easily thrown into deep water. Wearing very high boots, my overcoat buttoned and belted outside with two pistols, I came very near sinking. Being only twenty years old, and knowing that I was being introduced to death, I was full of panic but had sense enough not to try to reach shore or struggle in any way. I finally got my face clear, the alarm was given, a rope was thrown to me, which I caught at last and was pulled out. When I reached the fire, I was sheathed in ice. This was soon melted off, and I kept my place in the column all day without ill effects either from the ducking or the bitter experience of the night before. My clothes dried during the day in spite of the cold.

This was November 20. On the twenty-first no buffalo were found. It was the first day that nothing was killed. We had now been marching eight days since leaving Fort Beecher. In spite of buffalo, the four days' rations were exhausted; the two days' forage had been forgotten, and a tobacco famine raged. The situation was critical, for we knew no more about objective than the day we crossed the Arkansas. The morning of the twenty-second, the usual hunting parties were sent out. No meat was left from the kill of the twentieth. All the forenoon the mountainous hills of the Cimarron loomed high, far in our front. Though marching steadily, hour after hour, toward them, they apparently approached no nearer. About 2:00 P.M. the overhead dome was lined with low clouds, and the hills were no longer there. A little later snow began to fall, silently, steadily, and copiously, restricting the vision to a radius of twenty yards and changing landmarks like magic. The column marched on in the gloom, suddenly appearing and disappearing, men and horses moving silently and white, like the sheeted ghosts of long dead cavalry. About dark, camp was made, with about five inches snow on the ground. Here we were sheltered by timber and built big fires. This stream was Sand Creek. Much anxiety was felt for the buffalo hunters. In the snow, they were like men blindfolded, and it was not likely that any of them had a compass. All reached camp, however, during the night.

At camp on Sand Creek, November 22, the crisis was reached. No buffalo had been seen for two days. The only food in camp was six barrels of coffee sugar in the officers' stores. Colonel Crawford ordered this issued. The sergeants of messes counted out to every man his share of the little cubes. One of the hardest fights of the winter was between two men of Troop L (Capt.

The 19th Kansas Cavalry caught in a blizzard.
NELSON A. MILES, *PERSONAL RECOLLECTIONS AND OBSERVATIONS.*

Charles H. Finch's) over a few extra cubes of this sugar. They were powerful
fellows and smashed each other beautifully till the guard interfered.

About 10:00 P.M. Capt. A. J. Plilcy left camp in the snow and darkness in
search of General Sheridan and relief. His escort was Lt. Jesse E. Parsons of
Troop C, with fifty picked men and horses. It was a difficult and dangerous
errand, but the safety, perhaps lives, of the command depended on his success
in finding Camp Supply. This was to have been located somewhere near the
forks of Beaver Creek and the North Canadian, but as a fact, it had not been
established when Crawford left Topeka. If it was hard to find in good weather,
Pliley's difficulties in a snowstorm were infinitely multiplied. The snow was
ten inches deep when he marched out and coming down steadily, though without wind.

The morning of November 23 found a foot of snow on the ground. The
blinding snow was still falling. Though there was not a scrap of food in camp,
it was impossible to move. All sense of direction was lost. All the cottonwood
trees in reach of camp were cut down during the day, and the starving horses
quickly stripped them of every twig and inch of bark, but among so many
horses, it was not much. There was much anxiety about the wind. If the snow
should begin drifting, the command would be forced to live on its expensive
mounts, thereby defeating the object for which the regiment was raised.

On the twenty-fourth the snow had ceased. The command moved out in a
foot and a half of snow, the men leading the now weakened horses. Each troop
took its turn breaking the trail. It was cloudy, and nothing could be seen more
than a mile or two in advance. Thus floundering through the deep white carpet,
in about five miles we came to the Cimarron Hills. Here the gloomy, crooked
canyons added greatly to the difficulties, but the grim march continued. A little before the sundown hour, the advance came upon a bunch of buffalo bulls.

They could not run in the deep snow, and all were killed. Camp was made about dark, ten miles from Sand Creek, in a snowfield surrounded by high hills and deep ravines. Buffalo for supper! How good it was! Few of these men had known hunger before. Hackberry trees grew on the hillsides, and though the fruit was all seed at best and now dried on the tree, it was sweet and agreeable and was eaten, seeds and all—appendicitis not yet being fashionable. The camp was officially named "Camp Hackberry Point" but became "Camp Starvation," and has never been alluded to otherwise by the members of the 19th.

The train did not reach camp until the morning of November 25. It was now seen that further march was impossible. The buffalo bulls proved that a little game might be found in these mountains. In order to reduce the number of men to feed, it was decided to divide the command. The sun now shone brightly, and the white landscape glittered and glistened. In pursuance of this decision, the strongest and hardiest men and horses were selected to the number of nearly five hundred and placed under the command of Lt. Col. Horace L. Moore. These were to march out of camp without tents, bed, or food and make their way to Supply, living as best as they could. The remainder of the regiment, over six hundred men, was placed under command of Maj. R. W. Jenkins. These included the sick, partially frozen, the dismounted, those weak physically from any cause, and the train, and were to remain in Camp Starvation, subsisting as they could till rescued. Colonel Crawford, of course, remained with Jenkins. It was hoped that Captain Pliley might reach camp early and send relief.

At 11:00 A.M. November 25, Moore led his column out of camp into a canyon leading to the Cimarron. The river here is two hundred yards wide, running through a gorge five hundred feet deep. There is no approach to the water except through equally deep tributary canyons. When the detachment debouched at the river, it was confronted by a lofty precipice opposite, offering no egress for half a mile up and downstream. The clear water looked black to the snow-dazzled eye, but the white cliff beyond loomed up like a gigantic wall. Marching downstream at the foot of the cliff, a narrow cleft was seen opposite whereby the uplands could be reached. Crossing here, the water was found of uniform depth, about three feet. Entering the mouth of the canyon a little after noon, marching in single file, the head of the column emerged from its rocky walls on the uplands just at dark. A full moon was rising and lighted up as desolate a landscape as this planet affords. A bivouac was made on a prairie brook, where big fires were built. We afterward learned that the temperature was twenty degrees below zero toward morning. Trees were cut for the horses wherever found. In their absence, the snow was dug away for two or three square feet, and the horses ate the frozen grass. Someone in Troop A killed a deer, and a quarter was sent to Lt. [B. D.] Wilson, Joe Peacock, and myself, for which our souls salaamed and kowtowed all night.

Next day, November 26, was Thanksgiving, but we didn't know it then. The sun thawed the snow on the twenty-fifth, and the cold nights made a crust that added to our tribulations. On the twenty-sixth the horses began to die of starvation. That night the bivouac was on a high prairie stream with wooded banks, and again the night was bitter cold. There was no food of any kind that night, so men literally "hung on hackberry trees." The finest racer was never nursed and coddled as were those starving troop horses. Men sat all night over fires to give their only blankets to the horses. The whole of the twenty-seventh was a struggle through the deep, crusted snow of the hilly prairies, and more horses perished. The trail of Captain Pliley was crossed during the day.

Camp on November 27 was in the timber of a large stream with wide, forest-covered bottoms. Oak and walnut trees were seen. This was undoubtedly the North Canadian. Camp Supply was still further west. The bivouac among these giant trees was encouraging. Besides big fires, there was venison and turkey enough to give everybody a fair taste. It was beginning to look like Camp Supply was no myth after all. Sheridan expected the regiment to make the march in four or five days, and it had marched straight on for fifteen days now, except the one day in camp on the twenty-third, and this was the first sign that there ever was such a place as the Canadian River.

The march of the twenty-eighth was for the most part up the river bottom in the edge of the timber. About midafternoon a roar broke out in the column and followed back to the guard. When it faded a little, it broke out again, clearer and louder every time. It was good, hearty, old-fashioned cheering, too. The occasion for the men having a conniption fit just there was, first, a stump whence the tree had recently been cut by the white man's axe; second, a wagon track since the snowstorm; third, some fresh chips on the snow! The fourth and last cheering was due to a messenger from the advance who informed Colonel Moore that Supply was in sight not five miles away.

The trail now cut across the uplands, and just at sundown, we reached the bluff overlooking a broad valley covered with timber, where two large streams evidently converged. There, almost at our feet, were the white tents of the long-lost cantonment not a mile away, and there was the most beautiful of all inanimate objects, the flag, silently floating in dignified power over the garrison. Even as we looked, a puff of white smoke appeared, the flag came fluttering down like a wounded bird, and in a moment or so the boom of the evening salute filled the whole valley. This was our objective.

This detachment of the 19th made the march from Topeka in twenty-four days on nine days' subsistence and seven days' forage. In twenty-two days of actual marching, it averaged over sixteen miles a day. Captain Pliley had arrived three days before, and General Sheridan had at once sent a suitable relief expedition to Camp Starvation. As soon as Sheridan heard Pliley's report, he set a large force at work clearing the snow from the level ground north of the garrison, had tents erected, with hay for bedding, and everything prepared for the sorely tried officers and men of the 19th. This was luxury!

General Sheridan and Colonel Custer had waited long for Crawford, but hearing nothing, Custer had gone out alone with the 7th. This was a great disappointment to the Kansas men, for they feared the enterprising Custer would strike so vigorously that the Indians would roar for peace. General Sheridan had a good round period of anxiety before he heard from the 19th, and suspense isn't edifying.

On November 29, the day after our arrival, a scout reached Camp Supply with news of the battle of the Washita on November 27 and the death of old Black Kettle, Little Rock, and most of their warriors, also the capture of the women and children of the band, accomplished at a loss of two distinguished officers—Maj. Joel H. Elliott and Capt. Louis M. Hamilton—and nineteen soldiers of the 7th Cavalry, including Sgt. Maj. Walter Kennedy, and the severe wounding of Capt. Albert Barnitz. Nearly one thousand Indian horses and vast quantities of property were destroyed.

December 1 Custer reached Supply, and his column was given the distinction of a review by the general commanding. About 10:00 A.M. the head of the column reached the top of the hill southwest of Supply and marched diagonally down the slope, in view of the entire cantonment. Though it was thirty-nine years ago, and though most of those gallant fellows have lain in their bloody graves for three decades, I can yet see that striking and dramatic parade as if it were yesterday: men and horses in bold relief against the glittering snow. First came the Osage scouts and trailers under Hard Robe and Little Beaver, in all their gaudy and barbaric finery, galloping in circles, discharging firearms in the air, chanting war songs, and at intervals giving shrill battle cries. Then came the silent citizen scouts of Pepoon, now recruited from their terrible losses at Beecher Island, marching in two platoons. Next came the splendid band of the 7th, playing "Garry Owen to Glory," riding abreast as one platoon, their instruments flashing and scintillating as they proudly rode by. Next in column, escorted by the whole body of the regiment, came the prisoners, the widows and orphans of the murderous Black Kettle's band, riding their own ponies, grouped and huddled as Indians always travel. After these, in platoon formation, came troop after troop, their lines perfectly dressed, intervals properly observed, marching with the precision of long service and perfect discipline—a splendid regiment—the train and the guard bringing up the rear. Five of Custer's troops lost their overcoats and overshoes during the battle. These men were wrapped in many-colored blankets with their feet tied up in grain sacks.

At the head of the column was a young man of medium height, slender, wearing buckskin hunting shirt and leggings much fringed. A worn hat with broad brim surmounted a tangle of curling yellow hair reaching below his shoulders. Across his saddle he carried a long rifle, with which he was expert. This was Custer at the age of twenty-nine, and this was about the last time he appeared in this garb on a public occasion. The next year he sacrificed his curls, and with them the dress of the old-time frontiersman. There was nothing in either figure or bearing to indicate the great physical strength and iron nerve that made him one of the most expert shots and horsemen in the whole world. Thus the 19th Kansas was introduced to its general.

The week that followed was a busy one. Colonel Crawford and Major Jenkins arrived December 1. The 19th had made its march of 355 miles from Topeka without losing a man, and having lost only seventy-five horses. Under the circumstances, this was remarkable. The march from Camp Supply to Fort Cobb and thence to Fort Sill has been well described by Colonel Moore,[4] by General Sheridan in his *Memoirs,* and Custer in his *Galaxy* papers.[5] All three speak of incidents and movements largely from the economic and strategic viewpoint, as seen at headquarters, while those who were "down in the troop" saw only the "human-interest" part. There was no time for the 19th and 7th to recuperate after their respective strenuous experiences. December 6 all the dismounted, the sick, wounded, frostbitten, and broken-down men of both regiments were detached from their several troops to be left as a garrison at Camp Supply. Maj. Charles Dimon[6] and four line officers were also detached. Capt. J. Q. A. Norton, with Troop D, having arrived that day with a train from the railroad, was ordered to the regiment, and Capt. Sargent Moody, with Troop M, took his place on escort duty.

The 19th and 7th regiments and nearly one hundred Indian and white scouts composed the column of Custer—about 1,800 effective horsemen. This was much the most formidable force ever sent against the Plains Indians. General Sheridan and his staff accompanied the column. There were over 300 six-mule wagons in the train. The Mexican Romeo was the principal interpreter. This man's name was Romero, but he was derisively called "Romeo" on account of his successful lovemaking. Though ugly as a millionaire's morals, the dried-up specimen of manhood had a squaw, sometimes several, in every tribe on the plains, or so it is said. Custer also carried two captive squaws, Mah-wis-sa (Black Kettle's sister) and Mo-nah-se-tah (Little Rock's daughter). These women had already exposed the secrets of the chiefs[7] and knew yet much of value to the commanders. They knew all the secret hiding places also. The snow had now settled a good deal, and a troop of the 10th Cavalry had been out on the trail two days' march to smooth the road.

Thus was the command hurled into the Indian country. The march December 7 was twelve miles. A special commissary had been detailed for the train, all picked men from the 7th. The men of the 19th chose to regard this as a reflection on the regimental integrity and decided to teach Custer a lesson. The snow had been so tracked by men and horses that the scheme was practicable. That night, when the midnight guard at the grain had been on post long enough, the relief approached and gave the countersign, and excused relieved sentinels from "falling in" in the rear. Then hidden confederates approached, emptied three or four wagons, and all silently disappeared in the darkness. When the real relief made its round, five posts were found vacant, the men sleeping calmly at the guard tent and a number of wagons emptied. The 19th was paraded at daylight and their camp searched. All the messes were well supplied, some unusually well, but the stores had been so skillfully divided that no evidence was obtained. A year later, at Topeka, a soldier, late of Troop

A, gave me the history of this raid on the train. It originated in Troop A, though "safe" men from others were taken in, chiefly from D and L, the troops of Norton and Finch. The night was so bitter cold that horse guards in each troop kept up big fires. All incriminating packages were burned there, and the darkness prevented the police guards seeing anything wrong. The best joke of all was that a generous supply of contraband food reached the headquarters mess. "Why," said my informant, "while the colonel was swearing, spitting blue vitriol and jumping stiff-legged around camp, he was picking the stolen rations out of his own teeth, and everybody knew that you fellows at the captain's mess lived on it for a week. Pliley, Norton, and Finch never knew why their stores lasted so confounded long." Lt. Charley Hoyt said one day, "It begins to look like the five loaves and two fishes business lately up our way." In the good-humored badinage between the men of the two regiments, the way the 7th shut up at mention of the commissary guard proved that it was a delicate subject with them.

The night of December 8 began that remarkable series of storms described in Sheridan's *Memoirs*.[8] Each was followed by zero weather. In a day or so it suddenly grew warmer, followed by another storm within an hour. The South Canadian was forded, with the temperature eighteen degrees below zero. The river was over half a mile wide, with four feet of water, covered with ice three or four inches thick, and the bed a dangerous quicksand. The ice was chopped out with axes, making two channels for column and trains. The night of December 10, the command camped in the Washita timber near Custer's battlefield of two weeks before. Elliott and his men were found where they fell fighting. Major Elliott's body was carried away with us, as were those of Mrs. Blinn and her little boy. This young woman was the daughter of W. T. Harrington of Ottawa, Kansas. Her husband, R. F. Blinn, was killed when she and the child, "Willie" Blinn, were captured on the Arkansas, in Colorado. They were wantonly murdered to prevent their rescue by Custer. The names of Mrs. Blinn and Major Elliott will always be synonyms for tragic death in the region once known as "the Plains."

The column forced its way down the Washita. The first twelve miles was over ground whence the wild tribes had fled in frantic haste the night after the battle. Tepee poles were left standing in places; everywhere wood was stacked around the dead campfires. Knives, revolvers, moccasins, bows and arrows overlooked in the flight were found by the soldiers. One trooper found a carefully wrapped package to contain nearly $400 in greenbacks, another a buckskin bag with $182 in gold coin. On through storm, deep snow, and arctic cold the column grimly marched, arriving at Fort Cobb December 18. By threatening to hang Lone Wolf[9] and the infamous Satanta, Sheridan got the Arapahos, Kiowas, and Comanches to camp under the carbines of the cavalry. The Kiowas met the command with a letter from Colonel Hazen, of the Indian Bureau, telling what good, peaceable folks the Kiowas were. Yet the dead girl and her baby in the wagon were captured by these same Kiowas not two months since, her husband killed and she and the two-year-old baby sold to the Cheyennes. A band of vagabond Comanches and Dog Soldiers ran away and were making for their desert stronghold in Texas when, on Christmas Day 1868, they were struck by the auxiliary column of Major Evans from New Mexico and practically exterminated. The Cheyennes got away to Texas in safety.

The time between December 18 and January 6 was spent comfortably camped in the heavy timber at Fort Cobb. Food was plentiful and forage fairly supplied, though the bad roads between Cobb and Fort Arbuckle made the hauling difficult. Christmas was a real, if rare, holiday. Eastern papers were received here, raking the army for making war on the "poor, peaceful Indians." One or two church papers were exceedingly bitter and demanded the "punishment" of Custer and all the officers and men of the 7th Cavalry for "deliberate, premeditated, and brutal murder of inoffensive and peaceful people."

Fort Cobb was to be dismantled and abandoned. Three days' march over a beautiful country brought us to Cache Creek, in the Wichita Mountains. Here Fort Sill[10] was established, twenty-eight miles south of Fort Cobb. Though Crawford had made the march from Supply to Cobb with a loss of only 150 horses, and though the weather greatly moderated about the first of the year, horses lined the trail to Sill with their carcasses. Captain Pliley was the only officer in both regiments who brought all his horses through the late storms. Every morning after going into cantonment at Medicine Rock, large numbers of horses were dead or dying at the cables. The veterinary surgeon, George Davidson of Topeka, "English George," exhausted his skill. The cold and starvation of the overland march was too much for these fine creatures, and though they received now a ration of grain, and grass was growing green, they died. At last the scattering survivors were turned in to Capt. Luther A. Thrasher, the quartermaster, and taken to Fort Arbuckle.

It is a pity that I have not the space to tell the events at Medicine Rock, officially known as "Camp Twenty-one in the Field"; of the battle of cartridges and the great four-day storm that wrecked the camp and drove the regiment behind the riverbank and into holes and improvised caves; a storm that changed so quickly from summer heat that in four hours it froze up a rapid mountain stream!

General Sheridan, at Camp Supply, received orders on March 2, 1869, to proceed to Washington, and on his way, near Fort Hays, received of his appointment as lieutenant-general of the army. Colonel Crawford resigned the command on February 12 and soon left for the railroad, and Colonel Moore commanded the 19th from this on.

Many stirring things happened here. The parklike country was alive with deer and turkeys—very tame. Chester Thomas, Sr., of Topeka, visited camp. He was "Uncle Chester" to all the Topeka men. The 19th had a battle with rattlesnakes but never dared tell the real truth about it, for fear their friends would put them in asylums. Lt. Charles H. Champney of Troop B told a mild and abridged edition to a party at the old statehouse at Topeka the following summer. His auditors maintain a shocked silence till Archie Williams, then attorney general, kindly but gravely said, "Champney, for your friends' sake you should value your health and avoid taking large quantities of liquid nourishment at a time." I entered, and when I confirmed his statements, they "laughed us both to scorn," mentioned "conspiracy," "collusion," and other unwholesome and unseemly doings.

March 2, 1869, the now dismounted cavalry marched out of its pleasant camp near Fort Sill and, skirting the southern base of the Wichita Mountains, was on its way to stir up the Cheyennes. Mud was deep between Forts Sill and Arbuckle, so that, though there were plenty of wagons, it was impossible to collect any considerable surplus of subsistence. The field column therefore started out with only five days' rations. The 7th still had left about two hundred of the seasoned horses, but these and the train mules had little forage. There was always plenty of ammunition. Though marching as infantry was new to these men, they made a pretty fair stagger at it from the start. Custer's official report says the "19th put to the blush the best regular infantry." The second night out, the camp was at old Fort Radziminski, a distance of forty-six miles in two days. Here, before the Civil War, Earl Van Dorn, later of the Confederacy, wintered a squadron of the old 2nd Dragoons, now the 4th Cavalry. Blistered feet and sore muscles were fashionable at this camp. Next morning the column crossed [the North Fork of the] Red River. It was a bed of red sand, almost without banks, over which ran here and there creeks and brooks of very red water, some deeper and some more shallow, but all lazily seeking the lowest and easiest places. The same pace was kept up the next day, the men standing it pretty well.

On March 6 the column crossed Salt Fork [of the Red River] and all day marched through a level, silent, desert country. Rations had been cut down twice already, and the men were getting hungry. This day the pace increased, and the trail for several miles behind was marked with a fringe of men hobbling along, doing their best but unable to keep up. The train and the guard were miles in the rear, so some of these hungry soldiers tried to shoot prairie dogs, though against strict orders. One of these stray shots struck and killed William Gruber, chief bugler of the 19th, who had been unable to keep up. The body was brought in by the guards, and just before "Taps" that night was wrapped in his blanket and buried in the sand. Since then I have never heard "Taps," whether bugle, piano, or the human voice, without seeing that desolate grave in the Texas sand. The shots over the grave wakened derisive yelps from coyotes, and I was aroused sometime in the night by the snarls of quarreling wolves in the direction of the grave. A trail of the runaway and defiant Cheyennes had been struck that day, and though over a month old, Mah-wis-sa knew where they were going and asserted that they honestly believed no soldiers could cross these desert wastes. This was confirmed by the broad trail they left behind.

March 7, when the command began its weary march, it was less by many men. From the 19th, nearly 300 had been taken. These were the footsore, those crippled by the four days' march, and the barefoot, of which there were many. These reported to Lieutenant Bell of the 7th, who, with about 450 men and a large part of the train, including all the camp equipage and stores, aside from subsistence and ammunition, turned to the right and made straight for Major Inman's camp on the Washita.

After leaving this camp at Gypsum Creek, Custer literally camped on the trail of the Cheyennes. This turned slightly to the north until the Salt Fork was reached, which it followed from that on. Here the scanty rations were again cut in half, which, though preventing absolute starvation, was the same as no food at all. The silent march went grimly on. The level country was now so desolate and dreary that the prairie dog was its only inhabitant. Not a bird was in the air—not even a raven. Rattlesnakes and gray scorpions avoided it scornfully. It was a vast stretch of desolation. About four blades of coarse grass grew to a square yard, and between them the dry sand crawled tirelessly back and forth with the wind.

The pace was now that of the forced march of light cavalry. From the first dawn till dark, with a few minutes' stop two or three times a day, the march was steady. Always scores of men hobbled in the rear, staggering into camp during the night, only to limp off with the others at early dawn. The mules were starving, but having been in fairly good flesh at the start, they kept their feet pretty well till March 10. As long as one could be got into the next camp, its life was sacred—none might touch its tempting quarters. On the tenth, coffee and sugar, met at rare intervals hitherto, disappeared from society. Tobacco was a dream. On the twelfth, the worst calamity of all befell—the salt gave out. Day and night, it was bitter cold. A piercing wind penetrated the threadbare and ragged clothing, while an increasing number became barefooted daily. The short sleep at night was broken by cold.

At last the mules began to fall. Every morning, when it became evident that rest had not restored an animal, its throat was cut and it was used for food, while the remaining mules were "doubled" into complete teams, and the extra wagons and all belonging to them were burned. At first awakening, the fatigue, soreness, and cold of the night made it seem impossible to move. As there was no breakfast to cook, the command moved out at once. Everybody limped and staggered along the first mile, after which they warmed up, their legs got limber, and they fell into the long, swinging stride of infantry, forgetting their sore feet and legs in the more noisy clamor of their stomachs. At this time, some complained that the front lining of their stomachs was chewing the rear lining. George Davidson, the veterinarian, said one morning:

> I just now saw a strapping young fellow crying like a baby. I inquired, "What's the matter?" "Civil War," says he. "What's that?" says I. "In my insides," says he. "Yesterday I sent down a piece of mule. It was a

stranger, an' ever' organ inside leaped on it an' tore it to pieces. Now they're all fighting because one got more'n the rest, an' it hurts my feelin's." "Aw," says I, "brace up an' quit cryin'—be a man." "I will," says he, determined like, an' reached down an' pulled up the skin of his belly to wipe his eyes, an' when he did, I seen where it was all wore into holes rubbin' against his backbone.

In his string of service horses, Senior Maj. (afterwards lieutenant colonel) William C. Jones of Iola, a fine officer,[11] had a racer, Old Lightning, which he had brought along with the generous view of augmenting the regimental amusements, and doubtless with the thought of relieving the heathen of other commands and places of their superfluous shinplasters. Old Lightning now placed Jones in strong pickle, for he couldn't afford to lose the horse and had no way to separate him from the fate of the starving mules. He was surely sincere in his efforts to bring the horse through alive. The rest of his horses had gone to the land of spirit steeds, so Jones devoted his energies to Lightning so assiduously that the men who knew not Jones were puzzled. It was at last decided that the major was afraid to trust the treasured equine to an orderly for fear the latter would be overcome with curiosity to see if there was not a trace of meat on the too openly exposed framework of the racer. It was feared that Jones's own hunger had made him suspicious.

Jefferson Cohee of Topeka had been one of A Troop's cooks and had hidden away a little salt, to which he clung like sin to a swollen fortune. Selecting the fattest piece of mule he could find, Cohee wrapped it, well salted, in mud and sat up all night to bake it. With a warning for secrecy, he gave a haversack containing the undivided half of this to Captain Pliley and myself. It was a life preserver, and one or the other wore that haversack all day and night. Seeing Major Jones and Lightning sauntering along together at the right of the column, looking so destitute and friendless, it was decided to divide with them. Jones and Pliley got into a wagon, fastened the curtains down, and made the transfer in whispers. It was reputed to be "beef," and the major seized it as does a squirrel a nut, with both hands, tearing it and swallowing the last morsel. Licking his fingers, he said, "Yes, but that's not beef, and Lightning's never eaten anything common or unclean."

Day after day, the rapidly perishing mules left much property to destroy. By the sixteenth only a few wagons remained. Men bivouacked where the column halted. The meat was held in the fire in absence of cooking utensils and afterwards eaten, burned outside and raw inside. In a few minutes the smell of burning meat was all over camp. Ever since, this odor—even the chance smell of a broiling steak—makes me ill. As soon as it was light, sometimes before, the march was resumed in much the same order as before. The route was westward, right up the Salt Fork. Approaching its headwaters, we entered a "chico" country. Near streams and on hillsides the mesquite grew, but on the uplands the scant grass of the Red Plains still held sway.

Here the trail turned sharply to the north and followed along the base of the famous tableland, "El Llano Estacado" of the early Spaniards and "The Staked Plain" of the American soldier and freighter. At the angle of the trail, we were about twenty or twenty-five miles from the Texas–New Mexico line. Many streams of good water flowed out of the great plateau. On March 18 an accidental development was seized on by the line officers and men and treated as a joke. The weather was so cold, the marching so severe, and the mules were dying so rapidly that laughing had somehow lapsed recently. This event, though an accidental discharge, was fired off so like a gigantic siege gun that it tickled the men immensely, and after a general laugh everybody felt better. For ten days the rations issued were so rare and ethereal that ninety percent of the men had long since ceased to look for them and had placed their affections solely on the mule. Thus they were not exasperated by a thimbleful of anything. Gradually they ceased to remember that there were rations. There being no officers' stores, the officers shared with the men, and all lived alike. On this date, therefore, when it was announced that the rations were exhausted—as if it made a particle of difference—after seeking to keep it secret, too, it raised shouts of laughter. It certainly was like shooting at a mosquito with a heavy cannon. These five days' rations had lasted through seventeen days of hard marching, which might have been worse.

On the seventeenth another event had had a decided effect on the column. In the forenoon a fresh trail was discovered—of a few lodges only—which came in from the North Fork of Red River and joined the big trail we had been following for nearly two weeks. Later the same day, campfires were covered with live coals in them. Though marching for twelve days at the limit of endurance, after this the column pushed on practically without rest. We had now left the chico country and were again on the Red Plains, headed northeast. All brightened up. "Somebody has left a valuable package on our doorstep" is the way Pvt. Marmaduke Lazelle expressed the general rejoicing. There was to be soon a settling of old scores.

The night of the nineteenth, I fell asleep from fatigue where I halted, with my boots on and without covers. Next morning my feet were badly frosted, and marching was doubly painful. About 2:00 P.M. March 20, while silently marching on over the level plain in what is now Wheeler County, Texas, a bunch of Indian homes was discovered in our right advance, not over a mile away. At the same moment, Indians were seen running toward them right across our front. Colonel Moore led the column, and leaving the ponies and running bucks severely alone, turned toward a low hill or mound from which they had emerged. The pace was so increased that the rear of the column was constantly on the double-quick. The regiment was apparently approaching a watercourse, and this chain of slight eminences indicated the bluff just beyond which the village was located, out of sight from the plain.

The order was now given, "On left front into line," and was executed with such promptness and vigor that the troops on the left came into position on the dead run. There, almost at the feet of the 19th, were tepees representing from 1,200 to 1,500 Cheyennes.

As the thought of cold and hunger, of the hardships of the winter, passed before these men, and the ample causes they had for reprisals on these enemies, there was one picture that loomed before all else and eclipsed all else in the heart of every man in that long, ragged, faded line from Kansas: the picture of a young mother lying dead on an army blanket, and in her arms a pretty little boy but two years old; the blue spot in the forehead of the one and the crushed head of the other telling how they died at the hands of the people in yonder camp—butchered out of malice that was more than devilish. Widowed first, then tortured for months, suffering every horror, and then killed with the cheers of her own people in her ears. Every officer and man thought of that picture as they saw it in the deep snows of the Washita. "Now is the time, and this is the place!" They could hardly believe their good luck.

As the men gripped their repeating carbines and saw that each had a cartridge in the barrel and seven others in the magazine, an officer came from Custer with the order to Colonel Moore, "Don't fire on those Indians." The men, stupid with wonder, hardly realized what it meant, before another aide brought Moore the orders for his position. The 19th was marched into the valley at the upper end of the village and halted in column of troops to "rest in place." The men of the 19th, not knowing the reason for this and fearing their general had been tricked, as had so often been the case, were angry. Neither Custer nor Moore ever knew what a critical time it was for about ten minutes. It looked, at one time, like they could not be restrained. The line officers argued, begged, and cursed. The accidental discharge of a carbine, or the shout of a reckless soldier, would have precipitated a killing that could not have been stopped, and would have entailed consequences impossible to estimate. Nothing was known along the line of captive white women, and at general headquarters nothing but what Mah-wis-sa had told them. This, however, was seized as a diplomatic potion and administered to the men, who knew that if those young women were in that camp, the first shot would be their death signal.

The 19th was at the upper end of the town and the 7th at the lower, every soldier silently clinging to his arms. Having learned all the secrets of the tribe from the captive squaws, Custer had the upper hand. He was soon in the village with Romeo to interpret, the principal warriors around him. He listened diplomatically to their falsehoods till he could discover their real chiefs and fix their respective identities, meantime sending word to the officers of both regiments to arm themselves well and walk down unconcernedly as if to hear the powwow. About a dozen or fifteen from the 19th and a like number from the 7th strolled down, and as soon as the general saw them crowding around him, he suddenly stood up and said: "Arrest those men!" They struggled, but struggled in vain. In a minute or two, armed guards were over them.

Then ensued a dramatic scene. Warriors swarmed like angry bees! On their bony ponies, hundreds of them raced around their village and the two regiments in the most threatening manner. Around and around they galloped, brandishing their fine rifles, screaming with rage and baffled hate. Though taken by surprise, they were now already dressed for battle. Their gorgeous war bonnets, brilliant battle pennants, new, long-fringed leggings (stolen from some freighter's wagon, doubtless) were all in sharp contrast to their sheet-iron colored skin, for, cold as it was, few wore blankets. It seemed that they were in such a frenzy of hatred that they must throw themselves in sheer insane fury on "Yellow Hair" and his officers. But there was something ominous in the perfect silence of the motionless soldiers, their clothes faded and ragged, their faces almost black from campfire and storm, their eyes deep sunken, their teeth protruding, and their fleshless cheeks like lines of skeletons. More impressive still to the superstitious Indian was the fact that these soldiers had crossed what the Indians all regarded as an impassable desert—had crossed it without horses, tents, or food, and suddenly, in daylight, swooped down on them, captured their village, and made their chiefs prisoners.

The council went right on, but "Yellow Hair," who had only listened before, now "made talk" himself. He told the chiefs that he wanted the two captives, alive and unharmed. He coolly ignored their protestations that they had not even heard of white squaws among the tribes. He greatly disconcerted them by talking and acting as if they had not spoken, whenever they lied. As their statements had all been false, except in minor matters, they now began to tell the truth. In the face of the recent denials, they now admitted that two women were held by their tribe, but said the captives were at a camp fifteen miles down the river (the Sweetwater). Custer told them to pack up at once and move down to that camp, and he would come the next day and get the women. In an hour the last warrior galloped away to overtake the squaws and pack ponies. The chiefs seized as hostages were Dull Knife,[12] Medicine Arrow,[13] Fat Bear, and Big Head.[14]

That night hunger and cold were self-invited guests. In addition, suspense was there—a new visitor. Next morning, the twenty-first, the column was early in motion. The Indian trail was broad the first five miles, then, as expected, began to fade away, until in another five miles there was no trail at all. The Indians secretly laughed at Custer for letting them out of the trap so easily. "Yellow Hair big fool like all white men—believe Indian—never learn!" But Custer had been with Hancock when this same trick was played, and was prepared. At the end of ten miles was a camping place, but it had not been used since the year before. The chiefs were then taken to a cottonwood tree, and Dull Knife was drawn up with a rope around his neck till his toes barely touched the ground. In that position, Custer told the three that he would not stand their tricks; that they must produce the women next day an hour before sundown, or all three should be hanged till they were dead. Word was sent to the tribe, and thus matters rested during the night of the twenty-first. Again cold and hunger controlled camp.

On March 22 a number of warriors visited camp early, but none after 8:00 A.M. Preparations for the hanging went on, and it was evident that the chiefs were getting anxious. That afternoon, as the arrangements for the execution were all complete and the sun was dipping low, word came from the hilltops that the watchers there saw something unusual going on. A solitary Indian appeared on a distant hill and halted long enough to beckon some unseen person forward, and then rode to a hill nearer and repeated the signal. A second figure came in sight and beckoned as did the first, and the third figure appeared, until quite a little chain of bucks was in sight. Then a group of a dozen appeared in the distance, among them two persons on one horse. These proved to be the women. The Indians all stopped on top of a low bluff overlooking the valley, where they were met by Romeo. The women both dropped to the ground, and the interpreter told them to go on toward headquarters, which he pointed out to them. Custer requested Colonel Moore to go forward and receive them as the representative of Kansas. He did so, and was accompanied by Majors Jones and Jenkins. The officers met them at the foot of the hill as the two came slowly down, clinging to each other as if about to be separated by force. Here was a drama rarely excelled in tragic interest in American history. It was in plain view of over one thousand men, among whom was one citizen, brother of one of the women, who was temporarily under guard to prevent him spoiling the only chance to save his sister by insanely killing Indians out of revenge for her sufferings. Moore has placed on record what was said, as the distance was too great for the breathless spectators to hear. The older, when asked if she was Mrs. Morgan, replied in the affirmative, and said her companion was Miss White. Her next words were, "Are we free now?" On being told that they were, she said, "Where's my husband?" The colonel explained that Mr. Morgan was at Fort Hays, not yet recovered from the wounds received at the time she was taken the previous summer. She asked next, "Where is my brother?" She was informed that he was with the column, but was not told that he was under arrest for her sake and his own. Miss White asked no questions. She had seen her people all killed at the time she was carried away.

They were now conducted across the bottom to where Custer was awaiting them. Their dresses were made of flour sacks, and they wore leggings and moccasins. As the fact of their scanty clothing became apparent, officers hurriedly threw off their greatcoats, and the girls were quickly wrapped in the two nearest. As they approached the general, still clinging together in a dazed, bewildered manner, the band of the 7th played a suitable air, which was changed softly to "Home, Sweet Home," as they arrived at headquarters, received by Colonel Custer and surrounded by the officers and men of both regiments. This was repeated a little later, as the rescued women looked on with interest at the retreat guard mount, dressed in more suitable clothing supplied by Colonel Custer's cook, a white woman. Chance had placed a lot of calico, needles, and thread with the command, and with these they soon came out in attire more feminine than the folds of the coats, in which they were almost lost. Custer had brought along a single "A" tent to cover necessary records. This was given to the girls for their home, and they could have had for the asking anything in the command to be had.

Mrs. Morgan was about twenty-five years old and Miss White seventeen, and yet their bodies bore the marks of more hard and cruel usage than a century of ordinary hardship entails. Heavy burdens had been carried on their bare shoulders till the skin was as hard and callous as the palm of a laborer's hand. The jealous squaws, with their barbaric rawhides, had covered their backs with scars. Some of the more recent lashing left unhealed gashes as wide as a man's finger. At first they had been sold back and forth among the bucks for fifteen ponies each, but their last owners only paid two. For five or six months, these tender plants of the American home had borne distress, homesickness, grief, abuse, cold, hunger, and loss of hope, and still lived.

Maj. Henry Inman, with a large train and heavy escort, had established a supplementary supply depot on the Washita near Custer's battlefield of November, in order to be in reach of the field column at the earliest possible moment. When the latter left Fort Sill March 2, with only five days' supplies, it was not regarded as possible that it could remain out later than the twelfth. Inman was already becoming anxious when, on the fourteenth, Lt. Bell of the 7th arrived with most of the train and 400 footsore and barefooted men from Gypsum Creek, all nearly starved. As the days dragged on, anxiety turned to fear. The absence of all news was reported to the War Department on the eighteenth, by way of Fort Hays, and on the twenty-second an eastern newspaper published the letter of a correspondent giving as a probable, if not necessary, fact that the whole column had perished in the unknown wastes of north Texas. Every day added to the anxiety in official circles, and by the twenty-fourth the most hopeful began to fear that the long silence only mean a great calamity.

The morning of March 23, the column started for Inman's camp. There was no time to lose, for the horses and mules were nearly gone and the men growing weaker. That night for a few hours the column bivouacked in its tracks. The march began at 2:00 A.M. of the twenty-fourth. As men staggered along in the dark, talk was scarce. About the only words heard were frequent low-voiced orders along the column, "Close up, men! Close up!" Nothing but the grim discipline of necessity was now required. At daylight there was no halt. At 2:30 P.M. of the twenty-fourth, the column halted on the open plain; no water in sight, and every man off duty fell to the ground. Mule meat was now a rare article. I now suffered anguish at every step from my frozen feet. The marching aggravated the burns, and Doctor [Mahlon] Bailey had little to work with. I had not slept, from this cause, for two nights. During the march from 2:00 A.M. to 2:30 P.M., we had covered thirty-six miles. While lying here, a few horsemen were discovered hovering in the distance, evidently regarding us with curiosity and suspicion. After many attempts, they were finally tolled within hailing distance and proved to be scouts left back at Supply in December, wounded or partly frozen. They were from Inman's camp that morning on a trip to the Salt

Plains buffalo hunting. It was about forty miles to the camp from here. Colonel Custer mounted a messenger on one of these horses for a rapid ride to Inman, ordering a rescue train sent at once to his relief with some empty wagons for the men who could march no further, of which there were many.

Though Colonel Custer himself and the entire 7th would wait for relief, he left Colonel Moore free to decide whether his regiment could bear further marching or not. Moore knew that it could not, but offered troop commanders permission to go separately if their men were able. It was now 4:00 P.M., and in ten minutes the irrepressible men of Troop A were falling in for the march. I happened to be lying a few feet in front of the right center, my feet screaming with pain, and while they counted fours, Lieutenant Wilson asked what I was going to do. On my replying that I would lay in that spot till I died or was lifted into a rescue wagon, a number of the men cried out, "That won't do! Where Troop A goes, you go too! A Troop is coming in tonight, and so are you, if we have to carry you every step of the way!" I finally staggered to my feet, and all night and till noon next day, those worn and starving but generous and loyal men took turns in helping me along the weary trail.

All that moonless night, Captain Pliley led his troop over that black and desolate plain, the polar star for his compass. At daylight the troop struck the Washita River about eighteen miles above Inman's camp. The river was frozen over except a narrow strip in the center. The ice was broken with poles, and the men bathed their swollen and inflamed feet in ice water. Of the troop, now reduced to sixty, twenty-six were without boots. All such had their feet wrapped in blouses, shirts, and blankets torn up for that purpose—for the feet must be covered, whatever the man suffered otherwise. The halt was short. About 11:00 A.M. we marched across Custer's late battlefield, and at the bend below Black Kettle's village site forded the river waist-deep, the ice being broken by poles.

About noon, rounding a point of timber, a sentinel was encountered, and in the river bend beyond were the tents, horses, wagons, mules, and men of a big camp. In the eyes of the pilgrims, that sentinel, personally, was a monstrosity. His body appeared to be swollen, his cheeks were puffed, his eyes bulged, his face was white, his lips were large, loose, and covered his teeth altogether, while his clothes were a gaudy blue. He had a sickly, bloated, and dropsical look generally. I was astonished to see that all the men at Inman's camp had the same peculiarities, and it was some time before I understood that this was the normal man. We didn't realize that it was our appearance that had changed. It had come about gradually, and as all were alike, there was no contrast to attract attention. When we turned the left of the first line of tents and saw the bright mess fires with clean cooking utensils at the side, hard-bread boxes partly filled, and sides of raw bacon banking them around, the ranks were broken without ceremony, and officers and men without a word began to eat hard bread and raw bacon.

Inman's men stood gaping in silent astonishment while their rations were consumed. Among those looking on were at least thirty men of this troop, some of whom had left it only nineteen days before at Gypsum Creek, Texas, but not one recognized a face among us—not even their captain's and first sergeant's. They supposed it was a party of starving Mexicans, wrecked somewhere on the plains. As the clothing was black and brown and hanging in rags and tatters, it was little wonder. Though Custer's messenger had arrived in the night and a relief train was already gone, none looked for any part of the command to make the march. I was suffering with fever due to my frosted feet and was delirious much of the first twenty-four hours in camp, so remember little that occurred there. Another troop of the 19th marched in about six hours after Pliley's, but I do not know whose.

This ended the forced marching of the 19th Kansas and the 7th Cavalry. On March 27 the rear guard arrived, and with it the last member of the famous expedition. The command had lived nearly a month on five days' rations and had accomplished all its objects, recovering the captives without ransom and bringing away Dull Knife, Fat Bear, and Big Head to be held as thumbscrews on the treacherous Cheyennes. It had marched twenty-two miles for every day out, the weather always freezing, without tents, cooking utensils, beds, or salt—its sole subsistence two-thirds of that time mules that had starved to death.

Camp Supply was reached by easy marches, and there both regiments picked up the last of the men detached the previous December. One member of Troop A had died at Supply. Joseph Larama, a half-breed Pottawattomie, had broken down under the hardships and exposure of the overland march from Topeka and soon died.[15]

Though two-thirds of both regiments had but just returned from a 445-mile march, when the column moved out from Camp Supply on its 200-mile march to the railroad, the 19th was cheering and whooping as if going to a picnic. The column forded the Arkansas at Fort Dodge and headed straight for Fort Hays. Two years before, when the 18th Kansas marched up and down, to and fro, in this part of the country, it was a trackless waste between the two forts. Now the column marched all the way over a smooth, well-traveled wagon road.

April 10, a week out from Supply, the 19th went into camp on Big Creek, just below the fort and a quarter of a mile below the town, and opposite. Here at once began the work of making out the necessary rolls, officers' reports, invoices and receipts, and all the business incidental to turning in military property and getting the six months' pay due to officers and men.

At last, on April 18, 1869, the 19th Kansas passed into history. Few regiments of such short life have had so conspicuous a part in such decisive movements. Though no bloody battles were fought, the two short campaigns conquered the five wild tribes of the Southern Plains. The Cheyennes, Arapahos, Kiowas, Comanches, and the Plains Apaches [Kiowa-Apaches] were forever pledged to peace. The homes of Kansas, Nebraska, Texas, Colorado, and the Indian Territory were for the first time made as safe as those in Ohio or Indiana. For nearly forty years, these Indians have been free to learn the ways of peace, and the strides they have made in that period seem almost incredible to an old soldier who knew them both before and during that terrible winter.

Lieutenant General Sheridan, in discussing the winter's work privately four years later, said that for the difficulties surrounding it, and for the hardships and suffering involved, there was no parallel in the history of our army. He mentioned several of the worst cases in history and compared them with Custer's march in the desert to show that in all the other cases, there were natural resources that would have been luxuries to the 7th and 19th regiments. He said also that by means of this "tremendous drubbing," the Indians would settle down and in half a century become self-sustaining, and in less than a century would become Christian citizens. Sheridan's dream is realized in less than forty years.

In spite of these hardships and sufferings, the mortality record of the 19th is surprisingly small. Out of 50 officers and 1,300 men, but four men died of disease, the result of hunger and cold. One was killed and one seriously wounded on duty, and one killed by accident. The troops of Pliley and Lender (A and G) had not a single deserter, and in all the regiment, in spite of their sufferings and privations, there were but ninety deserters. Kansas has no reason to be ashamed of her 19th Cavalry and the work it left for succeeding generations to enjoy.

A Few Years' Experience on the Western Frontier

JOSEPH P. RODGERS[1]

Miscellaneous Collections, Manuscripts Department, Kansas State Historical Society, Topeka

I left my home in Clarionsburg, Clarion County, Pennsylvania, April 1, 1867. At the age of eight, my father died, leaving five children, one sister older than me. Owing to financial circumstances, it was necessary for me to leave school and go to work in order to help support the family to keep the wolf from the door.

During the Civil War, work was plentiful and wages good. I, being a strong boy, filled a man's place, so received good wages.

The war over and the men home, conditions changed. Wages dropped and work [was] hard to get. At this time, I read so much about the opportunities in the West and that mother could get 160 acres of land by living on it for five years, so west I started with forty dollars in my pocket. I finally landed in St. Louis broke. There I procured a job with the St. Louis Car Company, driving a horse car at two dollars a day. I stayed in St. Louis until I had a few dollars, then moved further west to where I had some relatives living in Kansas who had moved there in 1856. At Kansas City I took the Kansas Pacific for Manhattan, Kansas. Manhattan was built a short distance up the Smoky River above Junction City, Kansas. They only ran a mixed train; only ran when they got ready and stopped the same. I was informed that the train would arrive at Manhattan at daylight; instead it passed through Manhattan during the night.

On arrival at Ogden, I discovered that the train had passed Manhattan. I asked the conductor at Ogden how much further to Manhattan. He said you passed it last night, and I will be back sometime within the next twenty-four hours if no mishaps and I will take you back, or you can go along to the end of the road and come back with us. However, I preferred to await their return, as the roadbed was so rough, it felt like the caboose was on boulders or ties. Stepping out on the platform with my carpet sack, there was one man in sight with a big white hat and two revolvers strapped on.

He saluted me with, "Hello kid; do you want to go to work? Did you ever drive bulls?"

I replied, "No sir; I have driven horses and oxen."

He replied, "That is the same thing. I am going to start a wagon train for Santa Fe, New Mexico, right away. I will give you fifty dollars a month and board; you furnish your own arms and ammunition."

I replied, "How am I to get back."

The man replied, "I hire you for the round trip, which will take about six months."

My reply, "I'll go."

The man said, "Do you see those covered wagons down there? Go right down, breakfast will soon be ready. Go right in and make yourself at home; I will be down before long. Then he pulled out a passbook, wrote my name, saying, "You are on the payroll."

I walked to the camp and found a jolly bunch of men from different sections of the United States that had drifted west to make a home and better their conditions. When the wagon boss came, I told him I had intended to go to my cousin Leslie Pritner's home, a few miles from Manhattan. He said he was well acquainted with the Pritners, and it was only ten miles in a straight line across the prairie.

I asked him what were the chances to hire a horse, and I would go over and see them and come right back. He replied he would rather I not go, as if all went well, we would pull out early the next morning. So I told him, all right. He told me afterward, the main reason he did not want me to visit the Pritners was that men were scarce, and he was afraid that I might not return.

Well, off for Santa Fe the second day with ten wagons with trailers, making twenty wagons in the train. There were five yoke of oxen to a wagon—fifty head of bulls, as they were called, ten drivers, one cook, one night herder, and one extra man in case of emergency, also the wagon boss, Thomas Nixon.[2] The train belonged to Maxey Waxabloom, a wholesaler and retailer of Ogden. This wagon train was used to haul produce, etc., which was traded for furs; also for handling contracts for the government.

We experienced no difficulty on the trip to Santa Fe, or on the return trip to Ogden. However, at different places we saw where the Indians had destroyed wagon trains that summer. At one spot about ten miles east of Dodge, we found the Indians had murdered some emigrants and burned their wagons; women's clothing was scattered around. We found a child's foot with the shoe still on, and it was badly crimped from the fire. Further, in regard to the depredations by the Indians on the Santa Fe Trail and the western frontier in general: While a great deal has been written about the early days on the western frontier, less than one-half of the crimes by the Indians has been told and probably never will be.

On arrival at Ogden, I was paid off. The wagon boss, Mr. Nixon, proved to be a perfect gentleman the entire trip. Mr. Nixon told me if I went up to Fort Riley, about three miles from Ogden, I would find farmers from the Wild Cat Creek hauling supplies to the fort, so off I went. When I arrived at the fort, I met an officer who proved to be a quartermaster. He asked me if I would like to drive a team out to Fort Harker, wages fifty dollars a month. I said O.K. and said no more. The next day I was on the road driving a six-mule team. The mules knew more about the business than I did.

There was quite a large train loaded with infantry and supplies. At Fort Harker, it was all hustle and bustle to get ready to move the next morning. That evening the railroad train turned up with a few gentlemen passengers, but we did not find out much until late that evening—it was a commission going south to hold council with the Indians to furnish them with provisions for them for the winter as a reward for murdering settlers on the frontier, taking women prisoners, burning wagon trains and houses, [and] torturing men and children in the most brutal way.

From Fort Harker, which was located along the Kansas Pacific Railroad, then building toward Denver, Colorado, we traveled southwest to Fort Larned to the Santa Fe Trail. At Larned, we connected with a large freight train loaded with all kinds of supplies—including provisions, clothing, arms and ammunition, also reinforcements of troops, which included six pieces of light artillery. From there we marched to Medicine Lodge Creek in south-central Kansas.

In the forepart of October [1867], we met about five thousand warriors with their squaws and papooses with them. The Indians were very indignant and sassy. They would not consent to any proposition. The commission was ready to start the ball rolling with a fight. We had about three hundred men in the wagon train, including the drivers. Artillery kept ready. Men slept on their arms, not even taking their boots off, expecting to be charged at any time, day or night. In daytime the chiefs would come into camp for a war talk. At night they would hold a war dance, swinging their scalping knives and the scalps of men, women, and children. We kept a short distance away. We kept a bold front, which had a great deal to do with signing a treaty, a treaty in their favor. Of course, they were to stay south of the Arkansas River and stop killing the white people. Those Indians felt they had a right to change their minds and had always done so. The treaty also furnished them provisions for the winter. Also arms and ammunition so that they could continue their depredations, while the widows and orphans went hungry.

I will give you my opinion, and the opinion of many others. There were quite a few men who had secured trading privileges, illegally, with the Indians. No one else was allowed to trade with the Indians. Many a poor honest man was arrested and sent to prison for trading for a few buffalo robes. Yes, I traded for quite a number of buffalo robes and was fortunate enough to get away with it, and I gave the Indian more than twice as much as the appointed government traders.

I will give you some idea how it was carried on. The squaws tanned the hides and did all the trading. For a perfect tanned hide, the Indian received a one-pint tin of flour, one cup of low-grade coffee, one cup of brown sugar, and a cup of beans; or, for twelve robes, they gave the Indian an old army musket and a few rounds of ammunition.

Now the treaty was over, and I was paid off at Fort Riley. My next move was to go and hunt up my Pritner relations. As my clothes looked a little shabby, I went to Junction City about three miles to fit out. There I dropped in with some cattlemen who were going to Texas to come up the trail the next spring with a herd of cattle. So I decided to turn cowboy. I bought a pony and outfit, including spurs and revolver, so was ready for the trip. We threw together and bought four cheap ponies to carry our equipment. Shall say we had a fine and enjoyable trip. When we got to Sherman, Texas, I hired out at once to help to get a herd together. We would leave in the spring when the cattle were in condition. We started with four thousand head of big steers. With the exception of two or three stampedes, we arrived in Abilene, Kansas, in August 1868. That was the principle shipping point at that time. Then I went to visit some friends. I found them all well and nicely fixed. They had raised no crops. The hot winds had burned everything in that section of country.

I could get no work of any kind there. I saw by the papers they were grading and building a railroad from Ottawa to Fort Scott. To Ottawa I went and got work, but had only been there a short time when the government called for a regiment of volunteers to go out on the plains to fight and exterminate war tribes of the plains. That just struck me to the dot.

—•— ≍◆≍ —•—

Governor Crawford cabled for a regiment of 1,200 men to enlist for six months under the act of 1863. For a winter campaign, it was to be a cavalry regiment, commanded by a full quota of officers clothed and mounted, subject to the rules of the Civil War. I think the call was made about October 10 or 12, 1868.[3] I enlisted at Ottawa, which company, after being mustered in, became Company F, 19th Kansas Volunteer Cavalry. The horses, being bought up in a hurry, surely were a fine lot. However, many were not even halter broken. One of the horses was drawn by a young man with little experience as a rider. In two or three days, the horses became victors. I traded for the horse, and a few days later one of the officers wanted to trade with me.

Lt. Col. [Horace L.] Moore took charge of drilling and disciplining the regiment. That was soon and easily done, owing to many of them having served in the Civil War. As reports came in every day of depredations by the Indians, Companies D and G shipped by railroad to Fort Hays to do guard duty for trains hauling supplies to Camp Supply, two hundred miles south.

On November 4 Governor Crawford issued a Thanksgiving proclamation, then resigned and mustered in as colonel of the regiment. On the morning of the fifth, we broke camp and moved in as good order as any Regular army that had been drilled for years. The night of the fifth, we went into camp on a nice little stream, plenty of wood. We were comfortable.

The next morning, when the bugle sounded forward march, we moved out as the last note was sounded as [if] we had been drilled for months. We headed southwest, marching for miles, not a house in sight. We struck the Santa Fe

Trail; we followed it through the town of Burlingame. It began to rain after we broke camp that morning. It was only a short time until we were all soaking wet to the hide. We marched all day in that rain so heavy at times we could not see the man ahead and at dark, soaked to the skin. Camp was made on the Neosho River, east of Emporia town. The blankets in the wagon were all soaked. The wind blew so hard they could not keep the covers on the wagons, so everything was soaked. Fires failed to dry the blankets as the rain turned to snow. It was a wet, melting snow, [and] it came through our dog tents as it melted, although they would turn [away] rain. A great many of the men had sore throats for several days. We departed from Emporia, and the day was cloudy and cold. Men and horses suffered with the cold. For some distance there were scattered settlers, and we were able to get forage for the horses, and they were in good heart when we reached Fort Beecher, now called Wichita.

At Fort Beecher is where Colonel Crawford's troubles began. There had been a supply train with rations and forage sent from Fort Riley. There was a drunken lieutenant and a few troops of infantry there, but no rations or forage, as it was customary in those days to sell or trade government supplies for whiskey. They always claimed they lost the supplies in a fight with the Indians. They had not sobered up enough to carry out their plans, as they did not expect us for two or three weeks. This lieutenant was court-martialed and removed from the service. Not a pound of grain for the horses.

When the command left Fort Beecher, we entered a desolate country only known by the Indians after crossing Arkansas River, [which] took up most of the day. The barefooted horses that had lost their shoes in the mud were shod.

Here I wrote a letter to my mother, who lived at Collinsburg, Clarion County, Pennsylvania, as we were told it would probably be the last chance, as that was the end of civilization and few were known to come out alive that went south of the Arkansas River.

The two guides, Apache Bill [Seaman] and Johnny Stillwell, that had been hired had never been south of the river, although they were well posted north of the river. Now that shows you what little was known of the Southwest and Oklahoma, when not even a guide or scout could be procured by the U.S. Army. So we started on a trip, no telling what the outcome would be. We were unprepared for such a march through an unknown country. What maps we had were misleading and guesswork. The weather was cold, no rations or forage, and unreliable information gave us much trouble. Colonel Crawford was up against tough proposition, with about three days' rations and one day's corn to march through an unknown country. We march southwest for five or six days. As we had to make our own roads, some days we made about sixteen miles, and some days about twenty-five miles.

About five or six days from the Arkansas River, after most of the command had tied their horses to the picket line, something scared the horses and they tore out the stakes and stampeded, now one hundred horses tied to one line coming through the camp, tearing down the tents, overturning the wagons.

There was much confusion, the men trying to get out of the way. I think there were about six hundred horses in the stampede. I happened to be on rear guard that day[4] and just got off my horse and was going to unsaddle when here they came. Our own company horses tore loose the line, and before I had time was caught in the center of the line, my horse on the dead run, the cable around my back. I had presence of mind to keep the spurs in my horse, and as soon as I could get my knife out, I cut the cable and was free but kept right on with the stampede. Now and then a horse would fall when his halter strap would break. The next morning I found myself several miles from camp, rounding up what horses I could find. I soon had plenty of help, as about one hundred had not broken loose. I think every horse but six was found.

We then marched on for two days, everything going along as well as could be expected. Just as we were going into camp, black heavy clouds covered the sky, and in a few minutes the ground was covered with snow. The next morning we dug ourselves out from under eight inches of snow, snow still coming down. We led our horses out, kicking the snow off in spots so the horse could get a bit now and then. There was no letup to the storm. There we lost a day, with twenty-four hours of snow. After laying there thirty-six hours, we moved on. We marched all day and it snowed all day. It snowed all that day until it was about two feet deep. That afternoon[5] about 4:00 P.M., the storm slackened and we went into camp on a small stream. Cottonwood trees were plentiful, so we chopped down trees and trimmed the limbs. We piled the limbs for fodder for the horses. We had fed out the last of the corn, giving them a few grains out of our hand.

Our rations all gone, the snow had settled to about eighteen inches. The next morning it was below freezing point, with a crust on the snow. We had plenty of wood, so built big fires. There was no breakfast for men or beast. The horses neighing and mules braying. The sun came out bright and warm, just as though nothing had happened, all smiles.

When it warmed up a little, orders were given to march. Between 10:00 and 11:00 A.M., we moved out; had only gone a short distance when we came in sight of a large buffalo herd. We killed quite a number [and] loaded the wagons with what we could haul. From this time on, it was warm through the middle of the day, but very cold at night. In marching through the snow and slush, our feet were soaking wet all day, as we walked all the time and led our horses so as to save them for later, cutting cottonwood trees for them or anything they could eat. The men did not suffer; we had plenty of buffalo meat. But those poor horses and mules; it made one sick to see them begging.

I laid down one night with my feet to the fire and fell asleep. I woke up with my feet hurting; the fire had drawn the soles of my boots, cupped them over my feet so tight I had to cut them up to get them off. There to Camp Supply, I had to wrap my feet with gunnysack and buffalo hide.

There was still some snow on the ground when I came off guard one morning at daylight. As most of the company had fell into line, I asked what is up. They told me Tim, the Irishman, had been falling in for sick call with the chills and fever, and they treated [us] to a little quinine and a glass of whiskey, and the doctor, being a good fellow, assumed it would do no harm. I threw my carbine and belt down. As the morning was cold, about seventy of the company marched up. The old doctor went along the line. Doctor asked what is the matter with all of you; same answer—chills and fever. The doctor told the steward to bring out enough quinine for a horse or elephant, put it in the tumbler, filled it up with whiskey, stirred it, and handed it to Tim. He sized it up, put it to his lips several times, [and] would gag, saying, "I have taken so much I have turned against it." By that time the quinine had settled to the bottom, and just as Tim was going to drink the whiskey off the quinine, the Doc grabbed the glass, stirred it up, [and] handed it back with an oath, "You drink that!" I pulled my hat off, gave one yell, lit out for the company, [and] everyone followed suit.

The march continued day after day. Horses giving out were shot by the rear guard. We camped one night in a big hackberry grove.[6] Those trees looked like an apple tree and about the same size. They are loaded with berries about the size of cranberries, and they hold fast and don't drop from the tree until the next spring. They have a sweetish taste like a currant, but very little meat, three or four seeds in each one. Wild game is very fond of them when ripe. In the winter, I have seen the trees so thick with wild turkeys it looked like a turkey crop. We surely helped ourselves to the berries. The seeds being so hard, they would not digest. We had plenty of sand, but no craw like the birds. Some of the troop came near losing their lives, the supply of castor oil and salts was in demand. If you ever run across 19th troops, ask them about Hackberry Camp.

We finally struck the Cimarron River, where camp was made. A great many horses and mules were not able to go further without rest. Colonel Crawford ordered Captain Pliley of Company A to take the best and strongest horses of his company and march for Camp Supply and have rations and forage sent out at once.[7] Here we found more buffalo, but the horses and mules were suffering by the cold and lack of forage.

The next day after Captain Pliley left, the colonel marched with what men that were able to move on. About three men with sore and frozen feet and disabled horses were left in camp. We pushed on to Camp Supply. We missed Captain Pliley on his return with supplies. We arrived at Camp Supply November 28, 1868. When Captain Pliley arrived at Hackberry with supplies and forage, the march was continued for Camp Supply.

Major [R. W.] Jenkins in command arrived on November 29.[8] Strange to say, we had not lost a man, but lost many horses. From Wichita to Camp Supply, we made the trip in twelve days, being about two hundred miles in a direct line. When we arrived, General Sheridan congratulated us on our pluck and energy, saying under all circumstances we had surely made a wonderful march. We had marched nine days without sufficient rations and forage. We had gone through one of the worst snowstorms known.

If General Sheridan had known anything about the country and what we were to encounter that time of year, he would never have given the order to make that march. He had been misinformed by his scouts, who had never been in that part of the country.

At Camp Supply, we learned that Colonel Custer had been sent by General Sheridan on a scouting expedition with the 7th Cavalry to locate the winter camp of the Indians. He struck an Indian trail of about one hundred fifty warriors going south that were returning from the north, where they had been committing depredations. He followed their trail until a snowstorm came up and covered the ground about fifteen inches, and he kept on going in the direction they were going. He located them on the Washita Creek one night. The weather was clear and cold. He sent Major Elliott and Captain Hamilton with a squad of men to try to find out how large the Indian camp was and get what information they could and return before daylight. They found the Indian camp so large and strung so far along the creek [that] they did not return until after daylight. The major reported smoke was coming out of the tepees.

Custer gave the command to charge. The regiment band, standing about four hundred yards from the nearest tepees, surprised the Indians, but no more of a surprise than Custer received as he thought he was only charging about one hundred fifty Indians, and he found he had charged about four or five thousand warriors besides the squaws and children. Being surrounded by the Indians, he found the squaws more desperate than the bucks. Custer was compelled to get out of that situation the best he could and in short order, as warriors were coming from all directions. It was only a miracle and quick retreat that saved the troops. A few minutes' delay, and the command would have been overpowered and killed the same as in Montana on the Yellowstone in 1876. When the command fell back to the wagon train, they were fortunate enough to drive one old chief and a few warriors ahead of them with about forty squaws and a number of children. There was a herd of ponies between the Indian camps. Custer sent a detachment back to round up the herd and shoot them while the Indians looked on, afraid to attack the troops, and Custer knew better than to continue the fight or even to go and rescue the dead. As for the wounded, he knew there were none. As fast as they fell, the squaws cut them up with their scalping knives. As near as I could find out, they shot between seven hundred and one thousand ponies. Had the 19th Cavalry or 7th Cavalry not been sent out until the 19th Kansas arrived, so as to have joined with Custer's command on the Custer expedition, there would have been a different story told, and Indian treaties and depredations would have been stopped.

On Custer's return to Camp Supply, General Sheridan marched for the Washita River with both regiments[9]: the 7th Regulars and the 19th Volunteers that still had their mounts. Now I had lost my mount and was left behind to do guard duty with quite a number of others. I went to our captain about it; he said if I could find anyone to change with me, he would be glad to let me go. I tried to buy a mount but failed, as all the boys were anxious for a fight. I then concocted another plan. I went to the corral of the 7th Regulars, which was only a short distance, picked me out a good mount, "I," as that brand would be easy to convert into an "F," as every company's horse is branded on the hips with the letter of the company. I went to the lieutenant and asked him if I was mounted if he would put me on the roll to go the next morning. He said, "Sure, but you have no mount." I said, "I will have one," and the lieutenant smiled. I rustled around and got a saddle and blanket. When it got dark and most of the troops had turned in, I moved off to Company I of the 7th. The guard walked back and forth along the line every few minutes, stopping at one end to get warm, as it was very cold. I watched my chance, untied my horse, [and] led him out to our own company. All had retired, a light still in the captain's tent [and] Sgt. Bill Castle and Ed sitting by a little tent. Those two men had served as officers all through the Civil War on the Confederate side. They asked me if I had a horse, and I told them I had. I went to a wagon, got an iron rod, and it was hot by the time we had the horse's front foot tied up. I pulled off my coat and threw it over the horse's head; a quick trick and easy done.

The next morning we moved out just as it broke day, and I could see our officers smile every time they looked my way. So I am one that stole a horse and did not get my neck broken, as few ever escaped the rope for that offense in that section.

I think it was the fifth day out from Camp Supply[10] we got to the battle-ground where Custer had fought what they called the Black Kettle fight. The Indians kept out guards, determined not to be surprised again, and ready to do battle the next time the troops came, as they had always, on previous engagements sent against them, [managed] to hold their own in that section and many times gave the troops the worst of battle. When they laid eyes on such a force of troops, strung out for five miles or more, they moved out in a hurry, leaving several tepees and considerable plunder behind. In fact, one soldier found three or four hundred dollars in cash. I happened to be orderly for our captain that day, Capt. J. B. Jenness, and when the command halted, all officers and order-lies went to the front, going down into the timber where the charge had been made, I saw several dead soldiers lying there, badly cut up. We went a short distance, noticed General Sheridan, Custer, and other officers, all of their horses in a group. The captain and I dismounted. The captain left me to hold the horses. In a few minutes he returned and asked me if I wanted to look. I went and what did I see—a woman with her skull crushed in, laying on a cottonwood log, and her little boy laying on top of her. Both had been murdered by the squaws when the fight started, as the first thing the squaws do when they are attacked. This woman was Mrs. Blinn and Joe, about [two] years old. They had been captured in Kansas, her husband and some others killed at the time. I found out afterwards his folks lived close to Ottawa, Kansas. Her folks were named Harrington.

The Indians making a getaway made a forced march down the Washita to Fort Cobb for the Indian agent to protect them. The Cheyennes broke away from the other tribes when they broke camp, going southwest. The Cheyennes had two white women in their possession, and if they took the women to Cobb, they would have to give them up. These were the women they had captured on the Republican River, close to where Concordia now stands (which I will mention later on). These women's names were Mrs. Morgan and Miss White.

We camped all night at the battleground, the dead being gathered and roped in blankets and buried. The next morning, by daylight, we moved on the Indian trail. We found so many hollows in the ground we had to break up the ground to get the wagons over, so we turned up to the ridge where it was easier going. About 10:00 A.M. it commenced to rain, turning into a snowstorm. The ground was soon covered; travel became slow for the wagon train. We worked our way back to the creek, where there was timber for camp that night, as it had turned into a regular blizzard, with the snow piling up to fifteen and eighteen inches. It cleared up during the night, and the harnesses had to be dug out of the snow and ice, fires built, and the harnesses thawed out before they could be put on the mules, the wind blowing and temperatures below freezing, a heavy crust on the snow, so we did not get started until afternoon. We kept up the pursuit for six days until we drove the Indians into Fort Cobb. About twenty miles out from Fort Cobb, we overtook the Indians. General Sheridan formed the command into double column, closing on the Indians. It looked as though something was going to happen shortly, as we were close and gaining on them very fast. They were doing their best to get away. Sheridan, Custer, and quite a number of the field officers were in the lead but a short distance taking in the situation, making preparation how to charge.

Everyone keyed up to the highest pitch, their carbines across their saddles in front of them. Just then, as we were ready to form in a column to make the charge, some of Colonel Hazen's scouts came dashing with orders to General Sheridan not to fire on the Indians, as two or three chiefs had come in and surrendered, and he had promised to protect them. Colonel Hazen represented [the] Interior Department, so there you are. But Sheridan moved right up on them as though he was going to open battle, I think in hope some of the Indians would make a move so he could get an excuse to clean the outfit out, for the officers and men surely meant to fight. Sheridan gave orders to take those chiefs prisoners. Now the way their arms were taken away from them was not slow nor in a very gentle manner. A guard had been thrown around them, and they were told they were prisoners of war and [at] the first unfriendly move they would be shot. I will say that some strong language was used. General Sheridan gave the Indian chiefs to report to him on a certain day at Fort Cobb, which they all did except the Cheyennes. He ordered all the tribes to move south to Cache Creek, about sixty miles south. The 19th Kansas marched for Cache Creek January 1, 1869. Cache Creek is in the Washita Mountains. We went in camp there and Fort Sill is located there.

In a few days Custer and the 7th Cavalry arrived. So the 19th Kansas Cavalry was the regiment that first located and occupied the Fort Sill reservation on January 3, 1869, and guarded the Indian chiefs taken prisoners by General Sheridan. We remained there until March 2. When Colonel Custer arrived at Cache Creek, he proceeded to put everything in military shape, as General Sheridan would be there in a few days. Streets were laid out. A parade ground was laid out. On the parade ground were officers' tents, headquarters in the center. A guard was put in front of Custer's tent. My orders were not to let any-one cross the parade ground, halt them three times; if they did not stop—shoot. The Indians were camped thick all around. I had been pacing that beat all day with nothing to do, as nobody tried to cross the ground. About the time I got disgusted with my job for having nothing to do, along came an old buck on a spotted pony and working his heels and using his quirt to keep the horse on a slow lope. I kept my back to him as though I did not see him, one eye over my shoulder. After he got some distance from me, I hollered "Halt" twice, not very loud; the third time I yelled at the top of my voice and shot at the same time. I threw another cartridge in and was going to take a little better bead when Custer's tent flew open and he yelled, "Don't shoot." By that time, the Indian had got up some speed. The Indian was hunted up and brought back to headquarters; there had been no damage done, only a hole in the blanket. The next thing, I was questioned. I told of the orders given me by the sergeant. That sergeant was sent for. The sergeant was questioned; he said it was customary to give such an order. No more guards in front of Custer's tent.

The next problem was to find the Cheyenne camp and, if possible, rescue those two white women alive. How well I remember Colonel Crawford resigning as colonel of the 19th command. On February 14 Colonel Moore took command. On Cache Creek, just about where the fort now stands, we found a large snake den about a mile along the creek. A rocky cave was under this, with a table rock extending out to the creek. Talk about snakes! There were all kinds and sizes. The larger portion were rattlers, the black snakes the longest. Although some of these rattlers measured eight feet or longer and eighteen or twenty inches around, we made hooks on poles to pull them out, and threw them in the creek. There were thousands of them. The boys skinned them and stretched them over the belts, and so I made me a vest cut of them.

We were on short rations at that time. The rations consisted of a chunk of fat bacon, two inches square, and two hardtack [that] I think had been left over from the Mexican War, as they were all honeycombed, and what the worms did not want was left for the 19th Kansas.

We were looking for General Sheridan from Fort Cobb with a mule train of supplies that had come from Fort Hays, about four hundred miles in the middle of winter. If an average of fifteen miles a day was made, it was good time, as no graded roads or bridges were there. While waiting for supplies, Walter Cotingham of our company found a beehive in a tree right at camp. The tree was chopped down, and it was loaded with honey. Oh, what a treat! After Sheridan's supply train arrived, we were ready to march. Now I forgot to men-tion that after going into camp on Cache Creek, we turned what horses we had left over to Uncle Sam, as there were not many left and of no more use. They were taken to Smith Valley to winter by a detail. We finished our campaign on foot and were called Walk-a-heaps by the Indians. I was recognized many times years afterwards by old warriors coming up and shaking hands; they would say, "Walk-a-heap." As once an Indian sees you, he never forgets you, and he will be your best friend today and your enemy tomorrow. That was in the days gone by; things have changed, as I have lived among them since they have become peaceable, and they were the best of neighbors. I have had many visits with them, exchanging shots with them.

We marched across the Staked Plains and crossed the old Staked Plains freighter road at an angle, sticking to the Indian trail. We were not far from the New Mexico and Texas line, I found out afterwards. Good water was plentiful. March 18 the weather turned so cold, the marching so fast, and the mules dying fast, many commenced to have long and sober faces, as about ten days we had been without sufficient rations, even out of salt. It was enough to make the strongest man wonder how long this could last. They knew their existence depended on water and mules. They forgot about rations, officers and troops shared alike from this date. Five days' rations had lasted seventeen days, hard marching every day and part of the night, hobbling along, getting into camp late hours at night, only breaking up with a short rest to hobble along the next morning. The mules were starving, although they were in good condition when they started. We were roasting and eating mule meat, as that is all we had. The howl went up, if we only had tobacco, as if anybody could live on tobacco. Now another calamity struck us; nobody had any salt to go with the mule. It was cold, day and night, with a strong wind going right through our clothing. Many were barefooted. Could sleep but little at night because of the cold. The mules were giving out fast, so we had plenty of mule meat. If we stopped for a few minutes, we killed a mule, roasted it if we had time, otherwise ate it raw. As the mules dropped out, we burnt the wagons. In the morning when we got up, we were so sore and stiff we could hardly move. No tents and only one single blanket; some had lost their overcoats. Day after day the mules dropped out and much property had to be destroyed. By the sixteenth only four wagons remained. We were moving west up Salt Fork near its head.

Something happened on the seventeenth. We struck a fresh trail, and it was not large. [It] came from the direction of the North Fork of Red River [and] joined the big trail we had been following for nearly two weeks. Though marching for days, it looked as though we would have to turn back, but now the boys said we are going to get those red devils or leave our bones on the plains.

We now turned northeast over the Red Plains country, always of the opinion something was going to happen before long and old accounts settled. We got to camp on the evening of the nineteenth about 10:00 P.M. I was so tired I was soon sound asleep, as I had my supper out of raw mule meat. As I hobbled along, I pulled my shoes off to give my sore feet a rest. I woke up with a cold, having no cover whatever, my feet were so frostbitten I could not get my shoes on. I cut the tail off my overcoat and some other rags and wrapped my feet. I sorely suffered that day on the march. On the march about two or three days later, we discovered Indian horses about a mile distant. In a short time we were discovered by the Indians, and they started for their herd and were on the run right across our front. Here is where Colonel Custer and Colonel Moore showed their good judgment on a move. He paid no attention to the Indians or herd. He led the column directly to where the Indians had come out of the timber on the double quick, giving no command, only trying to keep out ahead. All wanted to get there first. There was a small mound close to the stream, and the camp was on the other side. Colonel Moore now gave the command left front into line and was executed with promptness and vigor. The troops on the left came into position on the dead run, forgetting all about their sore feet. Right there, within a few yards of the 19th, we looked down on fifteen hundred to two thousand Cheyennes, comfortably housed in their tepees.

As the boys thought nothing of the cold and hunger when they looked back on the years gone by, of the countless murders of the settlers that many had to bury—and a number were relatives—the troops wanted revenge.

In the heart of every man in that long and faded line of the 19th Kansas, their thoughts were of Mrs. Blinn and her little boy lying on the Washita battlefield, her husband murdered before her eyes, herself and child carried off to a worse death. If I could only forget it. Now they felt that this was the time and place to put a stop to the Indian depredations.

The men made sure that their carbines were in good shape and perfect order. These Spencer carbines held seven cartridges and one in the barrel. We were waiting for the order to fire when an officer came running from Colonel Custer to Colonel Moore with an order, "Don't fire, wait." The command could not understand what this meant, looking at one another. Another officer came hurrying up to Colonel Moore with orders to form his command in the valley at the upper end of the tepee village. The 19th obeyed the order, formed in column awaiting for the next move, not knowing the reason for the delay.

We had seen Colonel Custer go into a large tepee and thought the Indians had made him prisoner. We reached for our knives in case of a short scuffle. They were not looking for such a bold move. They were under armed guard in a minute or less time, then something happened that will never be forgotten by that command. The warriors were all mounted coming out of the timber, hundreds of them, riding in a circle in a threatening way, swinging their rifles over their heads, with one war whoop after another, as that was their mode of doing before a charge. Their bonnets painted up, fringed and beaded leggings, and once in a while one with a gaudy blanket over his shoulder. The troops stood there, anxious for the order to fire. The officers were watching every soldier to see that he did not fire. Our troops' faces [were] black with smoke from the campfires, their eyes deep sunk, and their teeth standing out like a skeleton's, their cheeks sunk in.

Those Indians could not understand how those troops could cross the plains on foot in the middle of winter. They thought it was impassable, as they had not crossed it without horses, tents, or provisions.

For a few minutes it was a critical time, the men wanting to fire, rifles in hand, many of them cocked. The officers in charge, begging and swearing, begging the men not to fire. It was not known yet whether the two women were alive or if they had been murdered. If the Indians still had them, the first shot fired would mean they would be murdered. They always made it a practice to kill prisoners as soon as attacked. It was a miracle that those two women were not killed at the battle of the Washita. The 7th Cavalry was stationed at the lower end of the tepees. Custer was now master of ceremonies with the camp surrounding. With Romero and himself in the middle of the warriors, they denied having the prisoners, but Custer was not to be misled; he knew the red men too well. About twenty or thirty officers walked down soon as they had assembled. Then Custer gave the command to arrest the chiefs.

The Indians were surprised that their chiefs were taken prisoners. The chiefs had the floor up to this time, talking very sassy and independent to Colonel Custer. Now Custer started to talk. He gave the chiefs that he had come to get the white women they had as prisoners. The chiefs contended they had no white women in camp [and] never had seen nor heard of any. Custer told them he knew they had the women and he wanted them alive and unharmed and he knew they were lying. That settled the controversy right then, and they admitted they had two white women captive, saying they were many miles away in another camp. Custer told the chiefs to have their tribe move to the other camp and lose no time in doing so. Said he would be there the next day to get the prisoners. Those squaws could give lessons on how to break camp and move out. They were gone in such a short time, it surprised all of us. Right here the chiefs received another surprise, as they thought they were going with the rest. Custer gave them to understand they were prisoners of war.

That night the same rations—roast mule over coals. It proved to be a cold night, but we had plenty of wood, and when we got too cold to sleep, we would build up the fire and warm up on one side while the other side got cold. We would fall asleep sitting up, while taking catnaps.

The morning of March 21, we felt rested up to some extent, as it was the first we had since starting from Cache Creek, now called Fort Sill. The camp moved out at daybreak for the camp where the chiefs claimed the women would be found. The trail was easily followed for several miles, then the trail got smaller. It began to scatter out, and in traveling several miles, the trail got dimmer, until finally they had scarcely left a track. Now those red devils thought they had pulled a sharp one on Custer and he never would get the white women.

The Indian camp was deserted when we arrived. Now there was another surprise for the whole command. The four chiefs were taken to a cottonwood tree, a rope put around one chief's neck, and the rope tight enough to make him gasp for his breath. After he was let down, Custer told him if those women were not brought in by sundown the next day, he would hang all four chiefs and kill the whole tribe. The chiefs sent a runner, as a few had hung around to contact the tribe. The runners had stayed behind, thinking the chiefs would be turned loose as they had on previous occasions. Then nothing but hunger and cold the night of the twenty-first.

One the morning of the twenty-second, quite a number of bucks came up to our camp but soon disappeared after holding a powwow with the chiefs. The chiefs now realized that something would happen, as every man that could rig up any kind of a rope wanted to be a hangman. The evening of the twenty-second, as the time of the hanging approached, everyone [was] ready and anxious to pull on the rope. Just then a few Indians made their appearance some distance from our camp, making signs. Then more Indians appeared and made more signals. Quite a number of bucks were now in sight. We did not know, and many thought they were getting ready to charge us if we started to hang the chiefs. Just then two persons on one horse came into sight; it was the white women. The Indians all stopped on the bluff where they could overlook our command.

Romero went out to meet the women; they dismounted. Romero pointed towards our camp, telling them to go home. Colonel Moore was ordered by Colonel Custer to meet them. He did so, accompanied by other officers; I have forgotten their names. They were coming very slowly, determined not to be separated. They were hanging onto each other.

Soldiers strained their eyes and held their breath for fear of making a noise. Oh what a sight, a thousand starved, hungry men. They had been paid a thousand times for what they had suffered and went through to know those women had been rescued from those murderous fiends and a life that was worse than any death.

With the command was a brother of Mrs. Morgan, who had been permitted to go with the troops. He had made threats he would kill the first Indian he laid eyes on, so Custer had put him under guard, as he knew the first shot fired meant death to the women. Colonel Moore asked if she was Mrs. Morgan. She answered and [said], "This is Miss White." Mrs. Morgan then asked about her husband, supposed dead. When told he was at Fort Hays, had been left for dead when she was taken prisoner but was getting well. She was told that her brother was with the troops and that she would see him in a few minutes. Miss White was quite sure all her folks were killed when she was taken prisoner. Her father at the time was plowing out in the field when he saw the Indians coming with his daughter. He made no fight, although he had his rifle. They took his rifle, then unhitched his team; hitching a horse to each one of his legs, pulled him in two. They tried to make his daughter look at her father as she covered her eyes and turned her back. The women were escorted to where Custer was; they were so scantily clothed that the officers took off their coats and put [them] around them, [the] two women still holding to one another, as though they did not realize they were among friends. The bugles played "Home, Sweet Home," as the women were received by Colonel Custer and other officers and men of both regiments. By this time, the women realized they had been rescued and were going home. Custer's small tent was turned over to the women. Mrs. Morgan was about twenty-seven years old. Miss White, eighteen when taken prisoner, was engaged to be married to a young man by the name of Brooks. He joined L Company of the 19th. They were married after we got to Fort Hays and lived for many years in Concordia, Kansas, having a family of six children. Mr. Brooks is dead. Mrs. Brooks is still living at Jamestown, Kansas. Those women were abused in the most brutal way; made beasts of burden by the squaws [and] were whipped with rawhide by the squaws. The squaws hated them. When first captured, they were traded to other bucks for twenty-five to thirty ponies, but they depreciated in value as time went on. They finally were traded for as little as two ponies, value $2.00. Just think; stop and think what hardship those two women went through.

On the March 23 the column marched for the supply camp on the Washita. Because of starvation and the raw meat without salt, many of the men had dysentery. That night we camped only a few hours, strung out along the trail. In the A.M. the men staggered to their feet, many cried with pain, no loud talking, in fact few words spoken, only by some of the more hopeful trying to cheer up their comrades. Once in a while you would hear some officer say, "Close up boys," trying to urge them on, and themselves so crippled up and weak they could hardly walk.

About 3:00 P.M.,[11] on a desolate looking plain [with] no water, every man laid down. My feet were not in as bad a condition as some of my comrades'. We had marched forty miles from 2:00 A.M. to 3:00 P.M. While resting here, objects appeared in the distance, then they became plainer. They spied us. They stopped in surprise, not knowing what to make of it, until they became satisfied it was not Indians, then they moved up close enough to see the motions from some of the men to come on. They were some troops that had been back at Camp Supply in December, not able to march further after being frosted on our march from Camp Beecher to Camp Supply. They were scouting for buffalo. They had come from the supply train on the Washita, where we were headed. [It was] about forty miles to the Washita River. Colonel Custer ordered one of their men mounted on one of the best horses, and sent him for a rescue train to be sent immediately with empty wagons, to be used to haul men who were unable to walk. When the brave boys knew that rations were coming, they could march no further. Colonel Custer said his troops would remain, as his men could not walk further. Custer and Moore held a parley. Custer told Moore he could use his own judgment about moving on. Then Moore gave the men a choice of laying there or moving on. Some of us moved on. We march all night, next day we struck the Washita several miles above the supply train.

When we struck the Washita, we first bathed our feet and then took a drink, the water being ice cold. Our feet were wrapped in pieces of blankets. We stopped only long enough to bathe our feet and tie them, then the march went on. We marched across Custer's battleground, but we looked neither right or left. We had to ford the river, which was about three feet deep. Shortly we came to a sharp turn and a nice timbered bottom. There we saw the tents of Camp Supply, men moving around. When we got our eye on those boxes of bread, I made straight for one, got a large chunk, saw a pile of bacon and made for that, cut off a chunk and ate only a little, when I spied a camp kettle boiling, I asked, "Have you any coffee?" Many voices said yes. They were probably wondering what animal that was. They brought me a quart cup of coffee [and] asked me if I wanted sugar. I said yes. I looked around, as I had forgot my manners and the rest. Everyone was helping himself just as though he had the right, and the men were hustling around to see that we had plenty.

Our clothes [were] all burnt. We had not made any attempt to wash, as we had no soap. Our hands and faces were all coated from eating mule. Dirt stuck to us. After filling up and resting for about two hours, I asked for a bar of soap. I went to the creek, which was partly frozen over, but off came my clothes, which had a louse on every inch of it. They were crawling thick in those Indian camps. After my bath, I took off my clothes and turned them inside out, and shook off what I could, then put them on again and went back to camp. One of the boys got me a kettle of hot water, and I washed until the skin got sore, and from that time on I felt better.

On the last day of the month of March 1869, the hardships of the 19th Kansas were over. The rear guard arrived with the last member of the command, including both regiments, which will be remembered by one and all. Never will forget they had lived a whole month on five days' short rations. Every soldier that has done service knows that short rations mean only enough to exist on a few days. They brought back with them four chiefs. We marched twenty-three miles a day. No tents, no beds, no cooking outfit, no salt. Alkali water at times. We were living on mule meat. When you read of this campaign, you will wonder how it was possible to carry on under such hardships. After a rest and plenty to eat, we marched to Camp Supply.

Camp Starvation

W. R. SMITH[1]

Winners of the West 3, no. 4 (March 1926): 8

E very Indian war veteran knows that there were worse perils encountered on the plains than those from wild savage Indians. The Western Plains sure had no welcome greeting for the 19th Kansas Cavalry in the latter part of November 1868. Scarcely had we reached this then-unknown pathless wilderness before old King Winter sent down his storms upon us. There was a succession of rain, sleet, hail storms, snows, raging blizzards, and intense freezing cold.

In the blinding storms, all trails and landmarks were lost sight of, and the regiment floundered about in the deep snow for two days before we reached Sand Creek, a tributary of the Cimarron River, where we went into camp. Some weeks later, *Harper's Weekly* published an illustration of our going into this camp. It was a wild and dreary scene.

"Camp Starvation," we called it, and that name gave a most correct idea of its fitness. Those sand hills along the north side of the Cimarron, among which our camp was located, were formed by the action of the wind in past ages by blowing the sand out of the riverbed. They were at that time covered by a growth of young timber, their only redeeming feature, as they supplied us with wood for fires.

Supplies for our regiment had been sent to Camp Beecher, now Wichita, but had been partly consumed by the troops stationed there. As it was urgent for us to reach General Sheridan at Camp Supply on the Canadian River, we had marched on with what rations and forage were left, scarcely half enough for the trip.

There we were, twelve hundred men and twice that many horses and mules, without food, forage, or tents, snowbound by winter storms among the sand dunes of the Cimarron, a bleak, desolate, and forsaken place. The continued storms had driven the buffalo far away, and only an occasional old stray stag could be found in some sheltered cove. They were killed and brought into camp, and the meat was ravenously devoured, without leaving a scrap. Even the bones were roasted and broken open for the marrow they contained.

The boys roamed over the brush-covered hills in search of anything that would sustain life, but game of all kinds was hard to find outside of their burrows under the deep snow. Large quantities of hackberries were gathered and eaten and made into tea by some of the half-starved boys, which afterward caused them much pain and trouble.

We had not received our full supply of clothing to protect us from the terrors of a winter on the plains, and some suffered greatly from lack of it, wrapping their feet in pieces of blankets or buffalo hides. Sheridan said afterward that he greatly feared the whole outfit had perished.

Our horses suffered terribly, some of them freezing to death, and in their starved condition acted like wild animals in their frenzy. We cut cottonwood poles and brush and carried it to them to gnaw the bark and twigs from. That was all there was for them to eat. Having gone nearly a week without much food, many died from starvation and cold. In after years, our line of march from this camp to Fort Sill could be followed by the bleaching bones of our noble horses.

A detail of fifty men with the best horses, under the command of Captain Pliley, was sent out in the storm over the snow-covered plains, without rations or forage, to find Sheridan's camp on the Canadian and send relief back to the regiment, which later we received, and then went on to Camp Supply. While at this cold, blizzard-swept, and starving camp, Thanksgiving Day was passed, but I fear few of the boys felt that they had anything to be thankful for.

When we went to the plains, we expected to fight Indians and maybe lose our scalps, but we never thought of those other worse enemies, cold and starvation. That ill fate followed us almost from first to last, without much glory, if any, for services rendered.

Lost in the Snow at Old Camp Supply

GEORGE B. JENNESS

Sturm's Oklahoma Magazine 4, no. 4 (December 1907): 52–57

When the writer first saw in the newspapers the suggestion that the old military post of Camp Supply was to be selected for the permanent location of an insane asylum in Oklahoma, the proposition appealed to him as preeminently appropriate by reason of its association with an insane incident there in the winter of 1868.

My first experience with this noted old post began that winter, and soon after its selection by General Sheridan as the base of supply for his operations against the hostile bands of Cheyennes and Arapahos, who had been committing depredations against the white settlers along the Kansas border the preceding summer and fall.

The pacifications and punishment of these marauding warriors had been placed in General Sheridan's hands, with unrestricted power from the general government to use any means necessary to bring this greatly desired result.

Reasoning from past experience that the cold months and absence of grazing for their ponies would prevent the Indians from making any extensive forays upon the settlements, and probably keep them in concentrated camps, the general decided upon a vigorous and relentless winter campaign. The army detachments stationed along our western border had usually remained inactive during the winter months, and this fact would give the bucks a sense of greater security and render them more liable to surprises and less vigilant in guarding their ponies.

Subsequent events proved the correctness of General Sheridan's reasoning, and a crushing campaign was waged against them, resulting in the recovery of several white women captives, the destruction of their ponies, aggregating over eight hundred, the capture of their villages and equipage, and final surrender of all the hostile bands of both tribes. In fact, it wound up the Indian Wars in the Southwest and forced the Indians back upon their reservations, where they have remained peacefully, if not contentedly, ever since, until now their descendants are about to become full-fledged citizens of this prolific state.

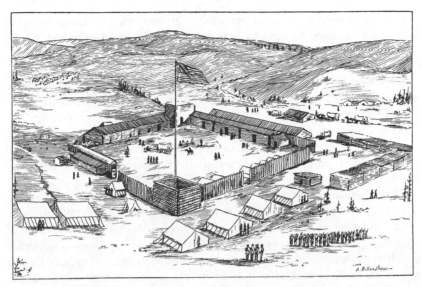

Camp Supply. CHARLES J. BRILL, *CONQUEST OF THE SOUTHERN PLAINS.*

But let us return to the subject of Camp Supply and the incident referred to above, wherein pandemonium reigned and nearly a thousand men were raging and yelling as though they were crazy or celebrating some heathen rite to the god of imbecility. It is this picture, conjured up again, that makes the insane asylum idea appear so peculiarly appropriate.

In order to give a correct understanding of the course of events and the scene of discord and disorder, we must go back some time and review a page of border history, the participants in which have nearly all passed over the "Great Divide."

At the time of his location of Camp Supply, General Sheridan had marched down from Fort Dodge, Kansas, accompanied by the 7th United States Cavalry, under command of Colonel Custer, a long wagon train loaded with supplies, and a small detachment of regular infantry. He had selected and named the camp, pitched the headquarter tents, had a few rough log buildings erected for the quartermaster and commissary depots, and unloaded the wagon train and sent it back to Fort Dodge for additional rations and forage.

In the meantime, the 7th Cavalry was putting in the time scouting southward in search of the winter rendezvous of the Indians, and had already encountered and wiped out Black Kettle's band on the banks of the Washita River.

At this period in our border history, the available force of regulars along the frontier posts was entirely inadequate for the duty of garrisoning these posts and at the same time conducting an effective campaign in the field.

To remedy this deficiency, authority had been given to the commanding general to call upon the governor of Kansas for a full regiment of cavalry. This fresh body of western men had been duly recruited, organized, and mustered into the service upon the same basis as volunteers during the Rebellion. Nearly all the officers and a large portion of the men were veterans of that "unpleasantness."

The regiment was designated the 19th Kansas Cavalry and was mounted upon the best horses that could be bought in central and western Kansas, regardless of cost.

The organization, 1,200 strong, had been perfected at Topeka, and upon the eve of the date fixed upon for its starting westward, Gov. S. J. Crawford had resigned his position as chief executive of Kansas and taken the colonelcy of the new regiment.

The command, with the exception of two companies, was ordered to march via the mouth of the Little Arkansas River, near where Wichita now stands, and thence southwestward to join General Sheridan at the new depot of supplies. It was the arrival of this strong reinforcement that he was anxiously awaiting, while accumulating the necessary rations, forage, and military impedimenta for the final onslaught upon the unruly savages in their winter camps.

The two companies excepted above were embarked upon the cars for Fort Dodge, there to become the escort for the wagon train upon its return to Camp Supply.

Colonel Crawford, an experienced regimental commander of the late war, marched his command by easy stages to the designated point on the Arkansas in order to gradually season his horses, as yet unaccustomed to the hard and steady grind of old cavalry mounts upon a long march. At this point, the government maintained a temporary, one-company post, and Colonel Crawford expected to obtain ample supplies for the continuance of his march to the general rendezvous, and to meet competent scouts to pilot him via the nearest and best course to our destination.

The scouts reported all right, and here the writer also joined the command, after a tiresome and lonely horseback ride from Salina, through a country infested by small bands of roving Indians. The expected forage and rations had not materialized, however, and no intelligence could be gained as to the whereabouts of the train of wagons, somewhere en route between that post and Fort Harker, and the colonel found himself in a very embarrassing situation.

After waiting two days, it was determined to push on with the scant five days' half rations on hand, the scouts agreeing that if the exceptionally fine weather then prevailing continued, Camp Supply could be reached within that time, or in six days at the outside.

"Man proposes and providence disposes," however, for on the morning of the third day after crossing the Arkansas, the most terrific blizzard ever experienced in that country, within the memory of the oldest trapper and buffalo hunter, came down upon us with bewildering suddenness. In a half hour's time the air was so filled with blinding, cutting sleet and snow that it was impossible to distinguish objects half a troop length away.

The command could be no worse off moving than bivouacked as we were, and after a scant, uncooked breakfast, the column pushed forward, led by the two scouts. It was a march impossible to adequately describe: horses stumbling and shrinking from the knifelike gale, men with heads down and covered with their overcoat capes, staggering after their file leaders, chilled to the bone and slapping, stamping, and pounding themselves in desperate endeavor to keep up a circulation of the blood. The country over which the command was struggling was one interminable succession of ravines and gullies, rough buttes, and frozen sand dunes, and through these the column wound in and out, up and down, changing direction until no one knew where we were.

This struggle was kept up until late in the afternoon, no pretense being made to partake of dinner, when the command was suddenly ordered to bivouac in a somewhat sheltered spot on the south of an overhanging bluff. Here the last of the forage was fed to the horses and wagon mules, while the men made shift to partially satisfy their hunger by eating what few rations were left, helped out by a distribution of the stores belonging to the officers' messes. What little fuel there was in the country consisted of "buffalo chips" and stunted cottonwoods, all now covered under a foot or more of snow. A few messes succeeded in digging out enough to boil water and make coffee, but the majority of the men were too tired and worn to attempt a fuel hunt.

The storm was still raging, the cold intense, and rolling themselves in their blankets, the men lay down fully dressed, and with their frozen boots rattling together like castanets, to pass the night in fitful sleep. By morning a heavy covering of snow marked the mounds where the men lay, but the bugle call at reveille brought them to their feet, shaking off the encrusted snow and icicles from hair and beard. It was a dreary prospect that they awoke to, as the storm continued to rage, rations and forage entirely exhausted, and the discovery was made that in nearly every troop, horses had been frozen to death at the picket lines, and many mules in the wagon train had succumbed during the terrible night. A search through the wagons by the commissary brought to light four barrels of cut loaf sugar, and these were opened and their contents equally divided among the officers and men, for all were alike rationless. To add to the desolation and discouragement of the aspect of affairs, the officers learned that the scouts had wandered from the old "Dutch Henry Trail," which they had attempted to follow from the Arkansas, and had no certain knowledge of our whereabouts. In fact, it was discovered that neither Apache Bill nor his mate[1] had ever been in this locality before, and had deceived General Sheridan by misrepresenting their knowledge of the country. Had this fact been made known to the men that morning, it is more than probable that they would have given the scouts a very unhappy half hour, if nothing more serious.

The day's march was a repetition of the previous day's experience. Facing the blinding snow, which now came in fitful gales, subsiding for a time to a gentle gust, then sweeping and roaring around us in savage fury, until horses and men were brought to a halt and turned tails and backs to the cold, bone-chilling blasts. At frequent intervals, details of men would be called for from the several troopers to go back and fish out some overturned wagon or ambulance from treacherous, snow-covered gullies or dig out and place upon his feet some debilitated and disgusted mule.

Sometime before dusk, the storm subsided and the sky cleared under a November sunset, but the cold increased in intensity, and many brave boys who would have charged a battery without unusual emotion were whining and crying like children from the intense pain of frozen feet or frostbitten hands, ears, and noses and hunger. It was the custom of the regiment to bivouac in a hollow square, the headquarters tents and wagon train upon one side and three battalions upon the other three sides, with the horses picketed inside the square, just behind their respective troops. About the time the several troops had unsaddled and the officers had started the men out with their horses, instructed to clear away the snow in spots, as well as possible, to enable the hungry animals to nibble the short buffalo grass beneath, the company wagons began to arrive and take positions on the left of each troop for unloading the mess kits and camp equipage.

Among the last of the train came a four-mule ambulance clattering through the square, with side curtains streaming out like slack sails on a "fore and after" running before a gale. In passing a six-mule team near the southwest corner of the square, the curtains blew into the faces of the wheelers, causing them to jump frantically to one side, startling the leaders and swing mules, and before the driver could regain his "jerk line," the team was away at full speed, jostling off camp kettles, mess pans, Dutch ovens, and coffeepots, making a rattle and din calculated to scare the life out of the most staid and faithful animal. They tore frantically down the west side of the square, frightening other mules and horses as they passed, until two-thirds of the steeds upon that side had joined the terror-stricken gang in a squealing, struggling, kicking mass that endangered the lives of officers and men.

Turning east at the next corner of the square, the demoniacal aggregation swept along the south battalion, taking with it every horse that could break away, and in less time than it takes to tell it, a large proportion of the mounts of seven troops and several mule teams were careening frantically over the prairie, taking the back trail over which we had marched during the day. It seemed impossible of belief that these rushing, snorting equines were the same dejected, staggering, lifeless beasts we had been nursing and favoring along, as though they were in the final stages of physical dissolution. Fear and panic had turned them into a bunch of galloping demons that had temporarily, at least, shaken off the controlling hand of man. Many of the troopers had been knocked down and run over, while the mule teams had cut through several company grounds, scattering men, carbines, and equipment in every direction, and it was a miracle indeed that no one was killed or seriously injured.

The runaway mule teams finally circled back towards the wagon park, where they were caught and quieted down, but the cavalry horses were showing their heels on the return trail a mile away before anything like order could be brought from the confusion and excitement in camp. Then there was hurrying to and fro; sharp, quick commands; a rush for the horses of the last-side battalion, which had escaped the vortex which had swept the other troops; mounting in haste; and hurried pursuit of the fleeing stampeders.

"Mount, mount your men," yelled the colonel as he came running toward these more fortunate companies. "Don't wait to saddle; slip on your watering bridles and round up those horses if you have to follow them all night." Cooler and more deliberate counsel prevailed, however, and some fifteen or twenty picked men and horses under command of Capt. A. J. Pliley of Troop A were soon in pursuit of the runaways.

It was late the next evening before the last of this detail returned, and out of a total of a few over four hundred that "made the run," they brought back all but about sixty of the escaped steeds. These stragglers had made good their freedom for a while, at least, but in years afterwards, we heard of thrifty Oklahoma settlers who had sturdy teams of horses bearing upon their left shoulder an obliterated brand, showing dimly the outlines of the familiar U.S. of the government Quartermaster's Department.

On the seventh day, the command found itself practically stranded amidst the interminable hillocks and deep gulches along the Canadian River, without food or forage. Many horses and mules had frozen to death, and the remainder were in no condition for continued service. Many of the men were in a debilitated condition, some badly frozen, nearly two hundred without mounts, and the remaining mule teams unable to pull the wagons or the heavy regimental blacksmith's forage, or even the light ambulances. Small hunting parties had been sent out from time to time, and one of these returned that evening with their horses laden with buffalo meat. They had luckily stumbled upon a group of four buffalos which had sought shelter in a partially protected coulee, where the blizzard had imprisoned them with drifted snow, which had banked the sides to a depth of five or six feet, while their continuous milling had trodden the center down, until they appeared to be bunched at the bottom of a dry cistern. They were too thoroughly chilled and subdued by the storm to attempt escape, and the men shot them with their revolvers with no trouble whatever. To men who had fasted for three days, this meat was like manna from heaven and was distributed equally among the officers and men. Quite a number of the men required the services of the surgeon during the night as a result of overeating the partially cooked meat.

To forage the horses was the most difficult problem, but by cutting young cottonwoods and allowing them to gnaw the bark, as Indian ponies are accustomed to do, with scant pickings of buffalo grass, the animals were kept from complete starvation. As we looked at their protruding hips and ribs, we could not avoid anticipating the comment by General Sheridan. He had reason to expect a reinforcement of able-bodied westerners, mounted upon the finest horses procurable, ready for an arduous campaign of rapid movements and endurance, and a storm, allied to a misconnection of supplies at the Arkansas post, had reduced the effectiveness of his command by at least twenty-five percent. The regiment was as badly demoralized as though it had passed through a severe engagement, sustaining a high percentage of loss both in men and animals, and it would require a month or more of rest and feeding to place the command upon an efficient campaign basis, while the loss of horses had permanently eliminated one-sixth of the effective force of the regiment, for all dismounted men must be left behind during active cavalry movements.

The problems immediately before us somewhat obscured these unpleasant considerations, however, and to arrive at some definite conclusion, the staff and line officers were called together for consultation. Of course, there was no danger of absolute starvation, for as a last resort there was always the prospect of horseflesh and mule meat. After a brief review of our difficulties, it was decided to mount as many able-bodied men as there were serviceable horses, abandon all the sick and dismounted men and disabled animals, and push on towards the supposed location of Camp Supply. The scouts had proved their uselessness, and the colonel was left to depend entirely upon his own resources and general knowledge, backed by the advice of a few men in the command who had hunted buffalo over the country between the Cimarron River and Beaver Creek, on which the scouts had reported Camp Supply located.

Some of the troopers, in felling cottonwoods along the small stream near our camp, had discovered large thickets of Indian or hackberry bushes, a palatable and nutritious wild fruit, and the men were gathering them in large quantities, and these, with a mule or two, if found necessary, would sustain the abandoned troopers until suitable supplies could be sent back to them. The assistant surgeon was also to remain in the camp to attend to the sick and frostbitten invalids. This camp was afterwards referred to by men in the regiment as Hackberry Camp, and for long years afterwards many of the Kansas boys remembered with a shudder their miseries and sufferings in this desolate and forbidding bivouac. The following morning the men and horses were duly selected, and by 8:00 A.M. the reduced command moved out upon its line of march, and with no wagons or other impedimenta to hinder its advance, made most excellent time, considering conditions. When camp was selected late in the evening, it was estimated that we had covered about twenty miles.

The next morning an early start was made, and in about two hours from camp, our advance guard reported a party of mounted men approaching from the front, and it was soon learned that the squad was a party of scouts, sent out by General Sheridan to find the lost 19th Kansas. The officers and men were greatly pleased to learn that we were then within three or four miles of our destination, and two of the well-mounted scouts were sent back to bear the good news to the abandoned men of Hackberry Camp.

Colonel Crawford's arrival with a part of the regiment was warmly welcomed by General Sheridan, though he was thoroughly exasperated to learn the extent of the disaster that had overtaken the command, and it was well for scout "Apache Bill" that he had discreetly disappeared during the preceding night.

When the detachment marched into Camp Supply and had been assigned a camping ground, the officers quickly found their way to the post sutlers in search of food and other needed refreshments. The men, as soon as they could picket their horses, began a wild rush to the other camps and the post commissary's depot, and before any of the officers realized the seriousness of the situation, they became a rushing, howling mob. All were clamoring for food, running here and there, tears streaming down their faces, and otherwise acting like a gang of lunatics just escaped from an asylum, and it was some time before they could be pacified.

That night the men left at Hackberry Camp came into Camp Supply, and again pandemonium reigned, and the scenes of the forenoon were reenacted with an increased intensity of feeling. As soon as they struck the camp, they began howling for something to satisfy their hunger, running from mess to mess in our own quarters, then circling about the other camps nearby. When rations were handed out to them, they would howl and fight like wolves to secure the greatest share. Several of these wild human beings had their arms full of hard bread and pockets full of bacon, yet they were clamoring for more, as though they never again expected to have an opportunity to procure anything to satisfy their hunger. It was a most remarkable exhibition of human weakness, and my first view of a body of full-grown, intelligent men thrown off their mental balance by emotional hysteria, probably intensified by the nervous shock during the stampede. I have often wished to learn the opinion of some competent alienist regarding the peculiar conditions surrounding the case, and the singular manner in which so many were affected.

As that picture presents itself to my mind, I imagine the orderly inmates of a state institution roaming quietly over the same grounds, well cared for by a liberal and benevolent state government, and difficult to distinguish in their ordinary behavior from any other citizens about their daily avocations or recreation. That old military post will always be associated in my mind with the craziest experience of my military life, and I doubt if ever again it contains as many wild and mentally irresponsible human beings as broke loose there that cold day in 1868.

Campaigning with the 19th Kansas Volunteer Cavalry

HENRY PEARSON[1]

Winners of the West 7, no. 1 (December 1926): 5

In the latter part of October 1868, the governor of Kansas issued a call for one volunteer regiment to fight Indians in Kansas, New Mexico, and the Indian Territory.

The regiment was soon formed, and the shipment of supplies to Topeka, Kansas, had arrived. After being mustered into service, the uniforms, ammunition, and equipment were drawn, and our horses had begun to arrive. After drawing the horses, bridles, and saddles, we were sent out to drill, and a greener, rawer bunch was never brought together. After drilling for two days, the emergency and haste being so great, we were prepared for the march into the Indian Territory.

On November 5 we marched up Kansas Avenue, four abreast, with bright shining equipment and well mounted on fine horses. A gayer-hearted bunch of boys certainly never marched up Kansas Avenue. Little did we realize what we were going into; we were supposed to fight Indians, but instead, to a great extent, we fought starvation and one of the worst blizzards ever known to Kansas.

Governor Crawford resigned his office as governor and was appointed colonel. He was loyal to his officers and kind to his men, and if they had hunted the territory of Kansas over, a better man for that position could not have been found.

After marching several days, we finally struck Fort Beecher, which is now known as Wichita. There we received orders to replenish our supplies enough to carry us on through to Camp Supply. As the wagon train from Fort Hays hadn't arrived, we decided it best to go on with half rations.

After staying in Fort Beecher a day and two nights, we marched out across the Arkansas River and bid good-bye to civilization. We marched on for two days, and on the third day, a rainstorm set in and we camped on a small stream.[2] Every fourth man was ordered to hold out four horses to graze until 9:00 P.M.

Our scouts had been on ahead finding the trail for us to follow the next day. About dark one of them came into camp and, jumping off his horse, hastily pulled off the bridle and saddle and started to lead his horse to where the others were feeding. The saddle had not been entirely unfastened and was dragging along the ground. The horse became scared at this and broke away from the scout, who ran as fast as he could toward the other horses, who became scared at the noise, and they started to run. It caused a stampede among all of them, and away they went over the prairie, four fastened together. The bugle sounded fall in, and we supposed the Indians were upon us and we would have to fight, but when we marched to the colonel's tent, we were informed that our horses were stampeded. For two days we searched for them and succeeded in finding all but 130 head.[3] The next morning we pushed on, 130 of the boys walking, but our provisions were becoming too short to wait longer.

For several days we marched, and then it began to snow. All the trails were covered, and the scouts had to go by their knowledge of the lay of the land. They disagreed about the location of Camp Supply from where we were located, but we tramped on, while all the time the snow was coming down faster and the thermometer registering lower and lower. We finally came to a small stream, and washing away the snow, we camped until morning. When morning came,[4] it was still snowing and steadily getting colder, so we pushed on, our supplies being nearly exhausted. At noon we were stopped and two hardtack was issued to each man, and that was all we had all that day. Just as night was coming on, we came to a small tributary of the Cimarron River, and here we went into camp.

The officers and scouts had a meeting, as something had to be done soon. They agreed there was no use in going further, as we didn't know where we were, so it was decided we stay here until the scouts could locate Camp Supply and bring back provisions.

One of the scouts believed Camp Supply lay due south of where we were camped, and the other one believed it lay southwest. They were told to pick out twenty-five men each and push on to where they believed Camp Supply lay and bring back provisions for man and beast. At 9:00 P.M. that night,[5] "Pancy Bill"[6] took twenty-five men and started south. Johnny Stillwell took two hundred rounds of cartridges, two carbines and two revolvers, an extra horse, and started southwest alone. About noon the next day, Pancy Bill returned to camp with his twenty-five men, but two of his horses died on the trip. He then decided that Camp Supply lay to the southwest.

There we were, nothing to cover us but the sky and snow, nothing to eat but hackberries, and wondering how long it would take us to starve or freeze to death. We found a little wood, with which we built a fire, and we cut down some trees so our horses could gnaw the bark.

The second day some of the boys began to talk about deserting and taking the back trail. The trail was completely obliterated and was almost impossible to be found, but about midnight about twenty-five of them gathered plenty of ammunition, picked out some of the best mules and horses, and started back. The rest of us decided we might as well stay there and starve or freeze, whichever it was to be, as to get lost and freeze out on the prairie. We were taking chances on Johnny Stillwell finding Camp Supply. We had a lot of confidence in Johnny Stillwell, even though he was but a boy of twenty years.

The morning of the third day, one of the boys from Company A and myself went out to see if we might find some animal or bird that we could use for food. After wandering around for quite a while, we found a sage hen, and the boy from Company A shot and killed it. Being reasonably close and with an ounce ball in his gun, and the sage hen being small, it was torn into pieces; but he gathered up all the parts he could find and took it to camp and cooked it, and God only knows how many hungry boys feasted on that little sage hen. On my return back to camp, a squirrel was unfortunate enough to let me see him run up a tree, and I shot him. When I took him into camp, we skinned him and put him in the camp kettle, but about all the boys got from that squirrel was about a pint of soup.

When the fourth day had dawned and we were still held prisoners, the boys began to talk about a suitable name for our camp. One of the boys, sitting with his head bowed, ready to meet death, said, "Let's call it Camp Starvation," and so it was named; a more suitable name could not have been procured had we had all the names in the book to select from.

Four days and nights we had been wondering if Johnny Stillwell had succeeded in finding Camp Supply or whether he had gotten lost and frozen to death, leaving us out on the prairie, away from all civilization and with no way to communicate with the camp, which was so near and yet so far away. But as if our thoughts were answered, we heard the squeaking of the wagon wheels on snow, and then we knew Johnny Stillwell had been successful and we would soon have food and provisions enough to carry us on to Camp Supply. We were so filled with joy and thanksgiving that some began to shoot off their guns, but the officers soon stopped that, for we would probably need all the ammunition we had before we were through with our campaign. The wagons drove in, one wagon for each company, and two guards were placed over each wagon. We were formed into company messes (about twelve in each mess), and each man was issued one hardtack and some coffee. We were told we could have more hardtack and coffee at midnight. Some of the boys refused to sleep for fear they would oversleep and not get their meager lunch at midnight. We stayed one more day, feeding our horses and letting them gain a little more strength so they could carry us on. We had only a few left, as the others had starved or frozen to death.

During the time that Stillwell had been gone, Captain Pliley and his company, with the best horses in the command, had started south. The rest of us, after resting and eating for a day and two nights, started for Camp Supply with two hundred of our horses dead and two hundred boys wading the snow, which was from sixteen to eighteen inches deep.

Custer had been waiting at Camp Supply for the 19th Regiment to reinforce him in his march to the Washita River, but fearing that we had all perished, he started on with his mounted men, and at Antelope Hill he met Black Kettle and his little band of Indians. He had quite a little battle with them and lost a few of his men but killed a good many Indians. As Custer looked down the valley, he saw it was red with Indians, so he decided he had better go back to Camp Supply, as we had probably arrived there by that time.

When he returned to Camp Supply, we were there and partly recuperated. He said there was no time to be lost, as the Indians would be getting further away. All of the 19th who had horses joined with Custer. We marched out of Camp Supply,[7] and after several days marching, we came to a small stream where the Indians were camping, supposing Custer had given up and that they could live there in peace, but when they saw Custer returning with reinforcements, they knew they had reckoned with the wrong men. They decided to fight, but when Custer was forming his lines, they soon changed their minds and thought it best to surrender without losing any more of their warriors.

We were very much disappointed to think that we had suffered starvation and laid out half frozen, many with their feet and hands frozen, and our uniforms in rags, and then we wouldn't get to fight those Indians after all.

From one camp to the other ran the messengers and interpreters with messages of truce. Custer finally went into the Indian camp and brought back four chiefs. They were asked many questions in regard to the white women who had been captured west of Concordia. They claimed the Sioux had them, and that they didn't know just where their camp was located. It was decided that the chiefs should be held in our camp until the white women were found and given to us. The Indian messenger was sent back to the Indian camp with the message that if the white women were not brought to us by sundown, the chiefs would be hung. The Indian came back and asked for one more day in which to bring the women. Custer granted one more day to them but told them no more time would be given them, that if they didn't bring the white women we would hang their chiefs. About 4:00 P.M. the next day, we could see an Indian ride up over the hill and look down into our camp and then ride back, and after a while another would ride up and look down to see if we still held the chiefs. Finally an Indian came into camp and asked for just one more day, but Custer said, "No, if those white women are not here by the time the sun is sending its last rays over that hill in the west, we will hang those four chiefs." Just as the sun was setting, a big chief riding a beautiful black horse came up over the hill, and following him came the two white women on a gray pony. The chief brought them up to our lines and surrendered them to us. Custer turned to Colonel Moore and said, "You are from Kansas, you receive and welcome those two women." We had prepared a tent for them and two guards had been placed over it, one at each end; the women were escorted to the tent, and everything was done for their comfort that was possible to be done out here in the wilderness.

The old chief who had brought back the women then demanded we give up to him the four chiefs, but Custer said, "No, we'll keep them awhile." He went back to camp, and the Indians began preparing for battle. We were much delighted to think we would get to fight them after all, but at the last moment we were disappointed, for they gave it up.

We stayed in the camp for a couple of days, as Custer thought maybe they would decide to start on the warpath, but they decided to let us keep the chiefs without a fight.

The time for the 19th to be discharged was drawing near, and so we were ordered to take the back trail for Fort Hays, where we duly received our honorable discharge. Custer determined to take the Indians to the reservation in the Wichita Mountains where they belonged.

The Washita Campaign

EDWARD S. GODFREY

Winners of the West 6, nos. 5–8 (April–July 1929)

During our return march to Fort Dodge from Brevet Brigadier General Sully's first expedition, September 1868, the general would at times relieve his mind by talking of his problems at the headquarters mess and camp-fires. One of the problems was a commander of his cavalry. For some reason he had come to the conclusion that Major Elliott, then in command of the troops of the 7th Cavalry, had not sufficient experience to trust him with an independent command.

Maj. Joel Elliott was younger than all the captains, most of whom had been field officers during the Civil War; some had commanded regiments and brigades. He was younger even than most of his lieutenants. In the Civil War, the highest rank held by him was that of captain, and his highest command had been a squadron (two troops) in his volunteer regiment of cavalry. After the war he taught school, and at the time he went before the Casey Board of Examiners for a commission, he was superintendent of the public schools of the city of Toledo, Ohio, intending eventually to study and practice law. He passed such a perfect mental examination that the board recommended his appointment as major of cavalry. He had anticipated an appointment as first lieutenant, or at most as captain.

He [Sully] mentioned the various field officers of cavalry within his jurisdiction as district commander and finally eliminated all of them. He several times mentioned the "Triumvirate of S's"—Sherman, division commander; Sheridan, department commander; and Sully, district commander—and seemed perfectly satisfied with the results of the expedition. For future operations, he intended to ask for a larger force, operate against the Indians till he chastised them, and then return to winter quarters.

On arrival at Fort Dodge, he asked for recruits and horses and equipment for the troops of the 7th Cavalry to the maximum (then 100) and for Colonel Custer to command the regiment.

A few days later General Sheridan arrived at the post. The plan of campaign was changed to establish a supply camp of a more permanent nature and to make a winter campaign. The supply cantonment was to be at the junction of the Beaver, or North Fork of the Canadian, and Wolf Creek, where Sully had abandoned pursuit of the hostiles.

Maj. Alfred Gibbs,[1] with the headquarters and band from Fort Leavenworth, joined the 7th Cavalry, and later the two troops stationed at Fort Harker arrived—eleven troops present. The regiment was sent out to Bluff Creek, about thirty miles southeast of Fort Dodge. Colonel Custer joined the regiment early in October and at once began aggressive operations against the hostiles who had repeatedly attacked the camp.

The troops of the 10th Cavalry were sent north to protect the frontier settlements on the Saline, Solomon, and Republican Rivers, which the Indians had been raiding since August 10.

General Sheridan established his field headquarters at Fort Hays,[2] where he could be in closer touch with communications and energize the forwarding of supplies for the coming campaign. Finding difficulty in getting transportation to forward supplies from Hays City to Fort Dodge, he ordered Number One Depot Train from Fort Leavenworth. This train was the pride of the Quartermaster's Department. It was composed of selected mules, as for many years the best mules sent to the department had been assigned to this train. That woke up the Quartermaster's Department!

While at Fort Dodge, he learned that the commissary of the post had asked the families and officers' messes to estimate the amount of officers' stores they wanted for the coming year. These were tabulated and sent to the chief commissary, department headquarters, as his annual requisition. When the supplies arrived, these canned goods were apportioned according to estimates, or if the garrison had been increased, according to the number of persons in the several messes. General Sheridan found some of the delicacies quite toothsome and drew on the stores until he was informed that he had his quota. He was surprised that there was a limit and that special requisitions were taboo. He ordered and approved a special requisition, and further ordered that in the future, special requisitions be honored. That woke up the Commissary Department!

In the meantime, Colonel Sully was busy with his requisitions for the new cantonment, or Camp Supply. Finding that mules were scarce, he estimated for a number of yokes of oxen, intending to use them to haul the supplies for the buildings at the supply camp on the army wagons with trailers to the new post, then use them to "snake" the logs for stockades, and subsequently kill them for beef. That horrified both departments! But he got his oxen, or "bulls," as they were called in the parlance of the West.

The outrages on the Kansas frontier settlers and the capture of women aroused the people of that state to appeal for protection. The Congress authorized the organization of the 18th and 19th Kansas Volunteer Cavalry.[3] The governor, Hon. S. J. Crawford, resigned to accept the colonelcy of the 19th, which rendezvoused at Topeka.

General Sheridan's plan for the winter campaign involved the operations of three columns:

Maj. A. W. Evans,[4] with six troops of the 3rd Cavalry and two companies of infantry, was to march from a base at Fort Bascom, New Mexico, establish a supply depot at Monument Creek, then scout the Canadian and the North Fork of the Red River Valleys as far as the Red River, the boundary of the Department of the Missouri.

A column of seven troops of the 5th Cavalry, under the command of Lt. Col. E. A. Carr, was to march southeast from Fort Lyon, Colorado, unite with Captain Penrose[5] with five troops of cavalry, then on the North Fork of the Canadian, and operate toward Antelope Hills on the Canadian.

The third column, at Fort Dodge under Colonel Sully, was to move southward and establish the cantonment at the fork of Beaver Creek and Wolf Creek. This column consisted of eleven troops of the 7th Cavalry and five companies of the 3rd Infantry. The 19th Kansas Volunteer Cavalry was organized at Topeka, Kansas, and was ordered to join this column at Camp Supply.

All these columns were to march November 1, but owing to the delays of supplies, the time was changed to November 12.

On October 28 the 7th Cavalry went into camp a short distance below Fort Dodge and named the camp "Camp Sandy Forsyth," in honor of Maj. George A. Forsyth, who, with fifty volunteer scouts, had withstood the attack of about seven hundred hostiles on the Arikaree Fork of the Republican. The arrival of about five hundred recruits and the same number of horses filled the organizations to the maximum. All the horses of the regiment were then arranged according to color on one long picket line, and each troop's commander, according to rank, was given choice of color for his troops. According to color, there were four troops of bay horses; three sorrel; one each black, brown, and gray; the band and trumpeters gray; and the eleventh troop the odds and ends of all colors, including roan, piebald, etc. For several years after this, before requisitions for colors were given considerations in purchases, I observed that these ratios obtained.

Drills and target practice were pushed to the limit. Forty of the best shots were selected for a separate organization under the command of Lieutenant Cooke. We youngsters named it the "Corps d'elite," and the name stuck throughout the campaign.

On November 12 the Fort Dodge column assembled on Mulberry Creek, the 7th Cavalry from Camp Sandy Forsyth on the Arkansas River, and the supply train of nearly four hundred army wagons, with its infantry escort, from Fort Dodge.

The next morning we had one of those tedious jobs of crossing a prairie creek: steep, deep banks, doubling of teams, breaking of coupling poles, amid the shouting and cursing of wagonmasters and teamsters. The wagon train was assembled in columns of fours—two troops of cavalry as advance guard, three troops with flankers on each flank, and two as rear guard. The infantry companies were distributed along the train, and the beef herd along the train, inside the flanking troops. The lading troops on the flanks would march to the head of the train, halt, and graze until the rear of the train had passed it, thus alternating so as to save dismounting and yet cover the flanks of the train. The advance guard of one day would be rear guard the next day. The details were by roster so as to equalize the functions. The slow travel of the "bull" train was a handicap to travel and to arrival in camp on a full day's march. The ensemble made an imposing cavalcade.

The march was without special incident till the last day's march down Beaver Creek,[6] when our Osage Indian trailers discovered the trail of a war party of 100 or more on their way north to raid the frontier. On arrival in camp, Colonel Custer requested permission to take the cavalry on the back trail of this war party and attack the village whence they came. Colonel Sully disapproved the proposal on the ground that since it was absurd to suppose the hostiles were unaware of our presence in the country, the village could not be surprised, but would be on the alert. He was obsessed with the idea that all our operations were under the constant surveillance of hostile scouts who kept the tribes fully informed.

On the sixth day of our march, we arrived at the fork of Beaver and Wolf Creeks. At once preparations began for the building of the cantonment, on which was bestowed the name "Camp Supply." This isolated post became the abode of many "Winners of the West." It was at this place that Sully had abandoned the pursuit of the hostiles about two months before.

The next day activities began in locating and laying out the cantonment, digging trenches for the stockade and for the quarters and barracks to house the personnel, and digging wells for [the] water supply. Outside parties, guarded by mounted troops, were sent to gather supplies and material for the post. The hum of the mowing machines was accompanied by the ring of the axe, punctuated by the crash of the falling timber. With axes and saws, these trees were made usable parts, which the bull teams snaked to convenient sites to load in wagons. The mulewhackers hauled them to the cantonment, where they were sorted for various uses as palisades, upright walls for buildings, rafters, etc. What a contrast these pioneer activities were to the centuries of quiet, wild life, yet to the participants, it was all in the day's work.

The 19th Kansas Volunteer Cavalry had been ordered to proceed from its rendezvous at Topeka on November 5. Two troops had gone to Fort Dodge to escort General Sheridan, and it was expected that the other eight troops would meet us at the fork of the Beaver and Wolf Creeks. Their absence created much concern.

On November 15, General Sheridan left Fort Hays to join the Fort Dodge column. He relates:

> The first night out a blizzard struck us and carried away our tents; and as the gale was so violent that they could not be put up again, the rain and snow drenched us to the skin. Shivering from the wet and cold, I took refuge under a wagon, and there spent such a miserable night

that when at last morning came, the gloomy predictions of Old Man Bridger and others rose up before me with greatly increased force.[7]

As we took the road, the sleet and snow were still falling, but we labored on to Dodge that day in spite of the fact that many mules played out on the way. We stayed only one night at Dodge, and then on the seventeenth, escorted by a troop of cavalry and Forsyth's scouts, now under the command of Lieutenant Pepoon, crossed the Arkansas and camped the night of the eighteenth at Bluff Creek, where the two troops of the 19th Kansas previously detailed as my escort were awaiting our coming.

As we approached this camp, some suspicious-looking objects were seen moving off at a long distance to the east of us, but as the scouts confidently pronounced them buffalo, we were unaware of their true character till next morning, when we became satisfied what we had seen were Indians, for immediately after crossing Beaver Creek, we struck a trail leading to the northeast of a war party that evidently came from the headwaters of the Washita River.

The evening of November 21, we arrived at the Camp Supply depot, having traveled all day in another snowstorm that did not end till twenty-four hours later.

Hearing of the near approach of General Sheridan, Colonel Custer mounted his horse and rode out to meet him.

The arrival of General Sheridan with two troops of the 19th Kansas Volunteers gave rise to an occurrence not mentioned by either General Sheridan or Colonel Custer in their published writings of this campaign. At that time, the Rules and Articles of War provided that when troops of the Regular army and volunteers came together, brevet rank took effect. Both Sully and Custer were lieutenant colonels. Colonel Crawford of the 19th Kansas was the senior in rank. Sully issued an order assuming command of the troops by virtue of his brevet rank of brigadier general, U.S.A. When this order reached Custer, he issued an order assuming command by virtue of his brevet rank of major general, U.S.A. Sully contended that as between officers of the Regular army, this should not obtain. General Sheridan decided in favor of Custer. Sully was relieved from duty with the expedition and ordered to Fort Harker to command the District of the Upper Arkansas. I heard Custer say that had the question not been raised, he would not have taken his stand and would have been perfectly satisfied to have served under Colonel Crawford. During the balance of the campaign, Custer exercised the immediate control of the troops.

⊶ ≍✦≍ ⊷

"November 22, 1868—The morning is cold; it snowed all night and is still snowing. Cleared up at noon and got warmer. We took our horses out to graze at noon and let them pick all they can this Sunday. Still it snows." (From the diary of Blacksmith W. S. Harvey, Troop K, 7th Cavalry, now living at Belle Vernon, Pennsylvania.)

We were grazing the horses in the sand hills on that day, when in the afternoon orders came to return to camp at once and prepare for thirty days' campaign. It is my recollection that three wagons were assigned to each troop, this for convenience for picket line—one for troop mess, one for officers' mess, and one for forage. Baggage was limited to necessities.

November 23—Reveille at 3:00 A.M. Snowed all night and still snowing very heavily.[8] The darkness and heavy snowfall made the packing of the wagons very difficult, but at dawn the wagons were assembled in the train, and daylight found us on the march, the band playing "The Girl I Left behind Me," but there was no woman there to interpret its significance. The snow was falling so heavily that vision was limited to a few rods. All landmarks were invisible, and the trails were lost. We didn't know where we were going, but we were on the way. Then Colonel Custer took the lead and became our guide.

As the day wore on, the weather became warmer, and I have never seen the snowflakes as large or fall so lazily as those that fell that day. Fortunately there was no wind to drift the snow to add to our discomfort. They melted on the clothing, so that every living thing was wet to the skin. The snow balled on the feet of our shod animals, causing much floundering and adding to the fatigue of travel. About 2:00 P.M. we came to Wolf Creek, crossed to the right side of the valley, and continued to march till we came to a clump of fallen timbers and there went into camp, with our wagon train far behind. As soon as the horses were unsaddled, everyone except the horse holders was gathering fuel for fires. The valley was alive with rabbits, and all messes were supplied with rabbit stew. Our rawhide-covered saddles were soaked. The unequal drying warped the saddletrees, which consequently caused that bane of cavalry— many sore backs. Snow, eighteen inches "on the level"; distance marched, about fifteen miles.

The snowfall ceased during the night. The sun rose on the twenty-fourth with clear skies and with warmer weather. The snow melted rapidly. The glare of the bright sunshine caused much discomfort and a number of cases of snow blindness. Some buffalo were killed and many rabbits. Some deer were seen. We camped on Wolf Creek. Distance marched, about eighteen miles.

November 25 we marched some distance up Wolf Creek, and then turned in a southerly direction toward the Canadian. As we approached the summit of the divide, the peaks of the Antelope Hills loomed up and became our marker for the rest of the day. We made camp late that evening on a small stream about a mile from the Canadian. The day's march had been tedious. The melting snows balled on our shod animals during the long pull to the divide. A number of horses and mules gave out but were brought in late that night. Wood was very scarce, but usually the quartermaster sergeants would load some wood in the cook wagon when parking, and they usually were on the lookout for fuel on the march.

At daybreak November 26, Major Elliott, with Troops G, H, and M, some white scouts, and Osage trailers, started up the north side of the Canadian to scout for a possible trail of war parties. The remainder of the command and the wagon train marched to the Canadian to cross to the south side. To California Joe had been given the task of finding a ford. The river was high and rising, current swift and full of floating snow and slush ice. After much floundering, he found a practical ford. The cavalry crossed first and assembled on the plain. Owing to the quicksand bottom, each wagon was double-teamed and rushed through without halting. A mounted man preceded each team, and other mounted men were alongside to "whoop 'em up."

While this tedious crossing and parking was going on, Colonel Custer and a number of officers went to the top of the hills to view the country. The highest peak was about three hundred feet above the plain. Suddenly we were enveloped in a cloud of frozen mist. Looking at the sun, we were astonished to see it surrounded by three ellipses with rainbow tints, the axes marked by sundogs, except the lower part of the third or outer ellipse, which seemingly below the horizon, . . . eleven sundogs. This phenomenon was not visible to those on the plain below.

As the last of the wagons had crossed and the rear guard was floundering, someone of our group on the hills called out, "Hello, here comes somebody." But Colonel Custer had already seen him and had focused his field glasses on the galloping scout, but he said nothing. It was a tense moment when Jack Corbin rode up and began his report.

Major Elliott had marched up the Canadian about twelve miles when he came to the abandoned camp of a war party of about one hundred fifty; he had crossed the river and was following the trail, which was not over twenty-four hours old, and asked for instructions. Corbin was given a fresh horse to return to Major Elliott with instructions to follow the trail till dark, then halt till the command joined him.

Officers' call was sound, and when assembled we were told the news and ordered to be prepared to move as soon as possible. One wagon was assigned to each squadron (two troops), one to Troop G and the teamsters, and one to headquarters; seven in all, and one ambulance under the quartermaster, Lt. James M. Bell. These were to carry light supplies and extra ammunition. I cannot recall of just what the limited supply consisted. Each trooper was ordered to carry 100 rounds of ammunition on his person. (They were armed with the Spencer magazine-carbine and Colt revolver, paper cartridges, and caps.) The main train, guarded by about eighty men under the command of the officer of the day, was to follow as rapidly as possible. For this guard, men with weak horses were selected. Capt. Louis M. Hamilton, a grandson of Alexander Hamilton, was officer of the day.[9] He was greatly distressed because this duty fell to him and begged to go along to command his squadron, but was refused unless he could get some officer to exchange with him. Lt. E. G. Mathey,[10] who was snow-blind, agreed to take his place.

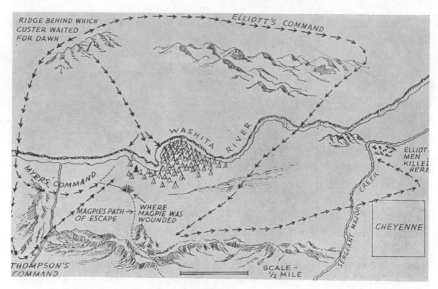

Movements of Custer's troops in the battle of the Washita.
CHARLES J. BRILL, *CONQUEST OF THE SOUTHERN PLAINS.*

Soon the regiment was ready to move, and we struck in a direction to intercept the trail of Elliott's advance. We pushed along almost without rest until about 9:00 P.M. before we came to Elliott's halting place. There we had coffee made, care being taken to conceal the fires as much as possible. Horses were unsaddled and fed. At 10:00 P.M. we were again in the saddle, with instructions to make as little noise as possible—no loud talking. No matches were to be lighted. Tobacco users were obliged to console themselves with the quid. Little Beaver, Osage chief, with one of his warriors had the lead, dismounted as trailers; then followed the other Indians and white scouts, with whom Custer rode to be near the advance. The cavalry followed at a distance of about a half mile. The snow had melted during the day, but at night the weather had turned cold, and the crunching noise could be heard for a considerable distance.

After a couple of hours' march, the trailers hurried back for the command to halt. Colonel Custer rode up to investigate, when Little Beaver informed him that he "smelled smoke." Cautious investigation disclosed the embers of a fire, which the guides decided from conditions had been made by the boy herders while grazing the pony herds, and from this deduced that the village could not be far distant.

The moon had risen, and there was little difficulty in following the trail. Colonel Custer rode behind the trailers to watch the developments. On nearing the crest of any rise, the trailer would crawl to the crest to reconnoiter, but seeing Little Beaver exercise greater caution than usual, and then shading his eyes from the moon, the colonel felt there was something unusual. On his return, Custer asked, "What is it?" Little Beaver replied, "Heap Injuns down there."

Dismounting and advancing with the same caution as the guide, he made his personal investigation, but could only see what appeared to be a herd of animals. Asking why he thought there were Indians down there, Little Beaver replied, "Me heard dog bark." Listening intently, they not only heard the bark of a dog, but the tinkling of a bell, indicating a pony herd, and then the cry of an infant.

Satisfied that a village had been located, Custer returned to the command, assembled the officers, and after removing sabers, took us all to the crest, where the situation was explained, or rather conjectured. The barking of the dogs and the occasional cry of infants located the direction of the village, and the tinkling of the bells gave the direction of the herd. Returning and resuming our sabers, Custer explained his plans and assigned squadron commanders their duties and places. Major Elliott, with Troops G, H, and M, was to march well to our left and approach the village from the northeast or easterly direction, as determined by the ground. Captain Thompson, with B and F, was to march well to our right, so as to approach from the southeast, connecting with Elliott. Captain Myers,[11] with E and I, was to move by the right, so as to approach from a southerly direction. The wagons under Lieutenant Bell and Captain Benteen's[12] squadron—[Troops] H and M—had been halted two or three miles on the trail to await the outcome of the investigations.

Just after dismissing the officers, and as we were separating, Colonel Custer called my name. On reporting, he directed me to take a detail, go back on the trail to where Captain Benteen and the wagons were, give his compliments to Captain Benteen, and instruct him to rejoin the command and Lieutenant Bell to hold the wagons where they were till he heard the attack, which would be about daybreak. "Tell the adjutant the number of men you want, and he will make the detail. How many do you want?" I replied, "One orderly." He then said, "Why do you say that? You can have all you want." I replied that one was all I wanted—to take more would increase chances of accident and delay.

I delivered my messages and returned with Captain Benteen's squadron. The camp guard remained with the wagons.

Upon the arrival of Captain Benteen's squadron, Major Elliott proceeded to take position, also Captain Thompson, and later Captain Myers.

Before the first streak of dawn, Colonel Custer's immediate command, as quietly as possible, moved into place facing nearly east, Lieutenant Cooke's sharpshooters in advance of the left, dismounted. Colonel Custer and staff were followed by the band, mounted. Captain West's squadron was on the right and Captain Hamilton's on the left, the standard guard in the center. Troop K (West's) was on the right flank, and I had command of the first platoon.

With the dawn, we were ordered to remove overcoats and haversacks, leaving one man of each organization in charge with orders to load them in the wagons when Lieutenant Bell came up. Following Custer, the command marched over the crest of the ridge and advanced some distance to another lower ridge. Waiting till sunrise, we began to feel that the village had been abandoned, although the dogs continued their furious barking. Then little by little we advanced. Captain West came to me with orders to charge through the village but not to stop, to continue through and round up the pony herds.

With all quiet in the early dawn, Major Elliott's command had reached a concealed position close to the village but was waiting for the signal from headquarters. The furious barking of the dogs aroused an Indian, who came from his lodge, ran to the bank of the Washita, looked about, and fired his rifle. I was told that a trooper had raised his head to take aim and was seen by this Indian. With the alarm thus given, the command opened fire. The trumpeters sounded the charge, and the band began to play "Garry Owen," but by the time they had played one strain, their instruments froze up.

My platoons advanced as rapidly as the brush and fallen timbers would permit until we reached the Washita, which I found with steep, high banks. I marched the platoon by the right flank a short distance, found a "pony crossing," re-formed on the right bank, galloped through the right of the village without contact with a warrior, and then proceeded to round up the pony herds.

As I passed out of the village, Captain Thompson and Captain Myers's squadrons came over the high ridge on my right. Both had lost their bearings during their night march and failed to make contact for the opening attack.

At the opening of the attack, the warriors rushed to the banks of the stream. Those in front of Custer's command were soon forced to retire among the tepees, and most of them being closely followed retreated to ravines and behind trees and logs, and in depressions, where they maintained their positions till the last one was killed. A few escaped down the valley. This desperate fighting was carried on mostly by sharpshooters, waiting for a head to show. Seventeen Indians were killed in one depression.

Lieutenant Bell, when he heard the firing, rushed his teams to join the command, and while loading the overcoats and haversacks was attacked by a superior force, and the greater part of them had to be abandoned. His arrival with the reserve ammunition was a welcome reinforcement.

While the fighting was going on, Major Elliott, seeing a group of dismounted Indians escaping down the valley, called for volunteers to make pursuit. Nineteen men, including Regimental Sergeant Major [Walter] Kennedy, responded. As his detachment moved away, he turned to Lieutenant Hale,[13] waved his hand, and said, "Here goes for a brevet or a coffin."

❖

After passing through the village, I went in pursuit of pony herds and found them scattered in groups about a mile below the village. I deployed my platoon to make the roundup and took a position for observation. While the roundup was progressing, I observed a group of dismounted Indians escaping down the opposite end of the valley. Completing the roundup and starting them toward the village, I turned the herd over to Lieutenant Law,[14] who had come with the second platoon of the troop, and told him to take them to the village, saying that I would take my platoon and go in pursuit of the group I had seen escaping down the valley.

Crossing the stream and striking the trail, I followed it till it came to a wooded draw, where there was a large pony herd. Here I found the group had mounted. Taking the trail, which was well up on the hillside of the valley, and following it about a couple of miles, I discovered a lone tepee, and soon after two Indians circling their ponies. A high promontory and ridge projected into the valley and shut off the view of the valley below the lone tepee. I knew the circling of the warriors meant an alarm and rally, but I wanted to see what was in the valley beyond them. Just then Sergeant Conrad, who had been a captain of Ohio volunteers, and Sergeant Hughes, who had served in the 4th U.S. Cavalry in that country before the Civil War, came to me and warned me of the danger of going ahead. I ordered them to halt the platoon and wait till I could go to the ridge to see what was beyond. Arriving at and peering over the ridge, I was amazed to find that as far as I could see down the well-wooded, tortuous valley, there were tepees. Not only could I see tepees, but mounted warriors scurrying in our direction. I hurried back to the platoon and returned at the trot till attacked by the hostiles, when I halted, opened fire, drove the hostiles to cover, and then deployed the platoon as skirmishers.

The hillsides were cut by rather deep ravines, and I planned to retreat from ridge to ridge. Under the cavalry tactics of 1841, the retreat of skirmishers was by the odd and even numbers, alternating in lines to the rear. I instructed the line in retreat to halt on the next ridge and cover the retreat of the advance line. This was successful for the first and second ridges, but at the third I found men had apparently forgotten their numbers and there was some confusion, so I divided the skirmishers into two groups, each under a sergeant, and thereafter had no trouble. When on the tactical board to devise new drill regulations (1881–90), this experience was instrumental in adopting the retreat and advance by alternating groups or units instead of by odd and even numbers.

Finally the hostiles left us, and we soon came to the pony herd, where the group we had started to pursue had mounted. I had not had a single casualty. During this retreat, we heard heavy firing on the opposite side of the valley, but being well up on the side hills, we could not see through the trees what was going on. There was a short lull, when the firing again became heavy and continued till long after we reached the village; in fact, nearly all day.

In rounding up the pony herd, I found Captain Barnitz's horse "General," saddled but no bridle. On reaching the village, I turned over the pony herd and at once reported to Colonel Custer what I had done and seen. When I mentioned the "big village," he exclaimed, "What's that?" and put me through a lot of rapid-fire questions. At the conclusion, I told him about finding Captain Barnitz's horse and asked what had happened. He told me that Captain Barnitz had been severely and probably mortally wounded.

Leaving Custer, I went to see my friend and former captain, Barnitz. I found him under a pile of blankets and buffalo robes, suffering and very quiet.

I hunted up Captain Lippincott, assistant surgeon,[15] and found him with his hands over his eyes, suffering intense pain from snow blindness. He was very pessimistic as to Barnitz's recovery and insisted that I tell him that there was no hope unless he could be kept perfectly quiet for several days, as he feared the bullet had passed through the bowels. I went back to Captain Barnitz and approached the momentous opinion of the surgeon as bravely as I could, and then blurted it out, when he exclaimed, "Oh hell! They think because my extremities are cold I am going to die, but if I could get warm I'm sure I'll be all right. These blankets and robes are so heavy I can hardly breathe." I informed the first sergeant, and the men were soon busy gathering fuel and building fires.

In the midst of this, Custer sent for me and again questioned me about the big village. At that time, many warriors were assembling on the high hills north of the valley overlooking the village, and Custer kept looking in that direction. At the conclusion of his inquiry, I told him that I had heard that Major Elliott had not returned and suggested that possibly the heavy firing I had heard on the opposite side of the valley might have been an attack on Elliott's party. He pondered this a bit and said slowly, "I hardly think so, as Captain Myers has been fighting down there all morning and probably would have reported it."

I left him, and a while later he sent for me again, and on reporting told me that he had Romeo, the interpreter, making inquiries of the squaw prisoners, and they confirmed my report of the lower village. He then ordered me to take Troop K and destroy all property and not allow any looting—but destroy everything.

I allowed the prisoners to get what they wanted. As I watched them, they only went to their own tepees. I began the destruction at the upper end of the village, tearing down tepees, and piling several together on the tepee poles, set fire to them. (All tepees were made of tanned buffalo hides.) As the fires made headway, all articles of personal property—buffalo robes, blankets, food, rifles, pistols, bows and arrows, lead and caps, bullet molds, etc.—were thrown in the fires and destroyed. I doubt but that many small curios went into the pockets of men engaged in this work. One man brought to me that which I learned was a bridal gown, a one-piece dress adorned all over with beadwork and elks' teeth on antelope skins as soft as the finest broadcloth. I started to show it to Colonel Custer and ask to keep it, but as I passed a big fire, I thought, "What's the use, orders is orders," and threw it in the blaze. I have never ceased to regret that destruction. All of the powder found I spilled on the ground and flashed.

I was present in August 1868 at Fort Larned, Kansas, when the annuities were issued, promised by the Medicine Lodge Peace Treaties of 1867, and saw the issue of rifles, pistols, caps, lead, and bullet molds to these same Cheyennes.

While this destruction was going on, warriors began to assemble on the hill slopes on the left side of the valley, facing the village, as if to make an attack. Two squadrons formed near the left bank of the stream and started on the charge, when the warriors scattered and fled. Later, a few groups were seen on the hilltops, but they made no hostile demonstrations.

As the last of the tepees and property was on fire, Colonel Custer ordered me to kill all the ponies except those authorized to be used by the prisoners and given to the scouts. We tried to rope them and cut their throats, but the ponies were frantic at the approach of a white man and fought viciously. My men were getting very tired, so I called for reinforcements, and details from other organizations were sent to complete the destruction of about 800 ponies. As the last of the ponies was being shot, nearly all the hostiles left. This was probably because they could see our prisoners and realized that any shooting they did might endanger them.

Searching parties were sent to look for dead and wounded, both of our own and hostiles. A scout having reported that he had seen Major Elliott and party in pursuit of some escapees down the right side of the valley, Captain Myers went down the valley about two miles, but found no trace.

A while before sunset, as the command was forming to march down the valley, Colonel Custer sent for me to ride with him to show him the place from which we could see the village below. There was no attempt to conceal our formation or the direction of our march. The command in column of fours covered by skirmishers, the prisoners[16] in the rear of the advance troops, standard and guidons "to the breeze," the chief trumpeter sounded the advance, and we were on our way, the band playing "Ain't I Glad to Get Out of the Wilderness." The observing warriors followed our movement till twilight but made no hostile demonstration. Then, as if they had divined our purpose, there was a commotion, and they departed down the valley.

When we came in sight of the promontory and ridge from which I had discovered the lower villages, I pointed them out to Colonel Custer. With the departure of the hostiles, our march was slowed down till after dark, when the command was halted, the skirmishers were quietly withdrawn to rejoin their troops, the advance countermarched, joined successively by the organizations in the rear, and we were on our back trail. We marched briskly till long after midnight, when we bivouacked till daylight, with the exception of one squadron, which was detached to hurry on to our supply train, the safety of which caused great anxiety. I was detailed to command the prisoners and special guard.

(One day on the march through a mesquite forest, Mah-wis-sa,[17] who was my go-between for the prisoners, came to me for permission for a squaw to fall out. This I granted and detailed a guard to remain with her. To this she objected, and Mah-wis-sa strenuously sustained the objection and assured me it would be all right to let the woman go alone. With great reluctance I consented. At our next halt, I was pacing back and forth with anxious looks on the back trail. I was perturbed not only with the prospective loss of a prisoner, but official action in consequence. Mah-wis-sa came to me as if to reassure me, but receiving scant attention, she turned away with a look of disappointment. Soon there was a shout from the prisoners, and looking at the back trail, to my great relief I saw my prisoner galloping toward us. Her countenance was beaming, and as she passed me, I saw the black head of a papoose in the folds of a blanket at her back, swaying with the motions of the galloping pony. The prisoners gave her a demonstrative welcome.)

At daylight next morning,[18] we were on the march to meet our supply train and encountered it sometime that forenoon. We were glad that it was safe but disappointed that Major Elliott and party had not come in. After supper in the evening, the officers were called together and each one questioned as to the casualties of enemy warriors, locations, etc. Every effort was made to avoid duplication. The total was found to be 103. Colonel Custer then informed us that he was going to write his report, and that couriers would leave that night for Camp Supply and would take mail. I visited Captain Barnitz and wrote a letter and telegram to Mrs. Barnitz that he had been seriously wounded but was improving. California Joe and Jack Corbin started with dispatches and mail after dark.

On November 30 California Joe, Jack Corbin, and another scout rejoined the command with mail and dispatches, including General Sheridan's General Field Order No. 6, which embodies the purport of Colonel Custer's official report. The command was formed as it reached camp on Wolf Creek, and this order was read:

Headquarters, Department of the Missouri, in the Field
Depot on the North Canadian, at the Junction
of Beaver Creek, Indian Territory,
November 29, 1868

General Field Orders No. 6

The major general commanding announces to this command the defeat by the 7th regiment of cavalry of a large force of Cheyenne Indians under the celebrated chief Black Kettle, reinforced by the Arapahos under Little Raven and the Kiowas under Satanta, on the morning of the twenty-seventh instant, on the Washita River near the Antelope Hills, Indian Territory, resulting in a loss to the savages of 103 warriors killed, including Black Kettle; the capture of 53 squaws and children, 875 ponies, 1,123 buffalo robes and skins, 535 pounds of powder, 1,050 pounds of lead, 4,000 arrows, 7,000 pounds of tobacco, besides rifles, pistols, saddles, bows, lariats, and immense quantities of dried and other winter provisions; the complete destruction of their village, and almost total annihilation of this Indian band.

The loss to the 7th Cavalry was two officers killed, Maj. Joel H. Elliott and Capt. Louis McL. Hamilton, and nineteen enlisted men; three officers wounded, Bvt. Lt. Col. Albert Barnitz (badly), Bvt. Lt. Col. T. W. Custer[19] and 2nd Lt. T. J. March[20] (slightly), and eleven enlisted men.

The energy and rapidity shown during one of the heaviest snow-storms that has visited this section of the country, with the temperature below freezing point, and the gallantry and bravery displayed, resulting in such signal success, reflects the highest credit upon both officers and enlisted men of the 7th Cavalry; and the major general commanding, while regretting the loss of such gallant officers as Major Elliott and Captain Hamilton, who fell while gallantly leading their men, desires to express his thanks to the officers and men engaged in the battle of the Washita, and his special congratulations to their distinguished commander, Bvt. Maj. Gen. George A. Custer, for the efficient services rendered, which have characterized the opening of the campaign against hostile Indians south of the Arkansas.

By command of Maj. Gen. P. H. Sheridan
(Signed) J. Schuyler Crosby, Brevet Colonel,
A.D.C. A.A.A. General

General Sheridan was informed as to the probable time of our arrival at Camp Supply and received us in review. Before we came in sight of the cantonment, the command was formed for the review of triumph. The Osage trailers, painted and in picturesque tribal garb, were at the head of the column, followed by the white scouts in motley frontier dress; then my prisoners, blanketed or in buffalo robes. At a distance in the rear came the band, followed by Lieutenant Cooke's sharpshooters, and the regiment in column of platoons, the wagon train in the rear. As we came in sight of the cantonment, the Osages began chanting their war songs and at intervals firing their guns and uttering war whoops, with some exhibitions of horsemanship. California Joe and scouts emulated the Osages' exuberance in western frontier style. The prisoners were awed and silent till the band began playing "Garry Owen" for the review of the regiment, when they awakened to conversation.

This pageant and review rivaled and no doubt was the prototype of the modern Wild West shows. It was the real thing. We camped on the Beaver, and that evening buried Captain Hamilton near the camp with all the formalities and solemnity of the military funeral, the 7th Cavalry and the 3rd Infantry present in formation. Hamilton had been an officer in the 3rd Infantry prior to promotion to the 7th Cavalry and had been its regimental quartermaster. General Sheridan, Colonel Custer, Captain Crosby, Captain Beebe,[21] and Lieutenants Cooke, Custer, and Joseph Hale (3rd Infantry) were the pallbearers.

We soon learned that the campaign was to be extended through the winter and began our preparations. I turned my prisoners over to the garrison. Later they were transferred to Fort Hays, where they were held for some months as hostages for the safety of white captives known to be in the villages of some of the tribes and to compel the tribes to go to their agencies.

We had the satisfaction that we had punished Black Kettle's band, whose warriors were the confessed perpetrators of the attacks and outrages on the Kansas frontier settlements of August 10—the originators of the Indian War of 1868.[22]

The Washita Campaign
and the Battle of the Washita

EDWARD G. MATHEY[1]

Special Collections and Manuscripts, Harold B. Lee Library, Brigham Young University

O n the evening of November 22, 1868, orders were issued to be in readiness to move promptly at daylight the following morning. It began snowing the evening of the twenty-second and continued all night, so that when the shrill notes of the trumpet broke the stillness of the morning air at reveille on the twenty-third, we awoke at 4:00 A.M. to find the ground covered with snow to a depth of over one foot, and the storm still raging in full force.

Surely this was anything but an inviting prospect, as we stepped from our frail canvas shelters and found ourselves standing in the constantly and rapidly increasing depth of snow which appeared in every direction.

Little grooming did the shivering horses receive from the equally uncomfortable troopers that morning. Breakfast was served and disposed of more as a matter of form and regulation than to satisfy the appetite. It still lacked some minutes of daylight when the command was in readiness to move, except the final act of saddling the horses. After the men had saddled their horses and were in readiness for the march, "To Horse" was sounded, and each trooper stood at his horse's head. Then followed the command, "Prepare to mount," and "Mount," when nothing but the signal "Advance" was required to put the column in motion.

The band took its place at the head of the column, preceded by the guides and scouts, and when the march began, it was to the familiar notes of that famous old marching tune "The Girl I Left behind Me."

The march of the 7th Cavalry was begun in the face of the blinding snowstorm, and before we had gone many miles, even the Indian guides owned that they had lost their way and could not recognize the country till it ceased to snow.

It had been intended to encamp at Wolf Creek, fifteen miles from Camp Supply, but the guides could not find it. Most men would have stopped in the face of such obstacles, but Colonel Custer did not stop. He took his course by the pocket compass, became his own guide, and reached Wolf Creek in the afternoon.

Marching in a blizzard. NELSON A. MILES, *PERSONAL RECOLLECTIONS AND OBSERVATIONS.*

Next morning at dawn, the column started, with eighteen inches of snow on the ground but a clear sky overhead, with a cold north wind. The march was continued with but little incident except the cold, through a country abounding in game, where was found plenty of buffalo. At last the column crossed the Canadian River. The crossing with the wagons occupied the best part of a day, and during that time Major Elliott, with three troops, was dispatched on a scout down the Canadian to hunt for Indian sign.

So far the column had not met any Indians. Bad as the storm was for the soldiers, the Indians had found it still worse. It had made them hug their lodges.

The last wagon of the 7th Cavalry had crossed the ford and parked on the plains to the south when a courier from Major Elliott came dashing in to report to Colonel Custer that Major Elliott had found the fresh trail of a war party, about 150 strong, leading nearly due south, with a trifle of easting. It was evidently that of the last war party of the season, going home. There was no more difficulty about finding the Indian village.

Lieutenant Colonel Custer's perseverance and pluck in marching away in the midst of a blinding snowstorm had been rewarded by "Custer's Luck." A little earlier start, and the war party would have probably found him, not he them. As it was, he had the advantage of a surprise. He was in the heart of the Indian country and as yet unperceived; the snow had proved his salvation.

The pursuit was almost immediately taken up. Colonel Custer gave the regiment just twenty minutes to prepare. Then, leaving eighty men with the poorest horses as a guard for the wagons, he started with the rest, provided only with what supplies could be carried on the horses, to intercept Major Elliott's party. The train was ordered to follow the trail of the regiment. Colonel Custer struck off at an angle to intercept Major Elliott's supposed course. That officer having started the Indian trail twelve miles down the river and at right angles thereto, it was probable that if Colonel Custer moved off to the southeast, he would cut the line of march.

Just about sunset he found it, but it was not till about 9:00 P.M. that the whole command overtook Major Elliott's party, in camp on the trail of the Indians. Then the whole regiment, about eight hundred strong, was reunited at last. They remained an hour in camp, getting supper and feeding the horses; at 10:00 P.M. resumed the march.[2]

Silently the command stretched out its long length, as the troopers filed off four abreast. First came two of the Osage scouts on foot. These were to follow the trail and lead the command. They were the guides of the main column, and the panther creeping upon its prey could not have advanced more cautiously than did these friendly Indians. The two scouts were directed to keep three or four hundred yards in advance of all others; then came, in single file, the remainder of the Osage guides and the white scouts. The cavalry followed in rear at the distance of about a quarter of a mile. Orders were given prohibiting even a word above a whisper. No one was permitted to strike a match or light a pipe. In this silent manner the column rode, mile after mile.

At last it was discovered that the two guides in front had halted and were awaiting the arrival of Colonel Custer. Word was quietly sent to halt the column until inquiry in front could be made.

One of the guides could speak broken English, and in answer to the question as to what was the matter, he replied, "Me don't know, but me smell fire." He was then directed, and his companion, to advance even more cautiously than before, and the column, keeping up the interval, resumed its march. After proceeding about a mile, perhaps further, again the guides halted, and looking in the direction indicated by them, [there] were to be seen the embers of a wasted fire.

From examining the fire and observing the great number of pony tracks in the snow, the Osages were convinced that the command was then on the ground used by the Indians for grazing their herds of ponies. The fire had been kindled by the Indian boys who attend to the herding, to warm themselves by, and in all probability the column was then within two or three miles of the village.

The two Osage guides advanced silently, and upon nearing the crest of each hill, one of the guides would hasten a few steps in advance and peer cautiously over the hill, and the same one who had discovered the fire returned to where Colonel Custer was and said, "Heap Injuns down there," pointing in the direction from which he had just come. Upon looking in the direction indicated, the presence of a large body of animals of some kind could be indistinctly recognized in the valley below, and at a distance which seemed not more than half a mile.

The Osage guide was asked why he thought there were Indians there. "Me heard dog bark," was the reply.

The two Osages having been ordered to keep a careful lookout, the main party of the scouts and Osages were halted, and the cavalry received a message from Colonel Custer to halt and keep complete silence, and directing every officer to report to him, after dismounting and collecting in a circle, they were informed of what had been seen and heard. In order that they might individually learn as much as possible of the character of the ground and the locations of the village, Custer proposed that all should proceed gently to the crest and there obtain a view of the valley beyond. This was done. Not a word was spoken until all crouched together and cast their eyes in the direction of the herd and village. In whispers Colonel Custer briefly pointed out everything that was to be seen, then motioned all to return to where they had left their horses, and standing in a group upon the ground or crust of snow, the plan of attack was explained to all, and each assigned his part.

The hour was past midnight. The general plan was to employ the hours between then and daylight to completely surround the village, and at daybreak, or as soon as it was barely light enough for the purpose, to attack the Indians from all sides.

The command, numbering, as has been stated, about eight hundred mounted men, was divided into four nearly equal detachments. Two of them set out at once, as they had each to make a circuitous march of several miles in order to arrive at the points assigned to them from which to make their attack. The third detachment moved to its position about an hour before day, and until that time remained with the main or fourth column. This last, whose movements were accompanied by Colonel Custer, was to make the attack from the point from which the herd and village had first been discovered.

Major Elliott commanded the column embracing Troops G, H, and M, 7th Cavalry, which moved around from the left of the main column to a position almost in rear of the village, while Captain Thompson commanded the one consisting of Troops B and F, which moved in a corresponding manner from the right of the main column to a position which was to connect with that of Major Elliott. Captain Myers commanded the third column, composed of Troops E and I, which was to take position in the valley and timber a little less than a mile to the right of the main column.

By this disposition it was hoped to prevent the escape of every inmate of the village. That portion of the command which Colonel Custer was to accompany consisted of Troops A, C, D, and K, 7th Cavalry; the Osages and scouts; and Lieutenant Cooke, with his forty sharpshooters. Captain Hamilton commanded one of the squadrons,[3] Captain West the other.

After the first two columns had departed for their position, it was still four hours before the hour of attack. The night grew extremely cold toward morning; no fires, of course, could be permitted. During all the long and weary hours of this terribly cold and comfortless night, each man sat, stood, or lay on the snow by his horse, holding to the rein of the latter. The officers, buttoning their huge overcoats closely about them, collected in knots of four or five, and seated or reclining upon the snow's hard crust, discussed the probabilities of the coming battle. Some, wrapping their capes about their heads, spread themselves at full length upon the snow and were apparently soon wrapped in deep slumber. The troopers were generally huddled at the feet of the horses in squads of three or four, in the endeavor to keep warm. The Osage warriors were wrapped up in their blankets, sitting in a circle, and it was plain to be seen that they regarded the occasion as a momentous one, and that the coming battle was the sole subject of their conference.

As the faint signs of approaching day were visible, the officers were collected. Those who slept were awakened. All were ordered to get ready to advance; not a word by officers or men was spoken above [an] undertone.

It began growing lighter in the east, and the column moved forward toward the crest of the hill. Up to this time, two of the officers and one of the Osages had remained on the hill overlooking the valley beyond, so as to detect any attempt at a movement on the part of the village below. These now rejoined the troops. Captain West's squadron was formed in line on the right, Captain Hamilton's squadron in line on the left, while Lieutenant Cooke, with his forty sharpshooters, was formed in advance of the left, dismounted. Although the early morning air was freezing cold, the men were directed to remove their overcoats, so as to render them free in their movements. Before advancing beyond the crest of the hill, strict orders were issued prohibiting the firing of a single shot until the signal to attack should be made.

The other three detachments had been informed before setting out that the main column would attack promptly at daylight, without waiting to ascertain whether they were in position or not. The plan was for each party to approach as closely to the village as possible without being discovered, and there await the approach of daylight. Captain Myers, commanding the third party, was also directed to move one-half of his detachment dismounted. In this order, they began to descend the slope leading down to the village.

Immediately in rear of Colonel Custer's horse the band followed, all mounted, and each man, with his instrument in readiness, to begin playing the moment their leader, who rode at their head, should receive the signal. As the main column was approaching near the village, a single rifle shot rang sharp and clear on the far side of the village from where the main column was. Colonel Custer then directed the bandleader to play "Garry Owen." At once the rollicking notes of that familiar marching and fighting air sounded forth throughout the valley, and in a moment were re-echoed back from the opposite sides by the loud and continued cheer of the men of the other detachments, who were there in readiness to pounce upon the Indians the moment the attack began. In this manner the battle of the Washita commenced.

The trumpet sounded the charge, and the entire command dashed rapidly into the village. The Indians were caught napping, but realizing at once the dangers of their situation, they quickly overcame their first surprise, in an instant seized their rifles, bows, and arrows, and sprang behind the nearest trees, while some leaped into the stream, nearly waist-deep, and using the bank as a rifle pit, began a vigorous and determined defense. Mingled with the exultant cheers of the soldiers could be heard the defiant war whoop of the warriors, who from the first fought with a desperation and courage which no race of men could surpass.

Our men had actual possession of the village and its lodges within a few moments after the charge was made, but this was an empty victory unless they could vanquish the late occupants, who were then pouring in a rapid and well-directed fire from their stations behind trees and banks.

At the first onset, a considerable number of the Indians rushed from the village in the direction from which Major Elliott's party had attacked. Some broke through the lines, while others came in contact with the mounted troopers and were killed or captured. Our men had gained the center of the village and were in the midst of the lodges, while on all sides could be heard the sharp crack of the Indian rifles and the responses from the carbines of the troopers.

As the Indians by this time had taken cover behind logs and trees, and under the banks of the stream which flowed through the center of the village, from which stronghold it was impracticable to dislodge them by the use of mounted men, a large portion of the command was then ordered to fight on foot, and the men were instructed to take advantage of the trees and other natural means of cover and fight the Indians in their own style. Lieutenant Cooke's sharpshooters had adopted this method from the first, and with telling effect.

Slowly but steadily the Indians were driven from behind the trees, and those who escaped the carbine bullets posted themselves with their companions who were already firing from the banks.

One party of troopers came upon a squaw endeavoring to make her escape, leading by the hand a little white boy, a prisoner in the hands of the Indians, and who doubtless had been captured by some of their war parties during a raid upon the settlements. Who or where the parents were, or whether still alive or murdered by the Indians, will never be known, as the squaw, finding herself and prisoner about to be surrounded by the troops and her escape cut off, determined, with savage malignity, that the triumph of the latter should not embrace the rescue of the white boy. Casting her eyes quickly in all directions to convince herself that escape was impossible, she drew from beneath her blanket a huge knife and plunged it into the almost naked body of her captive. The next moment retributive justice reached her in the shape of a well-directed bullet from one of the trooper's carbines. Before the men could reach them, life was extinct in the bodies of both the squaw and her unknown captive.

The desperation with which the Indians fought may be inferred from the following: Seventeen warriors had posted themselves in a depression in the ground, which enabled them to protect their bodies completely from the fire of our men, and it was only when the Indians raised their heads to fire that the troopers could aim with any prospect of success. All efforts to drive the warriors from this point proved abortive and resulted in a severe loss to the command.

They were only vanquished by our men securing positions under cover and picking them off by sharpshooting as they exposed themselves to get a shot at the troopers. Finally the last one was dispatched in this manner. In a deep ravine near the suburbs of the village, the dead bodies of thirty-eight warriors were reported after the fighting terminated. Many of the squaws and children had very prudently not attempted to leave the village when it was attacked, but remained concealed inside their lodges. All these escaped injury, although when surrounded by the din and wild excitement of the fight, and in close proximity to the contending parties, their fears overcame some of them, and they gave vent to their despair by singing the death song, a combination of weird-like sounds which were suggestions of anything but musical tone.

As soon as the warriors had been driven from the village, and the fighting pushed to the country outside, the interpreter went around to all the lodges and assured the squaws and children remaining in them that they would be unharmed and kindly cared for; at the same time, he assembled them in the large lodges designated for that purpose, which were standing near the center of the village. It was about 10:00 A.M., and the fight was still raging, when a small party of Indians were seen collected on a knoll a little over a mile below the village, and in the direction taken by those Indians who had effected an escape at the commencement of the attack. It was supposed that the Indians seen were those who had continued to escape, and having procured ponies from the herd, had mounted them and were anxious spectators of the fight. In the meantime, the herds of ponies belonging to the village, on being alarmed by the firing and shouts of the contestants, had from a sense of imagined security or custom rushed into the village, where details of troopers were made to receive them.

By this time the group of Indians already discovered had increased. One of the captured squaws was interrogated[4] as to who were the Indians to be seen assembling on the hill below the village. She gave the information that just below the village then occupied, and which was part of the Cheyenne tribe, were located in succession the winter villages of all the hostile tribes of the Southern Plains with which we were at war, including the Arapahos, Kiowas, the remaining band of Cheyennes, the Comanches, and a portion of the [Kiowa]-Apaches; that the nearest village was about two miles distant, and the others stretched along through the timbered valley to the one furthest off, which was not over ten miles. Only here and there, where some warrior still maintained his position, was the fight continued.

In the meantime, a temporary hospital had been established in the center of the village, where the wounded were receiving such surgical care as circumstances would permit.

Captain Hamilton, who was heard to caution his squadron, "Now men, keep cool, fire low, and not too rapidly," was among the first victims of the opening charge, having been shot from his saddle by a bullet from an Indian rifle. He died instantly. His lifeless remains were tenderly carried by some of his troopers to the vicinity of the hospital. Soon afterward, four troopers were seen coming from the front bearing between them, in a blanket, Captain Barnitz, another troop commander, who was almost in a dying condition, having been shot by a rifle bullet directly through the body in the vicinity of the heart. Of Major Elliott, the officer second in rank, nothing had been seen since the attack at daylight, when he rode with his detachment into the village. He too had evidently been killed, but as yet it was not known where or how he had fallen. Two other officers had received wounds, while the casualties among the enlisted men were also large. The sergeant major of the regiment, who was with Colonel Custer when the first shot was heard, had not been seen since that moment. The command was not in as effective condition by far as when the attack was made, yet it was soon to be called upon to contend against a force immensely superior to the one with which it had been engaged during the early hours of the day. The captured herds of ponies were carefully collected inside the lines and so guarded as to prevent their stampede or recapture by the Indians.

The wounded, and the immense amount of captured property in the way of ponies, lodges, etc., as well as the prisoners, were obstacles in the way of the command attempting an offensive movement against the lower villages. On all sides the Indians could now be seen in considerable numbers, so that from being the surrounding party, our men found themselves surrounded and occupying the position of defenders of the village. [As] it seemed that the Indians did not intend to press the attack, about two hundred men were ordered to pull down the lodges in the village and collect the captured property in huge piles preparatory to burning.

When everything had been collected, the torch was applied, and all that was left of the village were a few heaps of blackened ashes. Whether enraged at the sight of this destruction or from other causes, the attack soon became general along the entire line and was pressed with such vigor and audacity that every available trooper was required to aid in meeting these assaults.

The Indians would push a party of well-mounted warriors close up to the line in [an] endeavor to find a weak point through which they might venture, but in every attempt were driven back. Several of the squadrons were mounted and ordered to advance and attack the Indians wherever force sufficient was exposed to be a proper object of attack, but at the same time to be cautious as to ambuscades.

Captain Weir, who had succeeded to the command of Captain Hamilton's squadron; Captain Benteen and [Captain] Myers, with their respective squadrons, all mounted, advanced, and engaged the Indians, who resisted every step taken by the troops, while every charge made by the latter was met or followed by a charge from the Indians, who continued to appear in large numbers at unexpected times and places. The squadrons acting in support of each other, and the men in each being kept well in hand, were soon able to force the line held by the Indians to yield at any point assailed. This being followed up promptly, the Indians were driven at every point and forced to abandon the field. The Indians had suffered a telling defeat, involving great losses in life and valuable property.

By actual count, the command had in its possession 875 captured ponies, so wild and unused to white men that it was difficult to herd them.

The number of prisoners consisted of sixty squaws and children. The squaws were directed to proceed to the herd and select a suitable number of ponies to carry the prisoners on the march. The squaws having taken their ponies from the herd, the rest of the animals were shot. Search was then made for the killed, wounded, and missing of the command, of which all except Major Elliott and nineteen troopers were found. These last were never heard of again till their bodies were discovered some weeks later. It seems that a party of Indians, at the beginning of the attack on the village, had escaped through a gap in the lines of the cavalry; that Major Elliott had pursued them and ran into the large force that was then hovering around Custer, fearing to attack him.

Having fruitlessly searched for the major, it was rightly concluded that he and his party had been attacked and killed, and Custer prepared for his return march. Placing the prisoners in the center, he first deployed his forces and marched straight down the river at the threatening parties of Indians from the other villages, with colors displayed and band playing. His intention was to strike consternation into their hearts and make them think he was about to serve them as he had served Black Kettle's band. The movement had all the effect he desired. The Indians fled in confusion, leaving only a few warriors to hover around him and watch him. He did not start till within an hour of sunset, and his feint diverted Indian attention from his wagon train, which he knew must be pretty near him by this time.

About an hour after dark, he reached the abandoned villages of the alarmed tribes, where he halted at 10:00 P.M., retraced his steps, marching rapidly for the wagons. At 2:00 A.M. he halted in the valley of the Washita and went into bivouac, the men building huge fires to supply the loss of their overcoats, which the Indians had captured during the fight. They had been left in a heap on the ground. Secrecy was no longer necessary now, and the men enjoyed themselves hugely. Next day they reached the wagons and pushed on, encamping at night at the place where the regiment first struck Elliott's trail. From thence two scouts were dispatched to Camp Supply to carry the news to General Sheridan.

The two scouts made the journey in safety. The country was apparently denuded of Indians, the blow on the Washita having demoralized them. A scout met Colonel Custer's column with a return dispatch before the regiment could reach Camp Supply. It was read at the head of the troops, and repaid them for all their hardships. It was as follows:

HEADQUARTERS, DEPARTMENT OF THE MISSOURI,
In the field, depot on the North Canadian,
At the junction of Beaver Creek, Indian Territory
November 29, 1868

General Field Orders No. 6—

The major general commanding announces to this command the defeat by the 7th Regiment of Cavalry of a large force of Cheyenne Indians under the celebrated Chief Black Kettle, reinforced by the Arapahos under Little Raven and the Kiowas under Satanta, on the morning of the twenty-seventh instant, on the Washita River, near the Antelope Hills, Indian Territory, resulting in a loss to the savages of 103 warriors killed, including Black Kettle; the capture of 53 squaws and children; 875 ponies; 1,123 buffalo robes and skins; 535 pounds of power; 1,050 pounds of lead; 4,000 arrows; 700 pounds of tobacco; besides rifles, pistols, saddles, bows, lariats, and immense quantities of dried meat and other winter provisions; the complete destruction of their village and almost total annihilation of this Indian band.

The loss to the 7th Cavalry was two officers killed—Maj. Joel H. Elliott and Capt. Louis M. Hamilton—and nineteen enlisted men; three officers wounded—Bvt. Lt. Col. Albert Barnitz (badly), Bvt. Lt. Col. T. W. Custer, Lt. T. Z. March (slightly); and eleven enlisted men.

The energy and rapidity shown during one of the heaviest snow-storms that has visited this section of the country, with the temperature below freezing point, and the gallantry and bravery displayed, resulting in such signal success, reflects the highest credit upon both officers and enlisted men of the 7th Cavalry; and the major general commanding, while regretting the loss of such gallant officers as Major Elliott and Captain Hamilton, who fell while gallantly leading their men, desires to express his thanks to the officers and men engaged in the battle of the Washita, and his special congratulations to their distinguished commander, Bvt. Maj. Gen. George A. Custer, for the efficient services rendered, which have characterized the opening of the campaign against hostile Indians south of the Arkansas.

By command of Maj. Gen. P. H. Sheridan
(Signed) J. Schuyler Crosby, Brevet Lieutenant Colonel,
A.D.C. A.A.A. General

In many respects, the column formed was unique in appearance. First rode the Osage guides and trailers, dressed and pained in the [most] extreme fashions of war, according to their rude customs and ideas. As the column advanced, these warriors chanted their war songs, fired their guns in triumph, and at intervals gave utterance to their shrill war whoops. Next came the scouts, riding abreast. Immediately in rear of the scouts rode the Indian prisoners, under guard, all mounted on Indian ponies and in their dress conspicuous by its colors, many of them wearing the scarlet blanket so popular with the wild tribes, presenting quite a contrast to the dull and motley colors worn by the scouts. Some little distance in the rear came the troops formed in column of platoons, the leading platoon, preceded by the band playing "Garry Owen," being composed of the sharpshooters under Lieutenant Cooke, followed in succession by the squadrons in the regular order of march.

In this order and arrangement, the column marched proudly in front of General Sheridan, who, as the officers rode by, saluting him, returned their formal courtesy by a graceful lifting of his cap and a pleased look of recognition from his eyes, which spoke his approbation in language far more powerful than studied words could have done.

In speaking of the review afterwards, General Sheridan said the appearance of the troops, with the bright rays of the sun reflected from their burnished arms and equipment as they advanced in beautiful order and precision down the slope, the band playing, and the blue of the soldiers' uniforms slightly relieved by the gaudy colors of the Indians, both captives and Osages, the strangely fantastic part played by the Osage guides, their shouts, chanting their war songs and firing their guns in the air, all combined to render the scene one of the most beautiful and highly interesting he remembered ever having witnessed.

So closed the Washita campaign, December 2, 1868.

Our Washita Battle

FRANK M. GIBSON[1]

Little Bighorn National Monument Library, Crow Reservation, Montana

I n carrying the reader back a quarter of a century to the time when the 7th Cavalry left its winter quarters in the spring of 1868, I shall try to make rapid flights, and touch but momentarily here and there on the most salient points, hurrying him on as quickly as possible, into the midst of stirring and important events. The previous winter had been a quiet one for the troops, nothing having occurred in the way of Indian hostilities to disturb their tranquility, but the department commander, having a thorough knowledge of the habits and dominant characteristics of the nomadic tribes, felt reasonably sure they would be astir in the early spring, bent upon their usual evil designs, which were annually anticipated with dread forebodings by border settlers.

Therefore, to avert these yearly occurrences if possible, five of the six troops of the 7th Cavalry stationed at Leavenworth (A, D, E, G, K) were ordered into the field in April 1868, under command of Major Elliott, and marched westward nearly three hundred miles to Ellis Station, on the Kansas Pacific Railroad. There being, however, no necessity to engage in active operations for the present, the camp here established became one of cavalry instruction. The troops remained in this vicinity until the warpath demonstrations of the young ambitious bucks of the Cheyennes, Arapahos, Comanches, and Kiowas, who were thirsting for fame, made it expedient to shift our base to Fort Larned.

A word upon our Indian policy might interest the reader. Of course, the Indian commissioner at Washington was changed with each administration, and upon entering on the duties of his office, the new incumbent was invariably confronted with the same old knotty problems of Indian policy that had been left unsettled by all his predecessors; therefore, it was always a matter of speculation with the military, who generally got hold of the "hot end of the poker," whether the new commissioner would adopt a rigorous and just policy and acquiesce, at least, in the Indians being brought to book for their misdeeds and infractions of law and order, or whether he would assent to the conciliatory and pampering course so urgently recommended and insisted upon by the eastern philanthropists, whose humanity was always tempered with enough sagacity to suggest their remaining themselves well within the bounds of civilization, and thereby keeping their skins whole and heads covered. While the civil and military authorities were working with the same ends in view, i.e., peace between the whites and Indians, the methods employed to bring about this desirable result were so conflicting and pursued on lines so diametrically opposed that their efforts proved abortive. The former, who never even got a "sniff of the battle from afar," were comfortably ensconced well out of harm's way in luxuriously appointed offices, racking their brains and devising ways and means to reach the Indian's heart through his stomach, by flattering his vanity, and by catering to his love for gaily colored vestments and trumpery with which to cover his unwashed skin; and the army was taking the hard knocks incident to active campaigning in fair weather and foul, in order to bring the Indian down to a peace footing by meting out well and merited chastisement to those disposed to resist the power and supremacy of the government and disregarded the majesty of the law.

This yielding policy on the part of the Indian Bureau resulted only in exorbitant and ever-increasing demands, until it became necessary for the army to step in and effect a settlement. At the very time that the Indian Department and its agents were busy doling out annuities and presents, and protesting that peace and quiet reigned and that the Indians were all on their reservations, the young warriors of the Sioux and Northern Cheyennes were raiding the settlements on the Republican, Saline, Solomon, and Smoky Hill Rivers, and those of the Kiowas, Comanches, and Southern Cheyennes were industriously at work committing all kinds of depredations in the country south of the Arkansas. As a natural sequence to this state of affairs, the air soon became pregnant with rumors of war, and the troops in the Indian country were on the ragged edge of expectancy, and reports were daily received of attacks made by war parties from the very tribes whose chiefs were at the time professing the kindliest feelings for the whites. That the fact of these raids was well known to them, and that they were practicing their well-developed art of cunning, deceit, and deviltry, will hardly admit of a doubt. The Indian Department now suggested that the innocent and peaceably inclined be protected, and that the guilty be turned over to the military for punishment. To this suggestion General Sherman strenuously objected, on the ground that such a course as separating the good from the bad was neither feasible nor expedient, and that it was utterly impossible of accomplishment. The other part of the contract he was willing to take, and did. It is quite possible that some of these Indians had not themselves been guilty of murder, rape, and rapine, but neither had they attempted any restraining influence over those who had, nor did the chiefs comply with the agreement to surrender the criminals on demand. General Sherman considered that these Indians had flagrantly violated all treaty stipulations, and protested against any goods or clothing going to any portion of the tribes off their reservations, and solicited an order from the president declaring all such to be outlaws.

Facilities of communication in those days were not as good as now, and as the Indian question was absorbing the attention of the philanthropists in the East on the one hand, the military authorities in the West on the other, it was considered advisable to subdivide the military departments in which hostilities were apt to occur into districts, so that the troops might be kept more closely in hand, and dispatched on field service with the least possible delay. The country in which the 7th Cavalry was at that time serving was a part of the District of the Upper Arkansas, commanded by Lt. Col. Alfred Sully, U.S. Army, an officer who had long enjoyed a wide reputation as a successful Indian fighter. His district included, besides the frontier of Kansas, those military posts most contiguous to the hostile tribes. He had concentrated a portion of his command at points on the Arkansas River and caused scouting parties to be sent in pursuit of marauding bands; they, however, always managed to elude the troops and continued their raids and depredations without fear of substantial interference. The settlers of Kansas and Colorado, many of whom had suffered a total destruction of their homes, and in many instances of desecration of their firesides at the hands of the wild and wily "wards" of our government, had become enraged, desperate, and determined that rigorous measures of a most aggressive nature should be taken, to rid them and the country of this disturbing element whose ever-recurring depredations were leaving death and destruction in their wake, and were so menacing to the welfare of the sparsely settled districts that husbandry was practically abandoned, and self-defense and the protection of property and happiness became necessary substitutes for yeomanry. So intense became the excitement among these people, so frequent the massacres, and so numerous the nameless atrocities committed upon their wives and daughters, that the hatred existing between them and the savages was characterized by deadly bitterness. The governor of Kansas had appealed to the general government to give protection to the settlers, or if this could not be granted, authority was asked to permit the people to take the matter in hand themselves and institute retaliatory measures.

Between August and November 1868, the settlers of the borders of Kansas and Colorado sustained the following losses: murdered, 117; wounded, 16; scalped, 32; women outraged, 14; women captured, 4; children captured, 2; horses and mules stolen, 619; stock cattle stolen, 958. With these unsettled scores rankling in their breasts, is it any wonder that the hardy yeomen grew impatient for the day of reckoning and the dawn of a brighter future? But I have enumerated at some length, and in greater detail than I had intended, some of the causes which led to the Indian War of over five and twenty years ago, and will pass on to other events.

Matters reached the stage previously described, when General Sheridan, who commanded the Department of the Missouri, with headquarters at Fort Leavenworth, Kansas, and upon whom the responsibility of affairs in his department rested, decided to take an active part himself. This meant to those who had been in touch with General Sheridan in military matters, and it was his guiding hand that led to the move of the 7th Cavalry to Fort Larned, where I shall resume the thread of the story. We camped very close to Larned, within a few miles of which were also located large camps of Arapahos, Comanches, and Kiowas. With these Indians we at first sustained quite cordial relations, interchange of visits being frequent between the two camps. But this apparent friendliness was short-lived, and even its semblance ceased on the report of well-authenticated reports of raiding parties from their bands. The Indians were not slow to notice our changed manner, and doubtless suspected the cause, but of course feigned innocence. Seeing, however, that ruse would not answer, they evidently concluded it would be wise to make themselves as scarce as possible, and very soon evaporated. Their disappearance was like the touch of a magician's wand—presto, they were gone. We tarried but a short time after their departure, for now war was practically declared, and we were ordered to proceed to Fort Dodge, to participate in an expedition there being fitted out under the personal supervision of Colonel Sully to operate south of the Arkansas.

After being thoroughly equipped and amply supplied, this expedition, composed of eight troops of the 7th Cavalry (A, B, C, D, E, F, G, I) and three or four companies of the 3rd Infantry, with Colonel Sully in command, crossed the Arkansas River near Fort Dodge about September 1 and directed its march southerly toward the Cimarron River, at which point the first encounter occurred. The Indians on this occasion manifested no desire for a general engagement, but seemed satisfied for the present to oppose our progress by vigorously harassing our flanks, advance and rear, and by keeping up a constant running fire, which was more annoying than effective; but when the command got to Beaver Creek, it became apparent that their forces had been considerably augmented, and that some daring spirits among them must have inspired the others with extraordinary boldness and courage, for they opened fire on our camp during the night, a procedure on their part quite out of the ordinary. Such an unusual occurrence, it must be admitted, took the troops very much by surprise, and as everybody, except the camp guard, had turned in for the night, considerable confusion prevailed before the soldiers got down to business in the real army style. This nocturnal demonstration did not last long, and as nothing was accomplished on their side, this mode of attack was not repeated, and it is supposed they paid a good price for their temerity.

As we proceeded down the valley of Beaver Creek, the ever-increasing number of Indians and the stubbornness of their opposition led to the conclusion that we must be in the vicinity of their villages, and on the afternoon of our fifth day out, and while penetrating a range of sand hills near the site where Camp Supply was located later, we encountered the combined resistance of several hundred Arapahos, Cheyennes, Kiowas, and Comanches. These hills were steep and sandy, and of such a character that mounted troops could not be used to advantage, so, as the infantry was in the rear with the train, we were dismounted to fight on foot, and had our attack been made with as much vigor and determination as the Indians displayed in their resistance, the hills could easily have been taken by the dismounted cavalry, and leaving the infantry to guard the train, we could have pushed on to their villages, which we afterward learned were but a short distance beyond, and the Washita campaign would in all probability never have been necessary.

Colonel Sully, for some reason, did not consider this plan feasible. He feared the train could not be pulled through such country, opposed by so many Indians; but considering that not more than half of our cavalry was engaged in the fight, and that the enemy was driven at every point, it is reasonable to suppose that with all the cavalry taken into action, and what could be spared of the infantry, we had quite an important victory within easy reach, had we chosen to seize it. However, we were ordered to withdraw and retrace our steps to Bluff Creek. The casualty list was a short one and the loss sustained by the Indians was never learned. Our march back to Dodge could hardly be called a triumphal one, but we got there in fairly good condition. Colonel Sully with the infantry crossed the river to the post, and the cavalry was ordered to proceed to Bluff Creek, some thirty miles southeast, and there establish a sort of observation camp; and thus our little campaign ended, quite barren of results.

General Sheridan's idea was to have two expeditions in the field at the same time, so as to settle the Indian troubles, if possible, before the snow began to fly, a result much to be desired. The majority of the available troops had been concentrated on the Arkansas River to take part in Colonel Sully's expedition, thus leaving the valleys of the Republican, Solomon, and Smoky Hill Rivers comparatively unprotected; and these were the favorite raiding places of the Sioux, Northern Cheyennes, Arapahos, and the Dog Soldiers. The latter was a band of warriors composed principally of Cheyennes, but made up of the most brutal, vicious, and turbulent of all the tribes. They were the most warlike and troublesome of all the Plains Indians, and at the same time, the most attractive in appearance, and resembled more closely than any others the ideal "brave" as depicted by Cooper. These bands were quite in evidence in their favorite haunts, and had been made to increase the size of Sully's expedition.

General Sheridan was without the necessary troops to place in the field against them. Therefore, he decided to avail himself of authority granted by Congress for the employment of frontiersmen as scouts, and recruited them from that class of adventurous spirits sure to be met with on the border.

Fifty men of this character were employed to operate against these unruly bands, and Maj. George A. Forsyth was selected to command them. The choice was well made, for Forsyth was a zealous man and a hard worker, and while the task was difficult and the obstacles many, he had his men engaged and equipped for field service in a remarkably short time. The object of this little command was to find the trail and follow it to the camp as soon as possible, for it was supposed that when the issue was brought to a head, or in other words, when the Indians were well and severely punished, the settlers would be able, at least for a time, to enjoy the peace and quiet so necessary to the farmer, and so highly prized by him. The Indian is a veritable "artful dodger," and in border parlance, "If he aims not to be caught, you must rise earlier than the lark to catch him, but if, on the other hand, he shows any indifference about it, you may look for a very large crop of Indians in the immediate neighborhood."

Forsyth's command was outfitted at Fort Hays, Kansas, and left that post August 28, 1868, so his and Colonel Sully's expeditions took the field about the same time, just as General Sheridan had planned. Forsyth scouted the country between Fort Hays and Fort Wallace, and leaving Wallace early in September, he headed for the town of Sheridan, and from there proceeded northward to the Republican River, where he struck the trail of a small war party. As he followed this trail, it grew in size rapidly and led to the Arikaree Fork of the Republican. Here the indications were such as to convince these experienced plainsmen that they were in close proximity of their enemy, who were evidently well supplied with warpath paraphernalia of all descriptions.

On September 18 Forsyth camped his men near a small island in the river, and at the crack of dawn on the following morning, all hands were suddenly aroused by the sentinel's loud and warning cry, "Indians." The little camp was wide awake in an instant, and the practiced eye of each man soon saw that the best fighting of which he was capable, and the most sterling qualities he possessed, would be put to the test that day. I shall not go into the details of this stubborn and gallant fight, further than to mention briefly the general results. Forsyth's killed and wounded numbered nearly half of his little band. He himself was severely wounded twice, Lt. F. H. Beecher, 3rd U.S. Infantry, was killed, and Acting Assistant Surgeon J. H. Mooers was mortally wounded; hence the other sufferers were deprived of surgical or medical aid. All their animals were killed or captured, and their supply ration was about exhausted, and in this plight Capt. L. H. Carpenter, U.S. Army, who commanded the relief party from Fort Wallace, found what was left of Forsyth's scouts on the morning of September 25. The loss to the Indians was large, but never accurately ascertained. This fight and the demonstration made by Colonel Sully's expedition may be said to be the actual opening of the hostilities which inaugurated the Washita campaign.

At Bluff Creek, where we left the cavalry, there was little to break the monotony and humdrum of everyday camp life except the daily visits of the aborigines; these were no longer of that friendly nature which for a while characterized their visits to our camp near Larned, but on the contrary were marked by an entirely different tone and manner. They now contented themselves with simply sending us their compliments from harmless distances in the shape of Indian missiles, with which a considerate government kept them generously supplied. Their wonderful scattering ability and the apparent fewness of their numbers made it next to useless to send troops in pursuit, and furthermore, they not only did no damage, but they furnished a little daily diversion to what would otherwise have been a very dull camp, and we rather enjoyed their diurnal displays of good riding and poor marksmanship. The fall was coming on apace, and we began to wonder if we had been forgotten, and what the next move would be or lead to, upon which subject many wagers were made and a great deal of random speculation indulged in.

Our suspense was soon dispelled, for before the end of September, it was rumored that Colonel Custer, who had not been with the regiment that year, would join in a few days and resume command of the 7th Cavalry in camp on Bluff Creek. These rumors proved to be based on facts, as shown by the following telegram:

> In the field, Fort Hays, Kan., Sept. 24, 1868.
>
> General G. A. Custer,
> Monroe, Michigan.
>
> General Sherman, Sully, and myself and nearly all the officers of your regiment have asked for you, and I hope the application will be successful. Can you come at once? Eleven companies of your regiment will move about October 1 against the hostile Indians from Medicine Lodge toward the Washita Mountains.
>
> (Signed) P. H. Sheridan, Major General Commanding.

It was in response to the application mentioned in this dispatch that Colonel Custer joined [the regiment] on Bluff [Creek] about October 6. His arrival seemed to infuse new life in the command. We had unconsciously fallen into a state of inertia and appeared to be leading an aimless sort of existence, but with his coming, action, purpose, energy, and a general strengthening of the loose joints was the order of the day. Everybody was alert and ready to meet any emergency, and it was well that it was so, as all our resources were called into requisition the very afternoon of his arrival. The Indians had evidently concluded to treat us to a surprise, for an hour before sunset, they made the boldest dash into the camp they had yet attempted, and one of a character so threatening that it necessitated instant action.

Colonel Custer was in his element now; nothing could have happened more opportunely or more to his taste—even though he had squared himself to pay his respects to an ample meal after a thirty-mile ride. We turned out and formed a dismounted skirmish line in much less time than it takes to tell it. The warriors were more numerous and displayed much more courage than usual by keeping within range of our carbines. Their purpose doubtless was to encourage pursuit by a party of about equal strength, and when their pursuers were well out of reach of succor, to fall upon them with a largely augmented force and destroy them if possible; but this was too old a game to be worked successfully, and finding their efforts in that direction futile, they disappeared in their customary rapid and mysterious manner.

A rare view of George A. Custer in civilian attire.
PETER COZZENS COLLECTION.

After this initiation and insight into the prevailing conditions, Custer decided that the camp should be held in check no longer, and that aggressive action should commence at once. In accord with this decision, he ordered four mounted detachments, each one hundred strong and fully armed, to be ready to move immediately after dark. They scouted the country thoroughly in every direction but discovered no trace of Indians, their camp, or belongings. But these scouting trips were not fruitless, for the fact of penetrating the enemy's country inspired the troops with confidence and convinced the Indians that they were not yet the masters of the situation.

The many obstacles in the way of successful operations against hostile Indians in the summer months are obvious; for instance, the tribes can move their families hither and yon with comparative ease and safety, and practically without hindrance; they are at home wherever they find themselves; they live entirely upon the country; grass and game are abundant; wood and water sufficient; the weather just to their taste and most favorable to their nomadic tendencies. In the winter all these conditions are changed; the moving of a village is then attended with a great deal of trouble and discomfort, and these are factors despised quite as much, if not more, by the Indian than by the white man; grass is very scarce, and game not at all plenty; and to have a needful supply of water and wood, it is necessary to locate their village for the winter on the banks of some timbered stream, and after locating, they find it most conducive to their comfort and happiness to remain there if possible until spring opens.

For these and other reasons, a winter campaign against Indians is considered more satisfactory than one undertaken when the conditions would be much more favorable to them than to us. So, as the facilities for fitting out a winter campaign were near at hand, and such a move seemed to promise good results, we on Bluff Creek had to reconcile ourselves to a prospect of a winter in the saddle, and a canopy for a roof. There were many men in the 7th Cavalry at this time who were not familiar with this or, indeed, any kind of warfare and were inexperienced in nearly everything pertaining to their duties as soldiers; and while the encounters they had already had under Colonel Sully, together with some that followed his expedition, were unimportant and without definite result in themselves, yet they served a good purpose as a training school in practical and realistic methods, and were of great benefit in preparing these raw men for service.

We eventually broke camp on Bluff Creek and wended our way to Medicine Lodge Creek, thoroughly scouting the country en route; and during the few days we camped on Medicine Lodge, we ransacked every nook and cranny in that vicinity but found nothing except old weather-beaten Indian trails; nothing to indicate the presence of anything animate; so, concluding our search, we returned first to our old camp on Bluff Creek, and thence to camp on the north bank of the Arkansas, a few miles below Fort Dodge. By this time, the year 1868 had nearly spent itself, it being then the tail end of October, and Jack Frost soon became a very prominent factor in every plan considered and in every calculation made. He was hailed with delight yet detested for his presence; he was considered necessary to our success and yet regarded an obstacle in the way of it; he was welcomed as a harbinger of peace yet utilized as an element of war. The hostiles regarded Jack Frost as their natural protector, yet he was their real enemy; with him in their midst they felt that peace was assured, yet he was traitor to their cause and a spy in their camp, and upon such irreconcilable terms, who could tell whether he would serve as friend or foe. We were not yet prepared to face winter weather in the field but commenced our preparations at once with that end in view, for it was now pretty well understood that we were going to fight it out, regardless of time. Everything was now bustle and activity. Everybody was busy getting his command and himself ready for a winter campaign.

Prices at the trader's establishment went up even more rapidly than the mercury traveled in the opposite direction. The trader himself was the jolliest fellow about; he was busy as a beaver day and night, but cheerful withal, and everybody thought it was very considerate and obliging in him to accommodate us with blue flannel shirts at $9.00 apiece, and cotton socks at $1.00 a pair. The command was being newly organized, re-equipped, and generally brushed up; the halt, lame, and the blind, both man and beast, were culled out, and everything and everybody not of vital value to a fighting column was eliminated.

These preparations had been made on a scale indicative of a long campaign, and finally, everything being in readiness, the entire 7th Cavalry, save one troop (L), broke into the ice-covered Arkansas on November 12, 1868, and having turned our backs upon the border outskirts of civilization, we faced boldly toward the Wichita Mountains with an abiding faith in our ability to achieve success, and entirely unmindful of the discomforts, sufferings, and privations which we were to experience. Our eleven troops made a total strength of about eight hundred men, and out of these, forty sharpshooters were selected and organized as a separate troop, so that twelve organizations were made out of the eleven. At Mulberry Creek, we made our first camp from Dodge, and here we were joined by the infantry and the supply train, and here also the district commander, Colonel Sully, assumed command of the combined forces. Our march to the North Fork of the Canadian River, or Beaver Creek, where Camp Supply was then established, was an uneventful one.

Upon our arrival at Camp Supply, the infantry immediately went to work to make themselves as comfortable as circumstances and appliances would permit, in contemplation of being more or less permanently located there. We of the cavalry contented ourselves with the ordinary camp discomforts, for being but "birds of passage," we knew our stay would be short. While lying in camp at Supply, helping the infantry haul logs with which to build abiding places for their occupancy, we were very much surprised one day by the unexpected arrival of General Sheridan and staff. Being a restless spirit, full of action, impatient of delay, and anxious for the success and welfare of the troops, General Sheridan came, no doubt, to be more closely in touch with the purposes of the expedition and, in case of necessity, to personally direct and arrange the details of the campaign. However, whatever his motives, he was there, and his presence was no sooner known than felt. He had not been in camp long when he arranged to send the cavalry off to "do or die," and as our movements contemplated a field of operations extending beyond the jurisdiction of Colonel Sully's command, he was ordered to return to his headquarters at Fort Harker that he might devote his personal attention to matters of importance in his district.

Camp Supply now became, as its name would indicate, a base of supplies. In many respects, this turned out to be a misnomer, for while there was a partial supply of everything, there was not an adequate supply of anything, at least for such a prolonged and far-reaching campaign as this one proved to be. There was sufficient for present needs, or perhaps enough for any prospective demands, as far as was known or contemplated; but long before we headed for home, many suffered the pangs of hunger, or raiment was distressingly ragged, and our animals were dying by the scores from exhaustion begotten of toil and starvation. These facts are not alluded to in a spirit of complaint or censure, neither would I presume to place the blame if blame existed, but for the information of those who have so severely, and in the main unjustly, criticized the conduct of the Washita campaign. I wish to state emphatically that if there were any omissions that could have been avoided, and the results in the intense hardships, suffering, and bitter privations experienced by both officers and me, they cannot be laid to the charge of any officer of the 7th Cavalry, and with these few words of explanation I drop the matter.

As we were eager and ready for active work, it did not take long to prepare for leaving Camp Supply. Rations and forage for thirty days were soon loaded on the wagons, and as we were to cut loose from all communications with the outside world, most of us scribbled off a few lines to our friends in the faraway East, not knowing when, if ever, another such opportunity would present itself, and for some of our number they were the lines of farewell forever. As our preparations were few and quickly made, orders were issued on November 22 directing the cavalry to move at daylight the following morning.

Reveille was the signal for the cavalry to be up and doing, for in compliance with General Sheridan's orders issued the day before, the 7th was to resume its march and penetrate a region of country heretofore practically unknown. Our exact destination was problematical, the location of the hostile villages was purely a matter of conjecture, and while we all knew we were operating on a "warpath" basis, our movements seemed to be enveloped in an impenetrable cloud of mystery. Being perfectly convinced we were not booked for frolic, we were entirely at sea as to whether we were to fight or make terms of peace. At least, this was the question among the subordinates, who were not admitted to the war councils or taken into the confidence of the counselors. A cloud of uncertainty hung over all that concerned us, and the mysterious air of the knowing ones, or those who thought or wanted it to appear that they knew, only served to quicken the curiosity of the youngsters, who perforce had to take what little satisfaction they could find in the old mythical adage "Everything comes to those who wait."

Everyone was in prime condition as regards health and spirits, and the whole outfit was in for it, whether it turned out to be a fight, a fluke, or a frolic. We dispatched a very hasty and early breakfast that morning, so early in fact that it was like taking it the night before, and for all the good it did, it might as well have been left for the crows. At the proper intervals the different signals for breaking camp and packing up were sounded, and finally, everything being in readiness, the men mounted, the sharp notes of the advance cracked through the crisp air, and the column moved forward to that old tune whose inspiring strains have cheered the heart of many a weary soldier—"The Girl I Left behind Me." If each one had a girl, there were upwards of eight hundred of them left behind on that occasion.

Emerging from our camp in the woods on the bank of Beaver Creek, we entered upon a scene so impressively grand and picturesque that it has fixed itself indelibly in my memory. A snowstorm had set in during the night, and our camp being in the midst of massive sheltering cottonwoods, its magnitude was not fully realized until we broke camp and rode out into it. Looking toward the west, the appearance of the country, with its pure white coverlet extending much farther than the eye could penetrate, for the snow was still falling, was far too beautiful to admit of faithful description. To the south, the tall sand hills, which ordinarily were most unattractive, were now clad in a snowy garment which seemed to give them an air of stateliness and importance wholly foreign to them in their native state. As we rode by them, they seemed to be passing us in review with silent approval and with an air of "Bless you, my children," and a wish of "Godspeed." It was a kind of morning when everything was sharp and fresh, when every breath inhaled was invigorating, when every sound was clear and well defined, and when the twittering chorus of the snow birds filled the air with melody and our hearts with gladness. Our hearts were not only light, but in most cases free, for in those days there were but a few benedicts in the 7th Cavalry, therefore the great majority being free from that stress of responsibility that absorbs the thought and involves the affectionate solicitude of husband and father, they never burdened their heads with more than their heels could kick off, consequently a state of semi-indifference regarding personal welfare prevailed. All, however, were more than anxious for the success of the expedition and bent every energy toward its accomplishment. The firm friendships formed in the early days among these officers have never been broken, except when the grim specter death stepped in and severed the bond formed by affectionate regard and intimate association.

It is not intended, however, to indulge in fulsome praise of the old officers of the regiment; but those who had the privilege of knowing them will agree that they were an exceptionally fine lot of men—fine in character, in physiques, and in almost everything that goes to make up true manhood—and it is a matter of congratulation among their surviving associates that their lot was cast with that of these noble fellows, most of whom have met death on the field of action in the service of their country. It is pleasant to reflect that theirs and one's interests were identical, and that we and they were a part of the same unit. At the time of which I write, both those who have already rendered their last account and those who have yet to answer that last roll call were a band of loyal brothers, bound together by ties of such genuine affection that it was deemed a privilege to make a sacrifice for each other's benefit.

We must not, however, burden our hearts and weary the reader with sad recollections, but move on as swiftly as may be to the Washita River. With the collars of our greatcoats upturned and heads well protected from the storm, we rode forth into its blinding fury under the guidance of our Osage Indian scouts. These Indians had been friendly with the whites for years, but it was war to the knife between them and the hostile tribes that were now engaging our attention. They were well posted as to the country, which was entirely unknown to us, so they were allies to the government service, that we might have the benefit of their experience and native craftiness in locating the winter retreats of our common enemy. Our scouts were ordered to direct us to a point on Wolf Creek about fifteen miles distant, for as a rule the first march is always a short one; but the topography of the surrounding country was completely obscured by the storm, which was so dense that even the eagle eye of the Osage could not penetrate it. He was therefore useless as a guide for that day at least, for as he travels purely by sight, sometimes, however, like a dog by scent, and as neither of these faculties was now available, we found ourselves like a ship at sea without a rudder. In this emergency, as in many others, Colonel Custer rose to the occasion, guiding the column himself, and by the aid of his compass conducted us with as much dispatch as the circumstances would permit, to a camping place on Wolf Creek close to the point at first designated. Everyone was glad to reach a place to spend the night; it could hardly be called a camp just yet, for the equipage necessary to construct one was in the wagon train still far in the rear, moving its weary length along slowly through a good foot of snow and in the midst of an unabated storm.

Everyone was busy and kept his blood in circulation by helping to gather a needful supply of fuel, for our hurried breakfast and fatiguing march had given all an imperative appetite; so, after doing full justice to a bountiful dinner, we enjoyed the cheering glow of the campfire, over which we smoked our pipes, while the soft, warm waves of the calming heat induced a comfortable feeling of drowsiness, soon to be followed by "tired nature's sweet restorer, balmy sleep." At 4:00 A.M. the next morning, the unwelcome notes of the reveille recalled us from the blissful "Land of Nod." The storm fortunately had abated, and when old "Sol," who had not risen as early as we, shone upon us, he disclosed a clear blue sky and an expanse of snow.

The two succeeding days, during which our march continued up the valley of Wolf Creek, nothing worthy of note occurred, save the appearance of buffalo in large numbers. They had separated into bunches and sought shelter from the storm in the clumps of trees skirting the creek and its tributaries. This opportunity was improved by laying in a needed supply of fresh meat, and that night found the camp stocked with an abundance of it. After the storm passed, the Indian scouts of course resumed their duties as guides, and being told to conduct the command to a point on the Canadian River in the neighborhood of the Antelope Hills, they changed our course on the fourth day to nearly due south, and at the end of a long and tiresome march, we made camp on the north bank of the Canadian. From information collected by Colonel Custer, he had every reason to believe that the hostile villages were located not very far south of the Canadian, and that the trail of a war party discovered some time before would lead to them. He also naturally concluded that if they had remained absent from their camp long enough to be overtaken by the storm, their trail could easily be found and followed, and therefore decided to send a reconnoitering party to look for it. In order to carry into effect this plan, he directed Maj. Joel H. Elliott to proceed with three troops to a point about fifteen miles up the north bank of the river. His orders were to follow any trail he discovered, and to send back to Colonel Custer every item of information.

Elliott's command left us before dawn the following morning, and we commenced our preparations for crossing this treacherous stream. The current was strong, and the water filled with immense cakes of ice, so considerable time was spent before a suitable ford for wagons was found. Fording a river of this character is, at best, attended with more or less danger, as its bed is quicksand; so the obstacles to be overcome under present trying circumstances can be better imagined than described; however, at the end of about three hours, the rear guard, following closely upon the heels of the last wagon, found itself on the south bank, and the crossing had been successfully made. Just as the command, which had halted on the high ground to see the last wagon safely over, was about to resume the march, Colonel Custer, who had been eagerly and anxiously scanning the country in the direction from which tidings might be hoped for from Major Elliott, was at that instant rewarded. Contrary to the old saying "A watched pot never boils," the colonel discovered in the distance a lone horseman approaching as rapidly as his overtaxed beast could carry him through the heavy snow. Before the arrival of this messenger, there was plenty of time for conjecture, and the vague guesses and tumbled thoughts which doubtless flashed through Colonel Custer's brain during these moments of suspense have most likely never been recorded. The man turned out to be [Jack] Corbin, one of the scouts who had accompanied Major Elliott. In broken and hurried sentences, and in a manner indicative of great excitement, he reported that Elliott had struck a trail of a war party of probably a hundred strong about ten miles up the river; that it was less than a day old, that it crossed to the south bank, taking from there a southerly direction, and that Elliott was following it as rapidly as possible. At last, then, the trail was found; now, at least, there was something tangible upon which to base future action. Corbin's excitement was communicated in a modified degree to [the] others. He was asked if, provided with a fresh mount, he could overtake Elliott, and upon replying that he could, he was sent after him with instructions for him to push the pursuit vigorously, while Custer would cross lots, as it were, and strike the trail further along. Elliott, in the meantime, was to keep Custer informed of any change of direction on the part of the Indians. In case we did not overtake him before, Elliott was to halt his command not later than 8:00 P.M. and await our arrival.

After starting Corbin off, Colonel Custer instantly turned his attention to stripping the command of every hindrance to rapid transit, as we were now to take part in the chase ourselves. We were to cut loose from the wagon train and take with us just as little in the way of rations, forage, blankets, and the like as it was possible to get along with. An ample supply of ammunition of course was necessary, for there was now no doubt of our being on a hot trail, which would certainly lead to a battle in a very few hours. The train, which was to follow in our tracks as rapidly as it could, was abandoned to the charge of Lt. E. G. Mathey, an experienced officer, with a detail of men sufficiently strong to afford it proper protection, and in less than half an hour after Corbin's departure, our hurried preparations were completed, and we were in our saddles and gone. Certainty and definite purpose now took the place of partial doubt and questionable wisdom. In all large commands are to be found "many men of many minds," consequently there is generally a conflict of opinion as to the best way of accomplishing the greatest good, but just now all were of one mind, all were eager to hurry on. The manifold discomforts incident to a very limited larder, a single robe and the sky as a covering, in the midst of a severe winter, will linger in the memories of the surviving participants of that memorable march, and the cheerfulness with which these discouraging conditions were accepted by everyone in the command only serves to intensify the strong bond of unity that characterized the officers and men of the 7th Cavalry.

The march was a long and rough one, every horse was urged to the top notch of his endurance, and as we hurried on hour after hour without a halt, without the slightest slackening of the forced pace, through unbroken snow, which had not commenced to soften under the powerful rays of the midday sun, every eye and ear were strained, and every faculty alert for some fresh development. The column was riding hard for Elliott's trail, and on and on it pushed until midday was past and the afternoon had more than half spent itself. Yet nothing occurred to indicate to the weary rider that he had lessened the distance between himself and the desired goal. The shades of night found us still moving at the same unchecked gait, 7:00 P.M. came, and a feeling of suppressed anxiety seemed to prevail, for there was still no sign of the trail. Some expressed the belief that the Indians had discovered that they were pursued, and hence had separated into small bands to elude their pursuers, thus leaving Elliott to choose between the horns of a dilemma, and in such an event there was no telling which direction either he or the Indians had taken; but as we heard nothing further from him, we continued to urge our tired steeds on their wearisome tramp. The scouts and guides had kept well out from the column in search of the trail, and about 8:00 P.M., when weary, disappointed, and somewhat depressed, we almost despaired of news, we saw one of them making frantic gyrations to attract attention, this being his mode of signaling that he had found the trail. We were not long reaching it, and upon examination, it turned out to be not only the trail of the war party, but also that of Elliott's command in pursuit.

The discovery of this long looked-for road to "ruin or renown" lightened our hearts and encouraged wearied men and jaded horses to renewed effort. The traveling was easier now, for the trail was well broken down, and it was like changing from a heavy to a compact road. Not a rein had been drawn since morning, not a moment of rest taken; not a morsel of food had passed our lips. But we were on the trail, which largely compensated for a great deal of suffering endured in our fatiguing chase. We had now but one thought, and that was to overtake Elliott's command. The night was clear, the country nearly level, and we could see over the snow-covered surface for several miles, but nothing of Elliott, who must be still far in the lead. Finally, as we rounded the crest of a rise, we saw in the distance a strip of timber probably a couple of miles away, and upon nearer approach found Elliott's command carefully tucked away under the leafless branches, seeking much-needed refreshment and rest on the banks of a stream of clear water. The joy and satisfaction of knowing that rest was at hand can no more be expressed in words than can the hardships our small army frequently experiences be appreciated by the general public, in whose interest they are borne. The hand of the dial pointed to the hour of nine when we arrived. One hour was the time allotted to food and rest, and at its expiration we were to be up and off again. To climb on top of a horse again with only one short hour's rest after such an exhausting ride was not the pleasantest thing imaginable. Personally, I would just then have given all I possessed for permission to sleep till "doomsday."

The horses had been unsaddled and given every care and attention possible. Our repast consisted of hard bread washed down by boiling hot coffee, drunk out of red-hot tin cups that blistered the lips every time they came in contact. Much of our hour had been consumed before the coffee was prepared, so we had to drink it more or less hastily. Many of my readers, I know, have had a hard tussle with a tin cup of hot coffee after the "general" was sounded, and finally had to dilute it almost beyond recognition with cold water if they hoped to drink it at all. That was our experience here. Hard luck, but there was no help for it at such a time.

At 10:00 P.M. we were again on the move, but we took things a little more quietly now, for it was necessary to exercise much caution. The trail grew fresher as we progressed, and it might at any time terminate at the threshold of an Indian village. It would not do to flush the game now, for that would certainly spoil the hunt. No trumpet signals were used, and no talking permitted except in suppressed whispers; even the tramp of the horses as they broke through the top crust that had formed on the snow since sundown made a noise that caused dismay in the command, lest the hostiles should be aroused by it. The Osage scouts had been dismounted and sent ahead on foot, that we might have timely warning of the proximity of the village. It now became necessary to "make haste slowly"; frequent halts were made, necessitated by the very deliberate, stealthy, and cautious progress of the scouts in advance, who had evidently no intention of walking into a trap or ambush. It was their peculiar knowledge of Indian traits and trails, together with their native cunning, caution, and sagacity, that made their services particularly valuable at this time. About midnight we came to a more sudden halt than usual, and all exchanged inquiring glances, for ever since we had left our temporary bivouac, all seemed to be conscious of an air of mystery in regard to our movements. Of course, there was no real mystery, but those who have never been in a position where it was their duty to follow blindly one in authority can form no conception of how the imagination can discount the judgment under extraordinary circumstances such as these. As to this last halt, our suspense was short-lived. Colonel Custer had found two Osage scouts who had been about half a mile in advance, halted and apparently rooted to the spot. He quickly sent back word for the cavalry to halt, and the Indians, in the best English they could muster, told him they smelt fire. All present sniffed the air and failed to detect the odor, but the scouts stood firm in their belief, and upon intimation from Colonel Custer reluctantly resumed the trail. In less than a mile beyond, they again came to an abrupt halt, this time to vindicate the perceptive powers of their nasal organs, for there, near at hand, were the remains of what was originally a very small fire. This, the Indians explained, had not been made by the war party we were following, but by the boy herders from the village who had been tending the ponies. Upon closely examining the ground about the fire, it was found to be covered by innumerable pony tracks in all directions, so the Indian theory was accepted as correct, and as a natural sequence, also the fact that we were now very near the hostile camp.

Absolute silence was enjoined upon all; no word was to be spoken except in a whisper, and only when necessary to communicate an order. Much fear was entertained lest some of the horses should neigh, or the dogs commence to bay at the moon, whose light was intensified by the great expanse of snow surrounding us, and might thus discover our presence to the enemy. The crest of each hill was cautiously approached, and the surrounding country critically examined, before the command was permitted to pass over it, and finally the scout who first detected the odor of fire was seen to flatten himself in the snow a short distance in front, on top of a slight rise, and after gazing long and intently, crawled stealthily back to where Colonel Custer was awaiting. He reported the hostile village down in the valley nearby. The colonel dismounted and, accompanied by the scout, hastened to the top of the hill to satisfy himself in regard to the matter, and although unable to see anything but heavy timber, he heard the barking of a dog and the tinkling of a bell supposed to be on the neck of a pony and coming from the direction indicated by the scout. But the sound that reached his ear most distinctly, and convinced him that the village had practically been reached, was, to use his own words, "the distant cry of an infant."

The command had been halted, and all officers were ordered forward to report to Colonel Custer. He informed them briefly of what he had seen and heard, and suggested that they should all proceed as noiselessly as possible to the crest with him, and he would point out the location of the village and the features of the country surrounding it. This was done, and the general plan of attack was explained. The design was to surround the village as completely as was possible for eight hundred men to do so, and at daylight, at a given signal, to make a simultaneous attack from all sides. There were still several hours before daylight, and ample time for the attacking columns to get into position. The dispositions were made as follows: Major Elliott commanded the battalion composed of G, H, and M Troops, which was to move well around to the left, to a position as near the village as possible. The officers with this column, besides Major Elliott, were Brevet Colonels Albert Barnitz [and] F. W. Benteen, troop commanders, and Lieutenants T. J. March and H. W. Smith.

Capt. William Thompson commanded Band F troops, which were to march to a corresponding position to the right, to connect if possible and cooperate with Elliott's battalion, but the distance necessary to be covered made it impracticable to get within communicating distance, and furthermore, it could not have been accomplished without disclosing the presence of Thompson's command to the Indians. The officers of this command were Bvt. Col. William Thompson and Capt. George W. Yates, troop commanders, and Lieutenants D. W. Wallingford[2] and F. M. Gibson.

E and I troops were commanded by Captain Myers and were posted down in the woods along the valley, about three-quarters of a mile to the right of the center. With this command were Bvt. Lt. Col. Edward Myers and Bvt. Capt. Charles Brewster, troop commanders, and Lt. J. M. Johnson,[3] but the latter before the close of the engagement was ordered to succeed Captain Myers in command of E Troop, he having been incapacitated by snow blindness.

The center column consisted of the Osage scouts, Bvt. Lt. Col. W. W. Cooke with his detachment of sharpshooters, and Troops A, G, D, and K, commanded by Capt. Louis McL. Hamilton (grandson of Alexander Hamilton), Bvt. Capt. M[atthew] Berry, Bvt. Lt. Col. T. B. Weir,[4] and Bvt. Col. R. M. West; the lieutenants were Bvt. Lt. Col. T. W. Custer, S. M. Robbins,[5] E. S. Godfrey, and Edward Law. Bvt. Capt. A. E. Smith, who was acting regimental commissary, also went into action with this portion of the command. Colonel Custer, accompanied by Lt. M[yles] Moylan, the regimental adjutant, personally conducted this column into the fight. The medical officers present were Assistant Surgeon Henry Lippincott, U.S. Army, and Assistant Surgeon William H. Renick, and both had their hands full soon after the first shot was fired and rendered efficient and valuable services. The different columns reached their respective positions in due season, and there silently awaited the coming of the morn. The weary vigil of that night left an impression that never can be effaced by the lapse of time. Daylight never seemed so long in coming, and the cold never so penetrating. It was an infraction of orders to talk or move about, so there was nothing left to do but to remain perfectly quiet and immovable, thus maintaining a deathlike silence, while spending the night in moody meditation, broken occasionally by spasmodic shivers and involuntary shakes. At break of day, the band, which was with the main column, was to strike up "Garry Owen," the signal for each command to charge the village. At last the first faint signs of dawn appeared, while the morning star still shone in majestic splendor like a beacon light, as if to warn the silent village with its sleeping braves of approaching danger.

And now we listened intently for the signal notes of "Garry Owen," our charging call, and the death march as well of many a comrade and friend. At last the inspiring strains of this rollicking tune broke forth, filling the early morning air with joyous music. The profound silence that had reigned through the night was suddenly changed to a pandemonium of tumult and excitement; the wild notes of "Garry Owen," which had resounded from hill to hill, were answered by wilder shouts of exultation from the charging columns. On rushed those surging cavalcades from all directions, a mass of Uncle Sam's cavalry-men thirsting for glory and feeling the flush of coming victory at every bound, and in their impetuous eagerness, spurring their steeds to still greater effort and giving voice to their long pent-up emotions. There was no hope of escape for the surrounded savages; their pony herd had been effectually cut off and their slumbering village entered from all sides before they had time to realize the extent of their peril, but they fought with courage and desperation.

After charging into the village and taking possession of it, the battle began. The troops were quickly dismounted, the horses sent to the safest place of shel-ter, and a desperate hand-to-hand battle ensued. The command had practically exchanged place with the Indians. It was now *our* camp, and they were the sur-rounding party, but the victory was surely ours, while death and destruction were inevitably the lot of the savages. They sought cover behind every available tree, along the steep riverbanks, indeed, behind anything that would afford the slightest protection, and as we were at very close quarters and had exchanged places with them, the soldiers were in constant danger of hostile bullets fired from all directions. Every man was kept as busy as a bee, and everyone knew he was fighting for his life. The repeated caution to the new men not to waste their ammunition had no effect at all on the excitement of such a hazardous conflict, and had it not been for the timely arrival of Bvt. Maj. J. M. Bell, the regimental quartermaster, who gallantly fought his way to the battlefield about half an hour after the battle began, with a fresh supply, the troops might have been required to husband their ammunition greatly to their disadvantage.

The rattle of the constant fusillade, and the din of its answering chorus as it echoed through the hill and dale and across to open plain, seemed to infuse new ardor and enthusiasm into the already fired souls of those zealous cavalry-men, and as the desperate fight progressed, the fury increased, and wilder and wilder grew the intense excitement, while louder and louder sounded the crack of our bullets, as they sped on their unerring flight, like a shower of hail, into the very midst of our enemy. The desperation displayed by both sides in this bloody conflict beggars description, and the marked bravery of both friend and foe was beyond praise.

And so the battle raged with relentless and overwhelming fury, until its death-dealing hand had sent to the "Happy Hunting Ground" their chief, Black Kettle, and the great majority of his ill-fated band of Cheyennes. This victory was as complete as it was possible to make it; Black Kettle's band had been swept from the face of the earth, the remnant being too small a nucleus upon which to rebuilt it. His village happened to be on the extreme west end of a number of hostile camps that had located for the winter on the banks of the Washita River, the remaining portion of the Cheyennes, and large bands of

Arapahos, Comanches, and Kiowas, and a small contingent of [Kiowa]-Apaches, occupying those further down the stream. Just as we were taking a respite from our day's hard work, it was necessary to resume hostilities and meet the combined attack of the other bands, made for the supposed purpose of rehabilitation, and incidentally to rescue survivors of their conquered allies, and also to recapture the large and valuable pony herd, in addition to numerous supplies of all kinds that had fallen into our hands. Their idea evidently was that after such success, and the capture of so much booty, our vigilance would be somewhat relaxed and they could take us unawares, but the eagle eye of watchfulness had marked their every move, and when their daring rush [came] upon our lines, they found the troops more than ready to give them the warmest kind of reception, and were soon convinced that it was too hot a place to tarry in; so, quickly scattering as only Indians can, they retreated in ignominious haste and perched themselves on top of the high hills overlooking the valley, and watched intently our preparations for departure. After the failure of this bold attack, they were no doubt much sadder, but possibly wiser, men, and the experience it afforded should have furnished them with abundant food for reflection. The last shot was fired; the battle was over, the victory ours. The iron hand of death had claimed as its victims two officers who had brilliant records for themselves on many a hard-fought field, and with them others who had, but a few short hours before, been in the prime of vigorous healthy manhood. Many a joyous heart turned sad, and after the wild tumult of bloody conflict had ceased, there came a peaceful lull, and an impressive and solemn silence prevailed, as we turned our backs upon that deserted valley of death. The battle of the Washita had been desperately fought and won, and its recital forms fitting close to this narrative, which shall be prolonged only in order to give some final details, together with official records.

＊　≍◊≍　＊

The herd captured numbered in all between eight and nine hundred animals, and after selecting a sufficient number of the best upon whom [to] mount our prisoners and to replace our own broken-down horses, the remainder had unfortunately to be shot, as Colonel Custer deemed it impracticable to take them along, especially as the Indians simply swarmed on the hilltops over which we had to pass, and as the ponies were more or less unmanageable, he did not care to incur the risk of their recapture. By 4:00 P.M., or possibly somewhat earlier, everything that could not be put to immediate use having been destroyed, we left the charred remains of Black Kettle's village, with every reason to expect a harder fight than the one just ended, but to our great surprise, as we approached the positions occupied by this overwhelming mass of savages, they disappeared like chaff before the wind; a few shots were exchanged, but no damage was done.

On leaving the site of the battle, our march was directed down the valley toward the other hostile camps, or rather toward where they had been, for it

Black Kettle. CHARLES J. BRILL, *CONQUEST OF THE SOUTHERN PLAINS.*

was afterwards learned that those villages had decamped and gotten their women and children out of harm's way while the fight was going on.

We proceeded down the valley until after dark; this was a "blind," I think, on Colonel Custer's part, his purpose being most likely to mislead the Indians as to his real intentions, for as soon as darkness covered our movements, we turned back on our tracks, passed by our field of strife, and on to our trail made the day before.

Our return march was necessarily slow, for besides Captain Hamilton's remains, we had a number of wounded, including Captain Barnitz, who it was supposed had received his death wound. These were put in the three or four wagons with which, as before stated, Lieutenant Bell so opportunely arrived early in the fight. We reached our wagon train during the forenoon of our second day's march, and making camp early that afternoon, got a little breathing spell and time to attend to such bodily comforts as were possible under such unfavorable circumstances; ample time also to sum up the results of the battle, which, briefly stated and from the best information obtainable, are as follows: The total destruction of Black Kettle's village and all it contained, including the eight or nine hundred animals before mentioned. One hundred and three warriors, including Chief Black Kettle, were killed, and fifty-three squaws and children were made prisoners. Our own casualties were Maj. Joel H. Elliott, Capt. Louis McLane Hamilton, and twenty-one enlisted men killed, and the wounded were Bvt. Lt. Col. Albert Barnitz, seriously, and Bvt. Lt. Col. T. W. Custer and 2nd Lt. T. J. Marsh slightly, and eleven enlisted men.

The circumstances attending the loss of Major Elliott, Sergeant Major Kennedy, and the seventeen enlisted men who accompanied them have never, to my knowledge, become a matter of official record; the details have never been known, only surmised. The cause which led to their separation from the main command was attributed to the fact that a number of Indians were seen escaping from the village, through the gap between the left of his squadron and the right of Thompson's squadron, and that Elliott and his party, who went in pursuit, were cut off and killed by the hostiles from the villages below. In the excess of commotion and consequent excitement incident to a desperate hand-to-hand conflict such as this, their absence was not noted for a long time, and when the bodies of these brave fellows were found some time later, about two miles or more from the scene of the battle, there was every evidence that they had made a gallant stand against vastly superior odds. The Indians had practiced upon their bodies the usual nameless atrocities that could only be suggested to minds depraved, and only resorted to by those trained to the vicious cruelty that characterizes the inhumanity of the Indian, and which has so indelibly and deservedly stamped upon him the title of savage. In most instances, the trunks of their ill-fated victims had been dismembered, and in a few cases, mutilated beyond recognition.

So perished this gallant little band. Hamilton was shot through the heart while gallantly leading his squadron into the hostile village, and it is said of him that he remained mounted and rode many yards after death ensued. The death of Captain Hamilton was particularly sad, for aside from the fact that he was a thorough soldier and exceedingly popular, he should not have been a participant in the battle of the Washita and was there only through courtesy, as I shall explain. When it was decided to abandon our wagon train, it became necessary to detail an officer to remain with it, and Colonel Custer well knew there was not an officer of the regiment who would be left behind if he could avoid it, so realizing the futility of calling for a volunteer for this duty, he very naturally decided that the officer of the day and his guard, with an additional detail, should remain with the wagons. When the adjutant, Lieutenant Moylan, communicated this order to Captain Hamilton, who happened to be officer of the day, it simply crushed him. He was in command of the squadron composed of A and D Troops, and the thought of it going into action without him was a blow to his soldierly pride and sensitiveness that almost stunned him, so he hastened to Colonel Custer and made such a strong and manly appeal to be permitted to lead his squadron that the colonel acquiesced, provided he could find another officer willing to take his place. As these were the best terms he could make, he hurried off to Lieutenant Mathey, who he remembered was suffering from snow blindness, and pleaded and reasoned with him until Mathey very unwillingly, and entirely out of consideration and respect for Hamilton, consented to relieve him as officer of the day and take charge of the wagon train. Thus Hamilton, through the courtesy and kindness of a brother officer, rode to his death.

Both Elliott and Hamilton were able and gallant officers, devoted to their profession, and zealous and thorough in discharging every duty devolving upon them. Captain Barnitz, who it was supposed had received a fatal shot, dispatched two warriors before he fell and bravely killed the buck who so seriously wounded him. He was later retired from active service in consequence of the disabling effects of that wound.

It was originally intended in narrating this story to depict at some length the special part played by each of the different columns in this engagement, and to describe some of the many personal encounters that took place, wherein great courage on the part of both friend and foe were conspicuously displayed, but so many years have rolled by since then that it is impossible now to collect the data necessary to a faithful account of such details; besides, after the columns had converged upon and charged into the village, they were all confronted by the same elements of danger, and all called upon to face the same peril, and therefore, the conditions being identical in all parts of the field, there was nothing to distinguish the success and good fighting qualities of one column from those of another, and where all did so well, comparison would not only be odious but unjust.

One incident of courage and coolness on the one side, pluck and impudence on the other, of which Colonel Custer speaks in his book is, I think, well worthy of repetition here. He says, in effect, that Captain Benteen, while leading his squadron to the attack, encountered an Indian boy, well mounted and about fourteen years of age, who rode toward him in a very threatening manner and, drawing a revolver, fired twice at him. Benteen, on account of the boy's youth, was disposed to regard him as a noncombatant and made signs of peace, but these were rejected with scorn, and the plucky little fellow dashed at Benteen's horse. After this, Captain Benteen made a final appeal to the youngster to surrender, but seeing him draw a second revolver, he was forced in self-defense to dispatch him.

The opportune arrival of the regimental quartermaster, Bvt. Maj. J. M. Bell, with two or three wagons and an abundant supply of ammunition is worthy, I think, of further mention. He was not expected to come to the battlefield, but he boldly pushed on to it, thinking that an additional supply of ammunition, which he had thoughtfully collected, might be useful, and he reckoned wisely; and luckily for himself and us, he reached us in the nick of time, for had he delayed a few moments longer, he would have been effectually cut off by the hordes of Indians who took possession of the surrounding hills, and doubtless he and his little escort would have met the fate of Elliott and his party; as it was, he had to fight his way through the timber skirting the Washita River and had a number of mules killed before he reached us.

From the camp where we resumed our wagon train, Colonel Custer forwarded his report of the fight to General Sheridan at Camp Supply; this he entrusted to two scouts who had repeatedly shown their worth and reliability since our departure from Camp Supply, California Joe and Jack Corbin. This mission necessitated a ride of some sixty miles through the heart of a hostile country, but the risk and danger it entailed made the journey a pleasure, rather than a duty, to these two plainsmen.

In concluding this story, which is much longer than intended, and yet largely abbreviated, it only remains to mention briefly some of the good results of the labors of the troops during the trying winter of 1868–69. The 7th Cavalry, in the first place, destroyed a band of notoriously hostile Indians, and with them all their property, as has already been told. It kept the other hostile tribes of that section constantly moving from place to place with their entire possessions and in a state of trepidation and uncertainty all winter long, and thus, through the discomforts, exposure, and suffering to which the warriors and their families were incessantly subjected, several of the bands were forced to sue for peace.

The campaign also resulted in bringing to the border settlers who had suffered incalculable misery at the hands of the savages, an era of comparative peace such as had never existed before. But the crowning achievement of the troops, and the one which was the most gratifying to the 7th Cavalry, was the rescue from the Cheyennes of the two white women whom they had held captive for many months. The joy of those women at their deliverance was boundless, but the story of their cruel captivity was too full of horror to relate, and their return to their homes from which they had been ruthlessly torn was as speedy as it was possible to make it.

The Washita campaign was a success from start to finish, and if the writer has been fortunate enough in his portrayal of its main features to make it even momentarily interesting to the reader, he will be amply rewarded for his effort.

Battle of Washita

CHARLES BREWSTER[1]

National Tribune, May 18, 1899

I n the autumn of 1868, General Sheridan, commanding the Department of
the Missouri, planned a winter campaign against the refractory and troublesome Indians of the plains. The state of Kansas raised the 19th Kansas Volunteer Cavalry, which was accepted by the government. With it, the 7th U.S.
Cavalry, and a few companies of infantry was formed the command which
started from Fort Hays and Fort Dodge, Kansas, in September of that year. A
number of scouts from friendly Indian tribes accompanied us. A large wagon
train carried supplies and equipage. Marching to the wilds of the Southwest,
the appearance of the command was quite imposing and was somewhat magnified by the wind, which constantly kept a cloud of dust above the column.

Whoever has route-marched with cavalry knows of the diversions that
troopers find to while away the time, when stories, songs, jokes, and conun-
drums are all in order.

On the first day out from Fort Dodge, while riding up along the column at
a slightly more rapid gait than it marched, my attention was directed, while
within hearing distance, to the musical voice—softened by the wind—of a
trooper, whose song and refrain was a paraphrase of "Out of the Wilderness,"
as follows:

> *If you want to smell hell, then join the cavalry, join the cavalry;*
> *Oh, if you want to smell hell, just join the cavalry, join the cavalry,*
> *for we are not going home.*

Lt. Col. Alfred Sully was in command of the expedition. The hostile Indians gyrated about us on their ponies at a safe distance on either side of the
moving column. For days they kept up a skirmish, galloping in circles around
us, hanging on the safe side of their ponies and firing under their necks. We
continued our march, paying but little attention to them, but once in a while a
few would feel emboldened and circle near enough to draw some of the troop-

ers' fire and get knocked out of the saddle or have a pony killed, in which case the mounted Indian nearest to the unfortunate rode rapidly to the dismounted Indian, who instantly sprang up behind his succor, when both would urge and belabor the pony.

We finally reached a spot which was selected for the post of Camp Supply, which was afterward Fort Supply. Here the Indians made a stand among the sand hills on the south side of the stream, but became discouraged and withdrew as evening approached. At this point, Colonel Custer arrived and succeeded to the command.

The 7th Cavalry, in light marching order, was soon thereafter started southward in quest of Indians. A fall of snow one night and a warm sun the following day aided the alert scouts in the trailing of a number of mounted hostiles returning to their tribes and families in their intended winter home on the Washita River. These scouts which accompanied the command belonged to the Osage and Delaware tribes and were partly civilized, yet with enough native instinct to enjoy the warpath and scalp-lifting privilege, abundant food, and authority to seize all hostiles' property. At night their tents were separated a little from the main camp, and the monotonous sound of beating the tom-tom was heard at all hours.

The day on which the hostiles' trail was struck was made about noon.[2] An officer with a detachment was designated to remain with the wagons, and we soon moved on, leaving, by orders, all sabers and all dogs behind. The trail in the snow was about twenty-four hours old and easy to follow.

A rapid march was kept up until about 5:30 P.M., when we halted in the timbered valley of the Washita to take coffee and food and to feed the horses. Here Colonel Custer announced that the troop which should report first as ready to move would be accorded the right of the line—the head of the column. This was an incentive for all to be expeditious during the halt for refreshments, and it was not very long before Colonel Custer showed surprise, while eating with his brother Thomas and Adjutant Cooke, when the officer commanding Troop I[3] reported it ready to move. Soon the march was resumed.

A little before dark, silence was enjoined, and there was no talking above a whisper. Seen from an elevation as night approached, what a weird, serpentine specter was this body, outlined upon the white snow. As it wound around the tortuous valley, it had the semblance of a huge reptile, stealthily creeping to destroy its victim or foe. The silence was oppressive. Even the horses, by their rapid gait, showed that they, too, nervously partook of the quiet excitement and were imbued with the portent of some anticipated event. It was an experience long to be remembered. The colder atmosphere of the evening made the snow firmer. The moon was not quite visible, as the sky was overcast with fleecy clouds.

About 11:00 P.M. the column's gait was slackened and moved very slowly, and finally halted with its head at the base of a hill. The adjutant rode down the line and gave the order silently to the troop commanders to dismount, and for all officers to walk forward quietly to the crest of the hill and join Colonel Custer, whom we found lying upon the crust-covered snow near the ridge.

The Indian scouts—always a few miles in advance—had kept Colonel Custer advised of every sign of proximity to the hostiles' camp, and we had already passed two smoldering fires made by Indian boys while herding ponies during the previous day.

After we assembled where Colonel Custer lay prostrate, peering over the top of the hill with a field or marine glass, he called our attention to an occasional faint tinkling sound like that of a bell upon some animals, also to the sound of a barking dog. It was finally discovered that we were close to the upper end of the camp of Black Kettle's band. The other bands were successively camped down along the valley and stream in the woods, although we could then see but little more than the general contour of the valley. It is remembered that while waiting here, Lt. Edward Law, while conversing upon the possibilities of the next few hours, reached out his hand to the writer and said, "Well, let us shake hands, and it will be good-bye if we don't meet again." This was declined as being too much preparation for an undesired end.

Colonel Custer indicated to us his plan of attack, which was by squadron from the other side of the camp. Crouching there upon the snow, in the dim light, with that group of fellow officers, this thought came to me: "How many of us will be together tomorrow evening? Probably some of us will be no more. Is it the last time we are all to meet?" Finally, evidences of approaching day became visible, and each squadron moved slowly and quietly to its appointed place of attack.

At last, with earliest light of morning, there resounded, echoed, and re-echoed over the valley the bugle call of the "Charge," and we braced ourselves in the saddles for the conflict.

We were now to avenge the slaughter of the poor, helpless settlers of the Republican, Solomon, and Saline Rivers and the scattered laborers on railroad construction far to the north.

Soon the muffled sound of cavalry horses' feet was heard, and it increased to a subdued roar, then instantly came the rapid discharge of arms. Fleeing from their lodges, tepees, and fighting as they fled from successive covers of knoll, bush, brush, ravine, and riverbank were the retreating Indians, pursued and falling. Amid the din was heard the mounted regimental band playing Colonel Custer's favorite battle tune, "Garry Owen."

The Indian boys and squaws fought as fiercely as did the bucks. They promptly killed all white prisoners. During the battle, one squaw was seen to kill a young white child by ripping open its abdomen.[4] Another white infant was found mangled beside its dead captive mother with bullet holes in her head.[5] It was a pathetic sight, which told of revengeful squaws.

With the first rush of the charge, Chief Black Kettle sprang out from his lodge and shouted loudly to his people, reproaching them for disregarding his warnings in the past, that the whites were now upon them and that he was glad—then he fell with a bullet through his heart. He was not a bad Indian, but he could not control his warriors. Down through the valley for many miles the camps extended, consisting of a number of tribes and bands, and as they heard and learned of the progressing battle, they hastily mounted ponies and hurried toward the fray, continuously keeping along the hilltops, where they swarmed until the fight was over. But many had no pony to mount, because of Custer's precaution to have them surrounded and herded by soldiers. They remained there to witness the destruction of hundreds of ponies, horses, mules, tepees, buffalo robes, dried meat, and a large amount of general plunder.

The Indian tribes which were scattered through the valley were the Arapahos, Kiowas, Cheyennes, Comanches, and some [Kiowa-]Apaches. Colonel Custer's official report gave the number killed as 103, the number of prisoners taken 53, including squaws and children. We captured 875 ponies, 1,123 buffalo robes and skins, 535 pounds of powder, 1,030 pounds of lead, 4,000 arrows, 700 pounds of tobacco, an immense amount of dried meat, thousands of lodge poles, and an endless number of cooking utensils.

The number of officers killed was two, and three were wounded. Twenty-one enlisted men were killed, and eleven wounded. That night the moon shone down upon the bodies of many who had not yet been found upon the battlefield.

Capt. Louis Hamilton, a grandson of Alexander Hamilton, was killed in the first charge. He was the officer detailed to remain with the wagons and supplies when the Indian trail was first struck, but his brave, restless spirit drooped at the thought of remaining away from an open engagement of his regiment, and he persuaded Lieutenant Mathey to serve as his substitute, which he did with the consent of Colonel Custer. Before the close of the War of the Rebellion, the sentiment became prevalent in the Union army that an officer did his duty sufficiently who served when and where ordered, instead of volunteering, whereby many lost their lives. But for this brave act, Captain Hamilton would perhaps be living today.

Lieutenants Custer and March were slightly wounded. Major Elliott and the sergeant major, with nineteen men who had become separated and cut off from the majority during the fight, were surrounded and killed by the Indians after a most desperate fight, their plight not being discovered by others of the command. Captain Barnitz was shot through the body and his death was expected, but he lived. A silk handkerchief was drawn through his body where the bullet made an opening or orifice.

The Indian War—
Battle of the Washita—
Report of General Custer

GEORGE A. CUSTER[1]

Army and Navy Journal, December 12, 1868

HEADQUARTERS, 7TH U.S. CAVALRY,
IN THE FIELD, ON THE WASHITA RIVER,
November 28, 1868

Maj. Gen. P. H. Sheridan, commanding Department of the Missouri.

GENERAL: On the morning of the twenty-sixth inst., this command, comprising eleven troops of the 7th Cavalry, struck the trail of an Indian war party numbering about one hundred warriors. The trail was not quite twenty-four hours old and was first discovered near the point where the Texas boundary line crosses the Canadian River. The direction was toward the southeast. The ground being covered by over twelve inches of snow, no difficulty was experienced in following the trail.

A vigorous pursuit was at once instituted. Wagons, tents, and all other impediments to a rapid march were abandoned. From daylight until 9:00 P.M., the pursuit was unchecked. Horses and men were then allowed one hour for refreshment, and at 10:00 P.M. the march was resumed and continued until 1:30 A.M., when our Osage trailers reported a village within less than a mile from our advance. The column was countermarched and withdrawn to a retired point to prevent discovery.

After reconnoitering with all the officers of the command the location of the village, which was situated in a strip of heavy timber, I divided the command into four columns of nearly equal strength: The first, consisting of three companies under Major Elliott, was to attack in the timber from below the village; the second column, under [Brevet] Lieutenant Colonel Myers, was to move down the Washita and attack in the timber from above; Brevet Colonel Thompson, in command of the third column, was to attack from the crest north of the village; while the fourth column was to charge the village from the crest overlooking it, on the left bank of the Washita. The hour at

The battle for the Washita. CHARLES J. BRILL, *CONQUEST OF THE SOUTHERN PLAINS.*

which the four columns were to charge simultaneously was the first
dawn of day, and notwithstanding the fact that two of the columns
were compelled to march several miles to reach their positions, three
of them made the attack so near together as to make it appear like one
charge. The other column was only a few moments late.

There was never a more complete surprise. My men charged the
village and reached the lodges before the Indians were aware of our
presence. The moment the charge was ordered, the band struck up
"Garry Owen," and with cheers that strongly reminded me of scenes
during the war, every trooper, led by his officer, rushed toward the
village.

The warriors were caught napping for once, and the warriors
rushed from their lodges and posted themselves behind trees and in
the deep ravines, from which they began a most determined defense.
The lodges and all their contents were in our possession within a few
minutes after the charge was ordered. But the real fighting, such as
has rarely if ever been equaled in Indian warfare, began when
attempting to clear out or kill the warriors posted in ravines or
underbrush. Charge after charge was made, and most gallantly too,
but the Indians had resolved to sell their lives [as] dearly as possible.
After a desperate conflict of several hours, our efforts were crowned
with the most complete and gratifying success. The entire village,
numbering forty-seven lodges of Black Kettle's band of Cheyennes,
two lodges of Arapahos, and two lodges of Sioux—fifty-one lodges

in all, under the command of their principal chief, Black Kettle—fell into our hands.

By a strict and careful examination after the battle, the following figures give some of the fruits of our victory: The Indians left on the ground and in our possession the bodies of 103 of their warriors, including Black Kettle himself, whose scalp is now in possession of one of our Osage guides.[2] We captured in good condition 875 horses, ponies, and mules; 241 saddles, some of very fine and costly work-manship; 523 buffalo robes, 210 axes, 140 hatchets, 35 revolvers, 47 rifles, 535 pounds of powder, 1,050 pounds of lead, 4,000 arrows, 90 bullet molds, 35 bows and quivers, 12 shields, 300 pounds of bullets, 775 lariats, 940 buckskin saddlebags, 470 blankets, 93 coats, [and] 700 pounds of tobacco. In addition, we captured all their winter sup-ply of dry buffalo meat, all their meal flour, and other provisions, and in fact everything they possessed, even driving the warriors from the village with little or no clothing. We destroyed everything of value to the Indians and have now in our possession as prisoners of war fifty-three squaws and their children. Among the prisoners are the sur-vivors of Black Kettle and the family of Little Rock.

We also secured two white children held captive by the Indians. One white woman who was in their possession was murdered by her captors the moment we attacked.[3] A white boy held captive, about ten years old, when about to be secured, was brutally murdered by a squaw, who ripped out his entrails with a knife.[4]

The Kiowas under Satanta and Arapahos under Little Raven were encamped six miles below Black Kettle's village, and the warriors from these two villages came to attempt the rescue of the Cheyennes. They attacked my command from all sides about noon, hoping to recover the squaws and herds of the Cheyennes. In their attack, they displayed great boldness and compelled me to use all my force to repel them, but the countercharge of the cavalry was more than they could stand; by 3:00 P.M. we drove them in all direc-tions, pursuing them several miles. I then moved my entire com-mand in search of the village of the Kiowas and Arapahos, but after a march of eight miles discovered they had taken alarm at the fate of the Cheyenne village and had fled.

It was then three days' march from where I had left my train of supplies, and [I] knew that wagons could not follow me, as the trail had led me over a section of country so cut up by ravines and other obstructions that cavalry could with difficulty move over it. The sup-plies carried from the train on the persons of the men were exhausted. My men, from loss of sleep and hard service, were wea-ried out; my horses were in the same condition for want of forage. I therefore began my return march about 8:00 P.M. and found my train of supplies at this point (it having accomplished only sixteen miles since I left it). In the excitement of the fight, as well as in self-defense, it so happened that some of the squaws and a few children were killed and wounded. The latter I have brought with me, and they received all the needed attention the circumstances of the case permit. Many of the squaws were taken with arms in their hands, and several of my command are known to have been wounded by them. The desperate character of the combat may be inferred from the fact that after the battle, the bodies of thirty-eight dead warriors were found in a small ravine near the village in which they had posted themselves.

I have now to report the loss suffered by my own command. I regret to mention among the killed Maj. Joel H. Elliott and Capt. Louis M. Hamilton, and nineteen enlisted men; [the] wounded includes three officers and eleven enlisted men, in all thirty-five men. Of the officers, Bvt. Lt. Col. Albert Barnitz, captain 7th Cavalry, is seriously if not mortally wounded. Bvt. Lt. Col. T. W. Custer and 2nd Lt. T. J. March are slightly wounded. Bvt. Lt. Col. F. W. Benteen had his horse shot under him by a son of Black Kettle, whom he afterward killed. [Brevet Lieutenant] Colonel Barnitz, before receiving his wound, killed two warriors.

I cannot sufficiently commend the admirable conduct of the officers and men. This command had marched constantly five days amid terrible snowstorms and over a rough country covered by more than twelve inches of snow. Officers and men have slept in the snow without tents. The night preceding the attack, officers and men stood at their horses' heads for hours, awaiting the moment of attack, and this too when the temperature was far below the freezing point. They have endured every privation and fought with unsurpassed gallantry against a powerful and well-armed foe, and from first to last I have not heard a single murmur; but on the contrary, the officers and men of the several squadrons and companies seemed to vie with each other in their attention to duty and their patience and perseverance under difficulties. Every officer, man, scout, and Indian guide did their full duty. I only regret the loss of the gallant spirits who fell in the "battle of the Washita." Those whose loss we are called upon to deplore were among our bravest and best.

Respectfully subscribed,

G. A. CUSTER,
Lieutenant Colonel 7th Cavalry,
Brevet Major General U.S. Army.

She-Wolf's Account of
the Death of Major Elliot

GEORGE BENT[1]

Collections of the Kansas State Historical Society 10 (1907–8): 441–42

T he following letter was written to Robert M. Peck of Whittier, California,
who favored the Kansas Historical Society with this copy. Mr. Bent has
been invited by this society to write a statement of the Indian side of the con-
troversies happening in Kansas. She-Wolf's account of the death of Maj. Joel
H. Elliott, as told to George Bent, is as follows:

> Your letter of December 7 received. First I will tell you what
> Cheyennes say about killing of Major Elliott and his men at the bat-
> tle of Washita.
> She-Wolf, Cheyenne Indian, Little Rock, Cheyenne, and a Kiowa
> Indian were running down Washita River with squaws and children
> after Custer's attack on Black Kettle's village. She-Wolf, who is here
> now living, tells me this. He says they all came to a very deep hole
> of water, and high banks on each side of it, so they all had to get out
> of the creek bottom into an open place to get around this deep hole.
> Soon as they came up in open view, Elliott and his men seen them
> and charged towards them. Little Rock told the squaws and children
> to fight for them. Elliott and his men charged upon them and com-
> menced firing into them. Here Little Rock was killed. The Kiowa
> Indian, now living, ran to Little Rock and picked up his arrows (this
> Kiowa only had two arrows left); he picked up six arrows of Little
> Rock. Understand, these people were running from Black Kettle's
> camp or village. A Cheyenne woman called White-Buffalo-Woman,
> now living with her sister, had been running so long [that] the girl
> gave out here. One soldier rode up to them and made motion to them
> to walk back towards the camp. The soldier got off his horse and
> walked behind them. Just in front of them, a lot of warriors running
> from Black Kettle's village rode up out of the creek timber. The sol-
> dier fired at the Indians as they were charging toward [him]. This
> soldier, White-Buffalo-Woman says, shot at the warriors two times

and then got a cartridge fast in his carbine. Bob-Tail-Bear rode up to the soldier and tomahawked him.

Elliott and his men were still chasing She-Wolf and the women and children down Washita River when these warriors cut him off from Custer. Bob-Tail-Bear and his warriors pushed Elliott and his men right into a lot of warriors that were coming up from the big village of Cheyennes and Arapahos. When Elliott saw he was surrounded, they turned all their horses loose, then himself and his men got in among high grass and were all lying down when the Indians rode around them. Touching-the-Sky tells me he got off his horse and crawled up towards them in small ravine and could see them lying down. When he motioned to Indians to bring their guns, he says several came running, stooping down. These opened fire on Elliott and his men and must have hit several of them, as it was very close. Those Indians on horses commenced to close in on Elliott, and those in the ravine kept shooting at [him]. In a little while, Roman-Nose-Thunder, Cheyenne, now living, was first to ride over Elliott and his men. Then the Indians all made charge on them. Elliott and his men did not do much shooting for some reason, and Elliott and his men were all killed inside of two hours. She-Wolf and squaws then went to where Elliott and his men were killed. They had stopped in the creek soon to rest up as Elliott had left them. The warriors, after killing Elliott and his men, went on up to where Custer's command was and fought him again.

Ben Clark, now interpreter at Fort Reno, was with Custer at the battle of Washita. He told me that Custer's officers told him that Custer ordered Major Elliott to take some of his men and drive those Indians out of the creek [Washita] that were firing at his men. Only one Indian was killed in this fight with Elliott; several were wounded. Black Kettle's village was further up Washita River. Other villages were down the river. Indians in these villages heard the firing, so the men ran for their herds of ponies and ran them into the villages. Meantime, Indians from Black Kettle's village began to come to the first village next to Black Kettle's village. Of course, they told what took place. Most all women got on horses and carried the news to other villages. All the men, fast as they got on their warhorses, rode for the battlefield. They met men and women and children of those that had got away. She-Wolf and Little Rock's party were the last ones coming down from the creek, and Elliott and his men lost their lives by following them too far down.

I knew Major Elliott and Captain Hamilton. Hamilton was also killed in Black Kettle's fight. I met both these officers in 1867, at the treaty in Medicine Lodge Creek. They were there with four companies to guard the annuity goods. Fourteen months afterwards, they were both killed. I was camped south side of Medicine Lodge Creek at that time. They were on the north side. Both these officers and Doctor Renick,[2] whom I went to school with in St. Louis, used to come over to my lodge every day and smoke with Black Kettle. I was then married to Black Kettle's stepdaughter. She died some years ago. I suppose you saw my picture in the *Frontier Magazine*. She had elk-teeth dress on.

Ben Clark told me that at the Black Kettle fight, a Mexican that used to live with my father came up with a little girl in his arms to give her to someone to save. A sergeant took the little girl, then told the Mexican to run, then shot him in the back as he ran. Ben Clark says this was a cowardly act. He said he would have stopped this or else had a fuss over it, but did not see it done. He was told of it by teamsters or packers. Ben Clark has an Indian wife and has a large family of half-breeds.

Respectfully,

GEO. BENT

To ROBERT M. PECK, Whittier, California

Another Side of the Washita Story

FREDERICK W. BENTEEN[1]

(St. Louis) *Missouri Democrat,* February 8, 1869[2]

Fort Cobb, Indian Territory, December 22, 1868

My Dear Friend:

I wrote to you from Camp Supply, which place was left on the seventh, arriving at this post on the evening of the eighteenth. On the eleventh we camped within a few miles of our "battle of the Washita," and Generals Sheridan and Custer, with a detail of 100 men, mounted as escort, went out with the view of searching for the bodies of our nineteen missing comrades, including Major Elliott.

The bodies were found in a small circle, stripped as naked as when born, and frozen stiff. Their heads had been battered in, and some of them had had the Adam's apple cut out of their throats; some had their hands and feet cut off, and nearly all were mangled in a way delicacy forbids me to mention. They lay scarcely two miles from the scene of the fight, and all we know of the manner they were killed we have learned from Indian sources. It seems that Major Elliott's party was pursuing a well-mounted party of Cheyennes in the direction of the Grand Village, where nearly all the tribes were encamped, and were surrounded by the reinforcements coming to the rescue of the pursued, before the major was aware of their position. They were out of sight and hearing of the 7th Cavalry, which had remained at and around the captured village, about two miles away. As soon as Major Elliott found that he was surrounded, he caused his men to dismount and did some execution among the Indians, which added to the mortification they must have felt at the loss of the village and herds of their friends and allies, and enraged them so that they determined upon the destruction of the entire little band.

Who can describe the feeling of that brave band, as with anxious, beating hearts they strained their yearning eyes in the direction whence help should come? What must have been the despair that, when all hopes of succor died out, nerved their stout arms to do or

die? Round and round rush the red fiends, smaller and smaller
shrinks the circle, but the aim of that devoted, gallant knot of heroes
is steadier than ever, and the death howl of the murderous redskin is
more frequent. But on they come in masses grim, with glittering
lance and one long, loud, exulting whoop, as if the gates of hell had
opened and loosened the whole infernal host. A well-directed volley
from their trusty carbines makes some of the miscreants reel and
fall, but their death rattles are drowned in the greater din. Soon every
voice in that little band is still as death; but the hellish work of the
savages is scarcely begun, and their ingenuities are taxed to invent
barbarities to practice on the bodies of the fallen brave, the relation
of which is scarcely necessary to the completion of this tale.

And now, to learn why the anxiously looked for succor did not
come, let us view the scene in the captured village, scarce two short
miles away. Light skirmishing is going on all around. Savages on
flying steeds, with shields and feathers gay, are circling everywhere,
riding like devils incarnate. The troops are on all sides of the village,
looking on and seizing every opportunity of picking off those daring
riders with their carbines. But does no one think of the welfare of
Major Elliott and party? It seems not. But yes, a squadron of cavalry
is in motion. They trot; they gallop. Now they charge! The cowardly
redskins flee the coming shock and scatter here and there among the
hills [to] scurry away. But it is the true line—will the cavalry keep
it? No! no! They turn! Ah, 'tis only to intercept the wily foe. See! a
gray troop goes on in the direction again. One more short mile, and
they will be saved. Oh, for a mother's prayers! Will not some good
angel prompt them? They charge the mound—a few scattering shots,
and the murderous pirates of the plains go unhurt away. There is no
hope for that brave little band, the death doom is theirs, for the cavalry halt and rest their panting steeds.

And now return with me to the village. Officers and soldiers are
watching, resting, eating, and sleeping. In an hour or so they will be
refreshed, and then scour the hills and plains for their missing comrades. The commander occupies himself taking an inventory of the
captured property, which he had promised the officers shall be distributed among the enlisted men of the command if they falter or
halt not in the charge.

The day is drawing to a close, and but little has been done save
the work of the first hour. A great deal remains to be done. That
which cannot be taken away must be destroyed. Eight hundred
ponies are to be put to death. Our chief exhibits his close sharp-
shooting and terrifies the crowd of frightened, captured squaws and
papooses by dropping the straggling ponies in death near them. Ah!
he is a clever marksman. Not even do the poor dogs of the Indians

escape his eye and aim as they drop or limp howling away. But are not those our men on guard on the other side of the creek? Will he not hit them? "My troop is on guard, general, just over there," says an officer. "Well, bullets will not go through and around hills, and you see there is a hill between us," was the reply, and the exhibition goes on. No one will come that way intentionally—certainly not. Now commences the slaughter of the ponies. Volley on volley is poured into them by too hasty men, and they, limping, get away only to meet death from a surer hand. The work progresses! The plunder, having been culled over, is hastily piled; the wigwams are pulled down and thrown on it, and soon the whole of it is one blazing mass. Occasionally a startling report is heard, and a steamlike volume of smoke ascends as the fire reaches a powder bag, and thus the glorious deeds of valor done in the morning are celebrated by the flaming bonfire of the afternoon. The last pony is killed. The huge fire dies out; our wounded and dead comrades—heroes of a bloody day—are carefully laid on ready ambulances, and as the brave band of the 7th Cavalry strikes up the air "Ain't I Glad I've Got Out of the Wilderness," we slowly pick our way across the creek over which we charged so gallantly in the early morn. Take care! Do not trample on the dead bodies of that woman and child lying there! In a short time, we shall be far from the scene of our daring dash, and night will have thrown her dark mantle over the scene. But surely some search will be made for our missing comrades. No, they are forgotten. Over them and the poor ponies, the wolves will hold high carnival, and their howling will be their only requiem. Slowly trudging, we return to our train some twenty miles away and, with bold, exulting hearts, learn from one another how many dead Indians have been seen.

Two weeks elapse—a larger force returns that way. A search is made, and the bodies are found strewn round that little circle, frozen stiff and hard. Who shall write their eulogy?

This, my dear friend, is the story of the "battle of the Washita," poorly told.

Colonel Evans's Indian Expedition

[EDWARD HUNTER][1]

Army and Navy Journal 6, no. 20 (March 13, 1869): 470

To the Editor of the Army and Navy Journal,

SIR: I send for publication a brief account of the march and operations of an expedition fitted out at Fort Bascom in November last and intended to operate down the Canadian River against hostile Kiowa and Comanche Indians.

The expedition organized as follows: Maj. A. W. Evans, 3rd Cavalry, brevet lieutenant colonel U.S. Army, commanding; 1st Lt. Edward Hunter, 12th Infantry, acting assistant adjutant general District of New Mexico, adjutant; 2nd Lt. A. A. Von Luettwitz, 3rd Cavalry, acting assistant quartermaster and assistant commissary of subsistence; Acting Assistant Surgeon L. H. Longwill, medical officer; Company A, 3rd Cavalry, Capt. [William] Hawley; Company C, 3rd Cavalry, Capt. [William J.] Cain; Company D, 3rd Cavalry, Lt. [Samuel] Hildeburn; Company F, 3rd Cavalry, Capt. [Howard B.] Cushing; Company G, 3rd Cavalry, Capt. [Deane] Monahan and Lt. [Lambert L.] Mulford; Company I, 3rd Cavalry, Bvt. Maj. [Elisha] Tarlton and Lt. [Albert D.] King; Company I, 37th Infantry, Capt. [James H.] Gageby and Lt. [George W.] Baird; and a battery of mountain howitzers, Lt. J. K. Sullivan.

The expedition left Fort Bascom, New Mexico, November 18 [1868], and proceeding down the Canadian on its north bank, established, December 7, a depot of supplies on Monument Creek, Texas—a point 185 miles below Fort Bascom, where a small redoubt was constructed, well arranged for defense, upon a strong natural site in close proximity to wood and water. From this depot, December 18, Major Evans cut loose without tents and with but three wagons, which he was forced to take along to carry his ammunition. He marched his command forty-two miles down the river, where a trail was struck, made by a village of Cheyennes moving from the north. Here the Canadian was crossed, and this trail followed to a point thirteen miles south of the western edge of the Washita Mountains, where, not being able to find water,[2] a detour was made to the east and north, and a dry camp made near the mountains, where was spent a Christmas Eve that will not soon be forgotten.

The next morning, Christmas, in snow and in the face of an intensely cold north wind, Major Evans started to move his command to a stream which was known to flow through these mountains, at the same time sending out scouts to see if there were any fresh signs of Indians. A scout returned and reported that he had seen and talked with two Indians. Major Evans at once detached Captain Tarlton[3] and company with instructions to pursue and capture those Indians, and with the rest of his command, moved on to make a camp.

Captain Tarlton had not gone far when he engaged a considerable band of Comanches at the mouth of a canyon, the passage of which they tried hard to prevent, and he, not having men enough to dislodge them, sent back for reinforcements. Two companies of cavalry and two mountain howitzers were sent up,[4] and the Indians pushed back on their village, from which they fled, going off two and three on a horse, when two shells from a little mountain howitzer burst in their midst. They left in our hands sixty lodges containing dried buffalo meat, corn, flour, tobacco, coffee, sugar, salt, axes, hammers, hatchets, knives, powder, lead, bullet molds, saddles, lariats, bows and arrows, and some very fine arms; also a great many buffalo robes and, as General Sheridan telegraphed, "all the paraphernalia of a rich Indian camp." Major Evans, coming up with the rest of his command, burned the village and pursued the Indians until dark, some of them galloping off in the direction of Fort Cobb, and others to the west toward the Staked Plains.

The general direction of large trails in this vicinity, and the course the Indian runners took during the fight, indicated plainly that Indians in considerable numbers were located in the canyons at the eastern border of the Staked Plains. It was Major Evans's desire to go after them there and punish them, but he had now marched his command 180 miles from his depot without forage, over a country whose grass the Indians had destroyed with fire; there were but few rations left, and his orders read for him to go down the Canadian as far as possible. So it was determined, in the absence of any information that there were troops so far south as the Canadian River, to push northwest to [the] Antelope Hills, which brought us on December 28 to the Washita River, and within twenty miles of Fort Cobb.

In the meantime, the Indians whose village was destroyed[5] had a part of them gone to Fort Cobb and reported that their lodges had been burned, their chief shot, and their stock killed or scattered over the country by Texans, who were some on foot and others mounted and driving cattle (having reference to our fresh beef that was driven along on the hoof). General Sheridan, upon their report, sent out four scouts, two whites and two friendly Indians, in the direction of the Washita Mountains, with orders to take our trail and find out what troops we were. As these men had no papers, they found it difficult to get into our lines, and the two Indians told at Cobb the next day that every man they saw had it in his face to kill them.

The writer, with these scouts and a few men, started on the evening of December 29 to Fort Cobb[6] but, getting lost, was obliged to pass a rainy night

The last trip in. CENTURY MAGAZINE 1891.

on the prairie and did not reach Cobb until noon of the next day. General Sheridan was happy to hear that it was the little column from New Mexico that had traveled so far and dealt so severe a blow to a notoriously bad and desperate band of Indians.

That night the Cheyennes and Arapahos sent their women in with a bragging message that they would be in in the morning, prepared to make a treaty or to fight. They came (twenty of them) on foot, but when they saw the soldier they had to deal with was no treaty man, the fight was out of them; they surrendered their tribes unconditionally and simply asked for a paper to protect them from the troops.

This surrender without any condition, and complete demoralization of the last of the hostile tribes,[7] rendered further military operations unnecessary, and Major Evans was informed that he could go back to his depot, where he arrived January 13 with almost his entire command on foot, so great had been the strain on his animals. Twenty-nine days was the time consumed in this scout, and nearly four hundred miles the distance traveled.

When General Sheridan entered upon this winter campaign, I suppose there were many doubts and misgivings in the minds of most people as to what would be accomplished, but I can assure your readers that these Indians are badly whipped and, I believe, ready to submit to whatever punishment or policy may be decided upon. I do not say that they have received or that they will receive a just measure of punishment, but I do believe, if General Sheridan is let alone, we will have a peace that will last longer than a single summer.

SANTA FE, N.M., Feb. 12, 1869

The Story of an Indian Campaign: Carr's Republican River Expedition of 1869

EDWARD M. HAYES[1]

Order of the Indian Wars Collection, U.S. Army Military History Institute, Carlisle Barracks, Pennsylvania

Early in October 1868, seven troops of the 5th Cavalry, under command of Maj. W. B. Royall,[2] left Fort Hays, Kansas, on a campaign against Roman Nose's band of Cheyenne Indians, who were supposed to be on Beaver Creek, a tributary of the Republican River, northwest of Fort Hays.

This campaign was bare of results, but later the same command under [Bvt. Maj.] Gen. E. A. Carr, who relieved Major Royall in command, was very successful.[3] I was at that time quartermaster of the expedition and had a wagon train of about seventy-six mule teams and a half dozen ambulances under my charge. The trail covered was partly over the same ground as the first expedition, but more directly toward the headwaters of Beaver Creek, as Major Carr had information that the Indians were located in that vicinity.

Orders were given for forced marches, and on the third or fourth day out,[4] late in the afternoon, my wagon train, which was about three miles in the rear of the column of cavalry, owing to its inability to keep up on account of inexperienced teamsters and the poor condition of the mules, was suddenly attacked by a band of three or four hundred warriors, who had apparently risen, as by magic, from the prairie and formed line on a slight ridge bordering on a small stream, and in a perfectly open country about three-quarters of a mile from the train.

The wagon train was in two columns, about one hundred yards apart, and somewhat lengthened out on account of the rapid gait and poor condition of the mules, but the sight of the Indians had a startling effect, and the straggling wagons closed up almost at a run.

The Indians presented a gorgeous spectacle, with their war bonnets, arms, and so forth glistening in the blinding rays of the setting sun. This impressive sight was only momentary, when the larger part of the Indians, composed of young warriors, I suppose, dashed forward to the charge, the others remaining apparently as a support to their charging brothers. The time given, however, was sufficient to get the train and guard in position to meet the attack. Two scouts were sent forward on the run to notify Major Carr of the condition of

A Cheyenne medicine man.
CYRUS T. BRADY, *INDIAN FIGHTS AND FIGHTERS.*

affairs, and succeeded in reaching him. The escort of the train, including con-
valescents, numbered about forty men and was divided into advance, rear
guard, and flankers, covering the open space between the columns of wagons,
front and rear of the teams, and forming a line of flankers on the side next to
the enemy.

The whole was kept moving all the time during the maneuvers and attack
and never once halted. The flankers were in charge of an old sergeant whose
name, unfortunately, I cannot recall, but whose coolness, bravery, and judgment was far above the average.[5] The men were dismounted, their horses being
sent to the shelter of the wagon train, the line marching in open order so as to
cover the flank of the train on which the attack was expected to fall. This line
was reinforced by a part of the teamsters, who, after having tied their lead
mules to the rear of the proceeding wagons, were ordered to join the flankers.
These men were armed with old-fashioned muzzle-loading Springfield rifles
and did good service.

Orders were given to reserve fire until the Indians were within fifty yards,
and then "fire at will." The charge was repulsed with considerable loss to the
Indians in both warriors and ponies.

In the meantime, Major Carr had detached three troops to the assistance of the train. The Indians, discovering the reinforcement before we did, drew away to confront the cavalry. Then took place one of the most interesting and exciting engagements of Indian warfare ever witnessed, the Indians receiving the charge of the cavalry and vigorously returning it. For a time it was charge and countercharge, and doubtful as to which would give way, until finally a determined charge of the troops drove them back again across the stream—both Indians and cavalry disappearing over the ridge.[6]

The train continued to move on and joined the remaining troops with Major Carr, who had gone into camp about four miles beyond. This was at sundown; the firing of the three troops and the Indians could be heard until dark, when Major Carr sent orders for the troops to withdraw and return to camp. The Indians followed, opening fire on the camp, which continued about two hours but with little effect on account of the darkness and poor marksmanship.[7] This was the first and only time in my experience that I witnessed a night attack by Indians.

Before starting early next morning, Major Carr decided to burn up a number of wagons, all the forage and camp equipage, in order to lighten the train and increase the number of mules to the teams of the remaining wagons.

The pursuit was then taken up and continued from early morning till late at night, the Indians being in plain view on all sides of the command and fighting desperately with the advance guard to retard our progress and give their village of women and children, which was only a few miles ahead and our objective, an opportunity for escape. Dark had overtaken us when we went into camp, the Indians skirmishing with us all the way. That night their small campfires were discernible a short distance from us, but no attack was made.

Before daybreak next morning,[8] Major Carr started out with the cavalry, directing me to follow with the wagon train, the troops pressing the village so closely that the Indians were forced to throw away all their belongings, including bundles of buffalo robes, dried meat, tepees and tepee poles, and abandon many of their ponies.[9] The pursuit was kept up by the cavalry for two days and nights, until the Indians scattered in every direction, leaving no trail to follow.

On the third day, the train rejoined Major Carr, and all marched back to Fort Wallace, Kansas, where the campaign ended. This campaign cleared the country of nearly all hostile Indians between the Platte and Arkansas Rivers, their favorite hunting ground, and practically ended the Indian troubles in that section.[10]

Col. W. F. Cody[11] was our guide on this occasion and had his first experience as a government scout, displaying all the well-known qualities of bravery and skill which later made him the most famous scout of the United States Army.

The hardships endured, the courage and perseverance displayed by the officers and men, can only be fully understood by those having had similar experiences.

The Capture of a Cheyenne Village [Summit Springs]

ANONYMOUS

Army and Navy Journal 6, no. 50 (July 31, 1869): 791–92

An officer of the 5th Cavalry, in a letter to a friend, gives the following account of the capture of a Cheyenne camp by the 5th Cavalry, under Major Carr, of which brief particulars were received by telegraph:

NEAR FORT SEDGWICK, Nebraska, July 14, 1869

We left Fort McPherson on June 9, traveling south and east until we reached a point opposite the mouth of Beaver Creek, arriving on the fifteenth. Up to this time, our passage through the country resembled a picnic excursion more than a military expedition. The weather was pleasant and forage luxuriant, and the grass thick and soft; and the day's march over, we lolled at our ease on the banks of some shady little stream, free from care or trouble.

But here our work began, for on this afternoon, as our herds were in the river, they were attacked by a small band of Indians, who endeavored to stampede them. In this, however, they were foiled, and so they hurried off. In a very few minutes, three companies were after them,[1] but it soon becoming dark, and there being no moon, they were obliged to give up the chase.

Early the next morning, however, the whole command, having been duly rationed, left the wagon train and started on the trail. This we followed until we reached the Solomon River, where we were overtaken by a very severe thunderstorm, which, all our shelter having been left behind, drenched every one of us through and through, but what was far worse was the loss of the trail. We followed down the Solomon for some distance, but finding nothing to encourage us, turned our faces to the north again, meeting in the evening our wagon train, which was on the road to join us. Arriving at Prairie Dog Creek, we traveled westward, scouting first the country between the Beaver and the Republican, until we arrived at a point on the latter stream nearly south of [Fort] McPherson, and where we expected to meet a train of provisions and forage. The train arrived the next day, and with the loss of only twenty-four hours, we continued our westward march.

The day before we reached this place,[2] a trail was discovered running northwest. The party making it was evidently a large one, and Major Royall, with three companies, was sent to follow it up. The major was unsuccessful in catching them but came across a band of thirteen, whom we have since learned were sent out to decoy the troops from the pursuit, and in this they succeeded, but at the cost of three men killed and eight ponies captured. After this the major retraced his steps and joined the main command.

Attached to our regiment are about one hundred fifty Pawnee Indians,[3] some thirty of whom accompanied Major Royall. It is the custom of the Indians, after making a successful raid, to enter their own camp singing and shouting at the top of their voices. They also fire off their guns and pistols at quite a rapid rate, and so, when on their return, they came into our camp in their wonderful manner, our sentries did not know what to make of it, and the whole command, alarmed at the cry of Indians, sprang to arms, and no little excitement ensued. The Pawnees, luckily, were recognized in time to prevent any mischief, and our little scare ended in rejoicings. These thirty Indians, after parading themselves through our camp, proceeded to their own, where they soon inaugurated a scalp dance, much to the disgust of the remaining 120, who, not having been engaged in the action, could not participate in the dance.

While Major Royall was thus employed, Major Carr, with the rest of the command, continued the westward march, and by the time Major Royall rejoined us, had scouted all that portion of the country in which the North Fork of the Republican River takes its rise. The country, to us, did not seem enticing enough even for an Indian; at any rate, neither Indian nor Indian sign was found, and the command took up the line of march for the big trail. For the first day and night, nothing occurred, but about 11:30 P.M. the second night out, the Pawnee camp was fired into by about fifteen or twenty hostile Indians, who, having fired their volley, decamped without awaiting a return. They inflicted no damage, however, and the next day we pursued our march as though nothing had occurred. The next evening brought us to the scene of Major Royall's encounter with the thirteen. The next day's march showed us several camps, each of which seemed fresher than the last, and [which] raised our hopes considerably.

Finally, on the evening of July 10, we reached the camp which they had left only that morning, and here we too rested. We now realized the size of the party we had to deal with and anticipated a grand capture, for the evident leisure with which they traveled plainly indicated their ignorance of our whereabouts. The morning of the eleventh saw the wagon train again left behind and the whole command, excepting such men whose horses were not fit for very hard marching, on the road a little after daylight. Out of the 150 Pawnees, only 50 accompanied us, the rest having used up their ponies.

Our march this day for the first twenty-seven or twenty-eight miles was westward, and this brought us nearly to the South Platte. At this point, all indications being very fresh, we took up the march at a gallop, uphill and downhill, through sand which covered our horses' fetlocks, and we kept it up for about ten miles. At this point, the Pawnees, who were in the lead, suddenly halted. The command halted,[4] and the majority of the officers, advancing to the top of the hill which we had been ascending, could plainly see the Indian camp between three and four miles off. A few minutes' rest here for the horses, and off we went again, this time at a full gallop. It wanted here twenty minutes to 2:00 P.M., and 2:00 P.M. saw us in possession of the Indian camp, and the Indians, with nothing but a portion of their herds, fleeing for their lives away over the hills.

Never before was a surprise so complete. A brisk wind blowing from the south prevented the noise we made from reaching them, and the first indication they had of our presence was when they saw us a few hundred yards off. Our men behaved nobly, and on they went right into the midst of them, nor stopped while one remained to meet their charge.

I append the results of the charge: fifty-two Indians killed, 450 head of stock captured, 7,000 or 8,000 pounds of dried beef destroyed, 650 buffalo robes destroyed, [and] 86 wigwams destroyed.

To this add all their cooking utensils, all their jewelry and finery of all kinds, many guns, pistols, bows and arrows, fourteen captive women and children, and you have some idea of their loss. Not one of our men was wounded.[5] They had with them two white women, captured at Salina last May. One of these was killed, and the other, though wounded, will in all likelihood recover.[6] At any rate, we have her, and the surgeon is doing what he can to save her for her friends. About $700 or $800 in greenbacks, and about $100 in gold form an interesting item in the list of captured property, for it is all being collected and is to be donated to the rescued woman.

                    Yours, etc.,
                        L

PART FIVE

Mackenzie and the Texas Frontier, 1866–73

One Wagon-Train Boss of Texas

WILLIAM M. EDGAR

Outing 39, no. 4 (January 1902): 381–83

During the latter days of February 1866, I left San Antonio with a train of twenty-five wagons, each drawn by a ten-mule team. We were freighted with merchandise bound for El Paso, about 640 miles of plain and mountain and desert away. Nothing of unusual interest marked our progress until we reached the Pecos River, except an extreme scarcity of water and grass, no rain having fallen for months past. Travel had been almost abandoned during the four years of our Civil War, in consequence of which the roads had been washed out by former rains, which rendered our progress slow and difficult; to make the journey even worse, we were overtaken by a frightful storm, which held us three days in camp without wood and killed 105 mules.

The return trip was pleasant, or as pleasant as the ceaseless grind of a caravan can be, jingling down an arroyo and straining up the other bank, slowly plodding over the deep sand of the flats, tightening nuts and throwing mule shoes until we pulled into old Fort Davis, an abandoned soldier camp. Here we were detained a day, awaiting the arrival of corn which I had ordered to meet us from Presidio del Norte, a Mexican town on the Rio Grande, eighty miles off our line of travel.

On the morning of June 1, I noticed several large smokes rising in the canyon below me, which cut my route through the mountains. I gave it little attention, supposing that some of the trains preceding me had set fire to the grass. We pulled out as usual and made ten miles down the canyon to a noonday camp. The grass was good and plentiful, but I found the water badly stirred up and almost unfit for use. Consequently, I gave orders not to fill the kegs here, intending to make a short afternoon drive to Wild Rose Pass over an ugly intervening hill. At 2:00 P.M. we left camp, and by 4:00 P.M. had passed the hill. The wagons were massed on the eastern slope, in a narrow gorge. The road ran for a mile, when it turned abruptly into Wild Rose Pass, my proposed camping place.

Wishing to select my spot for the night, I rode ahead of the wagons, accompanied by my cook and an old man by the name of Forbes. This latter

A race for the wagon train. HARPER'S NEW MONTHLY MAGAZINE 1895.

was mounted on a fine American horse, while myself and the cook were riding mules. The cook was leading a very spirited horse which I had purchased at El Paso.

When about a thousand yards in advance of the train, my cook pulled up, saying, "Look at the Indian!"

There he was, sure enough, a mounted Indian gazing steadily at us. In less than a second, he was joined by four, who then bore down upon us at full speed.

Old Man Forbes, becoming alarmed, broke for the train. My horse, led by the cook, started to follow, and being much fleeter than the mule, he drew the cook's saddle, to which he was securely tied, upon the mule's neck, throwing the cook violently to the ground. I feared he was seriously injured and tried to get him up behind me.

While thus preoccupied, I heard shots from the direction of the train, and glancing that way, saw the wagons corralling while swarms of warriors circled them. Seeing it was folly to attempt reaching the train riding double on a mule, I directed the cook to go on foot, keeping well to the left of the Indians, holding his gun in readiness but not to fire so long as he could avoid it. I told him quickly that when an Indian started toward him, to cover him with the gun while I would ride down the road directly to the train, thus drawing their attention. We bade each other good-bye and started in on our hurried and desperate strategy. Our plan seemed well devised, since the cook was not molested. The entire force of Indians, some sixty or seventy of them, left the train and made for me. They closed in on all sides, using their arms freely, and why the mule or myself never received a scratch remains to me an unexplained miracle to this day. I had no arms save an army six-shooter, though anything else would have been in my way. They continued to close in on me until the circle around me could not have exceeded forty feet in diameter.

Not succeeding in dismounting me, two of them more daring than the rest closed in on my right and left, trying to catch my bridle. I threw my pistol down on one and fired my first shot. It was almost touching the Indian's breast. He shrugged his shoulders and left for the Happy Hunting Grounds. Mr. Number Two made the same attempt from the other side, and my second shot sent him lining out after his brother. This target practice drove the entire bunch to my rear, leaving my road open to the wagons, but I was no more fearful than before. I expected them to lance me through the back. None too soon I threw myself forward on my mule's neck and, glancing back, saw two warriors mounted on quick ponies, with lances almost touching my back. Like a thought, I covered them with my six-shooter, causing them to rein up heavily, throwing their horses onto their haunches. Before they could recover, I was out of reach.

On arriving at the train, my men, after witnessing what they had, seemed to look upon me as superhuman. The cook had successfully run the gauntlet, but in looking to the rear of the train, I perceived Old Man Forbes, about half a mile distant, coming at full speed, hotly pursued by two Indians, all of their horses much jaded.

Instantly grasping a rifle, I ran down the road to his assistance. When near enough, I fired at the first Indian, who immediately gave up the chase, though apparently unhurt. Reloading, I drew down on the second, and he fell dead in the middle of the road. This freed the old man, who lathered into the wagons directly, safe and sound. It was a very narrow pass we three had come through. After leaving me in front of the train, I had supposed Forbes had gone direct to the train, but seeing so many Indians, he had left the road, passed around a small mountain or butte, coming back into the road considerably in rear of the wagons, thus giving him a rough and rugged run of about four miles.

Having now got everything safely in keeping, I looked around and found the corral had been disadvantageously located. I concluded to change it by moving directly towards the water, where there was vantage ground. We fought our way to a sag, with high ground on all sides affording good shelter, and again halted the train.

All night long the Indians harassed us. They crept up close to the wagons and wounded many of our mules with arrows. To our right and not more than one hundred yards away was a deep washout where the Indians were secreted before making the first assault, and from this point they mostly made their advance. Morning did not mend our situation. The Indians seemed determined to take the train, yelling from the washout that if we did not leave the wagons and go to the hills, that they would surely kill us all. My men were all Mexicans, the majority of whom were clamorous to abandon the property in order to save their lives. I talked to them at length and prevailed on them to remain, promising to acquiesce in their wishes if no succor reached us by the end of the following day.

We were now completely surrounded, the Indians firing from every direction, though I must say with little effect because the men were well protected, but they were maiming and killing mules. The wagons were close together except in the front and rear, which were well secured with ropes hung with blankets, the better to conceal our movements in the corral. I caused rifle pits to be dug under the wagons, and on the second day began to dig a well, which, when abandoned, was thirty-four feet deep with water in sight. We could have reached water on the second day had we been able to work steadily. There was no moon. By night the Indians approached very close and showered us with arrows, and by day we were prevented from moving about.

For four days and three long, weary nights the siege lasted, during which we had no time to prepare food, were without water, and could not sleep. This privation was particularly true of myself, being in command and having to be constantly on the alert for both my own men and the enemy.

The Indians lay about us beyond rifle fire—some herding horses in plain view while a few held favorable positions, keeping up a continuous fire. I soon discovered that in order to reach my men in the pits, they were forced to expose themselves by getting on the back of the arroyo or washout, and by putting some of my best shots in the wagons, raising the cover just enough to see the Indians as they drew above the bank to fire, we were able to kill a few.

After a little of this, they quit their positions and began to make overtures for a big peace talk. They invited us into the arroyo for this purpose, but I was familiar enough with Indians to know that it would only invite treachery on their part. I told them that if they wanted to talk, they must come out of their hiding and talk on the plain. One of them finally did so, stating that they were very poor, were in fact in a starving condition, and that if I would give up a little corn, they would give up the water and leave us. This I agreed to do, much against my will.

On the morning of the fourth day, they marshaled all their forces in our front, in groups of from twenty to fifty. One chief appeared with a fiery red blanket, and as you have seen cattle going to water, they started off in single file, at a snail's pace. They passed behind a little butte, and as they emerged on the opposite side we counted 218 bucks.

At a water hole on our left there were eighteen others on foot, and at another water hole in our front we counted twenty-five others, making 251 Indians in sight at one time.

They were Mescalero and Lipan Apaches under Chief Gordo, and on the second day were joined by as many Navajos from Bosque Redondo Reservation in New Mexico. They were well clothed, well armed, and well mounted. They crossed the road about two hundred yards in our front, where they began to pass around the train. I now felt that our only hope lay in a determined fight, so I prepared for what seemed the final struggle. Going to each rifle pit, I cautioned my men to be calm and to hold their fire until they were sure to kill. During all this time, everything was as silent as the grave. The Indians kept moving until they were lost in the washout. I expected a charge, but after a time they came out and said they would take the corn and give up the fight. We accordingly placed the corn fifty yards in front of our wagons, telling them that twenty men could come up and remove it, but that more would be fired on. They made an attempt to come *en masse,* but I ordered a halt, and Gordo prevailed upon them to do so. They finally got the corn, which they distributed, and then, to our satisfaction, they left. I drove my mules to water, but while drinking, I so much distrusted them that I rode back to have a look down the valley. I saw them returning, as I mistrusted they would, but I waved my hat, and again they bore away from us, disappearing, to be seen no more.

My whole force in the fight was twenty-six men and two boys. We had as passengers two women and two children belonging to two of my teamsters. These I used to good advantage in working on the feelings of my men, saying that no one but cowards would abandon women and children to savages.

In the Limpio Canyon, which was the scene of this fight, we afterwards found ample evidence that Chief Gordo's *hombres de armas* had suffered heavily, which undoubtedly made them fainthearted and willing to quit, but they had us in a very bad way before they did and might have conquered us with a little more persistence.

Recollections of the Kiowas and Comanches

BRITTON DAVIS[1]

Papers of the Order of the Indian Wars, U.S. Army Military History Institute, Carlisle Barracks, Pennsylvania

East San Diego, California
December 17, 1925

Lt. Col. C. A. Bach, U.S.A.,
Chief, Historical Section, Army War College
War Department, Washington, D.C.

My dear Colonel Bach:

By a queer coincidence, I am able to add a little to your records of Satanta. Of the two tribes—Comanches and Kiowas—the Kiowas were best disposed toward the whites. They fought the Comanches as frequently as they did the white settlers. In my boyhood days, their habitat was north-central Texas, the vicinity of what is now Fort Worth. But they ranged as far south as the Nueces River, and far enough north to come in contact with the Sioux. As a boy, I was with a party of my father's friends hunting on the Pedrinales River, some thirty or forty miles from Austin, Texas, when a war party of Kiowas camped less than two miles from us on the same stream. Fortunately, they missed us. This was about the year 1870 and was the last raid of these people. The war party numbered only seven, and the Kiowa chiefs claimed that it was composed of Kickapoos and two or three outlawed Kiowas.

In 1869 my father was appointed provisional governor of Texas.[2] Shortly after his inauguration, he went to the penitentiary at Huntsville for an inspection, taking my mother, brother, and myself with him.[3] We were in the superintendent's office, where my father was hearing complaints and pleas for clemency. Two Indians were brought in. They were Satanta and a subchief of the Comanches known to the whites as Big Tree. Satanta was of medium height and about fifty years of age. Big Tree[4] was a magnificent specimen of a man—fully six feet tall, broad of shoulder, and straight as an arrow. Compared to Satanta, he was of quite dark complexion.

The Indians had been in the penitentiary for about two and a half years. They claimed that they had gone into a white settlement on a peaceful errand [and] had been captured and sent to the prison without a chance to defend themselves.

My father had evidently investigated their case before our visit, for he informed them through the interpreter that he was going to pardon them and send them back to their people. They say the Indian is stoical. There was nothing stoical in these two. Big Tree said something to the interpreter. Satanta looked dazed. The interpreter evidently repeated what my father had said. In a moment, tears were streaming down the faces of the two Indians; they fell on their knees before my father and were prevented from kissing his feet only through the interference of the deputy sheriffs. They were led away sobbing.

Another incident relating to the Comanches may be of interest to your section. It illustrates the Indian point of view, so little understood by the white interested only in his destruction and the acquisition of his lands.

After the Huntsville trip, my father went to Fort Worth, then a mere "cow town," to establish peace with the Comanches and Kiowas. After the formalities of [the] peace pact were completed, the head chiefs of the Comanches brought to my father as a present a robe made of six skins of the big prairie wolf, the gray lobo. The robe was about eight or nine feet long and about four or five feet wide. Two sides of it and one end were adorned with human scalps set about a foot apart, three of the scalps being those of women.

The chief apologized that one end was unfinished and assured my father that he would have finished it out for him had the peace council been held a little later. He further explained that the scalps were none of them of white people, only Indians and Mexicans; therefore, my father need have no objections to receiving the robe. My father replied diplomatically that he knew that scalps were the proof of prowess of a great warrior, and therefore he could not think of depriving him of them, but that he would be pleased to accept the robe if the big chief would remove and retain the scalps, which was duly carried out.

Yours very truly,
Britton Davis

With the 6th U.S. Cavalry in Texas

[BENJAMIN T. HUTCHINS][1]

Army and Navy Journal 4, no. 10 (October 27, 1866): 154

To the Editor of the Army and Navy Journal:

SIR: Perhaps it may not be uninteresting to you to hear from matters in this part of the world. The 6th Cavalry has now been scattered over the northern portion of Texas, with the exception of three companies, which still remain with the headquarters at Austin, and orders have been expected to remove to the extreme frontier and occupy some of the posts held before the war. The regiment is at present, however, but indifferently supplied with good horses, and authority has been received to purchase six hundred additional, which will be the number necessary before much can be done against the Indians. Average horses are now selling here for about $150 in currency.

Brevet Major Claflin of the 6th Cavalry,[2] with his company (H) and a company of the 4th Cavalry under Lieutenant Porter,[3] has just returned from an expedition, the object of which was to inspect and report upon the condition of Forts Chadbourne, McKavett,[4] and other old posts, and the amount of work necessary to place them in repair. Captain Claflin traveled over 1,400 miles and was absent three months, having marched on an average over sixteen miles a day, including all the stoppages and delays. According to his report, many of the posts have been nearly demolished, but others are only partially damaged, and troops could occupy several of the stations at once.[5]

The Comanches have been unusually bold lately, and by their raids have driven off large quantities of cattle and murdered many, and have greatly retarded progress upon the frontiers. Some of these incursions have been made to within 150 miles of Austin. White men are said to lead these bands, and the Indians are reported to be well armed with six-shooters and rifles. Several men were killed and scalped lately close to Jacksboro, where Captain Cram[6] and two companies of the 6th Cavalry are stationed. General Heintzelman[7] seems to think that it will be better to break up the small posts and establish larger ones, with at least four companies of cavalry in each. This arrangement will not, however, be made until spring unless horses can be obtained sooner than is anticipated.

A Comanche warrior. CENTURY MAGAZINE 1889.

We have had but few desertions in the regiment of late, although we have received many recruits. It is a noticeable fact, however, that the new additions are composed of a much better class of men than those received about the time the 6th Cavalry was stationed at Frederick, Maryland.[8] A very large number of those deserted, but most of them were of very bad character and had evidently belonged to the class of bounty jumpers during the war.

H.

CAMP SIXTH U.S. CAVALRY,
AUSTIN, TEXAS, October 1, 1866

An Indian Attack in 1868

WILLIAM J. MILLER

Kansas City *Star,* December 29, 1901[1]

To be surrounded by hostile Indians at such close quarters that the twang of their bowstrings can be heard, to be shot with arrows until one's body is pierced with twenty-three wounds, and then to escape and live to an old age is an experience that comes to few men. But this is what happened to William J. Miller, a ranchman who lives on the Sweetwater in Wheeler County, Texas, and is familiarly known in western Oklahoma and the Panhandle as "Uncle Billy" Miller. He has lived for years with an iron arrowhead in one of his lungs, but in spite of it is a man of large physique and robust appearance. Surgeons in Kansas City have located the arrowhead several times with an X-ray machine but declined to remove it, saying that the operation would be more dangerous than to allow the arrowhead to remain.

Miller comes frequently to Cheyenne, where several of his relatives live. To him an Indian is the incarnation of all that is fiendish and bloodthirsty. "If I had the power of lightning, I would not let it thunder till I had killed every one of them," said he. To a group of listeners in front of "Smoky Joe" Miller's hotel, Uncle Billy told this story of his memorable fight:

> In 1868 I lived in San Saba County, Texas. On the night of January 17 in that year, A. W. Morrow, a neighbor now dead, and myself encamped near the watermill of Maj. A. J. Rose, where Brady Creek empties into the Colorado River. There had been no trouble with marauding Comanches, and when we started home early the next morning with a four-horse team, we were armed with only two dragoon pistols. We were traveling a main road, between two settlements, and had gone about eight miles when we heard the running of horses in our rear. Morrow was walking and, calling to me, said, "Wait, a lot of cowboys are trying to overtake us; they must have bad news." A herd of cattle close by had led him to believe that our followers were cowboys.

I saw that Indians, instead of cowboys, were coming, and shouted to Morrow to jump into the wagon or he would be shot full of holes. Our wagon cover was up and tightly drawn. I whipped our horses into a run, but the Indians soon overtook us. Morrow crouched in the rear end of the wagon and began to fight. He shot one Indian, whose horse whirled and threw him to the ground. This caused the Indians to fall back a little and enabled us to see that there were about fifteen in the party. They were a dirty, greasy bunch of wretches, much of their war paint having been off since they started on their raid. Several women were among them, riding astride and fighting as viciously as the men. Our horses ran away and went at breakneck speed for about three miles. The Indians kept close to our rear and fired at us with Winchesters, pistols, and two old Long Tom rifles, doing little damage, however, as they were poor marksmen with firearms. They killed one of our horses, and then, luckily or unluckily for us, ran out of ammunition.

We could see them unsling their bows and shift their arrow quivers into position, and knew that the worst of the fight was yet to come. The first arrow struck Morrow in the hand; the Indian who shot it tumbled, yelling, from his horse with a bullet in his chest. In the runaway, our horses threw the wagon into a ditch, where we stuck fast. We were reduced to less than a dozen cartridges and saw that we must make every bullet count. We never fired at any Indian more than ten feet away. The Indians charged us time and again, often coming within eight or ten feet of the wagon. We could have hit them with clubs. They talked to each other in the sign language, making as little noise as possible, and pressing closer and closer upon us. Their leader came within six feet of me, and I shot him through the hips. He yelled, clutched his saddle, and galloped away.

A squaw shot me in the right cheek with an arrow that protruded from behind my ear. Six more struck me in the head, the points "kinking" against my skull, making it difficult and painful to pull them out. Seven more lodged in my body between my neck and waist. I pulled one arrowhead from my abdomen that was as long as my finger and so keen that a person could whittle with it.

The Indians were at too close range for their arrows to acquire speed, or else we would have been shot through and through. In pulling an arrow from my left side, the head slipped from the shaft and remained in my lung. It is still there. Another missed the femoral artery in my left leg by the width of a knife blade. I carried a steel barb in my right thigh till 1874, when Dr. Dowell at Galveston removed it. I presented the relic to Morrow as a souvenir. The cold, acid sting of an arrow plowing its way through your flesh is a sensation never to be forgotten. It is less painful than it is sickening.

The return of the runners. CENTURY MAGAZINE 1895.

Poor Morrow was as desperately wounded as myself. An arrow struck him squarely in the left ear, and while I was pulling it out, another went whizzing into his right ear. He could see both shafts and imagined that one arrow had passed entirely through his head. He groaned and said that he was killed. Before I could reassure him, an arrow hit him in the left eye and glanced under the skin to his ear. Blood poured down his face in a stream and covered my hands and arms. "They have shot my eye out," he exclaimed. "No, it glanced," I replied, pulling the arrow from the wound. Morrow was hit three or four times before I was touched. When the Indians got under good headway, the arrows came so rapidly that I couldn't pull them out as fast as they went in.

We were now in desperate straits, suffering from dreadful wounds, out of ammunition, save one load in Morrow's pistol, and our horses unable to pull the wagon from the ditch. The Indians, in their excitement, had shot away most of their arrows. The chuck box fastened to the end of the wagon bristled like a porcupine. I believe that a double armful of arrows was sticking in the wagon and ground. I told Morrow that our only hope of escape was to cut the traces and make a run on horseback. The Indians had withdrawn to parley, knowing that they only had a few arrows left in their quivers, and fearful that we might still have ammunition.

Morrow and I mounted a horse each and started. An arrow whizzed and struck his horse in the hip, causing the animal to pitch. Morrow was thrown fully ten feet high, falling on his head. He called to me that he was killed. I answered by pulling him up behind me, and was thankful to find that he still held to his pistol with its remaining load. We ran our horses as rapidly as possible toward a clump of trees. The Indians shot at us about twenty times while we were cutting the traces, but upon reaching the deserted wagon, they replenished their supply, and a stream of arrows poured after us. A friend afterward trailed us for 150 yards by the arrows sticking in the ground.

We rode about three-quarters of a mile before reaching cover in the timber. Then a singular thing happened. Whether it was due to their savage admiration of our pluck and seemingly charmed lives, I am unable to say. We had killed, as later reports showed, about seven Indians. The remainder of the band now galloped to within sixty feet of where we crouched in the timber, and stopped. Their leader rode out and looked steadily at us for a few seconds, without saying a word, and returned to his former position. Each Indian in turn did the same thing, and then the band rode away and disappeared over the ridge.

Although expecting death, we were too much in anguish to feel thankful for our immediate deliverance. Fearing that they would return, we secreted ourselves as closely as possible in the timber. Both of us were soon terribly nauseated and burning with fever. We remained hidden until about 9:00 A.M. next day.

Early in the morning of the fight, Jack Flood was cutting cedar posts in a canyon when he heard the Indians coming, secreted himself, and saw them pass by. The appearance of a Comanche Indian in Texas meant war. Flood ran to the farm of John Fleming, gave the alarm, and raised a posse of twelve men. They reached our wagon about an hour after the Indians had gone.

Morrow and I were wild with thirst and tried to reach Brady Creek, but I grew so sick that I could go no further. I told him to scan the country and fire the remaining shot in his pistol if he saw white men. He saw the posse, mistook our friends for Indians, and crept back to me with one of his boots full of water. I drank so much that I was unable to walk. The posse searched all day without finding us. Four of its members agreed to stay all night in an old log house nearby and resume the search next morning. Major Rose, now of Belton, Texas, and J. Z. Sloan of San Saba were two of these four volunteers.

About daylight on January 19, Sloan found an arrow sticking in the ground, and a few steps away another and another, which he followed till he came to the timber where we were hiding. He was within thirty yards of me before I saw and recognized him. Our rescuers got a wagon and hauled us home, reaching there about dusk. We recovered three of our horses. One of mine had three arrows in him. I cut down into his haunch eleven inches to remove an arrowhead.

Morrow and I were pitiable looking objects, covered with blood, gashed with wounds, and almost dead. Both recovered after a number of surgical operations. I was compelled to use crutches for two years.

The Indians escaped from Texas before they could be overtaken. They had stolen away from the Fort Sill reservation, in what is now Oklahoma, to burn, pillage, and murder. We brought suit against the government for losses due to their depredations, but lost through the delay of our lawyers in prosecuting the case.

The Indian I shot in the hips proved to be old Asaharber, who died in 1884. I saw him in 1883, for the first time after the fight, at a cow camp in the Panhandle, where I had gone to run horse races with the Comanches. He was in the grub shack eating when I entered. He stopped instantly and, watching me carefully, got up and went outside, keeping his face constantly toward me. Through an interpreter, he said that he knew me. I replied that there was no doubt of it and felt an itching to kill him. Next morning his camp at the mouth of the Sweetwater was gone; he had headed for Fort Sill as fast as his ponies could travel.

"I hate Indians like hell," said Uncle Billy, his eyes flashing with anger. Then, in great scorn:

The poor homeless man of the forest! I want to kill a man when he talks that way. These devils did enough in that raid to turn any white man against the whole race. They stole a ten-year-old boy, William Herter, in Mason County, carried him to the head of the Concho, then to Pueblo and New Mexico, finally trading him for a horse. The boy was old enough to tell his name, and the man who got him wrote to Sheriff Milligan, and the boy was restored to his father.

In Gillespie County, they killed two women by cutting off their heads, raised a baby by the heels and dashed its brains out against a tree. I saw blood on the tree a year later. In Llano County, they scalped a Mrs. Dancer four times. She had remarkable courage. The Indians jabbed arrows in her to see if she was dead, but she never flinched, and crawled away after the Indians left. In Burnet County, a farmer named Benson went about one hundred yards from his house to tie his horse, his eight-year-old boy following him. The Comanches surprised Benson and killed him, tied the boy, and left him on the ground near where they concealed themselves all day and night. The child saw the neighbors bury his father's body. He was taken to Fort Sill and exchanged four or five years afterward. He returned to the Comanches, married a squaw, and may be still living with the tribe.

Scouting with Mackenzie

W. A. THOMPSON[1]

Journal of the United States Cavalry Association 10 (1897): 429–33

The Llano Estacado, or Staked Plains of Texas, consist of a plateau 2,500 to 3,000 feet in altitude, 350 miles or more north and south, 250 or more east and west. To the eye perfectly level, but it is undulating, with long, imperceptible rolls that run north and south; a treeless plain covered with a carpet of very nutritious grasses. The great portion of this great plateau is dotted thickly with depressions in [the] shape of a washbowl that vary in size from 100 yards to half a mile in diameter. During the rainy season, July and August, these basins are filled to overflowing with water, which percolates through the sand and limestone that underlies the whole plateau, breaking out and flowing upon the surface at the heads of the many canyons that indent the whole eastern side of these plains, forming beautiful, limpid brooks, which are the headwaters of the Texas rivers.

This whole section of Texas was for ages the home and general rendezvous of that portion of the Comanche tribe of Indians known as the Kwahadis.[2] The Staked Plains had numerous and very large herds of antelope, and as Kwahadi is the Comanche name for antelope, it was known as the Kwahadi country, and the Indians as Kwahadis. These Kwahadi Indians are a bright, quick-witted race—brave, venturesome, bold, and dashing fighters, splendid horsemen, and not cruel to their prisoners. They had been for years raiding Texas, New Mexico, and Old Mexico, stealing horses and cattle, fighting and killing the frontier settlers. The United States forces, as well as the Texas Rangers had for a long time been fighting these Kwahadis, but with meager results, simply because the custom had been to follow these raiding parties to within fifty miles or less of the edge of the Staked Plains, and then return.

In 1870 Colonel Mackenzie[3] was transferred and assigned to the command of the 4th U.S. Cavalry. For some time previous to this transfer, he was colonel of the 40th U.S. Infantry, and owing to his superior soldierly qualifications, great talent, and untiring energy, both in the field and garrison, he left that regiment with a reputation as first-class soldier, and surpassed by no regiment in our army. The most important question in the Department of Texas was how to

Wounded on a scouting expedition. CENTURY MAGAZINE 1893.

subdue and rid Texas of these bold Kwahadi raiders. The department commander, General Augur, selected Colonel Mackenzie to accomplish it and authorized him to adopt such plans as he might see fit. At that time, 1870, the Staked Plain as a whole was an unknown country to the whites. Mackenzie's plan of operations was very simple, and it was to take a force strong enough into the enemy's country and attack him wherever he could be found.

The campaigns of 1870–1871 were mainly for exploration, for, as he expected, the Kwahadis would keep out of his reach and only stampede his horses at night whenever they could, and which they did do, with the loss to his command of eighty horses and several pack mules during 1870.

In 1872, with six troops of the 4th Cavalry,[4] having become acquainted with the topography of the northern portion of the plains, he made a night march that placed his command in a section of country which enabled him to discover and surprise a large camp of Kwahadis on McClellan's Creek, near its confluence with the North Fork of the Red River, Texas. The Indians saw the command three or four miles off, as it was passing over a ridge. But dust enveloped the column, so that they thought it was only a party of their own people driving a herd of buffalo towards camp for slaughter, as they were drying meat and making pemmican for their winter supplies. The command was thus enabled to reach within half a mile of the camp before the Indians discovered the true state of affairs.

The charge was made in echelon, troops in columns of fours. The colonel rode by the side of the commanding officer of A Troop, which was the base troop. When the troop was near the center of the camp and parallel with a small ridge thickly covered with high grass, about ten or fifteen yards off, about seventy-five Indians raised in line and gave the troops a volley, but fortunately, and what will be the case nine times out of ten, with very little damage, as the volley was high. Like all close Indian fighting, it then became general and more or less individual. The fight commenced on September 29 about 4:00 P.M., and by 5:00 P.M. the battle was over. It was one of the most satisfactory victories over Indians the colonel ever had, for it was complete.

He burned up all their winter supplies and at least 100 fine wigwams, captured 200 squaws and children, about 3,000 horses, and killed fifty-two warriors; all this with the loss of four or five men slightly wounded. It was the most terrible blow the Kwahadis had ever received. In making his official report of the engagement, Colonel Mackenzie reported seventeen dead warriors, as only that number was found and counted. The Kwahadi chiefs, after they had surrendered and were living at Fort Sill, Indian Territory, in talking over their fights, and this one on September 29 in particular, said that they lost fifty-two warriors.[5]

The commanding officer of A Troop cut off and enclosed about eighty warriors in a crescent-shaped ravine, through which ran a good-sized brook. About the center was a deep pool some twenty-five or thirty-foot long and eight or ten feet wide. When the troop was deployed, the flanks commanded the exit of both the lower and upper portion of this ravine. The fighting was close and desperate; the Indians charged the line twice but were driven back with great slaughter. As fast as the Indians were killed, their bodies were thrown into this deep pool, from the fact that almost all Indians have a perfect horror and dread of being scalped after death, as they do not want to appear in the "Happy Hunting Ground" scalpless. This particular portion of the fight can best be pictured by imagining a troop of men in line on a stage, firing into a crowded theater pit.

Until 1874 the colonel had carried on his campaigns against these Kwahadis during the spring, summer, and fall months. With the exception of his 1872 fight, he had not by any means subdued them or stopped the raiding. In 1874 he decided upon a winter's campaign and made his preparations accordingly. Fort Griffin, Texas, was his base. On September 12 he left there with six troops of the 4th Cavalry and thirty Indian scouts and established his sub-base of supplies in Cañon Blanco.[6] On September 27, after a night's march of some thirty miles from Tule Canyon, he discovered and surprised a number of large camps of Cheyenne Indians in Palo Duro Canyon. A running fight took place in which three Indians were killed. All the wigwams and supplies in the several camps were burned, and 1,800 head of horses were captured.[7]

A few days afterwards, he moved north and west of Palo Duro Canyon, and while scouting that section of the plains, his scouts captured a party of Mexicans from New Mexico, who had three or four ox teams loaded with supplies and ammunition that they intended to trade to the Kwahadis. The wagons were burned up, and the command had plenty of beef for some days. Among this party of Mexicans, it was discovered that two of them had been raised from children among these Kwahadis, and they agreed to pilot the colonel, for releasing the others, to where the Kwahadis had their winter camp.

The command returned to Cañon Blanco, and after resting and fitting out for the winter's work, left there on November 3, moving southwest into the center of the plains. It had been the custom for these Kwahadis to break up in small bands and establish their winter camps where water flowed. On November 5 his scouts discovered and surprised a party of these Indians, with a herd of twenty-eight horses, killing two of them and capturing twenty-seven horses. This party proved to be a raiding party that had just returned from the settlements with the stolen horses. As no white man had ever before been in that portion of the plains, an attack from that quarter was least expected. Night marches were of frequent occurrence, and a few days after the above-noted affair, he surprised a camp of Kwahadis, killing three warriors [and] capturing sixteen squaws and 155 warhorses.[8] The colonel was constantly on the move, from water to water, and while not being able to reach within shooting distance of any more bands of Kwahadis, he forced them to flee from their camps with the loss of their winter supplies, and this caused a great deal of suffering. The weather was very trying, a day or so of lovely, June-like weather followed by cold rains, sleet, and snow. His command was clothed and lived, so far as rations were concerned, with the most Spartan-like simplicity.

This method of scouting was continued for over two months, and when the horses were about worn out, the clothing about threadbare, and the food all gone, the command returned to Fort Griffin in the latter part of February 1875, where it was broken up and the troops returned to their different posts. As this was the first time the Kwahadis had ever been disturbed and routed out of their winter homes, and the first time the whites had ever explored and become acquainted with that portion of the plains, the moral effect, as well as the damage inflicted, was more than any kind of a human creature could stand. So the chiefs collected their scattered bands, numbering 1,500, marched to Fort Sill, and surrendered to the Indian agent in March 1875. Ever since this occurrence, the people of Texas have enjoyed the blessings of peace.[9]

A study of Colonel Mackenzie's Indian campaigns will show that the results were the perfect and complete subjugation of the Indians, and the frontier people ever afterwards enjoyed a permanent peace and security. Such has been the fact since he left Texas with his regiment, both in 1875 and 1879, when he put an end forever to Mexican cattle stealing and established law and order along our side of the Rio Grande. His winter's campaign, after a hard, close, and desperate fight against the Northern Cheyennes, 1876–77, ended in their complete and lasting subjugation. His expedition against the Ute Indians was a successful one, and while it partook more of diplomacy, it added much to his credit and reputation, for by his skill, decision, and wonderful energy, he subdued them completely without the loss of a life. The people of Colorado have him to thank for the peace and security they have enjoyed ever since.

Colonel Mackenzie endeared himself to all who ever had the honor to serve under his command. He possessed many noble traits of character. He had the faculty of imparting to all under him a high sense of duty, and by his own example educated his officers and men to a high state of discipline and efficiency. He was a man of very deep and intense feeling, of a high-strung and nervous temperament, and those who did not understand him fully gave him the credit of bordering upon the martinet; but all who did understand his character knew him to be a man of such a noble heart and of such courage that it was impossible for him to possess a particle of such a spirit.

On the Trail of Satanta

"EUREKA"

Army and Navy Journal 8, no. 48 (July 15, 1871): 767[1]

To the Editor of the Army and Navy Journal.

SIR: For years it has been denied that it was the Indians on the reservation north of Texas[2] that committed the cruel and brutal outrages we frequently heard of on the Texas frontier. At last the question has been definitely settled that it is almost invariably the Indians whom the government feeds, clothes, and protects that come across Red River from off the reservation and go in periodic raids into Texas to steal, ravish, and murder.

On May 18 last a train loaded with corn, owned by the contractor Mr. Henry Warren, of Weatherford, Texas, was on its way to Fort Griffin. When nearing Salt Creek, about twenty miles from Fort Richardson, this train was attacked by about one hundred well-armed and well-mounted Indians. They killed seven of the teamsters, including the wagonmaster, smashed the wagons, scattered what corn they could not carry off, and made off with all the mules except five that were killed in the fight. These worse than brutes in human form, not content with killing, scalping, etc., chained one of their victims to one of the wheels of a wagon and burned him to death; the manner in which they mutilated the dead cannot be described.

General Sherman[3] had only passed over the same road the day before, en route from Griffin to Richardson, and had a narrow escape from falling into the hands of this band of savages. A few of the men that escaped from the train, one severely wounded, made their way to Fort Richardson and told the story to General Sherman, who immediately ordered out Col. R. S. Mackenzie, 4th Cavalry, with every man that could be mounted to follow the trail of the savages. General Sherman drove back the same day to the place of the massacre and saw with his own eyes what had been done. The general sent an express to Fort Griffin, ordering out every man of the 4th Cavalry that could be mounted at that post.

Colonel Mackenzie started with four companies of the 4th Cavalry from Richardson, viz., A, B, E, and F, with thirty days' rations on pack mules, and struck for the headwaters of the Big and Little Wichita Rivers, and he was

433

Torturing a soldier.

NELSON A. MILES, *PERSONAL RECOLLECTIONS AND OBSERVATIONS.*

joined by the command from Fort Griffin under 1st Lt. Henry Sweeney, 4th Cavalry, at the Big Wichita. The march was exceedingly severe on both men and animals; rain fell without intermission almost for five consecutive days and nights, wetting everything through and keeping it so, in addition to which the trail could not be found. The streams were all more or less swollen, and difficulty was experienced in crossing them; several had to be waded by the men leading their horses. Altogether, the first week nearly wore out the patience of every man in the command, but pluck and endurance carried them through until Pease River was finally reached, where [the] trail of the mules taken by the Indians was discovered and followed across Red River, and from thence across the belt of country between it and the North Fork of Red River. The trail led distinctly across the North Fork of Red River and into the Indian reservation, striking the west end of the Wichita Mountains. The command camped that night on the North Fork of Red River, and unfortunately during the night we had one of the most tremendous rainstorms ever witnessed; the rain came down in a perfect deluge, and in the morning the face of the country was found to be washed clean; every vestige of the trail had disappeared. Parties of mounted men with officers and Tonkawa Indian scouts were sent in every direction during the day to try and find the trail once more, but the rain had totally effaced all signs, and the search was reluctantly abandoned.

The command was then headed for Fort Sill, and after marching east about seventy miles along the base of the Wichita Mountains, arrived on June 4 at Fort Sill, Indian Territory.

Although the stolen mules had been trailed onto the reservation, thereby leading to the conclusion that it was Indians off said reservation who had committed the outrage, yet upon our arrival at Fort Sill we found indisputable evidence that it *was* the reservation Indians and no other that had been guilty. Satanta and Satank,[4] the two head men of the Kiowas, with Big Tree, one of their greatest "braves," were in the guardhouse at Fort Sill in double irons, arrested and confined by General Sherman's order and at the request of Mr. Tatum, the Indian agent at that point.[5] Satanta and Satank confessed to the Indian agent that they and the Kiowas claimed all the credit of the last fight, and that it was he and Satank and no one else that captured the train, killed the men, and drove off the mules, and that he was now square with the Texans, as he had gotten a scalp for every one of his young men that had been killed the past year.

The headmen were called together at the quarters of Colonel Grierson,[6] 10th Cavalry, commanding Fort Sill, and in the powwow that ensued, this Satanta and Satank leveled their Spencer carbines at both General Sherman and Colonel Grierson, and but for the promptness with which they were seized, both officers might have been shot dead where they stood. Lone Wolf, another chief, promised that if General Sherman would let him go, he would bring in the herd of mules next day, to which Mr. Lone Wolf pledged his Indian honor! The general allowed him to depart, but neither he nor the mules have since been seen or heard of. Satanta, Satank, and Big Tree were turned over to Colonel Mackenzie and his command, with orders to take them, as prisoners accused of murder, to Fort Richardson, Texas, there to be held for trial by the civil authorities of the state at the town of Jacksboro, which is within half a mile of the post of Fort Richardson.

The day the command left Fort Sill,[7] Satank, with two guards, was placed in a wagon. He had shackles and handcuffs on. About one mile from the post, he managed to wrench his hands loose and sprang on one of the guards, who, in springing back, fell out of the wagon, Satank securing his carbine as the man went over the side of the wagon. Satank sprung the lever to load, and nothing saved the lives of one or more men but the fact that there was a cartridge already in the chamber. His determination to kill someone was evident; he worked rapidly at the gun, and his countenance was most ferocious. Every man was mounted, and time was precious. The order to fire was given, and Satank fell back, shot through. In about twenty minutes he breathed his last. Thus died one of the most cruel and cold-blooded savages that ever existed. He was so devilish that the worst savages of his own tribe (Kiowas) used to say that Satank was "heap bad man." For years he was the terror of the Kansas borders, as he has of late been to the Texas border, and it is said of Satank that he had committed more murders and outrages of all kinds than any other one Indian in existence.

During the whole of this, Satanta and Big Tree sat together in one wagon, perfectly still, and when Satank was shot, they both laughed and said, "Satank heap old fool." Colonel Mackenzie brought the other two Indians to Fort Richardson, where they are now in prison awaiting the action of the Texas civil authorities of Jack County.

The command arrived at Fort Richardson June 14, having marched 367 miles in twenty-three days, a portion of the time in very bad weather, fording and wading five rivers, wet through every day for a week and sleeping so every night, and yet not a case of sickness occurred during the whole scout.

Company D, 4th Cavalry, Lt. Sweeney commanding, returned from Fort Richardson to Fort Griffin, where it arrived June 19, after being out thirty-one days and having marched 439 miles. Thus the question whether it was or was not Indians from the reservation that were raiding Texas and devastating the frontier for the past three or four years, murdering men, women, and children, stealing horses, and driving off whole herds of cattle, has been settled, and the fact established beyond a question that the Indians on the reservation live there under the care and protection of the government, come to Texas bent on robbery and murder when they choose, perpetrate the most brutal outrages, even to burning their victims alive, and then return to the reservation in question and openly brag and boast of the deeds they have done "down in Texas."

Satanta has confessed that it was Indians off the reservation that fought Captain Bacon and Captain McClellan, 6th Cavalry, and boasted that they were whipped by the Indians. They collected together on the reservation and deliberately marched off to Texas to meet and fight McClellan, numbering about six to one. And after the fights with Captain Bacon, 9th Cavalry,[8] and Captain McClellan, the Indians coolly returned to the reservation and told of what they had done, but no notice was taken of it, and nothing was done until Mr. Lo had the temerity to raise his gun against the [commanding] general of the army and one of its leading colonels. There are any number of witnesses who heard Satanta confess.

We anxiously await further developments on the Indian reservation question and the hanging of Satanta and Big Tree.

EUREKA

Over the Border with Mackenzie

E. B. BEAUMONT[1]

United Service 12 (1885): 281–88

The close of the Rebellion found the 4th U.S. Cavalry in Macon, to which place it had followed [Maj.] Gen. J. H. Wilson in his brilliant campaign through Alabama and Georgia.

In November 1865 the regiment was ordered to Texas, and after nine years' arduous service in preserving law and order during Reconstruction and protecting the frontier from Indian incursions, the winter of 1872–73 found it garrisoning the posts of Richardson, Griffin, and Concho.

The 4th had won a high reputation for efficiency and gallantry during the war and acquired additional laurels under an active colonel, who never allowed its sabers to rust for want of employment. In spite of the disagreeable duties imposed upon the regiment during Reconstruction, both officers and men secured the respect, and in many cases the regard, of the citizens of Texas, and Colonel Mackenzie is deservedly popular through the state for his untiring efforts to protect the frontier.

In the spring of 1873, in consequence of frequent and disastrous raids by hostile Indians from Mexico, a portion of the regiment was ordered to concentrate at Clark, about thirty miles from the Rio Grande. Five companies left Fort Richardson on March 5 and, taking the road via Griffin, Phantom Hill, Concho, and McKavett, reached Fort Clark on April 1, having marched over four hundred miles. The wives and children of the officers and men, some sixty in number, accompanied the command during this pleasant march and lent an air of refinement and comfort to the monotony of camp life. The 9th Cavalry, under Colonel Merritt,[2] was relieved by four companies of the 4th, and two more of the same regiment were sent to Duncan on the Rio Grande, as there were no quarters for them at Clark.

Colonel Mackenzie arrived soon after, bringing with him the secretary of war[3] and General Sheridan. The latter inspected the troops equipped for scouting and expressed himself well pleased with their serviceable condition.

It is thought that the policy to be pursued in regard to border raids was determined upon during the presence of these distinguished officers, and the emphatic endorsement of the War Department of Colonel Mackenzie's invasion seems to confirm this opinion.

With the ostensible purpose of recuperating the horses, which had been somewhat reduced in flesh by long marches, the companies were sent out of the post to grazing camps from seven to fourteen miles, where the men were drilled, practiced at target firing, and subjected to rigid discipline. This dispersion of the companies would allow the command to move without discovering the object to the prying eyes at Clark, for without doubt the garrison was closely watched by those interested in stolen stock.

Fort Clark is situated on the bank of Las Moras Creek, which heads in a beautiful spring two hundred yards from the post. From a platform extending some distance from the bank, one can look down into the clear water ten or fifteen feet, when the view is closed by luxuriant water plants. Far down in the crystal depths, fine bass, sunfish, and catfish can be seen swimming among the plants, disdaining the most tempting baits of the disgusted angler. The pool of the spring is some sixty feet across, affording a volume of water about eight feet wide and two feet deep, with a swift current.

Clark stands about forty feet above the stream, on a ridge which terminates in the head of the creek and spreads out into a considerable plain, slightly undulating. There is scarcely any soil, but feeble patches of grass rest the eye, and a few stunted trees bear faithful testimony to the utter barrenness of the plateau. Windstorms of great violence visit this vicinity, breaking down lightframe buildings, and in the fall of 1873 literally made kindling wood of a cavalry stable, the horses being fortunately at the picket line at the time or many would have been killed, whereas but one was lost. Framed tents have been picked up and carried several yards by the wind, and then torn to ribbons.

West of Fort Clark and the Rio Grande, in the Mexican Territory, lies the Bolson de Mapimi, a dreary, waterless waste of mountains and trackless deserts. Secure in this wild region, the Apaches for three centuries defied the efforts of the Spanish troops, necessitating the presence of large garrisons on the route from New Mexico via Chihuahua to Monterrey, to protect the settlements and supply escorts for trains and travelers. So little is known of the region by whites that it appears on the maps as the Terreno Desconocido,[4] and a remnant of the once powerful Apaches[5] dwell among its mountains but had changed the scene of their depredations to the soil of Texas. They had a good market in Mexico for their stolen mules, horses, and cattle. This, however, is in strict obedience to the law of compensation, for it is not much over a quarter century since powerful bands of Comanches and kindred thieves, whose camps lined the banks of the Llano Sansaba and the Concho Rivers, plundered the frontier settlements of Mexico and found a market in Texas. Fredericksburg, a frontier settlement seventy-five miles northwest of San Antonio, was a regular horse mart, and there are living old citizens who have witnessed the return of bands of plunderers exulting in their fine show of horses and scalps of women and children, and whose drunken savage orgies have chilled the lifeblood of the peacefully disposed Germans.

It is related that a band of Indians once captured a German near Fredericksburg, and never having heard such a barbarous lingo before, actually released him without harm, probably believing him to be demented. A Fredericksburger is responsible for this statement.

Joined with the Apaches were bands of Lipans[6] and Kickapoos,[7] all actuated by deadly hostility to the Texans. Issuing from their mountain retreats, they traveled by night across the plains and mountains, hid by day among the ravines or cedar brakes which abound, suddenly swooped down upon some unprotected ranch, cruelly murdering its wretched inhabitants, drove off the stock, and sometimes carried women and children into captivity. Small parties drove off the horses and mules from different parts of the country and, assembling far out on the Staked Plains, where white men had never been, and where want of water makes it dangerous to penetrate without a guide, they rested and leisurely retreated into Mexico.

The Kickapoos were the most relentless, if possible, towards the Texans, by whom they were wantonly attacked while peacefully emigrating from Arkansas. The Texans were routed with severe loss, but from that day Texas has been considered fair ground for Kickapoo raids, and all murders there as justifiable retribution. Rumor says that the Texans fired on a flag of truce and killed a squaw, by whom it was carried. To the credit of the Texans, it is said that the command, to a large extent, were opposed to interfering with the peaceful march of the Kickapoos, who had committed no depredations, but some of the hotheaded men insisted upon fighting and fired upon the flag. It is to be hoped these latter bore the brunt of the fight and the punishment.

Against these Kickapoos and their allies all Mackenzie's efforts were directed, and he sought every means to discover their villages. Spies were sent into Mexico, stimulated by offers of a large reward, but weeks went by, until the thought of action was disappearing from the minds of the troopers, but they were quickly aroused from their fancied security.

The cozy camp of A and B Companies on the Piedras Pintas[8] Creek, nestling among the tall elms and luxuriant undergrowth, lay calmly sleeping in the soft light of a May moon,[9] when the sentinel over the guard heard the whirring rattle of wheels as they came rolling from the direction of Clark. A sharp challenge rang out in the midnight air, when a short, active officer[10] humped from the carriage, gave a few curt orders to the sergeant of the guard, and walked rapidly through the camp to the tent of his brother captain. Stepping into the open tent, before which a few smoldering embers marked the campfire, he bent forward and, placing his hand lightly on his comrade's shoulder, wakened the sleeper, saying, in half-serious and half-playful tones, "Wake up, old fellow; I have news for you. A courier has just arrived from Duncan, and we are to march as soon as possible. Pack up and saddle at once, for we must cross the San Felipe road before daylight. Take five days' rations, leave your property and tents standing in charge of one man; everything will be sent for from Clark in the morning."

In a moment the shrill notes of the assembly disturbed the sleepers. The companies were formed, the orders given, and the camp is all life and activity. Here the cooks are hastily preparing breakfast, the troopers saddling their horses or making hasty toilets, while the patient pack mules are receiving their loads and curses from sleepy soldiers. Our active friend from Clark is in the meantime restlessly moving about the camp, solving difficulties for the brave and subordinate soldiers, whose powers of analysis are limited. Then back to his brother officer's camp with the query, "All ready, old fellow? All ready, hombre? Well then, mount at once and follow my company, for we are bound over the border."

The moon sailed high in the heavens as the commands "Stand to horse! Lead out! Count fours and mount!" followed in quick succession.

No unnecessary noise marked the departure of the regulars from their beautiful camp, upon which they had spent so much labor, but they hardly think of it now, as the prospect of action stifles all regrets, and when the day broke, the column had crossed the San Felipe road and was wending its way along the little valleys which cut the country southwest of Clark. About 8:00 A.M., after a march of fifteen miles, the command reached the banks of Las Moras Creek, fourteen miles from Clark, where C Company was basking in the sun, for but few trees afforded grateful relief from the overpowering heat. Las Moras at this place had contracted into a narrow, shallow stream, choked with water plants spreading over a marshy bottom, difficult to approach and almost impossible to cross.

Halting here, the companies unpacked and unsaddled to await the other companies from Clark. Colonel Mackenzie arrived early, with I Company, and at noon E and M, with a detachment of Seminoles, under Lieutenant Bullis of the 24th Infantry,[11] made their appearance after a very fatiguing march, having gone some miles out of their way. The six companies of cavalry, guides, Seminoles, and detached men of other companies made a total force of nearly four hundred, well mounted and in fine fighting condition.

About 1:00 P.M., under a blazing sun, the march commenced, Bullis leading with his Seminoles, and the companies [following by] rank—I, B, C, A, M, E. Following the course of Las Moras, which gradually dwindled to a muddy ditch difficult to cross, the Rio Grande del Norte was reached about 8:00 P.M., the command having halted for half an hour to let night come before approaching the ford. The trail on the Mexican side had been washed by high water, and it was with difficulty that a place could be found where the column could get out of the river. The double line of horses made a living dam across the stream, while the treacherous quicksand would give way and allow the animals to sink to their girths, but in less than two hours all were assembled on the Mexican shore, in an open bottom surrounded by tall reeds and thick undergrowth. Dismounted and awaiting the signal to move, smoking their pipes or eating the lunch carried in the saddlebags, officers and men quietly discussed the object of their expedition and its chances of success.

At 10:00 P.M. the head of the column emerged from the river bottom and, winding though a rocky ravine, ascended to open, rolling ground, when the order to trot was given, and away sped the somber troops, startling the dwellers in the lonely ranches, when the dull thunder of tramping hoofs rose and fell as the rapid human torrent poured across plains or plunged into ravines. Lights disappeared from dwellings as if by magic, and perhaps many a devoted mother clasped her babe to her bosom in awful terror at this unusual and ominous roar at the dread hour of midnight. It soon became evident that the laden mules could not keep up at this gait, and the colonel ordered the companies to take what they could in their pockets and saddlebags and abandon the stores, his own packs sharing the fate of the rest. The halt occupied but a few minutes, and away dashed the column through blinding dust all night.

Once a part of the column was misled by a pack train, which had stopped to water without orders, and upon issuing from a ravine, the advance had disappeared. The moon had risen and looked blood red, but by its light a faint line of dust was seen, and following this at a gallop for two miles, the column was overtaken.

It seemed as though the long night of fatigue, discomfort, and thirst would never end, but daylight found the troops descending into the beautiful valley. When day breaks upon the prairie, nature appears the personification of death—cold, motionless, dreary, and hopeless; the faces of the worn troops are pallid and corpselike; but when the glorious sun pours its golden flood of light upon the plain, the earth smiles, and life and hope return.

Daybreak[12] disclosed a creek in the valley, which was followed for six miles, when four more [miles] in advance the hostile villages were discovered. Dropping out the pack trains and forming fours, the column took the gallop and, in an impetuous charge, rushed down upon the doomed villages of savage Kickapoos, Lipans, and Apaches. I Company, with its intrepid Captain McLaughlin[13] and fearless Lieutenant Hudson,[14] led the van, and with a wild hurrah dashed into the grass huts and shot right and left at the Indians, who, arms in hand, rushed out to escape. The Kickapoos were struck first, and the firing alarmed the other villages, whose inhabitants had time to escape to the ravines, thickets, and marshes which encircled their homes, but not before twenty of their warriors had paid the penalty of their brutal crimes. Two or three companies were deployed and, circling round the villages, captured some two hundred head of horses and forty squaws and children.

These villages were said to contain nearly four hundred fighting men, but at the time of the attack, a large party was absent on a thieving expedition and escaped punishment, for Mackenzie had hoped to find all at home and strike a blow that would paralyze these marauders forever. They were of the tribes who perpetrated the Howard Wells[15] massacre and deserved the worst punishment that could be inflicted. How many Indians were wounded is unknown,[16] as the country afforded excellent facilities for concealment. The troops had one man mortally wounded, one broke a leg, and one lost an arm.

Resting men and horses for some five hours while the captured stock, consisting largely of Texas brands, was gathered, litters were prepared for the wounded and ponies selected for the prisoners to ride. The torch was applied to the grass-roofed huts and canvas shelters, and in a short time the villages were reduced to ashes. At this moment two Seminoles brought in a mounted Indian whom they had not disarmed, but stupidly allowed to carry his rifle in his hand. Brought in the midst of the troops, the villages burning, women and children standing under guard, he suddenly realized that he was among enemies and, uttering a feeble yell, leveled his rifle at Captain Mauck, who had just ridden up. As quick as thought, the captain threw himself behind his horse's shoulder, when the Indian changed his aim and fired without effect at one of the Seminoles. The captive fell from his horse dead, pierced by three or four balls, for the men, horrified at their captain's imminent danger, fired at once. For a moment, Mauck's deadly peril seemed to paralyze all who witnessed the scene without being near enough to afford any assistance, and success would have been too dearly purchased by the sacrifice of so gallant and efficient an officer. But our army records will show scores of noble soldiers who, after years of usefulness to the country, have ignobly died in conflicts with these human lice. Witness the noble Canby's death.

Ruin and desolation marked the spot, and danger lurked in the homeward path, for a few hours' march distant was a town and a well-settled district, which would send their rancheros to avenge the insult to their territory. Mackenzie thoroughly understood the situation, but confident in the excellence of his troops, carefully and rapidly made his arrangements for the transport of the wounded and prisoners, and leisurely took up his march for the Rio Grande. During the afternoon a few ranches were passed, whose inhabitants appeared anything but pleased at seeing United States troops on their soil, and occasionally horsemen could be seen observing the column.

At sunset the troops halted for water, and then commenced another long night of fatigue to the troops and suffering for wounded and captives. The children, worn out with terror and fatigue, could hardly be kept on their ponies, and frequent halts had to be made to close up the column and arrange the litters. Officers and men, worn out by three nights' marches, would fall asleep in their saddles or, while awake, imagined they heard men conversing, and that they were passing through towns. Men became morose and quarrelsome, and lying down during a halt with arm through bridle rein, could with difficulty be roused, and the officers had to be constantly on the watch to prevent them from being lost. Woe betides any sleeper who might be left behind, for the road was dogged by raging, merciless foes, who had their homes and kindred to avenge.

Hour after hour dragged its slow length along, until fourteen had passed, and the rising sun of May 19 disclosed the welcome waters of the Rio Grande, which must be passed ere rest could be hoped for. Descending from the ridge which bounded the valley, the weary column wound by shaded roads and bordered by dense thickets until a Mexican ranch with a clearing to the river was reached, when, without the formality of "by your leave," the farm gate was opened, and following a narrow path, the horses soon buried their noses in the wide, rapid stream. Men and horses seemed to draw new strength from the refreshing waters and pushed forward with animation across the deep ford. The eastern bank was soon climbed, and the welcome order to go into camp given. The saddles were stripped from the jaded horses for the first time in forty-one hours, and while the scanty breakfast was preparing, the men thronged to the river to bathe. Supplies came from Duncan in a few hours, messengers having been sent to announce the arrival of the command. A shot or two from the Mexican shore caused a ripple of excitement, but the day and night passed without disturbance, though precaution was taken for fear of surprise, as reports from Duncan indicated great excitement in Piedras Negras, where drums had been beaten for two days to raise volunteers to intercept the return march.

The command slept in a circle with the animals in the center, and at noon next day started for Clark, where it arrived on the twenty-first. A and B Companies marched in forty-nine hours, including all halts, 125 miles without losing a horse or mule. In the meantime, the garrison at Clark had been full of rumors of disaster—the command had been surrounded and cut to pieces, or was retreating before overwhelming numbers and was in extreme peril. There was but little sleep for the anxious wives at Clark. The slightest noise in garrison would bring pale, frightened women to the doors to learn the cause, and the careless soldiers were anxious for their absent comrades. A courier from the camp brought letters, which dispelled all anxiety, and the garrison joyfully awaited the return of the successful troops. In a few days reports were brought that Mexicans or Indians, or both, meditated an attack on the post, and measures were taken for defense; but in a week or two, all thought of danger, if any existed, passed away, and quiet reigned on the banks of Las Moras.

This raid brought the Kickapoos to terms, and some months later a treaty was effected, by which they agreed to move to a reservation in the Indian Territory, where it is hoped they will forever remain at peace.

A Raid into Mexico

ROBERT G. CARTER[1]

Outing 12, no. 1 (April 1888): 1–9

F ort Clark, Texas, is situated in Kinney County at an approximate elevation of one thousand feet above the level of the sea. It is 125 miles west of San Antonio de Bexar and forty-five miles north of Fort Duncan, at Eagle Pass on the Rio Grande River. Its location is on a rocky ridge of limestone, at the foot of which is a magnificent live-oak grove. Amidst its cool, inviting shadows, bubbling and sparkling from a clear and crystal pool, a series of beautiful springs called the Las Moras (the Mulberries) emerge from their hidden sylvan retreat into a smooth and narrow but sluggish stream. It forms the source of the river bearing the same name, which, flowing on some twenty miles, mingles its waters with the Rio Grande del Norte.

Clark was an old infantry post in 1852. In May 1873 it was not yet rebuilt, and the dilapidated and limited quarters proved anything but inviting to the wearied troopers of the 4th U.S. Cavalry, just arrived after a four weeks' march from Fort Richardson, and now bivouacked among the delightful live oaks referred to, waiting for the 9th Cavalry to vacate the post.

The heat during the first hours of the day was overpowering, but in the early afternoon a cool, refreshing breeze from the Gulf of Mexico sprung up, tempering the air to a soft balminess, and from that time until midnight all lived out of doors under the low, broad, vine-covered verandas—built about all the quarters—from which our *tenajas,* or water coolers, swung in the air. The evenings were particularly fine, warm, and dry, requiring no outside wraps. We were indeed in a tropical climate. The water from the deep springs was cold and delicious, and the watercress, everywhere abundant on the banks of Las Moras, furnished us with a crisp and delicate salad for our morning and evening meals.

Opposite the post, beyond the creek, on a low, flat piece of land, almost in the mesquite chaparral, is a small town named Brackettsville, the county seat of Kinney County—the exact counterpart of Jacksboro, near Richardson, the *ulcer* of every garrison, an inevitable fungus growth, only improved or eradicated after much care and trouble. Its composition varied somewhat, but there were the inevitable adobe houses, Mexican ranches or jacales, and picket stores, profusely plastered with mud, used for whiskey shops, gambling saloons, etc. Mexican greasers, half-breeds of every hue and complexion, full-blooded descendants of the African persuasion, low-down whites, and discharged soldiers composed the population, and at night a fusillade of shots warned us that it was unsafe venturing over after dark on the one crooked, unlighted, and wretched street, Le Boulevard de Brackettsville.

On April 11 the secretary of war and General Sheridan arrived, which created no little stir in camp. The command was carefully inspected, and at night a brilliant hop was given, partly complimentary to our distinguished guests, and in honor of the arrival of the 4th Cavalry.

The regimental headquarters with I Troop were daily expected from Fort Concho, and pending their arrival and the adjutant, I was summoned rather unexpectedly one night by Colonel Mackenzie, who came to my door. He desired my presence at his quarters after I had made my rounds and patrolled the town. Upon arriving at his house, I found him nervous and uneasy. He frequently arose before stating his business—looked about the quarters and closely watched to see that there were no listeners. He then, in strictest confidence, informed me that through some renegade Mexicans and half-breeds, he was possessed of certain knowledge with reference to the Indians, who just previous to our arrival had raided up the Nueces Valley and committed the massacre at Howard Wells. Their trail, with stolen stock, led back across the Rio Grande. He had ascertained their exact locality, numbers, etc., and should immediately commence preparations for an expedition against them. He proposed to effectually check their raids in the future and punish them for the past.

At his dictation I wrote a detailed letter to the department commander—the nature of which it would be improper for me, even at this late day, to divulge; and having enjoined the strictest secrecy upon me until the expedition had proved a success or failure, I left his quarters a burdened soldier—for *my wife* was included in this sacred pledge. I was a *marked man* for four weeks. I was shown a reply from department headquarters authorizing the necessary supplies on requisitions for the expedition, the destination of which was only known to Colonel Mackenzie and myself.

Preparations went steadily on until May 15. Horses were carefully shod, pack animals and saddles got in readiness, ammunition obtained in larger quantities, sabers ground, etc. The companies were sent singly, or two or more together, into grazing camps near the post. McLain, the scout, had been in the Kickapoo and Lipan villages, reported his knowledge gained to the colonel, and all was now ripe for the start.[2]

Upon more than one occasion, I felt that my good faith was doubted. At stables one evening, the colonel beckoned me to him. "You have told Lawton[3] the secret I reposed in you?"

"I beg your pardon, sir, but I have not."

"You have, then, told your wife?"

"You are mistaken, sir; I have not told a soul, unless in my dreams."

"Well, but Lawton says *he* knows that *you* know, and says *he* can find it all out through *you* or your *wife!*"

"Yes, but colonel, *that* is an entirely different matter. He *has not* found out a thing, nor will he." And yet Lawton was his quartermaster, making every preparation to go—where, he knew not.

Our camp was upon the Piedras Pintas (Painted Stones) Creek; I had just returned from a moonlight tour among the luxuriant chaparral everywhere about our delightful camp, after an unsuccessful search for mescal and aguardiente (brandy) peddlers, who, knowing that the men had been paid, had ventured forth from the depths of Brackettsville to demoralize them. I had inspected the guard and was half drowsing by the side of my troop commander, Captain Beaumont, when Captain Mauck rode hurriedly into camp from Fort Clark and gave the orders to "pack up" and saddle immediately. The captain, turning to me, said, "What is the meaning of this—where are we going?" I quietly replied, "Across the Rio Grande."[4]

All was soon busy preparation, crackling campfires were at once started to see to pack by, and at early dawn,[5] led by Ike Cox, the guide, we filed out of camp and marched rapidly across the country to the lower Las Moras, where we arrived about 8:00 A.M. and, dismounting, awaited the arrival of Colonel Mackenzie, with two companies from Clark, and Troop M from Fort Duncan, which, having lost its way, did not arrive until nearly 1:00 P.M. In a few minutes after, the entire column of six companies—A, B, C, E, I, and M, and a detachment of Seminole Negroes or half-breed scouts under Lt. John L. Bullis, 24th Infantry—was moving rapidly for the "Rio Bravo."

In this extreme Southern latitude, the sun, now high in the heavens, beat down with burning force upon our heads, which it was found necessary to protect by wet sponges fastened in our hats. Several short halts were made, and at one Colonel Mackenzie briefly made known the objects of the expedition, the probable results, and the possible risks every man—officer and soldier—would incur in an invasion of Mexican soil. Capture meant hanging—the death of a felon. Notwithstanding the spectral ghost of a gibbet before our eyes and the tired condition of those who had already marched twenty miles, all were in excellent spirits. The river was reached shortly after 8:00 P.M., sufficiently dark to cross, and the passage commenced.

We waited in the middle of the river over an hour, waiting for the head of the column to gain the opposite bank, which, steep and treacherous, retarded its advance. Our reflections were only disturbed by the murmuring of the swift stream and the impatient splashing of our animals. All talking was prohibited. A low "Forward!" We stemmed the current and a few moments later scrambled over the low but steep bank, into the dense canebrake that borders the stream above and below the ford. We debouched from the chaparral upon open ground. It was now too dark to distinguish anything but the dim forms of the moving men. We were indeed upon the soil of Mexico, and without further delay, the start was made for a night's ride upon the distant villages.

The night was soft and warm. The moon soon rose but, partially hidden by a light haze, shed an uncertain light upon the column. We rode rapidly, going where we knew not, led by the half-breed guides on their fox-gaited beasts. They knew the importance of reaching the villages by daybreak in order to surprise them, also the distance, and spared not their horses. Our gait, therefore, was constantly increased from a fast walk to a trot, then a gallop, and again to a pushing trot and a rapid fox-gait (between a walk and trot)—sometimes the dust so obscured the column it was with the greatest difficulty the rear companies could be closed up, every break or "arroyo" would string the animals out by file, which required a gallop later to close up on the advance.

It becoming evident that our pack mules could no longer keep up such speed and would so impede our progress before morning as to make our arrival on time uncertain, I was urged to ride to the head of the column and suggest that the "packs be cut loose." I felt that it was a bold suggestion, to sacrifice all our rations at the outset of an Indian raid, and on foreign soil. But I also felt that it was absolutely necessary. I passed C, B, and I Troops at an easy gallop, until I reached Colonel Mackenzie. Up to this hour, he was ignorant of any difficulty in the rear, or that all was not going well. I modestly opened up the subject. Well, for about a minute, one would have surmised that the pack train had "turned loose." But my persuasive argument soon became convincing, and I was rewarded with "Yes, tell all the troop commanders I'll halt and give just five minutes to cut the packs loose. Tell the men to fill their pockets with hard bread."

Time was precious. The knives flashed, and the mules, freed of their burdens, trotted along like kittens the remainder of the night. We again moved forward. Sometimes crossing a ravine, and when the rear was delayed, the only general guide we had was the dust ahead, through which glimmered the moon's rays. Sleep almost overpowered us, and yet on, on we went—conversation had long ago begun to lag. Nothing was heard save the ceaseless pounding of the horses and the jingle of the saddle equipment.

The gray of dawn slowly crept upon us. Then the first faint gleam of daylight streaked the horizon. A dazed, exhausted feeling had begun to steal over our weary bodies, and we seemed sustained only by the exciting novelty of the occasion. For the first time we ascertained that the guides, notwithstanding our tremendous gait during the night, had miscalculated the distance, and we were still some miles from the villages. I suggested to the colonel to take a light gallop, but his judgment was opposed to it. He dared not wind the horses before making the final charge. The pace was increased, however, and mile after mile sped rapidly by.

At the head of the column, as the daylight gradually increased, was now beheld a curious sight—the half-breeds on their animals could be seen in their saddles, constantly plying their quirts, and with their heels vigorously helping the beasts along, never swerving a hair from the general direction taken the evening before; then the Seminole-Negro scouts, with ebony faces, flat noses, and full lips, but with the characteristic high cheekbones of the Indians, their long, crinkly hair plentifully powdered with dust. In the rear, the men—their bronzed faces also covered with dust; their slouched hats of every conceivable shape, plentifully sprinkled with the same. Their features, haggard with loss of sleep and the strain of the all-night ride, gave them a kind of hard, desperate appearance that would remind one of the pictures of Italian brigands in their raids for plunder and ransom money. An occasional laugh, the nervous shifting movements in the saddle to relieve the weary, aching limbs, the short pipe to console the tired frame and empty stomach, all went to make up a picture such as was not the good fortune of any of "our artist on the spot" to witness, much less to faithfully interpret. The exhilarating breezes from the mountains—cool, dry, and life giving—gave us new strength and action.

We now commenced winding down into a lovely valley, daylight streaming all over the land, and soon had the satisfaction of hearing tinkling bells and seeing several pony herds, which scampered off at our approach. Immediately after, we struck the rocky bed of a stream, thickly skirted with chaparral and small timber. Large, round stones, washed clean and smooth and thrown to the surface by many a flood, impeded our progress at every step.

The stream, a mere thread, soon became a series of large water holes, from which man and beast now drank in pleasurable companionship, washing the dust from their parched throats. This was the Remolina. We slipped from our horses and tightened the girths.

It was broad daylight. The sun tipped the mountains with its golden touch. The beautiful azure of a cloudless Mexican sky, a calm and peaceful morning, was full upon us. It was an inspiring sight as the column, again in motion, wound its way under cover of the fringe of bushes toward the object of its terrible mission.

We were rapidly approaching the Indian villages. All talking ceased, and the clatter of the horses' hoofs upon the stones, the jingling of spurs and rattle of equipment grew painful. The column was hurriedly but silently closed up. As we debouched from the dry bed of the stream and were beginning to wind around the base of the hill, we saw hurried preparations made ahead, which indicated our very near approach to the scene of death. Men began earnestly to look at their weapons and quietly prepare for the fight. The pack trains were turned out, "fours" were counted, [and] we commenced to descend a long slope, upon which, scattered here and there, were thick patches of prickly pear, many cacti of every variety, and the ever present mesquite. At the foot we could seem to see the huts and the general outline of an Indian abiding place. And as the fringe of chaparral grew thinner, the lodges burst suddenly upon our view. We listened almost breathlessly for the fight to begin. The head of the column, now lost to view, again reappeared, this time at a gallop. An order was passed hurriedly to the rear to prepare for a charge, to hold the horses well in hand, and not to scatter out.

A shot, followed by another, and a third, and the white horses of Troop I, in the lead, could be seen stretching down the slope upon the village, now in full view. "Left front into line! Gallop! March!" rang out from front to rear. "Charge!" And then there burst forth such a cheering and yelling from our gallant little column as that Kickapoo village never heard before. It was caught up from troop to troop and struck such dismay to the Indians' hearts that they were seen flying in every direction.

The sudden charge proved a complete surprise. The leading company was soon among the grass lodges. Carbines were banging, rifles were cracking. The men were incessantly cheering and scattering in pursuit; the warriors yelling and flying in every direction, half-naked, from their huts. It was a grand and impressive sight. Sharp and imperative commands alone held the men in ranks or kept them from dashing individually into the village.

Over bushes, rocks, prickly pear, and the long, daggerlike points of the Spanish bayonet dashed the mad, impetuous column. Here could be seen a horse gone crazy and unmanageable with fright and running off with its rider, who was wholly powerless to control him. Small mesquite trees had to be avoided, and what with controlling the men, dodging rocks, bushes, and handling our horses, a more reckless, daredevil ride we never had.

Soon the rear companies struck the village and, dismounting and fighting on foot, were at once engaged. It was short work. I Troop was pursuing the flying warriors across the low, swampy ground, everywhere cut up and intersected by irrigating ditches, and with fields of corn and grain. On the left were the pony herds, seemingly as intent upon getting away as their masters.

We quickly fired the villages. The fierce crackling of the flames mingled strangely with the carbines, rifles, cheers, and yells. Taking a part of Troop A, I struck across for the herds, and after much hard riding through the chaparral everywhere skirting the village, expecting momentarily to be ambushed by small parties of stampeded Indians, I succeeded in rounding up most of the animals and started back.

As I approached the small stream bordering the smoldering lodges, riding at a rapid walk, one of the men shouted, "Look out, Lieutenant, there are Indians under the bank!" Turning quickly, I saw under a large overhanging bunch of flags what appeared to be the form of a large Indian in the act of pointing a weapon. It stirred and gathered, apparently, to fire. My carbine cracked, and the Indian fell. The men then opened.

Dismounting and ordering the firing to cease, I approached the flags, and parting them, witnessed one of those most singular and pitiable spectacles incident to Indian warfare: A small but faithful cur-dog was at the entrance, savagely menacing our advance. Beneath him lay stretched the dead body of a gigantic squaw, and behind there seemed to be more bodies. It was necessary to kill the dog before we could proceed farther. The men, reaching in, then drew forth two small children, respectively two and four years of age, badly shot through their bodies. One was dead, the other nearly so. Opening the bush for further revelations, way in rear we saw the form of another squaw, apparently unhurt, but badly frightened. Her black, glittering eyes were fastened upon the group of soldiers with a fascinating stare, not unlike that of a snake. We made signs for her to come out, but as she refused, she was quietly and without harm dragged forth. We thought this was all, but almost covered up under the immense flags we found still a third child, a girl of about twelve, badly wounded. It was one of those cruel and unavoidable accidents of grim-visaged war.

Gathering up our prisoners, we found we had about forty, with nearly 200 ponies. About twenty warriors had been killed. Among the prisoners was old Costilietos, chief of the Lipans, who had been caught by a lariat thrown over his head by one of our Seminoles as he was darting through the bushes. He had been a precious old rascal. Another prisoner, brought in and not disarmed by his captor, nearly ended the life of Captain Mauck. As soon as he fairly realized, by the burning villages, prisoners, etc., what had happened, and how he had been duped, he brought his rifle down quickly upon the captain, but was immediately riddled by bullets as we jumped to his [Mauck's] rescue and took in the critical situation.

There were many thrilling incidents and adventures during the fight. Captain McLaughlin, that sturdy and intrepid old soldier, whose company led, pursued several Indians some distance, shot at and wounded one, who fell and permitted Captain McLaughlin to ride up to him. What was the captain's astonishment to see the Indian rise up, deliberately level his rifle, and make a close shot at his head. But a miss is as good as a mile. The next moment he fell by the captain's six-shooter. Another had his pony shot from under him. Quickly jumping from his body and running at full speed, he overtook and leaped up behind a mounted Indian and rode off under fire. Some of the men's horses bogging just at this moment, they both escaped.

Sergeant O'Brien of A Troop, a gray and grisly old soldier who knew no fear, was pursuing an Indian, both afoot. He [O'Brien] had fired and missed, when the savage, thinking he had no time to reload, turned suddenly, and whirling a large, brass-bound tomahawk, threw it with such precision as just to graze the sergeant's head. Walking deliberately up to him with his carbine, throwing a cartridge quickly, as he advanced, into the chamber from the magazine, O'Brien said, "I have you now, you old spalpane," and shot him dead at fifteen paces.

We unsaddled, and remaining just long enough to treat the wounded (one mortally), to amputate an arm and set a leg, to construct litters, and assign the prisoners to ponies for the ride back, we started. Beyond the Kickapoo village, about one-fourth of a mile, was that of the Lipans. Still farther beyond in the distance, sharply defined in the clear atmosphere, stretched the Santa Rosa Mountains, whose peaks were now bathed in the mellow sunlight, seeming only a few miles distant, towards which a great many of the Kickapoos and all of the Lipans fled when first aware of our hostile approach.

Colonel Mackenzie, when first informed of the relative strength of the two villages, was told he would be compelled to make his main attack upon the largest—the Kickapoo village. But before commencing the charge, one of the guides suggested dividing the force, sending a part around the Lipan village in the direction of the mountains, thus cutting off their escape in that direction, while the remaining companies made a vigorous attack upon the Kickapoos. But the colonel would not listen to it, owing to his belief that the latter were more numerous. Hence the escape of all the Lipans before they could be reached over the swamp approaches to their stronghold.

The sun was now high in the heavens; the heat was increasing in intensity. We mounted and commenced our retrograde march. Our course lay through the little Mexican settlement of Remolina. Everywhere we met the malignant scowls of El Mexicano. It was a novel and astonishing spectacle for them to behold a body of United States cavalry, with prisoners, swiftly traversing their territory for safety beyond "El Rio Bravo."[6]

Their occasional exclamations in muttered, incoherent Spanish, far from indicating a friendly spirit to Los Americanos, foreboded evil to us before striking American soil. It was a scalding day; not a breath of air stirred. The heat hung over the earth in tremulous waves, parching and roasting our brave little command till we could seem to endure it no longer. Had it not been for the numerous lagoons met frequently during the day, our suffering would have been intense.

Our trail had been discovered going in, and the results of our raid had been communicated by rapid couriers up and down the river. Even then the "long roll" was beating from Piedras Negras to the upper fords for the volunteers to intercept our march. It was ascertained that a short distance away was another Mescalero Apache village. These Indians, long resident in Mexico, were sworn allies to the Kickapoos and capable of sending five hundred warriors against us.

As darkness settled about us, our anxiety increased, which, added to the exhausted condition of the men and animals, left us in no cheerful frame of mind, or prepared for our long night ride and a possible fight in ambuscade. The moon, yellow and tropical, but dazzling bright, rose and illuminated our trail, now glittering with myriads of dewdrops that everywhere flashed like diamonds under our horses' feet.

We wearily rode on. The heavy, overpowering hand of sleep was upon every officer and man. This was the third night that many of us had been absolutely without sleep. The Indian prisoners were heavily guarded in the rear, and our Seminole scouts stealthily hovered about our flanks to guard against ambush or surprise, while our advance guard slowly felt its way ahead.

It was a long, long night. Everywhere in the column, men drowsed and swayed in their saddles. Officers, obliged to forego even this luxury, were on the alert to keep them awake, and at every halt to urge them to renewed efforts. We had read stories of the execution of Chinese criminals by sentinels keeping them awake with bayonets until death relieved their sufferings. The eyes seemed strained out of our heads. The tension was so great that the head seemed full to bursting. The physical pain endured cannot be conceived. The imagination pictured all kinds of tangible objects to our overstrained minds. Now, in the bright moonlight, a huge boulder loomed up before our bewildered eyes, and the horses [were] guided around the obstacle. Again we passed through hamlets and large towns, all commenting upon the extravagant illumination which the people had resorted to. We were at all times dodging and stooping to avoid imaginary objects. One man, wandering from the column a short distance while it was at [a] halt to enjoy an undisturbed rest, awoke, only to find the column gone and a Mexican standing over him. He jumped up, fired his pistol, ran through the bushes, and following our trail until morning, finally crossed the river and joined the command. Such was our mental condition—a hallucination of the mind bordering upon the insane.

Towards morning the Indian papooses and children—in some cases mounted in threes and fours upon the ponies—began to be troublesome by falling fast asleep and tumbling off, which occasioned frequent halts in order to have the rear closed up for safety. They were finally lashed on with lariats.

Several times the Seminoles in the rear reported the enemy in sight. At these times word was passed along to keep the men waked up. But we were not attacked.

The gray of dawn found us still dodging about the winding paths and roads among the mesquites leading to the river. At daylight the heavier timber that skirts the Rio Grande was seen, and soon we were upon the banks of the stream. The interminable night of horror, of nightmare, had passed. We made many long, tedious halts in the canebrake. I looked about me. Scenes which neither pen nor tongue can describe were everywhere about. Some of the men were asleep with their arms about their horses' necks, others were drowsing and nodding bolt upright. Some, by persistent efforts to smoke and talk, barely held their drooping lids from closing.

The condition of the prisoners, although ludicrous, was pitiful. They were riding double and by threes on the captured ponies. The children, half naked and streaked with dust and sweat, deprived, by being lashed, even of the privilege of lying upon their ponies' necks, were fast asleep, and their black heads and swarthy skins presenting a striking contrast to the blue-coated troopers that surrounded them. Here was a child of but five or six years; his head was shaved smooth, except a tuft or stiff scalp lock running from his forehead over to his neck. His face was painted in particolored stripes. His infantile warrior spirit had given way. The tears had coursed over the paint and sweat, and the dust adhering, gave him a very ludicrous, yet strangely touching expression. All faces wore that gray, ashy, deathlike appearance indicative of overworked nature and the approach of exhaustion. It took some time to get the wounded in the horse litters across. But at last the rear of the column stood upon American soil, and we gave vent to our pent-up feelings with a hearty Amen!

We bivouacked upon the land of Capt. Green Van, a ranchero of some notoriety along that line of the Rio Bravo, who with undaunted courage had volunteered to guide us on this hazardous expedition, and of course now would travel with his life in his hand, as the Mexicans would turn upon him for revenge.

Our stay here was one of continued excitement, as shots were heard and threats were sent over that a large body was gathering to attack us that night.

Our position was on a small plateau or tableland, completely surrounded by dense canebrakes. We slept in a circle, with pickets thrown out and selected sleeping parties in the brakes. We turned in for sleep. The field proved to be an immense ant heap, which persecuted and tortured us until early morning, when we moved to a more secure spot, and after recuperating man and beast with rations and forage dispatched from Fort Clark, we took up the march for the post, arriving about noon on May 21, there to meet the anxious garrison, who had purposely been kept in ignorance of even our destination, and after a terrible suspense now rejoiced at our safe return.

On the twenty-fourth Colonel Mackenzie, hearing well-founded rumors that a large body of Indians and Mexicans were making threatening demonstrations on the opposite bank, took two companies and scouted in the direction of Villa Nueva and other points, and returned on the twenty-sixth without seeing or hearing anything. Our scouts, however, reported during the day that we might expect an attack at any time.

The night of May 26 closed in dark, and with every indication of one of those terrible thunderstorms peculiar to the tropics. All was gloom and inky blackness. The eye could distinguish nothing a foot away. The anxiety was intense all over the garrison. Pickets had been thrown about the entire post. Ladies and children gathered in groups in each other's quarters or on the porches and breathlessly discussed the chances of coming battle, of massacre, and all the attendant horrors of Indian retaliation. The hoarse boom-boom of the thunder, the incessant flash of the lightning glared about the little plateau, bringing out the buildings with startling clearness one moment, only to be succeeded by impenetrable gloom the next. It rattled and roared in angry succession. It was just such a night as would set an atheist to thinking whether there was really a God in Heaven who now controlled the elements, and if he was prepared to meet this Unknown Power.

The entire garrison was deeply impressed with the awful sublimity of the scene, when a carbine shot, another, and another in quick succession, and a spluttering rattle by the pickets caused all to start to their feet, and the ladies and children, with blanched cheeks, to gather and huddle for protection. The long roll on the drum vied with the rattling, booming thunder. The cavalry bugles sounded their loudest assembly. Every flash showed the gallant troopers pouring out of the barracks in the dreadful storm, carbine in hand. Officers, with a last word of cheer to the companions of their lives in this far-off wild, buckled on sabers and pistol and hurried to the companies now falling in to the music of the drummers. A few moments and every man was under arms. We awaited further developments from the pickets, who had now ceased firing and maintained an almost provoking silence. In a moment or two, however, it was ascertained that one of the pickets had discharged his piece at a hog, and was, of course, followed by a fusillade from the others. All of the officers were immediately summoned to headquarters, where verbal instructions were given to be carried out in case of another alarm or bona-fide attack. One set of stone quarters was designated for the ladies to repair to. The citizens of the town were notified, and thus ended the Mexican scare. The suspense was over. The attack never came, and quiet and peace reigned for many a day on this border of the Rio Grande.

With the Buffalo Soldiers on the Texas Frontier

"RECORDER"

Army and Navy Journal 11, no. 8 (October 4, 1873): 117

An expedition left Fort Sill, Indian Territory, on August 19, 1873, consisting of Companies G, H, K, and M, 10th Cavalry, and C, 11th Infantry, commanded by [Brig.] Gen. J. W. Davidson, lieutenant colonel, 10th Cavalry. In addition to this force, two companies of the 9th Cavalry[1] were ordered to join from Fort Richardson, Texas, making altogether six companies of cavalry and one of infantry.

This command was assembled for the purpose of moving around the reservation of the Comanche and Kiowa Indians, in order to pursue and punish, if possible, any savages upon marauding expeditions outside. The arrangements were made as quietly as could be, and every care was taken to conceal the departure of the scout from the Indians, who are always in the neighborhood of their agency, which is located close to Fort Sill.

The troops marched on August 19 for Gilbert's ranch, on the Red River, by a circuitous route in order to deceive the savages still further. At Gilbert's ranch, the companies from Fort Richardson joined, and the entire force continued the march up the Red River. Upon crossing the Pease River, the country changed in its appearance for the worse, the grass became poor, and the water was affected more or less by gypsum, which occurs in vast quantities in this region. The water of the Pease seemed to be worse than any other, perfectly salty and nauseating, and the Red River was very little better. Recent rains enabled the command to obtain fresh water in holes and did much in this way for the welfare of horses and men.

The companies from Fort Richardson were under the command of Captain Baldwin.[2] The officers brought with them a young gentleman from New York named Hoxie, a brother of Richard L. Hoxie of the Engineer Corps,[3] who had journeyed to Texas for the benefit of his health, impaired to some extent by hard study in his profession of the law. The day after the scout passed the mouth of Pease River, Mr. Hoxie was found to be missing. For two days nothing was heard of him, and the greatest anxiety was felt for his safety. Colonel Davidson halted his command and dispatched two companies to search for

him. After looking in every direction without success, this party finally concluded to proceed up the Pease River for a distance. Just as they were about to
give up and return, some observing eye discovered a figure, evidently human,
upon an adjacent sand hill, close to the banks of the river. To the joy and surprise of everyone, this was found to be the lost one for whom they were
searching. He had lost his way while wandering from the column and had mistaken the wide, sandy bed of the Pease for the Red River; and after two days of
unavailing efforts to find the troops or their trail, had thrown himself down to
die, overcome by hunger and fatigue. Upon the pommel of his saddle he had
written his story—his name, a statement that he had been lost on such a date
from Lieutenant Colonel Davidson's column, and had perished—with his
address in New York City. Everybody was delighted to see him safe again, and
Mr. Hoxie did not indulge in any further curiosity regarding the nature of the
country out of sight of the troops.

On August 28 the scout passed over Groesbeck Creek. Just to the left of
the crossing, a newly made grave was discovered. Everyone pressed forward to
examine it. A stone was placed at the head, and roughly engraved upon it were
these words: "Hank Medley, killed by Indians, August 25, 1873." It was
known that a party of surveyors had started in this direction, and it was therefore surmised that Hank Medley belonged to their party. A number of cartridge
papers lying around testified that the party ahead was preparing for the future,
alarmed probably by the death of their comrade.

Here was one more outrage added to the long list committed by the savage
marauder upon the frontier of Texas, for which no redress had been obtained
or can be. The Indian is reported to be at peace by the Indian agent, and very
few place credence in these tales from the border of his crimes and robberies.
Lieutenant Myer of the 11th Infantry,[4] with a small force, was sent forward by
Lieutenant Colonel Davidson upon the trail of the surveyors, with instructions
to communicate with them. The troops then proceeded more to the north and
then to the west up the Red River, until the 100-degree meridian longitude was
passed, when the course was changed to the north, the 100-degree meridian
being the boundary of the reservation.

Some delay was caused by the failure of Lieutenant Myer to make his
appearance when expected, but finally he returned, having ridden ninety-five
miles in carrying out his orders. The surveyors were found, and Mr. Maddox,
their chief, accompanied Myer into our camp. As we supposed, Hank Medley
was one of their party. Eight Indians had suddenly surrounded him while he
was hunting buffalo and shot him down before assistance could be rendered,
although the Indians were forced to flee without scalping him on account of
the approach of the party of surveyors.

The scout proceeded to the north, crossing Buck Creek, the Salt Fork of
Red River, and finally the North Fork of Red River. Companies were continually kept on detached service, scouting the right, left, and advance of the column, and occasionally detachments were left behind at the camps, when
vacated, lying *perdu* in order to catch any savages who might be following on

Buffalo soldiers in action on the Texas frontier. W. F. BEYER, *DEEDS OF VALOR.*

our trail, and who might exercise any curiosity regarding our camps after we left them. Several trails were seen, but none of any consequence or very recent.

After crossing the North Fork, the command moved to the east, into the Kiowa and Comanche reservation. Very high bluffs are to be seen in this vicinity along the north bank of the North Fork, with a stratum of gypsum near the summit in some places twenty feet in thickness—a most remarkable geological formation. Plaster of paris could be obtained from this single stratum of gypsum sufficient to supply the commercial demands of the continent. A number of Cheyenne Indians followed the column for two or three days and seemed to show some signs of hostility. They were off their reservation, and Colonel Davidson finally succeeded in effecting an interview with three or four of them. He warned them to return to their reservation, and we did not see them afterwards.

The scout returned to Fort Sill by the north side of the Wichita Mountains, through a beautiful country covered with fine grass and supplied with an abundance of good water, and on September 14 arrived at the post. During the absence of the command, a report had been spread through the country that Fort Sill had been attacked and the women and children massacred. This was without any truth. The Indians are now on their good behavior, as Satanta and Big Tree have been sent here as prisoners, and a great council is to be held in a few days to determine their fate, at which Governor Davis of Texas and the secretary of the interior intend to be present. The scout marched four hundred miles without loss of animals.

Buffalo Days

J. WRIGHT MOOAR[1] (as told to James Winford Hunt)

Holland's: The Magazine of the South 52, nos. 1–4 (January–April 1933)

THE SHARPS RIFLE

The buffalo threw up his shaggy head and looked at the hunter, who, crouching on the prairie seven hundred yards away, immediately froze into immobility. The seconds passed. Man and beast regarded each other intently. On a distant knoll, another wild figure appeared—an Indian on his pony. His sharp eyes took in the picture on the plain below. He too paused and sat as if carved from stone. The miles-wide sward of dun prairie grass broke against the red bluffs of an arroyo and the low, rocky hills marking the foot of the great Staked Plains of Texas. It was a picture for Remington.

At last the buffalo moved uneasily and, in doing so, turned broadside to the hunter. The distant watcher saw the white man settle himself for the shot. He had some experience with the terrible range of the great gun of the buffalo hunters, but it seemed incredible to him that any weapon could be effective at such a distance. The very wind seemed to pause as the sights were adjusted and the great muzzle rose to the proper elevation and steadied. An instant later the smoke streamed from the gun, and the astonished Indian saw the buffalo sink to his haunches, rock sidewise, roll over, thresh the ground for a moment, and grow still in death.

The red man waited for no more. Whirling his cayuse [pony], he lashed him into top speed and fled like a shadow over the hills, where his renegade band awaited him.

Years afterward, Quanah Parker, the Indian, and Wright Mooar, the hunter, met at a peaceable reunion of early settlers and Indians, tamed on their reservations, and had an interesting discussion of the incident. Years later still, I had the story from Wright Mooar's lips, and the rugged old frontiersman, among the very last of the buffalo hunters, laughed heartily over the Indian's amazement and frantic flight.

"Where did that happen?" I asked.

"Somewhere in Garza County, Texas, not far from where [the] post is now."

Josiah Wright Mooar. HOLLAND'S: THE MAGAZINE OF THE SOUTH 1933.

The night came slowly, as it does in West Texas, as I sat with the old frontiersman on the veranda of his rank home, and to my eager questions came the recital of the stirring days of the buffalo, which constitutes these chronicles to follow. Mooar, now nearly eighty years of age, a sturdy old New Englander from the green hills of Vermont, a far-wandering son of the old frontiers of Kansas, Oklahoma, and Texas—but wait.

Here is an odyssey of hairbreadth escapes from death with wild Indians, wilder white men, and thundering herds of wild buffalo. Here is the story of the beginning and the end of a great commercial enterprise, peculiar to a period of American history that has no parallel in any other country on earth. You shall have his story, as he told it to me.

—MR. HUNT'S NOTE

A NEW BUSINESS ENTERPRISE

My Scotch ancestors, were a sturdy, God-fearing race who came to America and settled in the wilds of Vermont. At nineteen years of age I left home, just as they had done, and turned my face west. I arrived at Fort Hays, Kansas, a government outpost on Big Creek, a tributary of the Smoky [Hill] River, in the fall of 1870, and soon after began cutting cordwood for a government contractor on Walnut Creek, thirty miles south of the fort.[2]

Those were wild days. The Civil War had left a restless spirit among the young men that began to express itself in a quest after new enterprises and adventures. At this time, W. C. Lobenstein was engaged in the fur-trading business at Fort Leavenworth, Kansas. Charley Rath and Charlie Myers, buffalo hunters and adventurers, acting as agents, delivered the furs of the Indians, trappers, and hunters to Lobenstein and were busily engaged in building up a vast fur trade, not the least of which consisted of the trade in buffalo hides, which at this time were being made up into buffalo robes.

In the winter of 1871 and the spring of 1872, Lobenstein apprised Charley Rath of the fact that an English firm had asked for five hundred buffalo hides, to be used as an experiment in making leather; and if successful, they would take an unlimited number of the hides, which would open up an immense trade in a new kind of leather to be placed on the markets of the world. Among others, I was now killing buffalo for the meat and became interested in the enterprise, and agreed to enter actively into the work of killing buffalo, and thus furnish my pro rata of the first five hundred hides.

The days that followed were days of constant adventure, hanging on the skirts of the great buffalo herd, the mighty victims falling before the deadly marksmanship of the pathfinders to the Golden West. Thus it came about that I furnished my quota of the five hundred buffalo hides which were daily turned over to Charley Rath, sold to Lobenstein, and eventually sent to the tanners of England. In making up my total, I discovered that I had fifty-seven hides left over. Packing those for shipment, I wrote my brother John Wesley Mooar, who was a clerk in a jewelry store in New York,[3] and to my brother-in-law, John W. Combs, who worked for a silk-importing company at 81st Pine Street, New York City, and notified them that I was consigning to their care the fifty-seven hides, and suggested that they undertake to sell them to the tanners of New England. When the hides arrived in the city, the novelty of the sight created a diversion that amounted to a mild sensation in the immediate group around them. On their way up to the jewelry store, they were marked by a number of fur dealers, who followed the wagon and entered into negotiations with the boys, with the result that those fifty-seven hides were sold to the tanners, made up into leather, and the experiment proved immediately successful.[4]

Even before the English firm had reported its success in the treatment of the buffalo hides and asked for a large number of them, I was apprised of the fact that the American tanners were ready to open negotiations for all the buffalo hides I could deliver. The moment it became known that here was a new industry promising great returns to those engaged in it, Charlie Myers opened a business at Fort Dodge, dealing in furs and in furnishings supplied to the trappers and hunters covering a vast section of the territory.

HELL-ROARING DAYS

The spring of 1872 was an epochal period in the history of Kansas and the western states generally. The Santa Fe Railroad began building west from Emporia, Kansas, and the railroad grading camps were strung along the new right-of-way for 160 miles.

Following the Civil War, the soldiers of the North and South returning to their homes drove the lawless bushwhackers, who had terrorized noncombatants of both factions, out of the settled communities and into the new frontiers. The lawless element took up residence and established towns along the route of the railroad. Saloons, gambling dens, brothels, and every rendezvous of vice flourished. Murders, robberies, and all sorts of crimes prospered unrebuked, and a man lived by his wits, courage, and ability to "draw first."

The first tent pitched in Dodge City was a saloon established by George Hoover and Jack MacDonald, half brothers who came into the country from Toronto. Within one month after the opening of the saloon, thirty-three graves adorned the hillside.

While the site of Dodge City was being surveyed and its first buildings erected, I was killing buffalo and selling the meat to the railroad graders and hides to such dealers as Rath and Myers. In pursuit of this enterprise, I joined with "Prairie Dog Dave" Morrow, a middle-aged man who had drifted in from Michigan, and a younger man from Maine named Charley Dunn. Each had a wagon and team and was armed with the famous Sharps rifle, which the Indians described as "shoots today and kills tomorrow" because of its superior range over all other firearms of the period.

A RACE FOR LIFE

In the early summer, in company with a man much older than myself and a boy two years younger, I set out up the Arkansas to establish a new buffalo camp. My older companion and I each had a wagon and team. The younger boy had no outfit, but went along as a helper. A hundred miles up the river, we came to an old, abandoned rock house, which had been a station on the Pony Express. This was remodeled, and enough hay for a permanent camp was cut and stacked.

The older man suggested that he and I take a load of meat to a trading post about seventy-five miles north and bring back more supplies. The younger boy was to keep camp during our absence. All agreed to this, and our plans were quickly matured. The night before the trip was to be begun, we had some final discussion, and then got into our bunks.

I lay there listening to the rising wind among the branches of the trees down by the river and around the corners of the house. Soon the usual serenade of the dwellers of the wilderness began. The coyotes opened with their yapping, and the deep, sustained howl of a lobo suddenly broke in. A crescent moon climbed above a cloud bank in the east and bathed the terrain of bluff and valley with a ghostly light. The water from the spring branch flowing near the house added its liquid voice to a thousand mysterious whisperings of the wilderness night. Presently I fell asleep.

Some sense of danger awakened me. Already I was becoming inured to the life of that lonely land and lay perfectly quiet, listening. The murmur of low voices came from somewhere, but the words were indistinguishable. In a moment, however, I recognized my younger companion's voice raised on a high note of fear and protest. Slipping quietly from my blankets, I crept to the small opening serving for a window. The moon had passed meridian height considerably, which showed I had been asleep for some hours.

From the deep shadow of the building and near a corner farthest from where I slept, I heard the voice of my older companion low and tense, saying, "Shhh—not so loud!"

Several minutes of utter silence followed, and then the speaker began again. "He's asleep. Get this. There ain't goin' to be no danger. During this trip he is goin' to jest disappear, see? That will give us his outfit. Nobody will know about it for months, and then we will tell all about how the Indians got him. See?"

"What about me?"

"Nothin'. Jest stay here and keep quiet. I'll handle the rest, and we get a good outfit."

There followed some whispering that I did not get. But I had heard enough to realize the horrible truth—that I was to be the victim of a murder plot. I crept back to my blankets and lay perfectly quiet, and shortly the two conspirators came in, softly as shadows. The older man called to me in a low voice, but I did not answer. Satisfied that I was locked in slumber, he lay down.

There was no more sleep for me that night. I lay wide awake, counter-scheming to save my life and to get away from that deadly neighborhood. At daybreak my plan was perfected. During the preparation of the breakfast, I feigned illness and ate nothing. As soon as the meal was over, I got my team and hitched it to the wagon without a word, as though I was going on with our trip as originally planned. Then, with my gun in my hands, I announced that I was sick and homesick, and was going to go back to Dodge.

My companions looked at each other, and the boy's face had a guilty expression, but the older scoundrel preserved his pose of friendliness and expressed his sympathy.

"Never mind, kid," he said. "I don't blame you. We will divide the stuff and you can go back. Sorry to lose you, but you air yore own boss."

The supplies were divided so as to give me a sufficiency for my return journey. During these preparations, I was constantly alert for any sign of treachery. But after a final friendly farewell, I drove away on the backtrack, keeping a wary eye on the treacherous pair until I had placed a safe distance between them and me. I drove hard, and coming to the bank of the river, where the water was swift and deep, dumped all the provisions into the river, not daring to eat lest I be poisoned. Pushing on as rapidly as possible, I stopped only long enough to kill a buffalo. That evening I met a great herd of cattle on the trail and quickly gained permission from the men to camp with the outfit that night.

FORAGING FOR A LIVING

Knowing that the passing of the herd had effectually effaced my tracks, I turned aside the next day, made camp in the timber along the river, and began killing buffalo, skinning them and living on their meat and on river water for seven days. Forty-two fell to my marksmanship, and their hides were secured. From eight of the fallen animals I cut the hams, hoping to trade them for groceries at the trading camps. Here disappointment met me. The trading camps for miles were those of a contractor by the name of Gunning, a Missourian who hated and mistrusted Kansans. He had laid on his employees a binding injunction that, supplies being precious and transportation slow and hazardous, strangers were not to be fed or allowed to barter for food. At the first camp I sold a buffalo ham, but when I tried to buy bread my request was peremptorily refused. At another camp, having sold a ham, I offered ten dollars for ten pounds of flour but was told I could not purchase anything at the camp for love or money.

WHEN A MAN WAS A MAN

Thus for seven days I wandered on, living on a straight diet of buffalo meat. At last, as I turned away from a camp, a man came out and asked to ride with me down to the next camp. All the buffalo hams had been sold but one, and the man, espying this, immediately offered to buy it.

"What do you get for a ham?" he asked.

"Two dollars."

"I'll give you two dollars."

"No, I won't sell it."

"I'll give you three dollars."

"It's not for sale."

"I'll give you five dollars."

"No, sir, but I will trade it to you for supper and breakfast at camp."

"Nothing doing."

Thus we traveled on down to the next camp.

A WOMAN AND A BOY

I pitched my lonely camp on the opposite side of a high railroad dump from the trader's camp, and having kindled a fire, was about to fry a piece of meat when a woman appeared on the high grade and hailed me: "Son, you come over to the camp and get your supper. A fellow who has lived for seven days on nothing but meat shall never be turned away from my table, rules or no rules."

"I'll give you this ham for supper."

"You come on, ham or no ham."

With alacrity I shouldered my ham and accompanied the good woman to the camp, where her husband, my erstwhile traveling companion, scowled and predicted they would all be fired.

I was given a wonderful supper, and the woman thankfully received the ham, as fresh meat was low in her larder. In spite of the man's protests, I was invited back the next morning and given a bountiful breakfast, and went on my lonely way, cheered and refreshed, coming at last to Dodge City, where I resumed my occupation of killing buffalo from among the small scattered herds in the vicinity of the fort.

THE COMING OF THE GREAT HERD

August 10, 1872, was my twenty-first birthday. On that morning there occurred the strangest event in the history of the West. No student of natural history has ever been able to account for the trek of the buffalo herd.

On the morning of August 10, 1872, I, in company with other wondering beholders standing on the north side of the Arkansas River, saw a sight perhaps never seen before, and surely never seen since. For seven miles from the south bank of the Arkansas, clear back to the hills marking the southern boundaries of the valley, and as far as the eye could reach up and down the river, was a living mass of buffalo, pressing in countless thousands upon each other, the foremost platoons drinking from the yellow flood now seven hundred yards wide, swollen by the melting snows of its mountain sources and presenting a barrier to the strangest migration in history. During the night of the ninth, this herd had pressed into the valley after crossing the sixty-five-mile divide between the Cimarron and the Arkansas. Somewhere in the hills, after the dry passage over the divide, the scent of water had come to the wild wanderers, and a stampede to the banks of the river had taken place. The thunder of its advance had aroused and stampeded the horses in the trading camps north of the river, and in some instances the traders themselves fled through the night in terror.

This vast herd of millions consisted entirely of prime animals—no old or very young in the herd. Later they began crossing the river in small but ever-growing relays, and finally the countless thousands poured across and pressed on to Montana, where they wintered. The following summer they trekked over the great watershed between the Missouri, Mississippi, and the Red River of the North, to the Hudson's Bay basin. Here, trapped in the rigors of an artic winter of blizzards and snows, they perished. The greater part of that vast herd, therefore, was destroyed not by the hunters' alleged wanton rapacity, but by its own unaccountable transcontinental urge and northward march.[5]

The herd was six or seven weeks crossing the Arkansas, and as the relays came over, the buffalo hunters swarmed upon their flanks. Men whose names became famous were numbered among the hunters. George Causey left the camps of Gunnings' graders to become a killer of big game, hunting the buffalo until the last straggler fell. Causey Hill, in Lubbock County, Texas, the highest sand ridge on the plains for miles, and also a landmark of early pioneers to that section of the plains, was named for George Causey.

HARPER'S WEEKLY.

A JOURNAL OF CIVILIZATION

Vol. XVIII.—No. 937.]   NEW YORK, SATURDAY, DECEMBER 12, 1874.   [WITH A SUPPLEMENT.
PRICE TEN CENTS.

Entered according to Act of Congress, in the Year 1874, by Harper & Brothers, in the Office of the Librarian of Congress, at Washington.

Slaughtered for the hide. HARPER'S WEEKLY 1874.

I hired an Irishman named Mike McCabe as a skinner, and I found an active place among the hunters. We killed thousands of the mighty animals and sold the hides to Rath and Myers, who relayed them through Lobenstein of Fort Leavenworth to the tanneries of the world.

>─┼─◆>─◦─‹◆─┼─◂

In November [1872], following the coming of the great herd, my brother John came west to join me in the new enterprise of buffalo killing. Upon his arrival in Dodge City, he went to Rath's store and asked, "Do you know a fellow by the name of J. Wright Mooar?"

"Yes," said Rath, "I know him. He is out a few miles at his camp but will be here in about three days with a load of hides and meat."

"Well, I'm his brother."

"All right. Glad to meet you. Hang around."

While waiting for me, John put up at the little hotel and spent the time seeing the strange sights of the frontier town. The tough, heavily six-shootered men, wagons loaded with hides and meat, long trail outfits with supplies, railroad gangs, desperadoes, officers of the law, soldiers, cowboys, and Indians made a motley, moving show that held his attention and caused the hours to pass quickly.

One day he noticed a claim house on the prairie some distance from the edge of town. He wandered out to it and heard voices inside. Being a tenderfoot, he did not realize the danger of "butting in" on other people's affairs in a land of outlaws, and getting no response to his knock, he pushed open the door and looked in on a strange performance. Two men were busily engaged in the peculiar occupation of painting a white horse black.

The tenderfoot immediately gave voice to his amazement. "What are you doing?"

The men, startled, looked upon the intruder with a deadly intentness for a moment but saw he was a harmless tenderfoot. This probably saved his life. Finally, one of the men answered, "We stole this horse down on Rattlesnake Creek last night, and we are going to paint him black and sell him back to his owner."

This they actually did.

Three days later, I came in with thirty-six hundred pounds of meat, which I sold for three cents per pound. I camped on the prairie about a mile from town, and John came out to the wagon with me after we had had supper at the hotel. As we talked, I made down my bed in the grass and crept between the blankets. John, after some questions and misgivings because this was his first night in the open, pulled off his shoes and crept in beside me. The camp bed of the frontiersman was a thing of art. A tarp was spread upon the grass, the blankets spread upon it, and the tarp was drawn back over the top and carefully folded in at the sides. The sleeper then crawled in at the head of his bed and drew the tarp end entirely over his head, thus encasing him [and] shutting out the cold and prowling animals or snakes.

John crept in with his trousers on but soon found the bed so snug and warm, in spite of the November chill, that he had to shed them. Two inches of snow fell during the night, and when the tarp was thrown back the next morning, we looked upon a white world.

My buffalo camp was at the point of what was known as Three-Mile Ride, twelve miles west of Dodge. We drove out to the buffalo camp. John stayed at this camp, getting his first taste of roughing it, while I traveled back to Dodge with the next load of hides and meat. Here I met my cousin Charles Wright, and since both John and Charles wanted to get into the buffalo-hunting business, I hired them and Mike McCabe at $50 per month. We headed an expedition southeast, crossing the Arkansas River at Fort Dodge and pushing on for forty miles to Kiowa Creek, west of Medicine Lodge. Here we were in camp a month and took 305 buffalo hides and 20,000 pounds of short-cut hams. The meat brought two and one-half cents per pound, and I gave half of the proceeds to freighters for hauling it to market. The hides I hauled myself. These hides were sold for $3.05 each.

THE GREAT BLIZZARD

On one of these trips to the hide market at Dodge City, John and I, each driving a team, joined the [Thomas C.] Nixon freight outfit, loaded with meat, at Kiowa Creek and traveled with it to Mulberry Creek, where we struck the old government road from Dodge City to Camp Supply. On the way, a blinding blizzard of wind and snow swooped down from the north, and men and animals were soon white with frost and struggling in an icy gale that became a real threat to life itself. At Mulberry Creek, we held a brief council and decided to press on to Dodge City. The government road along here for miles was a wide and deeply beaten trench from one to two feet deep. The howling gale drove the snow across this, banking it on the other side and leaving a plain trail for the teams to follow, but at length we came to the mouth of the creek valley, as it debouched into the wide valley of the Arkansas, and the trail shallowed and was soon apparently lost.

Another council was held, and it was agreed to stick together and try to reach John Hunt's ranch at a point on the trail. Here a saloon, store, and ranch houses would afford shelter, which was rapidly becoming a necessity if we were to survive. Ice formed on our beards, eyebrows, and eyelashes until we could scarcely see our way.

At last the lead team, driven by Levi Richardson, stopped, bringing the whole cavalcade to a halt. Staggering back through the howling gale to the other drivers, he announced that one of his lead mules was frozen to death. John Mooar saw that Richardson was completely blinded by the ice that had formed on his beard and eyelashes. Cupping his hands around his own mouth and over Richardson's eyes, he blew his warm breath on the matted ice until he could brush it away and Richardson could see.

Pat Baker, who was driving the second team, volunteered to go forward and drive the lead team. "I can make those blankety-blanked leaders move," he shouted above the storm, and a few moments later was cracking his blacksnake whip over their backs. But they would not move. He then went forward and seized one lead mule by the bridle bits and strove to drag them around from the drive of the gale. As he struggled with the stubborn animals, he staggered against a wall—and found that the mules had reached the ranch and were standing with their heads against a door! Snow had drifted entirely over it.

In a short time we were inside, and while the teams munched their food under the windbreaks, we, half frozen, were gathered about the fires and steaming food and drinks, inside the houses. Only the unerring instinct of the faithful mules had brought us to safety.

One of the drivers was Bat Masterson, who later gained considerable fame.[6] Years afterward, I was in New York City and called at the Astoria Building, inquiring for Bat Masterson. A polite clerk answered that Mr. Masterson was in and went to inform him that he had a visitor.

In a moment Masterson appeared and said, "Do you want to see me?"

"If you are Bat Masterson, I do."

"Well, I'm what's left of him."

"Do you remember being with Nixon's wagon train on January 27, 1873?"

"I was right there."

"Who drove the front wagon?"

"Pat Baker."

"No, it was driven by Levi Richardson. Pat Baker was next."

"Well, who drove the next wagon?"

"I did."

"And who drove the next?"

"Columbus."

"Yes, sir; and who came next?"

"Jimmie."

"And who was next?"

"The Mooar brothers."

"Right again. I am Wright Mooar, driver of the last wagon."

From that moment, we two comrades of the old frontier sat down to live again, for a time, the experiences of those stirring days and pay tribute to the faithful dumb animals whose unerring sense of direction and surroundings, superior to any man's intelligence in such an exigency as that of the blizzard, had saved our lives.

MOOAR BROTHERS AND WRIGHT

Mike celebrated our return to Dodge City by getting on a protracted spree and was left at Dodge. We three boys formed a partnership. I loaned my brother John and cousin Charles two hundred fifty dollars each, to enter the firm on an equal footing with me. Under the new arrangement, I shot the game, and the other boys did the freighting and marketing and looked after the camp. Three men were hired for skinners, and again we turned toward Kiowa Creek. Spring had come—the spring of 1873. All nature had awakened from the sleep of winter; the prairies grew green and lush with grass and sparkled with flowers; the voice of mighty achievement called to the spirit of adventure. For a time all went well, and profits piled up rapidly. Every day we saw some new and thrilling brush with big game.

And then the shadow of death hovered near. John was stricken with pneumonia, and I took him to the Dodge City hospital, where for weeks he struggled in the grip of the dread disease. At last good medical care and youthful courage and strength prevailed, the shadow passed, and the outfit which had been in Dodge for six weeks, waiting for John's recovery, again turned to the big-game country, this time trekking to the Cimarron River and remaining there all summer. Other outfits joined us for protection against roving bands of Indians, who looked with bitter foreboding upon their vanishing meat supply. At this time the Cimarron was believed to be the boundary line between Kansas and the Indian Territory.

MILLIONS UPON MILLIONS

A general belief better grew and prevailed that the great buffalo herd was extinct; but some argued there must be another herd, as the herd that had gone north consisted entirely of prime animals. At last a neighbor hunter, John Webb, and I determined upon a scouting trip to ascertain the truth of the situation. Saddling our favorite mounts and carrying no supplies but a sack of salt and plenty of ammunition, we turned our faces to the unknown wilderness.

Our direction of travel was south, and we crossed the north prong of the North Canadian River, known as Beaver Creek, at a point about twenty miles east of where Beaver City, Oklahoma, is now. Continuing south across Wolf Creek, another prong of the North Canadian, we turned west on the divide between the North and South Canadian Rivers; and somewhere in this lonely land, now the Panhandle country of Texas, we found the great herd, millions upon millions, fattening on the grass of those mighty uplands. Pushing on westward through living lanes opening before us as we advanced, and camping at night in the midst of browsing, drowsing thousands, we came in sight of the breaks of Blue River or the South Canadian. Tascosa, Texas, is now at the mouth of Blue River. Here we turned north. For five days we had ridden through and camped in a mobile sea of living buffalo.

THE COUNCIL OF WAR

On our return, the buffalo hunters held a council and listened to our report. Differences of opinion marked the council. There was considerable doubt as to the government's attitude toward the hunters should they go out of the Indian Territory into Texas, a sovereign state. A hunter by the name of [Steele] Frazier united the council by a proposal that a conference be held with Major Dodge, commander at Fort Dodge.[7] Frazier and I were chosen as envoys. Returning to Dodge City, we dressed for the occasion in new shirts, trousers, and hats and went down to Fort Dodge, six miles distant from Dodge City, for the interview.

The major was gracious in his reception and fired volleys of questions at us. We did not get their import at the time, but the information thus obtained later appeared in an article on the habits and history of the buffalo, written by the major. Finally, I asked the all-important question. "Major, if we cross into Texas, what will be the government's attitude toward us?"

"Boys," replied the major, "if I were a buffalo hunter, I would hunt buffalo where the buffalo are."

That settled the question.

TEXAS OR BUST

Charley Wright now withdrew from the partnership, and in September 1873, John and I, with four teams and ten men, set out for the wilds of Texas, crossing the Neutral Strip, now Beaver County, Oklahoma. We hunted awhile on the South Canadian, and then turned back, pitching camp on the Palo Duro Creek, in Hansford County. On this trip to the Canadian, we made our own trail, striking four miles west of the old ruins of the John C. Fremont and Kit Carson Adobe Walls. Upon our return to Dodge City, we followed the old Fort Bascom government trail across the Arkansas River.

BUILDING ADOBE WALLS POST

So passed the winter of 1873. In March 1874 A. C. (Charlie) Myers, Dodge City dealer in hides and hunters' supplies, bought Hank Sutler's outfit or eight six-yoke teams and moved a branch store south to Hutchinson County, Texas. He too crossed the Neutral Strip at the mouth of the Hansford County Palo Duro Creek, and followed the creek up to a point four miles below the ruins of some old adobe walls, supposed to have been built some years before by Brent's Fort traders. He located his new trading post on this site and called it Adobe Walls.

About forty hunters and teamsters in the party erected a stockade corral and built in one corner of the corral a storehouse of cottonwood logs.

In April Charles Rath, a competitor, moved a branch store down and built a sod house a short distance south. It faced east, as did Myers's store. James Hanrahan then came with a stock of whiskey and built a saloon between the two stores, close to Myers's stockade. Tom O'Keefe erected a picket house for a blacksmith shop between Hanrahan's saloon and Rath's store. All were established and doing business by May 1.

John and I moved our supply of hides and meat to Dodge City and our camp to the new trading post. John, in company with a Mr. Warren, who had a family in Dodge, and a freighter known as Dirty Face Jones, hauled supplies to the new stores at Adobe Walls. Each drove a six-mule team and two wagons.

EXCHANGING LEADEN COMPLIMENTS
Early in May I made a trip south of the Canadian River with Mart Galloway, Philip Sisk, Lem Wilson,[8] Dave Campbell, and John Hughes. Six men, three teams, and three saddle horses composed the group. We went down the river to the mouth of Red Deer Creek, crossed the river, and went up Red Deer, south to the head of the Washita, moving on the middle Washita to Gageby Creek. While in camp here, a small party of Indians came near the camp, but would not accept an invitation to come in and soon passed on. The same day, we moved several miles up the creek and camped in a wide flat. Next morning, at the first sign of day, the Indians charged the camp from the south, lying on the right side of their horses and shooting under the horses' necks at the beds of the hunters as they galloped through. John Hughes and I slept on the east side of the east wagon in the camp. Hughes was next to the wagon; his gun was standing against a wagon, and my gun was under the top blanket to protect it from dew. At the first sound of the charge, Hughes sat up, seized his gun, and shot the lead horse as he came opposite. The big ball tore through the horse and his rider, who hung on the opposite side and whistled for more victims.

The rest of the Indians rode furiously by and circled to the west, taking cover in a thicket and shooting at the camp, but were too far away to do any damage. It was still pretty dark, but we could see the flash of their guns and replied with the deadly precision of trained marksmen, with the best rifle in the world in our hands. This soon smoked the Indians out of the thicket. But even in the face of such rifle fire, two Indians made a run past the camp, reached down as their ponies sped, picked up their dead companion's body, and bore it off, joining their comrades. Then all rode away and were seen no more. Does history furnish any real parallel in horsemanship for these daringly savage Comanche and Cheyenne Indians?

Next day we crossed the North Fork of Red River and camped on Salt Fork. Buffalo were coming from the south in great numbers, and ten days of uninterrupted hunting followed, in which 666 bison hides were taken, and Philip Sisk was sent to Adobe Walls to get John Mooar and others to haul in the hides.

At about the time my companions and I had left Adobe Walls on this hunting trip, John Mooar, Warren, and Jones were in Dodge City after more supplies for the new post, and rumors were flying that Indians were leaving the reservations to fight buffalo hunters.

Jones asked Warren if he was going back, and the latter replied, "No, if you and Mooar are fools enough to go down among the Indians, you can go, but I am going to stay at home."

Jones replied, "If you were born to be killed by Indians, you would be killed by Indians if you went to New York. That wouldn't make any difference."

John Mooar and Jones loaded and trailed back to Adobe Walls, and on arriving, heard reports of Indians on the range and accounts of encounters. Jones returned to Dodge City alone. John Mooar remained, and the next day Sisk came in with the request for his services to bring in the hides.

Thus the daily humdrum of events moved on to the battle of Adobe Walls, marking a crisis, a climax, and a new beginning in the history of the Panhandle of Texas.

>-+-+>-+-O-+-<+-+-+-<

While Sisk and John Mooar were preparing to come out to our camp, a sergeant and four soldiers, with Amos Chapman, a half-breed Cheyenne Indian employed by the government as a scout, came to Adobe Walls from Camp Supply. Their mission was a mystery, and on being asked, one of the soldiers very indiscreetly replied that they were looking for horse thieves—a statement which was quickly resented by the hunters present, and especially by a band headed by Red Loomis, and there were muttered threats. During the day, the soldiers went up the river a few miles to look for trails and did not come back until the next morning. Amos, the scout, stayed and had a secret conference with Myers, Rath, and Hanrahan.

The hunters became more suspicious and by night were drinking considerably and itching for mischief, because they believed that Amos was an Indian spy. They finally confided to Hanrahan that they were going to hang Amos. Hanrahan began to scheme to save him, knowing he had brought news of grave importance as a government spy, and yet news of such a character that he dared not divulge it to save the breed.

Dark came at last, and Amos came to the back door of the saloon. Hanrahan took him aside and showed him John Mooar's wagon back of Rath's store, and told him to slip out to the wagon and get into bed with John, as no one would think of looking for him there. Amos went into the saloon, got a drink, loudly announced he was going over to Myers's, and went boldly out the front door. Once under cover of the darkness, he fled to John Mooar's wagon and explained the necessity of sanctuary, which was immediately granted. He crept in and pulled the tarp over his head. As he had left the saloon, announcing his intention of going to Myers's, he had also stated he was coming back to the saloon to sleep.

"All right," said Hanrahan. "Come back."

To cover the scout's getaway, the saloonkeeper called all hands to the bar for a drink. Later, they hunted for Amos in vain. When all quieted down, he slipped away; but while in the wagon, he told John what his mission was. Lee and Reynolds, post sutlers at Camp Supply, were friends of R. M. Wright, post sutler at Fort Dodge, and Wright was a partner of Charles Rath. Learning the day and the hour that the Indians had planned to attack Adobe Walls and massacre the traders, they had sent Amos to warn the post of impending disaster. The soldiers had been sent as escort to Amos at the request of Lee and Reynolds.

A CLOSE CALL

Amos told John he would have plenty of time to warn me and my companions, and the next morning John took three more teams and two extra men and left for our camp on Red River. With Sisk as pilot, they made forced drives. Arriving at our camp, John took me aside and told me of the impending Indian invasion. He brought news also that the buffalo had got as far north as the Canadian River, so we lost no time loading up and starting to Adobe Walls. All were anxious to kill buffaloes near the stores.

The second day of the homeward journey, it began raining. Noon camp was made near the head of Red Deer, on a flat between two lakes. The horses and mules were grazing, about half the number in each lake. The perspective was good, and many buffalo were in sight. Suddenly a large band of Indians showed up about a mile back, following our trail. A rush was made to get the horses and mules to the wagons. I ran toward the stock on the left. The Indians came on like soldiers, one in the right column blowing a bugle.

Philip Sisk and Lem Wilson were just ahead of me. They had left their rifles uncleaned since the last buffalo kill and were unarmed. It became evident that something had to be done to halt the oncoming attack, or we should be cut off from our teams.

As he ran, Wilson looked back at me and yelled, "Is your gun ready, Mooar?"

"Yes," I replied, "and I have forty rounds of ammunition."

"Well, for God's sake, hold 'em back, and Sisk and I will get the stock."

The situation was desperate and seemed all but hopeless.

I dropped on one knee and, taking aim, sent a big .50 ball screaming across the front of the charging column. Instantly the horses were jerked to their haunches, and the Indians stopped in a confused huddle. They didn't like my music. Seeing my advantage, I sent bullet after bullet whistling and skittering along, each one a little closer to the Indians than the last. They became more disconcerted and fell back. Precious time was gained. A glance showed me my companions still running toward the horses and mules. Would they have time to make it? I took careful aim and brought down a horse, his redskin rider going over his head and flinging himself flat on the prairie. The bugler tried to rally his followers. They swung back and started forward again. Again the old .50 spoke in deadly language, and the group broke up and fell back. A wild yell arose, and some began shooting, but their shots fell short.

Again glancing around, I saw that the boys had reached our teams and were rounding them up. In a few moments they came thundering by me and reached the wagon. I continued the bombardment until the boys got the teams hitched, and we drove furiously on to Red Deer Creek a mile away and crossed it near its head at upper Cottonwood Tree.

As we were crossing, a fearful bolt of lightning split a black cloud above us, and a crash of thunder seemed to jar the world. Hardly had we gained the opposite bank when a cloudburst sent a wall of water roaring down the channel and out into the valley, flooding the crossing twenty feet deep and completely cutting the Indians off from immediate pursuit.

Sisk and Wilson never allowed their rifle barrels to become foul again on that trip.

RACING FOR LIFE

We now cut through by the most direct route to the Adobe Walls crossing on the Canadian River, arriving about the middle of the afternoon of the third day. Philip Sisk and John swam the river and engaged Myers's ox teams to get the wagons across the river. While they were gone, the Indians arrived and charged our camp, riding between the wagons and over the fire, knocking over the coffeepots and skillets.

Next morning, John Webb, wagonmaster, came across with forty-eight yokes of oxen, two big Murphy seven-foot-wheel wagons, and eight drivers. The river was about seven hundred yards wide and from three to seven feet deep, being at flood from melting snows in the Rockies. The wagons had large frames like hay frames, with twenty-four yokes of oxen to each wagon. The hides were loaded and lashed down, and the hunters' smaller wagons were trailed. The horses and mules were driven in and swam the river, the oxen being more reliable in deep, swift water with the load. The ox teams were now strung along beside the river, with the pointers' feet at the edge of the water. Then five or six men approached the leaders and, with a concerted shove, pushed them into the river. Then, working down the line, they pushed the string oxen in.

Several horsemen rode into the water below the wagons to keep the teams headed across the river, and as the oxen's feet struck bottom, they began pulling with all their might, dragging the swimming oxen and wagons along until the passage was made. The long string of oxen made it possible for some of them to be wading and pulling all the time, while men on both sides of the river kept guard, and men in the river urged on the awkward cavalcade. No Indians appeared during this performance.

Camp was made on the north side of the river, while Webb took the ox teams up to the stockade for the night. Supper was in preparation when a whooping band of redskins dashed through the camp, shooting right and left. They got a warm reception, the roar of our big rifles mingling with the popping of the Indians' lighter arms and the savage yells of both reds and whites. No hunters were hurt, and the invaders carried away their own dead and wounded.

Next morning the entire hunting outfit arrived at the Adobe Walls post.

That day Joe Plummer came in and reported his two men, Dave Dudley and Tommie Wallace, killed by the Indians at the mouth of Red Deer Creek. Anderson Moore came in and reported two men killed south of the river. They were Antelope Jack and Blue Billie. Both camps had been destroyed.

Next day Myers began loading his wagons with hides to be hauled to Dodge City. John and I loaded our wagons to go along also and lent our extra rifles to Myers's outfit so his drivers could all be armed. I asked Myers and Rath if they were going to stay, and they said they were. However, I did not believe their assertion, as I knew that they had kept information of the prospective Indian attack on Adobe Walls from the hunters, and that only Myers, Rath, Hanrahan, John, and I, and possibly one or two others, knew of the report the scout Amos had brought, or what his mission was. This was done to keep the hunters and helpers around the post for protection.

The last trek from Adobe Walls to Dodge was begun the next morning. Eight miles out, the freighters met Dirty Face Jones, along with six mules loaded with powder, lead, and guns. He had driven ninety miles without sleeping himself or unharnessing his mules. He drove on to the post, discharged his load, slept five hours, put on a half load of hides, and overtook the big caravan the next day at Palo Duro Creek. I was driving the rear team of the long train. Jones said, "I can now drive as slow as need be."

PROPHECIES

The next day we met Ike Shadler with four six-yoke teams at Rifle Pits on the Palo Duro. John Webb said, "Ike, you hurry back, or the Indians will get your scalp."

On the Beaver the next morning, Myers and Rath came into camp on good horses. They stayed with the train one day and made a night ride into Dodge. Myers left Fred Leonard in charge of his store, and Rath left James Langton in charge of his.

At Sharp's Creek, the wagon train met a hunter named Burr with four men. Billy Tyler, one of the four, told of a fight they had with the Indians the day before on the Cimarron, and Burr remarked, "Yes, Billy, and you are going to fall early in this war."

The prophecies of Webb and Burr were soon fulfilled. Shadler and Tyler were both killed at Adobe Walls June 28, and this was the date that Amos had given for the attack.

Arriving in Dodge June 29, the first news the caravan heard was that Warren, to whom Dirty Face Jones had made his fatalistic statement that if he was "born to be killed by the Indians, he would be killed by Indians if he went to New York," had been slain and scalped by Indians just on the outskirts of Dodge.

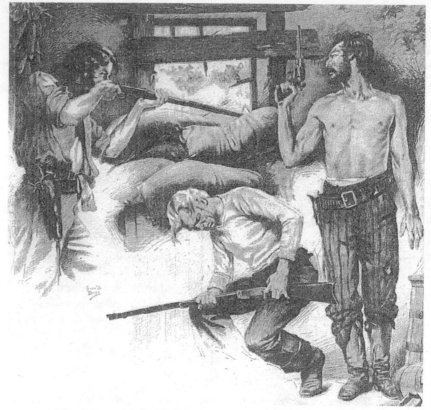

The fight at Adobe Walls. HOLLAND'S: THE MAGAZINE OF THE SOUTH 1933.

BATTLE OF ADOBE WALLS

As I was not a participant in the battle of Adobe Walls, I will not give a detailed account of it. In the *Life of Billy Dixon,* by his wife, Mrs. Olive Dixon,[9] there appears the best account of this fight I have ever seen. As a cool and daring participant, Dixon seemed to see the whole fight and was able to give a true and coherent account of it. His story agrees with the best accounts I got from the lips of other survivors.

The battle may be called the "Alamo of the Panhandle," with this difference: that of the twenty-eight men and one woman who defended the post, only four were slain, and a fifth lost his life as the result of the accidental discharge of his own rifle some days after the fight, while the historic Texas Alamo had no survivor among the defenders.

The odds against the defenders of Adobe Walls were overwhelming. The Indians' numbers have been variously estimated at from seven hundred to one thousand, but Chief Whirlwind of the Cheyennes[10] told me, when I saw him some years after the battle, that there were more.

Myers's store, with Leonard in charge, had eleven men; Hanrahan's saloon had nine men; Rath's store, with Langton in charge, had eight men and the one woman referred to, a Mrs. Olds.[11] All testified that she was as brave and efficient in the battle as any of the men.

The Indians fought under the famous Comanche Chief Quanah Parker. Quanah's mother, Cynthia Ann Parker, was a white woman who had been kidnapped in infancy by the Indians and had married the brave Comanche Chief Nocona, who later was killed in battle by Sul Ross and his Texas Rangers while Quanah was still a very young brave.

In all former accounts of the battle, much has been made of the providential cracking of the ridgepole in Hanrahan's saloon. The real cause for the night alarm was kept a secret by a group of men, including myself, who knew the truth. Under a solemn oath, we agreed to keep this secret until there should be but one survivor. He was then to be released from his oath. I am that survivor and will give the facts.

Rath, Myers, and Hanrahan knew the day and the hour of the Indian attack, thanks to the information of Amos the scout, but they kept the information to themselves, knowing that if the hunters should learn the truth, they would retire to Dodge and leave Adobe Walls post to be destroyed. The matter was kept secret after the fight because of the fears of Rath and Myers and a few close friends that the buffalo hunters might bitterly resent not having been warned and take reprisals.

Hanrahan, brave Irishman, stayed at the post and bore his part in the fight. It is possible that he told gallant Billy Dixon; but if so, Dixon, though no party to the deception, gamely stayed and is the outstanding hero of the battle. If he knew it, as I think he did, he kept his oath and died with his lips sealed.

NO RIDGEPOLE EVER CRACKED

The noise was a pistol shot, fired as a signal agreed upon between Hanrahan and someone else. At the sound, Hanrahan jumped up, shouting, "Clear out! The ridgepole is breaking!"

It was about 2:00 A.M. The alarm quickly spread. A slender little prop found conveniently cut at the woodpile exactly fitted under the ridgepole. The prop was utterly inadequate. The ridgepole was two and one-half feet in diameter, and the prop was but eight inches. But in the ensuing excitement, it answered the purpose in carrying out the deception.

Dixon says in his book: "We never could find a single thing wrong with the log."

All hands being aroused, they gathered at the bar, took a few drinks, and most of them decided to remain awake. Consequently, at 4:00 A.M. they were up, and the surprise attack, so carefully planned by the Indians, met with a counter-surprise.

For all that, the Indians had planned well. Most of the hunters were supposed to be south of the river, and ordinarily but eight or ten people would have been at the post; taken unawares, they would have fallen an easy prey to the warriors.

The attack came at daybreak. Out of the fading shadows of the night, shattering the air with blood-curdling yells, the Indians rushed upon the post, catching the Shadler brothers and killing and scalping them in their wagon, and nearly catching Billy Dixon and Billy Ogg, who were outside the post trying to round up the horses.

All the hunters agreed that the Indians charged desperately and showed great daring. They surrounded the buildings and in some instances dismounted and tried to break in the doors. At Myers's store, they even shot through the portholes into the store. Those inside hastily made new portholes through the fresh chinking, which was not yet seasoned. There was no chinking in the corral walls, and the Indians killed all the stock in the enclosure as well as on the outside. The Indians had many horses killed under them in the fight, which lasted most of the day. Billy Tyler was killed in Myers's store, at the door to the corral, during the early part of the battle.

There was a mysterious bugler, who was said to be a Negro deserter from the United States Army. He had inspired great confidence among the Indians. He was killed as he was leaving the Shadler wagon with all the groceries he could carry. The Indians showed great bravery in dragging their dead and wounded off the field, but left about a score of those that lay closest to the building.

Next day several hunters came in with hides, and men went out at night on horseback to spread the news of the attack among the camps, until all the hunters came in to the post.

The Indians had so many to care for, with their chief wounded, their medicine man and bugler dead,[12] and other heavy losses, that they never molested the hunters who came in later.

Leonard, Langton, and Hanrahan were very anxious to get news of the fight to Dodge, as it was evident there would be no more buffalo hunting for a long time. Henry Leas was the bearer of the tidings. Leaving on a dark night, he slipped away, leading his horse at the end of a forty-foot lasso, avoiding the road and going south to near the river. There he mounted and rode upriver several miles, finally turning north and traveling without mishap to Dodge.

It was some time before a relief party was organized, and the men at Adobe Walls grew impatient and began leaving in parties strong enough to feel safe. Finally, in August, a large train of teams was sent to bring to Dodge the remaining hides and supplies. All hides south of the river were lost and Adobe Walls abandoned, and the Indians later razed the place. They even tore up the foundation logs. Thus ended, in September, with a great financial loss to all parties concerned, an enterprise that had begun with such great prospects of success in March.

However, the fearful drubbing the Indians received had a more salutary effect on them, and did more to open the Panhandle of Texas for occupation, than did the government's activities and all other expeditions that ever went against the Indians in Texas. For this reason, the battle of Adobe Walls is recognized as epochal and decisive in the settlement of the Panhandle and northwest Texas.

During the months of August, while the hunters and traders were staying close around Dodge and checking up their losses, Col. Nelson A. Miles led a military expedition in pursuit of the marauding Indians for the purpose of rounding them up and driving them back to their reservations. For scouts he took Billy Dixon, Tobe Robison, Lem Wilson, and others of the buffalo hunters.

Dixon remained in the government service for several years and distinguished himself for courage and skill of a high order. Chief Whirlwind's account of what happened to Miles's expedition occurs later in this chronicle.

>→⊱→○→⊰→←

And now, while the hunters herded their horses by day and stood guard at night with the animals penned in Tom Nixon's corral, they planned a sort of experimental hunt, sending out a small contingent of their number, among whom were Steele Frazier and I. Each man had a saddle horse, and Frazier and I had a wagon and team besides. The company of adventurers had twelve teams made up in the same way.

Traveling cautiously down to the Cimarron, we found the buffalo herd had turned south, and immediately fell upon its rear and flanks, soon killing four hundred head. The hides were staked down, meat side up, and left near the river, while we followed the herd to Beaver Creek in No Man's Land, where a large number more fell to our big rifles.

At a council, it was determined to send two outfits back to Dodge with the hides left on the Cimarron, the others to follow later with the final returns from the hunt. I volunteered to be one of the two outfits to return. Frazier stayed with the main body after vainly trying to persuade me to remain. A man by the name of McCabe and his partner took their outfit and accompanied me. I soon regretted not having taken Frazier's advice when I saw the carelessness of my companions, who were continually wasting their ammunition on small game, though I urged them to save it for Indians. They laughed at my advice, so I said no more, but kept my rifle and a generous supply of cartridges ready for instant use.

A RENDEZVOUS WITH DEATH

The morning we arrived on the Cimarron and started to load the hides, a howling sandstorm struck us, and McCabe wanted to delay the loading until the gale had spent its fury; but I prevailed upon him to proceed as rapidly as possible, and to push on for night camp at a spring on the head of a stream called Stumpy Royer, in what is now Mead County, Kansas. The spring was about a half mile off the main trail we were following. Camping near the spring, I suggested to McCabe that I would get my rifle and cover his trip down to the spring for water for the camp. He resented the idea that there was any danger; but nevertheless, I kept my rifle and four hundred rounds of ammunition at hand, and aroused my sleeping companions by the rising of the morning star.

We were back on the main trail by daybreak. The trail ran for several miles along a ridge and just under its crest, on the way down to Crooked Creek. As we pressed along the way during the morning, we suddenly heard distant shooting, the sound of which drew nearer, and at one time was near enough that we could hear the bullets hit. McCabe now became alarmed, but as the reports of the guns revealed them to be of small caliber, I suggested that perhaps "Dog Kelly" and his party were out shooting small game.

Nevertheless, we pushed on as rapidly as possible, arriving at Crooked Creek near sundown, and McCabe, who was in the lead, pulled up at a good camping place and began unhitching his team. I, however, pressed on, and to McCabe's angry protest, said I was going on to Mulberry Creek. Protesting, McCabe hooked up and followed. We learned later that this decision saved us from a horrible fate. The shooting heard that day had been a battle between a band of some twenty-five or thirty Indians and a small surveying party led by Captain Short, camped on Crooked Creek. In a running fight, Short and his men were killed and scalped.[13]

Four days later, the hunters on Beaver came to the spring on Stumpy River and found a compass and other impedimenta of the surveyors, which the Indians had carried there and thrown aside.

Here the hunters discovered that my companions and I had also camped. Fearing the worst, a party led by Frazier pushed on to Crooked Creek on horseback and discovered that the Indians had also been there, and had ridden around the spot where McCabe had driven out to camp for the night, but after milling around for a time had taken another direction than the road to Mulberry. Nevertheless, not knowing that we had ever reached Mulberry, the hunters became more alarmed and pushed on to Dodge, where they were rejoiced to find us safe.

One other curious incident connected with this event was the finding of a postal card near the compass discarded by the Indians at the spring, on which was a crude picture of six human bodies lying in certain postures and at certain intervals; and on the bodies were dots, which later proved to be exact representations of the positions and postures of Captain Short and his men, the dots marking the wounds they had received as they were shot down. Some Indian artist had thus left a record of the massacre. No eyewitness of the tragedy, save the Indians, lived to give any account of the last struggle of six brave men for life. Their mutilated bodies were found as the artist had drawn them, and imagination based on the knowledge of the characteristics of Indian warfare was left to picture the scene. Perhaps surprised as they worked, inadequately armed and hopelessly outnumbered, they kept their rendezvous with death and fell as they fought, one at a time, the last survivor firing his last shot in a desperate attempt to sell his life as dearly as possible.

In the midst of such conditions, it is strange that men like my reckless companions should have become so careless.

THE TRAIL LEADS TO TEXAS

With the arrival of the main body of the hunting expedition, the hides taken were sold, and the pool was divided.

In November, I with others trekked to Francisco Creek in the Panhandle and engaged in a successful hunt, dropping back to Beaver Creek, in the Neutral Strip, in December. Here we wintered, and carried our hides to Dodge City in March. At Wichita, Kansas, and El Dorado, we sold the meat.

From El Dorado, we turned south into Texas, our object being to get on the south side of the big herd. On the last day of April, the lumbering wagons and wild-looking riders arrived at Colbert's Ferry and crossed Red River to Denison, Texas. Camping on the creek between the river and the town of Denison, we traded some of our mules for oxen and bought some wagons. July came and found us still in camp there.

At last we were ready to go. Half the wagons were loaded with government freight, and the rest with supplies for the expedition—twelve wagons in all. One of the drivers had been over the road and knew the best camping places.

After passing Decatur, the caravan rolled onward through a country where stone chimneys stood by the trail, silent monuments to the tragedies of ambitious attempts at frontier settlements snuffed out by Indian raids. The driver, who knew the road, told us of the horrors of each separate case with which he was familiar. Whooping bands of Indians fell upon these outlying homes and settlements, burning, killing, scalping, and taking prisoners to suffer a more horrible fate than those who fell in the massacre. The log cabins were burned to the ground, and only the stone chimneys were left.

When one traces the route as briefly outlined in the above account, he will find our party in the end reached the Brazos River, in Haskell and Stonewall Counties. A winter camp was finally made on Mule Creek, near where the town of Weinert now stands.

The hunting was fine, and in November John conducted a return expedition to Denison, carrying four thousand hides. It took eighteen teams of six yokes of oxen, and three wagons to each team, to haul this enormous shipment. As the wagons, piled high with hides, passed through Sherman, they created a sensation; people crowded the streets along the routes of travel. Arriving at Denison, John found no market there, and the banks would not advance a dollar. He thereupon telegraphed Lobenstein at Leavenworth, who bought the entire shipment, wiring the necessary remittance. With the money, John purchased six months' supplies for all the hunters, bringing each his correct balance in money. The party now consisted of the Mooar brothers, White and Russell,

Mike O'Brien, and John Goff. This transaction caused Lobenstein to establish a branch office at Fort Griffin, which carried the market to the frontier.

JUSTICE FOR THE HUNTER

Because he has been criticized as a destroyer, a ruthless killer, and wastrel of a great game resource of the nation, the hunter appeals to the bar of history for his vindication, and the incidents of this chapter are typical of his factual statement.

On leaving Fort Richardson, which is now Jacksboro, Texas, our hunting party was on Salt Creek Prairie, where, two years before, Indians had massacred the drivers of Long's train of six ten-mule teams and burned the wagons and such goods as they could not carry away. Ten men were killed and scalped—one escaped. The government could not control these marauding bands, and settlement was unable to advance or supplies reach the outposts until the hunters came, killed the redskin's meat supply, and transformed him from a bloody raider to a meek ward.

That same fall, other hunters came from Dodge, and a dozen different outfits of various sizes hunted out of Fort Griffin.

These hunting expeditions ended for all time the Indian depredations on the settlers, as the redskins had their hands full with the hunters. One small raiding party went to the settlements in 1877; but some of them never came back, and that ended the war on the settlements.

For years it had been the custom of the Indians to cross Salt Creek Prairie between Forts Griffin and Richardson, raid the settlers, collect a few scalps, and steal horses, sometimes going as far as Parker County in small bands and assembling at a given point to begin raiding.

Before the alarm could reach the forts, rangers sometimes got on their trail; but by the time the citizens could organize, or the forts order out a detail—with a requisition on the commissary for supplies, and twenty rounds of ammunition per man with his pack made up—the Indians had slipped away, and were so far ahead of their pursuers that they could obliterate their trail by merging it in those of the buffalo herd. There they broke into small parties, to come together again at a point a hundred to a hundred and fifty miles away. There was nothing for the pursuers to do but return home, sad and disappointed.

With the hunters, it was quite different. We lived with the buffalo and had plenty of ammunition and a gun far superior to any the Indians had any knowledge of. Within four years, we opened up a vast empire to settlement and put the Indians forever out of Texas.

As the buffalo hunters drove the Indian out, the cowman, alert to see his opportunity, followed into the newly opened ground so closely that some of the big herds of cattle were within hearing of the roar of the "big .50," and by the time the buffalo was gone, the country was stocked with cattle.

Buffalo hunting was a business and not a sport. It required capital, management, and a lot of hard work. Magazine writers and others who claim that

Chief Whirlwind. SMITHSONIAN INSTITUTION.

the killing of the buffalo was a national calamity and was accomplished by vandals simply expose their ignorance, and I resent such an unjust judgment upon us.

On June 28, 1874, for instance, twenty-eight buffalo hunters killed more Indians at Adobe Walls in three hours' time than ever did all other forces in the Panhandle of Texas! And if it had not been for the work of the buffalo hunters, the wild bison would still graze where Amarillo now is, and the red man would still reign supreme over the pampas of the Panhandle of Texas.

And I want to state that any one of the families killed and homes destroyed by the Indians would have been worth more to Texas and to civilization than all the millions of buffalo that ever roamed from the Pecos River on the south to the Platte River on the north.

CHIEF WHIRLWIND

Meanwhile, over at Dodge City, Rath, Wright, Lee, and Reynolds had formed a combination and dispatched their business manager, W. H. West, and Russell, chief wagonmaster, on a trip to find a direct route to Fort Griffin, establish contact with us, and locate other trading posts in the buffalo range.

These trade emissaries reached the camp on Mule Creek in April 1876. Among other things, they bought 450 selected hides for buffalo robes from John and me for delivery to the Cheyenne Agency in the Indian Territory, where Chief Whirlwind had a camp. The chief's tribe, for a stipend, dressed the hides for robes. A curious kind of circulating medium was employed by the merchants. It was a brass coin, twenty-five of which were accepted by them in payment for a horse. Thus the Indians were recuperating [*sic*] their losses in horses occasioned by their encounters with the hunters by tanning hides for brass coins, which were paid back to the merchants for horses.

I started from my camp with the hides on May 1, and upon my arrival, turned the hides over to Chief Whirlwind and remained among the Indians for several days. It was during my stay that I got Chief Whirlwind's version of events beginning with the battle of Adobe Walls and concluding with the raid of Colonel Miles.

One day I asked, "How many Indians were in the Adobe Walls fight?"

"More than twelve hundred," replied Whirlwind.

"What were your losses?"

"One hundred and fifteen."

"Why did you get whipped so badly?"

The Cheyenne chief replied, "Comanche medicine man no good."

"What did you do when Miles got after you?"

Whirlwind laughed, "Miles no good. Me lead 'um on long trail, round and round. Braves make trail for him to follow, then slip back behind and scalp stragglers and shoot up rear."

"Where did you lead him?"

"Palo Duro Canyon."

"Where next?"

"Got him down in breaks on gyp water. Soldiers got sick. Braves get on bluffs and throw rocks at 'um. Too sick to move."

"Why didn't you kill them?"

"Ugh! Ugh! Washington!"

"You weren't afraid of Miles?"

"No. Sundown, shoot big gun, *boom!* Tell every Indian for fifty miles where he camped. Every morning shoot big gun, *boom!* Tell every Indian fifty miles he still there. Humph! Heap big bull!"

So much for Whirlwind's opinion of United States military regulations. The old chief assured me his days of fighting the palefaces were over, as he pointed to his gray hair. But it was not long until he had slipped out again and gone north to help Sitting Bull.

An Adobe Walls Defender

W. K. MYERS

Chase County (Nebraska) *Leader,* June 13, 1934

W. K. Myers, who passed his eightieth birthday anniversary last week, is one of the few defenders of Adobe Walls now living.

Mr. Myers, at the time of the battle, was a youth of twenty years. He had gone west with two older men to hunt buffalo and was hired to hunt and skin animals. His principal work was skinning and doing the camp cooking.

On the morning of the attack on Adobe Walls, Mr. Myers, who had slept outside of the building with many others and had arisen early, was getting breakfast for his party. One or two other men had gone out from the camp to round up the horses, and the first he knew of the attack was the sound of a pistol shot, given as a warning by one man who went after the horses. The man was riding at breakneck speed ahead of the Indians. Mr. Myers, with the others, rushed inside the stockade. There were, however, two men who were not awakened by the noise. They were sleeping in a wagon, and these men were killed,[1] and later their bodies were found in the remains of the wagon, which had been burned. A large dog which these men had with them in the wagon was scalped by the Indians.

The attack, as Mr. Myers recalls, came just before daybreak. He says that [as] they looked off toward the direction from which the Indians were coming, they could make out what appeared to be a slowly rising cloud. The dust was kicked up by the Indian ponies. A few moments later, the camp was surrounded by howling Indians, who began pouring in a heavy fire.

Defenders of the camp kept inside until afternoon of the day of the attack. They could easily fight off the Indians, and there were few casualties and few of the men were injured.

History has it that the camp was saved from surprise by the cracking of the ridgepole, but Mr. Myers says that he does not recall the incident, nor does he remember that the ridgepole was broken. At any rate, he, with many other men of the camp, did not sleep in the stockade, but outside on the ground or in their wagons. The attack did not come until some of the men in the camp were up, and Mr. Myers was one of them. He had breakfast partly prepared for himself and two men he was working for when the alarm was given, but they did not partake of the meal.

It was not until almost night of the day of the attack that the Indians disappeared, and it was much longer before other than a scout or two were sent out from the camp.

PART SIX

The Red River War, 1874–75

My First Fight on the Plains

NELSON A. MILES[1]

Cosmopolitan 50 (January 1911): 792–802

During the time I was stationed [on the Plains], I had ample opportunity to study the history, traditions, customs, habits, and mode of life of the Native Americans. I found it a most interesting subject. What we know of the Indians, and what has been written concerning them, would fill many volumes. What we do not know of their origin and history would fill many more. Whence they came and when we know not, but if we were to judge from their stature, features, color, language, art, music, and many of their characteristics, we would be convinced that their ancestors were of Asiatic origin. There is evidence that they acquired control of this continent by conquest, rather than by peaceful means. Their displacement of the prehistoric races undoubtedly required centuries of time.

But whatever their history, their blood and experience produced a superior race. All the early explorers and historians speak of them as a strong, intelligent, honest, peaceful people. At first they welcomed the foreigners to their shores with cordial hospitality, and were repaid by their people being kidnapped and transported to foreign countries, doomed to a life of captivity and servitude. From the days of Columbus, there are many accounts of their being transported to European countries, but no record of their being returned. They were sold into slavery in the colonies of Massachusetts, Rhode Island, Connecticut, Virginia, and the Carolinas, and other parts of our country. They were hunted with hounds kept at public expense in Connecticut; were shipped to France to serve in the galleys.

Three hundred years of the cruelty, bigotry, and cupidity of the white race, and two hundred years of warfare, engendered hostility and hatred in both races. It was handed down from father to son, through generations, and became in our day as natural as it was universal. It was more intense with the Indians, as they were the unfortunate and subjugated people. Not only was their country overrun, but the vices and diseases brought among them by the white race were more destructive than war and swept whole tribes out of existence. Still, they maintained a courage and fortitude that was heroic. In vain might we

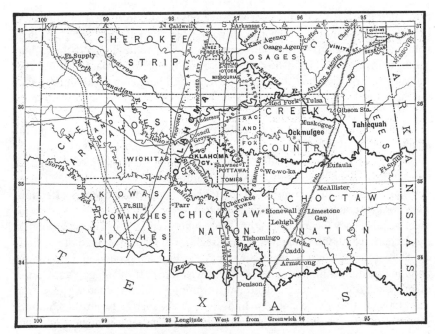

The Indian Territory. CENTURY MAGAZINE 1885.

search history for the record of a people who contended as valiantly against the overwhelming numbers of a superior race, and defended their country until finally driven toward the setting sun, a race practically annihilated.

The art of war among the white race is called strategy or tactics; when practiced by the Indians it is called treachery. They employed the art of deceiving, misleading, decoying, surprising the enemy, with great cleverness. The celerity and secrecy of their movements were never excelled by the warriors of any country. They exhibited courage, skill, sagacity, endurance, fortitude, and self-sacrifice of a high order. They had rules of civility in their intercourse among themselves or with strangers and in their councils. Some of these we could copy to our advantage.

With their enemies, they believed it right to take every advantage. If one of their own tribe committed a serious offense or crime, they believed it right for the victim to administer swift retribution, and the whole tribe approved. Within their own tribe and among their own people, they had a code of honor which all respected. An Indian could leave his horse, blanket, saddle, or rifle any place by night or day and it would not be disturbed, though the whole tribe might pass near. This could not be done in any community of white people.

An amusing incident occurred several years ago when Bishop Whipple[2] was sent by the government to hold an important counsel with the Sioux nation. The bishop was a most benevolent man and a good friend of the Indians, and had much influence with them. It was in midwinter, and a great multitude of Indians had gathered in South Dakota to receive this message from the Great Father at Washington. Before delivering his address to the Indians, the bishop asked the principal chief if he could put aside his fur overcoat in safety. The stalwart warrior straightened himself up to his full height and with dignity said that he could leave it there with perfect safety, "as there was not a white man within a day's march of the place."

The Indians believed that the Great Spirit had given them this beautiful country, with all its natural resources, advantages, and blessings, for their home; with deep emotion and profound reverence, they spoke of the sun as their father and the earth as their mother. Nature they worshipped, upon it they depended, with it they communed, they cherished it with deepest affection. They looked upon the white race as their inferiors, as a grasping, degraded, cruel people. They had no respect for those who lived by digging the ground or by trade, in which the traders were ever seeking to take advantage of the Indians. As for the miner, who went down into a hole in the ground in the morning and remained until night, his life to them was like that of the gopher. On the plains, their life was independent and most enjoyable. In whatever direction they moved, they were sure to find in a day's march beautiful camping grounds, plenty of timber and grass, pure water, and an abundance of food. Besides the flesh of animals, they had Indian corn, and wild vegetables, berries, fruit, and nuts were easily obtainable.

As the transcontinental railroad was constructed and the settlements advanced, the buffalo, deer, and antelope, the Indians' principal food supply, were destroyed. Enraged at the prospect of starvation, they gathered large war parties and raided the settlements of Colorado, Texas, and Kansas, and attacked surveying and working parties along the line of the railway. Against these powerful marauding bands, expeditions of troops were sent; one, under command of Maj. Eugene A. Carr, 5th Cavalry, made a forced march across the country and, on July 12, 1869, surprised and attacked a large camp of Indians who had congregated at Summit Springs, Colorado, killing and wounding a large number of Indians and recapturing one white woman. This achievement was well planned and executed by the able and experienced command and his gallant officers and soldiers. Another expedition of the same year was under command of Maj. George A. Forsyth. It was made up of fifty frontier riflemen noted for their courage and skilled marksmanship. This command, while bivouacked on the Arikaree, a small tributary of the Republican, in northern Kansas, was attacked September 17, 1869, by several hundred Indians. After a most desperate encounter, the Indians were repulsed with very severe loss, including their principal chief. The command of Major Forsyth lost, in killed and wounded, half its number, and was finally rescued by other troops after it had been besieged for nine days. The losses to the Indians did not dishearten them, but seemed to stir them to still stronger hatred for the white invaders of their country. This condition of affairs continued for several reasons until the

Adobe Wells after the siege.
NELSON A. MILES, *PERSONAL RECOLLECTIONS AND OBSERVATIONS.*

spring of 1874, when the Indians gathered in great numbers at a place known as Medicine Lodge, Indian Territory. This was a grand council of war, similar to those held in the days of the Six Nations, or the time of the conspiracy of Pontiac, or that confederation of the great tribes inspired by The Prophet and led by his brother, Tecumseh. The Indians of the Southwest, who had been accustomed to roam at will over Texas, New Mexico, Colorado, Kansas, and Indian Territory, were gathered at this great council. Their grievances and their woes were proclaimed and their final destruction predicted with vivid native eloquence. Their savage natures were aroused to the most intense ferocity. There was but one sentiment, and that was for revenge and relentless war upon the white race. The unanimous resolve of the warriors of the different tribes was the formation of a great war party to attack and destroy the buffalo hunters who were occupying a stockade at Adobe Walls on the Canadian River in the Panhandle of Texas. Fortunately, the Indian attack upon the hunters occurred on Sunday,[3] when they were all gathered together. The Indians displayed the greatest courage, some of them dashing up to the very gates of the stockade and trying to beat them down with their spears and tomahawks while their comrades kept up a sharp fire with their rifles. Their assault was repulsed with severe loss, a large number were killed and many wounded, and the government troops were called upon to suppress the Indian hostilities.

In August 1874 I was directed to organize a command at Fort Dodge and move south against the hostile Indians. Other commands were also ordered to move: one east from New Mexico, under Major Price[4]; one north from Texas, under Colonel Mackenzie; one west from Indian Territory, under Lieutenant Colonel Davidson.[5] My command consisted of two battalions of eight troops of cavalry, commanded by Majors Compton[6] and Biddle[7]; one battalion of four companies of infantry, commanded by Major Bristol[8]; a company of friendly Indians; a detachment of artillery; and a company of civilian scouts and guides. These were mostly hunters and expert riflemen, familiar with the country.

I resolved upon certain principles that I regarded as essential: Never, by day or night, to permit my command to be surprised; to hold it in such condition at all times, whether marching or camping, that it would be ever ready to encounter the enemy; to keep the divisions in communicating and supporting distance of each other whenever possible, and always ready to act on the offensive. There is an old saying that when an Indian wants food, he hunts game; when he wants sport, he hunts the white man. But no man, be he white or Indian, likes to be hunted, and if the hunt is continued, it will in time unnerve the stoutest-hearted. During that year, that country had been scourged by a most prolonged and consuming drought and, what was most unusual and more destructive, by a visitation of myriads of locusts, which devoured almost every green thing.

The command moved south to Camp Supply, Indian Territory, and thence southwest, crossing the Canadian River. We then continued that course until we struck the main heavy trail of the Indians near the headwaters of the Washita River. The detachments of the command had already had slight encounters with scattered bands of Indians. Some days we would not see an Indian, although we knew they were watching us and in close proximity; but a very good rule to observe, when one is in the Indian country, is this: "When you see Indians about, be careful; when you do not see them, be more careful."

On August 24 we followed the main body of the Indians south in the direction of the breaks of the Red River. Indians, when pursued, select with great care the roughest and most inaccessible places, and they could not have made a better selection than they did at this time. Concealed in the canyons and behind bluffs, they awaited the approach of the command.

On the morning of August 30, they made a wild dash and a furious charge against our advance guard. Some 250 came with the suddenness and fury of a whirlwind, but they were met by one of the coolest and ablest officers, Lt. Frank D. Baldwin,[9] who had made a distinguished record during the Civil War and afterward became a general officer. His command quickly dismounted and opened a destructive fire with their rifles, which checked the onslaught of the savages. As soon as the design of the Indians was developed, the cavalry of the command galloped into action. Then the artillery detachment, under Lieutenant Pope,[10] took position on favorable ground, and the entire force assumed the offensive, immediately making a countercharge. We drove the Indians from their chosen position, fighting over sand hills, bluffs, dry arroyos, and coulees, the roughest broken country I have ever seen fought over. It was a continuous

Indians fleeing their village toward the Staked Plains.
NELSON A. MILES, *PERSONAL RECOLLECTIONS AND OBSERVATIONS.*

advance, the officers leading with great gallantry and every soldier a hero. The Indians were pursued for nearly twenty miles, across the Red River, up the Grand Canyon of the Tule, and out on the Llano Estacado, or Staked Plains. It was the first serious engagement with the main body of the Indians, and while the loss was not serious on either side, it was a demonstration of the excellent fighting qualities of our troops, and the same fortitude and tenacity was maintained in all the subsequent encounters.

I have never known men to suffer as much as they did in this engagement. The heat was intense, the ground parched by the burning sun, and not a drop of refreshing water within twenty miles of the field. The Red River, which during the rainy season has water enough to float a steamboat, was at this time a bed of drifting white sand. What little water there was in the vicinity was so impregnated with alkali that it was impossible for it to be used by man or beast. One little realizes the suffering of men under such circumstances. In some instances they opened the veins of their arms to moisten their burning lips.

This country into which the command had been drawn is unlike any other section of this continent. The only country that I have ever seen like it is the steppes of Russian Siberia. It is high plateau or tableland, covered with short buffalo grass and as level as a billiard table, without a tree or shrub to be seen as far as the eye can reach. We marched over it sometimes for days, and it seemed like being in midocean in a dead calm. The canyons and broken country along its eastern border were a refuge for the Indians when pursued and a comparatively safe place to conceal their families and herds, and they undoubtedly thought they had made a fortunate escape.

The command was now some two hundred miles from any base of supplies, and to have returned to our base would have left the Indians in full occupation of the country. I therefore resolved to send for additional transportation, make my wagon train a movable base, and remain in that country until the Indians were subdued. I then made such dispositions of the troops as to make the country untenable for the Indians. Four troops of cavalry, under Major Price, joined mine and became a part of my command. Excellent service was rendered by the troops under Colonel Mackenzie and Davidson, but their forces were greatly embarrassed by the breaking down of their transportation. Our couriers, when sent on long journeys, were obliged to travel principally by night and conceal themselves during the day. Several instances of heroic daring on the part of these men occurred. Scout William F. Schmalsle dashed out from a besieged train at night, and although pursued by Indians, escaped by riding into a herd of buffaloes, and after that by concealing himself during the day and traveling at night. At another time a party of six—four soldiers and two scouts—under Sgt. [S. T.] Woodhall were surrounded by a large body of Indians on the open plains, but by getting into a buffalo wallow and partly entrenching, they repulsed the Indians, although outnumbered twenty to one. One was killed, two were severely wounded, and all were struck by the bullets of the enemy.

By a system of espionage at their agencies, and by friendly Indians with whom they were in communication, I was enabled to learn much of the condition and designs of the hostile Indians, and this valuable information enabled me to anticipate some of their movements. Wherever the Indians could be found, they were fought and pursued. This occurred in several engagements during the autumn months.

On November 8 a command under Lieutenant Baldwin surprised a camp of Gray Beard[11] on McClellan Creek, and after a spirited engagement, routed the Indians and recovered two little white girls, Julia and Adelaide German, aged seven and nine years, whom the Indians had held in captivity. They told us that their family had been journeying from Missouri to Colorado when they were attacked. Their father, mother, brother, and a sister were killed, and they, with two older sisters, were carried away by the Indians, but for several weeks they had not seen their sisters. When rescued, they were the most emaciated mortals I have ever seen. Their little hands were like birds' claws. They had been forced to travel rapidly by night and by day with the Indians in their long journeys, but with insufficient and coarse food. Their condition excited the deepest sympathy of the brave troops. When the officers and soldiers looked upon these poor unfortunates, warm tears could be seen coursing down their bronzed faces. It nerved every man to heroic endeavor to avenge the wrong and rescue those still in the hands of the savages.[12]

Thus the weeks and months wore away, with constant marching and hunting the enemy. We had an occasional rest while awaiting supplies, and as the country was well stocked with every kind of game, our larder was well supplied. The approach of winter was our best ally. Timely and ample provision was made for the comfort of our troops, but the cold blasts of what is known as a Texas norther added to the discomfort and destruction of the Indians. We drove them out of every place where they could be found, and finally across the Staked Plains to the valley of the Pecos River in New Mexico. Here a scarcity of food and the cold winter were most destructive and disheartening. I was convinced that the Indians were so reduced that they would surrender if an opportunity were granted them. I therefore equipped a small party of friendly Indians and sent them by a summons to the hostiles to surrender, making a condition of the surrender that they should bring in alive the two German girls they held in captivity, and adding that unless this was done, no terms would be granted and active measures would be continued until they were exterminated. In the meantime, the two little captives that we had rescued had been sent to Fort Leavenworth under charge of Doctor Powell, where the ladies of the garrison took care of them and nursed them back to health. The doctor, on returning to camp, brought me their photograph. It occurred to me to send it as a ray of hope to their unfortunate sisters, if they could be found. I therefore offered an Indian messenger a good reward if he would place it in their hands. On the back of the photograph, I wrote the following message:

HEADQUARTERS INDIAN TERRITORY EXPEDITION
In the Field, January 20, 1875
TO THE MISSES GERMAINE [*sic*]:
Your little sisters are well and in the hands of friends. Do not be discouraged. Every effort is being made for your welfare.
NELSON A. MILES,
Colonel and Brevet Major General,
U.S. Army,
Commanding Expedition

I placed the photograph in an envelope and especially charged the runner to put it in the hands of one of the unfortunate captives. He carried this message a distance of some four hundred miles over the snow-covered plains and frozen rivers, across the Staked Plains, until he finally reached the camp of the hostile Indians on the Pecos River, New Mexico. The blasts of winter had destroyed a great number of their horses and ponies, which the campaign had reduced to poor condition, and the Indians were most destitute and desperate, so that the demand for their surrender was opportune and was accepted on the imperative conditions named. The principal chief, Stone Calf,[13] sent for the two white girls, placed them with care and marked consideration. The morning following the receipt of the demand for surrender, the tribes commenced their difficult and laborious journey toward the agencies in the eastern part of the Indian Territory. They traveled mostly on foot, as the greater number of the horses and ponies with which they had commenced the campaign had been

Colonel Miles's envoy to the hostiles on the Staked Plains.

NELSON A. MILES, *PERSONAL RECOLLECTIONS AND OBSERVATIONS.*

captured or destroyed, and those that remained were scarcely sufficient to transport their limited supplies and baggage.

When a favorable opportunity occurred, the courier quietly handed the eldest girl my note on the back of her sisters' photograph, and as she told me afterward, she was overcome with joy and hope. It was the first information she had had that her sisters were alive, and that anyone knew of her existence or was interested in the rescue of herself and her sister.

After reaching the agencies, the Indians formally surrendered their arms, horses, and captives to the military authorities. The Indian warriors were paraded in line under the guns of the troops, and the two white girls passed along in front of them, pointing out the Indians who had murdered their family and committed other cruel atrocities. Seventy-five were taken out, placed under a strong guard, and sent to Florida. The two girls were sent to Fort Leavenworth, where they joined their younger sisters. They were all provided with a good guardian and a comfortable home. On my recommendation, $10,000 was deducted from the annuities to the Indian tribe, and $2,500 was placed to the credit of each of these unfortunate girls. In time, they grew up and married, and at last accounts were in comfortable homes in Kansas, Colorado, and California.

That campaign, lasting for many months, closed after most difficult and laborious efforts on the part of the troops, with the satisfactory result that the vast southwestern country has been free from the terrifying and devastating presence of hostile Indians, and the citizens of the states of Kansas, Colorado, Oklahoma, Texas, and New Mexico have enjoyed an era of peace. Scarcely a hostile shot has been heard in that country for the last thirty-five years.

A Terrible Ride through Indian Country

FRANK D. BALDWIN[1]

Box 21, Folder 23, William C. Brown Collection, University of Colorado Libraries, Boulder

Fort Leavenworth, Kansas
September 14, 1874

My Darling Wife,

You wanted me to give you a full and minute account of all my trips and engagements since I left Fort Dodge, Kansas, so here goes. I left Dodge on the eve of August 11 with twenty Delaware Indians and twelve white scouts, reporting to Major Compton, who was in command of a battalion (four companies) of cavalry. I marched with him until we reached the Brazos, crossing it between Kiowa [Creek] and some other small creek just above it. At this point, according to orders, I left Major Compton's command, having been reinforced by eighteen men from the cavalry under Lieutenant Henely, a very good officer and one that I requested be sent with me.

On the morning of August 16, with my small but picked command, I started for the Adobe Walls. My command now consisted of two commissioned officers and fifty men. Marched in a southwest course, striking the Palo Duro about twenty miles above its mouth, then up said stream for twenty miles, then south fifty miles, arriving at Adobe Walls at 10:00 P.M. of the nineteenth, having marched ninety miles in three days. The last fifty miles was marched in one day and without water; my command suffered very much for want of it.

The Adobe Walls are so called because a great many years ago the Mexicans built a trading post using the same adobe that all the old Mexican houses are built with. These old buildings are still standing, but in a very dilapidated condition; in fact, so much so that they can't be used. So much for the name of the place.

I went into camp when we arrived in what proved to be a very bad place, but could not discover this until daylight, as it was so dark. The next morning, not according to my old custom, I allowed

497

my camp to remain, as the men were all so very tired, as well as myself. Just imagine my condition, not having ridden for [some] time on a horse, then go out here, get into a saddle, ride fifty miles in a barren, desolate country, the sun as hot as a dutch oven. Your imaginative powers are good, so I will not tell you in plain English what did trouble the most.

Well, on the morning of August 19, about seventy-five Indians rode up on a hill about fifty yards from camp and fired into it. The cavalry was at arms, mounted, and I ordered Henely to follow at his utmost speed. My Indians were very slow, and it was some time before I could get them started, but when they did go, it was fun to see them, yelling and doing just as the wild dogs do.

The chase was continued for some time, a distance of about twelve miles through the sand hills and over a very rough country. We captured several ponies. There is no chance of ever being able to tell how many we killed or wounded, as they will run greater risks to take away the body of one of their slain than they will to get a scalp of a white man. We returned from the chase about 8:00 P.M. and moved into the stockade, which had been erected about eight miles from the old site of the Adobe Walls by a large party of buffalo hunters. When the Indians attacked them on June 27, and after fighting them all that day, the Indians were driven off, with a loss of fifteen killed and thirty-five wounded.

I remained here until the morning of the twentieth, when I started down the river to join the command under Colonel Miles. About 3:00 P.M. my advance guard ran into a party of Cheyennes, and so sudden was the charge that the entire party was either killed or wounded.[2] This was the first blood of the campaign and the first scalp. I see short accounts of it are in a good many of the papers.

From here I continued the march until I had marched thirty miles east. Went into camp expecting any moment to be charged by a large command of the noble red men, as they were hovering in the bluffs nearby all the evening. As to whether my Delaware Indians are brave men or not, also my white scouts, I have but one answer to make, and that is I never saw any men more brave—not one of them flinched.

Nothing more worthy of note occurred except that we were closely watched every hour of the day and night; but being constantly on the lookout and ready for them, they did not venture within range.

I rejoined the command on August 22 near Antelope Hills. I was welcomed by Colonel Miles in a manner showing that he was well pleased with my successful trip. After joining the command, and after commencing our onward march from the Canadian, I was con-

John W. Davidson, a rare pre–Civil War view.
COURTESY OF PERRY FROHNE.

stantly in advance or on the very extreme flanks, making extended detours in those directions, hunting for Indians. But whenever we did go out on such a trip, Colonel Miles always sent very soon after a detail of cavalry to support me in case I did get into trouble. So you see, he is not going to abandon me in case of trouble. On the twenty-eighth we struck a large trail and camp. This we followed with all the zeal of a foxhound after its game, and for three days the chase continued without rest, you may say.

On the morning of August 30 when, as usual, the extreme advance being the scouts, [we] were charged with all the fury that the [Indians] mounted, trying to break our lines. Desperately they fought for five minutes, and as desperately did my brave scouts fight and hold their ground. My flanks were uncovered, and I only had men enough to defend my front. Just at this time Hentig[3] came up and reported to me with a part of his company. As soon as his command came up, I ordered the entire line to charge, which they did quick, so quick driving everything before them. But on a range only about two hundred yards distant, [the] enemy had again posted themselves, and this ridge must be taken or we would lose many men. Again I gave the order to charge, and this time a most gallant fight was made and the hill taken. Here I halted until the command, which had moved up very promptly under Colonel Miles, came into action and I was ordered to take the extreme left. I went here and remained on the left all day until 2:00 P.M., when the battle closed.[4]

We had been fighting hard all day and were glad to rest. There were about six hundred Indians and the same number of us. Our victory was complete. I marched back two or three miles and reported to the colonel on the north bank of Red River that evening, and the next morning was ordered again to find the trail. After passing through an abandoned Indian village, we again struck their trail, followed it until dark, and went into camp to await the light of another day. The Indians had abandoned everything on their march, and we burned it all as we passed through. There must have been at least three hundred lodges destroyed.

This, my darling, takes us up to September 1, when I will commence again to relate our many adventures. I trust you will have not much trouble to decipher this.

Frank

Pampa (Texas) *Daily News,* March 20, 1932

Through the courtesy of Mrs. Juanita B. Williams-Foote [daughter of the late Maj. Gen. Frank D. Baldwin] and T. D. Hobart, the *News* presents a hitherto unpublished letter by Maj. Gen. Frank D. Baldwin, famous Indian fighter of the Panhandle's frontier days, to his wife. Mr. Hobart obtained the letter, describing a remarkable ride and continuous fighting by [then Lieutenant] Baldwin and three scouts, from Brig. Gen. W. C. Brown, retired, of Denver.

The letter, with deletions, follows:

Fort Dodge, Kansas
September 17, 1874

My Darling Wife:

I wish I could have gone east when I was at Leavenworth. You don't know how badly I hated to turn my back to the east when I was so near you, but General Pope told me yesterday that I should go east when we get through and stay as long as I wanted to, and you will not have me even ask to go during such times as these, and especially as I have such a conspicuous position, I could not leave without injuring myself very much. I think I have made a start, and with my usual good luck at Indian fighting will make something of a reputation.

I think my trip has been a good thing, though I never want to try it again. You will see an account of it in the paper I sent you today; this was put in by Hathaway, I believe.

I never was treated more politely or with more consideration [than] by General Pope himself and all his staff. I was with him three hours relating incidents of my perilous ride, as he called it, and

Brig. Gen. John Pope. U.S. ARMY MILITARY HISTORY INSTITUTE.

his last words were, "Baldwin, you have done well, and I don't want to lose such an officer by his running any unnecessary risk, and you must not attempt to make the return trip to your command without a good escort." I will not, and never again will I make such a trip without I am ordered, but I felt that my scouts needed an example set them, as they were a little backward about going on such trips. I have made it, and the most perilous journey it was.

Their chief has set them an example, and one worthy for them to emulate (if I do say it), and in the future not one of them must ever fail to attempt, at least, to go wherever ordered, and I don't think they will [fail].

I have had to answer more questions and repeat my story so often to the people I have met that I shall be glad to get back. Everybody on the train knew me and were asking all kinds of questions.

I left off with my narrative on August 31, the next day after the big fight at Red River. The battle is to be known as the battle of Red River.

On September 1, also on the second and third, I lay in camp, way up toward the head of Pleasant Valley; that is, my command was up there. I stayed down at headquarters, so I enjoyed the rest very much. On the fourth I scouted on the east side of the plains all day, and at 2:00 A.M. on the fifth started on the main trail across the Staked Plains, the command following about 5:00 A.M. We marched out on this barren level about thirty-five miles, when we came to good water and halted to rest, the main column not moving out seven miles as far as I had gone. Here I received orders to return to the command, which I did, rejoining it at 6:00 P.M. After a short rest of an hour, the colonel, Baird,[5] Wetmore,[6] and myself with two scouts and five orderlies started back to the camp we had left in the morning, where we arrived at 2:00 A.M. on the morning of September 6.

Here Major Biddle (6th Cavalry) provided us a good place to sleep. After taking breakfast, consisting of ham, bacon, coffee, and bread, without sugar, at 8:00 A.M. we started for the main supply camp, where Captain Bristol (5th Infantry) and Captain Ewers[7] were in camp. We reached the place at 1:00 P.M.; so you see, from 2:00 A.M. on the fifth to 1:00 P.M. on the sixth, I had ridden about ninety miles, and all on one poor horse. At 4:00 P.M. the colonel intimated that he wanted someone of us to go to [Camp] Supply with important dispatches, and asked me if I did not want to go. I of course could not say no, and at 8:00 P.M. my orders were handed to me, and to my surprise I was ordered into Leavenworth with not only written but verbal messages for General Pope in person.

At 8:30 P.M. I was ready, had chosen three of my best men, who had proven the bravest of my scouts,[8] and we started off with light hearts, although not without some doubt of a perfectly safe journey. The entire night was spent on the road, and not until 4:30 A.M. on the seventh did we pull bridle rein. We had made over forty miles from the command, and tired and hungry, we sought to find a place where we would be secreted from our wily enemy, that we might have a day of quiet, which both man and beast required, before continuing our journey; in fact, we did not intend traveling during the day at all.[9]

You know that when I am in an Indian country, I am always on the lookout, and I was not napping this morning. As soon as I had got into camp, I sent a man to a high point nearby while the balance of the party unsaddled. I got a cup of coffee. This man had not been on post more than half an hour before the alarm of "They are coming" was given by him in a low tone of voice. This was enough; we all knew what was coming. Each of us grasped his rifle, clambered up the almost precipitate bank, got into a good position, and then only had to wait fifteen minutes before twenty-six (counted them myself) came dashing over the hill and within fifty yards of us. I cannot describe my feelings. There were twenty-six Indians at least, and there was many another not far away, to my little band of four, including myself, but braver and more determined men than those three who were with me never leveled a rifle on an enemy, as they came over the hill and got in full view.

Each man singled out his Indian, and three of the red devils fell from their horses never again to rise; two of us had fired at the same

Indian, which accounts for there not having been four killed. My men are all good shots, and you know I can do that kind of work very well, but this was what they did not expect—the Indians thought to make easy prey of us and without loss to themselves. They fell back out of sight and gathered around us, occupying all of the bluffs within range, but very careful not to expose their worthless carcasses to the unerring aim of my party. We remained here for an hour after the first onset, and finding that we were surrounded and our enemy was in such concealed places, I gave the order to saddle up and get out. This was done with promptness. Then we had to lead the horses out, as the banks were too precipitous to ride up, and all must be done under very heavy fire, but I am glad to say not well-directed fire. When we gained the crest of the hill, we were fully exposed to their concentrated fire.

We mounted, and I gave the order to draw pistols and charge through their line, which was done, and it will seem like egotism for me to say this, but it was done as only brave men can do such desperate acts.

After we had finally cleared ourselves from them, we brought our horses down to a trot and did not increase this gait, rather trusting to our rifles to keep our already pursuing friends at proper distance than to tire our horses out on the start. After going about two miles, keeping up a brisk fire from on horseback, they had so gained on us that we were compelled to dismount and again try them on foot, which was done and successfully, for we drove them back to our rear over a mile.

But while they were retreating at our immediate rear, another party got in our front again. We mounted and charged through the screeching hounds, killing two or three on this charge with revolvers. Again we galloped off for two miles or more, when they came up with us, but more cautiously than before; they had learned the almost deadly results of shots from our rifles. Here we made another stand, dismounted. This was the last, for after we emptied more saddles, they would not venture nearer than 1,500 yards. After we mounted again, they continued to follow us, but at such a distance that their shots fell short every time.

We made for the level plain, and when I found a good place where they could not come nearer than two thousand yards without exposing themselves, halted and secured our horses, determined to remain there and fight until darkness could cover our retreat, but after remaining in the place for an hour, and our friends not coming to accept our challenge (but keeping in sight all the time), we concluded that inasmuch as the plain was about dead level and there would be no chance for them to ambush us, and having every confidence in my men and their trusty rifles, I started taking a course due north over a barren, trackless country.

To add to our discomfort, it was raining as only it can when it gets started on the western deserts, and during the fight we had lost everything in the shape of wrappings, and all we did save was our rifles, ammunition, and six pieces of hard bread, each [of] which was reduced to a dough by the rain, and for two days and nights we were without a mouthful of anything but grapes and acorns. Not for one minute did it stop raining. I can't give any idea about the journey. The Indians were on our trail and all around us constantly. I trust I shall never be called on to perform another such journey, but this was not the end.

On the morning of the eighth, as we neared the banks of the dry Washita, I ran into a camp of Comanches, numbering about one hundred, and we had got within three-quarters of a mile and had been discovered by their outpost, but this time we were up to snuff. As we all had blankets on, we looked more like Indians than white men, and taking it regular Indian style, lay down on our horses and galloped right ahead. We had not gone very far before we ran onto their picket, who had two horses, both of which we captured, and the Indian too, and turned them off into the timber, which was about half a mile away.

This was the climax. The idea of four men on worn-out horses dashing through a camp of one hundred wild Indians, capturing and carrying off one of their men and two Indian ponies! But we had all grown desperate, and not having any thought of getting through, we were bound to put on a bold front and sell out for all we were worth. After gaining the timber, before doing which we had to swim the river three times, all felt relieved, for in the timber we could defend ourselves against their camp until dark.

We continued our journey down the Washita for about fifteen miles, or until dark, being careful not to leave the timber, and after dark crossed over the divide onto the Canadian, striking it about sixteen miles west of Antelope Hills.

Here I found Captain Lyman[10] in camp with the supply train for Colonel Miles's command. Here I got fresh horses and turned my Indian (who proved to be a white man who had lived with the Indians since he was six years old)[11] over to Captain Lyman, and increased my number by two men, making five scouts and myself.

We dug holes in the sand and lay there all day waiting for night to come. Captain Lyman had gone and left us early in the morning. Nothing of interest happened during the day of September 9, and as soon as it was dark, I started on for Supply, a distance of seventy-five miles, where I arrived next morning at 10:00 A.M.

Philip H. Sheridan near the end of his career.
RAY D. SMITH COLLECTION, KNOX COLLEGE ARCHIVES.

I have made some terribly hard rides in my life, but never did I make one that could in any way compare with this one. I rode from 8:00 P.M. on the sixth until 10:00 A.M. on the tenth, with only about fourteen hours' rest, and that was after the first sixty hours, riding a distance not far from four hundred miles. I hope I shall never have another such ride to make, and not only the ride, but we had to fight our way through for two days.

I left Camp Supply on the morning of the eleventh and am writing here (Fort Dodge, Kansas) at 12:00 P.M. on the twelfth; remained here until 4:00 P.M. of the thirteenth, proceeded to Leavenworth by rail, where I arrived on September 14 at 3:00 P.M. and was received with hearty welcomes from all. I have already quoted the general (Pope) and what he said about being careful. I shall not go anyplace again without a strong escort.

You can realize without anticipating all the danger in the world that we will have lots of hard work to do yet, and you must not expect that I shall be clear from joining it as a matter of duty, if nothing more. On September 16 I started to Dodge, where I arrived today (seventeenth). Tomorrow I start for Supply with a good strong escort.

The reports from the front this morning are that Captain Lyman's train was surrounded by four hundred Indians and he could not get out for four days. He lost one killed and three wounded.[12] Lieutenant [Granville] Lewis of our regiment was shot through the knee and will lose his leg. You had better retain my letters, as I keep a limited diary, and on my up-trip lost it. So what I have written contains all of my diary.

Yours truly and forever,
Frank

Scouting with Baldwin on the Texas Panhandle

LEMUEL T. WILSON[1]

Pampa (Texas) *Daily News,* September 29, 1933

I had hunted buffalo for about two years, so I was familiar with all of that western frontier country. In the spring of 1874, we had considerable trouble with the Indians. Twenty-three of us (buffalo hunters) were corralled by Indians at Adobe Walls for about three months. I helped to build the stockade there for our protection and was in the battle of Adobe Walls on June 27, 1874.

In August 1874 Colonel Miles heard adverse reports about us and sent Lt. Frank Baldwin with a detachment of soldiers down to Adobe Walls to investigate. Lt. Baldwin and his command arrived at Adobe Walls on the evening of August 18 and camped about one-half mile west of the stockade. Next morning, the Indians attacked us and one of our hunters, George Huffman, was killed and scalped. As soon as Baldwin heard the shooting, he came to our assistance. He took after the Indians and had a running fight with them for about ten miles. When he returned, we asked permission to leave there under his escort, as we could not go by ourselves on account of the Indians. As he needed more scouts, he hired Ira Wing, Tobe Robison, and myself as scouts. We left Adobe Walls on the morning of August 20.

Water was very scarce, and in the afternoon Lieutenant Baldwin came back to where we hunters were and asked if any of us knew where there was water. The men and horses were nearly famished. I said, "I know a place where we have always found water." He sent Charles Morrow and me to look for it. When we reached "Gallina," or Chicken Creek, we found water, also two Indian scouts camped by a small fire with meat roasting on a stick. When they heard us, one got away, the other one I killed.

I shot at the other several times but missed him. We learned afterward that the one I killed was a subchief and a great warrior named "Whizzing Arrow." He came from behind a stump, and we met face to face not over six feet apart, and it had to be a finish. I beat him to it, and I took his scalp. It may have been against military orders, but when I was about ten years old back in Iowa, we got word that the Indians had killed and scalped my favorite uncle, and I promised my grandmother that when I grew to be a man, I would go west and kill an Indian to avenge Uncle Jim, and this was the first one that I was sure I had killed, so I took his scalp.

Lieutenant Baldwin let me keep his trinkets, such as rings, knives, bows, and arrows. But his ponies were turned over to Colonel Miles when we reached his camp August 21, on the Canadian River west of Antelope Hills. Lieutenant Baldwin made his report to Colonel Miles, after which Miles sent for me, to have me give my version of the affair, which I did.

<hr/>

Pampa (Texas) *Daily News,* October 1, 1933

On the morning of August 22 or 23, we left with Miles's command and were with him in the battle of August 30 (on Byrnes Creek in the northeast corner of Briscoe County). At one time during this battle, when Miles had his command deployed in a skirmish line, a small band of Indian sharpshooters had gained a point where the troops could not get action on them. He sent word to Lieutenant Baldwin to send a couple of scouts over a small flat to dislodge them. He sent W. F. Schmalsle and myself. We had to crawl about two hundred yards in plain sight of the entire skirmish line to keep out of sight of the Indians. On the left, the soldiers did not understand the orders, thought we were Indians crawling away, and commenced firing on us. Lieutenant Baldwin saw our plight and tried to stop the firing, but couldn't make them understand. We were between two fires—the troops' and the Indians'.

I said, "Let's get up and run for it," so we made a dash across the plateau and gained the point. When we got started, it did not take us long to put the Indians on the run. After we got back, Miles kept moving his troops from one hill to another, keeping it up all day, and advanced right along. At one place, when the Indians made a stand in front of Baldwin's command, the eighteen scouts, I among them, made a charge on the point against Baldwin's orders. Schmalsle was near Baldwin, and he stopped him, saying, "I'll keep one of you back, anyway." Schmalsle moved away from Baldwin a few feet, and then made a dash up the hill after us. When we got to that point, the Indians had gone to another point. But I forgot to stop and went on to the point where the Indians were. By this time, Baldwin's command had come up from the rear, and seeing the danger I was in, [Baldwin] ordered a charge. By sheer luck, they relieved me. As I recall it, we fought them all day. They finally drew off to a hill about a mile away.

Lieutenant Baldwin's command of soldiers and scouts was always near Colonel Miles. The Indians had collected on a hill and seemed to be holding a council. Colonel Miles ordered the artillery to put in a nine-pounder and told the gunner to aim to hit the bunch of Indians. I was close and heard the command. It seemed to me a long time before the shell hit. It struck right in the middle of the bunch. That was the last we saw of the Indians that day.

In the evening Miles ordered us to take the back track, and we went back to camp. Next morning we took up the main trail and followed them to Tule Canyon. As I recall it, Miles took the cavalry and scouts and followed the trail to where it left the canyon and went out on the Staked Plains. We scouted around there for a while, then returned to headquarters on the afternoon of September 6. Colonel Miles asked Lieutenant Baldwin to take what men he needed and carry a dispatch to Camp Supply. He selected W. F. Schmalsle, Ira Wing, and myself.

We left Colonel Miles's headquarters about 4:00 P.M. September 6, and that evening we rode into the camp of Major Biddle, in command of a supply train on the Salt Fork of Red River (a few miles north of Clarendon, Donley County). I needed a remount, as my horse was played out. I was ordered to the picket line to select a horse from the 6th Cavalry. I chose a horse of Canadian breed, one of the best I have ever ridden.

We left Major Biddle's camp just before dark. We planned to travel by night and hide away during the day. Just at daylight, September 7, we made camp on the head of Whitefish Creek (near where the Santa Fe crosses it in the southern part of Gray County). Here we had our first encounter with Indians on that memorable ride of September 6–10, 1874. I was the scout on guard that morning when the Indians discovered us. We had traveled all night and of course were all worn out. I was so drowsy I could hardly keep my eyes open. I chewed tobacco at that time, and I put tobacco spittle in my eyes to keep awake, and it was well I did or I would not have seen that Indian who was looking for us. I slipped back down the hill and gave the alarm to the others, who were just finishing breakfast, and we were ready for them. He had not seen me, and when he came over the rim of the draw looking for us, we all took a shot, and I guess we all hit him. In the attack by the rest of the band, which took place at once, they killed our pack mule, and we lost all our food supply and everything but what we had on our persons or in our saddlebags. We held a council and decided to dash through them. If we stayed there, [we] would surely be killed, and we decided we had better die in trying at least to get away.

The four of us held council, which took but a few minutes. Wing said, "We will dig rifle pits and hold them off." I said, "What will you dig rifle pits with?" He said, "Our butcher knives." I said, "While we are digging a pit half big enough to hide one man, they will kill every one of us. We will have to make a dash and fight our way through." Lieutenant Baldwin and Schmalsle voted with me. We mounted our horses and made a dash up out of the draw four abreast, onto the level right among the Indians, who were all off their ponies looking for us. Our dash was such a surprise to them that they tumbled over each other trying to get away from us. On we rode, firing as we went. As soon as they could get their ponies, they took after us. As our horses were jaded, they soon came within shooting distance. Then we stopped, dismounted, and beat them back. We didn't stop to see how many we had killed, but we knew we had emptied a number of saddles. This fighting kept up all day. We would dash ahead and they would overtake us, then we would stop and fight them back. We had long-range army guns and were all good marksmen, which accounted for the fact that none of us were wounded. We were corralled three times by Indians and fought our way out each time.

━━ ☰◈☰ ━━

Pampa (Texas) *Daily News,* October 2, 1933

Late in the afternoon, after the last fight and the remaining Indians had been driven back, we were resting about one thousand yards out on the Staked Plains and out of range of the Indians' guns. Lieutenant Baldwin took from his jacket pocket a photograph of his wife and little daughter, gazed long at them, [and] shaking his head, he said, "I never expected to see you again."

We were tired and hungry, as we had not had a bit to eat since our scanty breakfast at early dawn. Fate befriended us. A sudden rain came up—almost a cloudburst, then a steady rain. The Indians bothered us no more. Then came night that we had longed for. We traveled as long as we could keep our course, then camped. Or rather, we just stopped, for we had lost our entire equipment back in the draw that morning. We picketed our horses to let them graze, and we laid down on the ground, using our saddles for pillows and saddle blankets for cover, the only protection we had.

Next morning (September 8), just at daylight, we started again, a little rested but still hungry. Late in the afternoon, near Sweetwater Creek, on which Fort Elliott was later built, we ran into an old buffalo which had been killed. We cut out a big chunk from his rump, which we ate raw. None of us had any matches, and if we had had any, we would not dare to use them, as we were afraid to build a fire. We rested for a while and let the horses rest and graze.

About 4:00 P.M., when we came to a ridge between Gageby Creek and the Washita, we saw spread out on a hill across the Washita a large herd of animals, about a mile away. We stopped for council. Lieutenant Baldwin said, "That must be a herd of buffalo." I said, "Lieutenant, did you ever see any white buffalo?" "No," he said, "then it must be mules and horses of Captain Lyman's train." I said, "Captain Lyman would have over one hundred wagons, that would mean about six hundred horses and mules. There must be at least fifteen hundred head of horses there." He said, "That's right, but what is it?" I said, "There are Indians near, and those are their ponies."

We went on about a quarter of a mile, and just over a little knoll, we looked down into a big camp. He said, "That is Captain Lyman's camp." I said, "That's an Indian camp." He said, "No, it can't be, there are not [that] many Indians behind Colonel Miles." We drew a little nearer, and I showed him they were tepees, and he was convinced they were Indians.

Then the question was, what shall we do? Lieutenant Baldwin said, "We will keep on and ride right through them and strike the plains beyond

Washita." I said, "No, there are too many of them. They will run right over us, tromp us into the ground, and kill us all without ever firing a shot." Baldwin said, "Well, what shall we do?" I said, "We will circle off to the right, work over, and strike the Washita farther down. If they discover us, we will separate—every man to himself—get into the swamp, and maybe some of us will get to Camp Supply."

The argument lasted several minutes. Lieutenant Baldwin said, "I am in command; follow me." I said, "I for one will not go. Lieutenant, you are in command, but you cannot make me go into certain death. I refuse to follow and will not put my head into a halter that means certain death." The lieutenant's eyes flashed fire. He surely was an angry man. Finally he said, "Come on, all who want to go to Camp Supply, follow me," and he mounted his horse. I said, "Come on, all who want to go to Camp Supply, follow me," and I mounted my horse. Baldwin started one way and Wing went with him. I started the other way and Schmalsle followed me. After going a few hundred yards, I said to Schmalsle, "Let's take the last look at Baldwin and Wing that we will ever have." We turned and looked, only to see that they had stopped also. When they saw we had stopped, they turned and came toward us. Upon reaching us, Lieutenant Baldwin, still angry and his voice trembling, said, "Wilson, if you are going to take command of this outfit, lead on." "Lieutenant," I said, "I don't wish to take command, but if you will follow me, I will take you to Camp Supply." He said, "All right, lead on. I'll follow." Thus we started my way, the scouts in the lead because they knew the way.

That was one of the occasions that he afterwards many times mentioned and said that I had saved his life. He said our good luck of the day before in fighting our way through had made him overconfident. We had not gone very far when I, who had the best horse, was riding a little in advance. In going over a little ridge, I saw an Indian, naked except for his G-string and moccasins, riding a pony and leading another, which was loaded with meat. He was riding along, singing his Ki-yi song with his head hanging forward, and he did not see me. I backed down, making signs to the others for silence and told them what I had seen, and that they would see him in a few minutes coming around the point. We held council and Baldwin said, "What will we do?" I said, "We can't shoot; we are too close to their camp. We will catch him, disarm him, and take him with us." So we waited till he appeared, then I rode right onto him, grabbed him by the neck, and choked him to silence. We both fell from our horses, but I hung onto him while Schmalsle and Wing disarmed him. We made signs to him that if he made a sound, we would kill him. It was later learned that he was a white man who had lived with the Indians since he was six years old. We cut the meat from both horses, turned one loose, and tied him to the other and took him with us.

At one time we had to pass in plain sight of the Indian camp some distance away. We rode single file, as Indians do. If they saw us, they probably thought we were Indians. As soon as we got out of sight, we rode as fast as we could for the Washita. We had to swim it. Wing's horse gave out, and when we got across, he couldn't make it up the bank, which was very steep. Wing jumped off and saved himself, but his horse fell back into the river. Not having any other horse we decided Wing should ride the Indian's pony and we would make the prisoner walk. He had to trot or run most of the way.

⊶ ⊰⊹⊱ ⊷

Pampa (Texas) *Daily News,* October 3, 1933

After crossing the Washita, the question was what to do now. I said, "We will travel down the river until dark. If we are attacked, we will scatter into the swamp and some may get through. I have the best horse. I will stay back and cover your retreat." When we would reach a little high ground, I would stop and watch while the others went ahead. Then I would catch up. We did this several times for four or five miles. It seemed like it would never get dark.

I caught up with them in a little cottonwood grove just before dark. We rested here about fifteen minutes, then we started northward through a draw toward the Canadian River, which we reached about midnight without further incident. The Canadian was much swollen from the recent rains. We had to swim it, and the Indian was dismounted. If we turned him loose, he would go back to camp and give the alarm. Had we made him swim, he would have been drowned. Wing wanted to kill him. I said, "No, that would be murder; he is unarmed and helpless." I solved the question by tying him to the tail of my horse. Schmalsle rode behind and a little downstream to watch the Indian. After crossing safely, we rested awhile and then took the old trail made by Colonel Miles during the first part of the expedition and followed it six or eight miles. We were traveling two abreast when, about 2:30 A.M. September 10, we were greeted by the most welcome sound I ever heard. "Halt, who goes there?" "A friend," answered Lieutenant Baldwin. "Advance friend and be recognized." We found that it was an outpost of Captain Lyman's supply train of thirty-six wagons. We were taken into camp, and Lieutenant Baldwin reported to Captain Lyman, who took him into his tent and directed the sentinel to take us scouts to the corral of the teamsters. The Indian was taken to the guard tent.

We three scouts began to hunt something to eat. I knew some of the teamsters. Wash Logan was the first name to come to my mind, and I began to look for him. I started around the corral calling for Wash Logan. I went clear around with no answer and came back to where I started. I was getting a little angry, so I kicked a fellow and said, "Get up, we are hungry; we haven't had a thing to eat for two or three days." Wash Logan, who happened to be the man I kicked, said, "Is that you, Lem?" "Yes," I said, "and I am as hungry as hell." He got up at once.

By this time the confusion had awakened the whole train, and it wasn't long until we had something to eat. While we were eating, I said to Schmalsle, "That Indian ought to be fed." Wash Logan said, "What Indian?" I said, "Boys, we'll show you something that will open your eyes." I went to Captain Lyman's tent and called for Lieutenant Baldwin. He said, "What is it, Wilson?" I said, "We are being fed. Don't you think we should feed that Indian, he must be hungry?" He said, "Yes, by all means."

Captain Lyman gave me an order to the sergeant of the guard for the Indian. Baldwin said he would guarantee that I would look after the Indian and return him to the guardhouse. I took him to the corral, and the teamsters surely did open their eyes at seeing a hostile Indian clad only with a G-string and moccasins. We fed him and returned him to the guard. Then we took a short sleep. (This captive professed a great joy in being again with the whites, and so completely deceived Lyman's men with whom Baldwin left him that when they were later besieged, he was given a gun. He joined a party going for water at night and made his escape.)

By daylight we were up and had our breakfast. Captain Lyman asked Lieutenant Baldwin to leave a scout to pilot him back to Colonel Miles, and he left Schmalsle. Wing and I went with Lieutenant Baldwin on to Camp Supply, which we reached without further incident.

— ·—◆—· —

Pampa (Texas) *Daily News,* October 4, 1933

Lieutenant Baldwin went on to Fort Leavenworth, leaving instructions with the commanding officer at Camp Supply that Wing and I were to remain there until his return. When Lieutenant Baldwin returned to Camp Supply late in September with an escort, we went with them to join Colonel Miles at the head of the Washita, where he established his winter quarters. Sometimes two of us were sent out to carry dispatches or as spies to investigate and report to him.

In October, I think it was, Colonel Miles, with a part of his command, went north to the Canadian River, followed along the Canadian to Adobe Walls, crossed the Canadian southwest from Adobe Walls out on the Staked Plains; there we made camp. On one occasion Colonel Miles sent for me and asked me if I would carry a dispatch to Lieutenant Baird at the head of the Washita. I said, "I'll try." He wanted the dispatch delivered as quickly as possible. He told me to eat my dinner and report to him for orders. I reported at 12:00 P.M. He gave me my orders and wished me good luck.

I started at noon and at 8:00 P.M. of the same day delivered the dispatch, after riding sixty-five miles alone, with Indians almost constantly in sight. When Lieutenant Baird read the dispatch, he said, "When did you leave Colonel Miles?" I said, "At noon." He said, "Yesterday?" I said, "No, today." He could hardly believe it.

The next day I piloted two companies of soldiers of the 6th Cavalry back to Colonel Miles. Early in November I would have been with the party who recaptured the two youngest German girls, but a few days before Lieutenant Baldwin was sent on that trip, Colonel Miles wanted to send a dispatch to

Soldiers opening veins to relieve thirst.
NELSON A. MILES, *PERSONAL RECOLLECTIONS AND OBSERVATIONS.*

Camp Supply. He first sent for scouts Robison and Shultz. He asked Robison
if they could carry a dispatch to Camp Supply. Robison asked, "How many
soldiers will you send along?" Miles said, "How many do you want?" He said,
"Six or eight." Miles asked him what for. He said, "We will need an escort for
protection." Miles told him to go to his quarters.

Later, he sent an orderly for Jim Dunlap and myself to report to him. He
said, "Wilson, do you think you and Dunlap could carry a dispatch to Camp
Supply for me? How many soldiers do you want?" "Not a one," I told him.
"Why?" "Well, the larger the party, the larger, plainer trail it would make, and
the more men, the more danger and harder to hide if necessary." "That's what I
thought. You and Dunlap get your equipment ready and report to me as soon
as possible."

At 4:00 P.M. we reported. He asked me what route I would take. I said we
would go north until we struck the Canadian, cross over, and follow the dividing range between the Canadian and the Beaver, as I thought we would be less
apt to encounter Indians. About dark we were following down a small stream
that empties into the Canadian near the mouth of the Big Blue. Many of the
streams in that country were filled with quicksand. We crossed and recrossed
this little stream. I can't recall its name. At one place my horse mired down in
the quicksand. My gun, which was carried in a sling on the saddle, was filled
with sand.

When we got on the bank, I told Dunlap I would have to stop and clean the
sand out of my gun. While doing it, Jim heard a noise and said, "What is that?"
We listened and learned it was Indians. They could not see us, as we were in

the brush down on the creek bed. But we could skylight them up on the ridge. We held the noses of our horses to keep them from making a noise and watched for three-quarters of an hour while about four hundred Indians passed by not over a hundred yards from us. We waited till the stragglers had all passed, then we took their back trail. We would travel at night and hide and rest by day. We afterwards learned that this was Gray Beard's band, which Lieutenant Baldwin had the fight with when he recaptured the two youngest German girls.[2] He also captured from them two fresh scalps of white men. The hair exactly corresponded with that of Dunlap and me, and as we had just gone the way they had come, of course they thought it was us, and we were reported killed.

We were gone nearly a month, and when we returned to Miles's command, he was still camped on the Washita in his winter headquarters. When we reported to him at his tent, he was surprised to see us and said, "Wilson, we thought you and Dunlap were dead. I am very glad to see you and to know you are alive." We learned afterwards that those two scalps were from two soldiers of the 8th Cavalry, Major Price in command. This was in November 1874.[3]

From this time till the spring of 1875, Colonel Miles kept the Indians continually on the move, and of course also kept the scouts on the go, carrying dispatches to or from his various commands. I was with Colonel Miles in the spring of 1875 when he established headquarters at Cantonment on the Sweetwater. We scouted all over the country along Red River and finally landed at Fort Sill. There we rested a few days, then started back towards Cantonment through the Wichita Mountains, following a general course between the Washita and South Canadian Rivers. He divided his command, sending one division one way and one the other. I was sent with Lieutenant Kingsbury of the 6th Cavalry.[4] We met Colonel Miles again when we arrived at Cantonment.

When Miles was relieved, he turned the command over to Major Biddle. There were eighteen scouts. Twelve went with Colonel Miles; six, I among them, were transferred to the command of Major Biddle and remained at [the] cantonment. I was sent with Major Forsyth when he was sent with surveyors to locate a site for a permanent post. They located it at the head of the Sweetwater and built the post known as Fort Elliott.[5]

When Major Biddle was relieved, I was transferred to Maj. H. C. Bankhead of the 4th Cavalry and continued in service until October 1876, when by order of the department, the scout force was cut down, [and] I was discharged.

A Fight with the Comanches and Kiowas

WYLLYS LYMAN[1]

Army and Navy Journal 12, no. 12 (October 31, 1874): 136–37

INDIAN TERRITORY EXPEDITION,
CAMP ON DRY FORK OF WASHITA RIVER,
TEXAS, September 25, 1874

Lieutenant G. W. Baird, U.S. Army, Acting Assistant Adjutant General:

SIR: In pursuance of orders, I have the honor to report the recent service of my company (I, 5th Infantry), having present with it thirty-eight rifles, and of a mounted detachment attached.

I moved, as directed, with thirty-six empty wagons to meet a train with supplies on September 1 at 2:00 P.M., from Battle Creek near Red River, Texas, on our trail to Oasis Creek at the Canadian River, 120 miles, arriving there on the morning of the fifth at 9:00 A.M. 2nd Lt. Frank West,[2] 6th Cavalry, with twenty troopers, horses much worn, joined me for escort duty on McClellan Creek. Before crossing the Canadian River, Lieutenant West sent me notice of the train and met me with it on the seventh. Seven dismounted men, 6th Cavalry, and one man, 5th Infantry, also joined me going to the front. The stores were transferred in the midst of a wild storm and rain. Indians were first seen while here, a party of fifteen [that] killed and scalped a teamster named Moore while hunting near camp on September 6, and quickly disappeared.

While on my return, and on the ninth at about 8:00 A.M., when we were crossing the divide between the Canadian and Washita Rivers, single Indian vedettes were seen at a great distance on the flanks and in front, and on approaching a ridge which crossed my route, a small party of mounted Indians appeared on its crest. Large bodies of Indians showed also at a distance on our right front. At about eight hundred yards from the ridge, the train was halted to close up. Fire was opened upon us by a few sharpshooters, when the infantry and dismounted men were deployed, right skirmishers in advance of the train and across its head, firing moderately, and the left skirmishers under 1st Lt. Granville Lewis,[3] 5th Infantry, on its left rear, the train being in two columns about twenty yards apart, prepared to corral.

Lieutenant West collected his mounted men, thirteen in number (the other horses being unserviceable), who had been covering the train as flankers, and deployed [them] as skirmishers on the right of the infantry in front. The command advanced, inclining to the left to gain the highest ground, the right skirmishers firing occasionally at long taw—say eight hundred yards. First Sergeant Mitchell of my company here dropped two ponies, whose bodies afterwards were seen still saddled. Lieutenant West advanced rapidly straight forward and soon drove the enemy from his ridge.

Reaching a water hole, the train was halted, mules watered, and kegs and canteens filled—a fortunate suggestion of Wagonmaster Callahan. Lieutenant West recovered his connection, which had become too remote, and the train went on, the skirmishers now moving parallel with the train, and at about one hundred yards from its right front and left rear respectively. Fire was soon reopened on us from commanding precipitous hills in front, when Lieutenant West advanced and, with his little party, charged up the hills to unseen ground, with a cheer and a rush which the enemy could not stand, and he fled.

Seeing that the train could not pass while these hills were occupied, I was about to direct Lieutenant West to attack there, when he proposed [it] himself. Though the number on the hills was not great, larger bodies were at hand, and the result was by no means certain. The enemy had apparently intended to make some stand here, from the articles found on the ground, such as bandages and haversacks. The movements of the Indians had been so contrary to their usual habit, in showing themselves openly and boldly like disciplined cavalry, though with something of their own uncertain and objectless riding about, that my impression is their design was to attack the command on the trail not far from the Canadian, and that the accident of our leaving the trail and diverging to our left disarranged their plan.

We now proceeded with our column some twelve miles; Lieutenant West in advance in skirmishing order and infantry skirmishers out, striking the trail again after some miles; the enemy threatening us in several distant bodies with observers near; when at 2:30 P.M. and at about a mile north from the Washita River, while the train was rising out of a very deep and bad ravine, which Lieutenant West had passed and had momentarily halted, a small party swiftly ran down from our right front upon the mounted advance, approaching it to within two hundred yards, I think, and seemed to be trying to gain the left of the train. They were driven off by the carbines and returned to their supports at some distance.

A large body had been for some time also hovering nearer on our right. The train having cleared the ravine, we were fiercely charged from the rear and right by a mass of some seventy Indians, about whom were as many more in open order. They rode within one hundred yards. This occurred in the rear, where Lieutenant Lewis had charge. He had skillfully handled his skirmishers according to his own judgment up to this time, and when this attack was making, he shifted his line to meet it to the right and rear of the train and opened fire. The enemy swerved around the rear of the train, and accordingly, Lieutenant Lewis removed his men across to cover it. Here he was subjected to a heavy fire from several directions. Sergeant de Armond, Company I, 5th Infantry, a gallant and experienced soldier and skillful shot, was here instantly killed while in the act of firing. Almost immediately after, Lieutenant Lewis was struck down by a shot through the left knee and wholly disabled. The charge was repulsed, but the fire continued. I regard the skillful management of Lieutenant Lewis as having perhaps decided the fate of the train. The corral was not yet completed, and the rear of the train was on the verge of a stampede!

The fall of Lieutenant Lewis, in whom the men had great confidence, somewhat disturbed the skirmishers here, but arriving here at this moment, the men were easily made to straighten their line and continue their fire. Sergeant Hay, Company I, 5th Infantry, was put in charge here. The enemy suffered, but their method of carrying off their injured on their ponies, which Lieutenant Lewis saw them practice, prevented our ascertaining to what extent; several riderless ponies were seen.

While all this last was going on, which, however, occupied but a few seconds, the right skirmishers with whom I was were faced toward the direction of this attack and opened fire, and they contributed to its repulse. The ground was such, however, that a part of them could not effectively aim their fire in this direction, and they engaged Indians on our right front. They all were subject at this time to a lively fire from our right and front, and as soon as relieved from the pressure at the rear, they gave their attention to this so effectually as to prevent much accuracy of aim by the enemy, though his fire continued very active till dark and was partly enfilading. The best practical disposition of them seemed to be to line a ridge which ran diagonally along our right not far from the train, and was to it as the right barb of a broad arrow.

The attack on Lyman's supply train.

NELSON A. MILES, *PERSONAL RECOLLECTIONS AND OBSERVATIONS.*

First Sergeant Mitchell, Company I, 5th Infantry, was now very active, and his pluck and skill were conspicuous. He is a pattern skirmisher. The latter part of the day, he had charge here. The enemy had opposite here a parallel ridge at about four hundred yards, and beyond, another and higher one running somewhat circularly at about nine hundred yards. He occupied these lines strongly, and his fire was constant and severe. He had also good positions at five hundred yards opposite the head of the arrow. Happily, he fired mostly too high, like other people.

The Indian practice of circling early began around our front and increased until it became a wonderful display of horsemanship. Savages, erect on their ponies with shining spears and flaming blankets and lofty fluttering headgear, dashed along the ridges with yells and defiant and insulting attitudes, appearing and swiftly disappearing, showing portentous against the sky in the bright sunlight. This wild entertainment appeared to be intended to divert attention from their dismounted firing parties.

Forming the impression that these riders were gathering on our left front, I took a few men away to that side, where most of the cavalrymen, dismounted, were engaged under Lieutenant West, and found the firing there so sharp that we had to lie close, the men getting in their shots along a slope we had there also. The line along here formed the left barb of the arrow, broken inward toward the rear of the corral so as to hold the ground that way. Of course, these lines on both sides were faulty in principle, but they were the only ones the circumstances and the ground permitted.

After seeing the men covered as well as practicable, I had dismounted. Opposite the left front lay a high ridge, behind which at five hundred yards was collected a noisy body of Indians, whose speeches and shouts seemed to indicate preparations to charge. We discussed this subject but could make nothing of it, and at sunset the ridge became quiet. Rascally high shots crossing also from beyond the train disturbed our equanimity here, striking among the prone blue figures, sparsely flecking the yellow grass, and conspicuous in the slanting sunlight. Lieutenant West was here, and I was told that earlier in the affair, he had to be active to preserve composure. Assistant Wagonmaster Sanford was dangerously wounded (stomach) while getting ammunition for this front, where he was actively engaged.

When the corral was first formed, Lieutenant West, who was then a little in advance, dismounted his men, placed his horses within, and formed his party as skirmishers along the left front of the corral, as above mentioned. The corral was imperfect. The right column was formed with the usual bulge, but the left column closed in so as to form with the right a concentric curved line, leaving hardly space within for the animals. This circumstance contributed on that particular ground to their security, I think, as the sloping ground swelled upward on the left hand.

When darkness set in, all fell to digging. The corral on the right, front, and rear was protected by a series of pits close upon the wagons, and forage sacks, etc., were used to fortify some of these. Four detached enclosed little works, one of which commanded nearly the whole vicinity, were made on the left and one on the right, at various short distances at points which seemed appropriate, and were occupied by small parties. Water was obtained from a pool about four hundred yards off. No firing occurred on this night. I cannot say if the Indians dug also, but during the next day it appeared that they had cover.

At dawn on the eleventh, the enemy resumed his fire, and it was actively continued on both sides, with lulls and short interruptions, and by spurts at night, until about 8:00 A.M. on the twelfth. In the darkness, Indians approached us more closely and addressed us in language more forcible than complimentary, and announcing that they had "heap Comanches and Kiowas." The replies of my men were even superior in Doric strength, however.

By day the enemy fired from cover, and from all sides, though occasional pony dashes were made until on the eleventh two savages were stretched, when this ceased.

Defending the supply train. W. F. BEYER, *DEEDS OF VALOR.*

On the night of September 10, there was some clamor for water, which had given out, but I declined to risk life for it till real suffering arose, and an unauthorized party of soldiers and teamsters which attempted to reach the pool was at once driven in by a volley. Thirty rifle pits covering this water were afterwards counted. Sergeant Singleton, Company A, 6th Cavalry, was severely wounded in the leg on this night at a pit he had charge of, and where he did good service. Next morning Private Buck, Company I, 5th Infantry, was painfully wounded on the head at Sergeant Hay's pit.

Lieutenant Lewis and Wagonmaster Sanford were suffering much from their hurts and the miserable surroundings and [were] without medical treatment. Considering their lives in great danger, and a brave and shrewd scout named W. F. Schmalsle volunteering to break through to Camp Supply, and finding it impossible to communicate with our headquarters, I sent Schmalsle on the night of the tenth to Colonel Lewis, 19th Infantry,[4] at Supply for relief. He was chased from the start, but his pluck and shrewdness carried him through to Supply at 9:00 A.M. on the twelfth.

During the morning of September 12, the enemy was seen to withdraw a part of his force—variously estimated at two hundred to four hundred warriors—across the Washita River and over the prairie beyond. A light fire, however, continued from small parties until it was decided to skirmish for water. Lieutenant West moved out his mounted men, and Sergeant Mitchell deployed an infantry party of fifteen men. They cleared the ridge beyond the water of Indians— Sergeant Mitchell leading and handling his men beautifully, and rapidly using his own deadly rifle—and the wounded and choking men and animals were relieved of their thirst.

Soon after, rain fell and a violent storm set in, which continued till the evening of the next day, and we were now [as] drenched as before we had been dry. The corral was a great puddle. Indians moved all day north and south along our front, singly and in distant parties. Some approached, observed us out of range, and passed on. Toward night on September 13, a large distant body of men moved in misty column northward in such order that we first took them for cavalry, but we signaled in vain, and mounted men sent out reported that they were Indians.

During this time, my sense of responsibility was enhanced by the fact that the whole command would have exhausted its supplies on the thirteenth, and was depending wholly on this train for rations and forage. I felt almost certain that the head of our column would appear next day, and it was decided not to move in the storm on account of the wounded, and as several horses had been hit and twenty-two mules had been killed or disabled, and the rest were tottering on their feet, I doubted if they could pull the wagons.

Late at night on September 13, Schmalsle and five other scouts appeared and announced the approach of Company K, 6th Cavalry, under Lieutenant Kingsbury, 6th Cavalry, with medical aid and an ambulance. They arrived at 2:30 A.M. next morning, after a most trying march of eighty miles through the storm. Lieutenant Colonel Lewis had most kindly hastened them off on getting my dispatch, and they marched to us without a rest. The skillful services of Dr. Gray, acting assistant surgeon, were an immense relief and benefit to our wounded. At 9:00 A.M. on the fourteenth, we moved out to join the command, and at the crossing of the Washita River met Major Chaffee[5] and Company I, 6th Cavalry, in the lead of our command, and went into camp.

The Indians whom we met were Comanches and Kiowas who had gone on the warpath from [the] Wichita agency. They were about four hundred in number, and it is believed they were directed by Lone Wolf. It is difficult to make certain of Indian casualties. There were thirteen ascertained cases of killed and badly wounded and, I believe, others.

A few of the teamsters were armed and did good service. Cartridge cases found in their rifle pits showed that the Indians had our own arms and ammunition, caliber .50, as well as Spencer, Sharps, and Henry rifles. They must have expended a great quantity of ammunition. They practiced volley firing at times. Over one hundred rifle pits were found, some single, some having capacity for several, many of which were well made and skillfully placed and covered, and at distances varying from six hundred to within three hundred yards—a few even nearer. Nine beef cattle which we had with us were stampeded and lost.

On September 9, at Oasis Creek, Lieutenant Baldwin, 5th Infantry, turned over to me a young white man who had been brought up with the Kiowas, and with Indian instincts and ideas, and whom he had made prisoner the day before while the man was on picket mounted on a mule near an Indian camp on the Washita River. Lieutenant Baldwin, moving with three scouts, had fallen unexpectedly upon this camp, and snatching the picket, made off, only escaping capture himself by great skill and daring. The prisoner cunningly made the guard believe, though warned, that he was delighted at his release from the Indians and somehow escaped by getting into the unauthorized night party which attempted to get water while I was engaged with Schmalsle, who was about to make for Supply.

Beside those persons above referred to, I beg leave to report the excellent service of Sgt. F. S. Hay, Sgt. W. Koelpin, Cpl. J. J. H. Kelly, Cpl. J. W. Knox, and Cpl. J. James, Company I, 5th Infantry, and that model soldier, Thomas Kelly, and I declare that, though some much excelled others, the steadiness and conduct of the whole company was admirable; also Sergeant Kitchen, Corporal Morris, and Corporal Sharpless, Company H, 6th Cavalry, and Sergeant Pensylle, Company M, 6th Cavalry.

My casualties are all above mentioned.

> Very respectfully, your obedient servant,
> WYLLYS LYMAN, Captain, 5th Infantry,
> Brevet Major U.S.A., Commanding Escort

———— ✠ ————

Army and Navy Journal 12, no. 8 (October 5, 1874): 117

The following is an extract from a private letter written by Captain Lyman. The letter is dated September 14, Camp on the Washita River, Texas:

I had a staving fight for three days, from the ninth to the twelfth, with four hundred Comanches. We made rifle pits and drove them away at last. If I had only had the Rice trowel bayonet, we would have beaten them off sooner. During the fight, thirteen men belonging to the escort and train were killed and wounded. Lieutenant Lewis of the 5th Infantry was badly wounded by a shot through the kneepan. Twenty-seven Indians were killed. The expedition was without water for forty-eight hours.

Billy Dixon, a Frontier Hero

E. A. BRININSTOOL[1]

Hunter-Trader-Trapper (March 1925): 11–13

One of the most thrilling experiences, combined with desperate fighting, in the annuals of frontier history, in which four enlisted soldiers and two army scouts successfully withstood for an entire day the combined attack of about 125 Kiowa and Comanche Indians, occurred on September 12, 1874, near the Washita River, in what today is Hemphill County, Texas, twenty-two miles south of the present town of Canadian, and twenty-five miles southeast of Miami. In 1874 this section was a howling wilderness, practically as unknown as the heart of Africa. These men were carrying dispatches from the camp of Col. Nelson A. Miles, on the McClellan Creek, to Camp Supply, Indian Territory.

In order that the reader may at the start intelligently understand the situation, I append herewith the official report of Colonel Miles relative to the affair:

> HEADQUARTERS INDIAN TERRITORY EXPEDITION
> Camp on Washita River, Texas, September 24, 1874
> ADJUTANT GENERAL U.S.A.
>
> (Through Office Assistant Adjutant General Headquarters, Department and Military District of the Missouri, and of the Army)
> GENERAL:
>
> I deem it but a duty to brave and heroic men and faithful soldiers to bring to the notice of the highest military authorities an instance of indomitable courage, skill, and true heroism on the part of a detachment from this command, with the request that the actors be rewarded, and their faithfulness and bravery recognized by pensions, Medals of Honor, or in such way as may be deemed most fitting.
>
> On the night of September 10, a party consisting of Sgt. Z. T. Woodall, Co. I; Privates Peter Rath, Company A, John Harrington, Company H, and George W. Smith, Company M, 6th Cavalry; and scouts Amos Chapman[2] and William Dixon[3] were sent as bearers of

dispatches from the camp of this command on McClellan Creek to Camp Supply, I.T.

At 6:00 A.M. on the twelfth, when approaching the Washita River, they were met and surrounded by a band of 125 Kiowas and Comanches, who had recently left their agency.[4] At the first attack all were struck, Private Smith mortally, and three others severely wounded. Although enclosed on all sides, and by overwhelming numbers, one of them succeeded, while they were under severe fire at short range, and while the others with their rifles were keeping the Indians at bay, in digging, with his knife and hands, a slight cover. After this had been secured, they placed themselves within it, the wounded walking with brave and painful effort, and Private Smith—though he had received a mortal wound—sitting upright within the trench, to conceal the crippled condition of the party from the Indians.

From early morning until dark, outnumbered twenty-five to one, under an almost constant fire, and at such short range that they sometimes used their pistols, retaining the last charge to prevent capture and torture, this little party of five men defended their lives and the person of their dying comrade without food, and their only drink that rainwater that collected in a pool mingled with their own blood. There is no doubt that they killed more than double their own number, besides those that were wounded. The Indians abandoned the attack on the twelfth at dark. The exposure and distance from the command, which were necessary incidents of their duty, were such that for twenty-five hours from the first attack, their condition could not be known, and not until midnight of the thirteenth could they received medical attention and food, exposed during this time to an incessant cold storm.

Sergeant Woodall, Private Harrington, and Scout Chapman were seriously wounded. Private Smith died of his wounds on the morning of September 13. Private Rath and Scout Dixon were struck but not disabled.

The simple recital of their deeds, and the mention of odds against which they fought—how the wounded defending the dying, and the dying aided the wounded by exposure to fresh wounds after the power of action had gone—these alone present a scene of cool courage, heroism, and self-sacrifice which duty, as well as inclination, prompts us to recognize, but which we cannot fitly honor.

Very respectfully, your obedient servant,

NELSON A. MILES,
Colonel and Brevet Major General,
U.S.A. Commanding

Two stories have been told in print of this desperate defense—one by Billy Dixon, one of the most courageous, hardy, cool, and renowned army scouts of the '70s, who died in 1913—and one by Amos Chapman, also a well-known army scout and a man of reputation as an Indian fighter. But in order that Billy Dixon may receive the proper credit due him, and his honor and reputation for truthfulness and veracity may be cleared, I propose to present herewith both stories. Amos Chapman is yet living today in Oklahoma, and for fifty years has posed as the real hero in the Buffalo Wallow fight. I offer an affidavit made by one of the four soldiers who were in the fight— Sergeant Woodall, in the form of a letter to Billy Dixon, written from Fort Wingate, N.M., in 1889. The reader must then draw his own conclusion as to who is the real hero in this thrilling engagement. Billy Dixon's account of the fight is furnished me by his wife, Mrs. Olive K. Dixon, today a well-known and brilliant newspaperwoman of Miami, Texas. It is as follows:

BILLY DIXON'S STORY

The most perilous adventure of my life occurred September 12, 1874, in what was known as the "Buffalo Wallow fight." My escape from death was miraculous. During that year, I came in contact with hostile Indians as frequently as the most devoted warrior might wish, and found that it was a serious business.

On September 10, 1874, Col. Nelson A. Miles, in command of the troops campaigning against the Indians in the Southwest, was on McClellan Creek, in the Texas Panhandle, when he ordered Amos Chapman and myself, scouts, and four enlisted men to carry dispatches to Fort Supply. The enlisted men were Sgt. Z. T. Woodall, Troop I; Pvt. Peter Rath, Troop A; Pvt. John Harrington, Troop H; and Pvt. George W. Smith, Troop M, 6th Cavalry. When Colonel Miles handed us the dispatches, he told us we could have all the soldiers we thought necessary for an escort. His command was short of rations. We preferred the smallest possible number.

Leaving camp, we traveled mostly at night, resting in secluded places during the day. War parties were moving in every direction, and there was danger of attack at every turn.

On the second day, just as the sun was rising, we were nearing a divide between the Washita River and Gageby Creek. Riding to the top of a little knoll, we found ourselves face to face with a large band of Kiowa and Comanche Indians. The Indians saw us at the same time, and circling quickly, surrounded us. We were in a trap. We knew that the best thing to do was to make a stand and fight for our lives, as there would be great danger of our becoming separated in the excitement of a running fight, after which the Indians could the more easily kill us one by one. We also realized that we could do better work on foot, so we dismounted and placed our horses in the care of George Smith. In a moment or two, poor Smith was shot down, and the horses stampeded.

When Smith was shot, he fell flat on his stomach, and his gun fell from his hands, far from reach. But no Indian was able to capture that gun. If one ventured near Smith, we never failed to bring him down. We thought Smith was dead when he fell, but he survived until about 11:00 P.M.

I realized at once that I was in closer quarters than I had ever been in my life, and I have always felt that I did some good work that day. I was fortunate enough not to become disabled at any stage of the fight, which left me free to do my best under the circumstances. I received one wound—a bullet in the calf of the leg. I was wearing a thin cashmere shirt, slightly bloused. This shirt was literally riddled with bullets. How a man could be shot so many times at close range and not be hit, I never could understand. The Indians seemed absolutely sure of getting us—so sure, in fact, that they delayed riding us down and killing us at once, which they could

Billy Dixon bringing in Private Smith.
W. F. BEYER, *DEEDS OF VALOR.*

easily have done, and prolonged the early stages of the fight merely to satisfy their desire to toy with an enemy, as a cat would play with a mouse before taking its life.

We saw that there was no show for us to survive on this little hillside, and decided that our best fighting ground was a small mesquite flat, several hundred yards distant. Before we undertook to shift our position, a bullet struck Amos Chapman. I was looking at him when he was shot. Amos said, "Billy, I am hit at last," and eased himself down. The fight was so hot that I did not have time to ask him how badly he was hurt. Every man, save Rath and myself, had been wounded. Our situation was growing more desperate every minute. I knew that something had to be done, and quickly, or else all of us in a short time would be dead or in the hands of the Indians, who would torture us in the most inhuman manner before taking our lives.

I could see where herds of buffalo had pawed and wallowed a depression commonly called a "buffalo wallow," and I ran for it at top speed. It seemed as if a bullet whizzed past me at every jump, but I got through unharmed. The wallow was about ten feet in diameter. I found that its depth, though slight, afforded some protection. I shouted to my comrades to try and come to me, which all of them, save Smith and Chapman, commenced trying to do. As each man reached the wallow, he drew his butcher knife and began digging desperately, with knife and hands, to throw up dirt around the sides. The land happened to be sandy, and we made good headway, though constantly interrupted by the necessity of firing at the Indians as they dashed within range.

Many times during that terrible day did I think that my last moment was at hand. Once, when the Indians were crowding us awfully hard, one of the boys raised up and yelled, "No use, boys; no use; we might as well give up!" We answered by shouting to him to lie down. At that moment, a bullet struck in the soft bank near him, filling his mouth with dirt. I was so amused that I laughed, though in a sickly way, for none of us felt like laughing.

By this time, however, I had recovered from the first excitement of battle and was perfectly cool, as were the rest of the men. We were keenly aware that the only thing to do was to sell our lives as dearly as possible. We fired deliberately, taking good aim, and were picking off an Indian at almost every round. The wounded men conducted themselves admirably, and greatly assisted in concealing our crippled condition by sitting upright, as if unhurt, after they reached the wallow. This made it impossible for the Indians to accurately guess what plight we were in. Had they known so many of us were wounded, undoubtedly they would have rode in and finished us.

After all had reached the wallow, with the exception of Chapman and Smith, all of us thinking that Smith was dead, somebody called to Chapman to come on in. We now learned for the first time that Chapman's leg was broken. He called back that he could not walk, as his left knee was shattered.

I made several efforts to reach him before I succeeded. Every time the Indians saw me stand, they would fire such a volley that I was forced to retreat, until finally I made a run and got to Chapman. I told him to climb on my back, my plan being to carry him as I would a little child. Drawing both his legs in front of me, and laying the broken one over the sound one to support it, I carried him to the wallow, though not without great difficulty, as he was a larger man than myself, and his body a dead weight. It taxed my strength to carry him.

We were now all in the wallow except Smith, and we felt that it would be foolish and useless to risk our lives in attempting to bring in his supposedly dead body. We had not seen him move since the moment he went down. We began digging like gophers with our hands and knives to make our little wall of earth higher, and shortly had heaped up quite a little wall of dirt around us. its protection was quickly felt, even though our danger was hardly lessened. When I look back and recall our situation, I always find myself wondering and thinking of the manner in which my wounded comrades acted—never complaining or faltering, but they fought as bravely as if a bullet had not touched them. Sometimes the Indians would ride toward us at headlong speed, with lances uplifted and poised, undoubtedly bent upon spearing us. Such moments made a man brace himself and grip his gun. Fortunately we were able to keep our heads, and to bring down or disable the leader. Such charges proved highly dangerous to the Indians and gradually grew less frequent.

Thus, all that long September day, the Indians circled around us or dashed past, yelling and cutting up all kinds of capers. All morning we had been without water, and the wounded were sorely in need of it. In the stress and excitement of such an encounter, even a man who has not been hurt grows painfully thirsty, and his tongue and lips are soon as dry as a whetstone. Ours was the courage of despair. We knew what would befall us if captured alive—we had seen too many naked and mangled bodies of white man who had been spreadeagle and tortured with steel and fire to forget what our own fate would be. So we were determined to fight to the end, not unmindful of the fact that every once in a while there was another dead or wounded Indian.

About 3:00 P.M. a black cloud came up in the west, and in a short time the sky shook and blazed with thunder and lightning. Rain fell in blinding sheets, drenching us to the skin. Water gathered quickly in the buffalo wallow, and our wounded men eagerly bent forward and drank from the muddy pool. It was more than muddy—the water was red with their own blood that had flowed from their wounds and lay clotting and dry in the hot September sun.

The storm and the rain proved our salvation. The wind had shifted to the north and was now drearily chilling us to the bone. An Indian dislikes rain, especially a cold rain, and those Kiowas and Comanches were no exception to the rule. We could see them in groups out of rifle range, sitting on their ponies, with their blankets drawn tightly around them. The plains country beats the world for quick changes in weather, and in less than an hour after the rain had fallen, the wind was bitter cold. Not a man in our crowd had a coat, and our thin shirts were scant protection. Our coats were tied behind our saddles when our horses stampeded and were lost beyond recovery. I was heartsick over the loss of my coat, for in the inside pocket was my dearest treasure—my mother's picture, which my father had given me shortly before his death. I was never able to recover it.

The water was gathering rapidly in the wallow and soon reached a depth of two inches, but not a man murmured. Not one thought of surrender, although the wounded were shivering as if they had the ague.

We now found that our ammunition was running low. This fact rather appalled us, as bullets—plenty of them—were our only protection. Necessity compelled us to husband every cartridge as long as possible, and not to fire at an Indian unless we could see that he meant business and was coming right into us.

Late in the afternoon, somebody suggested that we should go out and get Smith's belt and six-shooter, as he had been shot early in the fight, and his belt was undoubtedly loaded with cartridges.

Rath offered to go and soon returned with the startling information that Smith was still alive. This astonished us greatly and caused us deep regret that

Twenty-five to one.

NELSON A. MILES, *PERSONAL RECOLLECTIONS AND OTHER OBSERVATIONS.*

we had not known it earlier in the day. Rath and I at once got ready to bring poor Smith to the buffalo wallow. By supporting the wounded man between us, he managed to walk. We could see that there was no chance for him. He was shot through the left lung, and when he breathed, the wind sobbed out of his back under the left shoulder blade. Near the wallow, an Indian had dropped a stout willow switch with which he had been whipping his pony. Using this switch, a silk handkerchief was forced into the gaping hole in Smith's back to staunch the flow of blood, in a measure.

Night was approaching, and it looked blacker to me than any night I had ever seen. Ours was a forlorn and disheartening situation. The Indians were still all around us. The nearest relief was seventy-five miles away. Of the six men in the wallow, four were badly wounded and without anything to relieve their suffering. We were cold and hungry, with nothing to eat, and without a blanket, coat, or hat to protect us from the rain and biting wind. It was impossible to rest or sleep with two inches of water in the wallow. I remember that I threw my hat—a wide-brimmed sombrero—as far from me as I could when our horses stampeded. The hat was in my way, and further, was too good a target for the Indians to shoot at.

We were unable to get grass for bedding for the reason that the whole country had been burned over by the Indians. It was absolutely necessary, however, that the men should have some kind of bed to keep them off the cold, damp ground. Rath and I solved the problem by gathering tumbleweeds, which in that country the wind would drive for miles and miles. Many of them were bigger than a bushel basket apiece, and their sprigs so tough that the weeds had the spring of a wire mattress. We crushed the weeds down and lay down on them for the night, though not a man dared close his eyes in sleep.

By the time heavy darkness had fallen, every Indian had disappeared. Happily, they did not return to molest us during the night, although of course we had nothing to assure us that we would not be again attacked. There was a new moon, but so small and slender that in the clouded sky there was but little light. While there was yet a little daylight left, I took the willow switch, and sitting down on the edge of the improvised little fort, I carefully cleaned every gun.

While engaged in this occupation, we held a council to decide what was the best thing to do. We agreed that somebody must go for help. No journey could have been beset with greater danger. Rath and I both offered to go. In fact, the task was squarely up to us, as all the other men were too badly injured. I insisted that I should go, as I knew the country and felt confident that I could find the trail that led to Camp Supply. I was sure we were not far from the trail.

My insistence at once caused protest from the wounded. They were willing that Rath should go, but would not listen to my leaving them. Once I put my hand on my gun, with the intention of going anyway, then I yielded to their wishes against my better judgment and decided to remain through the night. The wounded men relied greatly on my skill as a marksman.

Rath, therefore, made ready for the journey, and then bidding us goodbye, he crawled away into the darkness. In about two hours, while we were hoping he had managed to get a good start without being detected, he returned, saying he could not locate the trail.

By this time, Smith had grown much worse and was begging us, in piteous tones, to shoot him and put an end to his terrible agony. We found it necessary to watch him closely to prevent his committing suicide.

There was not a man among us who had not thought of the same melancholy fate. When the fighting was at its worst, with the Indians closing in on all sides, and when it seemed that every minute would be our last, it was only by our great coolness and marksmanship that we kept the savages from getting in among us, which would probably have compelled us to use the last shot on ourselves. At that time, I was wearing my hair long, and as I had quite a crop of it, I knew it would be a great temptation to the Indians to get my scalp.

Hunter-Trader-Trapper (April 1925): 15–17

Poor Smith endured his agony like a brave soldier. Our hearts ached for him, and we longed to relieve his suffering, but there was absolutely nothing that we could do for him. About 1:00 A.M. that night, he fell asleep, and were glad of it, for in sleep he could forget his sufferings. Later in the night, one of the boys felt of him to see how he was getting along. Poor Smith! He was cold in death. Men commonly think of death as something to be shunned, but there are times when its hand falls as tenderly as the touch of a mother's, and when

Another view of the Buffalo Wallow fight.
NELSON A. MILES, *PERSONAL RECOLLECTIONS AND
OTHER OBSERVATIONS.*

its coming is welcomed by those to whom hopeless suffering had brought the last bitter dregs of life. We lifted the body of our dead comrade and gently laid it outside the buffalo wallow on the mesquite grass, covering the face with a white silk handkerchief.

That was a night to try men's souls! What fate would the morrow have in store for us? It was night that is indelibly stamped on my memory, and which time can never efface. Many a time since has its perils filled my dreams, until I awoke, startled and thrilled, with a feeling of most imminent danger. Every night the same starts are shining way out there in the lonely Panhandle country; the same winds sigh as mournfully as they did on that terrible night, and I often wonder if a single settler who passes the lonely spot knows how desperately six men once battled for their lives, where now, perhaps, plowed fields and safety, with all the comforts of civilizations, are on every hand.

Like everything else, the long dreary night at length came to an end, and the first rosy tints of dawn tinged the eastern sky, while the sun came out clear and warm. By this time, all the men were willing that I should go for help. Our perilous position was such that there must be no waiting for darkness to cover my movements; it was imperative that I start immediately, and bidding them all [to] be of good cheer, I started. Daylight exposed me to many dangers from which the night shielded me. By moving cautiously at night, it was possible to avoid an enemy, and even if surprised, there was a chance to escape in the darkness. But in the broad daylight, the enemy could lie in hiding and sweep the country with keen eyes in every direction. On the plains—especially in the fall, when the grass was short and there was no cover—the smallest moving object could be perceived by such trained eyes as hostile Indians possessed, at an astonishingly long distance. I knew I must proceed with the utmost caution, lest I fall into an ambush or be attacked in the open by superior numbers.

I had traveled scarcely more than half a mile from the wallow when I struck the plain trail leading to Camp Supply. Hurrying along as rapidly as possible, and keeping a constant lookout for Indians, I suddenly checked myself at the sight of moving objects about two miles to the northwest, which seemed to cover about an acre of ground. At first the objects did not appear to be moving, and I could not tell whether it was Indians or white men. I skulked to a growth of tall grass and lay in hiding for a brief time. My nerves, however, were too keen to endure this, so I cautiously raised myself and took another look. The outfit was moving toward me. Shortly, I was enabled to discern that it was a body of troops. Indians always traveled strung out in a line, but there were traveling abreast.

I never felt happier in all my life! I stepped out into the open and banged away with my rifle to attract their attention. The whole command suddenly came to a halt. I fired a second shot and present saw two men ride out from the command toward me. When they came up, I told them my story and reported the serious condition of my comrades. The soldiers rode rapidly back to the command and reported. It proved to be a detachment under the command of Major Price, accompanying Colonel Miles's supply train, which was on its way from Camp Supply to field headquarters.

It appeared that the same Indians we had been fighting had been holding this supply train corralled for four days near the Washita River. Major Price happened along and raised the siege. The Indians had just given up the attack on this train when we happened to run into them.

Major Price rode out where I was waiting, bringing his army surgeon with him. I described the condition of my comrades, after which the major instructed his surgeon and two soldiers to go and see what could be done for my wounded comrades. I pointed out the location, which was not more than a mile distant, and asked the surgeon if he thought he could find the place without my accompanying him, as Major Price wanted me to remain and tell him about the fight. He said he could, and they rode away.

I was describing in detail all that had happened, when I looked up and noted that the relief part was bearing too far toward the south. I fired my gun to attract their attention, and then waved it in the direction I intended they should go. By this time they were within gunshot of the wallow. Suddenly, to my astonishment, I saw a puff of smoke rise from the wallow, followed by the roar of a rifle—one of the men had fired at the approaching strangers and dropped a horse ridden by one of the soldiers.

I ran forward as rapidly as possible, not knowing what the men might do next. They were soon able to recognize me, and lowered their guns. When we got to them, the men said they heard shooting—the shots I had fired to attract the attention of the troops—and supposed the Indians had killed me and were coming back to renew the attack upon them. They were determined to take no chances, and not recognizing the surgeon and the two soldiers, had fired at them the minute they got within range.

Despite the sad plight of the wounded men, about all the surgeon did was to merely examine their wounds. The soldiers turned over a few bits of hardtack and some dried beef, which happened to be tied behind their saddles. Major Price further refused to leave any men with us. For this he was afterward severely censured—and justly. He would not even provide us with firearms. Our own ammunition was exhausted, and the soldiers carried weapons of a different make and caliber than our own. However, they said they would let Colonel Miles know of our condition. We were sure that help would come the instant the colonel heard the news.

We watched and waited until midnight of the second day after these troops had passed before help came. A long way off in the darkness, we heard the sound of a bugle. Never was there sweeter music than that to our suffering nerves. It made us swallow a big lump in our throats. Nearer and nearer came the bugle notes. We fired our guns with the few remaining cartridges we had, and soon the soldiers came riding to us out the darkness.

As soon as the wounded could be turned over to the surgeon, we placed the dead body of our comrade in the wallow where we had fought and suffered together, and covered it with the dirt which we had ridged up with our hands and butcher knives. Then we went down on the creek, where the soldiers had built a big fire and cooked a big meal for us.

Next day the wounded were sent to Camp Supply. Amos Chapman's leg was amputated above the knee. All the men eventually recovered and went right on with the army. Chapman could handle a gun and ride as well as ever, but had to mount his horse from the right side, Indian fashion.

When I last heard from Amos Chapman, he was living in Sailing, Oklahoma. In the early '80s, Col. Richard Irking Dodge, U.S.A., wrote a book entitled *Our Wild Indians*[5] in which he attempted to give a circumstantial account of the Buffalo Wallow fight. Sergeant Woodall was displeased with the statement of facts therein and resented the inaccuracies.

When Colonel Dodge was writing his book, he wrote to me and asked me to send him an account of the Buffalo Wallow fight. I neglected to do so, and he obtained his information from other sources. If my narrative differs from that related in Colonel Dodge's book, all I can say is that I have described the fight as I saw it. In saying this, I do not wish to place myself in the attitude of censuring Colonel Dodge. However, it should be reasonably apparent that a man with a broken leg cannot carry another man on his back. In correcting this bit of border warfare history, I wish to state that every one of my comrades conducted himself in the most heroic manner, bravely doing his part in every emergency.

Colonel Miles had both the heart and the accomplishments of a soldier, and Congress voted to each of us the Medal of Honor. He was delighted when the medals came from Washington, and with his own hands pinned mine on my coat when we were in camp on Carson Creek, five or six miles west of the ruins of the original Adobe Walls.

It was always my intention to return and mark the spot where the Buffalo Wallow fight took place, and where George Smith yet lies buried. Procrastination and remoteness of the place have prevented this.

Now for the story which appears on page 631 of Colonel Dodge's well-known book, *Our Wild Indians,* which was brought out in 1882:

Heroic as was the conduct of all, that of Chapman deserves most special honor, for he received his wound while performing a deed than which the loftiest manhood can find nothing nobler.

The first intimation of the presence of Indians was a volley which wounded every man in the party. In an instant, the Indians appeared on all sides. Dismounting and abandoning their horses, the brave band moved together for a hundred yards to a buffalo wallow. Chapman and Dixon, being but slightly wounded, worked hard and fast to deepen this depression, and as soon as it was satisfactorily deep to afford some cover, it was occupied. Smith had fallen from his horse at the first fire, and was supposed to be dead. Now the supposed dead body was seen to move slightly. He was alive, though entirely disabled. Turning to his comrades, Chapman said, "Now, boys, keep those infernal redskins off of me, and I will run down and pick up Smith and bring him back before they can get at me."

Laying down his rifle, he sprang out of the buffalo wallow and ran with all speed to Smith and attempted to shoulder him. "Did any of you ever try to shoulder a wounded man?" asked Chapman, in relating the story. "Smith was not a large man—160 or 170 pounds—but I declare to you that he seemed to weigh a ton. Finally I laid down and got his chest across my back and his arms around my neck, and then got up with him. It was as much as I could do to stagger under him, for he couldn't help himself a bit. By the time I got twenty or thirty yards, about fifteen Indians came for me at full speed on their ponies. They all knew me and yelled, 'Amos, Amos, we have got you now!' I pulled my pistol, but I couldn't hold Smith on my back with one hand, so I let him drop. The boys in the buffalo wallow opened on the Indians just at the right time, and I opened on them with my pistol. There was a tumbling of ponies and a scattering of Indians, and in a minute they were gone. I got Smith up again and made the best possible time, but before I could reach the wallow, another gang came for me. I had only one or two shots in my pistol, so I didn't stop to fight, but ran for it. When I was within twenty yards of the wallow, a little old scoundrel that I had fed fifty times rode almost on me and fired. I fell, with Smith on top of me, but as I didn't feel any pain, I thought I stepped into a hole. I jumped up, picked up Smith, and got safe in the wallow. 'Amos,' said Dixon, 'you are badly hurt.' 'No, I am not,' said I. 'Why, look at your leg.' And sure enough, the leg was shot off just above the ankle joint, and I had been walking on the bone, dragging the foot behind me, and in the excitement I never knew it, nor have I ever had any pain in my leg to this day."

┅ ⹂⹌⹃ ┅

I had read this account of the buffalo wallow fight, as related by Amos Chapman, probably a hundred times when a small boy—in fact, it was one of my pet stories forty years ago, and I always marveled at the cool courage of a man who could pack a 170-pound wounded comrade on his back, with his own leg shot off at the ankle joint.

It was not until about 1900, however, that I read Billy Dixon's version of the Buffalo Wallow fight. There was such a vast difference between the two stories that I immediately became interested. I wondered if Amos Chapman was "stealing Billy Dixon's thunder," or vice versa, and I determined to do a little investigating. I secured the address of Amos Chapman in Oklahoma and wrote him, calling his attention to the difference between his own story of the Buffalo Wallow fight and that of Billy Dixon, and asked him if his story as related in *Our Wild Indians* was really true. I never received a reply. Not knowing but that Chapman might be dead, I wrote to an attorney in the town and received a reply that the attorney could tell me anything about Amos Chapman which I might want to know. I therefore called his attention to the two stories and asked if he would query Chapman about it. I never received any further communications from the attorney, although I wrote him once or twice more.

I then communicated with Mrs. Olive Dixon at Miami, Texas, wife of the noted scout, who is at present a well-known newspaperwoman of that section. She was at first loath to say anything on the subject, but I pressed the matter, insisting that for the sake of history [and] of the reputation of her dead husband, the actual facts should be made public. Mrs. Dixon thereupon sent me the following letter, which was written by Sergeant Woodall, one of the four soldiers in the fight, from Fort Wingate, N.M., where he was then stationed, under the date of January 4, 1889. This letter, it appears to me, disproves the Chapman story and proves conclusively that Billy Dixon, the intrepid scout, is the real hero of the famous Buffalo Wallow fight.

The reader, however, must form his own conclusion after reading Sergeant Woodall's communication:

Fort Windage, N.M.
January 4, 1889.

FRIEND DIXON:

Hearing that you were at Adobe Walls in the Panhandle of Texas, and as we both came near passing in our checks between the Gageby Creek and the Washita River on September 12, 1874, I thought it would not be out of place to drop you a few lines and revive old times. I hear from a man by the name of Shearer, who belonged to the 4th Cavalry, that you were there.

Do you ever see Amos, or any of the men who were with us then? I never have, and would very much like to see any of them and fight our old fights over again.

Did you read the account (in *Our Wild Indians*) where Amos carried Smith on his back, and did not know his leg was shot off until he got to the wallow? Did you ever hear tell of such a damn lie, when he knows very well that you carried both of them there yourself? I was surprised when I read the account in the book written by Colonel Dodge. To read it, you would think there was no one there but Chapman himself. The idea that a man could have his leg shot off and did not know it makes me tired. You can bet that I came very near knowing it when I was struck, and I know it and feel it to this day, and my leg was not shot off. When I read the book, I came very near contradicting it, as there were others who did just as much as Chapman, if not more. It seems that when he met Colonel Dodge, he took all the credit to himself. Dixon, don't fail to answer his letter because I would sooner hear from you than any man that I know of, and give me your opinion of the fight. I would have written you before, but did not know where you were. I will close this letter with my best wishes for your welfare.

From your sincere friend, and one on whom you can depend under any and all circumstances.

(Signed) Z. T. WOODALL,
First Sergeant, Troop I, 6th Cavalry, Fort Windage, N.M.

━━ ≡✦≡ ━━

With no other desire save to give "honor to whom honor is due," and wishing to write only the true frontier history, I determined that it was high time—after a lapse of fifty years—that the reputation of Billy Dixon as the real hero of the famous Buffalo Wallow fight be sustained, and this noted frontiersman, who yet has hosts of friends throughout the country who remember him with only words of praise and commendations, be placed on the pinnacle of fame, where he rightly belongs.

Mackenzie's Expedition on the Staked Plains

GEORGE E. ALBEE[1]

New York *Herald,* October 16, 1874

> CAMP OF MACKENZIE'S EXPEDITION
> NEAR PALO DURO, Texas, September 29, 1874

The Llano Estacado, or Staked Plains, is an elevated plateau or tableland lying partly in Texas, New Mexico, and the Indian Territory. Not many years ago, it was designated as the Great American Desert upon the maps, and supposed to be a vast sandy waste like the Sahara of Africa. Now the geographers inform us it is "an elevated tableland without wood or water, across which a wagon route was formerly marked by stakes." The plain rises abruptly four or five hundred feet above the surrounding country and stretches for hundreds of miles an almost level prairie, covered with a heavy growth of buffalo grass, which remains green during the entire year and which, as may well be imagined, is the winter home of countless herds of bison, who come down from above the Canadian, and of well-mounted bands of Comanches and Kiowas, who, after drawing their annuities and supplies upon their reservations, make this a base from which to go on their raids after Texan herds and scalps. The eastern and southern sides of this great tableland are gashed and seamed by a succession of canyons and arroyos, the ruggedness and grandeur of which is beyond description. The edge of the Staked Plains is chaos itself. In these canyons rise all the important rivers of Texas—the Red, Washita, Pease, Brazos, Colorado, and Concho are fed by the drainage of the plateau, while their valleys furnish wood, water, grass, and shelter from wind—the only contributions that a red man asks from nature; with their help, he can feed, clothe, house, and mount himself, and have at all times plenty of Texan horses, women, and children to barter with friendly tribes and traders for red flannel and whiskey.

From the close of the Civil War until 1869, this region was an unknown land to the troops serving upon the Texas frontier, and it was fondly believed that twenty-five or thirty cavalrymen could ride over the country at pleasure and whip all the hostile tribes, one after the other. In September five years ago, Captains Carroll and Heyl of the 9th Cavalry,[2] with another officer, came around by the heads of the Colorado and Brazos with a command of ninety odd, and on the freshwater force of the Brazos were attacked by a strong force of Kiowas and Comanches, who were repulsed after a severe fight.[3] The next month Colonel Bacon,[4] of General Sherman's staff, went back to the same locality with seven officers and two hundred men; he was attacked in broad daylight by a very heavy force of Indians, whom, after a fight of four hours, he completely stampeded. Next day he founds the lodges, whipped the warriors, and captured their stock, camp equipage, and squaws.[5]

In 1871 Colonel Mackenzie, who commanded a division of Sheridan's troopers at Five Forks, having been assigned to command the 4th regiment of cavalry upon the reorganization of the army, took out an expedition from Fort Richardson across the Red River through the Washita Mountains and up the North Fork to McClellan's Creek, swinging around to the northeast and south, fording the Sweetwater near Antelope Hills, and thence back to Fort Griffin, having met with no large body of hostile Indians. Refitting and filling up with supplies, he came out to the scene of the Bacon and Carroll fight via Flat Top and Double Mountains. On the Fresh Fork, he had a skirmish with the Comanches in which he was himself wounded in the eye by an arrow, obliging him to relinquish the command and return to Fort Griffin.[6]

In 1872 Mackenzie came out again and established a supply camp on the Fresh Fork,[7] determined to stay on the plains until he could overrun the whole of the Indian stronghold. First he sent Captain McLaughlin with a column ninety miles southwest to Mucha Que, the head of the Brazos, developing the previously unknown fact that it was a well-watered region and a favorite camping place for Indians, where they would stop to rest and recruit their stolen stock while en route from the San Saba, Blanco, and Nueves ranches to their markets in the Indian Territory and New Mexico. On receiving McLaughlin's report that no Indians were below him, Colonel Mackenzie struck out again, crossing the Staked Plain at its widest part, through a region entirely unknown except to the red men and the New Mexican traders who supply them with whiskey and such other groceries as are not provided for them by the government, coming out at Fort Sumner in New Mexico, thence north to Fort Bascom, then across the plains again to Palo Duro, the head of Red River, down the Red River to Canoncito Blanco (Little White Canyon), thence across the heads of Washita and Pease to his supply camp on the Fresh Fork.

Capt. George E. Albee. COURTESY OF PERRY FROHNE.

As soon as the stock could be rested, he started north again across the Red River to its North Fork, where we found a large village of hostile Comanches, which was at once charged. About fifty were killed, a large number wounded, 200 squaws and 1,200 horses were captured, and the village burned.[8]

Last year the Indians were comparatively quiet, but as they seem to have had a general "digging up of little hatchets," another expedition became necessary in 1874. To make up a decent escort in the present economically depleted condition of the army, which reduction the *Herald* deprecated from the start, it is necessary to draw off all available men from a thousand miles of frontier. This command comprises men drawn from every post on the line, from Richardson, the most northerly, to Duncan, on the Rio Grande; and yet the available fighting force, exclusive of teamsters, train guard, and packers, is about 400 men. The gathering of the clans took place at the old supply camp on Fresh Water Fork and was completed by the arrival of the Seminoles from the Rio Grande, twenty-one strong, and seven Tonkawa braves from Fort Griffin, on the eighteenth of this month. Those friendly Indians are used as advance scouts and trailers, and are quite necessary to an expedition of this kind.

The command moved north, along the edge of the Staked Plains, on the morning of the nineteenth. On September 20 a party of four spies, who were one day's march in advance, were discovered and attacked by about twenty-five Comanches, and after a short, sharp fight were obliged to run for their lives. One of them had his horse shot under him, but he succeeded in getting safely upon another old animal, and the whole four reached the Seminole-Tonkawa camp in safety. Their pursuers took alarm and ran off their herd of about 100 animals in a southerly direction with all haste.

Captain McLaughlin was at once detached with part of the cavalry in pursuit, and he followed the trail more than thirty-five miles before dark, obliging the Indians to drop several horses and abandon considerable camp equipage in their hasty flight. When it became too dark to follow the trail, McLaughlin must have been close on their heels, but with another night's start, the race would have been hopeless, so he returned to the camp of the main command. Still marching almost due north, Mackenzie camped in Boehm's Canyon (named after a captain of the 4th Cavalry, the hero of many a fight and skirmish in northwestern Texas)[9] on the twenty-fifth, sending part of the command five miles ahead to camp in Tule Canyon, and return next day for the purpose of deceiving the spies who were known to be watching the column.

On September 26 a few Indians appeared and skirmished with the outposts at Tule Canyon, after which that detachment pulled up stakes and joined the main camp at Boehm's Canyon. That night everyone lay down to sleep with his clothes on, fully expecting an attack before morning—and it came. At 10:15 P.M. several parties of from ten to thirty Indians dashed up on different sides of the camp, firing in among the men and horses and yelling like bloodthirsty demons, as they are—peace commissioners and Indian agents to the contrary notwithstanding—in a vain attempt to stampede the stock; for every horse and pack mule was "staked, cross-sidelined, and hobbled," and could not run if they would. These terms may need some explanation. Each horse was "staked," or tied with a thirty-foot one-inch rope, to an iron stake or "picket pin," fifteen inches long, driven hard and fast in the ground. "Cross-sidelined" means that a forefoot was tied to the hind foot on the opposite side, leaving them the same distance apart as when the animals stand naturally. "Hobbled"—hoppled, more properly speaking, but the word is obsolete in the army—means that both forefeet are tied together. Imagine an animal running far under such discouraging conditions.

The Indians charged around the camp a few times until they found that the stock was not likely to change ownership, after which they selected a position below, in the canyon, from which they kept up a desultory fire until daylight, doing no damage, except shooting Lieutenant Thompson's horse through the neck and putting another ball through his saddle pockets, while the return fire killed and wounded several horses at least, for they were found in the ravine next morning.

Before it was fairly light, the Indians, who evidently had no idea of the strength of the column, came boldly out on the hill for a fight to the number of about 150. Captain Boehm, with his company, and Lieutenant Thompson, commanding the scouts and Indians (who is known to his messmates as "Hurricane Bill," from the plan of his attacks), were ordered to charge and drive them from the vicinity while the rest of the companies were saddling and packing.

Peter [Boehm] and his men went at them in the good old way, charging straight through their center in the most gallant manner, losing no men, but killing one Indian, while Hurricane Bill and his scouts acted as flankers on each side, killing another Comanche without loss to themselves. This Indian, one of the finest-looking fellows your correspondent ever saw, was going up the side of an arroyo when a Seminole jumped down from his saddle and, taking deliberate aim, killed the Comanche's horse, who, being thus suddenly dismounted, started off at a great rate across the prairie on foot. One of the Tonkawas then ran his horse upon him and gave the *coup de grace* with his six-shooter, the pistol being so near his head that the powder burned his skin.

The Comanches scattered in every direction, making no more fight, but after a little while gathering together again in plain sight, two or three miles in front of the prairie, and marched off to the eastward in close column, like a detachment of civilized troopers. But the cavalry did not follow the trail, of course. That device is getting a little threadbare; every step taken on that trail, which was meant with intent to deceive, would have carried the command away from their villages, and villages were what the column was after; for if their herds and homes are struck, it tells very seriously, but if you strike a moving party of warriors, a possible dead Indian or two represents the sum total of the harm done them.

The column remained quietly in camp until about 2:00 P.M.,[10] when it marched out a few miles in the direction the Comanches had gone and went into camp, as if for the night, at a water hole on the prairie. As soon as it was dusk, the command saddled up and started off almost due north at a great pace and, traveling all night, arrived on the brink of the big canyon near the head of Red River[11] just as day was breaking.

The canyon is from 500 to 800 feet deep, and at this point about half a mile wide. It was here that Colonel Mackenzie expected to find their villages, and he was not disappointed. Looking far down into the valley beneath their feet, the troopers could see the lodges stringing for miles down the river, and the Indian herds grazing in all directions, appearing to one looking from such a height like chickens and turkeys. Officers and men saw their enemies before—or rather, below—them, but how to get to them was the question. At last a narrow, dizzy, winding trail was found, such as a goat could hardly travel, and the cavalry started down the sides of the precipice. The Comanches took the alarm at once and began their retreat.

The descent took nearly an hour, but at last the soldiers were down, and Thompson, with his scouts, and the companies of Captain Beaumont, with Captain Boehm, charged the village with such impetuosity that the Indians ran in every direction. After a short but sharp fight, the companies charged on down the canyon through the village, which proved to be scattered along for about three miles to its end before halting. It was a running fight for the entire distance, but the command was very fortunate—but one man, Henry E. Hard, bugler of Captain Wint's[12] company, being shot, the ball passing through the body, leaving an ugly wound, but at this writing he is doing well, with a fair prospect of recovery.[13] Fourteen horses were also killed and wounded from all the companies engaged.

After driving them through the whole village, the colonel ordered the hedges burned and the captured stock to be driven up the sides of the canyon to the prairie above. While executing this order, some little sharp skirmishing occurred with straggling Indians who had secured places among the rocks high up the sides of the canyon, which they had reached by trails that could not be found by our men, and from which they delivered their fire with comparative impunity.

During the fight, five Indians were certainly killed, and probably ten or twelve were wounded. Fourteen hundred and six horses and mules were captured, from which 360 of the best were selected to be retained, and 1,046 were shot to prevent the possibility of their again falling into the hands of the hostile Indians, in case of any attempt at stampede.

All the lodges were burned, and the loss to this particular band of Indians is almost irreparable.[14] Taken all in all, this is believed to be the most effective blow dealt the Comanches and Kiowas on this frontier during the last two years. Some of the servants and Tonkawa squaws found time to do considerable plundering in the camp while the troops were at the front fighting and before it was burned, and the plunder they got is worth mentioning. There are bows and arrows, shields, robes with hair and robes without hair, curiously decorated and painted; new blankets, just from the reservation (and which, it is interesting to note, are about four feet by three in size, obliging them to run two together to make one of ordinary size), stone china, kettles, tools and implements of every description; the best breech-loading arms, with plenty of metallic cartridges, one mule being found packed with 500 rounds and another loaded with lead and powder in kegs; bales of calico and turkey red, sacks of

Minneapolis and Osage Mission flour, groceries of all kinds in profusion. Indeed, they seemed to be richer in everything than white
men who behave themselves.

Among the articles lost by the Indians in their flight were two
documents on which comment is unnecessary, and with true copies
of which I will close this letter, viz.:

OFFICE KIOWA AND COMANCHE AGENCY
INDIAN TERRITORY, April 9, 1874

Long Hungry is recognized as a chief among the Cochetethca
Comanche Indians and promises to use his influence for good
among his people, while continuing to conduct himself in a friendly
and peaceable manner. I ask for him kind treatment by all with
whom he may come in contact.

J. M. HAWORTH,
United States Indian Agent,
Kiowa, Comanche, and Apache Indians

No. 18—KIOWA AND COMANCHE AGENCY,
INDIAN TERRITORY
August 6, 1874

Wah-Lung, of Sun Boy's band of Kiowa Indians, is registered and
will not be molested by troops unless engaged in acts of hostility or
away from his camp without special permission.

J. M. HAWORTH,
United States Indian Agent

Countersigned by
G. K. SANDERSON, Captain 11th Infantry

With Mackenzie
in the Texas Panhandle

CHARLES A. P. HATFIELD[1]

Order of the Indian Wars Collection, U.S. Army Military History Institute,
Carlisle Barracks, Pennsylvania[2]

In the early summer of 1875, five hundred warriors of the southern tribes—Comanches, Kiowas, Southern Cheyennes, and Arapahos, well armed with breech-loading rifles, with an ample supply of ammunition, and accompanied by their families, left the reservation at Fort Sill and moved out to the Panhandle of Texas, three hundred miles to the west, where they joined forces and operated as a unit.

Several expeditions were ordered out to take part in a general campaign against the hostiles. One command came from New Mexico, one from Fort Sill, and Col. Nelson Miles with the 5th Infantry and 6th Cavalry from Fort Leavenworth, all headed for that vast uninhabited and little-known Panhandle.

Col. R. S. Mackenzie, with the 4th Cavalry, was, at the time of the outbreak, on the distant Rio Grande and necessarily was late in entering the campaign.

His first objective was Fort Concho, Texas, about two hundred fifty miles north of his starting point, where he arrived with six troops of his regiment—A, F, H, I, K, and L—about the middle of August 1874. He had with his command five companies of the 10th Infantry under Maj. Thomas Anderson.[3]

Troop E, 4th Cavalry, of which I was second lieutenant, had just arrived at Fort Davis, Texas, 250 miles west of Fort Concho, with thirty-five Seminole-Negro Indian scouts under 1st Lt. John L. Bullis, 24th Infantry. They had completed a hard expedition against the Mescalero Apaches, Troop E starting the latter part of June from a camp fifty miles below Fort Duncan, Texas, and the horses were in worn condition. Troop E and the scouts received an order to proceed to Fort Concho and join Mackenzie's command.

We marched through Fort Stockton, crossed the Pecos River at Horse Head Crossing, passed over the Staked Plains seventy miles without water, except what was hauled in wagons, and arrived at Fort Concho several days before Mackenzie.

Col. R. S. Mackenzie, with six troops 4th Cavalry and five companies 5th Infantry, left Fort Concho on August 19, 1874, and marched north to establish

Christopher C. Augur as a major general of volunteers. LIBRARY OF CONGRESS.

his supply camp at the head of Catfish Fork of the Brazos River,[4] at the eastern edge of the Staked Plains, almost 175 miles due north from Concho.

Troop E, 4th Cavalry, and the Seminole scouts remained at the post ten days to rest and recuperate, and left the post, following the trail of the main command, on August 29, 1874. The route followed was up the North Concho River, thirty-six miles to Rendlebrook Spring, to Colorado River, to Culver's Creek, to Hemphill's Creek, to Double Mountain Fork, to Brazos River, to supply camp.

On arriving at Double Mountain Fork, Troop E (Captain Boehm), with the Seminole scouts, moved to the west thirty miles to scout the country near the head of Double Mountain Fork, on the eastern edge of the Staked Plains.

On September 11 the Double Mountain, a prominent landmark, was thirty miles southeast of us, and the supply camp was supposed to be forty-five miles northeast. On the morning of September 14, a party of three Indians, mounted, apparently unaware of our presence, came within a third of a mile from our camp. Captain Boehm, with seven Seminoles and six men of Troop E, gave chase for several miles, but the Indians escaped. On September 15 we began marching in direction of the supply camp, keeping up scouting and looking for Indian trails. On the sixteenth we came to the road made by the main command thirty miles south of supply camp. On September 18 we arrived at the cavalry camp, ten miles from supply camp.

First Lieutenants W. A. Thompson, Louis Warrington,[5] and Wentz C. Miller,[6] 4th Cavalry, who had been relieved from recruiting duty in the East to join the expedition, arrived in camp from Fort Griffin, Texas, on the night of September 18.

Our supply camp was furnished with supplies from Fort Griffin, 125 miles to the east of us, by long wagon trains under infantry guard. The cavalry and scouts were finally assembled and ready to march north against the hostiles. The following officers of the 4th Cavalry were present for duty with Colonel Mackenzie:

Captains—Napoleon N. McLaughlin (Troop I); Eugene Beaumont (A); Sebastian Gunther (H); E. M. Heyl (K); Theodore Wint (L); and Peter Boehm (E).

First Lieutenants—H. W. Lawton, Regimental Quartermaster; David Irwin, Assistant Quartermaster; W. A. Thompson (A); C. M. Callahan (E); Louis Warrington (L); W. C. Miller (I); H. Crews (K); and H. Sweeny (H).

Second Lieutenants—John A. McKinney (K); Abram Wood (F); C. A. P. Hatfield (E); Joseph Dorst (A); A. C. Tyler (L); and Mathew Leeper (I).

By 1916, of these officers, I was the only survivor.

Lieutenant Bullis had been left sick at Fort Concho, and Lieutenant Thompson was finally assigned to command the scouts till end of campaign.

On the night of September 19, five selected scouts, mounted and each leading an extra horse, were sent to the north on reconnaissance. On the morning of September 20, the entire cavalry and scouts, with one infantry company as guard to wagon train, marched north, following the trail of the five scouts for fifteen miles, and went into camp.

At 2:00 P.M. a horseman appeared, coming over the hillcrest a mile to the north of us at full speed; presently a second appeared, then a third, fourth, and fifth. Directly on the heels of our five scouts came a bunch of Indians, which withdrew in sight of our camp. It seems that our scouts, arriving at a place of springs, small stream, and much broken ground, called Quita Que, thirty miles north of the supply camp, found themselves surrounded by about forty Kiowas. A hot fight ensued. Only two of the scouts, Seminoles named Adam Payne and George Washington, managed to shift their saddles and equipment from their riding to their lead horses. A running fight followed for fifteen miles back to our camp, with the loss only of five horses. It was a hunting party of Kiowas with their families. We broke camp and moved north to Quita Que at a trot and went into camp.

On the morning of September 21 (Monday), our wagon train caught up. Captain McLaughlin, with 1st Squadron (called battalion in my diary), was sent in pursuit on Indian trail. Colonel Mackenzie, with 2nd Squadron, moved north on old road.

On September 22 we were in camp at Pease River, the first sweet, fresh water we had found, the rest being gypsum or salt. On September 23 (Wednesday) we left Pease River and climbed five hundred feet onto the Staked Plains, keeping our wagon train with us.

The eastern edge of the Staked Plains, extending for more than one hundred miles, from a few degrees west of north to a little east of south, is abrupt and difficult of ascent. Viewed from ten miles east, it appears like a mountain range. From its eastern edge spring nearly all the rivers flowing through Texas. Late today Captain McLaughlin, with 1st Squadron, came into camp; after three days' forced marches, he had not overtaken the Indians.

September 24 the rainy season had commenced. The country was deluged with water. Marching was difficult. Remained in camp. On September 25 we broke camp and marched west twenty-five miles and camped on a shallow rain-water lake.[7] There was evidence of many Indians in the country; they appeared on distant horizons, but the condition of horses did not permit pursuit.

On September 26 Colonel Mackenzie, with the 2nd Squadron—Troop A (Beaumont), Troop E (Boehm), Troop H (Gunther), Troop L (Wint), and the scouts—left the wagon train, guarded by 1st Squadron and company of infantry (Captain Parks, 10th Infantry), and marched west. An hour before sundown, we came to Tule Canyon, where an old road crossed where it was shallow and wide, and intended to camp but found insufficient grass.

While we were still mounted, a party of thirty or forty Indians came over a slight ridge one thousand yards to [the] south of us as a challenge. Doubtless the main body of Indians were waiting for us just over the ridge. Colonel Mackenzie, an experienced Indian fighter, had another scheme than [a] desultory fight in the open, and marched the squadron back five miles to good grass on a small, rainy-season stream. Expecting a night attack, the horses were doubly secured on full lariats, with hobbles and sidelines. All of us went to rest on our blankets outside of the horses.

Colonel Mackenzie had sent out a spy, a half-breed Mexican named Johnson, several days before to locate the main winter camp of the Indians. Johnson found the permanent camp thirty miles to the northwest of us, in the Deep Palo Duro Canyon of Red River, and had returned to report only twenty minutes before the night attack commenced.

A few hundred yards to the west of camp began the breaks, which extended in increasing size down to Tule Canyon, several miles to the west. The Indians assembled [as] near as possible in the breaks—broken ground—and sent a large charging party to form behind a small butte about one hundred fifty yards north of Troop A. It was known what was going on. The men of Troop A, lying on their stomachs, wide awake with carbines loaded, waited for the assault. Presently it came with a rush en masse at 10:15 P.M. Of course, the Indian idea was to rush through camp and stampede our horses. When the charging party had arrived at about thirty yards, Troop A opened fire and, but for the total lack of target practice in those days, would have emptied many saddles.

The Indians, so taken by surprise, hesitated and turned in flight, but soon began to circle the compact camp, firing into it, while little attention was given to them. After their mounted work had lasted about a half hour, they collected in the near breaks—one party [of] about thirty behind a bank only two hundred yards away—and kept firing till 2:30 A.M. It was remarkable that with so many shots fired into camp, only about a dozen horses and none of the men should

Col. Ranald Mackenzie. NATIONAL ARCHIVES.

have been struck. After the charge on Troop A, none of the Indian fire was returned.

There was a full moon; I could see a man walking at one hundred yards. To test the light, I got from my saddle pocket a part of an old New York *Herald* and could read the small type readily.

At midnight, the wagon train, 1st Squadron, and infantry arrived and went into camp three-quarters of a mile north of us.

At the earliest daylight September 27, the Indians renewed their fire, when Colonel Mackenzie came over to Troop E on south side of camp and ordered Captain Boehm to mount, charge, and dislodge the Indians, saying to the captain that he must go only two miles in pursuit and that Troop L (Captain Wint) and the scouts would support him on the right.

Troop E, preceded by a troop guard of a corporal and nine men in column of fours, went at a trot and gallop on the Indian position. A party of a dozen Indians intercepted our guard, and a hand-to-hand fight ensued. Just before the arrival of the troops, the Indians broke and ran. The troop, in column of fours, kept at a steady rapid gait on passable ground to the south of the breaks. Troop L, off to the right of us, became entangled in the heavy breaks and ravines and made no progress.

The Indians, in rapid flight, were scampering up and down the ravines, going to the west. At times we were at thirty yards from them, but the troops did no firing. Shortly after heading [up] a deep ravine, from which many Indians were escaping, we came onto the open level country, when there before us was the Indian skirmish line. It was about twelve hundred yards in length and contained at least five hundred men retreating rapidly. It seemed marvelous. I do not believe our soldiers could have extricated themselves from the deep, rough ravines, debouched, and formed such an excellent line in face of a rapid pursuit.

When we reached our two-mile limit, our guard of ten men was close up to the Indians and six hundred yards to our left; Troop E was one hundred fifty yards behind the center of the Indian line, and the scouts were several hundred yards to our right. Fearing our guard would be lost if we stopped pursuit, we kept on two miles further. One Comanche who had lost his horse and was on foot was shot by the scouts.

The Indians who were well armed continually turned in their saddles and fired at us. If target practice had been developed as it was fifteen years later, we could have killed many Indians; but since a man could enlist in those days, serve five years, and get discharged without firing his piece, not much damage was done. It was just as well and possibly better, for the final result was the same.

It was the custom of these Indians to attack a command when their camp was threatened; we expected it. This was the Indians' grand effort. Mounted on their best war ponies, painted and strung with sleigh bells, in full regalia, with everything to impress the imagination, it was highly spectacular.

A brilliant sun came up behind us as Troop E was thumping along in rapid pursuit. The line of Indians was clearly defined. Their gorgeous headdresses, otter-skin scabbards, with bows and arrows, and occasional decorated spears held aloft as guidons, and rifles held in their hands, were plainly visible. As I rode, I thought of the rush of immigration into the West, and that I had better look and take it all in, for I would never see the same sight again, and how true my prophecy.

We halted; the Indians gradually assembled at several large bunches of loose stock a mile to the west, to exchange their war steeds for those for transportation, and we returned to camp.

Preparations were made for moving out with a pack train, which was a complicated business in those days, before the advent of the aparejo and diamond hitch.

At 1:00 P.M. six troops and scouts started with several days' rations, leaving Troop F with the wagons. We marched west five miles and took the large trail of the Indians, which led a little west of south. The Indians expected us to follow, to break down our horses, to lead us away from their camp. We followed leisurely, stopping occasionally to graze our horses until dark, when we changed our course to the right and started for their main winter camp thirty miles to the north of us.

At 1:00 A.M. on September 28, we came onto the great fresh trail of the Indians returning to their camp. Being a little ahead of time, we halted at 2:00 A.M. and bivouacked till 4:00 A.M. Then we mounted and moved north on the wide trail. At the first gray dawn, we came up against the eastern edge of a large, deep, black-looking canyon—the Cañon Cito Blanco—and presently we saw in front of us what seemed a wide black streak from west to east on the gray prairie—the Cañon Palo Duro, the head of Red River. At the junction of these two immense canyons, we dismounted to lead down a well-worn trail. A year later I was informed by a couple of engineers, surveying the line of the Texas Pacific Railway, that they had found the depth of the canyon at this point to be 1,450 feet.

Troop E was in the lead, followed by Troop A.[8] Very soon we came to an Indian sentinel, dismounted, with his horse saddled. Probably he had been asleep until we were within a hundred yards of him, when he fired his rifle, waved a red blanket, and disappeared. The effect was immediate, from perfect quiet to pandemonium.

From our position on the trail where the Indian sentinel had been, we had a fine view looking west up the grand canyon. The camps, about a dozen belonging to different chiefs, stretched up the stream for two miles. The first camp of about thirty tepees was directly under us. I could have dropped a stone into it, but so far below, the tepee seemed no larger than a five-cent piece, and the ponies smaller than sheep. From all the camps, Indians were streaming west in noisy, disorderly flight. Running, stumbling, and leading our horses down the trail, it was a half hour before we reached bottom. Troops E and A formed a skirmish line and started in pursuit, with the scouts ahead.

The Palo Duro Canyon opposite the mouth of Cañon Cito Blanco is about a mile wide, with the main Red River—twenty feet wide, two inches deep, clear and salty—meandering through its bottom.

Our advance up the canyon was impeded by large boulders and clumps of willow and cottonwood, but we soon came under fire from bunches of Indians, high up on both sides of the canyon. By 9:00 A.M. we had ascended the canyon three miles, and the four remaining troops, with the pack mules, had come down the trail and joined us. The Indians had too good a start of us; the squaws and children had escaped, and many of the Indians had climbed out of the canyon onto the plain. From their elevated positions—where they looked no larger than insects—they kept up a continual fire on us below.

We were halted and ordered to return. We destroyed completely everything, including provisions, collected nearly two thousand Indian horses and small Spanish mules, drove them up the long trail, and all of us arrived on the level plain by 1:00 P.M. We had killed five, and probably more, Indians.[9] A trumpeter of L Troop was shot through the body but survived. Three horses of Troop H were shot and killed by the Indians. At 2:00 P.M. we started back to our wagon train, driving the immense herd of captured stock with us.

At 2:00 A.M. September 29, we arrived at the wagon train [and] camped in Tule Canyon, where the old road crossed. We remained in camp September 29, disposing of the captured animals. The Mexican Johnson, who had located the Indian camp, was allowed to select forty from the herd as his reward, and five each were given to the most prominent of the Seminole scouts. Of the balance, many of the best horses and mules were assigned to the troops to replace broken-down animals. The balance—about 1,425—were driven to a confined central place in the canyon and shot by four firing parties. I understand that this large pile of bones remains until today.

With the total destruction of the permanent Indian camp at the approach of winter and the loss of nearly all of their horses and mules, the campaign of Colonel Mackenzie had accomplished its object and was virtually at an end.

My diary was kept daily up to October 24, 1874, but shows nothing material—only marches, camps, and following small trails. The cavalry marched around the extreme head of Red River and down its northern side. We came to many Indian trails, but all were heading for the Fort Sill reservation. We returned to the supply camp on Catfish Fork of the Brazos on October 24, 1874, and shortly afterwards the expedition was broken up, the troops and companies being ordered to different army posts for the winter.

I certify this statement conforms to a diary kept by me at the time of the operations and now in my possession.

Charles A. P. Hatfield,
Colonel U.S. Army, retired

2833 St. Paul Street
Baltimore, Maryland
May 7, 1925

Battle of Palo Duro Canyon

JOHN B. CHARLTON[1]

Frontier Times 1, no. 8 (May 1924): 367–71

During the summer of 1874, while Colonel Mackenzie's command was in quarters at Fort Clark, Texas, rumors became rife of unrest among certain tribes of Indians on the government reservations. These rumors were soon verified by a threatened outbreak. Shortly after this news reached post, I was sent by Colonel Mackenzie with dispatches to Fort Sill, and my orders were to travel by night only, as the country at that time was infested by numerous small bands of Indians; so by traveling at night, much delay was avoided and many dangers evaded. By changing horses at each army post on the route, I was able to make the ride, a distance of about 580 miles, in six nights. Upon my return, I found the colonel's command at Fort Concho, Texas, and there learned that the threatened outbreak had occurred—that Lone Wolf's band, strengthened by warriors from other tribes, had left the reservations and, with their families, had established themselves in winter quarters somewhere well within the border of northwest Texas, and that Colonel Mackenzie had been ordered out with his command, consisting of seven troops of cavalry, to intercept them and break up their camp.

I reported to the colonel and was placed with the scouting party then being formed. This party consisted of six white men, thirteen Seminoles, and twelve Tonkawa Indians; Lt. William Thompson was made chief of the scouts.

The command left Fort Concho immediately, moving in the direction of what was then called Cañon Blanco, but is now known as Yellow House Canyon. The supply trains, accompanied by four companies of infantry from Fort Concho, followed. After several days' marching, we reached this canyon, where a supply camp was established. Rain fell in torrents that night, and a "norther" blew up, which added greatly to the discomfort of the troops. The next morning, September 26, 1874, with fifteen days' rations for each man, the troops were on the march again, this time the objective being Tule Canyon, about a day's march ahead of us. After reaching the level of the plains, the scouts were ordered out on duty, as we were nearing that part of the country where, it was hoped, reliable information might be gathered as to the location of the main body of Indians. Lieutenant Thompson had orders to travel in a direction deviating somewhat from that taken by the command. We rode all morning without any sign of Indians, but about noon came to a slight break in the plains, where we drew rein to make a survey of the landscape. I noticed what appeared to be [a] herd of about a hundred buffalo. I called Lieutenant Thompson's attention to them. Looking through his field glasses for a moment, he exclaimed, "They are Indians, Sergeant, and they are going to attack us. Get your men ready for action."

I dismounted the men, placing six of them in charge of the horses, and the remainder was formed in line of battle around the horses. Lieutenant Thompson watched the approaching savages intently until they were near enough to make sure of their approximate number, then he rode over to us and gave orders to fall back toward the command, as we were outnumbered four to one. "Hold steady, men, and reserve your fire until they are within easy reach," said the lieutenant.

They were approaching rapidly, about 120 of them, and yelling like demons. The scouts numbered thirty-one men, all told. When the Indians reached a point about sixty yards from our defense line, they suddenly turned to the right and began circling us. Then we opened fire. Step by step our scouts fell back, fighting every inch of the way and hoping meanwhile that we were traveling in the direction of the command. One Indian buck, mounted on a white horse, kept riding toward us, firing and yelling, then riding back into line. Each trip he grew bolder and approached nearer to our men. Just how many of the scouts decided to stop his bluff I cannot say, but this Comanche soon went down with several bullet holes in his carcass. The Indians continued to harass us until about sundown, when luckily we reached the trail of the command. Our foes, realizing from the size of the trail the presence of a large body of troops in that vicinity, disappeared as if by magic. We then mounted our horses, took up the trail, and reached camp about 10:00 P.M. Several Indians were killed by our men, but by good luck we had no casualties to report.

When Colonel Mackenzie heard of our skirmish with the Indians, he ordered about one-third of the company, including the scouts, placed on guard that night, as he, with the rest of us, strongly suspected that we would be attacked before daylight. His suspicion proved correct, for at "moon up" they were upon us, this time several hundred strong. That portion of the men not on guard rested on their guns, so at the first alarm from vedettes, we were up and ready for them. At the first fire from our men, the Indians withdrew, no doubt somewhat surprised at the number of troops. At no time during the night did they approach so closely again, but kept circling the camp skirmishing, presumably for an opening to stampede our horses. Ten wagons, in charge of Wagonmaster James O'Neal, arrived at camp during the night. These wagons were loaded with forage and ammunition and were accompanied by one company of infantry, the other three companies having been left to guard the supplies at Yellow House Canyon. It is a mystery why this train of ten wagons was not attacked, for owing, no doubt, to some atmospheric condition peculiar to the plains, the drivers heard none of the firing and came noisily into camp, cracking their whips and yelling at their mules, which were floundering in the mud.

At dawn the following day,[2] the Indians left us. A laughable incident occurred about this time. As the Indians disappeared, the attention of the troops was attracted by the sight of a solitary Comanche riding a brown pony. He was on a little rise out of range of our rifles, and appeared nonplussed as to the direction taken by his companions, from whom he had evidently been cut off. He scanned the horizon for a moment, then attempted a shortcut in the direction taken by the other Indians. This brought him in range of our rifles, when Henry, a Tonkawa, shot his horse dead, and the horse, in falling, threw the rider. Henry then rode forth against his fallen foe. Now, in those days, an Indian wore his blanket in this fashion: Taking the blanket lengthwise, he wrapped it around his body. His cartridge belt, with pistol in holster, was buckled around his waist, and the top part of the blanket then turned down over the belt.

The Comanche had risen to his feet, but was somewhat dazed from the fall when Henry arrived upon the scene. Henry's rifle was strapped to his saddle, and he was so sure of victory that he had neglected to draw it until it was too late. He fumbled desperately for his pistol, which still remained entangled in the folds of his blanket. In the meantime, the Comanche, fully recovered, had made a spring for the Tonkawa, dragged him from his horse, and drawing his bow, began to give him the trouncing of his life. At every cut of the bow, Henry leaped about three feet in the air, making frantic gestures toward the troops and yelling, "Why you no shoot? Why you no shoot?" The whole command was laughing, but we had enjoyed the fun long enough, so somebody shot the Comanche, and Henry took his scalp with great satisfaction, but he nursed a grudge against the whole bunch of us for several days.

After the troops had breakfasted, Colonel Mackenzie sent for me and told me to take two Indians and follow the trail of those who had attacked the command the night before. So, accompanied by two Tonkawas—"Johnson" and "Job"—I took up the trail at once, and we rode rapidly for several miles before I began to notice numerous other trails, all converging and fresh. The country over which we rode appeared level as far as the eye could see and was covered with undulating waves of rich grass.

Suddenly and unexpectedly, we came in view of Palo Duro Canyon, a colossal crevice which breaks the plains of northwest Texas for a distance of sixty miles. I dismounted at once, left Job in charge of the horses, and with Johnson, crept on hands and knees to the edge of the canyon precipice. I felt overawed at the depth of the walls of the canyon, which at this point had a sheer drop of about 1,500 feet, the distance from wall to wall being about a half mile. A small stream of water was running through the canyon. Flecks of valley land were visible, intermingled with dark cedar tops, which cast shadows on the ground. In the open, hundreds of horses were grazing. Viewed from our immense height, the horses appeared as tiny moving objects. Tepees thickly dotted the banks of the stream as far down the canyon as I could see. I afterward learned that this Indian camp was three miles long. At any rate, from my vantage point, I had gotten a pretty comprehensive view of the whole situation. Time was pressing, and there was a ride of twenty-five miles back to the main command. "Heap Injun!" grunted Johnson, close to my ear. "You bet your life, old scout, and some canyon too," whispered I, as we backed off cautiously and made a run for our horses.

I lost no time in reporting to Colonel Mackenzie what I had seen. In a short time, the troops were again in the saddle, marching against Lone Wolf's stronghold, in the depths of Palo Duro Canyon, and its defense of 1,500 warriors. The colonel left one troop of cavalry with the remaining company of infantry to guard the wagons at Tule Canyon. This reduced the strength of the main command to less than six hundred men. After an all-night march, the command reached the Palo Duro Canyon at sunup on the morning of September 28, 1874. The scouts, as was their duty, were slightly in advance of the main column. As the rear of the column swung into line, Colonel Mackenzie rode over to us and said, "Mr. Thompson, take your men down and open the fight." "Very well, Sir," said the lieutenant.

Now the only means of ingress to the canyon available was a rocky and precipitous buffalo trail, down which the men were forced to go in single file. Lieutenant Thompson led us down here, and as we went over the brink, McCabe, an Irishman and one of the scouts, murmured dolefully, "And not even a cup o' coffee to sthay me stummick."

When we had reached a point about two-thirds of the way down, an Indian sentinel to our left leaped to his feet from behind a rock and uttered a war whoop that awoke the echoes far and near. That yell, with the shot that finished his earthly career, aroused the multitude of Indians below.[3] The din became terrific.

And then we went down into the inferno of howling redskins. Kiowas, Comanches, Arapahos, and Cheyennes attacked us from every quarter, first by dozens, later by hundreds, as the warriors gathered from the lower part of the camp. Many were concealed behind rocks, while others were ambushed in the foliage of the cedars. We were being reinforced as rapidly as the troops could make the descent of the tortuous and precipitous trail. The smoke from our rifles settled down, adding further obscurity to the darkness of the canyon. But I could hear Colonel Mackenzie's voice giving orders somewhere in the thickest of the fray.

The Indian warriors held their ground for a time, fighting desperately to cover the exit of their squaws and pack animals, but under the persistent fire of the troops, they soon began falling back, slowly at first, toward the head of the canyon.

The herd of Indian ponies, frightened by the uproar, fled first to one pass and then to another, only to have their leader shot down by a trooper, thereby blocking the trail. The main body of the Indians retreated in the open along the

The battle of Palo Duro Canyon. W. F. BEYER, *DEEDS OF VALOR.*

banks of the stream. Here the troops suffered their greatest casualties, being subjected to a crossfire from numerous snipers hidden in the timber on both sides. It was about five miles to the pass where the squaws left the canyon, and it was well toward sunset when the warriors, now in full retreat, reached that point. The command followed closely the going out of the Indians, but long before the rear troops had reached the level of the plains, Lone Wolf's magnificent band of warriors had fled. We followed them for a short distance; but as the men had been twenty-four hours without food, and as our dead and wounded were in need of attention, Colonel Mackenzie thought it best to turn back.

Upon reentering the canyon, we passed over dead Indians everywhere. Their wounded they took with them. After a careful search, we found our casualties to be two dead and quite a number wounded.[4] One man was shot through the bowels, but he got well. His recovery, said the doctor, was due to the fact that he had been without food so long.

The Indians, although no doubt apprised of the approach of the troops after the attack at Tule Canyon, were evidently not looking for a pitched battle so soon; otherwise they would have gathered their ponies and packed their tepees, all of which were left behind. Colonel Mackenzie ordered the tepees and everything of value to the Indians burned. This was done, after which the horses—about 2,200 in all—were rounded up and driven out of the canyon, when the main command started on the return trip to Tule Canyon. Everybody was tired and hungry, but the scouts, who had done extra-hard duty the preceding forty-eight hours, were utterly worn out; so try as I would, I could not keep awake. Several times during the night, as I slept in the saddle, I felt Colonel Mackenzie's hand on my shoulder, shaking me. "Wake up, Sergeant," he would say. "Wake up your men and look after your horses." This I did, rousing the other weary scouts and rounding up the straggling ponies, only to fall asleep again immediately myself.

The command reached Tule Canyon in the early morning, when the colonel ordered the captured horses shot. Some questioned the wisdom of this act, but it was the only thing to be done, as there were too many horses in this herd to be taken care of by the limited number of men in the command.

The Sappa Creek Fight

AUSTIN HENELY[1]

Winners of the West 7, no. 1 (December 20, 1929): 6–7[2]

Fort Wallace, Kansas,
April 26, 1875

The Post Adjutant,
Fort Wallace, Kansas,
SIR:

I have the honor to submit the following report of operations performed in compliance with Special Orders No. 38, dated Headquarters Fort Wallace, Kansas, April 18, 1875.

On the morning of April 19, with forty men of H Company, 6th Cavalry, Lt. C. C. Hewitt, 19th Infantry, engineer officer,[3] Acting Assistant Surgeon F. H. Atkins, and Mr. Homer Wheeler, post trader of Fort Wallace, as guide,[4] fifteen days' rations, ten days' forage, and two six-mule teams, I started for Punished Woman's Fork to strike the trail of a party of Indians reported there.

My transportation, all that was at Fort Wallace, was so inadequate that I made only thirteen miles that day. The next day I directed my wagons, with a suitable guard, under command of Sgt. [George K.] Kitchen, to proceed directly to Hackberry Creek, while I scouted Twin Butte and Hackberry to find a trail. Cpl. [William W.] Morris, commanding the advance, about noon discovered a trail of twelve lodges. I then hunted up my wagons, abandoned one wagon and half my forage, rations, and camp equipage, notified the commanding officer at Fort Wallace of the fact, in order that they might be recovered, and started on the trail at the rate of nearly five miles an hour, reaching the Smoky Hill River that night. During the night it rained, and the trail was followed with difficulty the next day to the Kansas Pacific Railroad, near Monument Station.

The Indians scattered after crossing the road, and a single trail was followed for several miles, when it was lost entirely. I then struck directly for the headwaters of the Solomon River, camped on it that night, and deliberated with Lieutenant Hewitt, Dr. Atkins, and Mr. Wheeler as to the best course to pursue.

Three plans were proposed. One was to turn back and try and strike some one of the other bands that we had reason to believe were crossing north. Another [was] to strike Sappa Creek, follow it for a day or two, and then march south to Grinnell Station, and if we failed to find a trail on Sappa, we still had a chance to strike one of the other bands, which might cross the Kansas Pacific Road near Grinnell. The last plan, and the one that was finally adopted, was to march in a northeast course to the North Beaver and follow it to its head, as it was believed the Indians would collect there, and follow it down for the purpose of hunting.

Shortly after daylight,[5] a hunter trail was discovered, which was followed until we met a party of hunters, who informed me that the Indians I was after were on the North Fork of Sappa Creek and had robbed their camp the day before while they were absent, and that they were going into Wallace, as they had reason to believe the Indians would attack them. Three of the hunters, Henry Campbell, Charles Schroeder, and Samuel B. Srack, volunteered to conduct me to the vicinity of the Indian camp, which they thought was about seventeen miles from where I met them. We marched about six miles and camped in a ravine until sundown, when the march was continued to within about five miles of Sappa Creek. I then halted and went into camp on the prairie, and the three hunters, accompanied by Mr. Wheeler, started to find the camp. Their efforts were successful, and we arrived at the North Fork of Sappa Creek in the gray dawn of the morning, about three-quarters of a mile above the camp, guided by the sight of a number of ponies grazing. I could not immediately discover the camp, as I could not tell whether it was above or below the herd. Mr. Wheeler, who had ridden off some distance to the right, galloped furiously back, swinging his hat and shouting at the top of his voice. I immediately galloped toward him with my command, and the camp was displayed to view.

My plan for the attack had been arranged as follows: Sergeant Kitchen was detailed with ten men to surround the herd, kill the herders, round it up as near to the main command as possible, stay in charge of it with half his men, and send the rest to join me. Cpl. [Edward C.] Sharpless, with five men, was left with the wagon with instructions to keep as near me as the very ragged and broken nature of the country would permit, always occupying high ground. With the rest of my command, I intended to intrude myself between the Indians and their herd and attack them if they did not surrender.

I will state here that the North Fork of Sappa Creek at this point is exceedingly crooked, is bordered by high and precipitous bluffs,

The Sappa Creek fight. W. F. BEYER, *DEEDS OF VALOR.*

and flows sluggishly through a marshy bottom, making it difficult to reach and almost impossible to cross.

As we charged down the side of the bluff, I could see about ten or twelve Indians running rapidly up the bluff to a small herd of ponies—others escaped down the creek to another herd, while the remainder, the last to be awakened probably, seeing that they could not escape, prepared for a desperate defense. By this time, I had reached the creek, which looked alarmingly deep and marshy. Knowing that no time was to be lost in hunting a crossing, I plunged in with my horse, Mr. Wheeler with me. By extraordinary efforts, our horses floundered through. A corporal who followed became mired, but by desperate efforts, all managed to cross, just as a number of dusky figures with long rifles confronted us, their heads appearing over a peculiarly shaped bank, made so by the creek in high water. This bank, with the portion of the creek and bluffs in the immediate vicinity, possesses remarkable topographical features, and I will endeavor to describe them. As we approach the creek from the south, it is observed that it makes a sharp bend to the northeast, and then turns south for a short distance. The ground slopes from the top of the ridge to near the creek, where it terminates abruptly in a semicircular crest concave toward it, and about five feet above another small slope which terminates at the creek. We crossed the creek at the termination of the southern arc; the Indian camp was at its northern termination. A number of holes dug in the ground were on the chord of the arc. Some of the Indians took refuge in these holes; others lined the banks, with their rifles resting on the crest. I formed my men rapidly into line and motioned the Indians to come in, as did Mr. Wheeler, who was on my left and a few feet in advance. One Indian, who appeared to be a chief, made some rapid gesticulations, which I at first thought was for a parley, but soon discovered it was directed to those in rear. I gave the command to fight on foot, which was obeyed with extraordinary promptness. As the men dismounted, the Indians fired, but excitedly. Fortunately no one was hit. I then ordered my men to fire and posted them around the crest in skirmish line. If we imagine the dress circle of a theater to be lowered to within about five feet of the pit, the men to be deployed about the edge, and the Indians down among the orchestra chairs, it will give some idea of our relative positions. The most exposed part was near the center of the arc, corresponding to that part of the dress circle opposite the entrance. Here Sgt. Theodore Papier and Pvt. Robert Theims, Company H, 6th Cavalry, were instantly killed while fighting with extraordinary courage. They did not appear to be more than fifteen or twenty feet from the Indians when they fell. After firing for about twenty minutes, and the Indians having ceased firing, I withdrew my men and their horses for the purpose of pursuing the Indians who had escaped. Hardly had we mounted when two Indians ran up to the two bodies, which had been carried some distance up the ridge. I immediately detached three or four men at a gallop to charge them, and the Indians retreated, accomplishing nothing. Just then an Indian, gaudily decked, jumped from a hole and, with peculiar sidelong leaps, attempted to escape, which he did not. I then posted my men at the two ends of the crest, avoiding the center, and began again, the Indians returning the fire from their holes without any damage for some time, when the firing again ceased and I concluded all were dead. Seeing a herd of ponies on the hill behind me, I sent two men to bring them in. A number of Indians tried to cut them off. I mounted and went to their assistance, driving the Indians off and bringing in the herd. Coming back to burn the camp, a solitary shot was fired from the holes, striking the horse of Trumpeter [Michael] Dawson through the body. I then concluded to make a sure finish, ordering Corporal Morris with a detachment to advance to the edge of the crest, keeping up a continual fire, so that the Indians would not dare to show themselves above the crest; another detachment went to the left and rear, and all advanced together; some few shots were fired from the holes without any damage. Nearly all the Indians by this time were dead; occasionally a wounded Indian would thrust the barrel of a rifle from one of the holes and fire, discovering himself to be dispatched. I have not been able to determine the original object of these holes or pits, but judge they were originally made for the shelter of those Indians who had no lodges and were deepened and enlarged during the fight.

Nineteen dead warriors were counted; eight squaws and children were unavoidably killed by shots intended for the warriors.[6] From the war bonnets and rich ornaments, I judged two were chiefs, and one, whose bonnet was surmounted by two horns, to be a medicine man.[7] The Indians were nearly all armed with rifles and carbines, the Spencer carbine predominating. A number of muzzle-loading rifles and one Springfield breech-loading rifle-musket, caliber .50, were found.

I then burned all their lodges and effects and threw some of the arms into the fire, destroying also a quantity of ammunition. There were twelve lodges, five or six covered with skins, and the other were the frames [*sic*], composed of new hackberry poles. Eight rifles and carbines were brought to the post of Fort Wallace and have been turned in.

I then withdrew with the captured stock, numbering 134 animals, to my wagon, which I could discern during the whole fight on a high bluff about a mile distant.

I judge the fight lasted about three hours. Feeling certain that other bands were in the vicinity who would soon concentrate and attack me, and at least recapture the stock, I marched to Monument Station, thirty-eight miles distant, reaching it about 8:00 A.M. next morning. The march was continued to Sheridan Station that day, where we were overtaken by a terrible norther, and I was forced to camp under a bank. The storm was so severe that it was impossible to herd the captured stock, our whole attention being directed to save ourselves and horses from freezing to death. After a night of intense suffering among horses and men, the men having but one blanket each and no tents—some of the men being frozen, and others who had dug holes in the bank for shelter requiring to be dug out of the snow by their comrades—the storm abated, and we split up in small squads to search for the captured stock. After a wearisome ride, occupying nearly all day, in which the faces and eyes of the men were injured by the reflection of the sun from the snow to such an extent as to necessitate medical treatment, eighty-nine ponies, one horse—branded "M" and recognized by some of the men as having been ridden by Pvt. [James H.] Pettyjohn, Company M, Sixth Cavalry, who was killed on McClellan Creek, Texas—seven mules, and one Spanish burro were recovered. Some of the rest may have perished by the storm, and some I believe will be picked up by citizens who have started, I understand, in search of them. One thing is certain, they will never be of any service to the Indians.

I cannot find words to express the courage, patience, endurance, and intelligence exhibited by all under my command. Lt. C. C. Hewitt, 19th Infantry, although by his duties not required to be at the front, was under fire continually, exhibited great courage, and performed important service. Dr. F. H. Atkins gave proof of the greatest courage and fortitude, going up to the bodies of Sergeant Papier and Private Theims to examine them, when such an action appeared to be almost certain death; and again daring the terrible suffering amidst the storm of the 25th, he was cheerful and full of words of encouragement to us all, exhibiting the greatest nerve when the stoutest heart despaired. I respectfully recommend that Doctor Atkins's important services receive the consideration to which they are entitled. All the men behaved with great gallantry. The following deserve special mention: Sgt. Richard L. Tea, Sgt. Frederick Plattner, Cpl. William M. Morris, Trumpeter Michael Dawson, Privates James F. Ayres, Patrick J. Coyle, James Lawthers, Markus M. Robbins, Simpson Hornaday, and Peter W. Gardner, all of Company H, 6th Cavalry.

Mr. Homer Wheeler, post trader of Fort Wallace, left his business and volunteered to accompany the detachment as a guide. His knowledge of the country and of Indian habits was of the utmost service. He risked his life to find the Indian camp; was the first to discover it in the morning; and although not expected to take part in the fight, was always on the skirmish line and showed the greatest courage and activity. The three hunters, Henry Campbell, Charles Schroeder, and Samuel B. Srack, who, with Mr. Wheeler, found the camp, performed important services; they participated in a portion of the fight and drove in a herd of ponies which otherwise would not have been captured. When these men turned back with me, I promised that they would be suitably rewarded if they found the camp. I respectfully request that their services, as well as those of Mr. Wheeler, be substantially acknowledged.

I brought to the post, for interment with the honors of war, the bodies of Sergeant Papier and Private Theims.

Although none were wounded, a number of the men had balls pass through their clothing, and one ball passed through the cartridge box (which had been moved to the front) of Pvt. Patrick Coyle. One horse was abandoned, having been lamed, another was shot in the engagement, and fifteen are now temporarily unserviceable, rendered so by the storm; nearly all of the men require medical treatment for the same reason.

There was found in the camp of the Indians a memorandum book containing rude though expressive sketches, made by themselves, of their exploits. Among a great number were the following, as I interpret them: the charge on the scouts at the battle of Red River; the attack on Adobe Walls and on Major Lyman's train[8]; the killing of Private Pettyjohn; and another (which I am not certain) representing the murder of the German family.

The following has been demonstrated to my entire satisfaction on this trip:

1st. The security of horses tied to the picket line by one of the forefeet. For the first night, my horses (nearly all new ones) became frightened and made a desperate effort to stampede, which I believe would have been successful had they been tied by the halter shank.

2nd. That a short, stout strap attached to the halter and terminated by a snap is better to link horses than tying them with the reins while fighting on foot.

> Very respectfully,
> (Signed) AUSTIN HENELY,
> Second Lieutenant, 6th Cavalry

PART SEVEN

Raids and Reprisals, 1865–81

Railroad Grading among Indians

ADOLPH ROENIGK[1]

Collections of the Kansas State Historical Society 8 (1903–4): 384–389

The year of 1868 was a busy time in western Kansas, especially at the army posts. Forts Harker and Hays were active. Indians had committed many depredations on the Solomon River and at other places. The 19th Kansas Cavalry was being organized. This regiment, with Lieutenant Colonel Custer and the 7th Cavalry, was getting ready for an Indian campaign. Horses, mules, wagons, and other freight were shipped by rail to these military posts. From here, soldiers and wagon trains followed the Indians south to the Indian Territory. After a battle, they were brought to terms and then fed by the government at a place called Camp Supply. I had been working for the government and came to Fossil Creek Station[2] in November to work on the railroad.

Ellsworth and Hays City were small frontier towns, with no others between or west of Hays to Sheridan, a small place at the end of the road near the state line. From there, freight was hauled by wagon train to Denver.

Fossil Creek Station had no depot or telegraph office. A water tank and a small frame box house the shape of a freight car were the only buildings. The sidetrack was about one mile west of the station. I think it had been built for the purpose of loading building stone for culverts and bridges.

A man named John Cook was in charge of the station, pumping water for locomotives by horse power (one horse). He and his wife also boarded the section men, generally six or seven. Several small dugouts were the quarters of the men, and a large one was occupied by the boarding boss and his wife, which was also the dining room for all. It had small windows on all four sides and could be used as a fort in time of need. Large herds of buffalo were in sight many times, and other game was plenty.

The railroad had been built the year before and was named Union Pacific Eastern Division; afterwards the name was changed to Kansas Pacific. There were no regular passenger trains running; only a mixed train, one day each way, and once in a while an extra. Indians had been troublesome more or less ever since the road was built, and men had been killed along the line. The company had armed its men with guns for their protection, six or seven of which belonged to the equipment of each section gang, the same as tools. We called

Railroading in a Southern Plains "norther." HARPER'S WEEKLY 1870.

them railroad guns, and we carried them with us when going to work; but seeing no Indians, some of the boys would get careless and leave them at home. They were breech-loading rifles of an unusual caliber. The ammunition could not be found for sale anywhere, and it was furnished by the railroad companies in such limited quantities as to allow no practice, and we were generally out, or nearly so.

Three of us—George Seeley (the boss), Charles Sylvester, and myself—intended to stay together and with the job at the station for some time. Each had brought a Spencer carbine, a seven-shot repeating rifle which has the magazine in the butt of the gun and was one of the best at that time.

About May 20, or a week before the raid, a man on horseback was passing through and stopped with us for dinner. I think he was a scout or some kind of government employee. He told us the report at Fort Hays was that the Indians had broken out at Camp Supply and were coming north, and we had better be on the lookout.

On May 28 there were seven of us. Besides us three who had the Spencers, there were George Taylor, Alexander McKeefer, John Lynch, and a man whose name I have forgotten. The latter had his gun with him, but had forgotten his ammunition and left it at home. The other three were unarmed.

I was the youngest man among them, but the oldest hand on the job at the time, and can say for myself that I was the most careful. Only a few days before, I had urged one of the men who was killed to take his gun with him when going to work. I had sixty rounds of ammunition, and the other two men about thirty rounds each. We were working on the track about one and three-fourths miles west of the station and about three hundred yards east of a large ravine running north to the Saline River; a branch of this one heads about a quarter of a mile east of where we were at work, and so we were between the two.

While busy at work in the forenoon, I overheard an argument between two of the men about Indians. They were looking north, and one contended that he had seen Indians; the other said they were not. On looking up, I had seen what might have been a bay animal. It had dropped out of sight, and the distance was too far to be sure. The handcar was standing on the track, with guns in the rack. I started for the car to load my gun. Charles Sylvester, who was our funny man, always full of stories and jokes, made fun of me, calling me a coward because I had done the same thing once or twice before when it turned out to be nothing but antelope, or something of that kind. I laid down my gun without loading it and went back to work. About an hour later, and when we had forgotten about it, one of the men shouted, "Yes, they *are* Indians." It flashed through my head as another of Charlie's jokes, but [at] the same instant, I saw Indians on their ponies coming out of the ravine west of us, yelling like demons.

I ran for my gun and, seizing my cartridge box, grabbed a handful, but loading in haste, got one too many in the gun. I could not shut down the magazine and had to pull it out and take out one. This occupied several moments. The Indians were right on our heels, firing at us, and the bullets made the dust fly all around me. Someone called, "Come on." Looking up, I saw the boys on the car leaving me. I ran and got on the car. We tried to get the car under headway but had gone only a short distance when Indians came out of the ravine ahead of us, and the next minute we were surrounded and they were firing into us from all sides. We had to take to our guns.

The Indians were also in danger of hitting one another. They opened out in front and let us pass, keeping up the fire from both sides and behind. I thought it impossible to reach the station alive. A culvert was ahead of us. I called to the boys, "Let's go into that culvert." Someone said, "No." I think it was one who had no gun. These words, and "Oh, God!" by one of the men killed, were the only ones spoken during the run. On we went. It was impossible to get the car under headway, as the Indians came so close we had to take to our guns, which slackened the speed of the car; but before we could get them to our shoulders, like circus riders the Indians would slip on the other side of their ponies, and we would let drive at them now and then.

About halfway, Alexander McKeefer and John Lynch were killed and fell from the car a few hundred yards apart. Each time, a crowd of Indians jumped off their ponies and gathered round. The last one exclaimed, "Oh God!" I turned to look at him and saw he was struck. The Indians were pressing us hard. I turned back towards them, and the next moment I saw him lying on the track behind us. Again the Indians gathered round, and I fired a shot into the crowd. When their guns were empty, we received a shower of arrows. One struck George Seeley in the thigh. He jerked it out the next moment. About one-half mile from our dugout, the Indians turned and left us. When within a few yards of the station, we met John Cook, with his rifle, coming toward us.

All got into the large dugout with our guns, placed the ammunition on the table in the center of the room, where it was handy, and waited for the Indians to come. We expected to be attacked. As none appeared, we spread some quilts on the floor, and four of us who were wounded—George Seeley, Charlie Sylvester, George Taylor, and myself—laid down, while the man that was not hurt kept watch outside in turn with John Cook. Nothing was seen for several hours. In the afternoon twenty-eight Indians passed that station on the south but out of our range, walking one behind the other, leading their ponies to a point on the road about two miles east, where they tore up the track by breaking off the heads of spikes and setting fire to the joint ties. They were the old-fashioned chair rails. In that way they removed some rails. The smoke was plainly seen from the station, and we suspected what they were doing.

Both trains were due at midnight to pass one another on the sidetrack one mile west. The one from the west came first and found the roadbed damaged, but a wreck was prevented on account of the train going slow to go onto the sidetrack. John Cook intended to flag the train from the east but would not venture out to the other side of the damaged track. When the train came in sight, he made a fire in the center of the track at the station by burning a bale of hay, but the signal was not understood by the engineer on account of the distance, and the train ran into the ditch.

The nearest telegraph station was Bunker Hill. A wrecking train to arrive and repair the track required nearly two days. We were taken to the government hospital at Fort Harker, later to Ellsworth, and treated by a doctor in the employ of the railroad company from Salina.

In the fall I went back to Fossil Creek Station. Things had changed. The place was a busy tie camp. The railroad was being extended from the state line to Denver. Woodchoppers were making ties and chopping cordwood on Paradise Creek for the new extension, and teams were hauling them to the station. Locomotives then burned wood. We had a telegraph office. The name of the operator was John J. Burns. A squad of soldiers were stationed here, as at every other station along the line. They were of Colonel Nelson A. Miles's regiment, the 5th Cavalry, with headquarters at Fort Harker. Twice more we saw Indians, one time a mile west at nearly the same place. Eight were coming from the south. Seeing us, they turned and took a course west and were soon out of sight. We were feeling all right that time and would have just as soon had a round or two with them. The soldiers at the station had also seen them and were coming to where we were. It was not known whether there were any more in the vicinity or not.

In the spring of 1870, I left the station. At the time of the raid, we were criticized by some, claiming that we acted cowardly in taking to our heels; that we should have made a stand; that we could have whipped them, and so on.

For myself, I will say at the time I had no other thought than my gun. Although we had plenty of warning, we were completely surprised. In a very short time, the prairie seemed swarming with Indians, and the majority of us were without means of defense. By the way the firing commenced, we knew they were well armed. The place there is level, and hardly any ditch for us to get into. But this was not all. Leaving myself out, I will say the boys had reason to believe we could outrun the Indian ponies, as we had done once before when we had a race with some of the best horses of Fort Hays. This can best be told by relating the whole story.

About February, I think it was, we had a blizzard that filled ravines and railroad cuts full of snow and left very little on the prairie. The sun came out warm, and we were shoveling to clear the track. We had had no train for a week. We had our section clear except one cut six miles west. While going there one afternoon to finish, a few miles from the station we met a big, burly looking fellow with a pair of six-shooters strapped to his side coming on foot. Answering a few questions as to the distance to the station, we passed on and forgot about him. Arriving at the cut, we shoveled snow on the east end, when one of the boys had occasion to go up on the high ground. He came down immediately with the report, "Indians are coming." Another went, to know the truth of the statement. He also came down with the same report.

All seemed to think the dugout would be the best place for us; so without argument, we pulled for home. We had gone but a short distance when horsemen appeared on the high ground behind us, and one of them fired a shot. Here the railroad makes a long bend. Four or five of the best mounted on the north side took off across the prairie to head us off. A lively race followed. We had a good car and downgrade, and I might say we fairly made her fly. The bend in the road was not short enough, and we easily outwinded the horses.

Being out of reach, we took it moderately. Getting home, we all got into the large dugout with our guns and got things ready for a reception. A while later, those horsemen who had run the race with us came in sight. One was carrying a stick with a white handkerchief attached to it as a flag of truce. Coming nearer, we saw that they were army officers, and later there came about thirty privates of the 10th Cavalry. They were Negroes and [were] those our men had taken for Indians.

They were following the track in the snow of the man whom we had met in the afternoon. He was said to be a horse thief, and when they saw the car going, they thought he was on and tried to head us off. On reaching the station, they took a circle around the place looking for his tracks, to see that he had not left; then the darkies made a search of our dugout with drawn guns. Finally they located him up in the water tank, made him hand down his guns and come down. The officers then had him tied by his wrists with the rope over the beam in the tank building and made him stand on his tiptoes. In that way they tried to get a confession out of him as to who his pals were. They worked with him all night.

An organized gang of horse thieves was about Hays City, and some of the best horses and mules had been taken from the government corral. The snow came at the wrong time, and it got too hot for the thieves, and this one tried to get away on foot. One of the soldiers told me the thief must have traveled forty miles that day, but the snow was not melted enough but what they could track him. The next morning all started back to Fort Hays. The man had to walk with his hands tied and a rope to the saddle of one of the Negroes. Later we heard that he never reached the fort, but that he was found in an abandoned sod house on the way, with bullet holes through him and some sod thrown over him. Our supposition was that the officers rode on ahead and left him to his fate in the hands of the soldiers, who killed him.

In conclusion, I will say that I believe the chances taken in getting on that car were greater than otherwise, and don't think I would have been in favor of it; but as soon as we started and saw Indians coming out of the ravine ahead of us, I thought it was a mistake, and I hardly expected to reach the station alive. Hundreds and hundreds of shots were fired at us, and twenty-eight bullet marks were counted on us and the handcar. It was a wonder we were not all killed. On the other hand, if the car had been off the track, there would have been no time to get it on, and it might have been better for us, as we would have been compelled to make a stand. We three were fairly good shots, and they could not have got us without our getting some of them, perhaps a large number, and after killing a few, they might have left us alone. Being near the railroad, we would have had relief.

The trouble was, we were not organized. Those who had no guns would not depend on us three; but in justice to the boys, I will say they were not cowards, any more than the average citizen. They expected to outrun the Indians, as we had the army officers, and could we have gotten the car under good headway, they could have done us little if any harm. When it was over, we did not know that we hit anyone, but the next day one pony was found dead in its tracks on the south side, and the carcass of another was found later some distance north and west.

When the train that had been on the sidetrack during the night came down to the station the next morning, the trainmen picked up the dead bodies on the way. They were stripped of clothing and horribly butchered up. They were scalped, rings of telegraph wire were through the calves of their legs and fleshy parts of their bodies, and arrows stuck into them. Being hurt myself, I was advised not to see them. They were wrapped in blankets and buried about three hundred yards south of the railroad track and a little east of the water tank, somewhere near what is now the main street of Russell. In the winter of 1869, I cut their names, native states, and the words "Killed by Indians, May 28, 1868." Alexander McKeefer was a Canadian, and John Lynch a New Yorker of Irish descent. Both were between thirty and thirty-five years of age.

A Gallant Stand on the Little Blue River

ANONYMOUS

Army and Navy Journal 7, no. 43 (June 11, 1870): 674

To the Editor of the Army and Navy Journal.

SIR: As deeds of daring are not of such common occurrence nowadays, I conclude you would like to hear one of those little episodes of army life on the frontier which brings out the higher qualities of the soldier and develops the more perfect man.

Company C, 2nd Cavalry, is stationed on the Little Blue, the frontier of southwestern Nebraska. It has been customary for Indians—it is hardly known what tribe, so swift have been their movements—to make annual raids through this section, kill what settlers they could without endangering their own lives, carry off what stock they could obtain easily, and create a general panic among the pioneers. Company C was sent here this spring to check these incursions, give confidence to the settlers, and induce emigration, so that the region, by virtue of numbers, could in a short time protect itself. Up to May 17, it was not supposed that there was a hostile Indian this side of the Platte; but as is usually the case, when you least expect them, they are sure to make a sudden appearance. On that day a settler came running into camp with the news that the Indians were near here and had stolen some horses from him. In a short time after, and just as the command had mounted to give chase, a boy came in with the sad intelligence that his father had been killed by "ye gentle savage" some four miles above camp. The command started on a vigorous pursuit but returned at midnight after a gallop of twenty-five miles, without having been able to overtake them.

On May 15 Sgt. [Patrick] Leonard had been detached with four men to hunt for two horses which had stampeded the day before. At about 11:00 A.M. of the seventeenth, he discovered the two horses which he had been looking for, quietly grazing on the prairie at a distance of a mile and a half, and unsuspectingly galloped toward them. The Indians (fifty in number) had previously secured these horses and tied them down for the purpose of drawing our party into ambush. They had concealed themselves in a ravine nearby, and when the sergeant and his party arrived within a hundred yards, discovered themselves, and with a wild war whoop charged, firing rapidly.

Almost at the first fire, Private Hubbard was severely wounded, as also were two horses. It was a moment of intense and thrilling excitement, well calculated to upset the oldest and steadiest head. Although the little party felt acutely its situation, yet never for a moment was its leader unnerved, as is shown in the fact that although the Indians were coming with a wild whirl, well mounted, armed, and ten to one, and although he himself was well mounted, as were two others of his men, and could easily have escaped, he comprehended fully the situation of his party and made his dispositions with such rapidity that by the time the Indians had got up to within twenty-five yards, they were ready for them and delivered their fire with such precision and coolness as to empty four saddles and kill one outright.

The sergeant had dismounted his men, killed his horses for a breastwork, and as before stated, had placed four of the enemy *hors de combat* in a twinkling. The effect of so fatal a volley entirely disconcerted our friends of the scalp lock persuasion, and they retreated to a neighboring ravine and held a very excited council of war. They concluded, however, to avenge the death of their comrade and came again and again to the charge with unwonted bravery, getting so close as twenty yards, but the fire of our little besieged party was so steady and effective as to finally wear out their courage and desperation, and after continuing the struggle for about two hours and a half, they retired sullenly, strapping onto their ponies three or four of their dead or dying comrades. Taking everything into consideration—the disparity of numbers, the surprise, etc.—I doubt if there is an instance in the whole annals of Indian fighting where a more heroic defense was made.[1]

CAMP BINGHAM, LITTLE BLUE RIVER, NEBRASKA, May 24

Indians at Ogallala Station, Union Pacific Railroad

"BUFORD"

Army and Navy Journal 7, no. 46 (July 2, 1870): 724

To the Editor of the Army and Navy Journal:

SIR: On the night of June 14, about 12:00 A.M., as the passenger train was on its way east, about five miles from the station, a large band or village of Indians were crossing from the south side of the South Platte, going north from the Republican and the country further south, evidently Cheyennes and without doubt the same party that have committed the numerous outrages and murders on the Kansas Pacific Railroad.

Where the Indians landed after fording the river, there is a strip of fine land between the railroad and river covered with luxuriant grass, a spot to make tired stock forget fatigue and pitch in to satisfy hunger and, as old man Bridger would say, grass till you can't rest. I suppose for nearly one-half mile east and west where they landed, the track has wide and very deep ditches on both sides. The freight train bound west passed before the Indians commenced crossing, and without doubt they thought no other train would pass, as they started, and I think succeeded in crossing, the whole village, when the passenger train unceremoniously burst upon them with its bright headlight.

Many animals were on the track, the engineer not dreaming of Indians, and it was impossible to check the train. Then commenced the work of destruction; some sixteen horses and mules were killed or had their legs broken and were afterward shot by employees at the station.

While the engine was plowing through on its work of destruction, and confusion reigned supreme, the Indians fired into the passing train. The engine providentially continued on the track; if it had turned into the ditch, this would have been a chapter of horrors. But the good angels were guarding the slumberers in the Pullman, the moon lent her silvery light to the scene, and on sped the locomotive with the train to bear the news to Alkali Station, to arouse the slumbering cavalry, only five miles away, to mount fiery and untamed steeds and pursue the poor discomfited Indian.

It happened about 12:00 A.M.; news reached Ogallala soon after. As Captain Wells,[1] commanding Company E, 2nd U.S. Cavalry, was nearest it, he was notified at once on its receipt. Men of courage are generally modest and truthful, and his official report does not convey the least idea of the heavy amount of work accomplished in twenty hours. The company, hurriedly mounted, consisted of Captain Wells, Lieutenant Norwood,[2] and thirty-seven men, with a soldier's ration, sixty rounds of carbine and thirty of pistol, with but a mouthful of food. They moved rapidly but cautiously along the road. Some 250 Indians were reported, and when near the scene, men were deployed front and on the flanks until we reached there to find that the Indians had fled. Animals were found in the ditch, and others limping around with broken legs. After some delay in hunting for the trail, it was struck; then a rapid pursuit began. Following a trail by the moonbeam's misty light is uncertain work, and the advance would often shout, "Trail lost."

The reader, if he ever followed hounds pursuing fox or deer, may have some idea of the excitement of this pursuit. Up hill and down steep ravine we followed in pursuit, and after many delays, we reached the North Platte to find no Indians, but a few jaded ponies struggling to reach the opposite shore of that deep and treacherous stream. Daylight had broken over the eastern hills, but the sun had not risen when we reached the Platte. The stream looked dubious; a number of Indians began to appear on the opposite bluffs, and a trail— the largest I ever saw—indicated a heavy body of Indians. After some little consultation, the captain decided to enter the stream, cross if possible, and move on the Indians. After many efforts, we finally succeeded in getting through quicksand and numerous swims, and reached the opposite bank without encountering the Indians. Strange thoughts flitted through our brains— something about Phil Kearny massacres—and you can judge of the mysteries beyond and around the heights we had to possess.

Skirmishers were deployed, gallop ordered, and soon we reached the hills to find the Indians gone. We continued on in rapid pursuit. Not an Indian to be seen. Horses, mules, ponies, and colts were strewn along the trail for fifteen miles. I never saw such demoralization.

The property that fell into possession of Captain Wells's command sums up as follows: thirty animals, twenty-seven lodges, fifty-six pack saddles with complete packs, any amount of buffalo robes, meat, cooking utensils, and many trinkets—enough to fill a couple of cars. Rather a disastrous move for the Indians. I think the command deserve much credit for their great amount of perseverance and courage. They started out without rations, followed a trail at night, and at daylight swam a stream full from bank to bank, with strong indications that an overwhelming force would drive them back. I hope if more of those parties pass other commands along the road, they may be equally successful in punishing them; if so, they will find farming on reservations the best for them.

A Fearful March
on the Staked Plains

[NICHOLAS NOLAN][1]

Army and Navy Journal 15, no. 6 (September 15, 1877): 54–55

We are enabled, through the courtesy of the headquarters, Department of Texas, to publish the following very interesting report of a scout under circumstances of the greatest suffering made by Capt. Nicholas Nolan, with Company A [10th Cavalry] from Fort Concho, Texas, July 10, 1877.[2]

The company left Fort Concho at 9:00 A.M., marched up the North Concho River, a distance of twenty miles, and camped.

July 11—At 7:00 A.M. left camp and continued up the North Concho River to camp at a point known as Camp Hudson, a distance of twenty-five miles. This day one man was sunstruck but soon recovered from its effects.

July 12—Left camp at 7:00 A.M. and marched up the North Concho River to its head, a distance of fifteen miles.

July 13—At 6:30 A.M. left camp and continued the march, leaving the North Concho, taking a trail leading to Big Springs, a distance of thirty-five miles, and went into camp. The command was compelled to make this march on account of not finding White Springs in the vicinity of the Four Mountains.

July 14—Left camp at 7:00 A.M. and marched to Wild Horse Springs, a distance of seventeen miles. Wild Horse Springs are supposed to be the headwaters of what is known as Morgan's Creek and lie in a northeasterly direction from Big Springs.

July 15—Left camp at 6:30 A.M. and marched twenty miles to the main Colorado River.

July 16—Was compelled to make a ford in order to cross the wagons to the north side of the river; this done, at 7:00 A.M. broke camp, crossed, and marched up the river twenty miles. It was intended in this day's march to find a suitable point to establish a supply camp, in which the command was unsuccessful.

July 17—At 6:30 A.M. left camp and marched in a northeasterly direction to Bull Creek, a distance of fifteen miles, where a suitable location was found and the supply camp established. This point is about seven miles to the northeast of Mucha Que Mountains. Here was found a party of twenty-eight men encamped, formed into a company for the purpose of following and recovering stock stolen by Indians from them, from buffalo camps and other points. We had with us for a guide a Mexican by the name of Jose Anaya [Tafoya], who had an extensive knowledge of the Staked Plains and who had formerly been a guide with Colonel Mackenzie in his scouts through this country. The party requested me to accompany them in their search for Indians, and having no guide with his command, I was only too happy to accede to their request, the object of the scout being to assist civilians and to find and punish all marauding Indians.

July 18—Both parties remained in camp. When Company A left Fort Concho, the transportation consisted of four six-mule teams, although the orders were for eight pack mules in addition; but owing to the few mules then at post, the company could not obtain any pack mules. That morning the eight leaders were taken from the teams and the four wagons sent with four mules each to Fort Concho for an additional supply of rations and forage. During all this day, the command was actively engaged in making preparations for a twenty days' scout.

July 19—At about 5:00 P.M., all arrangements having been completed, Company A left camp. The command now consisted of I, 1st Lt. C. L. Cooper and forty enlisted men, and a few of the citizens, taking care of their own transportation. This day the company marched to the main prong of the Colorado River, a distance of fifteen miles, where we made a dry camp for the night.

July 20—At 5:00 A.M. started and marched to the head of Tobacco Creek, a distance of fifteen miles.

July 21—At 7:00 A.M. the command left camp and marched eight miles to a point on Tobacco Creek, where we halted and were deciding to make a night march to Laguna Sabinas. At about 4:00 P.M. Quanah [Parker], a Kwahadi chief of the Comanche tribe, came into camp and produced a pass from the Indian agent at Fort Sill, Indian Territory, dated July 12, 1877, which was countersigned by Col. R. S. Mackenzie, 4th Cavalry, commanding Fort Sill. The pass authorized him and party to be absent from the reservation forty days, the purport of the pass seeming to indicate that they were on a mission to bring back Indians that had left the reservation. Being perfectly satisfied that the pass was genuine, and finding that he and party were liberally supplied with government horses, equipment, arms, ammunition, and rations, I did not feel authorized to detain him. At 7:30 P.M. the company left this halting place and proceeded on to Laguna Sabinas, a distance of fifty miles, arriving there at 8:00 A.M. on July 22 and going into camp on the ground where Lt. Col. [William R.] Shafter, 24th Infantry, had his supply camp in 1875. Great difficulty was found in obtaining water for the command, the men being compelled to dig several holes and dip out the water with small tin cups, securing it in camp kettles, in order to obtain enough for men and animals. This was a long and tedious job, and the command remained in camp during this day.

July 23—The guide Jose and a party of the citizens left camp for the purpose of ascertaining if there were any signs of Indians and if water was to be found in the vicinity of the five wells. At about 11:00 A.M. Quanah and party again visited camp, where they remained until about 5:00 P.M., when he left, taking a westerly direction. This was the last seen of them.

July 24—Jose and party returned and reported that they had found a trail of a few Indians some twenty miles to the west of our camp, and that it ran in a northeasterly direction towards Double Lakes. The guide also said that his party had traveled forty miles without water, having found none during the entire trip, which occupied thirty hours. At 4:30 P.M. the command left camp and started for Double Lakes, marched twenty-five miles, and made a dry camp for the night.

July 25—At 6:00 A.M. left camp and marched to Double Lakes, a distance of about fifteen miles, camping on the ground occupied by Colonel Shafter in 1875. Here the same difficulties in obtaining water were encountered as at Laguna Sabinas. At this point, no fresh signs of Indians were discovered. During the day, the guide Jose and a party of citizens made a scout directly west and went to Dry Lake, seventeen miles, for the purpose of ascertaining if there was water there and if any signs of Indians could be found.

July 26—The command remained in camp awaiting the return of guide and party. At about 11:00 A.M. two of the party returned and reported that the guide had seen forty Indians pass that morning at 8:30 A.M., about three miles west of Dry Lake, and that they were traveling in a northeasterly direction. At 1:00 P.M. the command was saddled up and ready to start, but owing to the tardiness of the two scouts, was unable to get off until 3:00 P.M. Marched to Dry Lake, arriving there a little before sundown, finding the guide and balance of his party. At this place, no water could be found, either for men or horses. I then asked Jose how far it was to water; he said fifteen or not more than twenty miles. The command continued on in a direct westerly course to strike the trail. Darkness coming on, the guide informed us that he was unable to proceed further until morning, so that the command unsaddled and made a dry camp.

July 27—At daylight, the command was saddled up, left camp, and followed on the trail until about 2:00 P.M., at which time we were compelled to abandon it on account of the ponies of the guide and citizens giving out. We were now in the immediate vicinity of the Sand Hills.

The command now commenced to suffer exceedingly for water. One of the men at this time fell from his horse from the effects of sunstroke, and I asked the guide how far it was to water. He replied six or seven miles; his pony being now completely broken down and unable to go further, the captain gave him one of his own private horses, in order that we might find water as soon as possible.

We then continued on in a westerly course and marched two miles, when the guide suddenly changed his course to a northeasterly direction. He, being mounted on a fresh horse, could make better headway than the command, owing to the exhausted condition of the men. He pushed ahead, the command

A tumble from the trail. CENTURY MAGAZINE 1889.

following him on the trail as fast as we could but, being continually detained by sick men, were unable to keep up with him without abandoning their sick men.

In this way we followed on after him for fifteen miles, until dark. During the last march of fifteen miles, a great portion of the command, being recruits, commenced to give out, continually falling from their horses. Up to this time, there were three men sunstruck. Owing now to the exhausted condition of the men, I was compelled to halt for a while, fully expecting that the guide had found water and would soon join us. Previous to marching the last six miles, I selected eight of my men (old soldiers) and directed them to continue on after the guide. I gave them nearly all the canteens, with instructions as soon as they found water to fill them and return to the command without delay.

Up to this time, the company had marched about fifty miles under a broiling sun, over a barren sandy plain, without a drop of water. From the statements of the guide, we fully expected to have found water during the early part of the day. I did not again see the eight men who I sent after the guide until my arrival at the supply camp on August 6.

At this point, the command remained in camp overnight. Before going into this camp, about a mile on the back trail, I left two sick men, detailing Sgt. William L. Umbles to remain with them, with instructions, as soon as they were able, to bring them into camp. This sergeant, instead of doing as directed, during the early part of the evening, with the two sick men, came up and passed on by the camp within easy hailing distance, without halting, although challenged by the captain and one of the command who had been sent back to show them, thus disgracefully deserting the command. This Sergeant Umbles is one of the party who afterwards went into Fort Concho and circulated the false reports of I and command being lost on the Staked Plains, and that the command had all abandoned the captain.

July 28—At daylight, the guide and the eight men not returning, I saddled up, but had great difficulty in getting the mules packed. Sergeant Umbles, the evening previous, having ordered to accompany him the only man with the competence to pack, the captain had to do most of the packing himself. When ready to start, all the citizens were scattered over the plains, their ponies gone. One of the citizens, Mr. Benson, advised that a northeasterly direction be taken, this being the course the guide had taken when last seen.

I then left camp on this course and marched about fifteen miles, when I came to the conclusion that, as no trace of the guide could be found, and as the Casa Maria was a small water hole and the distance to it unknown, so that a large command might easily pass within a short distance of it without its being discovered, it was best to return to Double Lakes. This decision was based on the fact that he was now between his trail of the previous day, which lay to the west, and that of Colonel Shafter of 1875, which was to the east, and consequently could not possibly miss the lakes. This is the course the ponies of the citizens had taken after stampeding, and [they] were afterwards found on this trail and at the lakes.

I now became convinced that the evening previous, the guide was completely lost, and that he had omitted taking bearings over the route traveled. In this he is supported by the statements of the men who had followed him after water during the night, and who informed him it was not found until the morning of the next day at about noon. The captain attributes his getting lost to the zeal he displayed in following the trail, he being largely interested in finding Indians, having lost stock himself, and cannot, under the circumstances, attach any blame to him.

The command now changed its course in the direction of Double Lakes and marched about fifteen miles when, owing to the men becoming completely exhausted, continually falling from their horses, they had much difficulty in making progress. At last we were compelled to halt until the sun went down. Just before making this halt, about a mile back, one of the men fainted. I directed Corporal Gilmore and one man to remain with him and bring him up as soon as he recovered. This corporal, instead of obeying orders by rejoining the command as soon as the man was able, deserted with [the] sick man, and the man left with him. He is one of the parties who accompanied Sergeant Umbles to Fort Concho and propagated the false reports. This corporal and the two privates lost their horses and equipment. Soon after this halt, Lance Corporal [George] Fremont, without any authority, together with two men, took their horses and two pack mules and deserted the command, which was at this time suffering intensely for want of water. One of Lieutenant Cooper's private horses had become so exhausted he was killed and his blood distributed among the men. Previous to this, the command were suffering so much for water we were compelled to drink our own and our horses' urine, as also did the horses and mules. Having sugar along, I issued a liberal supply to the men, which tended to make the urine palatable.

At this halt, we remained until about 11:00 P.M., when the command commenced packing and to saddle up, but owing to the exhausted condition of the men, it occupied at least three hours to get ready and to start. At this point, a large portion of the rations had to be abandoned. I was also compelled to abandon one horse, unable to move.

At about 2:00 A.M. of July 29, [the command] got started and marched twenty-five miles, but owing to the intense heat and fearful condition of the men, was compelled to halt in a scrub mesquite flat and obtain such little shelter as a saddle blanket would afford. During the last march, one horse and equipment were abandoned. Thus we remained here, powerless to move, until after sundown, when we again got started and marched a distance of fifteen miles to Double Lakes, arriving there at about 4:00 A.M. July 30. At the last halting place, we were obliged to abandon a private horse of Lieutenant Cooper and seven company horses; three of these horses were killed and their blood distributed among the men; all surplus rations and property that could not be taken was abandoned. At this halt, two mules stampeded.

Up to the arrival at Double Lakes, the command had been without water eighty-six hours. On arrival at Double Lakes, we found Sergeant Thompson and six men, who the day previous had been sent in advance to Double Lakes. Five horses of this party dropped dead on the way. As soon as the company reached this water, two men were sent back on the trail with canteens filled to meet three men who had straggled, and when last seen were in the vicinity of Double Lakes. They also had instructions to render assistance to other men coming in. These two men, sent out with water, returned and reported that they were unable to find any trace of the three stragglers. I immediately sent out other parties in different directions, who made diligent search for them, but without success. In the evening of this day, two men who had straggled from the command came into camp. One of these men had lost his horse and equipment. During the day, a party was sent to the last camp to bring in some of the rations which had been abandoned. This party allowed the pack mule to escape from them, but it afterwards came back to camp, the men returning without accomplishing their mission.

July 31—The command remained in camp. At about daylight, I sent a detail with two pack mules back to the last camp for rations; they returned in the afternoon with an abundant supply. About 11:00 A.M. this day, Capt. P. L. Lee, with his company (G), 10th Cavalry, [and] a party of Tonkawa Indian scouts, came into camp, and upon learning my situation, immediately tendered all the assistance in his power. One of his wagons was at once unloaded and, with a party of men and Indians, dispatched on the back trail with an abundant supply of water, in order to pick up stragglers and all abandoned property. The scouts were particularly instructed to scatter and use all possible means to find lost men and property.

August 1—The command remained in camp awaiting the return of the parties sent out, who returned in the afternoon, bringing with them Lance Corporal Fremont and Private Gaddie, whom they found about ten miles from camp, having lost their horses and equipment and two pack mules with packs.[3] This Corporal Fremont is the party referred to as having deserted on the evening of July 28, taking with him the two men and two pack mules. This corporal reported that one of his party, Pvt. [Isaac] Derwin, had died and that the three horses they had with them had also died, and that the equipments had been abandoned as they could not carry them. This day a horse, ridden by Private Rose, died in camp from the effects of a gunshot wound while out as a flanker near Dry Lake. The shot was supposed to have been fired by an Indian. The Tonkawa scouts, who returned by Dry Lake, about seventeen miles west from camp, reported that they had found the body of a soldier. In the evening a detail with a wagon was again sent out on the back trail to make a more thorough search for men and property.

August 2—Remained in camp. Corporal Roberts, with a detail, was sent to bury the man found by the Indian scouts. Upon their return, they reported that they had found the body, which proved to be that of Pvt. J. F. Gordon, which they buried. This was one of the three stragglers before referred to as last seen in the vicinity of camp. Corporal Roberts and party had also instructions to make a thorough search at Dry Lake and vicinity to discover any stragglers and property, but found no signs. The party with the wagon, sent out on the back trail, returned without finding any men or property.

August 3—The command still remained in camp. I sent out a wagon and party to bury the man Derwin, reported by Corporal Fremont as dead. The corporal accompanied the party. On arriving in the vicinity of the place where it had been reported the man had died, a most diligent search was made by the scouts and men, but no trace of his remains could be found. This morning Captain Lee sent a scout to Laguna Sabinas to search for signs of Indians.

August 4—Sergeant Allsup and fifteen men of the command who had been left in charge of supply camp arrived in search of the command, the sergeant having been informed by Sergeant Umbles that the command had all perished. I now learned for the first time that this Sergeant Umbles's party, and Corporal Gilmore and party, had reached supply camp in safety, and that Sergeant Umbles had ordered Private Johnson to accompany himself and Corporal Gilmore to Fort Concho, they taking fresh horses belonging to the men left at supply camp. Sergeant Allsup also reported that Sergeant Umbles stated to him at the time of leaving supply camp for Fort Concho that his object in going there was to get a commissioned officer to come out and take charge of the remnant of the company. Immediately after hearing this report, I sent two couriers to Fort Concho by way of supply camp with a penciled communication to the post adjutant, giving a rough statement as to the condition of the command, and that all statements made by Sergeant Umbles to the contrary would be false. In the afternoon of the day, the scout sent out yesterday by Captain Lee to Laguna Sabinas returned and reported signs of Indians, which were supposed to be that of Quanah and party returning to Fort Sill.

August 5—At 6:00 A.M. broke camp and proceeded towards supply camp, being accompanied by Captain Lee's command. Marched to the breaks of Double Mountain Fork of the Brazos, a distance of thirty-three miles, arriving there at sundown. Owing to the guides missing the water hole, the men were compelled to make a dry camp.

August 6—At 6:00 A.M. left camp and marched to supply camp on Bull Creek, where we arrived at 12:00 A.M., a distance of twenty miles. During this march—from Double Lake to supply camp—the animals were without water twenty-eight hours. This afternoon Assistant Surgeon J. H. T. King, Lt. R. G. Smither, adjutant, 10th Cavalry,[4] and Lt. Wallace Tear, 25th Infantry,[5] with a portion of the 10th Cavalry band [and] two ambulances, arrived from Fort Concho in search of the command and to render any assistance in their power, they having acted upon the false statements and reports of Sergeant Umbles and Corporal Gilmore when they came into Fort Concho. On my arrival at supply camp, I received a telegram dated headquarters, Fort Griffin, Texas, July 31, 1877, directing me, pursuant to telegraphic instructions from headquarters, Department of Texas, dated July 31, to return to Fort Concho; accordingly, at about 6:00 A.M. on August 7, I broke up the supply camp and marched to the Colorado River, a distance of fifteen miles, Captain Lee's command accompanying me, when I camped for the night. That morning, Assistant Surgeon King and Lieutenant Tear, with a four-mule ambulance, were sent to Fort Concho, their services not being required, Lieutenant Smither and band detachment remaining with the company.

August 8—At 6:30 A.M. left camp and marched to Davis Creek, a distance of thirteen miles. I was here informed that I would have to march twenty-five miles without reaching water, so I went into camp until 4:00 P.M., when I again started and marched to Morgan's Creek, a distance of ten miles, and made a dry camp. At this place, a horse was shot, having glanders. This morning Captain Lee and his command separated from me and proceeded to Fort Griffin.

August 9—We left camp at 5:40 A.M. and marched to Deep Creek, a distance of seventeen miles, where we found excellent rainwater and went into camp. At this camp, one horse died from blind staggers.

August 10—At 3:30 P.M. left camp and marched twelve miles to Rock Springs.

August 11—Left camp at 4:30 A.M., marched to Hackberry Springs, a distance of four miles, halted until 3:30 P.M., and then continued on to Willow Creek, a distance of twelve miles.

August 12—Left camp at 5:30 A.M., marched down the North Concho River to three miles east of Monumental Park, a distance of twenty miles.

August 13—Left camp at 5:30 A.M., marched down the North Concho to Grape Creek, a distance of twenty-four miles.

August 14—Left camp at 5:15 A.M., marched twelve miles into Fort Concho, arriving there at about 9:00 A.M.

I think that had water been found in places where former scouts found it in abundance, without a doubt this scout would have been successful, resulting in the capture of not only the Indians on whose trail I was, but possibly other marauders.

At the points before referred to as having been the camps of Colonel Shafter in 1875, and when at that time large bodies of fresh water existed, on this scout it was obtained only by great labor in digging, and then brackish and unfit to drink.

The command, after leaving the head of Concho River, encountered many difficulties in finding water, as all the springs and water holes, where heretofore plenty could be found, were dried up. From these facts and other signs observed during this scout, I am of the opinion that but very few Indians are east of the Staked Plains, and those only in parties of from two to four.

During the absence of the command from supply camp, Sergeant Allsup says that on four occasions three Indians attempted to steal the stock but, owing to his vigilance, were unsuccessful.

The conduct of the men generally was exemplary, with the exception of the three noncommissioned officers already referred to.

The missing men, had they obeyed orders, would have reached water as soon as the command did, and under the circumstance, no blame can be attached to anyone but themselves. After reaching water, every effort was made to rescue them. I think that, had the men been able to remain on their horses, I could have reached water at least thirty-six hours sooner, and that all the men and horses would have been saved.

I learned from the guide, on arrival at Dry Lake, that the party of forty Indians he reported before leaving Double Lakes turned out to be a party of eight only. The loss to the command during the scout was four men—two of whom died, and two that are still missing[6]—twenty-three public horses, two private horses, and four pack mules.

A Brief Account of the Sufferings of a Detachment of United States Cavalry from Deprivation of Water during a Period of Eighty-six Hours while Scouting on the Staked Plains of Texas

J. H. T. KING[1]

Fort Davis, Texas: Charles Krull, post printer, [1877]

On the evening of August 4, 1877, two noncommissioned officers and one private belonging to Company A, 10th Cavalry, came into Fort Concho, Texas, reporting that Captain Nolan and Lieutenant Cooper, with twenty-six soldiers, while in pursuit of marauding Indians, had wandered amongst the sand hills on the Staked Plains; that no water could be found; and that when last seen, the whole command was exhausted and dying of thirst.

A relieving party, to which the writer was attached, was organized at once and left immediately in search of the missing men. After a rapid march of sixty-two hours, we reached Captain Nolan's supply camp, situated seven miles northeast of the Mucha Koway Mountains and 140 miles from Concho, where we learned that Captain Nolan, Lieutenant Cooper, and all the men except four had just come in safely one hour previously. As the lost men advanced toward us, we remarked their changed appearance since we had last seen them a few weeks before; their aged and careworn faces portrayed the hardships they had undergone, while additional gray locks and other indications of suffering were visible. The following is the painful history which they narrated.

Captain Nolan, Lt. Charles L. Cooper, and forty troopers of Company A, 10th Cavalry, with eight pack mules, had for some days been scouting in the region of Double Lakes and Cedar Lake, looking for Indians. On July 26, 1877, a rumor was brought into camp at Double Lakes that a band of hostile Indians had recently been seen passing Dry Lake; Captain Nolan forthwith prepared to follow them and broke camp at 1:00 P.M. July 26. The Indian trail was struck west of Dry Lake and pursued until dark, being then no longer discernible. The guide, in his anxiety to keep the Indian trail, had neglected his landmarks and was unable to find water when the halt was sounded. The party was compelled therefore to make a dry camp and so pass the night. On leaving Double Lakes, each man's canteen had been filled, but in consequence of the intense heat, they were emptied in the early part of the march, and what little water Dry Lake contained was so strongly alkaline that neither man nor beast could drink it.

At dawn the trail was again taken up and followed perseveringly, not only with a view of capturing the Indians, but also with hopes that it might conduct them to some lake or water hole. Their course lay over a gently undulating country, the soil dry [and] mostly of a reddish color, covered with bunches of short grass, here and there a stunted mesquite bush ten or fifteen inches high, and occasional twigs of scrub oak of similar size. The heat was excessive—*coup de soleil* had prostrated two men, and all were suffering severely from thirst.

Towards sunset, the trail commenced to spread, breaking into a multitude of ill-defined tracks, rendering further pursuit useless, and the chase was given up. Men had been thrown out on the flanks all day to seek for water, and for the same purpose, the guide explored every valley and depression in view. Matters were assuming a grave aspect; many were faint and exhausted; some fell from their saddles. The horses needed water equally with their riders. After adopting all customary methods to extricate his command from this critical position, Captain Nolan finally mounted the guide on his private horse, a tough animal, and ordered him to traverse the country, ranging wherever he thought it possible to find water. This guide was never seen afterwards; Captain Nolan awaited for a time his return, and then determined to fall back upon Double Lakes, which were supposed to be seventy-five or one hundred miles distant, where he felt confident of obtaining water.

Another day was drawing to a close, and as night came on, advantage was taken of the cooler atmosphere, and every nerve was strained to reach Double Lakes.

The next day found them still marching onwards, and the midday tropical heat causing great suffering. The desire for water now became uncontrollable. The most loathsome fluid would now have been accepted to moisten their swollen tongues and supply their inward craving. The salivary and mucous secretions had long been absent; their mouths and throats were so parched that they could not swallow the government hard bread; after being masticated, it accumulated between the teeth and in the palate, from whence it had to be extracted with the fingers; the same occurred with mesquite beans and whatever else they attempted to eat. The sensibility of the lingual and buccal mucous membranes was so much impaired that they could not perceive when anything was in their mouths. The condition of the *primae via* may in a degree be realized when it is

explained that brown sugar would not dissolve in their mouths, and
that it was impossible for them to swallow it. Vertigo and dimness of
vision affected all. They had difficulty in speaking, voices weak and
strange sounding, and they were troubled with deafness, appearing
stupid to reach other, questions having to be repeated several times
before they could be understood; they were also very feeble and had
a tottering gait. Many were delirious. What little sleep they were
able to get was disturbed with ever recurring dreams of banquets,
feasts, and similar scenes in which they were enjoying every kind of
dainty food and delicious drink. At this stage, they would in all likelihood have perished had they not resorted to the use of horse blood.
As they gave out, they cut them open and drank their blood. The
horses had been so long deprived of every kind of fluid that their
blood was thick and coagulated instantly on exposure; nevertheless,
at the time it appeared more delicious than anything they had ever
tasted; in fact, everyone was so eager to obtain it that discipline
alone prevented them from struggling for more than the stinted share
allowable to each. The heart and other viscera were grasped and
sucked as if to secure even the semblance of moisture. At first they
could not swallow the clotted blood but had to hold it in their
mouths, moving it to and fro between the teeth until it became somewhat broken up, after which they were enabled to force it down their
parched throats. This horse blood quickly developed diarrhea, passing through the bowels almost as soon as taken; their own urine,
which was very scanty and deep colored, they drank thankfully, first
sweetening it with sugar. The inclination to urinate was absent, and
micturition performed with difficulty. A few drank the horse urine,
although at times it was caught in cups and given to the animals
themselves. They became oppressed with dyspnea and a feeling of
suffocation, as though the sides of the trachea were adhering, to
relieve which they closed the lips and breathed through the nose,
prolonging the intervals between each inspiration as much as possible. Gazing at each other, their lips thus closed were observed to be
covered with a whitish, dry froth and had a ghostly, pale, lifeless
appearance, as though they would never be opened again. Their fingers and the palms of their hands looked shriveled and pale; some,
who had removed their boots, suffered from swollen feet and legs.

The situation was now desperate, and feelings akin to despair
took possession of them—suspicious ideas toward each other came
over them, and they all lost confidence in each other. They again saw
the sun set, and another night was spent on these untrodden wastes
without alleviation of their misery. Persistent wakefulness now
aggravated their mental anguish, and in vain at every halt they lay
down and tried to sleep.

Their deplorable condition continued to gradually grow worse
until 5:00 A.M. July 30, 1877, when, providentially, part of the command succeeded in making Double Lakes. At this time, a number of
men were missing, some having been unable to keep up with the
main column, while others had strayed for water.

Both officers and men were almost helpless on reaching Double
Lakes, and the wished-for water did not greatly benefit any of them
this day. Canteens of water were at once strapped to the horses, and
two or three men sent on the trail back to succor and help on the
stragglers. Fortunately, the following morning, Captain Lee, 10th
Cavalry,[2] with a detachment of Tonkawa[3] scouts, touched at Double
Lake and rendered most valuable assistance to Captain Nolan's
party, dispatching scouts on all sides to hunt for men and horses, and
furnishing rations and some delicacies which the sufferers were in
absolute need of. The demands of their systems were so imperative
that the inclination to drink was irresistible; it seemed impossible to
refrain from pouring down water, notwithstanding that their stomachs would not retain it. As they kept filling themselves with water,
it was vomited up; the same thing occurred when they endeavored to
eat food. Warm coffee was the only thing they had that revived them
at all until after Captain Lee met them.

Although water was imbibed again and again, even to repletion of
the stomach, it did not assuage their insatiable thirst, thus demon-
strating that the sense of thirst is like the sense of hunger, located in
the general system, [such] that it could not be relieved until the
remote tissues were supplied. Moreover, the activity of this regener-
ating process was prevented by the deficiency of water in the
absorbent vessels themselves. The same cause is competent to
explain the overpowering dyspnea which threatened the existence of
these men; for only moist membranes allow the free passage of
gases that must take place in respiration. The lungs of these men
were filled with the purest air, yet they appreciated an almost overwhelming sense of suffocation. Another point worthy of our attention is the loss these men must have sustained by integumentary and
pulmonary exhalations. The mean daily exhalation of watery vapor
in expired air Valentin estimates at one and one-fifth pounds average, and the daily loss by coetaneous transpiration at about two
pounds; in the case before us, the quantities were influenced and
increased by the conditions of temperature, exercise, etc.

The superior endurance of the mule over the horse was obviously
manifested on this scout. The horses' tongues were swollen, mouths
and systems generally affected in the same manner as the men's; they
could not chew or swallow grass, [and] many gave out completely.
On the other hand, the mules were comparatively unfatigued [and]

would crop the grass and graze at every halt. It is essential to remember that the sensation of thirst to which these cavalrymen almost succumbed was intensified by the dry state of the atmosphere.

They were toiling over arid plains and elevated plateaus in a climate noted for its lack of moisture. On August 1, 1877, Captain Nolan heard that fourteen of his followers had managed to get all right as far as the supply camp. His total loss, therefore, after this dangerous scout, only consisted of two men dead and two missing, supposed to be dead. Captain Nolan remained five or six days at Double Lakes to recuperate, and then retraced his steps to the supply camp, arriving there on August 7, 1877.

> (*signed*) J. H. T. King,
> Captain and Assistant Surgeon,
> U.S.A.
> Post Surgeon,
> Fort Concho, Texas

A true copy of report to the medical director, Department of Texas, September 1877.

> (*signed*) J. H. T. King,
> Captain and Assistant Surgeon,
> U.S.A.

Last Indian Raid
in Southwest Texas

[MRS. CHARLES M. HARPOLE, ET AL.]

San Antonio *Evening News,* May 25, 1924

Texas's last Indian raid took a toll of two lives. United States troops followed the raiders into Mexico, whence the Indians had come, and killed six of the seven bucks in the raiding party. In April 1881 a party of Lipan Indians looted the house of John M. McLaurin, about 10 miles north of Leakey, and killed his wife and Allen Lease, a sixteen-year-old boy. United States soldiers at Fort Clark, now Brackettville, under Lieutenant Bullis, were notified, and they followed the band into Mexico, surprised them in camp near the Santa Rosa Mountains, killed six braves, and captured a small boy and a squaw. Mrs. Charles M. Harpole of San Antonio, a girl of five at the time of the murder of her mother, tells of the tragedy, which was indelibly stamped upon her memory:

My father left home early on the morning of April 19 to go to what was then called The Ditch, now Rio Frio, where there was a general store, for supplies and medicine. After noon my mother took my two little brothers and me with her to the garden to oversee some planting that she wanted done. After a while she heard a noise at the house, and thinking that some hogs had gotten into the yard, sent Allen Lease, a boy working for us, to the house to run them out.

Allen started up the hill, and whether he saw the Indians or turned to close the garden gate, I do not know. He was shot through the head from the back and died instantly. My mother was shot through the hip, so she called to me to take my little three-year-old brother and run to the fence and try to get away. She reached the fence and climbed on it in her attempt to get over it and down into the riverbed, but was shot again. The Indians seemed to think she was dead and did not notice us children, but continued robbing the house.

Soon my mother raised up to see where we were, and an Indian shot her twice more, making five wounds she had received. When the Indians left, I went to the house and brought a dipper of water for her. I then started to the nearest house for help. I came upon George

Fisher and his wife down the river a little way, where they were fishing. Mr. Fisher took me to a neighbor's house, where he left me with the women and children who had gathered there to remain while the men went on the trail of the redskins.

My father returned at sundown to find my mother still lying in the garden as I had left her with the two little boys. She lived only a few minutes after Father found her. At the house everything had been taken or broken.

Toby Edwards, then a boy of seventeen, was one of the company of white settlers who followed the Indians for several miles, and then surrendered its task to Lieutenant Bullis and his men, who had been notified at Brackettville. He tells the story of the Indians:

I heard of the killing of Mrs. McLaurin and Lease when I returned from Uvalde, and was told to meet at the McLaurin place that night and take the trail from there. When I arrived at the house, a company of men was already preparing to take the trail. We saw where the house had been plundered, all the mattresses emptied of feathers, and every bit of clothing had been taken away by the Indians. Upon investigation, we saw signs which proved that they had been around the place for several days. Up on the bluff in front of the house, we found signs of their camp.

This bluff overlooks the surrounding country for miles on every side, and from the top, the Indians had been able to keep watch for a great distance both up and down the river. They had seen McLaurin leave home, had also watched as Frank Sanders and another man rode up the canyon later in the day, and then when they saw Mrs. McLaurin go with the three children and Lease to the garden, they descended.

Our men trailed the Indians from the top of the bluff in front of the house, and for several miles they were rather hard to trail. We had found a deck of cards, a cow's tail, and a woman's dress. At the mouth of Joy Creek, near the Nueces River, we found where they had killed a beef. A man known as Old Man Joy, who lived in a cave near there and for whom the creek and cave were named, told us that he had heard the shot but had not gone to see who had fired it. The Indians stole some horses at Spring Creek, which made them much easier to trail.

Up to this time, there had been sixteen men in our party, but here we separated into groups of four and went in different directions. In my bunch, there were Bill McLaurin, brother-in-law of the woman who was killed, Hugh Colston, a man named Coryell, and myself. Four other men joined our party over on the Nueces—Nick Colston, Sam Rainey, Jim Waldy, and his brother, whose name I can not recall.

We came to a little church out in the woods, where they were hold-ing services. When we rode up, Parson Edwards came out to learn what we wanted. He turned to his congregation and said, "Friends, I sure hate to disappoint you, but these Indians have got to be followed, so we will just put off this meeting till some other time." A meeting place was arranged for the men who volunteered to help us, but the four mentioned in the foregoing paragraph were the only ones who appeared.

Someone proposed that we notify Lieutenant Bullis at Fort Clark, so we sent a man with instructions to report to him that night. He stopped on the way, however, so Bullis did not get word until the day following. We waited there all day and until 2:00 P.M. the next day without food, so when the soldiers did not come, we went to hunt something to eat. While we were gone, the troops came and took up the trail where we left it.

Lieutenant Bullis and his men followed the Indians into Mexico, surprised them in camp, killed six warriors, [and] captured a squaw and a little boy.[1] One of the Indians escaped, however, so the soldiers hurried back across the border to avoid a fight with neighboring Indi-ans who might be notified by him. The old squaw told the soldiers that she had come regularly with this band of Indians to that country every moon for twenty years. These raids, she said, were primarily for the purpose of stealing horses. They kept her captive for months and finally sent her to the Indian reservation in Oklahoma. She also told the men that had it not been for her, the children would also have been killed.

I was only seventeen when the raid took place. I thought when we started out on the trail that I could whip the world, for I was carrying a dandy new, improved center-fire rifle. They had just come out. The rest of the men were carrying those old government guns which had been issued to the minute company of which I was a member. This company was for the purpose of protecting the settlers against the Indians. John Avants, who was lieutenant of our company, was gone at the time, so I appropriated his gun and saddle for the pursuit. My bunch was gone fourteen days. It was ten days after we returned before we got word of what Bullis had done.

On April 25, 1881, the San Antonio *Express* published in its news columns the following account of this raid:

Rio Frio Texas, April 25, 1881. On yesterday about forty Indians vis-ited the upper part of this canyon, fifteen miles above the point, and killed Mrs. John McLaurin and Allen Lease of Uvalde while in her garden near the house at work. When they discovered the Indians, Mr.

Lease started to the house to get his gun, but was shot down before he could reach it. Mrs. McLaurin started to run for her life and was shot down also. Her three little children were with her, and the oldest, six or seven years old, when her mother fell, ran to the house, and taking a pillow from the bed, placed it under the lady's head, and then placed the two small children by her side, and started for G. W. Fisher's house to give the alarm. Little Maud, when she was in the house after the pillow, says that it was full of men, "big black men." They did not seem to take any notice of the child. They destroyed everything in the house of any value, even the sewing machine.

PART EIGHT

The Ute War,
1879

Incidents of the Recent Campaign against the Utes

J. SCOTT PAYNE[1]

United Service 2, no. 1 (1880): 114–29

Concerning the engagement fought September 29, 1879, in western Colorado between three companies of United States cavalry and several hundred Ute Indians, some things have been written that are true and many more that are the merest fiction. The writer entertains no hope of disabusing the public mind of the many erroneous impressions of that affair conveyed through the columns of the daily and illustrated press. That indeed were a useless task, and this paper is ventured simply with the desire of laying before the military readers of the *United Service* a narrative of events, beginning with the departure of the White River expedition from Fort Fred Steele, Wyoming, September 21, 1879, and concluding with the relief of the besieged command by General Merritt, colonel of the 5th Cavalry,[2] at daybreak of October 5. The command was composed of three troops of cavalry—E of the 3rd, and D and F of the 5th—and one company of infantry, E of the 4th, the total fighting strength being about one hundred and eighty men. A train of twenty-five wagons accompanied us, upon which rations and grain for thirty days were transported.

The officers with the expedition were Maj. T. T. Thornburgh,[3] 4th Infantry, commanding; Lt. S. A. Cherry, 5th Cavalry, adjutant; Lt. S. A. Wolf, 4th Infantry, quartermaster and commissary; Dr. R. B. Grimes, acting assistant surgeon, U.S.A., surgeon; Capt. J. S. Payne and Lt. J. V. S. Paddock, 5th Cavalry; Capt. Joseph Lawson, 3rd Cavalry; and Lt. B. D. Price, 4th Infantry; the four last named being company commanders. The expedition left Fort Steele Sunday morning, September 21, and after a dusty march of fifteen miles over the high, rolling plateau lying between the post and Rawlins, reached that place during the early afternoon and went into camp for the night. This town, which has a population of perhaps eight hundred souls, is situated in a cleft of the Rocky Mountains and presents, when seen from a distant point, quite a picturesque appearance. The Union Pacific Railroad Company have located machine shops here, and it is the point from which supplies are shipped by wagon transportation to the Indians at White River Agency and to Fort

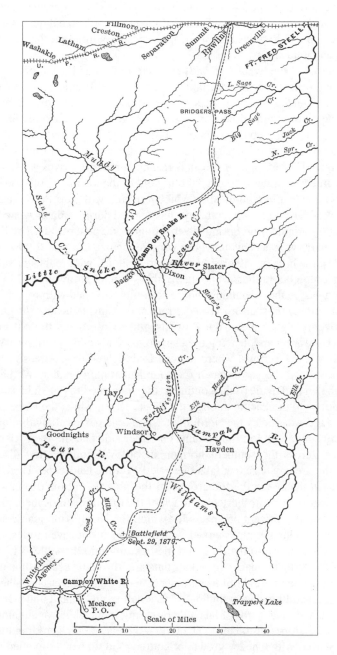

The Ute War.

HARPER'S NEW MONTHLY MAGAZINE 1890.

Washakie, a military post in northwestern Wyoming. In its earlier days it was, in western phrase, a "live town," with all the term implies; but quiet times have long ago come to Rawlins, and its people, mostly railroad mechanics, are law-abiding and industrious.

At dawn of the twenty-second, we were in the saddle and on our way to the agency over a road which, taking a course nearly due south, traverses a country unequaled for dreariness of aspect and, so far as the observer can determine, utterly unfit either for pastoral or agricultural pursuits. Sagebrush, filling the air with its pungent odor and covering the ground so thickly as to render travel almost impossible except over the well-beaten trail, is the only vegetation to be seen, and no stream is reached until one arrives at Mud Spring, where pure, clear water is found bubbling out of the top of a knoll, and running down, is soon lost in a little valley which, covered with nutritious grass, is the only spot of verdure on which the eye has feasted during a day's weary march. The country around Mud Spring is very rugged and picturesque. The little val-ley soon narrows to a canyon, whose winding course the road follows for sev-eral miles, the hills on either side being precipitous, with ledges of sandstone standing out in bold relief, while the foothills extend far away until lost to the south and east in the mountains, whose summits, crowned with foliage already rich in autumnal tints, afford vistas of rare and exquisite beauty. At Lambert's ranch, twenty-eight miles from Rawlins, the road crosses the old emigrant route to California and, leaving the canyon, ascends a high hill, over which it winds to Willow Springs, where the eye is delighted to see trees in leaf and green grass, and the ear to catch the sound of running water. We have now passed the Great Divide of the continent, the watershed to our right sending its contributions to the Pacific through the Snake River, whilst the streams on the left reach the Atlantic by the North Platte. The road passes along through sage-brush and sand, with lofty mountains on either side and the Bear River chain stretching across the southern horizon in billowy outline, first discernible through the dreamy haze that falls like a veil over the landscape. There was lit-tle to charm the eye in the foreground of the picture; but the distant expanse brought near by the foreshortening touch of the dry, rare atmosphere presented one of those magnificent prospects for which the North American cordilleras are noted. Leaving the plateau over which it has run for seven miles, the road makes a sudden turn to the right and, descending into the valley of Mud[dy] Creek, follows that stream over alkali flats and through sagebrush and grease weed for eighteen miles until its confluence with Snake River is reached. Here we found several ranches, a trading store, small tracts of land under fence and cultivation, and large herds of fat cattle browsing in the valley or sunning them-selves on the slopes of the hills. The river—a clear, rapid, sparkling mountain stream, skirted with a heavy growth of cottonwood timber—is named from its serpentine course and winds through a charming valley, narrow and produc-tive—a very strip of fertility in a region sterile and desolate.

After leaving Snake River and crossing the Colorado-Wyoming boundary line, two miles out, our route lay to the southwest over rolling ground, from which we observed for the first time heavy clouds of smoke ascending from fires set by the Indians in the mountains on our left. This, with the debris of tepees and traces of recent Indian campfires, easily distinguishable from those lighted by white men, reminded us that we were indeed approaching the land of the Utes. These evidences of the propinquity of the gentle savage excited, at the time, no apprehensions of trouble, as for months past the grass and timberlands of northern Colorado had been burning, and vast volumes of smoke, borne before the prevailing winds from the west, had been drifting across the Medicine Bow range and hanging like a pall over the plains at the eastern base of the Rocky Mountains.

Fortification Creek we found a pretty stream, issuing from a bold, picturesque canyon, with fringes of willows along its banks, the water excellent, and the grass in the valley nutritious and abundant.

Leaving Price with his company of infantry to establish a supply camp at this point, the command resumed its march next morning and followed Fortification Creek for eighteen miles, crossing and recrossing it several times, and at 2:00 P.M. went into camp in the fertile and beautiful valley of the Bear or, as the Indians call it, the Yampa River. Here again we found ranches, herds of cattle and horses, and other reminders of frontier settlement.

We were now in the very confines of the neutral territory lying between the white settlements and the Ute reservation, and as our first acquaintance with members of this tribe was formed in our camp on the Yampa, a digression may be indulged in at this point, in order that attention may be called to some incidents of our interview.

The Indians visiting us here were Saarwick[4]; a chief of prominence, "Ute" Jack[5]; a subchief, Unque[6]; an Uncompahgre who had a pass from the agent at Los Piños, in which he was represented as being a good Indian; and several others whose names I cannot recall. Jack, who, were he a white man, would take to politics, has for a long time been an agitator and stirrer-up of strife. Endowed with the powers of oratory—erroneously supposed to be a gift not at all rare among Indians—a good judge of savage character, and ambitious of reaching that eminence in his tribe for which he fancied himself fitted by nature and education, he has been, for a year or more gone by, endeavoring to arouse a feeling of distrust among his people, well knowing that by catering to their taste for blood, the avenue to success would be opened. For the accomplishment of his ends, he brought every art to bear, and finally has succeeded in bringing about an Indian war which has set the border ablaze and aroused in the public mind and conscience a feeling of deep resentment against his race. He talked quite freely with us, using broken but easily understood English, telling us of his travels in the East and the impressions made upon his mind by the great cities he had visited and the multitudes of people he had seen, his standard of excellence for each place being the theatre. When asked how he liked New York, his reply was laconic and expressive: "New York pretty good; pretty good theatre in New York," and so on through the list, varying the adjective to suit the impressions made by the performances he had witnessed in different cities.

Although apparently friendly, it was evident that his mind was not at ease, for while conversing upon any topic, he would turn suddenly to some one of the officers and ask, "What you come for? What's the matter? What soldiers going to do?" Notwithstanding assurances of our pacific intentions, and despite our most engaging efforts to divert his mind from a subject on which it morbidly dwelt, with that distrust which is so marked and prominent a trait of Indian character, he would revert to it and ask the same questions over and over again.

When speaking of Mr. Meeker,[7] the agent at White River, he was very abusive, and when asked what Mr. Meeker had done or failed to do, he said the agent had promised him a wagon "with a heap of red paint on it," but the one offered him he had indignantly rejected because of the want of lurid embell-ishment so attractive to the savage eye. What a cause for bloody war, and what a commentary on all efforts to bring these barbarous people under the influ-ences and forces of civilization!

It is easy to see, in the light of experience, that the Indian problem is one whose solution presents many difficulties. The great trouble is to be found in the teachings of men—benevolent, but totally ignorant of the subject with which they are dealing—who, in a spirit of evangelism, desire to civilize the savage by filling his stomach with food and his heart with religion, both processes to be carried on without the constant presence of force, the only thing for which the Indian entertains respect.

The truth is that by force and force alone, tempered, to be sure, by mercy, but that mercy exercised judiciously and sparingly, can his wild nature be kept under control. But persons clinging to the evangelical theory are active and make proselytes among various classes of people, thus smothering public opin-ion and creating for the red man a sympathy entirely undeserved. Sentimental-ists, whose ideas of aboriginal character are derived from Cooper's novels, have here an object on which to expend that surplus of inexpensive sympathy with which such natures endowed, and the philanthropists whose charity is too far-reaching to fall within the horizon of the communities in which they live find an opportunity to make a display of their virtuous opinions, at once osten-tatious and cheap. These "humanitarians" complacently gaze—safely from afar off—at slaughtered officers and men, and hear unmoved of murdered chil-dren and outraged women; but let the savages be thoroughly punished for their acts of atrocity, and the vials of wrath are opened upon the heads of the mili-tary. Better fifty dead officers and soldiers and nameless outrage to a score of women than one Indian corpse.

Many reasons for the outbreak of the White River Utes have been given. The encroachments of the miners may have had some effect, the effort of the agent to make them tillers of the soil doubtless had its influence, but the real cause goes back before all minor troubles and is to be found in the Indian's thirst for blood and love of rapine. Be their reasons ever so good, there can be no excuse for their treachery before the beginning of hostilities. They came to us, not "as an army with banners," their feathered plumes waving in the autumn breezes, their trappings gleaming with barbaric splendor, and their arms glinting back the bright rays of the sun, thus giving warning of their hostile intent and throwing the gage of battle at our feet; but with duplicity in their hearts. Whilst their countenances wore the signals of peace, they visited our camps, professed friendship, and having learned our force, departed, feeling no doubt full assurance of an early massacre, a species of amusement which commends itself to aboriginal minds as the most pleasurable of innocent and fanciful pursuits.

After leaving Bear River, the country improves greatly, and eight miles from the crossing, the road enters one of the most beautiful canyons I have ever seen. Through this it winds for four miles, constantly ascending, with sierra after sierra bursting into view, until the crest of the divide between the Yampa and Williams Fort is reached. Thence it descends for an equal distance, the canyon narrowing until it debouches into an exquisite valley three to five hundred yards wide, through which courses the sparkling stream last named. The scenery here was full of wild beauty. The mountains, springing from the vale abruptly to an altitude of a thousand feet above the creek bed, were covered with cedars, spruce, and lichens; the banks of the stream were fringed with willows, and the grass in the valley grew luxuriantly. Here we camped on the night of the twenty-seventh and received a visit from "Colorow," a White River chief of bad reputation[8]; Henry [Jim] the agency interpreter; and three other Indians who came in from the agency with Mr. [Wilmer] Eskridge, an employee, who had been sent by Mr. Meeker with a communication to Major Thornburgh. These Indians were not disposed to be sociable at first, but their reserve seemed to wear off, and they laughed and talked among themselves, listening the while to whatever was said by any of the officers; for be it known that among these people, it is unusual to find one who does not understand the English tongue sufficiently well to catch the drift of conversation on any subject with which they are familiar. Colorado [Colorow] was exceedingly surly, shaking hands with little cordiality, and in response to an invitation to smoke, saying, "Colorado big chief, no sabe smoke pipe," a remark which we interpreted at the time as conveying a rebuke for our want of hospitality in offering an individual of his power and celebrity anything less excellent than a *Reina Victoria*. However, we had no Havanas left; for his fellow citizen Jack, when offered one the night before, had shown his high appreciation of our courtesy by taking every cigar in the only box of our mess.

From Williams Fort, the road, still going south, enters the canyon of a small mountain rivulet, and at a distance of three miles bears sharply off to the right, when in a pretty little park we found several sweet springs overhung by masses of red sandstone, in some places eroded by the action of wind and water into forms of fantastic beauty; in others piled rock upon rock in inextricable confusion, as if the Titans had been playing at bowls in the long, long ago. On our right, a mountain, grim, brown, bare, rose to an altitude of three thousand foot; on the left, the peaks shot skyward, their crests wearing the foliated aspect of cathedral spires, and the feathery plumes of smoke from the burning timber floating between us and the sun were beautiful with the tints of golden bronze.

The divide was crossed at an altitude of eight thousand feet, and we camped two miles from the top in a fine canyon, where good water and grass were found for our animals. My beautiful bays! How little did we think you were bearing brave men to death, and that ere the shades of another night should lower, "stable call" would have no music for your ears!

We left camp at 6:30 A.M. of September 29 and emerged from the gloom of the canyon just as the first pencils of sunlight were gilding a lofty pinnacle, surmounted with a leaning rock strikingly resembling a man's form.

At 9:30 A.M. we reached the high ground overlooking Milk River. Descending the hill, a fine landscape lay before us. A small stream running softly down a narrow valley; on the right hand, a mile off, a line of bluffs continuous and inaccessible, with broken ridges nearer the creek; on the left, rounded knolls and what our English friends call "downs," furrowed with arroyos and running back to the high hills which form the advance guard of the White River Mountains. The air was soft and balmy, and the bright sunshine shooting in broad flashes across the hilltops filled the valley. Save in the long column which, dismounted, was winding its way down the hill, not a living creature was in sight. Earth and sky were fair to behold, and the pictured calm seemed the very symbol of peace.

The command was halted and the horses watered at the river, after which the march was resumed, E Troop of the 3rd Cavalry and F of the 5th proceeding, under the immediate command of Major Thornburgh, while D of the 5th remained with the wagons.

Following the river for a thousand yards, the troops crossed and took a trail going over the hills to the left, with the view of cutting off the elbow made by the road. A good deal of nonsense has been written in the newspapers to the effect that the command pursued this route by the advice of a guide who, knowing the Indians were lying in ambush in the canyon, took us this way to avoid annihilation. Major Thornburgh turned off the road to shorten his march. Neither he nor I were apprehensive of trouble at this time, and the first intimation of it came from Lieutenant Cherry,[9] who, with the advance guard, had proceeded over some high ground between the trail and road, and had discovered the Indians drawn up in line of battle, or more correctly speaking, lying in ambush along the ridges which covered and commanded the road.

With a quick and soldierly perception of the situation, Lieutenant Cherry turned back and made signals for the command to retrace its steps just as the leading company (F, 5th Cavalry) was descending the ridge into the valley beyond. Company F was immediately conducted to the side of the hill on its left flank, while E, 3rd Cavalry, was halted on the high ground it occupied, and both companies at once dismounted and deployed, by Major Thornburgh's orders, as skirmishers, E, 3rd Cavalry on the right, along the crest of the ridge, and F Company, 5th Cavalry, as well up the side of the hill, which, constantly ascending, stretched away indefinitely, as the nature of the ground would permit. Our line at this time resembled the letter V, the point towards the Indians, and that portion of it formed by F Company, 5th Cavalry, projecting considerably beyond the point of junction, and being deflected to the left so as to prevent the enemy from turning our flank.

At this time, attempts were made by Major Thornburgh in person, and by Lieutenant Cherry, to communicate with the Indians, but efforts in that direction were met by a shot,[10] and at once a hot fire was opened upon us, and the fight began all along our lines. The Indians had displayed admirable skill in the selection of the ground upon which to give us battle. We were enveloped by high hills from which they were enabled to pour a plunging fire upon us whilst they were enabled to keep well under cover, and it soon became evident that our position, in the face of an enemy greatly superior in numerical force and superbly armed, was untenable. In the exercise of sound judgment and a perfect appreciation of the situation, Major Thornburgh determined to make a junction with the troop at the train, and with that object in view, directed the companies engaged to retire slowly. In the meantime, a hot fight had been raging, two men of my company being killed and a number wounded at other parts of the line. The command retired as directed in perfect order, the led horses being well protected between the skirmish lines of the two companies, while a heavy and effective fire did great execution among the savages and prevented an attempt on their part to break through our lines. Failing in their efforts in front, the Indians endeavored to cut the command off from the train, which had, by Major Thornburgh's order, gone into park on the right bank of Milk River, and to accomplish this purpose, passed around our left flank, beyond carbine range, and concentrated in great force upon a knoll to the left of us and completely commanding our line of retreat. Major Thornburgh, upon discovering this new danger, directed me to charge the knoll with twenty men of my company to sweep the Indians off, and then at once, without attempting to hold the hill, to fall back upon the train and take measures for its protection. This duty being performed, and a way opened for the return of the led horses, I repaired to the wagon train and at once took steps looking to its defense.

Major Thornburgh no doubt started for the train just after giving me the order referred to and was killed after crossing the creek, within five hundred yards of the wagons.[11] He saw but three-quarters of an hour of the fight, but during this brief period displayed his ability to command and that superb courage under fire which always inspires confidence and admiration. He was one of nature's noblemen, simple, frank, and generous. He leaves a heritage of honor to wife, children, and brother, and to the army an example worthy of emulation.

I trust I may be pardoned for referring here to an incident personal to myself; but as it illustrates the quiet heroism of two humble men, one living, the other dead, I cannot pass it by unnoticed. When charging the knoll which I have referred, my horse was shot, and falling, broke his girth and threw me violently to the earth. When I got to my feet, I saw that my detachment had swept over the hill and was rapidly disappearing in clouds of dust and smoke. Just as I discovered an Indian within fifty yards of me—I was completely at his mercy, having neither gun nor pistol—1st Sgt. [John] Dolan of my company, who had missed me from his side, turned back and, dismounting, offered me his horse. Brave old man, all unconscious of the heroism of his act, he thought not of his own but of his captain's safety. He died, as a brave man would choose to die, two hours later, but not until I had thanked him for the offer I could not accept. As it was, he would not leave my side until a gallant young recruit named Carpenter brought me a led horse, when we three left for the corral together. While these events were taking place, Captain Lawson,[12] with E Company, 3rd Cavalry, and Lieutenant Cherry, with a detachment from E Company, 3rd, and "F," 5th Cavalry, gallantly held the Indians in check in front, gradually retiring, Lieutenant Cherry, with his detachment, covering the retreat.

Upon reaching the train, I found it parked on the right bank of Milk River about two hundred yards from the water, the wagons forming the north side of a corral elliptical in shape, its long axis running east and west, and the south side exposed to a fierce fire from the Indians, who, passing in ravines along the river and upon commanding heights, were making a determined effort to capture and destroy the train before it could be placed in position for defense. The animals were crowded within the area indicated, and I at once directed some twenty or more of those wounded to be led out and shot along the open space referred to, thus making a continuous line of defense and affording cover for our sharpshooters.

The wagons were now unloaded, and bundles of bedding, grain and flour sacks, and mess boxes were used for the construction of breastworks. About this time, Lieutenant Paddock,[13] who displayed in this his maiden fight the intrepidity of a veteran, was painfully wounded in the hip, and I received through the left arm a gentle hint that the enemy were not disposed to discontinue their attentions.

Captain Lawson and Lieutenant Cherry, with their commands, had now reached the corral, and we were entertaining the hope that our greatest danger was passed, when a new and startling peril threatened us. The savages, disappointed in their efforts to prevent the concentration of the command at the train or to drive us into the open field, where certain death awaited, took advantage of a high wind blowing towards the corral and set fire to the dry grass and sagebrush down the river.

At the moment this danger was realized, we observed that the Indian supply train, which we had passed on the hill a mile back on the road, was parked within seventy-five yards of our position and so situated as to command the approach to water. Apprehensive that the Indians might, under cover of the smoke, make a lodgment in this train, and with the further purpose of burning the grass on the north side of the corral so as to present as little surface as possible to the Indian fire when it should approach, orders were given to fire the grass on that side; and in a few minutes, we were gratified to see Gordon's train in flames. The fire from below was now approaching with frightful rapidity, volumes of black smoke rolling before it, through which the angry, lurid tongues of flame shot high into the air, giving to the scene an aspect appalling and grand.

Now the fire reached the exposed salient or the corral; some of the wagons were set on fire, and the utmost effort was required to extinguish the flames. At this critical juncture, the Indians made their most furious attack. Not one could be seen, but the incessant crack of their rifles dealt destruction to man and beast. In every ravine the red devils were lurking, and from every sagebush came the messenger of death.

The fire extinguished, our greatest peril passed, but the danger had been averted at great loss. Wagonmaster [William] McKinstry, Teamster [Thomas] McGuire, Sergeant Dolan, and Pvt. [Samuel] McKee, of my company, and Pvt. [Thomas] Mooney, of D Company, were killed, and not less than a dozen men wounded. It was now that Dr. Grimes was shot whilst gallantly ministering to the wounded, and I received my second reminder of Indian malignity.

From this time—about 2:45 P.M.—until nightfall, the Indians kept up a furious fire, doing great damage to our stock, fully three-fourths of them being killed, or so severely wounded that they were killed by my order. At dark a large body of Indians charged down beyond Gordon's burning train, delivering volley after volley. They were repulsed easily and fled, suffering a loss of several warriors, who were distinctly seen to drop from their saddles.

When night had come and we were enabled to look our situation in the face, the prospect, though certainly unpleasant, was not discouraging. We had thirty days' rations, were within two hundred yards of water, and although we had lost our gallant commander and two men killed in the fight in the field and ten more in the corral, besides having forty-two wounded to look after, we had ninety brave fellows unhurt and felt confident of holding out until help should come.

During the night, the dead animals were removed, a full supply of water was procured for twenty-four hours, the wounded were cared for, entrenchments were dug, and by daylight, the corral was in good condition for defense.

Couriers had been sent out at midnight with dispatches to the military authorities, ammunition and rations distributed in the several trenches, and that sense of security was felt for the command which sprang from a knowledge of its gallantry and fortitude.

The cartridge bag. CENTURY MAGAZINE 1891.

Next day the Indians kept up an almost incessant fire, killing nearly all our animals but doing no other damage. We were unmolested during the night of the thirtieth, but after that time, the enemy gave us no rest. On the night of October 1, our water party was fired on at short range and one man shot in the face. The guard for the water party returned this fire, killing one savage.

At daylight of October 2, Captain Dodge and Lieutenant Hughes,[14] with D Company, 9th Cavalry, came into our camp, the first intimation of their approach being given by an Indian lying in the ravine, who called out as a warning, no doubt, to his copper-colored companions, "Soldiers coming." Recognizing the voice as that of a savage, the men were directed to lie low and keep a sharp lookout, as we suspected the alarm was a ruse to get the troops out of the trenches in order that the enemy might fire upon them from their places of concealment. In a few minutes, however, brave John Gordon,[15] who with Rankin[16] and Corporals [George] Moquin and [Thomas F.] Murphy had taken out dispatches at midnight of September 29, called to us in his cheery tones, and he and his companions were admitted.

We had now a material addition to our fighting force and heard with joy that our courier had gone through with safety. No words can convey our sense of appreciation of the gallantry of Captain Dodge and his command; but it is gratifying to know that from their superiors and the public, they have received the praise such courage deserves.

All this time, our minds were full of conjectures as to the fate of the people at the agency. We feared the worst for all concerned; but the savages, as afterwards learned, having wreaked their vengeance upon the agent and all male employees, made captives of the women and children. This can hardly be attributed to any feeling of humanity in the breasts of the Indians in general, but is doubtless due to the influence of Ouray,[17] principal chief of the Ute nation and immediate head of the Uncompahgres. He is a man of marked ability, and realizing the necessity for his people to be on good terms with the whites, has always exerted his influence, hitherto potential, on the side of peace, and his recent efforts to avert war when imminent, and to stop it when flagrant, furnish abundant evidence of his sincere desire to accommodate himself and his followers to the changed condition of affairs brought about by their restriction to a limited territory and their dependence upon the government for subsistence. His friendship for the white people has made him unpopular with some of his tribe, and his life has been attempted more than once. Through all, however, he has remained firm, and to his power, exerted through his family connection, the females and children captured at White River owe their lives. Susan, wife of Johnson, a White River chief and sister to Ouray, was the fast friend of these unfortunates from the moment of their capture. Her appeals to her husband made him their friend also, and by the interposition of these two, the children were saved from death and the women from a fate nameless and more horrible. There is a flavor of romance in the devotion of this savage woman to her paleface sisters, and the blackness of the page devoted to the crimes of her race will be illuminated by the story of her efforts to protect innocence and shield virtue.

The history of one day of the siege is the history of every other day, the monotony being varied only by the diverse schemes for our annoyance evolved from the versatile brains of our neighbors. We were compelled to lie low, for the exposure of a head or arm would attract the fire of the Indians and remind us that the better part of valor is discretion. Fortunately the weather was fine. The beauty of the sky day and night surpassed description, and some of the atmospheric effects were peculiarly striking. One day, as Captain Lawson and myself were lying in a rifle pit, the mirage projected the whole valley against the heavens.

I was dozing, when an exclamation from the captain aroused me, and I saw the river bottom reflected in the sky, and the entrenchments which had seemed so secure apparently exposed to an enfilading fire. So perfect was the illusion that one fancied for a moment the danger real and not imaginary. As we always expected to be fired on when the moon rose, we watched that spectacle with deep interest. The first shimmer of her borrowed light, caught by the hilltops, would attract the attention of the Indians, and as the curtain of darkness would be uplifted and the flood of light stream over the landscape, they would gather in the shadowy ravines and pour volley after volley into the corral, the flashes from their rifles lighting up the dark places and lending to the scene an effect startling and weird.

Signal fires would, during the nights from time to time, burst into view, and the yells of the Indians holding their scalp dances, mingled with the howls of hundreds of coyotes, attracted by the decomposing animals, made the hours hideous with the discord of horrible sounds.

The stench arising from more than three hundred dead animals, lying within a hundred yards of us, was endurable by day, but at night, when the cold air descended into the pits, despite the fine training our olfactory nerves had received for this climax of bad smells which we all knew was approaching, the putrefying odor was almost stifling.

It was a sad sight to see these poor animals lying stark and cold under the stars.

One great cause of anxiety was the fear that the weather, variable and coquettish here as elsewhere, might change her mood and, instead of sending us warm sunshine by day and bright nights, open the sluices of the heavens and rain upon our uncovered heads from the abundance of her reservoirs; or that snow, which quite frequently falls at this altitude earlier than October, might descend, a calamity less to be dreaded than rain only because we might have shaken it from our persons and thrown it out of the trenches as it fell. In our condition, without sufficient clothing and without tents or wood, either of these misfortunes would greatly have augmented the sufferings of the command and taxed their patience and fortitude almost to the limits of human endurance. Fortunately we were spared both calamities, and I pass from what might have been to resume the chronicle of what was.

Tragic as the affair had been, it had its comic side, and ludicrous incidents were frequent. When the men took advantage of a cessation of the fire from the hills to stretch their cramped limbs in the area of the entrenchments, the sharp reports of Winchester rifles and the vicious whiz of a bullet would suddenly divert their minds from the delights of perambulatory exercises and cause them "to seek that seclusion which a (rifle pit) grants." They would clear the open space at a bound and, jumping over the breastworks, enter the pits in most informal and indecorous style, much to the diversion of those of their comrades whose heads, bodies, and limbs escaped striking proof of their hasty coming. Every half hour the time call—as, for instance, "Number one, ten o'clock, and all's well"—starting from the pit in which Lieutenant Cherry and myself had selected our quarters, was repeated from trench to trench; but frequently the regular call would swell, before it made half its elliptical journey, into a verbal bulletin containing news from all parts of the globe, as well as editorial comments on our status quo. This was hardly in accordance with strict military usage, but neither was the siege; so, as far as this breach of the customs of service was involved, the rules were relaxed. Moreover, the half-hourly bulletins came freighted with so much humor, sometimes dry, sometimes quaint, and again grim and loaded down with so many phrases damnatory of our savage enemies, that we heartily enjoyed the humorous part, and found the other so expressive of our own uncharitable anti-Ute views that no effort was made to suppress an inclination on the part of the men, the indulgence of which, speaking liberally, was innocent and entertaining. Besides, our opponents came down into the arroyos under safe cover of the banks, not fifty yards from the corral, and abused the entire command in the most vituperative terms. Having exhausted, apparently, in this vocal exercise the capabilities of the Ute dialect, they resorted to a language rich and copious in profane lore, and vociferated in English, hurling at us epithets which evinced a wonderful knowledge of the Anglo-Saxon tongue as a vehicle for one's disapprobation. Such phrases as these, "Come out with your cowardly cavalry and fight fair," and "We'll kill all soldiers pretty soon," were mild samples of their abjurations. There were many which would shock the sensibilities of your eastern readers, but with which we on the frontier are familiar, for it is a deplorable fact that the white denizens of the border draw as freely upon the exchequer of English profanity as their red brethren.

We did not care much for this abuse, which at one time was personally directed to myself, whom the Indians called by name and subjected to a more terrible cursing than was ever leveled at the head of a government mule. This, I confess, was a little exasperating, and although I did not myself reply in kind, I was greatly pleased to observe that I had some men in my command whose abilities in that line had never before been fully appreciated. Among the many valuables captured from our people by the Indians was an evening dress suit (citizen's), the property of a young officer of the command. The story runs that it was brought along by his striker through mistake; but by those to whom his gallantry among the divine sex is as well known as his conspicuous courage under fire, this statement is taken with a grain of salt. There be those who think he looks to the feminine possibilities of any place, and that when he started for the agency, with the probability of remaining all winter staring him in the face, he took his dress suit in order to provide for all emergencies.

Two nights before the battle, when several of the Utes came into our camp, they were struck with the size of three of the officers, among them the one referred to, and I recall the fact that two of them—the interpreter Henry, a magnificent-looking savage over six feet high, and another tall, vicious-looking rascal, whom the Indians, very happy in names indicative of character, called "Bummer Jim"—made these three officers stand up and measure statures. Is it not possible that even at that early moment they were taking the preliminary steps towards parceling out our apparel, having due regard for the accurate fit of the garments in which they were soon to display to admiring squaws the graces of their persons?

Be that as it may, they made extensive captures in that line of goods, and I have always fancied that in the distribution thereof the dress suit fell to Bummer Jim. What desecration! The shapely trousers, which aforetime whisked over the waxed floor whilst the legs therein were inspired by the sweet strains of music, to be "cut hostile," and that Hatfield coat, whose sleeve was wont to encompass palpitating and blushing beauty, to adorn a painted squaw!

The Indians found also in this officer's trunk a photograph of himself, and as a courteous acknowledgment of the acquaintance formed on the Yampa, left this picture lying on a stone, the top of it partly torn off, thus in savage style conveying the cheerful and reassuring suggestion that although they had been disappointed in their desire to have his scalp, they still entertained hopes of it. The commonly accepted belief that the Indian is under all circumstances a stoic is erroneous. He is a great joker, but his humor is of a sort which utterly fails to commend itself to the favorable consideration of the individual at whom it is directed. Of such a kind was the following remark addressed to us one day from the ravine: "Come out and harness up the rest of your mules for your own funeral." To men almost *in extremis,* few things could have been said wherein grim humor and deep malignity could be more horribly combined.

The author of this cheerful suggestion was all artist in his way. As we approached the boundary line of the reservation, someone found hanging from a bush a sheet of paper, whereon were traced rude pictures of dead men, with innumerable and immense bullet holes through them, and beneath, cabalistic characters running across the page after the manner of our writing. This riddle we failed to read at the time, but half an hour later, we had no doubt of its interpretation.

Under all the circumstances, the time did not drag as heavily as might be supposed. We had great faith in our early deliverance, for we knew neither man nor beast would be spared when Colonel Merritt started to the rescue. During the Sioux campaign of '76, whilst Captain Price and myself were making a forced night march to overtake the general, then on his way to overtake General Crook, at 3:00 A.M. in the morning we reached a point where we expected to find Merritt's command. Seeing no sign of camp, and tired out with the fatigue of constant riding for twenty-four hours, we sounded the "officers' call" with the hope that our comrades might, if in the vicinity, indicate their presence by a reply. Greatly to our delight, the response came, and the incident has passed into a regimental tradition.

While lying in the trenches on the night of October 4, this incident came to mind. Believing it *just* possible for Colonel Merritt to reach us next morning, and knowing that if possible, come he would, I directed one of my trumpeters to be on the alert for the expected signal.

And so it was. Just as the first gray of the dawn appeared, our listening ears caught the sound of officers' call breaking the silence of the morning and filling the valley with the sweetest music we had ever heard. Joyously the reply rang out from our corral, and the men rushing from the rifle pits made the welkin ring with their glad cheers. Deliverance had come, and their fortitude and courage had met with reward.

The scene beggared description. Brave men wept, and it was touching to see the gallant fellows hovering around to get a look at the colonel whose name had been on their lips for days, and who, as they heard from their comrades just arrived, had risen from a bed of sickness to make a march unparalleled in military annals.

The drama had been full of interest and well sustained. Comedy and pathos had moved to laughter and melted to tears; tragedy had stalked across the stage; and when the curtain fell upon it, the actors and audience were rejoiced that "the play had been played out."

The Outbreak of September 1879

H. W. SPOONER[1]

Journal of the United States Cavalry Association 20, no. 78 (May 1910):
1124–28

An outbreak occurred in September 1879 at the White River agency in Colorado which was brought about by local causes.

The agent wished the Utes to cultivate the soil, and as they would not labor, an issue was soon raised between them, which culminated in an open rupture when the agent attempted to plow a piece of land which they desired to preserve for grazing purposes. The agent then asked for military assistance, and Major Thornburgh of the 4th Infantry, who was commanding Fort Frederick Steele, Wyoming, was instructed to proceed to the agency with a sufficient force and restore order. When it came to the knowledge of the Utes that troops were marching towards the agency, they became greatly excited and threatened to attack the soldiers if they crossed the boundary line of the reservation.

On September 19 Captain Payne, with Companies D and F, 5th U.S. Cavalry, moved by rail from Fort D. A. Russell to Fort Steele and joined Captain Lawson's company of the 3rd U.S. Cavalry and Lieutenant Price, who commanded a company of the 4th U.S. Infantry, and on the twenty-first the troops, under Major Thornburgh, set out for the agency. The infantry company was detached at Fortification Creek and encamped to await further orders. The command, now reduced to six officers and 125 enlisted men,[2] then marched southward to Deer Creek and encamped on the twenty-eighth.

A number of the Ute chiefs visited Major Thornburgh at the camps at Bear River and Williams Fork and were informed that he was going to the agency for the sole purpose of restoring order, and that they had nothing to fear from the presence of the soldiers. Although the chiefs were dissatisfied and objected to the presence of any troops at their agency, they accepted presents from the officers and departed with protestations of friendship.

The march was resumed on September 29, and about 10:00 A.M. the command arrived at Milk Creek, about twenty miles north of the agency. At this place Captains Payne and Lawson, with their companies, turned off the road, taking a trail that led to the left, while Company D, under Lieutenant Paddock, remained with the wagon train, which was about one mile to the rear. There was no serious apprehension of an attack, but it was deemed prudent to advance with caution, as the command was approaching a deep canyon, through which the wagons must pass. Lieutenant Cherry was in the advance with a small escort and, while passing over some high ground, discovered the Indians lying in ambush along the ridges that commanded the road. With a quick perception of the situation, he turned and warned the companies, and the men were at once dismounted and deployed as skirmishers. Major Thornburgh and Lieutenant Cherry then rode forward and attempted to communicate with the Utes, but they refused to talk and at once opened a rapid and galling fire upon the troops. It was soon apparent that the exposed position of the troops in the face of an enemy well armed and in superior force was untenable, and the men were directed to retire slowly and effect a junction with Company D, which was protecting the wagon train. The men retired in excellent order, and the enemy, having been foiled in their purpose to ambuscade the command, moved around the left flank beyond carbine range and concentrated on a knoll to the left of and commanding the line of retreat for the purpose of cutting off the companies from the wagon train, which had begun to park on the right bank of Milk Creek. Captain Payne, with a part of his company, charged the knoll and dispersed the enemy, and then retired to the train and adopted measures for its defense. Major Thornburgh started for the train just as Captain Payne made the charge and was shot and instantly killed after crossing the creek, and within 500 yards of the wagons.

The command then devolved upon Captain Payne. The train was parked about two hundred yards from the water. The wagons formed the north side of a corral, elliptical in shape, its long axis running east and west. The south side was exposed to the enemy, who massed in the ravines along the stream and upon the heights, and made a determined effort to captured and destroy the train before the wagons could be placed in a position for defense. A number of wounded animals were led out to the exposed space and shot down, thus making a continuous line of defense and affording a cover for the sharpshooters. The bedding, boxes, and sacks of grain and flour were then taken from the wagons and used for breastworks, and in a short time the train was in as good a state of defense as the means at hand would permit.

In the meantime, Captain Lawson and Lieutenant Cherry, by their superb fighting, had held the enemy in check until this much had been accomplished, when they entered the corral, bringing all the wounded with them. The enemy, having been defeated in their efforts to prevent the concentration of the command and the parking of the train, took advantage of a high wind and set fire to the tall grass and sagebrush down the creek. An agency supply train was encamped within seventy-five yards of the corral and commanded the approach to the water, and Captain Payne, fearing that under cover of the smoke the enemy might make a lodgment in the train, ordered the grass on the north side to be fired, and in a short time the train was in flames. The fire, which had started down the creek, now approached with great rapidity and

Fighting for water. HARPER'S NEW MONTHLY MAGAZINE 1890.

threatened to destroy the exposed part of the corral. The officers and men, at this critical moment, when the enemy made their most furious attack, displayed great courage. Several lives were lost and a number of the men were wounded, but the flames were extinguished and the enemy was again repulsed.

From this time, 3:00 P.M., until midnight, the enemy kept sharpshooters at work, and three-fourths of the animals were killed or so severely wounded that they were killed by the troopers. At dark the enemy charged the corral and delivered volley after volley. They finally retired with a loss of several warriors, who were seen to fall from their ponies. During the night, the dead animals were dragged beyond the corral, a full supply of water for twenty-four hours was secured, Dr. Grimes (wounded)[3] cared for the wounded, and by daybreak the corral was in a good condition for defense. Captain Payne, twice wounded, prepared his dispatches, and at midnight he started couriers to Rawlins, where they arrived on the thirtieth, when news of the disaster first reached the country.

During September 30, the enemy kept up an almost incessant fire and killed all the animals except fourteen mules. They withdrew at midnight and renewed the attack at daybreak. On the morning of October 2, Captain Dodge, with Lieutenant Hughes, thirty-five men of Company D, 9th U.S. Cavalry, and four citizens, rode into the besieged camp after a forced march of twenty-three hours. At Hayden's, on Bear River, a courier informed Captain Dodge of the disaster, and he never drew rein until he rode into the corral just at daybreak. Before dark, thirty-eight of his horses were killed and the others were wounded.

Meanwhile, a movement of troops such as had never been witnessed in the Department of the Platte—if, indeed, in any department—was in progress. The troops fairly leaped to the emergency and, moving from all points with the utmost dispatch, rapidly concentrated at Rawlins, where Colonel Merritt arrived at 5:30 A.M. on October 2 with Companies A, B, I, and M of the 5th Cavalry, and at 11:00 A.M. of the same day, he began, with two squadrons of cavalry and five companies of infantry, what has been appropriately named "a lightning march" of 175 miles to Milk Creek, where he arrived at 5:30 A.M. of October 5, and raised the siege and dispersed the enemy, who retreated through the canyon towards the agency.

Companies D and F, 5th Cavalry, had eight men killed, two officers (Captain Payne and Lieutenant Paddock) and fifteen men wounded, and 110 horses killed. Captain Lawson of the 3rd Cavalry had one man killed and seventeen men wounded, and nearly all his horses killed. The wagonmaster and four civilian employees were killed, as were nearly all the train mules.[4]

The commands encamped at Milk Creek until October 10 (other troops arriving daily, among the number H of the 5th Cavalry), when Companies D and F, with Captains Lawson's and Dodge's companies, moved by easy marches to Rawlins, whence, after a brief delay, they were moved by rail to their respective stations.

This is an exact account of the fight and relief at Milk Creek. I could give a very lengthy description of several personal experiences and name several of the officers and men who displayed much coolness and bravery, but I believe the foregoing facts cover the ground.

The exact reason, as given to the writer, why the Utes objected to the plow turning up the particular stretch of ground indicated by the agent (Meeker) to be worked was because it was the parade ground (so to speak) before the village, and the only open and level space left for the Indians to hold their dances, run their horses, etc. (so said "Ute John"), and although the Indians told Meeker he had no right to take that ground for planting, and gave their reasons, he was so pigheaded he would have his way. The Utes told him that if he plowed that ground, that would put the log chain, or plow chain, around his neck and plow the ground with him (they did so afterward, and pretty thoroughly too); still, he was determined to have his way, and he plowed the ground.

Although I lost many good comrades in the fight, still I cannot believe the Utes [are] altogether to blame for their loss; but Meeker is beyond blame, for all at the agency, fourteen in all, with the exception of the women, were killed.

Rescuing Payne's Command

WESLEY MERRITT[1]

Harper's New Monthly Magazine 80, no. 474 (April 1890): 732–37[2]

On October 1, 1879, the garrison at Fort Russell, Wyoming Territory,[3] was startled by the receipt of telegrams recounting a disaster that had overtaken the command of Major Thornburgh, who was known to be marching to the relief of the white inhabitants of the Ute Indian Agency. In this command, which had been attacked by the Utes, was part of the garrison of Fort Russell.

"Major Thornburgh is killed; Captain Payne and two other officers, including the surgeon of the command, are wounded. The command is surrounded and constantly pressed by the hostiles; fifty men are killed and wounded, and all the horses are killed." These were the fragments of news which dribbled through the wires, all too slowly for the impatient comrades of the small, beleaguered force in the wilds of Colorado. "You will proceed with all available troops in your command to the rescue of Payne and his sorely pressed command," said the dispatch from the commanding general of the department to the officer in command at Fort Russell.

Officers were assembled, and the orders for preparation given. No need to insist on haste; the dead, wounded, and beleaguered were kith and kin to those going to the rescue, endeared by hundreds of associations which make men stick closer than brothers. Each officer went about his work with the coolness and precision of the usual preparation for a routine service, though there were decision and promptitude which told of the serious work ahead.

In four hours from the time the news first reached Fort Russell, all the troops of cavalry, with their horses and equipments, for which there was transportation by rail, were on the cars and running as fast as steam could carry them toward Rawlins, a point two hundred miles distant on the Union Pacific Railroad, from which the march was to commence across the country to the scene of disaster.

By daylight on the following morning (October 2), a force of about 200 cavalry and less than 150 infantry had collected at Rawlins Station. The move to the relief of Payne and his command must be made as soon as sufficient force was collected. Payne had reported he was sorely pressed by the Indians on every side and had many wounded, among the rest, the medical officer. His supplies were sufficient to last for five days from September 29. The way to the scene of disaster was long, and succor must arrive in three days of the time still left for the troops at Rawlins. Other troops were being hurried forward, but they could not reach the railroad starting point for a day or two at least. Rumors were current that the Southern Utes had broken out, which would increase greatly the strength of the hostiles. The greater their strength, the less time remained for saving the shattered and maimed command. Even then the Ute Indians on the warpath had been largely augmented by the malcontents from kindred bands and were making every effort to destroy the weak remnant of Thornburgh's command.

In anticipation of the fewness of the available cavalry for the rescue, and with knowledge that no infantry unassisted could make the march in time to be of service, light wagons, with as good teams as the country could afford, had been ordered collected from the country around Rawlins, in which to transport the infantry. This was all done, and the supplies of every kind transferred to wagons and pack trains, so that the command marched out from Rawlins at eleven o'clock on the morning of October 2. There was a distance of 170 miles to be traversed before the fate of the besieged command could be determined.

The march was a case for calculation and judgment. A single dash of fifty or even seventy-five miles can be made by horses, as racing men say, on a breath, but at the end of this greatest distance, still a hundred more miles were left to be accomplished. Too much haste at first, wearing out the horses, would leave the command afoot and helpless. Would the command reach its destination in time was the one absorbing thought in the mind of every officer and trooper in the column.

It is difficult for one who has never marched on the plains to form a conception of the tedium and seeming slowness of the progress. The cavalry command scouting after Indians will see the landmarks, apparently a few miles off, made so by the clear atmosphere of the plains, stand out as though one could walk to them in a few hours, remain during days of marching in the same places and with the same appearance. Were it not that nearer objects conveyed the fact of distance gained, one might easily imagine that he was journeying in a land where the efforts at motion were nullified by the sorcerer's art, and progress was impossible. And if this is so when a usual march is being made, who can tell the exasperation at the want of apparent progress on the road the rate of travel on which means life or death to those whom it is one's duty to save! At the end of the first ten hours from the start, the relieving column had accomplished about forty-five miles. Everything was brought up, and the command was still in good condition. Here a halt was made till dawn of day, at break of which the onward march was resumed.

Let us now, while still marching forward, recall, as was done by everyone in the rescuing column hundreds of times, what had occurred to Thornburgh's command. Ten days before the news of his disaster reached Fort Russell,

Major Thornburgh left Rawlins Station with a force of cavalry and infantry to protect the agency and its white inhabitants from the Indians they were there to feed and instruct. The Indians had grown restless under the efforts of the agent to teach them farming and the other industries of the whites, and the agent became anxious for the safety of his family and himself. Thornburgh moved leisurely through the country, making convenient camps after usual marches, without molestation, and not until the sixth day were any Indians seen. In the camp, after it was established on this day, several Ute Indians of prominence visited Major Thornburgh in the afternoon, talked freely and pleasantly with him and his officers, and departed about nightfall, apparently in a most friendly mood. This was more than a hundred miles from the agency. After this, Thornburgh pursued his march without incident. On the morning of September 29, while his command was separated by a short distance, he came on the Utes in strong force near a pass in the mountains which bounded their reservation. Their attitude was extremely hostile. While incredulous of their intent to fight, he took the precaution to deploy the part of the command with him, at the same time by signs trying to open communication with the Indians. His over-tures were met by a volley from the Indians, which was at once replied to by the troops, the skirmish line being slowly withdrawn to connect with the rest of the command and to protect the wagons.

In battle, Indians always send warriors to the flanks and to the rear of the force with which they fight. This they do without reference to the strength of the enemy. It has therefore passed into a proverb that "there is no rear" in an Indian engagement. The Utes pursued these tactics with Thornburgh's com-mand, in the meantime violently engaging his skirmishers in front. While con-centrating his command, and when a few hundred yards from the wagons, Thornburgh was killed. The command was united at the wagons, and sur-rounded by the hostiles, hurried measures were taken for defense, the fighting on each side being continued with desperation. The wagons were formed in an irregular circle, and the contents, together with the dead animals which had fallen nearby, were used in constructing a sort of defensive work. Within this ghastly protection, the wounded men were conveyed, and soon, with the implements in the wagons, a circular rifle pit was constructed. And now a new danger threatened. A high wind arose soon after the commencement of the attack, and the Indians fired the dry grass and brush to the windward of the wagons, and taking advantage of the smoke and fire, made a furious attack in the hope of burning the defenders out. This was a terrible danger, but with coolness and courage, the troops combated the flames, and it was not long before their fury was expended. Later in the day, the Utes made a violent onslaught on the breastworks, but being repulsed, settled down to watch their prey in the hope that starvation or lack of water would finish the work.

During the night, the means of defense were strengthened, and water was obtained by force from the stream nearby for the famishing wounded and suf-fering defenders. Couriers were also sent out into the darkness in different

Utes watching for the relief column.
CENTURY MAGAZINE 1891.

directions with the hope that the distressful condition of the command could be made known and relief hurried to them. The couriers succeeded in passing out and carried the news that started the relief command from Fort Russell.

On the last day of September, and for four days in October, the command contended with the Indians, repulsing attacks made from time to time, answering shot with shot and taunt with taunt—for many of the Utes spoke English. Each night the defensive works were strengthened; and each day defended against renewed attacks. A deep, square pit was dug in the interior of the circle, in which the wounded were made comfortable, the medical officer, though wounded himself, dressing the wounds of those most needing attention. At night also, armed parties sent out for water succeeded in bringing in a supply, though at times meeting resistance and fighting for what was obtained. In this way, the time for five long days and nights was occupied, who can tell with what anxieties, gloomy forebodings, and doubting hopes!

In the meantime, the rescuing force was losing no time. Without drawing rein, save for a needed rest at intervals to conserve strength for the whole of the work, the command pressed on with unflagging energy, marching with advance guard, and at times flankers, to prevent the possibility of ambuscade

Tidings of the relief column; listening to officers' call.
CENTURY MAGAZINE 1891.

or surprise. The country was quiet, and no signs of Indians were discovered. A halt was made on the second night, after completion of little less than two thirds of the whole distance to be accomplished.

At dawn the morning of October 4, the march was resumed. The unfinished distance must be completed by the following dawn. About one hundred miles had already been accomplished in twenty-three marching hours. More than seventy miles, to be marched over in daylight and darkness, in the next twenty-four hours, was before the command. This would require little less, if all went well, than twenty hours' constant marching.

In these days of rapid transit, it is not easy for people to bring their ideas of travel down to the rate of march of a cavalry column. This, if long distances are marched, cannot safely exceed, including halts for rest, four miles per hour. A single horseman can do more than this, for he can regulate the rate according to the road, and he has not the dust and crowding of a mass of cavalry horses on a narrow road to contend with. Besides, the single horseman provides himself with the best of horses, while the march of a cavalry column must be regulated to meet the abilities of the least enduring animal. All these elements entered into the calculation of the march of the rescuing force. It must make the march, and that, too, with undiminished numbers.

On this day's march, several settlers were met by the command, fleeing for safety, and rumors of murders and depredations by the Indians were received from all quarters, At one point, the head of the column was approached by an excited party asking medical assistance, who led the medical officer to a wagon in which a citizen was lying on an improvised bed, who was an unsightly mass of wounds and had been left by the Indians for dead. His companion had been killed. When it was discovered that the wagon body in which he lay was nearly half full of loose cartridges, in which he had been trading with the Indians, sympathy for him was greatly diminished.

As night came on, the difficulties of marching were much increased by the darkness and rough roads. From time to time, halts had to be made and staff officers sent to the rear to direct the column in the darkness and see that all kept well closed. After a seemingly interminable season of marching by the uncertain light of a waning moon, in which objects were dimly defined and always distorted, the hour indicated to the weary though watchful horsemen that they were approaching the scene of the conflict. Not a sound broke the stillness of the chilly night save the steady tramp of the horses and the rattle and jingle of the equipments of the men. The infantry part of the command, owing to the darkness and difficulties of travel, had fallen behind. A blackened heap of ashes on the highway, with fragments of iron and chains and pieces of harness and rubbish, marked where a train loaded with stores for the agency had been burnt, and further on, the bodies of the slaughtered trainmen, with distorted features and staring eyes, told all too plainly of their short run for life—of the mercy they had pled for, and how their prayers had been answered by the merciless foe. These were not cheering omens. Had Payne and his men shared a like fate? No one had come to tell. But it would soon be known.

"It can't be far from here," said the guide for the third time, as the command was brought to a halt, and everyone strained eyes and ears for a sight of the surrounding country or a sound from the front. A bugler with his trumpet ready was close at hand to sound the call known as "officers' call" in the cavalry, a certain sign of recognition, that there might be no collision with friends who, hearing the tramp of horses, might mistake the force for foes. Presently the guide satisfied himself that the command was near the place, and the clear notes of the trumpet awakened the echoes of the night.

Captain Payne, in recounting the event, says: "Believing it just possible for help to reach us next morning, I directed one of my trumpeters to be on the alert for the expected signal. And so it was: just as the first gray of the dawn appeared, our listening ears caught the sound of officers' call breaking the silence of the morning, and filling the valley with the sweetest music we had ever heard. Joyously the reply rang out from our corral, and the men, rushing from their rifle pits, made the welkin ring with their glad cheers."

Besieged by the Utes

EDWIN V. SUMNER[1]

Century Magazine 42, no. 6 (October 1891): 837–47

In the summer of 1879, trouble occurred between the White River Utes and their agent, N. C. Meeker. The cause is not important, but the trouble finally became serious enough to warrant the call upon the secretary of war for the support of troops to repress turbulence and disorder amongst the Indians of that nation.

In September an expedition was organized in the Department of the Platte, and the following troops were ordered out: one company of the 4th Infantry under Lt. Butler D. Price[2]; Troop E, 3rd Cavalry, Captain Lawson commanding; and two troops, D (Lt. J. V. S. Paddock) and F (Capt. J. S. Payne), of the 5th Cavalry. Maj. T. T. Thornburgh, 4th Infantry, commanded the whole, and Acting Assistant Surgeon Grimes was the medical officer.

This command was concentrated at Fort Steele, Wyoming, on the Union Pacific Railroad, and marched south from that point towards White River agency about September 21. Nothing of an unusual character occurred during the first few days of the march, nor was it supposed that anything of a serious nature would happen. The agent had asked for one hundred soldiers, and more than double that number were in this column. The troops were en route to a certain point to preserve order, not expecting to make war. The Utes understood that, and the very evening preceding their attack upon the troops, the chiefs entered the soldiers' camp, partook of their hospitality, and assured them of their friendship. The report of General Crook says, "The last message Meeker ever sent to Thornburgh was to the effect that the Indians were friendly and were flying the United States flag. Yet in the face of all this, the very next morning these Indians, without provocation, treacherously lay in ambuscade and attacked the troops with the result already known." This, General Crook says, is not war, it is murder; and the general, as usual, is correct. But is it not strange that with all the horrible examples furnished us in past years, we have never been in the habit of preparing for murder as well as war? It seems at least unfortunate that all our Indian wars must of necessity be inaugurated with the massacre or defeat of the first detachment. It may be interesting, if not instructive, to give a few examples.

The Modoc War of 1872, in which so many valuable lives were lost, was begun by the advance of half a troop of the 1st Cavalry. This force rode up to the Indian camp, dismounted, and were standing to horse, with probably no thought of being murdered or of any serious trouble. It is reported that while the officer in command was talking to the chief, a rifle was discharged by an Indian, either accidentally or as a signal, and that instantly thereafter, firing on the troops took place and a number were killed and wounded. The Indians, about sixty in number, taking advantage of the confusion among the troops, retired to their stronghold in the Lava Beds, murdering every white man en route. In this stronghold, they defied the government, massacred a commission composed of prominent men sent to them in peace, and withstood the attacks of 1,300 soldiers for months, and until both food and water gave out.

The Nez Perce War in 1877 commenced in about the same way. Two small troops of cavalry, marching down a deep and long canyon, presented themselves before the camp of Chief Joseph, as if a display of this nature was all that was necessary to capture a force of two hundred fifty warriors. The Indian, always quick to see an advantage and to profit by it, was not slow in this instance, and the first few shots from the enemy on the left and rear of the line caused a hasty retreat of the soldiers, who no doubt up to that time thought there was to be nothing serious. The Little Bighorn fight in 1876, where Colonel Custer and most of his command were massacred, was surely the result of overestimating one's strength and underrating that of the enemy.

Other examples could be furnished, but are not these, with their attendant losses and failures, sufficient to prove that with the Indian as a foe we must always be prepared, and especially careful when he seems most friendly and still holds onto his rifle? On the other hand, many instances are known where troops have met and overcome at the start more serious obstacles than those mentioned above, and without a shot being fired. A column on the march, prepared to fight if necessary, is not likely to be disturbed, and it is almost certain that no Indians will be seen or heard from unless they have all the advantages, and unless certainty of success follows their efforts.

This Ute campaign was a repetition of all the other sad occurrences in Indian warfare. Major Thornburgh, the commander, as noble and brave a man as ever marched with troops, fell as others had, having ignored an enemy in the morning who had the power to defeat him before noon. The march through these mountains and into the valley of Milk River, as described, was made, as any march would be conducted, on a turnpike through a civilized country and among friends. No danger had threatened; on the contrary, the Indians appeared friendly, and assuring messages had been received from the agent.

Thornburgh, not having had experience with Indians and trusting to appearances, anticipated no trouble, and consequently was wholly unprepared when the attack was made. We can in a measure account for such action on the part of a commander when it is remembered that with some men, the desire to appear before their troops free from undue anxiety is greater than their sense of caution. Considering the number of troops in this command, and the fact that not half that number of Indians were opposed to them, it is fair to presume that with proper precaution, the command might have gone through to the agency without losing a life or even hearing a shot; but the officers and men following Thornburgh doubtless, like him, had no thought of danger to such a column; and had the major made sufficient preparation to secure his command, and reached his destination safely on that account, he would have been pronounced an "old granny" for having unduly harassed his troops when no enemy appeared.

The employment of the chiefs, ostensibly as guides, but really detaining them as hostages, would have insured the peace as well as the safety of the command beyond a doubt.

But to go more into details: Thornburgh, after leaving his infantry company at a supply camp, pushed on with his three troops of cavalry, and while on the march, on September 29 at 10:00 A.M., at the crossing of Milk River, the Indians opened fire on the column from all directions, and from what followed, it would appear that the command was completely surprised, or sufficiently so to make some confusion among the troops. F Troop, 5th Cavalry, and E Troop, 3rd Cavalry, were quickly brought into line and for some time fought well and bravely, but the superior tactics of the Indian, in his usual role of turning the flanks, and the loss of many brave men, including the commander, soon caused a retreat, and these two troops fell back perhaps half a mile to a point where Lieutenant Paddock, in command of D Troop, 5th Cavalry, and the wagon train, had corralled his train, formed his troop, and was prepared to receive and shelter his comrades. It is not known what orders Lieutenant Paddock had from his commanding officer as to his duties with the rear guard and wagon train, but it is supposed that as no precautions were being taken in front, none were ordered in rear, so that the prompt action of this young officer in arranging his wagon train and troops for a stand, and holding every man to his duty there, was praiseworthy, and was the means of saving many lives. This afforded shelter and a rallying place for the scattered troopers, then being outflanked and driven back by the enemy; indeed, Paddock's command was even receiving attention from the Indians in the way of rifle balls, for the Indians knew if they could get the train, they could capture or kill the rest of the command before it could escape from the valley. Here there was a halting place, and the whole command was concentrated behind and about the wagons. The Indians then surrounded the soldiers, fired upon them from all directions, and setting fire to the grass, advanced to within a short distance of the wagons, being screened by the thick smoke from the fire of the troops.

In this situation, the battle was carried on for the rest of that day, the troops being strictly on the defensive and keeping behind the wagons, while the Indians, lying close to the ground and concealed as much as possible, were able to kill most of the animals and occasionally to pick off a soldier or teamster.

The loss of the animals and the number of wounded men to be cared for and protected made any movement from this spot out of the question. There was nothing to do then but fight it out and hold on until reinforcements could reach them. However, the longest day must have an end, and the sun aided these harassed soldiers by disappearing behind the hills and affording them, under cover of darkness, an opportunity to prepare for the morrow. This first night was employed by the troops in building a breastwork near the water and in caring for the wounded.

There being no timber within reach, shelter had to be constructed from such material as was at hand. The wagons were unloaded and spare parts used, bundles of bedding, sacks of grain, cracker boxes, and bacon sides were piled up, but this not being sufficient, the bodies of dead horses and mules were dragged to the line and made use of for defense. A pit was sunk in the center of the square, and in this hole in the ground the surgeon placed his wounded, himself being one of the unfortunates. This, then, was the situation of a command of able-bodied, well-equipped soldiers, strong men every one, which, a few hours previously, had struck its camp and marched in all confidence into this valley of death. Where were now the flaunting guidons and the rude jokes about cowardly redskins? Instead thereof, many were mourning the sudden taking away of beloved comrades, whose bodies were left on the plain to the savage enemy, and all bemoaned the fate of their noble commander, also left on the field. He had proudly led them forward, and when the unlooked-for attack fell upon them, still kept at the front; perhaps, having recognized too late the error of overconfidence, he determined to repair the fault even at the sacrifice of his life.

Thornburgh was a noble man, and beloved by all. The troops following him were as good as any in the army, and would have proved more than a match for the enemy if they could have gone into the fight on anything like equal terms.

After dark on this first night, a volunteer was called for to take one of the horses yet left alive and, if possible, steal his way through the enemy's line to the nearest telegraph station. From several volunteers, Corporal Murphy of D Troop, 5th Cavalry, was selected to take this desperate ride, and he accomplished the distance of 170 miles to the railroad in less than 24 hours.[3]

The place selected, or rather, forced upon Captain Payne, 5th Cavalry, now the senior officer, for the defense of his command, was near the battlefield, and fortunately within reach of the stream called Milk River. It was in a small, round valley or opening in the mountains, and within easy rifle range of the tops of the nearest hills surrounding it. On these hills the Indians took position, and while being concealed and well protected themselves, the Indians were able to pick off any soldier showing himself above the breastwork, or while moving about inside of it. The soldiers returned the fire occasionally, but

Blowing officers' call. CENTURY MAGAZINE 1891.

it is not known that an Indian was injured during the siege. The enemy, however, was kept down close behind the ridge, and no advance or open attack on
the entrenchment was at any time attempted. The position taken was on a rise
or table, and was about 200 yards from the stream. No water could be obtained
during the day, but after dark a party started out to fill their buckets and canteens. They were almost immediately fired upon by the enemy, who, anticipating their necessities, had found concealment on the further side of the river in
the thick underbrush. As some of the party were wounded, they returned to the
breastwork unsuccessful. Water being an absolute necessity, even if it *cost* life,
another party was sent out, this time under escort of armed men. As soon as
the party was fired upon, the escort discharged their guns, and although firing in
the dark and at random, it is supposed that one or more of the enemy were
wounded; at any rate, the Indians fled, and the troops were not prevented after
that from getting water that night sufficient for the next day.

With the dawn of the second day commenced the firing upon the troops
from the hilltops. Not an Indian could be seen on whom to return the fire; only
a puff of white smoke indicated from time to time where the bullet came from;
and as there was little chance of finding the Indian at the spot from which he
had fired, there seemed to be no use wasting ammunition on space, and firing
by the troops was kept up only to prevent open attack.

On this day nearly all the animals remaining alive were easily disposed
of by the enemy, and some men were killed and wounded. Among the latter
were Lieutenant Paddock and Surgeon Grimes. The long, weary hours of this
day must have been trying indeed to the besieged. The suffering and groans of
the wounded seemed more terrible than the sight of the bodies of the dead,

which could not be removed except at the expense of other lives. It is said that after night, these bodies became part of the breastwork and were used to protect the living.

Exciting accounts have been published of the situation of a party of our countrymen held fast by the ice of the frozen north. It may be said that they had rations, were comparatively comfortable, and had only to wait for a return of the sun to thaw their prison doors and set them free. But these soldiers, although nearer home, were brought to a stand where a life was called for at every crack of the rifle, and where to them the light of day was the season of distress. From the number of lives already lost in this short time, and the number of wounded requiring care and increasing the anxiety, and considering the time that must elapse before help could possibly reach them, an hour here contained more real suffering than could be felt in many days of waiting only for the sun to shine.

Aside from being constantly harassed by the enemy from the outside, an incident occurred on the inside of the works this day that came near finishing the lives of some of the wounded. One of the horses was shot in such a manner as to make him frantic and unmanageable. He charged about the enclosure in a furious way until exhausted, and then fell into the pit among the wounded. Fortunately no one was injured, but some of the men said that in their nervous condition they thought the whole Ute nation had jumped from the tops of the hills to the bottom of the pit.

At an early hour on the morning of October 2, the sentinel heard the approach of a column of horsemen, and the besieged soon welcomed Captain Dodge, 9th Cavalry, at the head of his troop. The captain, having heard of the situation, came at once to the assistance of his comrades, and managed to get through to the entrenchment without losing any of his men. This reinforcement of two officers and fifty enlisted men added materially to the fighting strength of the command, and they brought with them also the cheering news that the courier had passed through safely. The horses upon which this party rode were soon disposed of by the enemy, and Dodge and his troop became as much of a fixture as any of the besieged. The gallant dash made by these colored troopers brought them into high favor with the rest of the command, and nothing was considered too good for the "Buffalo Soldiers" after that. Captain Dodge almost immediately received well-merited promotion and was the hero of the campaign.

Leaving the besieged to worry through the days and nights that are to pass before relief can reach them, we will go with the swiftly riding courier and see what follows his arrival at the railroad.

On the morning of October 1, our quiet garrison at Fort D. A. Russell, near Cheyenne, Wyoming, was aroused by the information received from department headquarters that Thornburgh and most of his command had been massacred by the Ute Indians, and that the few officers and men remaining were entrenched, protecting the wounded and fighting for their lives. The com-

manding officer, Col. Wesley Merritt, fortunately possessing all the characteristics of a true cavalryman, always had his command well in hand. At this
time, he had four troops of the 5th Cavalry and one company of the 4th
Infantry, and when this sudden call reached him, all that was necessary was to
sound "Boots and Saddles" and go.

The order to take the field reached us about 8:00 A.M., and at 11:00 A.M.
we had saddled up, had marched two miles, and were loaded on the cars—
horses, equipments, pack mules, rations, and all—and were under way. We
reached Rawlins Station, our stopping place, about 1:00 A.M. next morning,
and met there four companies of the 4th Infantry, also ordered for field service
under Colonel Merritt. The rest of that night was spent in preparing for the
march. The infantry, in wagons, were on the road by 10:00 A.M.; the cavalry
marched a little later, but overtook the infantry about twenty-five miles out at
5:00 P.M. Then all pushed on together until 11:00 P.M., when it became necessary to halt and rest the animals. At 7:00 A.M. we were on the road again and
continued marching until 11:00 P.M., at that time reaching the camp of the
infantry company left behind by Major Thornburgh. Here a short rest was
taken, and at dawn of day we resumed the march, reaching the entrance to Big
Bear Canyon about 4:00 P.M. This was a rough, ugly-looking place to enter
with a command at night, especially with the knowledge of disaster in front
and not far off. But the situation called for the greatest exertion, as well as the
taking of all the chances, and although we had already made an unheard-of
march that day, and on previous days, every man was anxious to go on, and
even the animals seemed to be under the influence of the hour. While they
were being rubbed down and fed, the men had their coffee and hardtack, and
just at dusk we started off for the last march, hoping soon to reach those we
knew to be in distress, and who could only be saved by our coming. Getting
through that canyon at night was a desperate undertaking, leaving the Indians
entirely out of the question, and on looking at the breakneck places afterwards
by daylight, over which we had passed, it seemed a miracle that we succeeded
in getting through without losing all the wagons carrying the infantry, and
some of the horsemen as well.

The cavalry was in the lead, but the "charioteers," as the infantry were
called, followed close behind, and on the downgrade occasionally ran into the
rear of the cavalry column. On the ascent, the infantrymen jumped from their
wagons and pushed horses, wagons, and all up the grades. On reaching the
summit, each party boarded its wagon, and with a cheer, away they went down
the grade on the run. All were under so much of a strain that fatigue or sleep
was not thought of. Thus it was, up one hill and down another all night, and no
light artillerymen were ever more expert at mounting their limbers than these
infantrymen in getting out of and into those wagons on the run.

Between 4:00 and 5:00 A.M., we reached a point about four miles from the
entrenchment, and at that hour saw a sight that made the blood run cold. A citizen wagon train, hauling supplies to the agency, had been captured by the

Indians, and every man belonging to it had been murdered, stripped, and partly burned.[4] As we had had no news from the front since leaving the railroad, this was something of a surprise, and as may be imagined, at that hour in the morning, not a pleasant opening for the day. The wagon train, for the last few miles, had been stretching out a little, but on reaching this spot, it was observed that all intervals were rapidly closed up and kept closed. But notwithstanding this depressing sight, some rude jokes were made, as usual, by the old soldiers in passing, and recruits were made to fear that before another sun should rise, they would be broiled in like manner.

Colonel Merritt at this time was some distance ahead with the cavalry, and crossing the last hill, he entered the valley just at dawn of day. It was yet too dark to see the entrenchment, but the column, while pressing on, was soon brought to a halt by a challenge from the besieged. A trumpeter was then summoned and officers' call sounded. This brought all hands to the top of the breastwork, and a lively cheer answered the last note on the trumpet. A wild scene followed this coming together of old comrades, and while it was going on, the enemy, although at their posts within easy range, did not fire a shot. Nor did they seem to be alarmed by the arrival of this overpowering force, but were for the time being quiet spectators of this grand reunion, their portion of the fun probably being in the supposition of "more horses, more shoot him."

The colonel, having the responsibility, was probably the only one of the party in accord with the Indian idea, and consequently, not wasting much time on congratulations, he immediately set to work to prevent the loss of more men or horses. The rear was safe in the hands of the infantry, and the cavalry was ordered to take the nearest hills on the flanks. This accomplished, the colonel moved out a short distance to the front, having a troop of cavalry as escort, but did not advance half a mile before being fired upon. We, however, recovered the body of Major Thornburgh, which up to that time had lain upon the battle-field of the first day. Under existing circumstances, a civilized enemy, or such a one as we are taught to fight in textbooks and in field maneuvers, would have made a hasty retreat over the mountains, and any strategist in command could have made certain calculations, but these Ute Indians, instinctively brave and not at all instructed, had the utmost confidence in their power to resist any number of soldiers attacking them in their mountain homes.

The Sioux Indian, on the open plains, likes to show himself as much as possible, thinks to intimidate his foe by such display and, by showing himself in different points in a short space of time, to make several Sioux out of one. On the contrary, the whereabouts of the Ute Indians amongst the rocks of mountainside, nearly his own color, cannot easily be discovered; he is not known until the crack of his rifle is heard and his enemy falls, and even then the smoke covers a change of position. It is therefore impossible ever to get a Ute out on the plains for the same purpose.

Colonel Merritt, on seeing that the Indians were still determined and prepared to dispute any advance on the part of the soldiers, ordered three troops of cavalry and all the infantry deployed to the front at once. Notwithstanding the fatigue of the long march and no breakfast, the men sprang to their feet and moved forward as if for the first time that day. Quite an exciting skirmish resulted from this advance, and the enemy went dancing round on the hilltops like monkeys under the short-range fire of the cavalry carbines; but when the infantry battalion, which had deployed behind the crest, came up to the top and opened fire, a change of scene was at once perceptible. The first volley from the infantry rifles made a rolling sound through the mountains like artillery; the Utes ceased the ballet performance and disappeared behind the hill, but still kept up their fire on both infantry and cavalry. The troops, however, adopting the Ute tactics, kept quite well sheltered, and as it was not the intention to advance further that day, everybody being worn out, the tired soldiers actually went to sleep on the line of battle, a few men being on the lookout and firing occasionally.

About noon there seemed to be some excitement going on among the Indians, and a large white flag was displayed to view. Field glasses were at once brought to bear, and it was discovered that a white man was waving the flag. Firing on both sides ceased, and the bearer of the flag was allowed to cross the valley and enter our lines. He proved to be an employee of the Indian Department and had been sent up from the Uncompahgre agency to stop the war,[5] the White River Utes with whom we were fighting being in a way under the control of Colorow, the chief of the Uncompahgres. It is supposed the Indians were ready to stop anyhow, seeing the amount of force now on the ground and prepared to punish them.

This virtually raised the siege and ended the war. Leaving a light picket line to watch the enemy, the rest of the troops were withdrawn and marched back to the entrenchment, where a jollification was now in order. The wounded were taken out of the loathsome place where they had suffered so many days, and made comfortable. Those who had not been able to wash since the first day's fight now made themselves more presentable and showed their true faces.

The fearful stench from the entrenchment, owing to the material used in its construction, was such as to necessitate a change of camp, and the whole command, accompanied now by the rescued party, moved back on the road about one mile, to clean ground and plenty of pure water.

An unconquerable desire to sleep and rest then overtook these worn-out soldiers. All forms and ceremonies for the rest of that day were dispensed with, and the valley, lately ringing with the sound of men in combat, was now as quiet and still as was its wont. In this short campaign, there were 13 men killed and 48 wounded, out of a command 150 strong. The papers throughout the country mentioned it for a day or two as "the Ute affair," and there it rests, being one of several instances where the percentage of loss is greater than that experienced in battles of which monuments are being erected and elaborate memorials published to commemorate deeds of bravery.

After the command brought down by Colonel Merritt had been well rested and was ready for another advance, it proceeded through the mountains to White River and the agency. It was a beautiful bright morning in October when we bade good-bye to the rescued command under Captain Payne, whose faces were turned towards home, while we marched south to rescue the employees at the agency. The infantry and wagon train marched on the road, while the cavalry were well out on the flanks and in advance. The white horses of B Troop, 5th Cavalry, could be seen now and then winding along the crests of the hills on one side, while the blacks of A Troop kept pace with them on the other. No attack could have been made on that column without due warning, and the result was we crossed the high hills and wound through canyon after canyon, reaching the valley of White River and the agency without hearing a shot or, to my knowledge, seeing an Indian.

At the agency, a horrible sight presented itself. Every building had been burned, the bodies of all the male employees were stretched upon the ground where they had been murdered a few days before, and the women had been carried off into a captivity worse than death. After the dead had been buried, the command went into camp on White River.

The Indians had taken to the mountains, and in order to follow them, it was necessary to abandon wagon transportation and fit up pack trains. While these preparations were going on, we had still another sad experience, and a reminder that the Utes were still near us and relentless enough to take any advantage presenting itself. A party under Lieutenant Hall,[6] regimental quartermaster was sent out to reconnoiter and look for a trail across the mountains from White River to Grand River. With this party was Lt. William Bayard Weir[7] of the Ordnance Department, and his sergeant, [Paul] Humme. Weir went out as a volunteer to accompany Hall and to hunt. As the party were riding along on the trail, a small herd of deer was discovered off to the left in a ravine. Weir and Humme went after them, while Hall kept on to the front. He had not gone far, however, before he saw fresh Indian signs, and soon afterwards heard sharp firing to his left and rear. On turning back to ascertain the cause and to help Weir if he should be in trouble, he was fired upon himself, and discovered that he was surrounded by Indians. He covered his party as quickly as possible in the dry bed of a stream near at hand, and kept the Indians off until after dark. Then riding into camp, he first discovered that Weir had not come in, and reported that he was probably killed. The battalion of the 5th Cavalry was turned out at once, and as it was 10:00 P.M., we had an all-night march ahead of us. Just at dawn, we reached the place where Weir had left Hall, and we took his trail and followed it up until we found his dead body lying cold and stiff on the mountainside. This seemed indeed an unnecessary sacrifice. Weir was a noble fellow, beloved by all, and the gathering of that sorrowing crowd of soldiers about his body was a sad experience even to the oldest of them. His face still bore the familiar and kindly expression we knew so

Infantry covering the withdrawal of cavalry. CENTURY MAGAZINE 1891.

well. An overcoat was wrapped around the body, and it was then strapped on a cavalry horse. We returned to camp as sad a funeral procession as one could well imagine.

The country through which we were then operating was a howling wilderness; it is now traversed by railroads and covered with villages and farms. Children at play unwittingly trample the grass over the graves of soldiers who gave their lives that they might live and thrive, and communities throughout the West generally send representatives to Congress, some of whom, in the peace and plenty of their comfortable homes, fail to recognize in Washington the hardships, privations, and sacrifice of life suffered by the army before their prosperity could be possible or the lives of their constituents assured. In this the simple duty of soldiers was performed, and no credit is claimed, but should not the record of past deeds such as these, accompanied by the prosperity that has followed, at least guarantee a more generous feeling for the army by all citizens, more especially by those who are called upon to support it?

The White River Campaign

LEWIS D. GREENE[1]

Order of Indian Wars Collection, U.S. Army Military History Institute,
Carlisle Barracks, Pennsylvania

Fort Snelling, Minnesota, still stands on the bluff looking down on the Father of Waters as it stood for over one hundred years, and in 1879, it was the home station of the 7th Infantry.

The afternoon of October 1, 1879, was one of peace and hazy autumnal sunshine until about 4:00 P.M., when the rattle of drums sounding the "long roll" abolished the first of these conditions. (The bugle had not superseded the drum at this time.) Officers and enlisted men came running; companies were formed promptly; all were asking, "Where is the fire? What's the row?" but all were equally ignorant as to the cause of the alarm.

In a few minutes came orders from the post commander to pack for field service: "Each man will wear a full cartridge belt and carry three days' travel rations, overcoat, blanket, and change of underwear. Ten days' field rations and one hundred rounds of rifle ammunition will be packed with tentage and field cooking outfits. All officers and men will hold themselves in readiness to fall in on ten minutes' notice." Several officers and men of the regiment were on pass in St. Paul and Minneapolis respectively six and seven miles north of the fort. The chiefs of police in each of those cities were wired to notify all officers and men who could be found to return to the post at once.

The quartermaster at St. Paul had been ordered to provide transportation for the expedition, and an hour or so later, a long troop train had arrived on the siding below the precipitous bluffs on which stood the Martello Tower, forming the easterly angle of the old walled fort.

By 6:00 P.M. all but about half a dozen of the strays had been rounded up. The companies were formed with full field service equipment, which, beside the rifle and full cartridge belt, included a haversack containing cooked rations for the journey; coffee was ordered by wire from conveniently located station restaurants, a shoulder roll made by each man spreading his blanket and rolling therein a change of underclothing, simple toilet articles, and the overcoat. The experienced old-timer carries less than the new man. He had learned by the ache-and-blister experience system to travel light. The rookie, ignorant of the game, frequently overloads himself and suffers therefore, but he quickly learns to cut out every ounce in excess of what his marching, camping, fighting, and eating make necessary, not merely desirable.

Occasionally the rookie takes along a book or two to pass the evenings pleasantly in camp. It has been noticed, however, that visitors to an abandoned first-night camp of a marching organization are frequently able to collect the beginnings of extensive private libraries from the abandoned books and magazines. Blistered feet, lame shoulders, and aching muscles seem not to synchronize with literary habits on campaign. Reading matter after the first day seems to be limited to that carried by the other fellow. There is no doubt that the human military animal often envies the professional pack mule; the latter has a much thicker hide and twice as many legs on which to distribute the load.

Again the drums followed hurried farewells with weeping women and children; again the bugle, "Attention," then "Fours right—March!" (The command "Squads right" had not yet arrived.) The six companies swung into column,[2] marched down the hill, boarded the train and off we rolled.

From the Omaha papers next morning, we learned the cause of the sudden call. It appeared that there had been unrest at the White River Indian Agency in Colorado for some time. The agent, Mr. Meeker, a most conscientious man, was filled with a desire to civilize the Indians. He tried by various means to wean them away from their wild customs, but they would have none of it; they resented his efforts to make them quit their nomadic habits and take an interest in schools and farming, occupations which, from their viewpoints, were degrading to a warrior.

The Indians finally became so impudent and surly that the agent sent word to the commanding officer at Fort Fred Steele, the nearest military post on the Union Pacific, sixteen miles east of Rawlins, Wyoming Territory, asking that a military force be sent to exercise a quieting influence on his charges. As a result of this request, the commanding general at department headquarters in Omaha ordered Companies D and F, 5th Cavalry, and E, 3rd Cavalry (at this time the word "company" applied to both mounted and foot troop units), under command of Major Thornburgh, to proceed to the White River agency and by their presence suggest a more pacific attitude on the part of the Indians. A few days before this, a subchief known as Johnson had viciously assaulted Agent Meeker on some trivial pretext and had beaten him so severely that Mr. Meeker was disabled for several days. This affair occurred in the presence of a small mob of other Indians, who laughed and jeered at the agent, showing their entire lack of respect and rebellious attitude.[3]

In accordance with his orders, Major Thornburgh took the field. On September 28, he had gone into camp near the northern boundary of the White River reservation. Then the head chief of the White River Utes, Colorow, with several minor chiefs, called on him most formally arrayed in their full dress paint and feathers. They were duly welcomed by Major Thornburgh, and the meeting resolved itself into a most dignified function, governed by the native

Infantry on the march.
RUFUS F. ZOGBAUM, *HORSE,*
FOOT, AND DRAGOONS.

rules of procedure, as formal as those of a European court. After the several preliminary formalities, Colorow asked Major Thornburgh the reason for his visit; the latter replied that he was on his way to the agency to call on the agent and the chiefs to discuss matters of mutual interest.

Colorow replied with proper gravity, expressing the high regard that he and his people had for the major and his people, but suggested that it would be wiser not to bring so many soldiers upon the reservation, as his people would not understand it and would be alarmed and disturbed. The major replied in polite phrase, assuring his visitors of his utmost friendliness, and the meeting came to an end, the Indians leaving with great formality.

Although I cannot vouch for the truth of the statement, I was told, and all our command believed, that Colorow, as he was leaving, turned to Major Thornburgh and said he would welcome a visit to his reservation and his house by the major and two or three of his young men, but that the major must not come upon the lands of his people with so many soldiers, significantly adding, "You have too many soldiers for peace but not enough for war."

Major Thornburgh, while holding a rank which implied many years' service in the army and corresponding experience and knowledge of Indians, was really lacking these qualifications, because he had never had any experience in Indian warfare.

The next morning, September 29, the column resumed its march. Near the entrance to a defile known as "Bad Canyon," the command was fired on, and several men and horses were hit. Major Thornburgh found that the Indians were in his rear as well as his front, and that he was being cut off from his wagon train about half a mile to the rear. He immediately called on a group of his men close by, ordered them to follow him, and charged the Indians in the rear. The party cut its way through, but in the skirmish, Thornburgh was killed.

Before the Indians could rally, Captain Payne, on whom the command then devolved, led the whole force through with a rush and got back to the wagon train. Meanwhile, the wagon train had been corralled in an irregular circle, each team being within and alongside the preceding wagon and so somewhat protected from enemy fire. With the command inside this corral, they could not be ridden down by the horde of mounted Indians.

The situation in which the command found itself was very serious. The road ran here in a shallow valley between two long, low hills with gentle slopes, scantily covered with sagebrush, the crests of the hills being three or four hundred yards apart. Between the ridges flowed an insignificant stream called Milk River, or Creek.

The men within the wagon corral dug in as fast as possible, but the resulting pits were mere hollows, giving very poor protection. It was very evident that they could not hope to successfully cope with the many times greater number of their assailants, and that help must reach them soon or their doom was sealed.

The government guide, an old-time frontiersman named Joe Rankin, volunteered to try to get through the enemy lines at Rawlins with dispatches. The chances were heavily against him, but the job had to be done, and shortly after dark he slipped away with his tough little bronco and managed to get through, though not without being fired on. This was Monday, September 29, and early on the morning of October 1, he reached Rawlins and filed his dispatches. He had ridden 150 miles on a single horse in less than thirty-six hours, over twenty of which were dark, two-thirds of the distance being in enemy country.

At Fort D. A. Russell, near Cheyenne, Wyoming, something over two hundred miles east of Rawlins, was the headquarters of the 5th Cavalry, commanded by Col. Wesley Merritt, who had been a major general of volunteers in the Civil War at the age of thirty-two, and who was to reach the same grade in the Regular army twenty-nine years later. He reached Rawlins on the second with four companies of his own regiment and, after gathering his transportation and supplies, left on Friday morning, October 3, with the four companies of the 5th Cavalry and four companies of the 4th Infantry in wagons. He reached Milk Creek on Sunday morning, October 5th, after a night march of over fifty miles and drove off the hostile Indians. It was one of the greatest forced marches of our military history and was successful in saving most of the besieged troops.

On the second night of the six-day siege of the Thornburgh command, the defense was startled by a call from a cavalry bugle and a voice calling, "My friends, don't fire." A few minutes later, in came a company of the 9th Cavalry commanded by Captain Dodge. They had been exploring in the main range of the Rockies and, hearing of the attack at Milk Creek, hurried to the rescue. It is probable that the Indians permitted this reinforcement to join the beleaguered force because they were sure of annihilating the entire force and were glad to have more victims. Their arrival, however, was a great encouragement to the besieged force, because it showed them that their situation was known and that help might be expected.

Up to the time when relief reached Milk Creek, thirteen enlisted men had been killed, and many were wounded. Captain Payne, Lieutenant Paddock, and Dr. Grimes were all wounded.

Of all the organizations ordered out for this campaign, the 7th Infantry at Fort Snelling were the farthest away. We did not reach Rawlins until Saturday, October 4, and then had to assemble and organize our wagon train, draw rations, forage, and additional ammunition. We left Rawlins Monday morning, October 6.

The first day's march of our command will never be forgotten by anyone who participated. The route lay across the Continental Divide and was all uphill. The road was hard and covered with a coating of fine gravel and sharp sand well mixed with alkali dust, which mixture was driven by a howling gale into our eyes, noses, and mouths and every crevice of our clothing. The wind was so strong as to frequently stop one in his tracks, and moving against it involved a continuous struggle.

We marched about twenty-one miles, when approaching night brought a halt and we went into camp, nearly everybody being about all in. In addition to exhaustion, I suffered from a badly blistered foot caused by an ill-fitting shoe, which could not be worn again for several days. I marched the next hundred miles wearing an old carpet slipper held on by a woolen stocking pulled over it.

On the third night out, we camped on Snake Creek on the westerly side of the Continental Divide, seventy miles from Rawlins. On Saturday, October 11, in a small valley surrounded by steep mountains, our column was halted and formed in line at the side of and facing the road. Soon another column emerged from the canyon a few hundred yards away. It proved to be the funeral cortège of Major Thornburgh and a wagon train carrying the wounded of the Milk Creek fight, escorted by the remains of what had been three fine companions of the 5th Cavalry, all on foot with not enough horses left to mount the three or four officers still fit for duty. It was an impressive moment, as our ingoing force lined up along the road at attention with hats off in respect for the dead as ambulances and wagons and the dismounted remnants of the cavalry moved on.

The following day saw another heel-blistering, heartbreaking march, just one steep hill after another. There was one canyon said to be fourteen miles long, and we believed every mile of it, and also that at least one-third of them were vertical. Our poor mules, half fed and driven to the limit, every day were becoming very weak. They had some grain each day, but no hay could be carried, and both cavalry horses and mules had only the scanty pickings of grass and brush to be gleaned between halting time and dark, and nearly half the time there was no such period.

The steepest hill and longest hill that day came after dark, and with our fagged-out mules, we had to double two and sometimes three or four mule teams to get one wagon to the crest. The last four miles before reaching a camping place that night took nearly as many hours, and we went into camp by starlight too tired to eat. We soon discovered by our olfactory nerves that we were on the Milk Creek battlefield, where nearly three hundred horses and mules, dead for ten days, sufficiently advertised their presence.

This march of about 150 miles was made in seven days under the most difficult conditions by infantry taken from garrison duty and with inadequate animal transportation.

The next morning, life was made still more pleasant by a cold drizzling rain; breakfast was characterized by soggy bread and half-cooked bacon, but we had hot coffee, which was a lifesaver. We pulled out, slipping here and there in the soft mud, and only made twelve miles in some six hours. We camped in the mud only eight miles from White River, where we arrived the following forenoon. Colonel Merritt's command was in camp at the agency but left the next morning in pursuit of the fugitive Utes who had killed the agent and all the white employees, except one who escaped, and also had burned the agency buildings. They had fled southward over the mountains toward Grand River.

The pursuit was brief; a courier arriving from Rawlins the following day brought orders not to follow the fugitive Indians south of White River and for the whole command to remain where it was until further orders. A "peace commission" had been arranged to talk it over and compromise the rebellion, arson, and murder. The expressed opinions of officers and enlisted men on receipt of this order were not suitable for publication.

On our arrival at the site of the burned agency, our commanding officer had reported our arrival to department headquarters and asked for orders. These orders arrived in due time, telling us to stay where we were.

The October nights were cold on the bare, windswept slopes of the Rocky Mountains at seven thousand feet elevation, and seemed especially so to our regiment from a comfortable post, which we left on a few hours' notice. We made ourselves as safe and comfortable as we could. We had our tentage, and the original camp was well deployed.

Winter was approaching, when living in tents would be unpleasant if not impracticable at this elevation, so we dug in. Dugouts, shacks built of the wreckage of the agency, and doubled tents with windbreaks were utilized. The enlisted men of my company used the dugout construction, while the quarters of the officers were quite palatial. I shared quarters with Captain Freeman and Captain Kirtland.[4] We dug a fireplace in the clay wall, and the chimney was a piece of the smokestack of the destroyed sawmill belonging to the agency. An outcrop of coal, found near the camp, furnished an ample fuel supply.

The winter was spent with outpost duty and infrequent trips with wagon trains (sleds) to Rawlins for mail and supplies. We were finally ordered back to Fort Snelling and left White River on June 10, 1880.

With Merritt's Command

JOHN F. FINERTY[1]

Chicago *Times,* October 30, 1879

THE KILLING OF LIEUTENANT WEIR
COLONEL MERRITT'S CAMP, WHITE RIVER, Colorado, October 21—
Since our retrograde movement from the direction of the Grand River on October 16 until today, we have been encamped in this place, within a few miles of the fatal agency, suffering all the ills of the monotonous existence which camp life entails upon military mortals. The weather has changed to the condition of the Indian summer, except at night, when it is bitterly cold. Our guides, some of whom have inhabited this region for twenty years, say that winter will close in fiercely pretty soon, which will, most certainly, not add to the comfort of campaigning in the Colorado wilds.

Meanwhile, governed by that national fiend called the Interior Department, Merritt and his men are reduced to inglorious inactivity while some of the infernally idiotic or knavish benevolists who afflict America with their humane balderdash are trying to patch up an ignominious peace with the murderous Utes. I know of no country that can stand so many kicks and cuffs from civilized and savage foes alike as this same America. It would appear that the persons suffered to have the national honor in their keeping are a pack of quaking cowards who deserve no consideration at the hands of the people whom they are alleged to govern. No wonder that in the light of recent events, the lieutenant general of the army very sensibly pronounces the Ute "war" a farce. By this time, had Merritt been permitted to proceed, although his command would have had to endure considerable privations, we should have been at the southern Ute agency and possibly might have had the pleasure of giving poor Meeker's assassins the whaling they deserve. As matters now remain, the soldiers are disappointed or disgusted, and the horses of the cavalry, destitute of forage—the country being badly provided with grass—are degenerating into the gaunt skeletons they were in 1876, when over five hundred of the poor animals had to be abandoned on the road between Tongue River and the Black Hills.[2]

With his hands securely tied by the Washington philanthropists, Merritt frets and fumes in vain. His latest orders are to vegetate here until it pleases

Col. Wesley Merritt. COURTESY OF PERRY FROHNE.

Carl Schurz[3] to let him loose. By that time, the country will be impassable, and the Utes can snap their fingers at the whole military power of the United States. All this is preliminary to the introduction of a horrible tragedy, which goes far to show how sincere the hostile savages are in their repeated desire for peace. I allude to the slaughter of Lieutenant Weir and his companion Paul Humme, late of the Palmer House, Chicago, the general news of which I sent you by courier to the telegraph office at Rawlins this morning.

Colonel Merritt has had very little faith in the successful issue of the peace commission and, not being familiar with the natural highways through the country, determined to send out a party to seek some better thoroughfare to Grand River than the one over which he attempted to move last Thursday.

Lt. W. P. Hall of the 5th Cavalry was desirous of acting as pioneer, and leave was granted him to take out the exploring party. Lt. William B. Weir, ordnance officer of the Department of the Platte, from the Cheyenne, Wyoming Territory, Depot, volunteered to accompany the expedition. With him went Paul Humme, also of the ordnance, and with Lieutenant Hall the veteran scout Jim Baker; Messrs. Drais, Oliver, and Martin, of the guides; and Private Sullivan of the 5th Cavalry.

Colonel Merritt decided to send two companies of the 3rd Cavalry under Captain Wessells[4] and Lieutenants Chase and Hunter,[5] as an escort. It is to be regretted that Messrs. Hall and Weir were not sufficiently impressed with the necessity of having a guard in the Indian country. No sign of Indians had been seen since Merritt relieved Payne, and the general impression was that all were south of Grand River and not disposed to hang around the scenes of their late atrocities. So general was this feeling of security that even officers of experience have been miles from camp deer and duck shooting since our return here. Lieutenant Hall is naturally indifferent to danger, and Lieutenant Weir, who was serving his first apprenticeship on the frontier, was like a schoolboy—full of life and health, and without the faintest idea of peril. His companion, Humme, an old frontiersman and a person of wonderful intrepidity, did much, no doubt, to inspire the young soldier with a love for adventure and an utter contempt for Indian prowess. Consequently, the youthful officers gave a cold shoulder to the escort, although Captain Wessells left camp an hour before they started, intending to join them on the road. Unfortunately for all concerned, Lieutenant Hall did not rendezvous with Wessells, taking a shortcut and leaving the officer of the escort in utter ignorance as to his whereabouts.

Lieutenant Hall went out to find a road. Lieutenant Weir went out with the double object of assisting Hall and having a hunt, as he was an enthusiast in pursuit of game. I saw the party start at 7:30 A.M. yesterday—Weir conspicuous in a complete suit of corduroys—little dreaming that I should never see some of them alive again.

At about 11:30 A.M. Lieutenant Chase came in from Captain Wessells, who was posted on a hill near the agency, waiting for the Hall party for instructions, as those who were to be escorted had not reported to the command. Colonel Merritt, through Lieutenant Swift,[6] his adjutant, directed Captain Wessells to move up the canyon about ten miles and wait there a reasonable time for Hall. If that officer did not report before nightfall, Captain Wessells was directed to return to camp.

Wessells moved up the canyon about twelve miles, striking Hall's trail about five miles from the agency and following it about seven miles. He halted at that point and waited for the exploring party until sundown, when, pursuant to orders, he returned, reaching camp at 8:30 A.M. Half an hour later, Lieutenant Hall, with all of his party except Lieutenant Weir and Paul Humme, reported at Colonel Merritt's headquarters that he had been "jumped" by Indians in the canyon, about twenty miles southward, on the Grand River divide, at about 1:00 P.M., and that Weir and Humme, having parted company to hunt some black-tail deer, were missing. This vastly alarmed the colonel, with whom Weir was an especial favorite, and he at once sent Major Sumner, with five companies of the 5th Cavalry, to hunt up the unfortunates. The night was intensely dark, and in crossing the river, and in the windings of the canyon, several companies got lost, but all kept on, forming a junction about daylight. Just as the sun rose, they reached the mouth of a small ravine, two miles this side of where Lieutenant Hall had been corralled, and discovered the lifeless body of Lieutenant Weir, stripped to the undershirt and frozen stiff by the cold of the preceding night. A bullet wound in the right cheek showed where the fatal messenger of Indian hatred had entered. The bullet ranged downward, passing through the neck to the left, where it made its exit, severing in its course the main arteries and breaking the vertebra column. Death was instantaneous—the handsome face wearing a tranquil expression, indicative of a painless passing away. In the dim morning light, owing to the blood which formed a dark pool around the head of the corpse, it was thought the Indians had battered the skull, but subsequent investigation showed that the savages had respected the dead, as no other wound than that which caused the death of the ill-fated officer could be discovered on the remains. Lieutenant Weir, while on horseback, unsuspicious of any danger, had evidently been shot from a rocky ledge above him, where the Indians lay concealed. In falling face downward from his horse, he suffered a few abrasions, but nothing of a disfiguring nature. When found, the body was lying partially on his side and face. Nearby lay his corduroy coat and pantaloons, crimson with his lifeblood. The garments were abandoned by the Utes. All else—his vest, blue campaigning shirt, watch, pocketbook, boots, hat, gloves, Springfield rifle and Colt's revolver, improved models, and fifty rounds of cartridges—were taken by his slayers. It was a horrible ending to a young, bright existence, and all who saw the corpse were deeply affected by the melancholy fate of Lieutenant Weir.

Diligent search was made for Paul Humme, but not a trace of him could be discovered. As he has not returned to camp, the chances are that he was wounded and made prisoner by the Indians, who doubtless carried him off for torture. Humme was by birth a Prussian and served when only seventeen years old in the memorable campaign of Sadowa. His father holds a position in the army of the German Empire, and his family is one of high respectability in the fatherland. Humme had a taste for the army and rose to be sergeant major of the 5th Cavalry. He was recommended for a commission, but owing to some carelessness, failed to obtain it. He retired from the cavalry and obtained a position as traveling man for a Milwaukee firm. Subsequently, through Colonel Merritt's influence, Potter Palmer appointed Paul Humme second steward of his hotel.[7] But the roving spoonful of suet was too strong in his veins to allow him to remain in civil life. He came west a few months ago and was received into the ordnance corps as chief tester of new arms. He accompanied Lieutenant Weir to the front and in all probability suffered a more cruel fate than the young man to whom he was vehemently devoted. Humme was a dead shot and a man of dauntless heart. He was pleasant of speech, and in youth received the benefit of a good education in his own country. Unhappily for himself and fellow victim, Humme's prudence was altogether dwarfed by his intrepidity and reckless humor. He has dearly paid the penalty of rashness. The death of Lieutenant Weir, under circumstances so painful, cannot fail to create a sensation in military circles. He was born in the army at West Point about twenty-seven years ago. His father was professor of drawing in that institution at the time of the lieutenant's birth. The family is numerous and well known throughout the country. Prof. John Weir of Yale College is half-brother of deceased. Mrs. Trueman Seymour and Mrs. Colonel Casey, whose husbands are of the army, are his sisters. Another sister—the youngest—kept house for the ill-starred soldier at Cheyenne depot. They were fondly attached to each other, and the deepest sympathy is felt for the poor young lady, who will have to meet the awful shock of a beloved brother's death all alone. Colonel Merritt feels dreadfully—the young man having accompanied him as a volunteer. During his stay with the column, the dead lieutenant made himself dear to everybody.

His personal beauty was remarkable, but he was entirely free from foppery, and his frank, pleasant manners carried sunshine wherever he went. He was a born hunter and a wonderfully expert angler. Personally, I am deeply sorry for his untimely doom, for I have rarely met, in either civil or military life, one more calculated to be a favorite with his kind. May the clay that enwraps him lie light upon his gallant breast.

The remains will be properly cared for until an opportunity presents itself for sending them to his afflicted relatives.

And now comes the wretched inquiry. Who is responsible? I do not propose to constitute myself into a censor but will give the statements of some of the principal actors in the calamity.

I asked Lieutenant Hall for his statement of the affair this afternoon, and he gave it substantially in the following words:

Our party, eight in all, left camp, anticipating no danger, at 7:30 A.M. on yesterday morning, Monday, October 20. Our business was to find a better road to Grand River than that over which we partially moved on October 16. We went by direction of Colonel Merritt. We moved south on the main trail south of the agency, going at a brisk pace until about noon, when we halted and lunched. During the ride, Lieutenant Weir saw some coyotes on the road and wished to fire at them. I asked him not to fire while we were advancing. He said there was no danger, but finally he desisted. When we were mounting after lunch, a band of black-tail deer passed near us. They crossed the road about three hundred yards in front of us, going toward the steep mountains on our left (the coast) hand. Lieutenant Weir and Paul Humme wanted to fire at them again, but I remonstrated, saying it would be better to wait until our return trip. The deer were too much for Weir and his companion, so they started off on the game trail, and I, with the rest of the party, continued south toward the Grand River divide. When I had gone about a mile, I heard the report of firearms, not in volleys, but one by one, as if Weir and Humme were shooting at deer. Thinking this, I kept on perhaps another mile, when I observed fresh pony tracks—I did not count how many—crossing my path. I immediately reached the conclusion that the Indians had "jumped" Weir and his friend. A spur of mountain lay between them and my party. I immediately resolved to join them and wheeled north, going eastward to where the firing was first heard at the same time.

We went as fast as we could go, and as we were rising on the ledge, mounted Indians to the number of fifteen or twenty opened fire upon us. I ordered my men to fall back into a small ravine two hundred yards distant, where the horses could find shelter. I was promptly obeyed and, strange to say, [we] reached there unhurt, horses and men, although the Indians kept up a hot fire as we retreated. On one side of the little ravine, the grass was burned off, and on the other, sagebrush grew in abundance. The Indians, while some of them blazed away at us from the heights on both sides, crept through the sagebrush and attempted to shoot down over the bank of the gully. It was then that the scouts, Jim Baker and young Drais, shot down two of them, which tamed their valor for a while. Our only chance was to stand them off until night; so we lay low, replying occasionally to the fire which they still kept up. After Drais fired, I saw one Indian throw his hands up. He also uttered a yell. I am convinced he was killed. I tell you, those were long hours we lay there under the guns of the Indians, and it was in my mind that a larger body might come down on us, but fortune favored us. As night was falling, I observed eight or ten Indians trying to get the ravine between us and our line of retreat. We opened on them in a lively manner, and they cleared out. I made up my mind that it was about time to be moving, if we intended to get away at all. So when it grew dark enough, I sent the horses down the ravine, while Drais and I, on foot, remained behind to cover the retreat. This was necessary so that the Indians should not suspect that we were on the move. Then Drais and myself stole down the ravine and joined our party. We mounted our horses and made a dash for it. None of us expected to get through without a fight, but stupidly enough, the Indians did not observe our flight, or else they had had enough and retired with their dead. It was too late to find poor Weir and his comrade, as darkness had settled down, and I hoped they had succeeded in standing off the Indians and escaped in the gloom. We made the best of our way to camp, which we reached at a little after 9:00 P.M., and reported to Colonel Merritt, who ordered out Sumner's battalion of the 5th, which I accompanied. In the last twenty-four hours, I have ridden eighty miles and feel pretty well used up, besides being horror struck at the unlooked-for fate of Weir and Humme. That is about all I have to say. The rest you know. I can only add that Lieutenant Weir knew nothing of Indian warfare, having been first in the artillery and then transferred to the ordnance. It was his ignorance of the savage character and his love for hunting that made the poor fellow leave my party. I assure you that I did all in my power to dissuade him, but I did not like to be too severe, as I could hardly consider him under my orders.

"You say, lieutenant," I observed, "that Weir was killed in the rear of where you were corralled?"

"Yes, two miles this side of it, and nearer to the mountains."

"How far did you go altogether southward on Monday?"

"I went about twenty miles, and Weir and Humme about eighteen."

In reply to a question as to why he did not consider it necessary to take an escort, Lieutenant Hall was understood to say that he did not believe there were any Indians this side of Grand River, and, furthermore, he wished to spare the cavalry horses as much as possible, there being no forage. He also said he doubted whether, had there been an escort, Lieutenant Weir could have been kept with the column, as the idea of danger from Indians could not be forced on either him or Humme, who had great influence with his chief.

At this point, an officer came up and said that Humme, when leaving headquarters, asked Lieutenant Weir to bring along a pack mule and they two would go to Grand River, being a match for any Utes they might meet on the way. The pack mule was taken and, with the horses of Weir and Humme, was captured by the Utes. All this only goes to show that no amount of bloody sacrifices will teach people to be cautious when campaigning in the Indian country.

I next interviewed old Jim Baker, a scout of seventy winters, who still retains the courage that has sustained him in the savage wilderness from boyhood up. He is a modified edition of the Leather Stocking.

Old Jim scratched his shaggy head when I asked him to tell me all about the "circus" in which he recently figured.

"Oh," said the old man, smiling grimly and shaking his long locks, "there 'ere 'rollickaboo' was but playing marbles aside of some of the scrapes I've bin in—not denyin' but what fur a time it did look uncommon lively. I know'd as what that young leftinant and his man would come to grief, they wor so wild about chasing the black-tail and sich like."

"Well, how did it all happen?" I interrupted.

"I'm agoin to opin the yarn if you only give me time," he answered.

When we were getting up from lunch near the divide, a bunch of black-tail crossed us, and the leftinant and Humme followed. Leftinant Hall wanted them not to go, but Weir laughed and said there wor no fear of Utes. They turned east toward the mountain, and Mr. Hall and the others kept on. Now, seeing they wor agoin' to make noise, I thought I'd have a rack at the black-tail myself, so I followed them a little way, but when I saw them agoin' up the steep ravine, I made up my mind 'twould be too hard on my pony, so I followed Hall, about half a mile behind him. Soon I heerd shootin—a kind of irregular like—and I said to myself, "Thim ere chaps have struck the black-tail sure." Then one of the scouts, I don't know his name, who had been off to one side, rode by me excited. I'm thinkin', and said, "Do ye hear that ere shootin' behind us? 'Tis a fight, I bet." I thought it worn't, and we kept on until we saw Hall and his men turnin' back. They had seen the pony tracks, as I found out afterward, and were goin' to see about Weir. As they wor risin' the ledge, I saw the Indi-

Lt. William B. Weir. COURTESY OF PERRY FROHNE.

ans a comin' at a hard gallop, and before I could think, they fired. I threw myself forward on the pony and shouted to the party, "Come along, boys." They came quick enough, and Leftinant Hall says, "Well, Jim, we're jumped, sure enough. What had we better do now?" "We must all stick together," says I. "Don't allow a man to stampede, or we'll all get left. Let us get into that hollow down there."

Leftinant Hall ordered the men to be steady, but the horses were wild at the noise of the firing, and we had some difficulty in gettin' into the hollow for shelter. We dismounted, and the Indians pegged into us lively, I tell you. I could see one fellow within twenty yards of me in the sagebrush. I was on my knees, trying to get a good sight at him. He blazed away at me, the ball just grazin' my hat. I returned his civility like, and I wasn't troubled by him no more. Another bull-headed varmint crept down nearer and fired right into us, tearin' up the ground between Drais's legs. The boy couldn't stand the pressure, so he rushed up the bank and, before Mr. Indian could get out of the way, let him have it full in the chest. There were one more good Indian after that. Drais did it like a brick. Well, this shootin' made the varmints cautious-like, so we put the horses down low and hugged the ground as a fellow hugs his sweetheart at a corn-huskin'—you've been thar, haven't you?—while they wasted their lead. I think them Utes is big cowards anyway, because we shifted once to get a better place, and they wor afeerd to charge in where we had been. Find' we didn't better ourselves, we went back to our hold and stood until night. I reckon as how some of them youngsters thought the sun would never set yesterday, altho' I must say to their credit, they all showed uncommon grit for green hands at the work. When night kem, we half fought and half stole our way out. I wonder myself why the Utes didn't jump us going in, but guess as how they got more than they bargained for. They are tricky varmints, but nothin' like the Cheyennes, or the Kiowas, or the Comanches for real fightin' qualities. If Cheyennes had been on to us yesterday, we'd all have been in the same box with Weir and Humme by this time.

I quite agreed with the old man, although I remember an occasion, very nearly similar, when even the Cheyennes were outwitted by a party of which I happened to be one. Such an escape could not occur a second time, however.

"Howsumdever," continued Baker, "I rayther guess thim ere Injuns were firing entirely at Leftinant Hall because he wore his shoulder straps. That's how they missed the bulk of us in the first place. How they missed him beats me. My eyes ain't what they were, an' we had no glass along. We were out on a scout, and so were the Injuns. They saw us first because they have better eyes and got the chance to jump us. Well, well, it can't be helped now, but I am real sorry for the poor boys thim red devils took in."

And the old man puffed savagely at his pipe, rose to his feet, and went his way.

Chicago *Times,* November 6, 1879

WITH MERRITT'S COMMAND
CAMP ON BEAR RIVER (Taylor's Branch Trail), Colorado, October 27— The desire of Colonel Merritt to find a shorter route for his supply trains than that hitherto used led him, on Saturday, to detach Capt. Guy Henry,[8] with A and D Companies of the 3rd Cavalry, for the purpose of opening and developing a new road, of which a good deal has been spoken of but very little actually known. Finding that the peace negotiations were liable to postpone military movements for the winter, and not wishing to be slowed in the mountains unprovided with an arctic outfit, I accompanied Captain Henry, with whom was my "mess" during the campaign, on his tour of discovery. His two companies mustered about sixty men all told, and Lieutenant Hardie[9] commanded D Company, under the captain. Bill Oliver, a well-posted scout who had been in the Hall scrape a few days before, acted as guide of the expedition.

We left Merritt's camp a little before noon—he was then posted on White River, five miles east of the new agency—and struck directly north, having five wagons in our train, through an opening in the mountains. The weather was bracing, clear, and breezy, and none of us were sorry to leave behind the insupportable monotony of camp life after the villainous saltpeter had ceased to burn. There was hardly a book to read in the outfit. There was nothing but water to drink, and the deep damnation of enforced idleness was strong upon all of us. The only event that broke the stagnation of the week was the arrival of Maj. Andrew Evans of the 3rd Cavalry, with I Company of his regiment under Lieutenant King,[10] after a march of thirteen days over miry roads in which the wagons stuck fast every half hour, from Rawlins. So scarce had the grass become that half the troopers had to take their horses out several miles every day to graze on the hillsides or in the pockets of the ravines. Perhaps the War Department has invented a method of keeping horses and mules alive on "wind pudding." Otherwise, it is difficult to explain the persistency with which they keep so many animals idle and starving on White River, when they must know, if they are not profoundly careless, that a few weeks will cover even the scanty vegetation that still remains in this region with snow, and nothing short of a miracle can save the suffering brutes from death by cold and lack of food. All the wagons at the disposal of the Department of the Platte can hardly supply Merritt's animals with half forage of grain for the winter. This, however, is something that the great war people should be more interested in than your correspondent.

But to my story. Our little column, after entering the mountain, was, by means of a somewhat tortuous and very romantic canyon, struck a blind trail, over which the guide had once driven a wagon from Rawlins to the agency. With the exception of a few "sidings," we found the road good until we had gone northward in the canyon some ten miles, when we struck a steep divide, which compelled us to "double up" on our mule teams. It was not, however, half as bad as some of the numerous grades we had to ascend and descend on the other route. Besides, the character of the pass is not so dangerous, the mountains being less abrupt and not of such altitude as those that bound the thoroughfare through Bear and Milk River Canyons. The valley is well supplied with grass and water, the Indians having unaccountably neglected to burn off the former. Timber, chiefly cedar, is found in many places, so that there is no difficulty in keeping well warmed up. I think there is hardly a section of one hundred rods in any part of the ravine that could not be easily protected by flankers on the hills. A couple of hours were consumed in accomplishing the divide, and then we found it downhill all the rest of the way. The day being far advanced, Captain Henry was compelled to halt and go into camp about fourteen miles down the canyon, where we found everything to make campaigning comfortable.

A little stretch of a few hundred yards, perhaps, immediately south of our encampment, might need corduroying for wet weather because the soil is rather marshy. In winter it will be as hard as a macadamized causeway. We found several large herds of Indian cattle on our line of march, all in excellent condition. Remnants of wickiups and traces of campfires showed where Indian hunting parties had been bivouacked some months before. The savages have a keen eye for good country, and the territory which belonged to the Northern Utes is one of the best game regions in the world. It absolutely swarms with black-tail deer, bears of different species, and wildfowl in perfect clouds.

A brilliant moon illuminated our tents on the night of the twenty-fifth, but the frost came down like a million razors, freezing solid the pails of water in our tepees and giving us, in spite of a Sibley stove and plenty of dry wood, some foretaste of what December will be up there among the highlands of Colorado. An immense pack of wolves sentineled the hills and chanted their dismal music at intervals until the morning bugle scared them off.

A soldier's toilet, especially when he has nothing but ice to wash with, is soon disposed of. The eyes and teeth are about all that demand particular attention, and the needful habits of sleeping in nearly all your clothing, including your honest breeches, which affected idiots term "unmentionables," enables you to jump out of your bunk with a celerity that would be truly astonishing to the average bellboy of a hotel. True, you feel a little greasy and itchy on back and breast, and you have suspicions, well grounded, mayhap, of a crawling plague under your armpits and other warm corners of your person, but all this is, after everything is considered, one-half of military glory. But lest I should shock the sentimental admirers of dashing young lieutenants, I'll dismiss the subject with a scratch—of my pencil. The girls never see the officers in tattered blouse and raveled shoulder straps. There is, however, one man in Merritt's column who defies dust, dirt, perspiration, and other ills of the frontier. I refer to Captain Babcock[11] of the 5th Cavalry, who always is newly shaved, sports a clean collar every day, keeps his boots highly polished, and has his buttons shined every morning. The captain—a handsome man with exquisite side-whiskers—is the envy of his corps. "Damn it," said Major Sumner the other day. "I wish I had Babcock's knack of dressing. He always looks as if he came out of a bandbox!" It is related of the dashing captain that on one occasion, while under fire from the Indians, a bullet covered his coat with dust. He immediately called his striker and directed him to brush it off, while he directed the movements of his company against the enemy. "Confound the savages," said he, "to spoil my best coat in that manner. Take your proper intervals men—five paces—and aim with a fine sight at the fellow who is popping up the dust all around me."

After a very hasty breakfast on Sunday morning, we mounted our chargers and moved right rapidly for [Eugene] Taylor's ranch, situated at the northern mouth of the canyon, expecting to find there something for the refreshment of man and beast. The ravine gradually widened out as we advanced, until at last the hills sank into mere rolling uplands, and before us lay a country that bears a striking resemblance to many parts of Dakota and Montana. We had cleared the canyon, placing its extreme length at eighteen miles, and looked around for the ranch, but none was to be seen. Some charred logs, broken boxes, and empty bottles showed how the Utes had employed their time, although Taylor had always been on the most friendly terms with the tribe.

Fortunately for him, he was absent the day of Thornburgh's misfortune, and so escaped a horrible death. The soldiers were happy in finding some potatoes and other vegetables, and three miles further on, we found a couple of haystacks, out of which the animals made a grand feast.

Captain Henry sent back two soldiers—Walsh and Bent—to Colonel Merritt with information about the road. The brave fellows started cheerfully, although the danger of being cut off by straggling savages was by no means small. I think detached service of that kind is more trying to a man's nerves than all the horrors of a well-fought battle.

We rested in camp most of Sunday, killing time as best we could under the circumstances. We observed four fresh pony tracks, which made the colonel rather uneasy about his two couriers. The stretch of country in the front showed a luxuriant growth of sagebrush as far as the eye could reach, and out of that unsightly but useful shrub we made our bed. The weather on Sunday night was rather milder than in the canyon, for which we were devoutly thankful. The moonlight was so lustrous that it would not be impossible to find a needle in a bundle of hay. One star in the east—could it be that of Bethlehem—blazed like a huge meteor, low in the horizon—one of the most entrancing objects that ever the eye of mortal rested upon. The air of Colorado is so rarified that all the heavenly bodies look larger and grander than they do in the regions bounding the Great Lakes.

Daylight[12] had not yet robbed Luna of her glory on Monday morning when we were on the march to Bear River on a very excellent natural road, over which even our gaunt mules found no difficulty in hauling the wagons. We had not moved more than a dozen miles when a long, silver line rose before us. "What stream is that, Oliver?" demanded the commandant. "Bear River," replied the scout. So it proved. We had made a cutoff of over thirty miles by coming the new route, and everyone felt delighted. We had to move a couple of miles down the river westward, for all these streams flow to the Pacific, to find a crossing. We found a splendid ford and went into camp on the north bank. We were disappointed at finding very little grass and no wood but willows of the smallest proportion on this part of the stream. Sagebrush is, however, abundant, and a brighter, sweeter body of water than Bear, or Yampah, River, as the Indians call it, is not be found on the continent. The soldiers found an Indian dugout, with paddles, and amused themselves by sailing in it all day. Several got upset, which of course delighted their comrades, who pulled them out, dripping, on the shore. The captain, in obedience to orders, sent back two more soldiers to Colonel Merritt. They left at 4:00 P.M. this afternoon, the distance to camp being roughly estimated at thirty-three miles, against sixty-five to Bear River by the old road.

At nightfall Walsh and Bent, the soldiers first detached, returned, bringing some letters from Colonel Merritt, who said he would send the wagons over our road in the future. He also directed that Captain Henry send a light party to Snake River, over fifty miles distant, in the morning, to look up that part of the road. The soldiers said they had met four suspicious-looking white men mounted on ponies in the canyon. They inquired whether the mail carrier came that way and were otherwise unduly curious. It is possible that the fellows were cattle thieves going after the Indian herds scattered among the mountains.

Captain Henry has decided that tomorrow Lieutenant Hardie, with the scout Oliver and two soldiers, must go to Snake River. I have decided to accompany the party, as otherwise I'd have to go back to White River and remain there for an indefinite period. We shall start at 5:00 A.M. and must do some hard riding to accomplish the march, with our tired horses, in one day.

THROUGH HOSTILE COUNTRY
LAMBERT'S RANCH, Bridger's Pass, Wyoming Territory, October 31—Two hours before sunrise on the morning of the twenty-eighth, Lieutenant Hardie's little party of five, including your correspondent, left Captain Henry's camp on Bear River and turned their faces to the north, knowing that a hard day's ride lay between us and Snake Creek. All were well armed, because we had to travel through a region comparatively unknown, where there might be any number of straggling Indians hunting the game which abounds in this wilderness of the West. The country—over which we moved at a brisk pace, our animals having been somewhat refreshed by the unusual treat of hay found at Taylor's ranch—presented the same general appearance as the major part of the great American desert, so called, seen from the portion of the Union Pacific Railroad which runs through the sagebrush and alkali lands. The horizon in nearly all directions was bounded by rugged bluffs, or buttes, whose crests were surmounted by natural walls, faced into almost artistic shape by the action of water during ages far remote. The soil, such as it was, bore the impress of the tracks of deer and antelope, whose chief nutriment is derived from the scant brush grass which grows at long intervals between the everlasting clumps of sage.

The road continued good until we reached a kind of gulch, well supplied with springs and grass, where a large drove of cattle roamed at will. A stack of hay and a little corral showed that the white man had been at work there before the outbreak. Not a human being, outside of ourselves, was to be seen as we passed through. McIntyre, one of the soldiers, picked up a memorandum book, which bore the name of Tom Morgan, a well-known ranchero of Utah who has been missing for some time. The gulch had a steep pitch, which will make it a heavy pull for wagons in bad weather, as the snow must be deep there when it comes down in the hard winter of that elevated region. The point to which I allude is distant some fifteen miles from Bear River and almost due north of Merritt's camp, fifty miles away, near the Ute agency. After passing the gulch, the country opened up better, and we struck a few spots of excellent grazing land but were rather astonished at finding some fresh pony tracks, with dog tracks intermingled, directly in our path and crossing us at right angles toward the west. As well as I remember, there were five ponies in that group, and subsequently we saw four other fresh trails, making nine in all. Oliver said the trails were made by an Indian hunting party, which was doubtless observing us from the bluffs on our left.

As we were moving over a rolling prairie, we felt very little apprehension of an attack. In any case, five well-armed men, in an open country, could whip a score of Utes. If, however, the latter caught us in a ravine, the chances of ever getting out would be dead against us. Ten miles north of the gulch, we found other springs, at which cattle, intermingled with deer and antelope, were drinking. All skedaddled as we approached, the bovine being quite as scary as the wild animals. Five miles further on, we crossed the divide, and the valley of Snake River lay stretched broad and picturesque at our feet. The river was still a full eight leagues away and hidden by the undulating ground lying between, although we had made a good thirty miles since morning. The road still followed the crest of the slopes as we began to descend, and on our right hand rose blue and beautiful, with snow piles lying like silver among the dark surroundings, Round Top and Battle Mountains, twenty long miles away. Our course changed a little to the northeast as we neared Four-Mile Creek, and ten miles from the Snake River, the trail we were on ran into the main wagon road used by Merritt's command during the earlier portion of the campaign. Near this junction we found, in the midst of alkali, pure fresh water, the place being known, according to the scout, as "Thousand Springs."

I think the weak point of the shortcut is the scarcity of fuel. It would be a necessity for wagon trains to carry wood with them from Snake River, or some other point, on their way out; coming back, they would have to cut timber in Taylor's Canyon, where it abounds. In every other particular, the cutoff is immeasurably superior to the ancient wagon road, for which the contractors claimed pay that was simply enormous. Agency freighters, in a country unsurveyed, bring the system of mileage charges down to a fine art. The same may be said of United States mail contractors. Uncle Sam has to pay the fifer always, no matter who may dance to the music.

On striking the old road, we saw a multitude of fresh mule and wheel tracks and knew that an empty train had just passed into Snake River. We met a bull train, loaded with army supplies, going north. It had five men, without arms, as a "guard." The bullwhackers must be crazy to go into an Indian country so carelessly as that. Lieutenant Hardie told them of the shortcut, but they chewed their tobacco with stolid indifference and never said whether they would follow it or not. Such surly idiots ought to get scalped as a warning to more of their kind.

At Four-Mile Creek, which was dried up when I came out, we found plenty of running water. From that stream into the Baggs ranch, on the Snake, we made fast time and found the train that brought in Lieutenant Weir's body—which had been taken to Rawlins that afternoon by a party sent out by the dead officer's relatives—there encamped. We, however, stopped at the ranch, which is run, in the absence of her husband, by Mrs. Baggs, who is one of the most remarkable females on the frontier. She keeps a very neat, clean place and sets a good table, but has a tongue like a Sheffield razor. She sailed for me the moment I alighted.

"You must all tumble into the same room, officers and men alike," says she. "There was a lieutenant here the other day who refused to eat with his soldiers! That's nice liberty, equality, and fraternity for you! Perhaps you'll refuse to eat with the soldiers too, eh? Let you all up, indeed! I think as much of the privates as I do of the officers. I'll have no second tables in a republican country. I'm a genuine frontier woman, that's what I am."

"My dear madam," said I, being utterly overwhelmed by all this eloquence. "I'm not a shoulder strap, but simply a journalist, and the most democratic of mankind. Arrange things to suit yourself, and they'll suit me. Have you got anything wherewith to cheer the inner man?"

"Oh, if you're not stuck up, all right." Said she, smiling, "I don't sell anything spirituous, but I have a private bottle for friends. Here, Ida, bring the gentleman some water."

By this time, Lieutenant Hardie and the two newspaper correspondents who had come with the train entered, and the eloquent lady treated all hands to some excellent whiskey—something we had not seen, tasted, or smelled for many weeks. Mr. Hardie professed himself, with ready tact, a leveler, and Mrs. Baggs was satisfied. She did not, thereafter, insist that all five of us should sleep together, and the two soldiers promptly refused to sit at the table with their officers. The men had too much respect for the necessary distance between their commander and themselves to take advantage of the situation. Neither would lay their blankets that night on the floor of the bedroom, but made their bivouac in an outhouse, although Lieutenant Hardie invited them to remain inside. Verily, I think the soldiers curried their ideas of respect too far, but such is discipline in the Regular army. I'd rather dig ditches in the city streets than be a noncommissioned officer or a private soldier in the best army of the world. An enlisted man has, generally speaking, a dog's life of it anyhow. In America, he enlists for soldiering, and he is forthwith converted into a laborer or cook, or anything but what he intended to be. Conducted as business now is in the American army, I call the whole system a failure and a farce. It is not the fault of the officers—neither are the men to blame. The system itself is responsible. The United States Army is a vast fatigue party—always doing heavy manual labor, which lowers the esprit of the troops, renders them heavy, awkward, miserably drilled, and, with few exceptions, entirely inferior on foot or horseback to the savage light cavalry who are periodically opposed to them in the field. This is plain speaking, but I challenge any officer or soldier in the army to controvert what I have here set down. If we are to have an army at all, let there be a pioneer corps, or a military train, to do the dirty work. Let us, then, have the companies filled up to the proper standard—an average of seventy-five men—and let our twenty-five thousand laboring hacks be drilled and set up so as to be efficient against any enemy they may have to encounter.

Some few regiments are pretty well taken care of by their field officers, but to drill men and work them like slaves, building and repairing forts and so forth, at the same time, does not fit the bill. No wonder that desertions are so frequent. It is infamous to enlist men to be shot at and not give them even a decent show to learn the use of their weapons, so as to be able to defend themselves properly when the hour of trial comes.

Lieutenant Hardie, with his little band, set out to rejoin Captain Henry on Wednesday morning, having to ride back that same weary road again. I rode with the returning train to Soldier Springs, where I, with two others, slept in the open air, waking in the morning to find our blankets hard and stiff as sheet from the severe frost, which had nipped our ears and noses in a charming manner. Several mules strayed off that night, which delayed us somewhat in the morning, but all were finally recovered. Near the wells, I met a supply train of thirty-three wagons with an infantry escort going out to Merritt. Lieutenant Reid, the quartermaster, accompanied the outfit and told me he would take the new road. I think his head was level.

Determined not to be caught out in the frost another night, your correspondent, with the New York *Herald* and Denver *Tribune* representatives, rode forward to this ranch—the train being too slow. We reached here at dark and found everything in confusion, the place having changed hands. We found good forage for the horses and had the good luck to secure some supper, which was much better than might have been expected under the circumstances. There were no spare beds at the ranch, but we procured a few armfuls of hay and made a regular shakedown, with saddles for pillows and horse blankets for covering. As the roof to our room was half off, and all the winds that howl through Bridger's Pass came whistling about our ears, you may be sure our lodgings were not what might be called comfortable. Half a dozen dogs, nearly famished, lay down beside us and helped to keep us warm. The animals, of course, left us a legacy of fleas, but I don't mind such trifles as that anymore. It is but thirty miles from here to Rawlins, and that I can easily do on horseback before 3:00 P.M. this afternoon.

BACK AMONG THE WHITES
RAWLINS, WYOMING TERRITORY, November 1—Here is something like civilization once more, although the little valley south of the town is filled with the tents of Colonel Brackett's[13] cavalry, 3rd and 5th combined. They are posted here as an army of observation. I found the officers all eager for war, of which, I now think, there is little likelihood this winter. Let me say a word about the length of a Colorado mile. Coming in from Lambert's, I made a bet with my two companions that no two persons we might happen to meet would agree as to distance. They took me up. The first man we met keeps what is known as the halfway ranch, which should be fifteen miles from Rawlins.

"How far do you call it in?" I asked.

"Oh, about eighteen miles," was the reply.

We went on and soon met a man driving a double team of mules. "How far to town?"

"Twenty miles; maybe more," he answered.

The next man we met was whacking a pair of bulls. He looked about as intellectual as the animals he was driving. About this time, mind you, we had ridden at least ten miles from the halfway ranch. "How far is it to Rawlins, friend?" I demanded of the bull baiter.

"Somewhar about seventeen mile," he responded sulkily.

We rode on another hour and met a fat man driving a buggy. "How far to Rawlins?"

He scratched his head and ruminated for a minute. "Well," he replied at last, "it is close on twelve miles."

This was rather consoling, and we kept on another half hour. Then we met a man on horseback. "How far to Rawlins?"

"Fifteen miles at least," he said shortly.

We grew desperate, and determined to assassinate the next man who increased the distance. We met an old fellow soon after and popped the question to him. "How far to Rawlins?"

"A good fourteen miles," said he.

That reply saved his life. We asked no more questions, but rode on doggedly. At last, toward evening, we struck the sagebrush town, convinced that the thirty miles between here and Lambert's are the longest ever measured by man or beast. Three dirtier-looking men than we were never came down upon the railroad. The sensation of positive filth was awful, and the necessity for a bath was never more keenly felt. Just now I am a little more presentable, but my face smarts as if I had suffered from a kerosene lamp explosion—the result of sun, wind, frost, and the eternally abominable alkaline dust of this vagabond stretch of country. So, now that the Ute War has been nipped in the bud by Carl Schurz, I will say farewell to camp and march for a while. Farewell to the blowing trumpet and the neighing steed. Farwell to cold and utter discomfort, such as only soldiers, or those who accompany a military column, ever experience. Farewell to the resonant profanity of the mule drivers, and to the kicking, biting, squealing, backing, jumping, and astonishingly artistic flatulency of the noble mule himself.

And this, for the present, winds up my experiences in the Ute country. If anyone desires to see more of it for himself, let him take the train to this post, and I'll vouch that before a month, he'll have swallowed more than his own weight of the vilest dust that ever cursed soldier or traveler on this earth.

NOTES

Introduction

1. *Annual Report of the Commissioner of Indian Affairs for the Year 1859*, 137–38.
2. William H. Leckie, *The Military Conquest of the Southern Plains* (Norman: University of Oklahoma Press, 1963), 23.
3. Nelson A. Miles, *Personal Recollections of General Nelson A. Miles* (Chicago: Werner Company, 1897), 139.
4. Leckie, *Military Conquest*, 29.
5. James L. Haley, *The Buffalo War* (New York: Doubleday, 1976), 10.
6. Stan Hoig, *The Battle of the Washita* (New York: Doubleday, 1976), 45.
7. Haley, *Buffalo War*, 12.
8. Ibid., 25.
9. Ibid., 38.
10. Leckie, *Military Conquest*, 234–35.

PART ONE: HANCOCK'S WAR AND THE MEDICINE LODGE TREATY, 1865–67

Julian R. Fitch and Isaac E. Eaton: The Smoky Hill Route

1. Julian R. Fitch enlisted as a private in the 6th Ohio Volunteer Infantry in 1861. He earned a regular commission in the 17th U.S. Infantry in February 1866 but was cashiered in January 1873. At the time that he wrote, Fitch was a brevet captain of volunteers in the Signal Corps.

Frank Doster: 11th Indiana Cavalry in Kansas in 1865

1. Frank Doster (1847–post-1922) enlisted in the 11th Indiana Volunteer Cavalry in 1864, at the age of seventeen. After muster out, he studied law and was admitted to practice in Illinois in 1870. Doster moved to Kansas the following year and in 1887 was appointed a district judge. In 1896 Doster was elected chief justice of the Kansas Supreme Court on a populist ticket. He was well known as a radical socialist. *Collections of the Kansas State Historical Society* (hereafter cited as *CKSHS*) 15 (1919–22): 524–25.
2. James R. Doolittle, a Republican senator from Wisconsin.
3. John B. Sanborn (1826–1904), a volunteer officer who rose to the rank of brigadier general during the Civil War and later became a distinguished Minnesota attorney.
4. Brig. Gen. John Pope, commander of the Military Department of the Missouri.
5. A reference to the Kiowa-Apaches, a small Athapascan tribe often mistaken for Apaches. Although they spoke a different language, the Kiowa-Apaches were closely associated with the Kiowas.

Winfield S. Hancock: The Indians

1. Winfield S. Hancock (1824–86), of the West Point Class of 1844, compiled a distinguished record as a corps commander during the Civil War. He became a major general in the Regular army in 1866.
2. Edward W. Wynkoop (1836–91) moved to Kansas Territory from Pennsylvania in 1858 and was appointed sheriff of Arapaho County. He served in the 1st Colorado Volunteer Cavalry during the Civil War and in 1864 conducted investigations into the Sand Creek massacre.
3. Henry Douglass of the 3rd U.S. Infantry, post commander at Fort Dodge, Kansas.
4. Henry E. Noyes (1839–1919) of the 2nd U.S. Cavalry, then assigned to department headquarters at Fort Leavenworth, Kansas.
5. Little Raven (c. 1810–89) was a hereditary chief of the Southern Arapahos. Little Raven visited Washington, D.C., in 1871, and held most of the Arapahos at peace during the Red River War of 1874–75.
6. Satanta (c. 1830–78) became a chief in his twenties by virtue of his ability as both a warrior and a diplomat. The Kiowas regarded him as one of their greatest men.
7. John H. Page entered the Civil War a volunteer private and ended his distinguished military career a brigadier general of volunteers after the Spanish-American War.
8. Edward O. C. Ord (1818–83), of the West Point Class of 1839, emerged from the Civil War a major general of volunteers. He commanded the Department of Arkansas from 1866 to 1867.
9. Herds of horses.
10. On May 23, 1867, Grant wrote Hancock as follows: "Reports from Indian agent Wynkoop to effect that Cheyennes have committed no hostilities against the whites to justify the destruction of their village. The Indian department desires to know if in good faith their losses should not be made good. Report by telegraph briefly reasons for destroying their property, whether they should be fed and equipped again, and reported at length by mail in reply to letters of Wynkoop and Leavenworth sent you by mail." John Y. Simon, ed., *The Papers of Ulysses S. Grant* (Carbondale: Southern Illinois University Press, 1967–), 17:162.
11. Jesse H. Leavenworth (1807–85), of the West Point Class of 1830, was the son of Brig. Gen. Henry Leavenworth, for whom Fort Leavenworth was named. Jesse H. Leavenworth resigned from the army in 1836 to follow a career as a civil engineer. He commanded the 2nd Colorado Volunteer Infantry during the Civil War and in 1864 was appointed agent for the Kiowas and Comanches.
12. George A. Custer (1839–76), of the West Point Class of 1861, had been named lieutenant colonel of the 7th U.S. Cavalry upon its organization after the Civil War.
13. Hancock also issued the following communiqué to his command before setting out, the belligerent tone of which contrasted sharply with his more conciliatory messages to Wynkoop and Leavenworth:

> It is uncertain whether war will be the result of the expedition or not; it will depend upon the temper and behavior of the Indians with whom we may come in contact. *We go prepared for war, and will make it if a proper occasion presents* [italics added]. We shall have war if the Indians are not well disposed towards us. If they are for peace, and no sufficient ground is presented for chastisement, we are restricted from punishing them for past grievances which are recorded against them; these matters have been left to the Indian Department for adjustment. No insolence will be tolerated from any bands of Indians whom we may encounter. We wish to show them that the government is ready and able to punish them if they are hostile, although it may not be disposed to invite war.

14. For each of the incidents he mentioned, Hancock enclosed affidavits from military officers and civilians that allegedly substantiated the guilt of the Cheyennes.
15. Maj. Wickliffe Cooper died on June 8, 1867. Lt. Matthew Berry commanded Troops B and C of the 7th Cavalry, which engaged the Cheyennes at Cimarron Crossing. Six Cheyennes were killed and one enlisted member of the 7th wounded in the affair.

James W. Dixon: Across the Plains with General Hancock

1. James W. Dixon received a direct commission as second lieutenant in the 3rd U.S. Cavalry in May 1866. He was brevetted captain the following year for gallantry as a volunteer officer during the Petersburg campaign. Dixon served until August 1870, when he was honorably discharged at his own request.
2. For a biographical sketch of Theodore R. Davis, see his "A Summer on the Plains," elsewhere in this volume.
3. The Dog Soldiers were a society of the most distinguished warriors of the Cheyenne tribe. The chiefs in question were Tall Bull and White Horse.
4. Tall Bull (c. 1830–69) was the most influential—and perhaps the most militant—of the Dog Soldier chiefs.
5. Pawnee Killer (fl. 1856–70) was not a chief, but rather a war leader of Little Wound's band of Oglala Sioux. Pawnee Killer participated in the Fetterman fight of December 1866 and led the war party that annihilated the Kidder party on July 12, 1867.
6. White Horse (fl. 1845–75) had been a prominent Dog Soldier since the mid-1840s, leading war parties between the Platte and Republican Rivers.
7. Bull Bear (c. 1835–post-1874) was a prominent Dog Soldier chief. He exercised considerable influence over fellow Dog Soldier Roman Nose.
8. It was not Hancock, but rather agent Wynkoop, who rode forward to calm the Indians. Wynkoop spoke with Roman Nose, who said he wanted peace and agreed to meet Hancock between the lines under a flag of truce.
9. Roman Nose (c. 1840–68) was not a chief; he owed his fame to his reputation among Plains tribes as a great warrior. Roman Nose was friendly toward the whites until after the Sand Creek massacre.
10. Hancock had concluded to burn the village as soon as he learned that the Indians had abandoned it. Only a stern protest from Wynkoop stayed his hand until word could be gotten from Custer. William H. Leckie, *The Military Conquest of the Southern Plains* (Norman: University of Oklahoma, 1963), 42–44.

Theodore R. Davis: A Summer on the Plains

1. Theodore R. Davis (1840–94) joined the staff of *Harper's Weekly* in 1861 and served that publication during the Civil War as a correspondent and illustrator, being twice wounded in action. Davis made numerous trips to the West on behalf of *Harper's* in the postwar years. One who knew him said that on his western tours Davis was "possessed of a buoyant and sunny disposition, and made friends wherever he went. No journey was too fatiguing to allay his interest in new sights and new experiences, and any danger added zest to all his numerous enterprises." Don L. Thrapp, *Encyclopedia of Frontier Biography* (Spokane: Arthur H. Clark Co., 1988–94, 1:381.
2. "Indian Village."
3. April 12, 1867.
4. There in fact were only two chiefs—Tall Bull and White Horse; the other Indians were Dog Soldier warriors.

5. Pawnee Killer of the Sioux and White Horse of the Cheyennes, with a small party of warriors.

6. Hancock left Fort Hays on May 5, 1867.

7. For a biographical sketch of Joel H. Elliott see "Sully's Expedition to the Canadian: A Huge Joke," elsewhere in this volume.

8. For a biographical sketch of Charles Brewster, see "Battle of Washita," elsewhere in this volume.

9. Christopher C. Augur (1821–98), of the West Point Class of 1843, ended the Civil War a major general of volunteers, with a strong record for quiet competence. He assumed command of the Department of the Platte in 1867; in 1871 he was transferred to command of the Department of Texas.

10. In the *Chronological List of Actions with Indians from January 15, 1837 to January 1891* (Washington, D.C.: Adjutant General's Office, 1891; reprint, n.p.: Old Army Press, 1979), 28, Indian losses are given as two killed and none wounded.

11. William W. Cooke (1846–76) was a volunteer officer during the Civil War and one of Custer's favorites in the 7th Cavalry.

12. Robert M. West, a brevet brigadier general of volunteers during the Civil War, and William Myers, a brigadier general of volunteers.

13. Albert T. S. Barnitz (1835–1912) began the Civil War a volunteer sergeant and ended the struggle a brevet lieutenant colonel. He was commissioned a captain in the 7th Cavalry in July 1866. His frontier diary and correspondence was published as Robert M. Utley, ed., *Life in Custer's Cavalry: Diaries and Letters of Albert and Jennie Barnitz, 1867–1868* (New Haven, CT: Yale University Press, 1977).

14. Six enlisted men were killed and six wounded in the fight near Fort Wallace; hostile losses are unknown. *Chronological List*, 28.

15. William A. Comstock (1842–68) was a grandnephew of James Fenimore Cooper. He was raised in Michigan and New York, but by the age of eighteen had found his way to Nebraska as an Indian trader. He had lived briefly with Arapahos and Cheyennes, who called him "Medicine Bill."

16. Charles Bent (c. 1847–68) was the son of the famous frontiersman and Indian agent William Bent and the Cheyenne Yellow Woman. After his schooling in St. Louis, he served briefly in the Confederate army, then joined Black Kettle's Cheyennes. He was present at the Sand Creek massacre.

17. Lyman S. Kidder (1842–67) saw extensive service on the frontier as a volunteer officer during the Civil War. He was commissioned a second lieutenant in the 2nd U.S. Cavalry in January 1867 and assigned to the Kansas-Colorado border.

Henderson L. Burgess: The 18th Kansas Volunteer Cavalry, and Some Incidents Connected with Its Service on the Plains

1. Henderson L. Burgess (1849–post-1929) settled at Olathe, Kansas, with his parents in 1866. After his service in the 18th Kansas Volunteer Cavalry, Burgess studied law in Olathe. He was admitted to the bar in 1874 and practiced law in Olathe for more than fifty years. *CKSHS* 13 (1913–1914): 535.

2. Burgess's article also appeared in *Winners of the West* 6, no. 9 (August 30, 1929): 6, with some additional paragraphs added pertaining to pension claims of the surviving members of the 18th and 19th Kansas Volunteer Cavalry regiments. The article was featured in *Winners of the West* just prior to the annual convention of the National Indian War Veterans in Topeka on September 9–12, 1929.

3. The 18th Kansas Volunteer Cavalry was a battalion-strength organization, numbering 353 officers and men.

4. For a biographical sketch of Horace L. Moore, see "An Indian Campaign," elsewhere in this volume.

5. George B. Jenness commanded Company C of the 18th Kansas Volunteer Cavalry.
6. For an account of the battle of Beaver Creek, fought August 22–23, 1867, see George B. Jenness, "The Battle on Beaver Creek."

George B. Jenness: The Battle on Beaver Creek

1. George B. Jenness continued his volunteer service into the campaign of 1868, commanding the Frontier Battalion as a major.
2. July 1, 1867.
3. For a biographical sketch of Horace L. Moore, see "An Indian Campaign," elsewhere in this volume.
4. George A. Armes rose from the ranks during the Civil War and was transferred to the 10th U.S. Cavalry in July 1866. He retired a captain in 1883.
5. For a materially different account of what transpired, see Allison J. Pliley, "Reminiscences of a Plainsman," elsewhere in this volume.
6. The lone warrior may have been Roman Nose; the attackers were predominantly Cheyenne Dog Soldiers.
7. August 28, 1867.

"Bart": Letter from Fort Dodge

1. Randolph B. Marcy (1812–87), of the West Point Class of 1832, saw wide service on the plains prior to the Civil War and authored several valuable books on the region.
2. The *Chronological List,* 30, locates the action on the Arkansas River, ten miles west of Cimarron Crossing, Kansas.
3. Members of the 10th U.S. Cavalry, the "Buffalo Soldiers."

Edward S. Godfrey: The Medicine Lodge Treaty, Sixty Years Ago

1. Edward S. Godfrey (1843–1932) had a distinguished military career, enlisting in the 21st Ohio Infantry in 1861 and retiring a brigadier general in the Regular army in 1907. He served on the frontier from 1867 until Wounded Knee in 1890, and was with Benteen at the Little Bighorn. Godfrey won the Medal of Honor for gallantry at the battle of Bear's Paw Mountain in 1877. He saw duty in Cuba and the Philippines, first with the 12th Cavalry, then as colonel of the 9th Cavalry. Godfrey wrote extensively of his frontier service, particularly of the Little Bighorn.
2. Thomas S. Wallace (d. 1878) of the 3rd U.S. Infantry.
3. William S. Harney (1800–89) had seen wider service against Indians than had any other active officer in the U.S. Army. He participated in the Black Hawk War of 1832, the Second Seminole War, and countless campaigns in the West prior to the Civil War.
4. The councils lasted from October 19 to 28, 1867, including the closing talks with the late Cheyenne arrivals.
5. Black Kettle and his Cheyenne band had met the commissioners on their arrival, and Black Kettle worked hard to bring in the more recalcitrant Cheyennes.
6. Stumbling Bear (1832–1903) was a cousin of Kicking Bird and a noted warrior who had led a decisive charge against Kit Carson's volunteers in the battle of Adobe Walls in 1865. After the Medicine Lodge Treaty, Stumbling Bear gradually became reconciled to the whites, and he visited Washington, D.C., in 1872. From 1877 until his death, Stumbling Bear lived in a government-built home on the Fort Sill reservation.

Henry Morton Stanley: The Medicine Lodge Peace Council

1. Henry Morton Stanley (1841–1904) was born John Rowlands, at Denbigh, Wales, the "illegitimate son of feckless Welsh-speaking parents." His youth was Dickensian in its hardships. Stanley's father died shortly after his birth, and his mother abandoned him when he was six. He shipped to Louisiana as a cabin boy in 1859, where he found work with a merchant, Henry Morton Stanley, whose name he adopted. Stanley enlisted in the Confederate army at the outbreak of the Civil War, but after imprisonment at Camp Douglas, Chicago, he joined the U.S. Navy. After the war he took up journalism, hiring on with the *Daily Missouri Democrat* in 1867. After filing the last of his Medicine Lodge stories, Stanley went to New York and was hired by the *Herald* to report on a British military expedition in Abyssinia. Two years later he went to Africa on behalf of the Herald to "find" Dr. David Livingstone. It was Stanley who labeled Africa the "Dark Continent." Thrapp, *Encyclopedia,* 4:489–90.
2. Not published in the *Democrat.*
3. Sen. John B. Henderson of Missouri had introduced the bill that established the peace commission.
4. Samuel F. Tappan (1830–1913) headed the army inquiry into the Sand Creek massacre. He was an ardent supporter of antislavery forces in Kansas before the Civil War, and during the war served as lieutenant colonel of the 1st Colorado Volunteer Cavalry. He took no part in the Sand Creek massacre and was a bitter foe of its perpetrator, Col. John M. Chivington. It was Tappan who later introduced Stanley to James G. Bennett, editor of the New York *Herald.*
5. Alfred H. Terry (1827–90) was commissioned colonel of the 2nd Connecticut Infantry in May 1861 and ended the Civil War a major general of volunteers. He was commissioned a brigadier general in the Regular army in January 1865 and held important commands on the western frontier until his retirement in 1888.
6. Meredith H. Kidd of the 10th U.S. Cavalry
7. William G. Rankin of the 31st U.S. Infantry.
8. Stanley is mistaken; the southern border of Kansas lay just twenty miles from the council site on Medicine Lodge Creek.
9. Joel H. Elliott of the 7th Cavalry.
10. Stanley neglected to record the response of the Cheyenne chiefs to Taylor's question in his next letter.
11. Mrs. Margaret Adams, a thirty-three-year-old French-Canadian and Arapaho woman, interpreted for Little Raven.
12. Mayne Reid (1818–83) was an English author of adventure stories.
13. Note this example of cultural differences between tribes.
14. John Evans of Colorado.
15. Edmund G. C. Guerrier (1840–1921) was a Cheyenne half-breed who survived the Sand Creek massacre and then scouted for the army. He later became a wealthy rancher in Oklahoma.
16. Owner of the famed Butterfield Stage Company.
17. John H. Page of the 3rd U.S. Infantry reportedly had received threats from the Indians camped near Fort Dodge.
18. Tosh-a-way, a Penateka Comanche chief, was generally well disposed toward the whites.
19. The Comanche signers were Ten Bears, Painted Lips, Silver Brooch, Standing Feather, Gap in the Woods, Horse's Back, Wolf's Name, Little Horn, Iron Mountain, and Dog Fat.
20. The treaty was dated October 21 but signed on the twenty-fifth.
21. George C. Snow was agent to the Osages in the Indian Territory.

22. October 28, 1867.
23. Heap of Birds and Curly Hair of the Cheyennes also signed.
24. The treaty stipulated annuity payments of ten, not twenty, years.

PART TWO: THE BATTLE OF BEECHER ISLAND, 1868

George A. Forsyth: A Frontier Fight

1. George A. "Sandy" Forsyth (1837–1915) was born in Pennsylvania, a ninth-generation descendant of William Brewster, who came to America aboard the *Mayflower.* Forsyth attended a prestigious preparatory school in upstate New York and later moved to Chicago, where he worked as a clerk alongside a young Marshall Field. He also studied law and passed the bar examination before the Civil War. Forsyth became a first lieutenant in the 8th Illinois Cavalry in September 1861 and ended the war a brevet brigadier general of volunteers. He became major of the 9th U.S. Cavalry in 1866. Forsyth took part in sixteen battles, two sieges, and sixty smaller engagements during his career.
2. Frederick H. Beecher (1841–68) was the son of a minister and the nephew of Henry Ward Beecher. He graduated from Bowdoin College in 1862 and immediately thereafter went to war, sustaining severe wounds in the battles of Fredericksburg and Gettysburg.
3. Sharp Grover (1825–69) had lived most of his adult life on the plains and was married to a Sioux woman.
4. Louis Farley (d. 1868) was a buffalo hunter and longtime resident of Kansas.
5. Hudson L. Farley (1849–1911) moved to Washington Territory after the battle of Beecher Island and worked as a carpenter.
6. Henry C. Bankhead (1829–94), of the West Point Class of 1850, retired a major in 1879.
7. Scouts Thomas Murphy and Jack Stillwell suggested to Forsyth that the command fall back to the island, a recommendation Forsyth wisely accepted.
8. The testimony of Native-American participants suggests that Forsyth greatly overstated the prevalence of repeating rifles among the hostiles. John H. Monnett, *The Battle of Beecher Island and the Indian War of 1867–1869* (Niwott: University of Colorado Press, 1992), 135–36.
9. In a footnote to his article, Forsyth described the Dog Soldiers thusly: "Dog Soldiers was a name given to about a hundred warriors of the various Sioux and other tribes that were for some reasons renegades and outcasts; in fact, bad men, generally criminals, who had been compelled to withdraw from association with their own people. Banded together, they were practically Indian highwaymen, and it was this band that the head men of the various tribes claimed they could not control, and upon whom they laid the blame for attacks upon the other settlements when they wished to avoid responsibility."
10. The Indian leading the charge was not Roman Nose, as Sharp Grover supposed and Forsyth here portrays so dramatically, but rather Bad Heart (d. 1875), a half-Sioux, half-Cheyenne war leader. I have replaced subsequent incorrect references to Roman Nose with [Bad Heart].
11. A possible reference to Weasel Bear, who was paralyzed with a severe wound but not killed.
12. This was the assault in which Roman Nose was mortally wounded.
13. Pierre Trudeau (d. 1869) was a French-Canadian trapper. His five-day journey from Beecher Island in quest of reinforcements cost him his health, and he died the next spring.

14. Simpson E. "Jack" Stillwell (1849–1903) moved with his family to Kansas and at the age of fourteen joined a wagon party bound for Santa Fe, remaining in New Mexico for ten years. He was a superb scout, serving under Custer, Miles, and Mackenzie for thirteen years following the battle of Beecher Island. He later was a U.S. deputy marshal and a police judge. Stillwell studied law and was admitted to the bar. He moved to Buffalo Bill Cody's ranch near Cody, Wyoming, late in life and died there.

15. There was no George W. Chalmers among the scouts; Forsyth evidently meant to write George W. Culver.

16. For a biographical sketch of Carpenter, see "The Story of a Rescue," elsewhere in this volume.

17. Forsyth's memory here failed him. The columns of Captain Bankhead and Major Brisbin arrived the day after that of Carpenter.

Fletcher Vilott: Withstood the Siege

1. Fletcher Vilott (1832–1912) came to Kansas from Indiana in 1856 and may have scouted for the 9th U.S. Cavalry before joining Forsyth's command. A paralytic stroke confined him to his bed in about 1908, and he died at his farm home three or four years later. Orvel A. Criqui, *Fifty Fearless Men: The Forsyth Scouts and Beecher Island* (Marceline, MS: Walsworth Publishing Company, 1993), 239–43. I have drawn this and other biographical sketches of the Forsyth scouts from Criqui's *Fifty Fearless Men,* a remarkable work, both as biography and social history, that I recommend heartily for those interested in the battle of Beecher Island or in the settlement of western Kansas.

2. The distance to Sheridan was closer to thirteen miles.

3. Nothing certain is known of scout John Wilson beyond the fact that he served at Beecher Island.

4. George Green, or Greene (1840–1913), came to Kansas in 1866. He settled in Lincoln County and in later life served as councilman and deputy sheriff; built a large hotel in Lincoln, a town he platted and founded; was a successful livestock dealer; and served in the state legislature.

5. John Lyden (1842–76) was an Irish immigrant who became a Lincoln County cattleman after the battle. He was robbed and murdered, apparently by a desperado named Pat Cleary.

6. Henry H. Tucker (1839–1908) was one of three scouts—the others being Chalmers Smith and James J. Peate—who returned to Beecher Island in September 1898 and started the reunions held annually at the battle site. Tucker served in the Union army from 1861 to 1864 and was mustered out as a brevet captain in the 143rd Illinois Infantry Volunteers. He settled in Kansas in April 1866. His wife, Charlotte Ingersoll, was a dynamic plainswoman who edited a weekly newspaper and was a national delegate of the Populist Party. Tucker held various public offices in Ottawa County.

7. Vilott's memory failed him. The mule carrying Surgeon Mooers's equipment was lost; the animal Vilott and his companions brought in carried ammunition.

8. If Grover thought the leader of the first morning charge was Roman Nose, he was mistaken. Roman Nose remained in the rear, having had his medicine "broken" a day or two before when he inadvertently ate fried bread served with an iron implement. Roman Nose had not had time to undergo a purification ritual to restore his medicine, so he was certain he would die if he took part in the fight against Forsyth. Bad Heart, a half-Cheyenne, half-Sioux warrior, led the assault and rode over the scouts' position and back again unscathed. Later in the morning, the Indians

unleashed a second, but less well organized, charge. A single mounted warrior—Dry Throat—galloped ahead of the rest, rode over the island, and was shot down by Jack Stillwell, apparently on the west end of the island. Vilott mistook this warrior for Roman Nose. John H. Monnett, *The Battle of Beecher Island and the Indian War of 1867–1869* (Niwot: University of Colorado Press, 1992), 137–38, 142.

9. This is the charge that Roman Nose led, and in which he was mortally wounded.
10. Allison J. Pliley and John J. Donovan.
11. September 20, 1868.
12. September 25, 1868.
13. Eli Zigler told a somewhat different story, saying that he and Vilott ran back to the island uncertain as to whether the approaching men were friend or foe. See Zigler's account elsewhere in this volume.
14. Zigler said that he and Vilott reached the island while the horsemen were still some distance away and their identity was as yet unknown; the accounts of John Hurst and other scouts support Zigler's version of events.
15. John Hurst recalled that it was John J. "Jack" Peate, a scout who had remained behind at Fort Wallace, and not Pliley, who rode with Carpenter in the vanguard. See Hurst's recollections elsewhere in this volume.
16. The trail Custer had blazed during Hancock's 1867 campaign.
17. There was no George Chalmers on the rolls of the Forsyth scouts; Vilott may have meant G. W. Culver, who was mortally wounded in the fight, when he wrote Chalmers. The only Chalmers on the rolls was Chalmers Smith. Criqui, *Fifty Fearless Men,* 198–99.
18. William Wilson was a former Confederate soldier whose past apparently was unknown to his fellow scouts.

Allison J. Pliley: Reminiscences of a Plainsman

1. Allison J. Pliley (1844–1917) moved with his family to Kansas in 1858. During the Civil War, he fought bushwhackers as a member of the 15th Kansas Cavalry. He settled in Kansas City, Kansas, after the Indian troubles and started a business supplying sand to city building contractors.
2. James A. Hadley. For a biographical sketch of Hadley, see "The 19th Kansas Cavalry and the Conquest of the Plains Indians," elsewhere in this volume.
3. A probable reference to George B. Jenness's, "The Battle on Beaver Creek," elsewhere in this volume.
4. Beaver Creek.
5. August 23, 1867.
6. Andrew J. Smith (1815–97) served in the West with the 1st Dragoons for twenty-three years before the Civil War. He attained the rank of major general of volunteers during the war, and in 1866 became colonel of the 7th Cavalry.
7. Thomas Murphy was the superintendent of Indian affairs for Kansas, not to be mistaken for Thomas B. Murphy, who was in charge of the ambulance train that brought the peace commissioners from Fort Larned to Medicine Lodge, and who later fought at Beecher Island.
8. Roman Nose was a Cheyenne.
9. Fort Larned, Kansas, was located on the right bank of Pawnee Fork, eight miles from its confluence with the Arkansas River, near the present town of Larned, Kansas. It had been built in 1859 to protect the Santa Fe Trail traffic.
10. Pliley repeated the misconception of Major Forsyth and others that Roman Nose led and fell in the morning charge.

Eli Zigler: The Story of the Beecher Island Battle

1. Eli Zigler, or Ziegler (1852–1916), was the youngest of the Forsyth scouts, being only sixteen at the time of the fight. He and his parents moved to Kansas in 1866 and were among the first settlers of Lincoln County. Zigler married in 1872 and had seven daughters. He spent most of his adult life farming.
2. In both "A Frontier Fight," elsewhere in this volume, and his *The Story of the Soldier* (New York: D. Appleton and Company, 1900), 220, Forsyth said that he received his second wound after Zigler and his comrades had carried him to the center of the island.
3. John Haley (1845–72) was born in Canada and came to Lincoln County, Kansas, in 1866 to homestead. He was murdered four years after Beecher Island by one Ezra Hubbard, with whom he had quarreled over a piece of timber.
4. Allison J. Pliley and Chauncey B. Whitney made the abortive effort to get through the Indian lines on the second night; Donovan and Pliley tried—and succeeded—on the third night.
5. September 22, 1868.
6. For a biographical sketch of Peate, see "The Relief of Beecher Island," elsewhere in this volume.
7. Captain Bankhead's column.

John Hurst: Scout John Hurst's Story of the Fight

1. John Hurst (1841–1920) lived on a farm in St. Lawrence County, New York, until 1859, when he set out for California. He penned his recollections in 1911, and they first appeared in the 1917 issue of the *Beecher Island Annual.*
2. Roman Nose was neither a chief nor a Sioux, but rather was a Cheyenne Dog Soldier.
3. Confederate major general Sterling Price staged an unsuccessful raid into Missouri with some twelve thousand troops in September–October 1864.
4. Forsyth said the men carried seven days' rations. Forsyth, *Story of the Soldier,* 211.
5. Monnett, *Battle of Beecher Island,* 125, gives the distance from Fort Wallace to Sheridan as thirteen miles.
6. For a biographical sketch of Thomas B. Murphy, see "The Battle of the Arikaree," elsewhere in this volume.
7. Nothing is known for certain of Walter Armstrong except that he fought at Beecher Island; his name may have been an alias.
8. Forsyth was recumbent when hit the second time.
9. Frank Harrington (c. 1827–1907) served in an Illinois regiment during the Civil War. He was discharged for disability in 1863 and moved to Kansas. In 1880 he resettled in Texas.
10. Martin Burke was an Irish immigrant who had served in India with the British Army and in the Civil War with a New York regiment.
11. Jack Donovan and Allison J. Pliley.

Walter M. Camp: An Interview with Scout John Hurst

1. Walter M. Camp (1867–1925) was a successful civil engineer who became interested in the Indian Wars as an avocation. He learned to speak Sioux and interviewed some 200 survivors of Indian Wars actions. Camp interviewed Hurst on September 11, 1916.

Sigmund Schlesinger: Scout Schlesinger's Story

1. Sigmund Schlesinger (1848–1928) immigrated to the United States from Hungary with his parents in 1864.
2. James Curry (c. 1840–90) was at Beecher's Island, but he also was an unsavory character who apparently did his share to shoot up Hays City, Kansas, during its early days. Among his supposed victims were an "inoffensive youth," several Buffalo Soldiers, and a prostitute.
3. William A. Comstock (1842–68) was a superb scout with an encyclopedic knowledge of the plains and its tribes. He was killed on August 16, 1868, while visiting the camp of Cheyenne chief Turkey Leg to gain information for Lieutenant Beecher on hostile intentions.
4. George B. Clark (1843–pre-1905) had grown up a neighbor of "Wild Bill" Hickok in Putnam County, Illinois, and served in the 7th Iowa Cavalry during the Civil War.
5. Silas Pepoon (1834–74) served as a lieutenant in the 1st Oregon Cavalry during the Civil War and was commissioned a second lieutenant in the Regular army in 1867.

Thomas B. Murphy: The Battle of the Arikaree

1. Thomas B. Murphy (1844–1929) drifted west after apparently having served in the 13th Missouri Infantry (Union) until at least December 1862. He took up farming in southern Kansas in the 1870s and prospered, earning a reputation as a leader in modern farming techniques and a breeder of prize-winning stock. He dictated his recollections of the battle of Beecher Island to his daughter, Dorothy Murphy, in July 1929, some five months before his death.
2. George B. Clark.
3. As with other survivors, Murphy mistook the warrior Bad Heart for Roman Nose.
4. No reliable estimate of Indian losses exists.
5. Murphy confuses Hudson Farley with Louis Farley, who had been mortally wounded during the fighting of September 17.
6. September 16; Murphy here refers to events just before the battle of Beecher Island.
7. Reuben Waller (b. 1840) was a former slave who had joined the 10th U.S. Cavalry in July 1867. He visited Murphy at his ranch in June 1929 to reminisce about the battle.
8. Henry Inman (d. 1899) joined the Regular army as a private in 1857 and earned brevets through the rank of lieutenant colonel for meritorious service during the Civil War and Indian campaigns. He was cashiered in July 1872.

Howard Morton: Wounded at Beecher Island

1. Howard Morton (1840–1925) was the son of a Massachusetts shipbuilder. As a boy, he circumnavigated the globe and worked on several ships. He enlisted in the 39th Massachusetts Infantry in December 1861 and rose to the rank of captain before the war's end. He lost an eye in the early hours of the Beecher Island battle but continued to fight throughout the entire siege. He lived in Beverly, Kansas, until about 1920, when he moved to Palo Alto, California. He died there, and his widow had his ashes scattered in the sea with military honors.

Chauncey B. Whitney: Beecher Island Diary

1. Little is known of the early life of Chauncey B. Whitney (1842–73). He was a first lieutenant in the 2nd Battalion of the Kansas militia during its brief service from July to November 1869. Whitney was elected sheriff of Ellsworth County, Kansas,

in November 1871. He was murdered while trying to stop a fight between two drunken, card-playing hooligans.

2. Joseph Lane (c. 1844–post-1908) was a saloonkeeper in Ellsworth, Kansas, prior to joining the Forsyth scouts. Scouts Chalmers Smith and Sigmund Schlesinger accused him of cowardice during the battle. That Lane behaved cowardly at Beecher Island is open to question. He served as a scout after Beecher Island and was paid a bonus of $50 in October 1868 "for special service in getting through with dispatches from General Carr's command." Lane unquestionably was a scoundrel; he was arrested in February 1869 for stealing horses and described in army dispatches as "a very desperate character." Lane settled in Pagosa Springs, Colorado, in 1876, and was living in Montana as late as 1908. Criqui, *Fifty Fearless Men*, 130–33.

3. George W. Culver served as a lieutenant in the 2nd Colorado Volunteer Cavalry during the Civil War. He worked as a watchmaker in Junction City, Kansas, then took a claim along the Saline River. In 1866 Culver became the first treasurer of Ottawa County, Kansas.

Louis H. Carpenter: The Story of a Rescue

1. Louis H. Carpenter (1839–1916) enlisted as a private in the 6th U.S. Cavalry in 1861 and ended the Civil War a colonel of volunteers. He earned two brevets during the Civil War, and a third brevet and the Medal of Honor for his conduct during the Indian campaigns of 1868. He retired a brigadier general in 1899.

2. Carpenter also wrote a letter to George W. Martin, the secretary of the Kansas State Historical Society, on April 22, 1912, describing the rescue of Forsyth's command. The letter was published in the *CKSHS* 12 (1911–12): 299–302 and differs slightly from Carpenter's account presented here, which originally appeared in *The Journal of the Military Service Institution* 17, no. 67 (September 1895). Significant differences are noted below.

3. In his letter to George W. Martin, Carpenter said he left Fort Wallace on September 21.

4. Carpenter told Martin that his command consisted of seventy men all told, of whom fourteen were civilians.

5. Charles Banzhaf was a German immigrant who had risen from the ranks. He was discharged at his own request in 1870.

6. Louis H. Orleman also was a German immigrant and former enlisted man. He retired a first lieutenant in 1879.

7. Luther P. Bradley (1822–1910) entered the Civil War as a lieutenant colonel of volunteers, rose to the rank of brigadier general of volunteers, and remained in the regular service after the conflict. He served widely on the frontier and retired a colonel in 1886.

8. In his letter to Martin, Carpenter said the corpse was later identified as Roman Nose.

9. James S. Brisbin (d. 1892) had risen to the rank of major general of volunteers during the Civil War. He died a colonel on active duty.

James J. Peate: The Relief of Beecher Island

1. James J. "Jack" Peate (1847–1932) of Pennsylvania was the son of a Methodist preacher. He ran away from home in 1866 and took employment as a scout in Kansas, quickly gaining a reputation for honesty and efficiency. He settled in Beverly, Kansas, after his scouting days and went into business. In September 1898 two survivors of the Beecher Island fight, H. H. Tucker and Chalmers Smith, met

Peate on the island to reminisce. They vowed to hold an annual reunion so long as there were living survivors. Thus was formed the Beecher Island Battle Memorial Association. Sandy Forsyth spoke at the dedication of a monument on the Arikaree during the 1905 reunion. That year Robert Lynam of Wray, Colorado, collected and published several of the scouts' recollections in the first number of *The Beecher Island Annual.*

2. Carpenter was awarded the Medal of Honor on March 26, 1898, for distinguished conduct during the Indian campaigns in Kansas and Colorado of September and October 1868, to include the relief of Forsyth.

PART THREE: SULLY'S NORTH CANADIAN EXPEDITION, 1868

Edward S. Godfrey: Some Reminiscences, Including an Account of General Sully's Expedition against the Southern Plains Indians, 1868

1. The perpetrators of these August 1868 raids were some two hundred Cheyennes under the command of Dog Soldier chief Red Nose and of The-Man-Who-Breaks-the-Marrow-Bones, a prominent member of Black Kettle's band. Depredations on the Smoky Hill and Santa Fe roads, as well as with raids near Fort Dodge, Kansas, followed. On August 23 General Sheridan ordered all Kiowas, Comanches, Arapahos, Cheyennes, and Kiowa-Apaches out of Kansas. Marvin H. Garfield, "Defense of the Kansas Frontier, 1868–1869," *Kansas Historical Quarterly* 1, no. 5 (November 1932): 454–57.

2. J. M. Bell began his distinguished military career in 1862 as a lieutenant in the 86th Ohio Volunteer Infantry. After the war he was commissioned a second lieutenant in the newly organized 7th U.S. Cavalry. Bell retired a brigadier general in 1901.

3. Alfred Sully (1821–79), of the West Point Class of 1841, served in the Seminole, Mexican, and Rogue River Wars. As commander of the 1st Minnesota Volunteer Infantry, he distinguished himself in the eastern theater of the Civil War before being transferred to the District of Dakota in 1863 to fight the Sioux. Sully led successful expeditions against them in 1864 and 1865. From 1869 to 1873 he served on boards at the War Department, then was assigned to command the 21st U.S. Infantry. Sully was known as a hard-swearing, short-tempered man who quarreled bitterly with many of his colleagues, among them George A. Custer. Thrapp, *Encyclopedia,* 3:1388–89.

4. Lewis Thompson (1839–76) rose from the ranks during the Civil War and was promoted to captain in the Regular army in 1866. He took part in Maj. Eugene M. Baker's controversial attack on a Piegan village on the Marias River in January 1870. Thompson committed suicide in the field shortly after the Little Bighorn campaign; he apparently had been drinking heavily just prior to taking his life. Thrapp, *Encyclopedia,* 4:1422.

5. Interestingly, Sully neglected to mention the night attack in his report of the expedition. Sully to Assistant Adjutant General, Department of the Missouri, September 16, 1868, Office of the Adjutant General, Letters Received, Record Group 393, National Archives.

6. September 11, 1868.

7. Algernon E. Smith (d. 1876) earned two brevets for gallantry during the Civil War. He was commissioned a second lieutenant in the 7th Cavalry in August 1867.

8. Myles W. Keogh (1840–76) was born in Ireland and served with distinction in the papal armies before emigrating from Italy in 1862. He won brevets through lieu-

tenant colonel for bravery as a cavalry officer in the Union army and earned a promotion to captain in the 7th Cavalry in 1866. Keogh tended toward depression and heavy drinking, but his courage was never questioned. Thrapp, *Encyclopedia*, 2:773.

9. Wolf Creek also was known as Middle River.
10. September 13, 1868.
11. Francis M. Gibson was commissioned a second lieutenant in the 7th Cavalry in October 1867; he retired a captain in 1891.

Anthony C. Rallya: Fighting Indians from an Ambulance

1. George W. Webb, commander in chief of the National Indian War Veterans and editor of *Winners of the West*.
2. April 1868.
3. Charles G. Cox (d. 1886) had risen from private to major of volunteers during the Civil War. His postwar career was abysmal, as Rallya suggests, and he was cashiered from the army in August 1870.
4. September 7, 1868.
5. California Joe was Moses E. Milner (1829–76), a Kentuckian who had spent time in the California gold fields before the Civil War. By the time of the Sully campaign, he had killed at least three white men—one for having kicked his dog.
6. Probably on the morning of September 11, 1868, near the confluence of the Cimarron River and Crooked Creek.

Joel H. Elliott: Sully's Expedition to the Canadian: A Huge Joke

1. Joel H. Elliott (1840–68) was appointed as the third major of the newly organized 7th Cavalry in March 1867, after a distinguished Civil War career as a company-grade officer. Custer himself urged the appointment, calling Elliott "a natural soldier improved by extensive experience and field service." Thrapp, *Encyclopedia*, 1:460.
2. Eugene A. Carr (1830–1910), of the West Point Class of 1850, ended the Civil War a brevet major general of volunteers and major of the 5th U.S. Cavalry, becoming a lieutenant colonel in the regiment in 1873. He became a brigadier general in 1892.
3. Fort Lyon, Colorado, built in 1860 near old Bent's Fort on the Arkansas River.
4. Edward Byrne, an Irish immigrant who had risen to the volunteer rank of lieutenant colonel during the Civil War.
5. Robert M. West (1834–69) won fame during the Civil War as colonel of the 5th Pennsylvania Cavalry, one of the best volunteer cavalry units in the Army of the Potomac. West later became an alcoholic, and he resigned his commission after the Washita campaign.
6. Custer and West had a feud that apparently began in May 1867, when Custer forced West to shave the heads of six troopers who had gone to the Fort Hays sutler's store without permission. West retaliated after the Republican River expedition of that summer. To the charges Custer then faced for absence without leave, West brought supplementary charges relating to two deserters from West's troop who had been shot on Custer's authority during the campaign. Utley, ed., *Life in Custer's Cavalry*, 281.

Anonymous: The Fight on Prairie Dog Creek

1. From the details he provides of General Sheridan's instructions to his quartermaster and chief commissary officer, it seems probable that the author of the article was a member of Sheridan's staff.
2. Also known as Buffalo Tank.
3. Maj. William B. Royall had been on a scout searching for Tall Bull's Cheyenne Dog Soldiers north of the Arkansas River with seven troops of the 5th Cavalry.
4. A reference to the battle of Beaver Creek, in which Troops H, I, and M of the 10th Cavalry under Capt. L. H. Carpenter, then escorting Maj. E. A. Carr to Fort Wallace, encountered a band of two hundred Cheyennes who were starting off on a buffalo hunt from a nearby village.
5. Thomas W. C. Moore (d. 1881) began the Civil War a private and ended the conflict a brevet lieutenant colonel of volunteers. He was discharged at his own request in 1870.
6. John H. Kane was an Irish immigrant who rose from the ranks during the Civil War; he resigned his commission in 1870.
7. Jules C. A. Schenofsky was a volunteer captain during the Civil War and was discharged at his own request in 1870. William C. Forbush, of the West Point Class of 1868, retired a colonel in 1903.

PART FOUR: THE CHEYENNE WAR, 1868–69

William C. Church: Sheridan's Indian Campaign

1. William C. Church (1836–1917) was the editor and cofounder, with his brother Francis P. Church, of the *Army and Navy Journal* and of *Galaxy Magazine,* which merged with the *Atlantic Monthly* in 1888. Church saw action as a volunteer aide and war correspondent during the Civil War and was wounded at the battle of Williamsburg. At the time of his death, he ranked as one of America's foremost journalists.
2. Philip H. Sheridan (1831–88), of the West Point Class of 1853, emerged from the Civil War with the rank of major general in the Regular army. He assumed command of the Department of the Missouri in February 1868. In March 1869 he was promoted to lieutenant general and given command of the Military Division of the Missouri, which he held until 1883, when he became the commanding general of the army.

"Soldat": General Sully's Winter Expedition

1. The "coloring of horses"—mounting the men of a troop on like-colored animals— was a practice that Custer introduced on this campaign; one that was to spread throughout the entire U.S. Cavalry.
2. Samuel J. Crawford (1835–1913) was a graduate of the Cincinnati College Law School, who migrated to Kansas in 1859. He saw action in the Civil War, first as a captain in the 2nd Kansas Cavalry, and later as colonel of the 83rd U.S. Colored Infantry, before resigning in November 1864 to assume the office of governor of Kansas. Crawford championed the removal of all Indians from Kansas to clear the way for white settlement.
3. A reference to the future Camp Supply, Indian Territory.
4. "Lo" was a sarcastic nickname for the Indian, from "Lo, the poor Indian," a phrase supposedly found in much humanitarian literature on the plight of the Western tribes.

Horace L. Moore: An Indian Campaign

1. Horace L. Moore (d. 1914) ended the Civil War as colonel of the 4th Arkansas Volunteer Cavalry (Union). He settled in Lawrence, Kansas, and was president of the Kansas State Historical Society in 1906.
2. An Indian Campaign was first printed as a pamphlet for apparent distribution to Colonel Moore's family and friends, and few copies survive. Moore also presented it as an address before the Twenty-first Annual Meeting of the Kansas State Historical Society on January 19, 1897. It was reprinted posthumously as "The 19th Kansas Cavalry in the Washita Campaign," *Chronicles of Oklahoma* 2, no. 4 (1914): 350–65.
3. The Pawnees were not hostile to the whites and figured in the campaign as victims of Cheyenne raids or as scouts for the army.
4. The number of warriors killed on the Washita is uncertain. The estimates of white participants range from Custer's high of 103 to that of J. S. Morrison, a scout sympathetic to the Indians, who said that not more than twenty warriors had been slain, the remainder of the casualties being women and children. Stan Hoig, *Battle of the Washita* (New York: Doubleday, 1976), 200–201.
5. Ben Clark (1842–1914) moved from St. Louis to Fort Bridger, Wyoming, where he became the post courier at the age of thirteen. He participated on the side of the federal government in the so-called Mormon War of 1857 and saw frontier service with the 6th Kansas Cavalry during the Civil War. Both the military and its Native American foes held Clark in high regard. He was fluent in several native languages and married a full-blood Cheyenne woman, by whom he had eleven children.
6. Sgt. Maj. Walter Kennedy was with Captain Hamilton's party. His body was found with one bullet hole in the right temple, seventeen in the back, and two in the legs; his head was partially severed from the body.
7. There was considerable disagreement among participants in the campaign regarding the circumstances surrounding the death of Clara Blinn and her child and the location of the bodies. Former Comanche-Kiowa agent Jesse Leavenworth testified before a Senate Committee on Indian Affairs that troops had shot Blinn accidentally at the start of the fight. For a full discussion of the subject, see Hoig, *The Battle of the Washita*, 211–13.
8. The army released Clara Blinn's letter to the press, and it was published in a number of Kansas and eastern newspapers.
9. William B. Hazen (1830–87) was a controversial, blunt-speaking officer who in 1880 assumed command of the Army Signal Corps as a brigadier general. He was detailed to the Bureau of Indian Affairs from 1868 to 1870.
10. James W. Forsyth (1834–1906), of the West Point Class of 1856. A Sheridan protégé, he rose to command of the 7th Cavalry in 1886 and ended his career a major general in the Regular army.
11. Crawford resigned his commission in order to go to Washington, D.C., and lobby for pay for his volunteers.
12. Four lesser Cheyenne chiefs—Lean Face, Big Head, Fat Bear, and another—were seized as hostages for the return of two white women held captive in the village of Medicine Arrow. Hoig, *Battle of the Washita*, 176–77.
13. Lean Face.
14. Romeo, or Romero, was a Mexican who had been raised among the Cheyennes.
15. Sarah White, a teenaged girl, had been seized in a raid on her parents' homestead near Concordia, Kansas; Mrs. James Morgan, married just one month, was taken from her homestead on the Solomon River. Both raids occurred in October 1868.
16. March 23, 1869.

James A. Hadley: The 19th Kansas Cavalry and the Conquest of the Plains Indians

1. James A. Hadley (1848–post-1908) came to Kansas from Indiana in 1866 and found work as a subsistence agent for the army. His father was a Quaker elder and one of the founders of Earlham College. Hadley served in the 18th Kansas Cavalry in 1867. In 1871 he was desperately wounded in an encounter with Indians near Sand Creek, Colorado. Twenty-four years later, he underwent a skull trephination to ward off total blindness from optical paralysis, a consequence of his wound. He married twice and settled in Indianapolis.

2. Brady probably was killed to settle a score with members of the regiment. Near the end of the term of service of the 19th, a drunken Brady refused to board the train that was to carry the regiment from Hays to Topeka. When the sergeant major tried to put him on a car, Brady shot him dead.

3. The 19th Kansas was not, strictly speaking, marching for Camp Supply in particular, but rather for its proposed site in the Indian Territory, as Camp Supply was not officially established until November 8, 1868, three days after the regiment left Topeka.

4. See Moore's "An Indian Campaign," elsewhere in this volume.

5. Custer wrote a series of articles about his experiences campaigning on the Southern Plains that appeared serially in *Galaxy* magazine between January 1872 and October 1874, under the title "My Life on the Plains." The articles were reprinted in book form under the same title.

6. The commanding officer of G Troop, 19th Kansas Volunteer Cavalry.

7. Mo-nah-se-tah may have revealed considerably more than the secrets of the chiefs to Custer. Captain Benteen later claimed that Custer kept her in camp as his mistress and was "seen many times in the very act of copulating with her." Custer's own description of Mo-nah-se-tah in *My Life on the Plains* certainly read like the words of one infatuated. Mo-nah-se-tah, said Custer, was "an exceedingly comely squaw, possessing a bright, cheery face, a countenance beaming with intelligence, and a disposition more inclined to be merry than one usually finds among the Indians. She was probably rather under than over twenty years of age. Added to bright, laughing eyes, a set of pearly teeth and a rich complexion, her well-shaped head was crowned with a luxuriant growth of the most beautiful silken tresses, rivaling in color the blackness of the raven and extending, when allowed to fall loosely over her shoulders, to below her waist." Charles K. Mills, *Harvest of Barren Regrets: The Army Career of Frederick William Benteen, 1834–1898* (Glendale: Arthur H. Clark Company, 1985), 178–79. Scout Ben Clark corroborated Benteen's claims, and several of Charles J. Brill's Cheyenne informants told him that Custer and Mo-nah-se-tah were lovers, and that the Cheyennes "had little use for her after her return to the tribe when Custer went north for good because she had displayed a preference for her captor so long as he would keep her with him." Brill, *Conquest of the Southern Plains*, 45–46; Sherry L. Smith, *The View from Officers' Row: Army Perceptions of Western Indians* (Tucson: University of Arizona Press, 1990), 82–83.

8. Philip H. Sheridan, *Personal Memoirs of P. H. Sheridan*, 2 vols. (New York: Charles L. Webster and Company, 1888), 2:325–27.

9. Lone Wolf (c. 1820–79) was a Kiowa chief and one of nine Native American signers of the Medicine Lodge Treaty of 1867.

10. First named Camp Wichita, Fort Sill was established on March 4, 1869, near the foot of the Wichita Mountains at the junction of Cache and Medicine Bluff Creeks. The post was renamed Fort Sill on July 2, 1869.

11. William C. Jones (1840–95) served as an officer in the 3rd Kansas Volunteer Infantry during the Civil War. He was warden of the Kansas State Penitentiary from 1883 to 1885 and U.S. marshal for Kansas from 1886 to 1890.
12. Not the famous Northern Cheyenne chief Dull Knife, but a Dog Soldier chief whom George Bent said was named Lean Face. Hoig, *Battle of the Washita,* 177.
13. Medicine Arrow, or Rock Forehead, as his Cheyenne name translated, was a lesser Cheyenne chief.
14. Big Head was a prominent Dog Soldier chief. Grinnell, *Fighting Cheyennes,* 114.
15. Name also given as Joseph Larimer. He died on February 23, 1869, at Camp Supply. Three other members of the 19th Kansas Cavalry—John J. Rogers of G Troop, and William Mills and William Libbitt of Company L—also died from exposure or disease during the regiment's term of service.

Joseph P. Rodgers: A Few Years' Experience on the Western Frontier
1. Joseph P. Rodgers (1850–1926), known as "Phelps" Rodgers, served as a private in the 19th Kansas Volunteer Cavalry. He died at the Sawtelle Old Soldiers Home near Los Angeles, California.
2. Thomas C. Nixon (1838–84) worked as a freighter in Kansas before becoming a prominent buffalo hunter in the early 1870s. He later ran a saloon and brothel in Dodge City and was named assistant city marshal. He was gunned down in a feud over a prostitute.
3. The call went out on October 11, 1868.
4. November 18, 1868.
5. November 22.
6. November 24.
7. Rodgers is mistaken as to the sequence of events; Captain Pliley set out on November 22.
8. James A. Hadley said Major Jenkins arrived on December 1. See "The 19th Kansas Cavalry and the Conquest of the Plains Indians," elsewhere in this volume.
9. The march began on December 7, 1868.
10. December 10, 1868.
11. March 24, 1869.

W. R. Smith: Camp Starvation
1. W. R. Smith served in Company F, 19th Kansas Volunteer Cavalry. Later in life he lived in Pryor, Oklahoma.

George B. Jenness: Lost in the Snow at Old Camp Supply
1. Apache Bill Seaman and Jack Stillwell, the latter of Beecher Island fame.

Henry Pearson: Campaigning with the 19th Kansas Volunteer Cavalry
1. Henry Pearson served as an enlisted man in Company I, 19th Kansas Volunteer Cavalry.
2. Pearson's recollection is faulty. The events he describes took place along Medicine Lodge Creek on the sixth day of the march, November 18, 1868.
3. Colonel Crawford maintained that all but six horses eventually were brought in.
4. November 20, 1868.
5. November 22.
6. Bill Seaman, also known as "Apache Bill."
7. March 2, 1869.

Edward S. Godfrey: The Washita Campaign

1. Alfred Gibbs (1823–68) was a regular officer who had served in the Mexican War and been wounded in action against the Apaches in 1857. He led a cavalry brigade in the Shenandoah Valley campaign of 1864. On December 26, 1868, he died suddenly of "congestion of the brain."

2. Fort Hays originally was located on Big Creek, a branch of the Smoky Hill River. It was built in October 1865 to protect construction crews of the Kansas Pacific Railroad. In June 1867 it was relocated fifteen miles to the west on the Big Creek.

3. Godfrey implies that the two Kansas units were recruited simultaneously; they were not. The 18th Kansas Cavalry was recruited for service during the so-called Hancock War of 1867, and the 19th Kansas Cavalry was mustered in the following year for service during Sheridan's winter campaign.

4. Andrew W. Evans (1829–1906), of the West Point Class of 1852, saw distinguished service in both the Civil and Indian Wars. He retired a lieutenant colonel in 1883 and was brevetted a brigadier general for gallantry at the July 1882 battle of the Big Dry Wash.

5. William H. Penrose earned brevets through the rank of brigadier general for service during the Civil War. He retired a colonel in 1896.

6. November 18, 1868.

7. Mountain man Jim Bridger had tried to dissuade Sheridan from undertaking a winter campaign.

8. It is unclear from the original *Winners of the West* article whether this passage also comes from Blacksmith Harvey's diary, and if it did, at what point Godfrey resumes his own narrative.

9. Louis M. Hamilton (1844–68) enlisted in July 1862 and won brevets for gallantry at Chancellorsville and Gettysburg during the Civil War.

10. For a biographical sketch of Edward G. Mathey, see "The Washita Campaign and the Battle of the Washita," elsewhere in this volume.

11. Edward Myers (1830–71) was a German immigrant who had enlisted in the 1st Dragoons before the Civil War. He earned brevets through lieutenant colonel during the Civil War and in 1866 received a captaincy in the new 7th U.S. Cavalry.

12. For a biographical sketch of Frederick W. Benteen, see "Another Side of the Washita Story," elsewhere in this volume.

13. A descendent of patriot Nathan Hale, Owen Hale (1843–77) was appointed a first lieutenant in the 7th Cavalry in 1866 and was killed in action during the battle of Bear Paw Mountain.

14. Edward Law (1847–81) was educated in Europe and at Harvard University. He was appointed a second lieutenant in the 7th Cavalry in August 1867 but resigned in 1870 to study law.

15. Henry Lippincott (1839–1908) served with the 7th Cavalry until 1871, and thereafter rose in the Medical Department to the rank of colonel and assistant surgeon general before his retirement in 1903.

16. Fifty-three Cheyenne women and children were taken prisoner in the Washita massacre.

17. Upon her capture, Mah-wis-sa claimed to be the sister of Black Kettle.

18. November 28, 1868.

19. Thomas W. Custer (1845–76) enlisted as a sixteen-year-old in the 21st Ohio Infantry and earned two Medals of Honor for gallantry during the Civil War. With his brother George A. Custer's help, he received a Regular army commission in 1866.

20. Thomas J. Marsh, of the West Point Class of 1868, resigned his commission in 1872.

21. William M. Beebe, Jr. (d. 1883), of the 38th U.S. Infantry.
22. The culpability of Black Kettle, directly or otherwise, in the attacks by a Cheyenne war party on the Saline and Solomon River settlements in August 1868 has never been conclusively demonstrated.

Edward G. Mathey: The Washita Campaign and the Battle of the Washita

1. Edward G. Mathey (1837–1915) fled his native France in 1845, after his family insisted he enter the priesthood. He emerged from the Civil War a major of volunteers and was appointed a second lieutenant in the 7th Cavalry in 1867, retiring with the rank of major in 1896. Mathey was known in the 7th Cavalry as "Bible-thumper" because of his dubious reputation as the "star blasphemy-hurler of the regiment." The ever-critical Captain Benteen said of Mathey, "Of all the nonentities with which a troop of cavalry could be damned, head and front, Capt. E. G. M. fills the bill." Mathey was in charge of the regimental pack train both at the battle of the Washita and the Little Bighorn; his apparent mediocrity kept him from losing his scalp with Custer in the latter battle. Utley, *Life in Custer's Cavalry,* 267–68.
2. November 26, 1868.
3. Hamilton had been ordered to command the regimental train but swapped places with Mathey, who apparently was suffering from snow blindness.
4. Mah-wis-sa, a sister of the slain Black Kettle.

Francis M. Gibson: Our Washita Battle

1. Francis M. Gibson (1847–1919) was a civilian clerk in the army Pay Department in Washington, D.C., before receiving a regular commission in the 7th Cavalry in October 1867. He retired a captain in 1890 on disability for chronic gastroenteritis.
2. Perhaps the most disliked officer in the 7th Cavalry, David W. Wallingford (1837–83) was an unsavory character who pillaged civilians during the Civil War and who associated with "prostitutes and lewd women" on the frontier. Dismissed from the army in 1870, he later landed in the Kansas Penitentiary for horse stealing.
3. John M. Johnson, of the West Point Class of 1867, was honorably discharged at his own request in 1870.
4. Thomas B. Weir (1838–76) was a loyal member of the Custer clique in the 7th Cavalry. He died in December 1876 of "congestion of the brain."
5. Samuel M. Robbins (1832–78) was a good officer when sober, but because of frequent public drunkenness, a court-martial recommended his dismissal from the army in 1871. He was permitted to resign.

Charles Brewster: Battle of Washita

1. Charles Brewster (1836–1904) was a law office clerk before the Civil War and served on Custer's staff during the Shenandoah Valley campaign of 1864. He was appointed a second lieutenant in the 7th Cavalry in July 1866. Col. S. D. Sturgis called him "constitutionally inefficient" and recommended his dismissal in 1870, but Brewster was allowed to resign honorably. He tried for the next thirty years to secure reinstatement in the army, each time failing. On one such occasion in 1878, 7th Cavalry officers Benteen, Mathey, Godfrey, Moylan, and Bell signed a letter to the Senate Military Committee maintaining that Brewster was "totally unfit, in every way, to be an army officer. He lacks decision, force of character, self-respect, and indeed everything that is noble and manly, and fails utterly to command the respect of troops." Utley, *Life in Custer's Cavalry,* 251–52.

2. November 26, 1868.
3. Here Brewster refers to himself. He may be lying about having been given the lead spot in the march; Colonel Sturgis said Brewster never hesitated to tell a lie when it suited his purpose. Utley, *Life in Custer's Cavalry,* 252.
4. More probably a Cheyenne woman who took her own life, and that of her infant, rather than fall captive. Hoig, *Battle of the Washita,* 134.
5. A reference to Clara Blinn and her child.

George A. Custer: The Indian War—Battle of the Washita—Report of General Custer

1. George A. Custer (1839–76), of the West Point Class of 1861, emerged from the Civil War a brevet major general in the Regular army. He was assigned to the 7th Cavalry as lieutenant colonel in 1866.
2. Cheyenne survivors admitted to losing only two chiefs—Black Kettle and Little Rock—and eleven warriors killed. Given that the 7th Cavalry lost only one officer—Captain Hamilton—and three enlisted men killed or mortally wounded during the fighting in and around the village itself, Custer's calculation of 103 warriors killed or wounded seems high, and undoubtedly the correct total, whatever it may be, included many women and children. Charles J. Brill, *Conquest of the Southern Plains* (Oklahoma City: Golden Saga Publishers, 1938), 161; Hoig, *Battle of the Washita,* 200–201.
3. Custer makes no further mention of these white captives, either in later correspondence or in his book, *My Life on the Plains,* and as historian Stan Hoig noted, no one has ever clarified these references. Hoig, *Battle of the Washita,* 140.
4. Probably a reference to the Cheyenne woman who was seen to kill herself and her child rather than be taken captive.

George Bent: She-Wolf's Account of the Death of Major Elliott

1. George Bent (1843–1918) was the son of the famous early frontiersman George Bent and Owl Woman, a Cheyenne. He grew up bilingual and was educated in St. Louis. He fought for the Confederacy during the Civil War and later went to live with his mother's people. Later in life, he became a prolific correspondent on Southern Plains Indian history and ethnology.
2. Lt. William Renick, acting assistant surgeon, 7th U.S. Cavalry.

Frederick W. Benteen: Another Side of the Washita Story

1. Frederick W. Benteen (1834–98) began the Civil War as a lieutenant in the 10th Missouri (Union) Cavalry and emerged from the conflict a lieutenant colonel of volunteers with two brevets. Commissioned a captain in the 7th U.S. Cavalry in July 1866, he developed an abiding distaste for Custer that began with Custer's perceived abandonment of Elliott's detachment at the Washita and continued until the day Benteen died. A heavy drinker, Benteen was sentenced to dismissal from the service by a court-martial. In light of Benteen's good combat record, President Grover Cleveland reduced the sentence to suspension from duty for a year. Benteen requested disability retirement to take effect at the end of his suspension. It was granted, and he retired in July 1888.
2. Benteen's unsigned letter to the St. Louis *Democrat* so infuriated Custer that he threatened to thrash its author, but he backed down when Benteen confessed responsibility.

[Edward Hunter]: Colonel Evans's Indian Expedition

1. Edward Hunter, of the West Point Class of 1865, served as adjutant for the 12th U.S. Infantry and later as quartermaster for the 1st U.S. Cavalry. In 1901 he was promoted to colonel and judge advocate.
2. Evans's command in fact found water—the North Fork of Red River, which they reached on December 23—but it was too heavily impregnated with gypsum and salt for human or animal consumption.
3. Elisha Tarlton (d. 1884) was commissioned a second lieutenant in the 3rd Cavalry in August 1861 and was honorably discharged at his own request in October 1870.
4. Lieutenant Hunter commanded the howitzer section.
5. The village may have belonged to the Nokoni Comanche Chief Horseback (or Horse's Back), whose warriors allegedly had raided Texas frontier settlements during the summer and fall of 1868. Leckie, *Military Conquest,* 117–18, identifies the village as that of Horseback's band; Rupert N. Richardson, *The Comanche Barrier to South Plains Settlement* (Abilene, TX: Hardin-Simmons University, 1981), 162–63, implies it belonged to another band.
6. It is this reference that enabled me to identify Hunter as the author of the article, as Major Evans, in his report of the expedition, states that he sent Hunter to Fort Cobb with dispatches for General Sheridan.
7. Hunter overstates Sheridan's success. Only two chiefs, Little Robe of the Cheyennes and Yellow Bear of the Arapahos, favored surrender. They parleyed with General Sheridan on January 1, 1869, and accompanied him and a small escort on a peace mission to the Arapaho band of Little Raven, who also capitulated. The powerful Dog Soldier band of Tall Bull remained defiant.

Edward M. Hayes: The Story of an Indian Campaign: Carr's Republican River Expedition of 1869

1. Edward M. Hayes (1842–1912) enlisted as a musician in the 5th U.S. Cavalry in 1856 and earned a volunteer brevet of major in the 10th Ohio Cavalry during the Civil War. He was commissioned a second lieutenant in the 5th Cavalry and assigned to frontier duty in 1868. He retired a brigadier general in 1903.
2. William B. Royall (1825–95) began his military service in 1846 as an officer in the Missouri Mounted Volunteers and saw action against New Mexican insurrectionists at Taos and later against the Comanches. Royall received six saber wounds in the Civil War and retired a colonel in 1887.
3. On June 9, 1869, Major Carr left Fort McPherson with eight troops of the 5th Cavalry and a three-company battalion of Pawnee scouts to track down the recalcitrant band of Cheyenne Dog Soldier Tall Bull, which had refused to make peace.
4. July 8, 1869.
5. Possibly Cpl. John Kile, Troop M, 5th U.S. Cavalry.
6. The engagement was more spectacular than sanguinary, as the cavalry suffered no losses and reported only two hostiles wounded. *Chronological List,* 41.
7. One cavalryman was wounded in the fray; hostile losses, if any, were unknown. Ibid., 41.
8. July 10, 1869.
9. Carr struck Tall Bull's main camp at Summit Springs, Colorado, in a narrow valley sixty miles up the South Platte River from Fort Sedgwick, on July 11, 1869. Tall Bull and fifty-one warriors were killed in the melee, while Carr reported only one man wounded.
10. The battle of Summit Springs also destroyed the Dog Soldiers as a cohesive fighting force.

11. William F. "Buffalo Bill" Cody (1846–1917) had moved with his family to Kansas in 1854. He rode for the Pony Express and during the Civil War served as a scout for the 9th Kansas Cavalry and later a private in the 7th Kansas Cavalry. His first employment as a government scout for the Regular army was not, as Hayes asserts, during the Republican River expedition; Cody began hiring out as a scout at Kansas frontier posts in 1866, and in August 1867 had a fight with hostiles while scouting for the 10th U.S. Cavalry.

Anonymous: The Capture of a Cheyenne Village [Summit Springs]

1. The three companies were under the command of Major Royall.
2. July 5, 1869.
3. The famed Pawnee Battalion of Maj. Frank J. North (1840–85), a plainsman who had long enjoyed firm and friendly relations with the Pawnees. After Pawnee scouts proved their worth guarding the Union Pacific Railroad during the Plains Indian uprising of 1864, North was authorized to enroll first one company, and later three companies of fifty men each, for Regular service. For an excellent history of the Pawnee Battalion, see George B. Grinnell, *Two Great Scouts and Their Pawnee Battalion* (Cleveland: Arthur H. Clark Company, 1928).
4. Carr halted his command about one mile north of Summit Springs, Colorado, at 1:30 P.M. on July 11.
5. Carr reported one enlisted man wounded. *Chronological List*, 41.
6. The women were carried off on May 30, 1869, during Tall Bull's raid through Republican County, Kansas. The soldiers found one, a Mrs. Alderdice, dead in one of the Indian lodges with her head crushed. The second woman, a Mrs. Weichel, managed to crawl toward Carr's troops despite a bullet wound in the breast. Cheyenne informants told George B. Grinnell that the women were Germans who spoke no English, and that Tall Bull shot them both. Leckie, *Military Conquest*, 128, 131; Grinnell, *Fighting Cheyennes*, 317.

PART FIVE: MACKENZIE AND THE TEXAS FRONTIER, 1866–73

Britton Davis: Recollections of the Kiowas and Comanches

1. Britton Davis (1860–1930), of the West Point Class of 1881, was given charge of renegade Chiricahuas who had surrendered after the Sierra Madre campaign and led Apache scouts ably during the early months of the Geronimo campaign of 1885–86. He resigned his commission in June 1886 to manage the Corralitos Mining and Cattle Company in western Chihuahua. During the next twenty years, Davis acquired a fortune of $750,000, only to see it swept away in the Mexican Revolution. After farming a time in New York, he settled in San Diego and there wrote *The Truth about Geronimo* (New Haven, CT: Yale University Press, 1929), one of the best accounts of the Apache wars.
2. Britton's father was Edmund Davis, the Republican Reconstruction governor of Texas from 1869 to 1873.
3. Britton Davis's recollection of dates is faulty. The event Davis describes occurred in October 1873.
4. Big Tree (c. 1845–1929) was a prominent Kiowa warrior who, with a large war party under Satanta, on May 17, 1871, attacked a wagon freight train on Salt Creek, Texas, belonging to government contractor Henry Warren, killing seven teamsters and running off with forty-one mules. Big Tree and Satanta boasted too freely of their exploits and were arrested at Fort Sill, Indian Territory, and taken to

Jacksboro, Texas, for trial. They were convicted of murder and sentenced to hang. The sentence was commuted to life in prison. Governor Davis released them after their tribe gave its pledge that they would behave. Big Tree and Satanta were again arrested during the Red River War. Satanta committed suicide in prison, but Big Tree was released after a short incarceration. He abided by his parole and in 1897 joined the Baptist church, serving for thirty years as a deacon.

[Benjamin T. Hutchins]: With the 6th U.S. Cavalry in Texas

1. Benjamin T. Hutchins was the only officer then serving with the 6th Cavalry whose surname began with the letter "H." As officers who contributed to the *Army and Navy Journal* often signed articles with their initials, I have attributed authorship to Hutchins. Captain Hutchins resigned from the Regular army in September 1869.
2. Ira W. Claflin (d. 1867), of the West Point Class of 1857.
3. David R. Porter (d. 1866), of the West Point Class of 1865.
4. Fort Chadbourne, Texas, was located on Oak Creek, thirty miles above its junction with the Colorado River. Fort McKavett was located on the south bank of the San Saba River, a branch of the Colorado.
5. Fort Chadbourne was reoccupied in May 1867 and abandoned permanently in December of that year. Fort McKavett was reoccupied in April 1868 and closed in June 1883.
6. George C. Cram (d. 1869), commissioned a captain in the Regular army in 1861.
7. Brig. Gen. Samuel P. Heintzelman (1805–80), commander of the Department of Texas.
8. The 6th Cavalry was posted to Frederick in June 1865 for a general reorganization, remaining there until mid-October 1865.

William J. Miller: An Indian Attack in 1868

1. Miller's account also appeared in the Alamogordo, New Mexico, *News,* January 16, 1936, and in *Frontier Times* 13, no. 6 (March 1936): 317–21.

W. A. Thompson: Scouting with Mackenzie

1. William A. Thompson served as an enlisted man during the Civil War. He was commissioned a second lieutenant in the 4th U.S. Cavalry in June 1867. Brevetted for gallantry during the Red River campaign of 1874–75, Thompson retired as a major in 1898.
2. Thompson spells the name of the tribal division as Twa-ha-da; I have replaced it with the more common spelling of Kwahadi.
3. Ranald S. Mackenzie (1840–89) graduated first in the West Point Class of 1862 and won four brevets for gallantry during the Civil War. After seventeen years of distinguished postwar frontier service, his mental health deteriorated, and the army retired him over his protests in 1884. He died of paresis two years later at his boyhood home in New Jersey.
4. Mackenzie led five troops of the 4th U.S. Cavalry and a detachment of Tonkawa scouts in the attack on the Kwahadi village along McClellan's Creek.
5. The army settled on a figure of 23 Kwahadis killed, 1 wounded, and 120 captured—most of the latter being women and children. Mackenzie lost four men wounded, one of them mortally. *Chronological List,* 52.
6. Mackenzie's full command consisted of eight troops of the 4th Cavalry and five companies of the 10th Infantry, all of which he had concentrated at Fort Concho,

Texas. The thirty scouts were Seminoles and Tonkawas under the command of Lieutenant Thompson.

7. The number of Cheyenne ponies captured—and subsequently killed—has been estimated at between 1,050 and 1,800. In his official report, Mackenzie simply said that "over one thousand" had been seized. Leckie, *Military Conquest,* 222.

8. The fight occurred on November 5, 1874, near the headwaters of the Double Mountain Fork of the Brazos River, Texas. Captain R. G. Carter, *On the Border with Mackenzie* (Mattituck, NY: J. M. Carroll, 1985), 506. Leckie, *Military Conquest,* 223, mistakenly gives the date of this action as November 3.

9. The last hostile Kwahadi band surrendered in June 1875.

"Eureka": On the Trail of Satanta

1. The article originally appeared under the prosaic title "Scout by the 4th Cavalry."

2. The Fort Sill Indian Agency, located in the Indian Territory.

3. William T. Sherman (1820–91), the commanding general of the army.

4. Satank (c. 1810–71), a Kiowa medicine man and war chief, also known as Setangya.

5. Lawrie Tatum (1822–1900), an Iowa farmer and prominent Quaker who became agent for the Kiowas and Comanches in July 1869.

6. Benjamin H. Grierson (1826–1911), an Illinois merchant who emerged from the Civil War a major general of volunteers. He became colonel of the 10th Cavalry in July 1866 and held a deep affection for his black troops.

7. June 6, 1871.

8. John M. Bacon was detached from the 9th Cavalry in 1871 to serve as aide-de-camp to General Sherman. He retired a colonel in 1899.

E. B. Beaumont: Over the Border with Mackenzie

1. Eugene B. Beaumont (1837–1926), of the West Point Class of 1861, was assigned to the 4th U.S. Cavalry during the Civil War and won a Medal of Honor for gallantry at Harpeth, Tennessee, in December 1864 and during the capture of Selma, Alabama, in April 1865. A year later he took command of A Troop, 4th Cavalry. Beaumont was a cavalry instructor at West Point from 1875 to 1879 and retired in 1892. A popular officer, Beaumont was a skilled raconteur, played the guitar, and wrote ballads in the field.

2. For a biographical sketch of Wesley Merritt, see "Rescuing Payne's Command," elsewhere in this volume.

3. William W. Belknap (1829–90) attended Princeton College, studied law at Georgetown, D.C., and began practicing law in Iowa in 1851. He ended the Civil War a brigadier general of volunteers. President Grant appointed him secretary of war in 1869. Belknap resigned in 1876 on charges of malfeasance arising from the sale of a post tradership in order to remove himself from the jurisdiction of a Senate impeachment trial. Belknap's guilt is uncertain; his wife may have arranged the deal without Belknap's knowledge.

4. In English, "unknown terrain."

5. Mescalero Apaches, so named for their custom of eating mescal. Less warlike than other Apaches, the Mescaleros ranged principally between the Rio Grande and the Pecos River in New Mexico.

6. The Lipans were an Apache people who roamed through Texas, depredating against whites, Mexicans, and other Native Americans. The Lipans maintained good relations with the Mescaleros.

7. The Kickapoos were of the central Algonquian group and had been pushed out of Wisconsin onto the Kansas plains, where in 1852 a large party broke from the principal group and migrated to Mexico.
8. "Painted Stones."
9. May 17, 1873.
10. Clarence Mauck (d. 1881) served with the 4th U.S. Cavalry from 1861 to 1879, when he was commissioned a major in the 9th Cavalry. He earned two brevets for gallantry during the Civil War.
11. John L. Bullis rose from the ranks during the Civil War. He earned four brevets for gallantry during the Indian Wars.
12. May 18, 1873.
13. Napoleon B. McLaughlin (d. 1887) began his military career in 1850 as a private in the 2nd Dragoons. He was appointed colonel of the 1st Massachusetts Volunteer Infantry in 1862 and earned brevets through the rank of brigadier general in the Regular army for gallantry at Chancellorsville, Gettysburg, Poplar Grove Church, and Fort Stedman. He retired a major in 1882.
14. Charles L. Hudson (d. 1874) was sergeant major of the 72nd Ohio Volunteer Infantry during the Civil War and was commissioned a second lieutenant in the Regular army in 1867.
15. The Kickapoos were not guilty of the April 20, 1871, attack on a civilian wagon train at Howard Wells that left sixteen whites dead; the perpetrators were Kiowas and Comanches. Richardson, *Comanche Barrier,* 177.
16. Hostile losses in the engagement near Remolina, Mexico, are given in the *Chronological List,* 54, as nineteen killed, two wounded, and forty-two captured.

Robert G. Carter: A Raid into Mexico

1. Robert G. Carter (1845–1936) served as an enlisted man in the Civil War and attended West Point afterward. Carter was compelled to retire in 1876 because of a disabling leg injury sustained when his horse fell against a rock five years earlier. He taught school, worked in book publishing, and wrote six booklets and three books on his Indian Wars experience, as well as the acclaimed *Four Brothers in Blue* (Washington, DC: Gibson Brothers, 1913), which chronicled the Civil War service of Carter and his brothers. His *On the Border with Mackenzie* (Washington, DC: Eynon, 1935) is one of the undisputed classics of the Indian Wars. Carter incorporated his *Outing* article—with numerous changes—into that book.
2. The scout McLain was a half-breed.
3. Henry W. Lawton (1843–99) enlisted in the 9th Indian Infantry in 1861 and ended the Civil War a lieutenant colonel. He studied law at Harvard briefly after the Civil War before accepting a Regular army commission. A major general of volunteers during the Spanish-American War, Lawton was killed in action in the Philippines.
4. In his *On the Border with Mackenzie,* 429, Carter said he replied, "Quien sabe? Perhaps across the Rio Grande."
5. May 17, 1873.
6. The Rio Grande.

"Recorder": With the Buffalo Soldiers on the Texas Frontier

1. Companies E and I, 10th Cavalry.
2. Theodore A. Baldwin began his army career as a private in the 19th U.S. Infantry in 1862 and retired a brigadier general in 1903.
3. Richard L. Hoxie enlisted in the 1st Iowa Volunteer Cavalry in 1861 and earned an appointment to the U.S. Military Academy in 1864.

4. Albert L. Myer enlisted in the 11th U.S. Infantry in October 1865. He was commissioned a second lieutenant in December 1867 and became colonel of the 11th Infantry in March 1903.

J. Wright Mooar: Buffalo Days
1. Josiah Wright Mooar (1851–1940) moved to the Arizona Territory in 1878. Two years later, he and his brother opened a livery business at Colorado, Texas. They also established a successful cattle-ranching enterprise.
2. Mooar moved first to Michigan, and then Chicago a year later, before drifting to Kansas.
3. John Wesley Mooar (1846–1918) retired from the Mooar cattle-ranching firm in 1905.
4. A Pennsylvania tanner bought the hides, paying $3.50 apiece.
5. A novel if unsubstantiated defense of wanton slaughter.
6. William Barclay "Bat" Masterson (1853–1921) was a noted lawman and sometime associate of Wyatt Earp.
7. Richard I. Dodge (d. 1895), of the West Point Class of 1848. He authored several works on the American West, among them *Our Wild Indians: Thirty Years' Personal Experience among the Red Men of the Great West* (Hartford, CT: Worthington and Co., 1882).
8. For a biographical sketch of Lemuel T. Wilson, see "Scouting with Baldwin on the Texas Panhandle," elsewhere in this volume.
9. Olive Dixon, *Life and Adventures of Billy Dixon, of Adobe Walls, Texas Panhandle* (Guthrie, OK: Frederick S. Barde, 1914). Billy Dixon dictated his memoirs to his wife shortly before his death in 1913.
10. An elder peace chief of the Cheyenne, better known as Old Whirlwind.
11. Mrs. Olds and her husband, William, operated a restaurant in Charlie Rath's store.
12. The Cheyenne medicine man Isa-Tai was not killed, but his pony was killed by a stray long-range shot that left Isa-Tai much impressed with the buffalo hunters' medicine.
13. Oliver F. Short led the ill-fated surveying party, which included his fourteen-year-old son, Daniel. The massacre occurred during the last week of July 1874.

W. K. Myers: An Adobe Walls Defender
1. Ike and Shorty Shadler.

PART SIX: THE RED RIVER WAR, 1874–75

Nelson A. Miles: My First Fight on the Plains
1. Nelson A. Miles (1839–1925) was commissioned a first lieutenant in the 22nd Massachusetts Volunteer Infantry in September 1861 and ended the Civil War a major general of volunteers. He was appointed colonel of the 40th U.S. Infantry in 1866 and ended his career as commanding general of the army in 1903.
2. Henry B. Whipple (1822–1901) was a prominent Episcopal clergyman and longtime friend of Native Americans. He championed their cause to every president from Van Buren to McKinley.
3. June 28, 1874.
4. William R. Price (1838–81) was commissioned a major of the 8th U.S. Cavalry in July 1866 after distinguished volunteer service in the Civil War.

5. John W. "Black Jack" Davidson (1825–81), of the West Point Class of 1845. He gained his sobriquet while commander of the 10th Cavalry Buffalo Soldiers.
6. Charles E. Compton began his military service as a sergeant in the 1st Iowa Volunteer Cavalry in 1861. He was promoted to the colonelcy of the 4th U.S. Cavalry in 1887.
7. James Biddle (1832–1910) saw wide service on the frontier, fighting in the Modoc and Red River Wars and in the Arizona Territory. He retired as colonel of the 9th Cavalry in 1896.
8. Henry B. Bristol had been commissioned a second lieutenant in the 5th U.S. Infantry in 1857; he saw service against the Navajo Indians during the Civil War.
9. For a biographical sketch of Frank D. Baldwin, see "A Terrible Ride through Indian Country," elsewhere in this volume.
10. James W. Pope, of the West Point Class of 1868.
11. Gray Beard was a Southern Cheyenne war chief.
12. Catherine and Sophia German remained captives of Medicine Water, a Cheyenne war chief.
13. Stone Calf was a Southern Cheyenne war chief who treated the captive German girls well and advocated their release.

Frank D. Baldwin: A Terrible Ride through Indian Country

1. Frank D. Baldwin (1842–1923) was commissioned a second lieutenant in the Michigan Horse Guards in September 1861. He won the Medal of Honor twice during his career and retired as a brigadier general in the Regular army. Baldwin was a favorite of Nelson A. Miles.
2. Four members of Baldwin's advance guard came upon two Indians on the west bank of Chicken Creek, killing one and mortally wounding the other. Frank D. Baldwin Diary, 3, box 21, folder 21, William C. Brown Papers, University of Colorado Libraries, Boulder.
3. Edmund C. Hentig of the 6th Cavalry was killed in action with Apache Indians at Cibicue Creek, Arizona, in 1881.
4. The battle of Palo Duro Canyon.
5. George W. Baird began his military career as a volunteer private in 1862 and retired a brigadier general in the Regular army in 1903.
6. William B. Wetmore, of the West Point Class of 1872.
7. Ezra P. Ewers entered the service as a private in the 19th U.S. Infantry in 1862. He retired a colonel in the Regular army in 1901.
8. Lemuel T. Wilson, William F. Schmalsle, and Ira G. Wing.
9. Baldwin and his scouts had ridden through the broken ravines along the base of Cap Rock, halting in what they thought was an isolated ravine to rest for the day.
10. For a biographical sketch of Wyllys Lyman, see "A Fight with the Comanches and Kiowas," elsewhere in this volume.
11. The white Indian whom Baldwin seized was named Tehan, or Tejana. The Kiowas had captured him in Texas, and then adopted him into their tribe.
12. Lyman lost one man killed and one officer and three enlisted men wounded.

Lemuel T. Wilson: Scouting with Baldwin on the Texas Panhandle

1. Lemuel T. Wilson (was carried as) a scout on the rolls of the Quartermaster Department from August 18, 1874, until October 31, 1881. He was living in Jacksonville, Oregon, in 1933, when the Pampa *Daily News* published his recollections.

2. Lieutenant Baldwin launched a surprise attack on Gray Beard's village on November 8, 1874. He discovered the girls in a lodge abandoned during the assault.
3. Evidently the scalps of two soldiers of Troop H, 8th U.S. Cavalry, killed in a fight along McClellan Creek, Texas, on November 6, 1874.
6. Henry P. Kingsbury, of the West Point Class of 1871.
5. Fort Elliott, Texas, was built to help open a route for Texas cattle that would avoid the settlements in the Indian Territory and Kansas. A temporary camp was first established on the North Fork of Red River in the Texas Panhandle in September 1874. In February 1875 Cantonment North Fork of Red River was built on the site. A new site, called Cantonment on the Sweetwater, was occupied on June 5, 1875. The post was named Fort Elliott in February 1876.

Wyllys Lyman: A Fight with the Comanches and Kiowas
1. Wyllys Lyman (1830–1900) entered the army as a lieutenant in the 10th Vermont Volunteer Infantry in 1862. He was commissioned a captain in the 40th U.S. Infantry in 1866 and retired a major in 1892.
2. Frank West, of the West Point Class of 1872, won the Medal of Honor for distinguished conduct during the battle of Big Dry Wash in July 1882.
3. Granville Lewis joined the army under an assumed name in 1855. He was commissioned a second lieutenant in the 5th U.S. Infantry in May 1866 and was retired for disability in November 1879.
4. William H. Lewis (d. 1878), of the West Point Class of 1849.
5. Adna R. Chaffee (1842–1914) enlisted in the 6th U.S. Cavalry in 1861. He commanded the relief contingent in the Boxer Rebellion of China and ended his distinguished career as a lieutenant general in the Regular army in 1906.

E. A. Brininstool: Billy Dixon, a Frontier Hero
1. Earl A. Brininstool (1870–1957) was a newspaperman who became a prolific author of books on frontier history.
2. Amos Chapman (1837–1925) began scouting for civilian wagon trains after the Civil War. In 1868 he scouted for Sully's Canadian River expedition, and in 1874 scouted for Colonel Miles. After recovering from his Buffalo Wallow wound, Chapman worked as post interpreter at Camp Sully and the Darlington Agency. Late in life, he lived at Siling, Oklahoma, adjacent to the Cheyenne and Arapaho agency.
3. William "Billy" Dixon (1850–1913) was a noted buffalo hunter and one of the first to work south of the Canadian River, in Comanche country. He was among the survivors of the Adobe Walls fight and in August 1874 Colonel Miles hired him on as a scout. Dixon scouted for the army until 1883, when he homesteaded on the site of Adobe Walls. He married Olive King in 1894 and was elected the first sheriff of Hutchinson County, Texas.
4. The Kiowas and Comanches who attacked the troopers and scouts were part of the larger war party then besieging Lyman's wagon train. Having grown tired of the wagon train fight, they were riding south to rejoin their families when they came upon the isolated dispatch bearers.
5. Richard I. Dodge, *Our Wild Indians: Thirty-three Years Personal Experience among the Red Men of the Great West* (Hartford, CT: A. D. Worthington and Company, 1882).

George E. Albee: Mackenzie's Expedition on the Staked Plains

1. George E. Albee won the Medal of Honor for distinguished gallantry in action during Captain Bacon's expedition against hostile Kiowas and Comanches on the Brazos River, Texas, October 28–29, 1869. He began the Civil War as a private in Col. Hiram Berdan's famous regiment of sharpshooters (Company G, 2nd U.S. Sharpshooters) and was wounded in the hip at Second Bull Run. Albee became an officer in the 36th Wisconsin Infantry and was also recommended for a Medal of Honor for Civil War service. Albee retired for disability in 1878 and had a long career in the arms industry.

2. Henry Carroll was a New Yorker who enlisted in the army in 1859 and rose through the ranks. He retired as colonel of the 7th Cavalry in 1899. Edward M. Heyl (d. 1895) rose through the ranks during the Civil War. He ended his career a colonel in the Inspector General Corps.

3. On September 16, 1869, Captains Carroll and Heyl, with nintey-five men of Troops B, E, F, and M of the 9th Cavalry, attacked a camp of two hundred Comanche and Kiowa lodges on the Salt Fork of the Brazos River, routing the Indians in an eight-mile running fight.

4. John M. Bacon served as aide-de-camp to General Sherman from 1871 to 1884. He retired a colonel in 1899.

5. Bacon led six troops of the 9th Cavalry and two troops of the 4th Cavalry from Fort Concho, Texas, on an expedition against the Comanches and Kiowas on October 10, 1869. Five hundred Kiowa and Comanche warriors attacked his field camp near the headwaters of the Brazos River on October 28 and, after a two-day fight, were routed. Bacon reported losses of 8 wounded (of 198 men engaged) and estimated hostile losses at 50 warriors killed and 7 women captured. Leckie, *Buffalo Soldiers,* 89–90; *Chronological List,* 43.

6. Mackenzie was the only man wounded in the October 19, 1871, skirmish on the Freshwater Fork of the Brazos. He reported two hostiles killed. *Chronolgocal List,* 49.

7. Also known as the Fresh Water Fork of the Brazos River.

8. Mackenzie reported 23 hostile Indians killed, 1 wounded, and 120 captured in the September 29, 1872, battle on the North Fork of Red River, at a loss of 1 enlisted man killed and 3 wounded. *Chronological List,* 52.

9. Peter M. Boehm enlisted as a bugler in the 2nd U.S. Cavalry in 1858 and won a Medal of Honor for gallantry in action at Dinwiddie Court House, March 13, 1865, while serving as aide-de-camp to General Custer.

10. September 27, 1874.

11. Palo Duro Canyon.

12. Theodore J. Wint enlisted in the 6th Pennsylvania Cavalry in 1861 and received a regular commission as a second lieutenant in the 4th U.S. Cavalry in November 1865. In 1902, after forty years of service, Wint was promoted to brigadier general in the Regular army.

13. Bugler Hard survived, said Lieutenant carter, "to sound bugle calls to many years after." Carter, *On the Border,* 490.

14. The most prominent Comanche chief at Palo Duro was O-ha-ma-tai; the Cheyenne villages were those of Chief Iron Shirt. Hadley, *Buffalo War,* 178.

Charles A. P. Hatfield: With Mackenzie in the Texas Panhandle

1. Charles A. P. Hatfield (1850–1931) joined the 4th U.S. Cavalry after graduating from West Point in 1872. He served on the Mexican border from 1912 to 1914, when he retired a colonel and settled in Baltimore.

2. Hatfield penned his recollections of service under Mackenzie in reply to a circular letter from Lt. Col. C. A. Bach, chief of the Historical Section, U.S. Army War College, Washington, D.C., to members of the Order of Indian Wars, soliciting material on the Indian campaigns.
3. Thomas M. Anderson began his military career as a private in the 6th Ohio Infantry during the Civil War. He retired a brigadier general in the Regular army in 1900.
4. Also known as White River or Running Water Draw. The campsite was about forty miles east of present-day Lubbock, Texas.
5. Louis Warrington (d. 1879) was commissioned a second lieutenant in the 4th Cavalry in 1867; he was awarded the Medal of Honor for gallantry in action during a skirmish in the Muchazur Valley, Texas, in December 1874.
6. Wentz C. Miller (d. 1892), of the West Point Class of 1869, had served as an enlisted man during the Civil War.
7. Tule Spring.
8. Carter said that Troop A led the way. Carter, *On the Border,* 489.
9. In the *Chronological List,* 58, hostile losses are given as four killed for the Tule Canyon and Palo Duro Canyon fights, an undoubtedly low estimate.

John B. Charlton: Battle of Palo Duro Canyon

1. John B. Charlton (1847–1922) enlisted in Battery K, 1st U.S. Light Artillery, in 1865. He reenlisted in 1870 in the 4th U.S. Cavalry and became an outstanding noncommissioned officer. Robert G. Carter credits him with killing Satank when the Kiowa chief attempted to escape while en route to Jacksboro, Texas, after the Warren wagon train raid. Charlton was recommended for a Medal of Honor for gallantry in the fight on McClellan's Creek, and in a later action saved the life of Lt. Peter M. Boehm, being himself badly wounded in the effort. Both Mackenzie and Carter thought highly of Charlton, who received a discharge—probably on account of his wounds—in 1876. Charlton roamed the world before settling down in Uvalde, Texas, to marry and become a stockman. In later years, Carter maintained a long correspondence with Charlton, which he published as *The Old Sergeant's Story* (New York: Frederick H. Hitchcock, 1926). Carter described Charlton in these terms: "I considered him one of the best noncommissioned officers in the regiment. While he had a free, rollicking, daredevil spirit, he was perfectly amenable to discipline. He was a very handsome, intelligent, active, energetic man—fully six feet, spare, sinewy, straight as an arrow, an athlete, one of the best riders, shots, and hunters." Quoted in Thrapp, *Encyclopedia,* 1:257.
2. September 27, 1874.
3. Many years afterward, Kiowa informants told Col. Wilbur S. Nye that the warrior, a minor Kiowa war chief named Red War Bonnet, was not killed, but fled to his tepee to put on war paint. Haley, *Buffalo War,* 177. Charles A. P. Hatfield, in his account elsewhere in this volume, implied that the troopers missed their mark, saying Red War Bonnet "disappeared immediately afterwards in a marvelous manner."
4. Charlton's recollection of troop casualties is at variance with official records, which claim only one soldier wounded and none killed in the action at Palo Duro Canyon.

Austin Henely: The Sappa Creek Fight

1. Austin Henely (1848–78), of the West Point Class of 1872. Henely drowned in a flash flood while on duty in Arizona.
2. Homer W. Wheeler contributed the copy of Henely's report that appeared in *Winners of the West.*
3. Christian C. Hewitt, of the West Point Class of 1874.

4. Homer W. Wheeler (1848–1930) traveled to Fort Wallace, Kansas, from New York in 1868. He made the acquaintance of Will Comstock, "Wild Bill" Hickok, and "Buffalo Bill" Cody, and from them learned the scouting trade. He accompanied Captain Bankhead's column to Beecher Island in September 1868. After the Sappa Creek fight, he was commissioned a second lieutenant in the 5th Cavalry on the recommendation of General Pope. He retired a colonel in 1911.
5. April 22, 1875.
6. Cheyenne sources agreed that twenty-eight Indians died in the fight, but placed the number of women and children at twenty, and the number of warriors slain as just seven.
7. The war bonnet in question belonged not to a medicine man, but to White Bear, a Cheyenne warrior. Chalfant, *Cheyennes,* 137.
8. Comanche and Kiowa war parties—and not Cheyenne—made the attack on Lyman's train; Henely consequently misinterpreted the sketches in this respect. Whether he correctly deduced the meaning of the others is unknown, as the book has never been found. Chalfant, *Cheyennes,* 138.

PART SEVEN: RAIDS AND REPRISALS, 1865–79

Adolph Roenigk: Railroad Grading among Indians
1. Adolph Roenigk (1847–post-1933) was born in Prussia and came to America as a young teen. He learned the trade of saddle and harness making in St. Louis, coming to Kansas in 1868 to work for the government. He settled in Clay County in 1870, engaged in the saddle and harness business, and grew wealthy. Roenigk also authored *Pioneer History of Kansas* (Kansas City: n.p., 1933).
2. Fossil Creek is a branch of the Smoky Hill River. The Fossil Creek Station became the town of Russell, Kansas, in April 1871.

Anonymous: A Gallant Stand on the Little Blue River
1. On his return to Camp Bingham, Sergeant Leonard took a settler's family of two women and a child under his charge. The department commander commended Sergeant Leonard for gallantry in action. Theodore F. Rodenbough and William L. Haskin, eds., *The Army of the United States* (New York: Argonaut Press, 1966), 181.

"Buford": Indians at Ogllala Station, Union Pacific Railroad
1. Elijah R. Wells (d. 1891) rose from the ranks of the 2nd Dragoons during the Civil War to the rank of major of volunteers.
2. Randolph Norwood (d. 1901) was brevetted major for gallantry in action on the Rosebud in May 1877 and at Camas Meadows in August 1877.

[Nicholas Nolan]: A Fearful March on the Staked Plains
1. Nicholas Nolan (d. 1883) was an Irish immigrant who joined the Regular army in 1852. Nolan served with the 10th Cavalry from 1866 to 1882 and died while on active duty. Leckie characterized him as "an able and humane officer." Leckie, *Buffalo Soldiers,* 162–63n.

2. In the spring of 1877, a large band of Comanches under Black Horse left their reservation and fled west to the Llano Estacado to prey on white buffalo hunters. Several small parties of Mescaleros also roamed the area, attacking stage stations. Colonel Grierson directed Captain Nolan to take Troop Λ, 10th Cavalry, and punish any of these marauders whom he might find on the Llano Estacado.
3. Corporal Fremont, the Fort Concho post librarian, subsequently was court-martialed, dishonorably discharged, and sentenced to a year in prison for desertion. Colonel Grierson, however, recommended leniency in Fremont's case.
4. Robert G. Smither was commissioned a first lieutenant in the 7th Indian Volunteer Cavalry in May 1865 after four years of enlisted service. He received a regular commission in the 10th Cavalry in June 1867 and retired a captain in May 1888.
5. Wallace Tear served as an enlisted man in the 96th Illinois Volunteer Infantry before being commissioned a second lieutenant in the 14th U.S. Colored Infantry in 1863. He was mustered out after the Civil War but was recommissioned a second lieutenant in the 40th U.S. Infantry in 1867. Tear resigned his commission in June 1883.
6. The missing men were Privates John Bond and John Isaacs.

J. H. T. King: A Brief Account of the Sufferings of a Detachment of United States Cavalry from Deprivation of Water

1. Joseph H. T. King joined the Regular army as an assistant surgeon in October 1867; he resigned June 30, 1881.
2. Phillip L. Lee (d. 1889), an enlisted volunteer during the Civil War who had been commissioned in the 10th U.S. Cavalry in 1866.
3. The Tonkawa was a once-prominent central Texas tribe that maintained peaceable relations with the Americans. By 1884 disease and incessant battles with unfriendly tribes had reduced their number to just ninety-two.

[Mrs. Charles M. Harpole, et al.]: Last Indian Raid in Southwest Texas

1. Lieutenant Bullis and his detachment of Seminole scouts engaged the hostiles in the Sierra Burras Mountains of Mexico on May 3, 1881. The *Chronological List* gives hostile losses as four killed and two captured.

PART EIGHT: THE UTE WAR, 1879

J. Scott Payne: Incidents of the Recent Campaign against the Utes

1. J. Scott Payne (1844–95), of the West Point Class of 1866. He left the military briefly to practice law but returned as a second lieutenant in the 6th Cavalry in 1873. He was retired for poor health in 1886.
2. Wesley Merritt. For a biographical sketch of Merritt, see "Rescuing Payne's Command," elsewhere in this volume.
3. Thomas T. Thornburgh (1843–79) was a well-regarded officer and native Tennessean who had enlisted in the Union army during the Civil War.
4. Also known as Sowawick, he was a subchief of the White River Utes.
5. Ute Jack, or Nicaagat, was one of three principal chiefs of the White River band of the Ute Indians.
6. Unque was a subchief of the Uncompahgre Utes from the Los Pinos agency.
7. Nathan C. Meeker (1817–79) had been an agricultural writer for the New York *Herald* and a devotee of cooperative farming before becoming agent to the Utes.

His tactlessness fatally marred his otherwise commendable efforts to better the Utes through farming.

8. Colorow was a Comanche who became a chief in the Ute tribe.
9. Samuel A. Cherry (d. 1881), of the West Point Class of 1875. He was murdered by a soldier two years after the Ute War.
10. Lieutenant Cherry gestured to the Utes with a friendly wave of his hat. He later claimed a nearby Ute fired the first shot in response to his gesture, while Ute participants asserted that either a soldier or some unknown party was at fault. Mark E. Miller, *Hollow Victory: The White River Expedition of 1879 and the Battle of Milk Creek* (Niwot: University of Colorado Press, 1997), 56–57.
11. Participants left widely varying versions of the precise circumstances surrounding the death of Major Thornburgh. For a discussion of the subject, see Miller, *Hollow Victory,* 64–66.
12. Joseph J. Lawson was a veteran Indian fighter who had served as a volunteer officer during the Civil War.
13. James V. S. Paddock, of the West Point Class of 1877.
14. Francis S. Dodge began his military service as a private during the Civil War. Martin B. Hughes was a member of the West Point Class of 1869 whose career was spent with the Buffalo Soldiers of the 9th and 10th Cavalry.
15. John Gordon was a questionable character who in 1874 had violated the 1868 Fort Laramie Treaty with the Sioux by leading a party of miners into the Black Hills.
16. Joe P. Rankin was a guide with the Thornburgh expedition.
17. Ouray was a chief of the Yampa and Grand River bands residing at the Los Pinos Agency.

H. W. Spooner: The Outbreak of September 1879
1. H. W. Spooner was the first sergeant of Troop E, 5th Cavalry.
2. Drawing upon unit muster rolls, Miller, *Hollow Victory,* 161–64, placed Thornburgh's command at 191 officers and enlisted men—of whom 30 were with the detached Company E, 4th Infantry—and sixteen civilians.
3. Acting Assistant Surgeon Robert B. Grimes was an Ohio native who had served with Crook's 1876 Bighorn and Yellowstone expeditions.
4. Miller, *Hollow Victory,* 171–80, gives the total casualty figures as follows: one officer, nine enlisted men, and three civilians killed; three officers (including Surgeon Grimes), thirty-six enlisted men, and five civilians wounded. Ute losses have been estimated at between twenty-five and thirty-nine killed and wounded.

Wesley Merritt: Rescuing Payne's Command
1. Wesley Merritt (1834–1910), of the West Point Class of 1860, rose to the rank of major general of volunteers during the Civil War and was a favorite of Phil Sheridan. He saw wide service on the postwar frontier, and in 1898 commanded the American military expedition to the Philippines. He retired a major general in 1900.
2. The material presented here is excerpted from an article by Merritt entitled, "Three Indian Campaigns."
3. Fort D. A. Russell was located at present-day Cheyenne, Wyoming, on the line of the Union Pacific Railroad.

Edwin V. Sumner: Besieged by the Utes

1. Edwin V. Sumner (1835–1912) was the son of a Civil War major general of the same name. The younger Sumner was commissioned a second lieutenant in the 1st U.S. Cavalry in August 1861. He served on the Pacific Coast from 1866 to 1880 and saw action in the Modoc, Nez Perce, and Bannock Wars. Sumner retired a brigadier general in March 1899.
2. Butler D. Price began his military career as a lieutenant in the 2nd Pennsylvania Cavalry in 1861. He was promoted to the colonelcy of the 16th U.S. Infantry in 1902.
3. Cpl. Edward F. Murphy, of Wayne County, Pennsylvania, received a Medal of Honor on April 23, 1880, for gallantry in action at the battle of Milk Creek.
4. Merritt's command came upon the debris of the wagon train of Rawlins resident George Gordon in Stinking Gulch, where Ute warriors had jumped it. Gordon was hauling a threshing machine for Meeker's use at the White River agency.
5. The employee was named Joe Brady. He came with a note from Chief Ouray—and not Colorow—ordering the "chief captains, headmen, and Utes at the White River agency" to cease their hostilities against the whites at once. Ouray was among the most influential, and perhaps the most diplomatic, of the Ute leaders.
6. William P. Hall, of the West Point Class of 1868. Hall was awarded the Medal of Honor for gallantry in action during the reconnaissance.
7. William B. Weir was a member of the West Point Class of 1870.

Lewis D. Greene: The White River Campaign

1. Lewis D. Greene, of the West Point Class of 1878, retired with the rank of captain in 1898.
2. Companies B, C, E, F, H, and K, under the command of Lt. Col. Charles C. Gilbert.
3. Johnson, a Ute medicine man whose Indian name was Canalla, got into an argument with Meeker over racehorses and the reservation irrigation ditch. They engaged in a brief fistfight, in which, says Miller, "Meeker's ego was bruised more than his body." Miller, *Hollow Victory,* 10.
4. Henry B. Freeman and Thaddeus S. Kirtland.

John F. Finerty: With Merritt's Command

1. John F. Finerty (1846–1908) was a veteran war correspondent who had earned the respect of Brig. Gen. George Crook and his officers for his conduct under fire during the battle of the Rosebud in the 1876 Sioux War. From that assignment came his highly regarded book, *Warpath and Bivouac.*
2. A reference to Crook's controversial "Horsemeat March," during the Sioux War of 1876.
3. Carl Schurz (1829–1906) was a Prussian immigrant who became a vigorous and eloquent spokesman for the German-American community and a staunch antislavery Republican. Schurz served as a major general of volunteers during the Civil War. As secretary of the interior, he became a champion of Native American rights.
4. Henry W. Wessells, Jr., left the U.S. Naval Academy in November 1864 and enlisted in the 7th U.S. Infantry. He was commissioned a second lieutenant in the 7th Infantry in July 1865 and transferred to the 3rd Cavalry in December 1870. Wessells retired a colonel in 1901.

5. George F. Chase, of the West Point Class of 1871, and George K. Hunter, of the West Point Class of 1877.
6. Samuel M. Swift retired as colonel of the 5th Cavalry in 1903.
7. The famous Palmer House Hotel in Chicago, which sometimes served as the lodging place of the commander of the Military District of the Missouri.
8. Guy V. Henry (1839–99) graduated with the West Point Class of 1861 and rose to the volunteer rank of colonel during the Civil War, earning a Medal of Honor for gallantry at Cold Harbor. A major general of volunteers during the war with Spain, he was military governor of Puerto Rico from December 1898 to May 1899.
9. Francis H. Hardie was commissioned a second lieutenant in the 3rd Cavalry in July 1876.
10. Albert D. King (d. 1900), a volunteer officer in the 2nd California Cavalry during the Civil War.
11. John B. Babcock began the Civil War a sergeant in the 37th New York State Militia and ended the conflict a major of volunteers. He received a regular commission as a second lieutenant in the 5th Cavalry in January 1867, served as a brigadier general of volunteers during the war with Spain, and returned to his regular rank of colonel in 1901. Babcock earned the Medal of Honor for gallantry in action at the battle of Spring Creek, Nebraska, May 16, 1869.
12. October 27, 1879.
13. Albert G. Brackett (d. 1896) began his military career as a lieutenant in the 4th Indiana Volunteer Infantry during the Mexican War. He commanded the 9th Illinois Cavalry during the Civil War and retired a colonel in the Regular army in 1891.

INDEX

Editor's Note: In preparing the index for *Eyewitnesses to the Indian Wars, 1865–1890: Conquering the Southern Plains*, I have deviated a bit from standard indexing practice. Where indexed items (names, places, concepts, etc.) appear more than once in the same article, I have cited only their first appearance in the article.

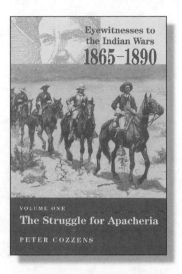

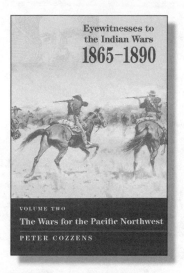

To Come in the Series:

EYEWITNESSES TO THE INDIAN WARS, 1865–1890
VOLUME IV: THE NORTHERN PLAINS

EYEWITNESSES TO THE INDIAN WARS, 1865–1890
VOLUME V: ARMY LIFE AND LEADERS

Peter Cozzens, editor

In the latter half of the nineteenth century, the American West was an untamed frontier, a fierce battleground where the preservation of law and order was a difficult task. Following the west coast mining boom, settlers from the east rapidly began to migrate to the abundance of land awaiting claim. The expansion of the United States, however, was barred by the unwillingness of the native peoples to give up the land that they had lived on for generations. Consequently, antagonism between the Indians and settlers led to bitter violence on several occasions, necessitating the intervention of the U.S. military, hence the so-called "Indian Wars."

WWW.STACKPOLEBOOKS.COM
1-800-732-3669

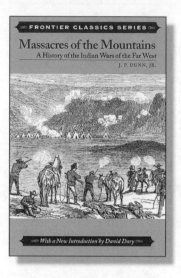

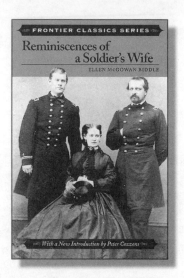

Arkansas River

Fort

Cimarron River

North Canadian River

Carr's Depot
△ 1868 – 1869

Third Cavalry
Depot
1868 – 1869
△

Fort Union
⬡

N E W   M E X I C O

Adobe
Walls
1874

Lyman 1874

Price 1874
⬡
Fort Elliot

South Canadian River

S T A K E D   P L A I N S

Fort Bascom
⬡

McClellan
Fight
187

McKenzie
1874

Palo
Duro

Miles
1874

Pecos River

Palo Duro

N

T

George Skoch